Space Radio Handbook

John Branegan, GM4IHJ

Radio Society of Great Britain

Published by the Radio Society of Great Britain, Cranborne Road, Potters Bar, Herts EN6 3JE.

ISBN 1 872309 05 4

Publisher's Note

No representation is made in this book as to the legality or otherwise of the reception of non-amateur radio signals described herein and, in case of doubt, the national telecommunications administration should be consulted. The attention of UK radio amateurs is also drawn to Note (c) in the Terms and Limitations booklet BR68 issued with the amateur radio licence.

Typography and cover design by Ray Eckersley, Seven Stars Publishing, Marlow.
Printed in Great Britain by Bath Press Ltd, Lower Bristol Road, Bath, BA2 3BL.

Contents

Preface

It is a common assumption that anything connected with space activity is complex. This is not true. Equipped with simple radio receivers, computers and telescopes, thousands of individuals, schools and clubs are following everything that goes on in space.

Do you want to listen to the cosmonauts as they go about their daily tasks in their space station?

Are you interested in space experiments or exploration? Would you, for instance, have been interested in monitoring the fallout from the Chernobyl nuclear accident, via a satellite reporting radiation over Chernobyl direct to your home?

Do you like the idea of satellite conversations with friends in Tokyo, unaccompanied by huge telephone bills? Indeed, is worldwide radio, television or data communications your objective?

Are you interested in a personal exploration of the mysteries of the universe, via your own radio astronomy station? Listening to the radio signals that have taken millions of years to come from distant galaxies?

Do you want to listen to the astronauts and cosmonauts as they set up bases on the Moon, and on Mars? In the past, the exploits of the great explorers like Columbus, Magellan, Cook and Livingstone could only be read about years or even decades after the event. Today, however, as the modern explorers open up the solar system, we can all follow in their footsteps as they reach towards the stars.

All these things, and a thousand others, are possible at no great expense from your own home, local club or classroom. Anyone who wants to participate can use this book to turn their home or school into a space observatory.

Space exploration is exciting and it is open to anyone. Come and join us.

John Branegan, GM4IHJ

Chapter 1

Space radio physics I

The Sun

Our parent star, the Sun, is the source of nearly all radio propagation variation, throughout both near-Earth space and the rest of the solar system.

The Sun is classified by astronomers as a G-type sub-dwarf star, a typical member of its type. G-type stars are not the most numerous of star types in our Milky Way galaxy, but none the less are very common.

The Sun is a rather unspectacular star: not among the brightest, and not among the most explosive. None the less it is in a class of stars which have one curious feature: spots.

All G-type stars seem to have spots. We cannot see this directly because of their enormous distance from us, but their light output, which we can examine closely, has features which are complementary to spots, visible as strong calcium lines. Regular checking of the calcium line in distant G-type cousins of the Sun suggests that they too vary cyclically. Like the Sun, the average G-type star has a spot cycle of 11 or 12 years duration. There are exceptions: some stars cycle their spots every three or four years, some take as long as 30 or 40 years for a spot cycle. But these slow and fast cycling G-types are rare.

Sunspot cycles are important in respect of radio propagation because they reveal that the Sun is losing material all the time. The loss peaks at solar cycle maximum and drops to a much smaller value five years later, before starting to climb to another maximum. Study of solar cycles reveal that they are half cycles of the Sun's magnetic field. Two spot cycles are necessary for the Sun to change the polarity of its magnetic field. One reversal of polarity takes 11 years. The full cycle back to the original polarity takes roughly 22 years.

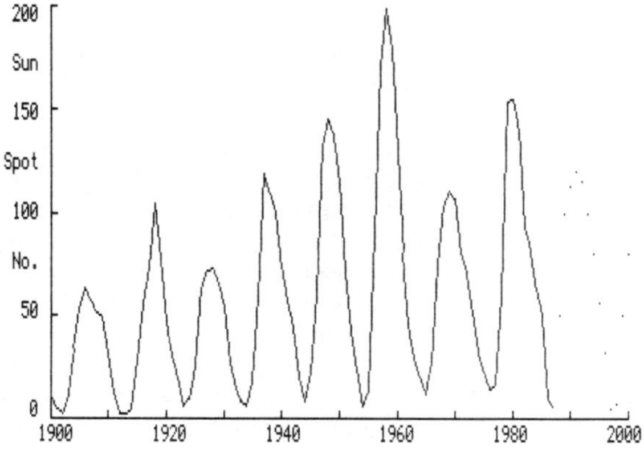

Fig 1.01: Sunspot cycles between 1900 and 1986 (estimate only after 1986)

This relationship between solar magnetic reversals and the sunspot cycle gives us an important clue as to what is happening. The Sun is a violent mass of extremely hot material. It retains its size and shape because gravity prevents most of the material escaping. However, the activity on the Sun often exceeds control by solar gravity and solar material would be quickly lost if it were not also restrained by solar magnetic fields. At solar cycle minimum, as the fields are changing polarity, their control on solar material is much reduced.

When the Sun is at sunspot cycle minimum it has few spots. So they are not a source of material loss at that time. None the less, there is a steady loss of material from another source. This is the coronal hole, a feature of solar cycle minimum. The coronal hole represents an area on the solar outer regions where the magnetic fields are particularly weak. Coronal holes start near the solar poles, but can extend down towards the solar equator and even across it and down to the opposite pole.

The material output of coronal holes is relatively weak, but they can last for months. As the Sun spins around once every 27 days the coronal holes steadily release material like a spray from a rotating garden hose. Every 27 days the Earth crosses the output spray from a particular coronal hole. The crossing may take two or three days if the hole is a broad one releasing a wide stream of material. In this way radio propagation on Earth can be seriously affected for several days, every 27 days, for several months.

Fig 1.02 shows the pattern of flow as seen from above one of the Sun's poles. The material released from the Sun is typical of the constituent material of the Sun's outer regions. Most of it is hydrogen, and it is ionised, so that it is split up into the separate components of hydrogen, the positively charged proton, and the negatively charged electron. Both components are free of one another.

Because of the spiral pattern of outward movement of the material, any planet in its path experiences it as a series of waves. These waves are referred to as the 'solar wind'. The solar wind never entirely disappears. Even at sunspot minimum, odd spots do appear from time to time, and disturbances around them add to the solar wind already being contributed by the coronal holes. As solar maximum approaches, the coronal holes disappear and more and bigger spots begin to appear on the solar disc. It is from these areas around sunspots that we get the enormously powerful releases of solar material which we call 'solar flares'. Also associated with sunspots are the second source of violent release of material, the solar filaments.

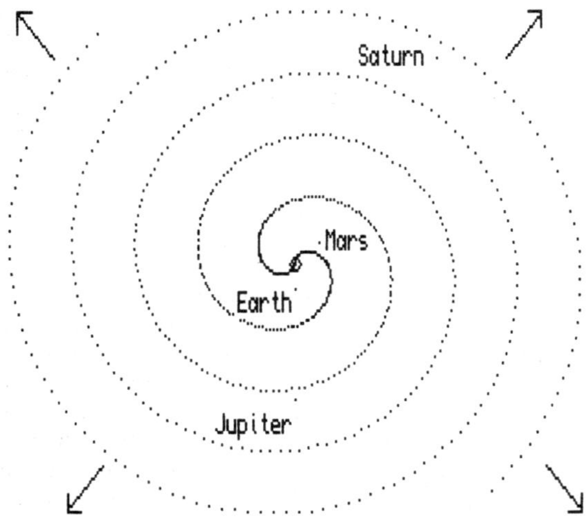

Fig 1.02: The outward motion of the solar wind

Satellite and spacecraft experiments have told us a great deal about the Sun's activity. Solar flare activity appears to be related to a cycle with a period of 152 days, but there is at present no consensus as to just why this is happening or whether it is a transient feature. Just why solar flares occur at all is something also awaiting explanation. However, certain features are obvious. We get more of them at solar maximum, and they are responsible for the very big disturbances of Earth radio propagation called 'sudden ionospheric disturbances' (SIDs).

Solar filament break-up can also cause large releases of solar material which can enormously enhance the solar wind, and in general they produce effects very similar to those which are produced by solar flares. Both flares and filament break-up are important, not just for the material they contribute to the solar wind, but also for their direct radiation contribution, mostly in the form of X-rays and gamma rays. Radiation from a flare can reach the Earth in nine minutes, and is often so powerful that it directly penetrates the day-side Earth ionosphere down to the D layer, where it produces so much temporary ionisation that all ionospheric propagation ceases, sometimes for minutes, sometimes for hours. These are the events we call 'SIDs'.

Following on behind the SID, but moving at a mere three or four million kilometres per hour, is the flare's enormously enhanced contribution to the solar wind. Some 36 to 48 hours after the SID, this arrives at the Earth, causing large magnetic storms and aurora, with all the accompanying disturbance of propagation which they bring in their wake.

Solar flares and filament break-up are transient features. Their association with large sunspot groups does mean that if, as often happens, a big sunspot group survives a full solar rotation period of 27 days, it can then be responsible for more flares and filament break-up, as it points at the Earth the second time around.

At any time in the solar cycle an observer above the solar pole would 'see' the solar wind as a series of waves expanding out into space from the Sun. Here and there, locally enhanced patches of high density would appear in the waves, the product of major flares. These high-density patches would be carrying their own magnetic fields with them, and would be travelling outwards faster than the mainstream waves, thus producing overlapping of fast-moving, relatively new material overtaking slower-moving, less dense material. Fortunately the Earth has a magnetic field of its own, and this is able to absorb the impact of much of the solar wind bombardment. Without the protective magnetic field, it is doubtful whether life as we know it on Earth would be possible. Using satellites and radio astronomy, it is possible to map both the day-to-day movement of the solar wind and to record its varying impact on the ionosphere and the atmosphere. For ionospheric propagation prediction purposes, we measure the solar radiation output in the microwaves. This solar flux measurement, as it is called, has been found to accurately describe the overall effect of the Sun's bombardment of the Earth, allowing prediction of its likely effects, both in the long and the short term.

The magnetosphere

The Earth with its protective magnetic field takes the full shock of the solar wind bombardment. Though seriously compressed on the sunward side, the magnetic field deflects the solar wind around the Earth and out behind it in a tail several million kilometres long. Fig 1.03 shows a side view of the Earth's magnetosphere and its magnetotail extension.

Much of the energy of the solar wind is deflected away, around the Earth and out beyond it, but a portion does leak through inside the magnetosphere, particularly over the Earth's polar regions. Even when the solar wind is weakest, this input is sufficient to replenish the Van Allen radiation belts which lie deep inside the magnetosphere. These belts are like magnetic bottles, restricting the radiation and generally confining it into two doughnut-shaped rings, a thin inner ring and a wider outer ring, which circle the Earth's magnetic equator. Fig 1.04 shows a side view of these belts named after their discoverer James Van Allen, whose Explorer 1 experiment was one of the most successful of early satellite experiments. Important features to note with the Van Allen belts are:

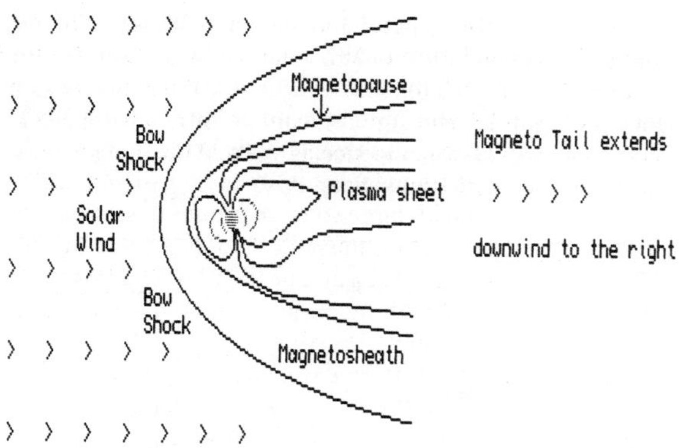

Fig 1.03: How the Earth's magnetosphere deflects the solar wind

(a) The belts do not extend above latitudes 60°N or 60°S. The regions above either pole of the Earth are clear.
(b) Radiation levels inside these belts are very high. So high in fact that residence in the belts for more than a day or repeated passages through the belts are fatal to both human beings and microelectronics.

The Van Allen belts are places to be avoided. Almost no satellites orbit in them. Low-altitude circular orbiters stay below 1500km and avoid most of the problems, although there are areas of the world such as the south Atlantic over which the Van Allen belts drop anomalous extensions down as low as 900km.

Manned flights in Earth orbit stay below 500km because it is too expensive in fuel to put them higher. But this has the effect of ensuring that their crews are safe from radiation problems, at least as far as the Van Allen belts are concerned, as solar flares can still be a problem to astronauts even in these low orbits.

Satellites which go much higher either keep a minimum height of about 24,000km to stay above the belts or, if elliptical orbiters, make very rapid transits through the belts at high inclinations, thereby spending most of their time high above the clear polar regions. The destruction of at least one radio amateur satellite computer is directly attributable to Van Allen belt radiation. Oscar 10's computer failed because the satellite did not get into a high inclination orbit. It therefore spent too much time in the thickest part of the Van Allen belts around the equator. Radiosport 8 at 1,600km also failed after a long life because it was too close to the bottom of the belts, and it eventually succumbed to radiation damage to its on-board computer.

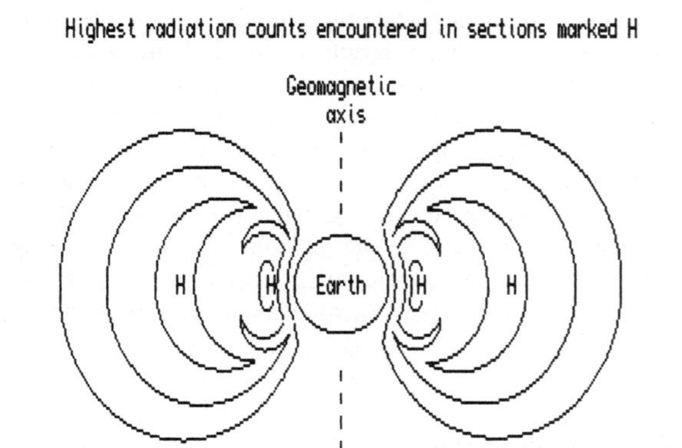

Fig 1.04: Cross section of the Van Allen radiation belts

Leakage downwards from the polar edges of the Van Allen belts is almost continuous, but it is not strong. It simply maintains low level auroral activity in the quiet location of the auroral oval at either pole. When the solar wind is enhanced by flares, filament break-up, or coronal hole discharge, the vastly increased precipitation of charged particles from the belt's sub-polar edges produces large auroral storms.

The magnetotail of the Earth

The deflection of the solar wind into a long tail down behind the Earth does not mean the end of its influence on the latter. Tremendous forces are released behind the Earth when the plasma shock waves of enhanced solar wind arrive there. Fig 1.05a shows the situation in the magnetotail in quiet undisturbed conditions. Far down tail behind the Earth, a neutral point is established in the magnetic field, and earthwards of this point a relatively stable situation prevails with a quiet magnetic field containing a long thin central plasma sheet.

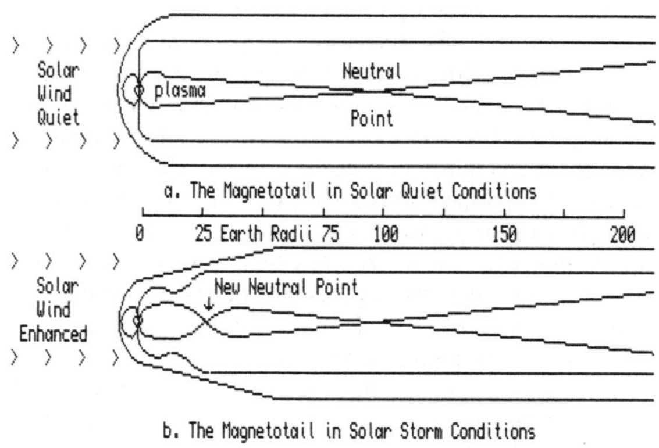

Fig 1.05: Solar storm induced changes in the Earth's magnetotail

Fig 1.05b shows the violent changes which occur when the enhanced solar wind storm hits the magnetosphere and overflows it into the magnetotail. There is a sudden explosive rearrangement of the magnetic field in the tail. The previously quiet plasma sheet down the centre line of the tail now finds itself cut into two separate sections either side of a new neutral point.

There was a tremendous amount of energy stored up in

the old quiet tail. Rearrangement of the magnetic field releases that energy, concentrating tremendous forces on the plasma in the tail. Some of this energy is used up firing the plasma now located beyond the new neutral point, further down tail at high speed. Meanwhile the plasma caught on the Earth side of the new neutral point is violently propelled up tail, back at the Earth. Guided by the Earth's magnetic field it comes in over the poles causing a tremendous magnetic storm. It takes three or four hours to reload this magnetic gun. So if the solar wind storm lasts more than four hours, the whole process is repeated.

Much of the information in the preceding paragraphs was obtained when the International Comet Explorer (ICE) space probe was using gravity-assisted manoeuvres to give it the correct trajectory and speed to take it to a rendezvous with Comet Giacobini Zinner. During these manoeuvres ICE made several high speed dashes down the magnetotail, swinging around the Earth and Moon at each end of its slingshot track. This gave it the high speed necessary to ride with the plasma of magnetic storms which coincided with its passage. There is as yet no clear consensus as to exactly how the magnetotail plasma is accelerated. Several explanations are currently available. One thing is sure, the magnetotail with its high-speed plasma is a very disturbed area. Several important communications paths cross the magnetotail at different times. Among these the EME path looks particularly vulnerable to propagation disturbance.

Plasma in deep space

The Pioneer and Voyager space probes have sent back a clear picture of the solar system out as far as Neptune. It reveals a situation very much like that around the Earth, although some of the activity is on a much bigger scale, commensurate with the large size of the gas giant planets.

Jupiter has a much bigger magnetosphere than the Earth, and its magnetotail extends at least as far as the next planet out, Saturn. In addition the curious volcanic moon of Jupiter, known as Io, produces so much debris in Io-Jupiter space that it forms a torus. The bridge of material between Jupiter and Io acts as a giant flux tube, carrying enormous current, and the density of charged material is sufficient to produce strong radio signals in the band 16 to 20MHz.

Saturn too has a long magnetotail, even though the solar wind has become far less dense by the time it has spread out to Saturn's orbit. Uranus has a strange offset magnetic field which, coupled with its spin axis pointing at the Sun, produces curious ionospheric conditions. Neptune has a weaker magnetic field than the Earth. The field is tilted at an angle and does not originate from the centre of the planet but a point near its magnetic south pole.

We are likely to remain ignorant of conditions at distant Pluto for several more decades. The Pioneer and Voyager probes will be continuing on out through the solar system. So far they are telling us that it is simply a question of the solar wind getting weaker and weaker with distance.

Long before the solar wind has faded away it is expected to collide with the general movement of plasma in our galaxy. This boundary should be marked by a plasma radio signal. Indeed the plasma receivers aboard the two Voyager space probes did detect signals at about 2kHz during 1984. There is, however, no evidence as yet that this means they are hearing the heliopause boundary.

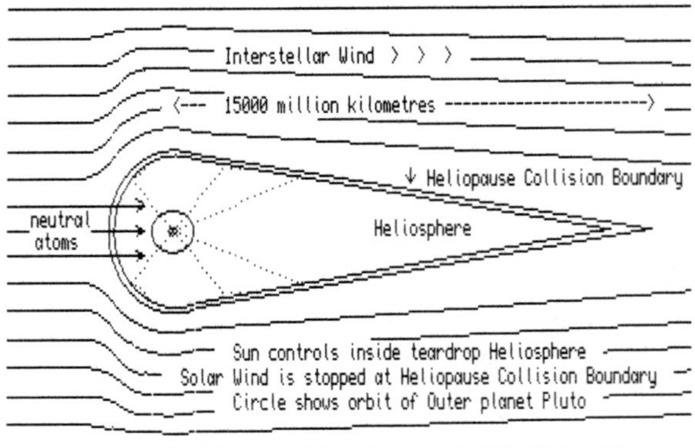

Fig 1.06: Collision of interstellar and solar winds creates the heliosphere

The heliopause is the collision zone of the solar and galactic winds. The 2kHz plasma signal that the Voyagers heard is at about the expected electron density/frequency anticipated in the collision zone, but there is also the possibility that what the Voyagers heard has another source. Eventually all four Pioneers and Voyagers should cross the heliopause boundary, and long before they do, if we can still hear their transmissions, we should have heard the increasing signal as they approach the collision point.

Other evidence from these spacecraft and the related Mariner spacecraft indicates that the whole solar system is bathed in a galactic stream of plasma. Composed of hydrogen and helium it is coming from the constellation of Centaurus and, after passing the Earth, is heading for the constellation of Cassiopeia. This stream of plasma is thought to drag out the heliopause into a long tear-drop, the same shape as our Earth's magnetosphere, but many million times larger. It seems that this most distant plasma we have found in our local area is the result of a stellar explosion somewhere in Centaurus or Ophiucus, one to ten million years ago, but this is sheer speculation. We must wait for quite a few decades before we can sort out what we have already found. Given that we could build remote-reporting plasma receivers and park them in space, there is no reason why radio amateurs should not participate in these exploratory studies.

The ionosphere

Every radio transmission from space must come down through the Earth's ionosphere, the zones of ionised plasma in the Earth's upper atmosphere. In this transit of the ionosphere the signal will suffer attenuation, scintillation, scattering, Faraday rotation of its plane of polarisation, and at times it will be reflected back into space.

Signals from the ionosphere or up above it can tell us a great deal about it. Satellites can be extremely valuable tools for understanding how and why the ionosphere behaves as it does, and the information we get from them can be used to optimise both satellite communications and use of ionospheric shortwave propagation for terrestrial communications.

The formation of the ionosphere

The atmosphere surrounding the Earth consists principally of two gases, oxygen and nitrogen, plus their various compounds. In addition there are much smaller amounts of hydrogen, helium and several other gases.

The undisturbed molecules and atoms of these gases are electrically neutral, but the atmosphere is never undisturbed. Ultra-violet radiation from the Sun bombards it by day, and cosmic and gamma radiation contribute a smaller bombardment throughout the day and night.

This continuous bombardment of high-energy radiation and particles from space seriously disturbs the ionosphere. The input of solar ultra-violet is sufficient to keep the daylight ionosphere continuously ionised; the UV strips electrons from atoms, allowing the electrons to go free, leaving behind positively charged ions formed from the now depleted atoms. Some of these positive ions will rapidly find electrons and combine with them, thus reverting to their electrically neutral state, but the solar UV is intense enough to maintain a high level of ions despite recombination and neutralisation. This excess of ions differs from zone to zone. Where the ionosphere is thin, ionised particles find it difficult to locate particles of opposite charge, so recombination is slow. Where the density of atoms or molecules is high, as it is in the lower levels of the ionosphere, finding a particle of the opposite polarity is easy, so recombination is swift and the overall excess of ions available at any time is reduced.

This physical arrangement of the ionosphere into zones of high and low ionisation is further aided by gravity. Heavy molecules do not reach the same altitude as atoms. Lighter atoms are found at higher altitude than heavy atoms and, given this vertical structuring, the bombarding UV produces ionised zones at various levels, depending on how far and with what intensity it penetrates through to a particular level and what it finds there in way of atmospheric composition at that height.

The end result of these factors working together is the production of zones of peak ionisation at various heights above the Earth. These zones are not usually sharply defined layers. There are generally no abrupt changes. Zones of ionisation grade into one another gradually. The positions of the zones and the state of individual zones is constantly changing and there is considerable movement vertically of the locations of peak ionisation.

In the plane tangential to the Earth there is much more irregularity. Stable structures rarely exist for more than a few hundred kilometres, and at times discrete horizontal structures can have dimensions of tens of kilometres only. Junctions between these platelets can show sharp gradients and individual regions can, horizontally, be very disturbed and turbulent.

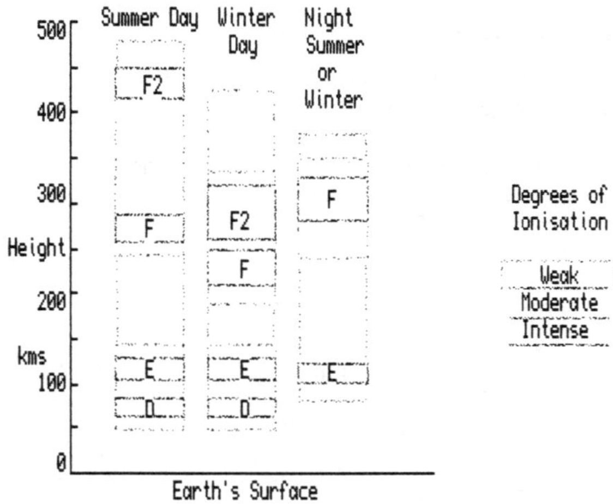

Fig 1.07: Daily and seasonal variations in the ionosphere

Fig 1.07 shows the broad distribution of the various ionised zones at different times of day and at different seasons of the year. The term 'layers' has been avoided in this description because it suggests sudden changes in vertical composition and ionisation. 'Zones' is a better word to describe the vertical differentiation of the ionosphere, because it suggests gradual change. Hereafter, however, the various zones of the ionosphere will be called layers because despite its inaccuracy it is the one most radio users are familiar with. Provided readers accept that layers are not sudden changes, like cream to cake to cream, no great harm will be done.

The D Layer

This layer forms during daylight around a central zone height of about 60 to 70km. Its ionisation is normally quite weak, because recombination is rapid at this height. At rare intervals it is subject to enormously enhanced UV input during SIDs. The UV and gamma ray output of these solar flares penetrates right down to the D layer and ionises it very heavily, so that for minutes or hours, depending on the duration of the flare storm, no HF propagation via the daylight ionosphere is possible.

At normal times the low ionisation of the D layer is incapable of propagating signals of frequency higher than about 400kHz. So it makes no normal useful contribution to HF ionospheric propagation. It does, however, have a negative effect on HF propagation, in that every time an HF signal transits the ionised D layer some of the signal energy is absorbed. At times therefore the D layer is a nuisance, sometimes restricting long-distance, low-frequency communications, eg 1.8MHz, which it confines to the sunset/ sunrise periods when the D layer is not sunlit and hence not ionised, but the much higher layers still in sunlight can propagate signals.

The E Layer

Next above the D layer, and a simple continuation from it, rather than a totally separate region, the E layer extends from about 90 to 125km altitude.

The E layer is more intensely ionised than the D. But none the less it is rarely able to support propagation of frequencies above 2 or 3MHz. It does, however, absorb energy from signals passing through it and its effects must therefore be considered when assessing HF propagation at any shortwave frequency.

The E layer above temperate latitudes is often subject to sporadic episodes of ionisation we call 'sporadic E' (SpE). This temporary enhancement of the E layer ionisation is local rather than general, and it displays markedly seasonal characteristics. Each temperate latitude zone north and south of the equator has a period of many days of strong E layer enhancement in the local summer, and a much shorter period of a few days of increased E layer enhancement in the local winter season. Propagation at these times can on rare days extend up to 144MHz, but only about one SpE event in 50 reaches this level, resulting in perhaps three or four events of this type each year at any given locality. On the other 150 days a year when some sporadic E enhancement of E layer ionisation is present, it is rarely capable of supporting propagation of frequency much above 50MHz. It can and does provide a useful propagation path for HF frequencies (particularly 28MHz), albeit restricted to about 2,500km extreme maximum range, because of the relatively low altitude (about 100km) of the refracting E propagating zone.

Both polar aurora and meteor scatter propagation centre around the E layer, with both these agencies capable of anomalous propagation of frequencies up to 400MHz. Peak performance in both these modes occurs around 50MHz.

Like the D layer, the E layer takes no positive roll in normal HF ionospheric propagation, but again like the D layer it has a negative role. The E layer absorbs energy from any signal going through it, either up or down. So, in company with the D layer, propagation, particularly at the lower HF frequencies (3,500kHz and 1,800kHz), is often restricted to the sunset/sunrise terminator line where the E layer is not ionised and cannot therefore attenuate signals going through it.

The F Layer

This is the region of the ionosphere most concerned with HF radio wave propagation. It is subject to daily changes, being strongest under the noon and early afternoon Sun. It does not completely disappear when it loses the Sun at night. During the night incoming cosmic radiation and gamma radiation is sufficient to maintain a low but useful level of ionisation.

The F layer follows straight on from the top of the E layer, gradually increasing in ion density up to a peak ionisation zone at about 300km, above which it declines in density, disappearing at about 350km at night. By day the height and vertical extent of the F layer is highly variable. On winter days peak ionisation at 300km is supplemented by a second peak ionisation zone at about 250km altitude. In summer the motion is reversed; the main zone of ionisation is around 300km but it has no lower sub-peak. Instead it has a much extended dense zone of ionisation going all the way up to a secondary peak at about 450km.

The pattern of F layer ionisation is an immensely complex one. In addition to the seasonal summer/winter variations, the sunspot cycle also has a marked effect. Indeed there is good evidence from satellites that the upper ionosphere at solar cycle peak is not Earth-derived at all, but hydrogen temporarily captured from the solar wind.

Propagation via the F layer is a subject we do not fully understand, but our knowledge is improving now that we are able to probe it with satellites which either observe from above or actually fly in the F layer.

Propagation via the ionosphere

All this discussion regarding the ionosphere would have little merit but for one thing. The Earth is a sphere, and in order to communicate by radio over large distances, we must bend signals around it.

The ionosphere is effectively a series of zones above the Earth's surface in which radio waves travel at speeds different from those they achieve in the neutral part of the atmosphere. Where there is a change of speed as a new zone is entered, there is bending of the wave front. Provided the correct frequency for the signal is used, the ionosphere will bend the signal back to Earth again.

When a radio signal enters an ionised medium, depending on the degree of ionisation, the part of the wave front which enters the medium first gets ahead of the rest still travelling slowly in the un-ionised medium. If the wave front encounters increasing ionisation, it goes faster still and bends further. With the appropriate density gradient in the ionised medium, the direction of propagation of the wave front can be redirected, slightly if the ion density gradient is slight, or totally reversed back on itself if the ion density gradient it encounters is big enough. The lower the signal frequency the more it turns.

Fig 1.08 shows how this bending occurs. The ionosphere is most useful at the shortwave frequencies, because it has just the right conditions to propagate them around the globe. Frequencies below the shortwave are bent so much in the ionosphere that they come almost straight back to Earth and propagate nowhere. Frequencies above shortwave are bent as they go through the ionosphere but this bending is slight

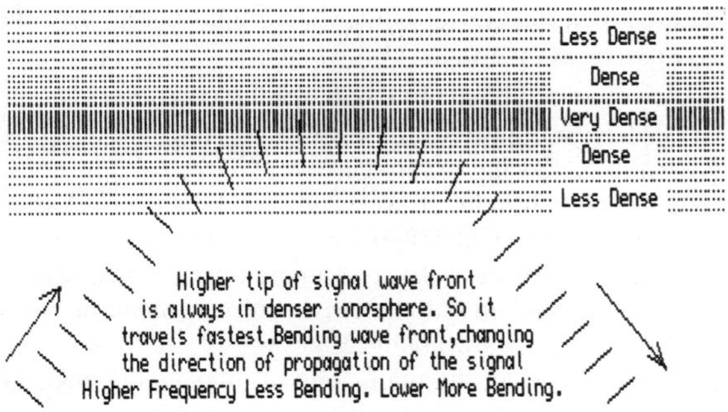

Fig 1.08: Ionospheric bending of radio signals

and is by no means sufficient to bring them back to Earth. So they carry on into space.

Probing the ionosphere

To efficiently utilise the ionosphere for communications, we must be able to predict and explain its general patterns. One of the first really useful tools for ionospheric research was the ionosonde. As Fig 1.09 shows, it allows us to examine the ionosphere directly above. We can measure the highest frequencies reflected by each of the D, E and F layers in turn, and use this data to estimate how the ionosphere will behave when we project a low-incidence oblique transmission at it.

The trouble with the ionosonde is that it is not really using the ionosphere in the way we want to use it for propagation. We do not want reflection of our signal; we want to propagate it forwards towards our distant target station, rather than back to us. For really long-distance communication we are interested in hitting the ionosphere as far away from us as possible. It is not the ionosphere over the UK we are interested in if we want to talk to Nigeria – we want to hit the ionosphere with our signal as far south as possible over, say, Gibraltar. So the ionosonde has been superseded by the oblique-incidence ionosonde.

The oblique incidence ionosonde is a useful tool, but it still suffers from the enormous defect that it relies on reflection, whereas the would-be HF communicator is looking for data on how a signal will be propagated forwards, not backwards. As Fig 1.10 shows, the true scale drawing of the relationship between the 6,380km radius Earth and its 330km ionosphere illustrates just how thin the ionospheric channel is. Efficient communication by HF propagation is a matter of forward propagation along the ionospheric channel, via the least number of bends/refractions, plus the least number of absorbing daylight transits (up or down) of the E and D layers. In order to predict what propagation we can expect, we need to know the forward propagation capability of the ionosphere at or near our horizon. For a station in Scotland wanting to put an HF signal into Africa, the ionosphere above southern Spain and Gibraltar is the problem. What is the maximum usable frequency (MUF) for forward propagation which will be supported by the ionosphere over that target region? A station in southern England will, by contrast, be interested in a region 600km further south.

There is only one way we can get this data. Unless someone is transmitting back along the path we want to use, we must use a satellite to check the path for us. Any satellite able to illuminate the underside of the ionosphere over this Spain-to-north Africa region will do. It would be nice if the satellite just flew down the signal path line at a height of about 330km, but this is not essential. Even if the satellite passes far to the south, as long as its radio signal gets to the underside of the ionosphere in the region of interest, we will know that forward communication at the satellite's beacon frequency is possible.

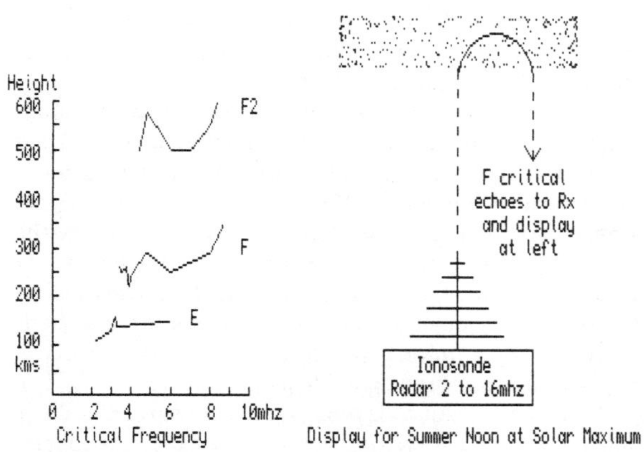

Fig 1.09: Ionosonde – vertical propagation radar

Maximum usable frequency

Using oblique-incidence ionosondes, it is possible to explore from the home location those places in the ionosphere roughly 1,500km away, where it is necessary to send our radio signals, so that they will be propagated by refraction/bending around the curvature of the Earth.

Before oblique-incidence probing was available, it was common practice to estimate the highest frequency the ionosphere would bend back to Earth by assuming it would be about three times the vertical incidence critical frequency found by an ordinary upward-looking ionosonde. This frequency was then referred to as the 'maximum usable frequency', or MUF for short.

The geometry of this situation is shown in Fig 1.10, where the low-incident-angle signal from Scotland reaches the F layer of the ionosphere over southern Spain. If the ionosphere at that point is dense enough, the signal will be forward refracted onwards and downwards to terrestrial stations deep in Africa.

A typical prediction chart based on ionosonde data is shown at Fig 1.11. The home station for this prediction is in Scotland, while the target station is at maximum single-refraction range in the Canary Islands, off the west coast of Africa. The halfway point in the ionosphere is just west of southern Spain as shown in Fig 1.10. This prediction is based on a computer program which stores data from ionosondes around the world, including this southern Spanish location. The chart produced from this data shows how the MUF at this halfway point, and hence the path from Scotland to the Canary Islands, varies with time of day.

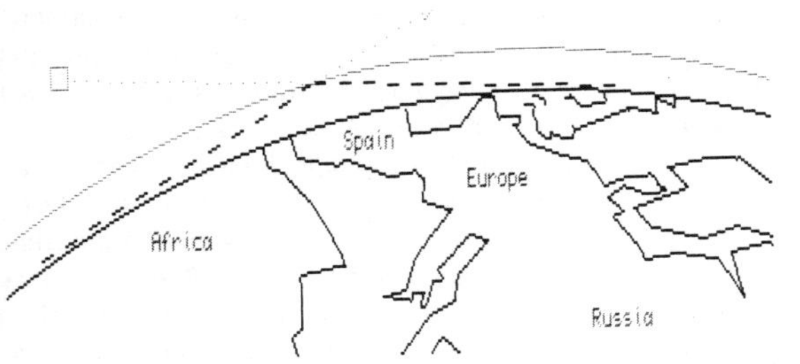

Fig 1.10: MUF via oblique incidence HF propagation

The chart used in Fig 1.11 is marked out in four-hour sections. Every hour the maximum usable frequency predicted is indicated by a circle, eg at 0000 UTC the MUF is just a little under 10MHz. So the ionosphere is predicted as having a critical frequency of about 10/3 = 3.3MHz, which should forward propagate a low-incident-angle signal if its frequency is less than 10MHz. The optimum frequency for best chance of communication is on or just below the predicted MUF.

At 1200 UTC the MUF is predicted as 21MHz, indicating an anticipated critical frequency of about 7MHz at the appropriate spot in the ionosphere. As solar radiation diminishes in the afternoon the MUF gradually drops back to the night-time low around 10MHz.

We can use this sort of data to predict how propagation to terrestrial stations will vary, and we can also use it to estimate likely propagation from HF satellites. We can similarly reverse the situation by listening to HF satellites, monitoring propagation of their signals, and then using this

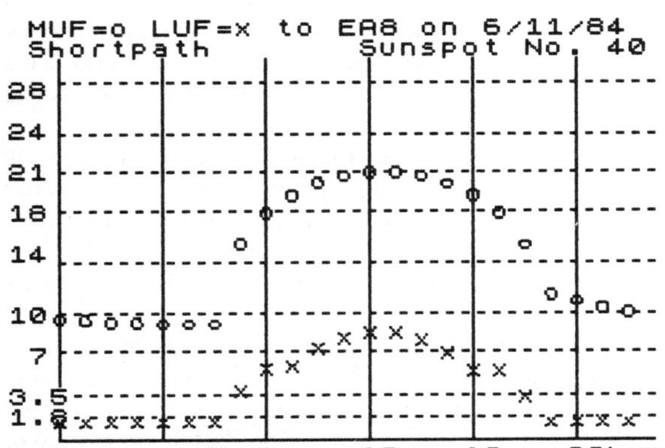

Fig 1.11: Maximum usable frequency prediction

data to predict terrestrial ionospheric propagation. There are five major points we can check and test:

(i) Is a signal from Scotland propagated to the Canary Islands as the prediction says at 1200 UTC on 21MHz?

(ii) Do signals below 21MHz get less far – are they bent more in the ionosphere?

(iii) Can a satellite in the ionosphere over southern Spain put a good signal at 21MHz into Scotland at 1200 UTC?

(iv) Can a satellite in the ionosphere well south of Spain illuminate the underside of the Spanish ionosphere and be propagated to Scotland? To be forward propagated to Scotland the satellite transmission must not be higher in frequency than the MUF over Spain, eg we would not expect a 19MHz satellite over Africa to be heard in Scotland at night, but it would be propagated to Scotland as soon as the MUF over Spain reached 19MHz.

(v) The situation for a satellite above the ionosphere is quite different. As Fig 1.10 suggests, if the Spanish ionosphere supports 21MHz propagation to the Canary Islands off its underside, its topside will send a 21MHz signal from a satellite arriving with similar incidence back into space.

Using a combination of predictions and signals heard, from both satellites and terrestrial stations, an experienced operator should be able to check his data against statements (i) to (v) above and arrive at a good appreciation of the real-time state of the ionosphere.

Terrestrial and satellite HF propagation

Before going on to describe the interaction between satellites and the ionosphere, a description of how the ionosphere propagates terrestrial signals is necessary. Fig 1.11 applies only to a specific signal path at a specific date and a specific sunspot number. Figs 1.12, 1.13 and 1.14 show diagrammatic side views of the simplest paths that a signal can take in the Earth-ionosphere signal channel.

Fig 1.12 shows the geometry for the part of the ionosphere above the transmitting station horizon. Points 3 and 3a on this diagram represent the station horizon in the ionosphere. This is not the coverage of the groundwave signal from station A. The so-called groundwave zone around the station is much more restricted than this. The actual extent of the groundwave is determined by the frequency used – the lower the frequency the further the extent of the groundwave coverage. Groundwave coverage is also governed by signal power transmitted and local geography.

To reach a station beyond its groundwave, the radio signal must be assisted by refraction in the ionosphere. Signal frequency must be adjusted to match the almost

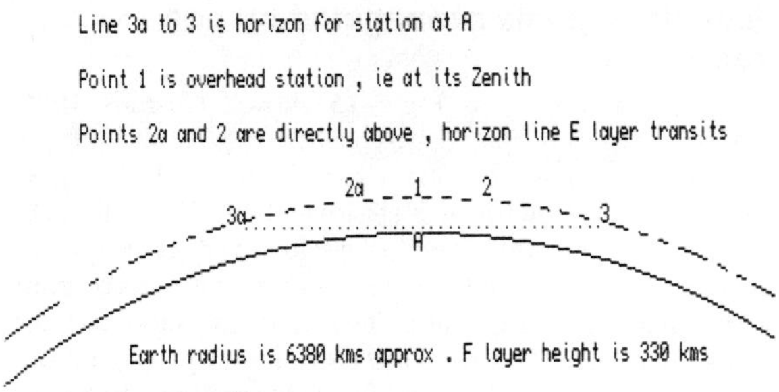

Fig 1.12: Earth and ionosphere – scale diagram

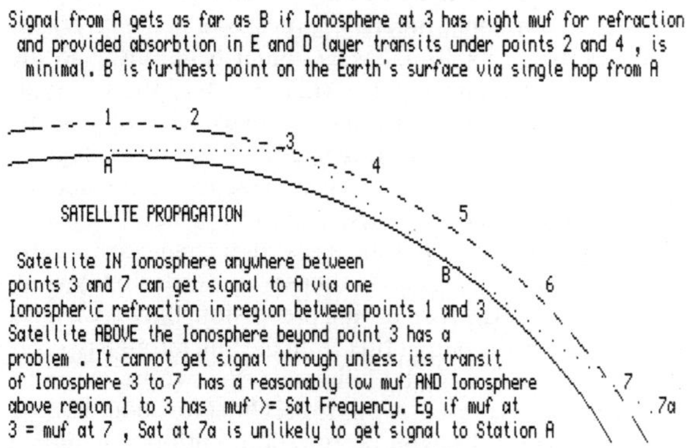

Fig 1.13: Earth and ionosphere – single-hop propagation

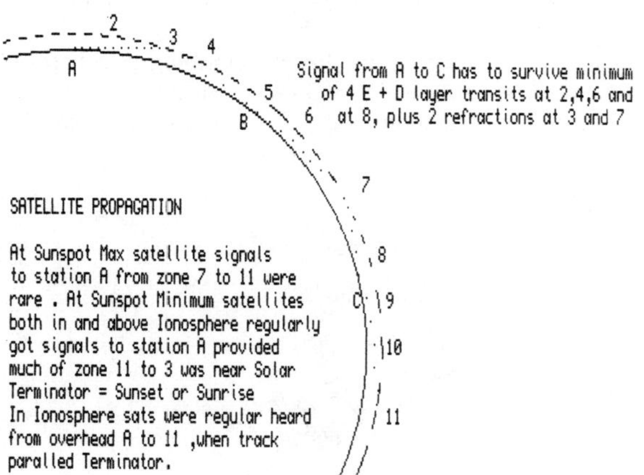

Fig 1.14: Earth and ionosphere – double-hop propagation

hourly changes of the ionosphere in order to ensure that the terrestrial signal is quickly bent back to a nearby station by using a low frequency, or, by using a higher frequency, be propagated somewhat further from the transmitter. The transmitted frequency should not greatly exceed the MUF but should be as high as possible, noting that for maximum efficiency no more than one refraction is desirable.

The new situation presented by the signal propagating beyond point 3 is shown in Fig 1.13. Station B is the furthest point that can be reached from station A via one forward refraction in the ionosphere.

If the signal is strong enough, it can of course go beyond point B, but it is now out of reach of the ground again, heading for another junction with the ionosphere somewhere near point 7. Provided the ionosphere is dense enough to refract a signal at that frequency, it can be forward refracted still further towards station C. Stations intermediate between B and C must use at least two refractions to get signals to and from station A.

Please note two important points about this simplified description of propagation paths. First, the MUF over places remote from station A is probably quite different from that at station A, and the MUFs at two separate refraction points thousands of kilometres apart are also likely to be very different one from another. This means that the lower of the two values of MUF at these points is the one which must be used.

The second important point concerns the signal ray path tracing. We must not forget the effects of the D and E layers. Each time the signal goes up to the F layer or down from it, it has to transit these layers. In daylight these transits subject the signal to absorption losses, which can be very important and cumulative on long signal paths with a lot of E and D layer transits occurring during local daylight when these layers are ionised.

HF satellite propagation

Satellites quoted in these paragraphs have the following characteristics:

Satellite	Operational	Height (km)	Frequency (MHz)	Remarks
Cosmos 1686	1985-1986	330	19.955	good solar min
Iskra 2 + 3	1982	340	29.577	end solar max
Salyut Cosmos	1986-1987	480	19.955	just above F
Radiosports	1981-1987	1,690	29.502	high above F

As these details show, these satellites had a wide range of characteristics. They transmitted on different frequencies, orbited at different heights, and operated at different times with respect to the sunspot cycle. For convenience their performance will be reported in four blocks:

(i) When they were above the station horizon.
(ii) When they were sub-horizon, propagating via one ionospheric refraction.
(iii) When sub-horizon propagating by two refractions.
(iv) When sub-horizon beyond the two refraction zone.

Satellites above the receiving station horizon

At sunspot minimum, as Fig 1.15 for Cosmos 1686 orbiting in the ionosphere shows, there was typical complete uninterrupted day and night reception when above the station

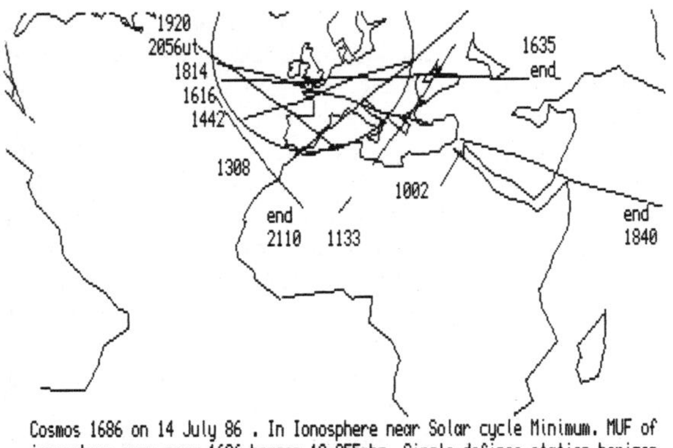

Fig 1.15: Propagation of Cosmos 1686 beacon on 14 July 1986

horizon. There was some reduction in signal strength when the satellite was at low elevation but this was not great.

The situation for a satellite orbiting above the ionosphere at this time was similar to the above. Salyut Cosmos at 480km and Radiosports 1 to 8 have given good signal reception whenever they were above the ground station horizon, both by day and by night.

At sunspot maximum, Fig 1.16 for the Iskra satellites shows a very different situation compared with cycle minimum. Although Iskra came above the UK horizon five times each day, its signal was not heard on three of these passes, and it was heard only part of the time on the other two passes. All Iskra passes were in daylight. The Iskra satellites did not survive long enough to make night-time passes.

The Radiosport satellites orbiting far above the ionosphere shortly after solar cycle maximum were not as badly attenuated as Iskra. None the less their daylight overhead UK orbits rarely if ever produced communications quality signals. The night-time orbits by the Radiosport satellites just after solar maximum were by contrast very useful, giving signals of reasonable communications quality.

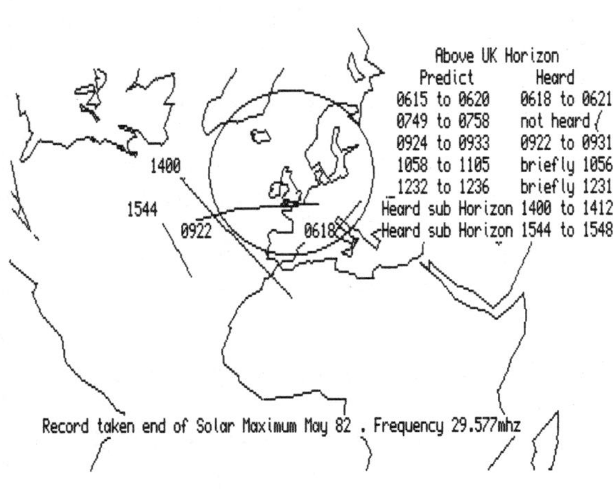

Fig 1.16: Reception map of Iskra 2 from British Isles

Satellite signals propagated by one refraction

At solar minimum, as Fig 1.15 shows, Cosmos 1686, orbiting in the ionosphere, was heard in the UK on some but not all days via one ionospheric refraction of its 19.955MHz signal when the satellite was at a lower latitude than the UK. Cosmos 1686 was restricted to these lower latitudes by its 50 degree inclination orbit, so it was not possible to check its performance from high latitudes but, given its low-latitude tracks, at least every other day it encountered propagation to the UK which made full use of one ionospheric refraction.

The two groups of satellites orbiting above the ionosphere behaved quite differently at solar minimum in this one refraction zone. Salyut Cosmos was actively propagated at times, its 19.955MHz signal being close to the average mid-latitude daytime MUF. Fig 1.17 shows a typical 60-day sequence for Salyut Cosmos, noting that the precession of the orbit of this satellite is about six degrees per day relative to the Sun, so that in 60 days it covered the full range of one day's local Sun time at a particular locality. This had the effect of putting its ascending and descending orbits into sunset and sunrise zones which drift slowly west.

In addition to its own orbital precession, Salyut Cosmos was looking at the output flux from the Sun through two 27-day solar rotations. Fig 1.17 illustrates the two effects of the Sun which were present at this time. Quiet for about 12 days with limited sub-horizon propagation, until the disturbed face of the Sun came around, at which point the enhanced solar output was visible in the records. Then, after 10 or 12 active days, back to the quiet Sun with little sub-horizon propagation.

As Fig 1.17 shows, solar flux was climbing quickly from 1 October onwards, and this too was reflected in increased single-hop propagation of the Salyut Cosmos signal. By

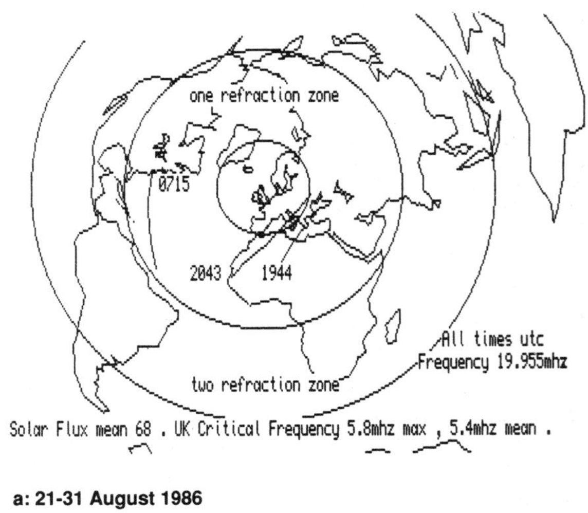

a: 21-31 August 1986

Fig 1.17a-g (above and on opposite page): Sixty-day sub-horizon reception sequence for Salyut Cosmos 19.955MHz signals during solar minimum. The spacecraft was flying at a height of 480km. All times are in UTC

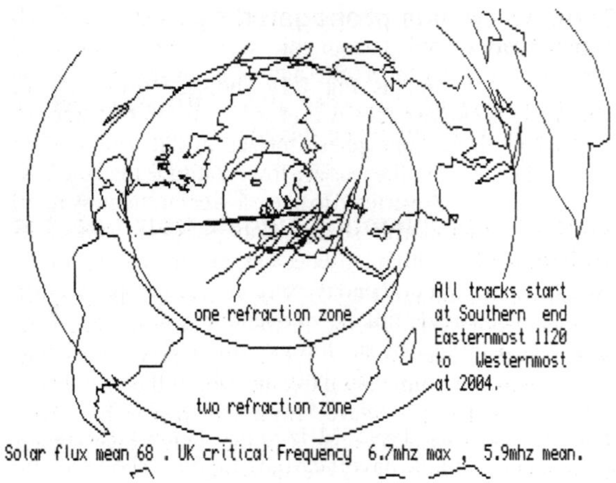

b: 1-10 September 1986

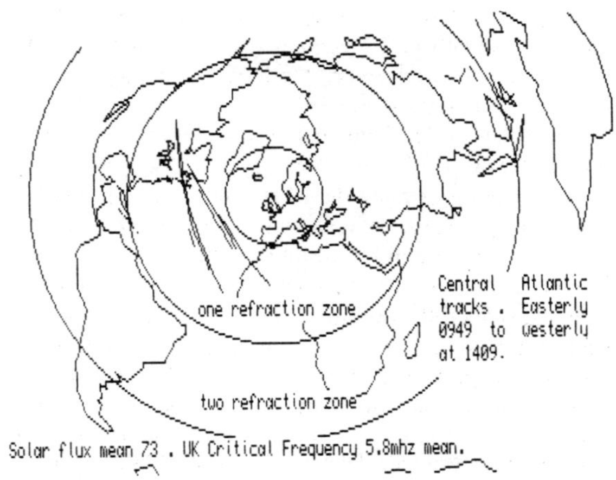

e: 1-10 October 1986

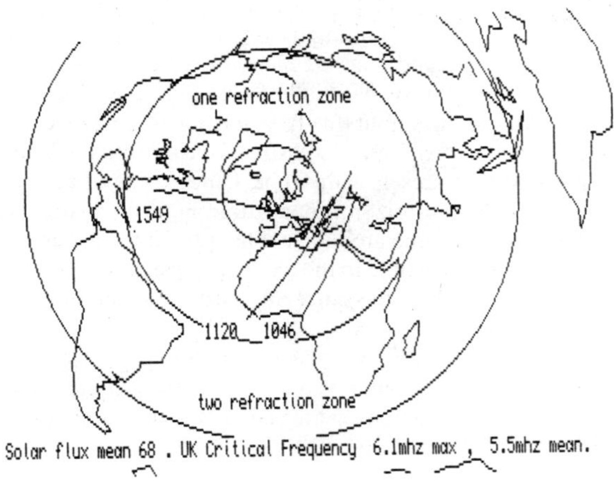

c: 11-20 September 1986

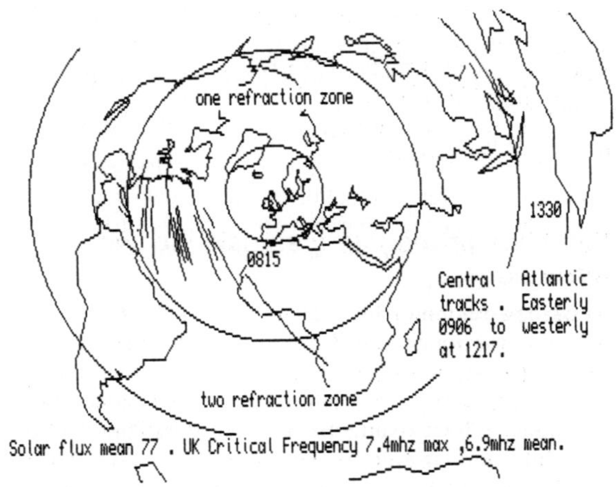

f: 11-20 October 1986

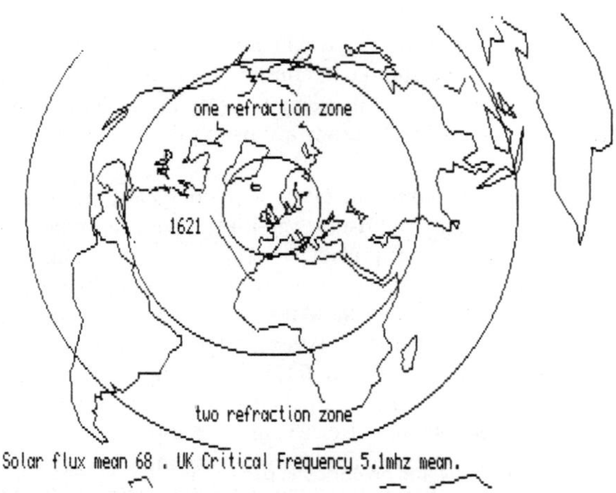

d: 21-30 September 1986

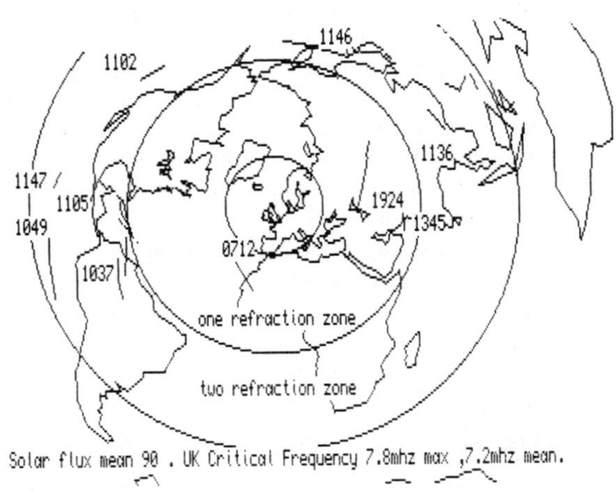

g: 21-31 October 1986

contrast with Salyut Cosmos propagation at 19.955MHz, there was virtually no F layer propagation of the 29.502MHz signals from the Radiosport satellites. Exactly as expected, the F layer did not support 29MHz propagation at this part of the solar cycle. Two incidents featuring sporadic E propagation of RS7 were noted.

At sunspot maximum the Iskra satellites were heard by single-hop propagation, as shown in Fig 1.16. The short life spans of these satellites resulted in their records being limited to their afternoon passages southwest of the UK.

In the years following solar cycle maximum, the Radiosport series of satellites orbiting above the ionosphere produced results like those of Salyut Cosmos at solar minimum as that satellite found the MUF of the ionosphere beneath it becoming less than its beacon frequency in the late afternoon towards the end of October 1986: Fig 1.17g refers.

In the years following solar cycle maximum, signals came in to the UK via sub-horizon propagation from RS satellites from scattered spots all around the world, but only in two or three minute bursts, just as the Salyut Cosmos signals did in late October 1986. Clearly, initial penetration of the ionosphere from above, before underside ionospheric propagation can commence, is the important feature for both these situations.

Satellites propagating signals via two refractions

At sunspot minimum, Fig 1.18 for Cosmos 1686 shows the typical sunset zone results from ranges out to the full extent sustainable by two ionospheric refractions from a signal source high (with a long viewpoint) above the ionosphere. In summer 1986, two afternoons out of three featured Cosmos 1686 propagation via two refractions, over an arc which shifted westward with satellite orbital precession, from the Indian Ocean east of Madagascar clockwise to South America.

Salyut Cosmos just above the ionosphere gives a quite different picture from this two-refraction zone. As Fig 1.17g shows, signals come from a wide arc at about 8,000km range in one or two minute bursts starting on the dawn or night side of the world. Again, ease of initial downward penetration of the night-time ionosphere appears to be the factor controlling whether propagation is possible, or is not, from this two-refraction zone.

It is of note that signals have a habit of appearing from over the same parts of the world repeatedly. The Hokkaido to Kamkatchka region and the region of the Pacific from California down to Peru are regular sources of two-refraction zone propagation observed over several years. These records apply to the Salyut Cosmos 19.955MHz beacon, but it is noteworthy that the only two records of propagation from this zone over this same period from the 29.502MHz Radiosport RS7 were both received whilst it was over Hokkaido in northern Japan.

At solar maximum no propagation of the Iskra 29.57MHz signals was recorded from this second refraction zone. Unfortunately, so far as the author is aware, no-one has reported checking Radiosport 29.502MHz signals in this zone in the years following solar maximum.

Satellites propagating signals from near the antipodes

At sunspot minimum Fig 1.17f shows a typical reception incident from west of Perth, Australia. This type of incident was recorded seven times in 1986, from both Cosmos 1686 in the ionosphere and Salyut Cosmos above the ionosphere. All these incidents occurred from a strip stretching from Perth in the west to Tasmania in the east. None of these incidents actually reached the antipodes.

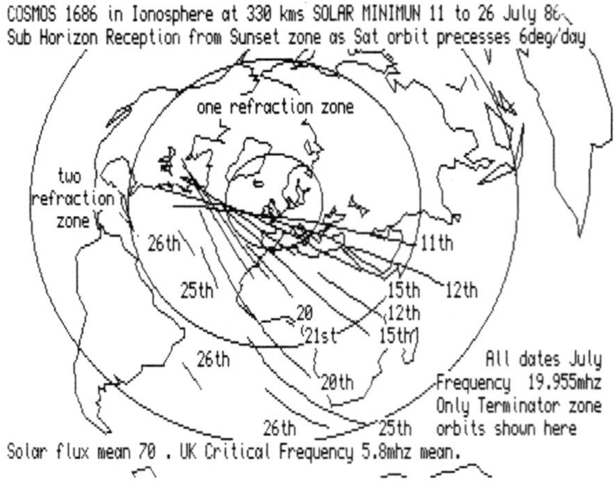

Fig 1.18: Ionospheric propagation of Cosmos 1686 at solar minimum

It is probably a coincidence that these incidents occurred as the satellite transmitted its 'furthest away from UK' point for that orbit, circa 128 degrees great circle. Only one Radiosport signal has been heard from this area at sunspot minimum.

At sunspot maximum Iskra was not heard from this distant zone. The Radiosport satellites have been reported as being heard 'antipodal' several years after sunspot maximum. None of these reports is detailed enough to allow a decision as to whether the satellite was actually antipodal as opposed to being in the Cosmos preferred strip west of the antipodes. Further to this point, there is ample data in late 1950s and 1960s IEEE journals, to substantiate reception reports of Sputnik and Oscar 5 signals antipodal.

This field of enquiry could prove very interesting as we go towards solar maximum, now that Radiosport 10/11 is in orbit.

The Doppler effect

Introduction

We all become familiar with the curious way that sound from a moving vehicle changes as the vehicle goes past us. Anyone riding on a vehicle has the impression that it is making the same steady sounds at constant frequency whenever the vehicle is moving steadily.

To a pedestrian standing beside the road, the sound from a passing vehicle appears to change in frequency in a very distinct way.

Both the vehicle driver and the pedestrian are correctly interpreting what they hear. We call this effect, where the sound appears to change to a detached observer as the vehicle speeds by, the 'Doppler effect'. Fig 1.19 examines this effect in detail.

In the situation shown in Fig 1.19a, the vehicle is stationary. So both the driver and the detached pedestrian hear the same vehicle sounds. In Fig 1.19b the vehicle is now moving towards the pedestrian, causing him to hear a higher frequency sound as the vehicle approaches, because the vehicle is in effect catching up on its own signal. The signal seems to be compressed, ie shorter in wavelength and therefore higher in frequency, as heard by the pedestrian.

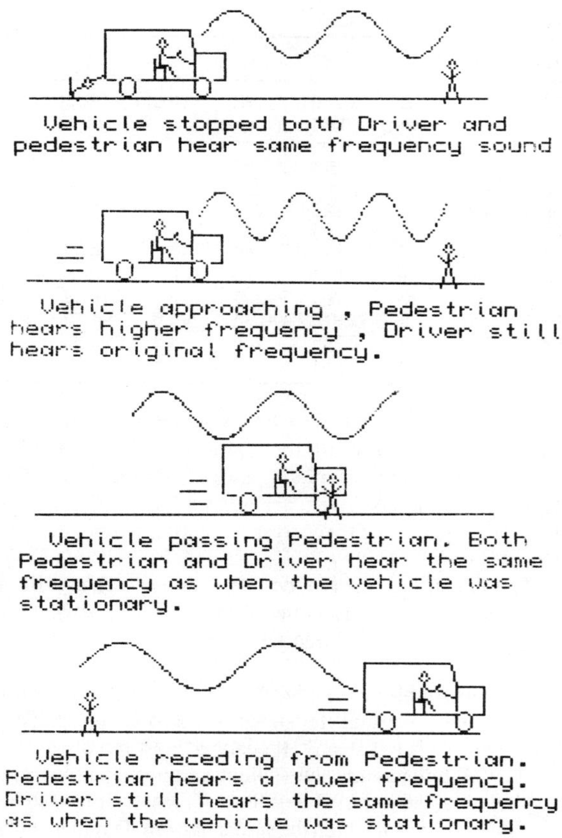

Fig 1.19a-d: Explanation of the Doppler effect

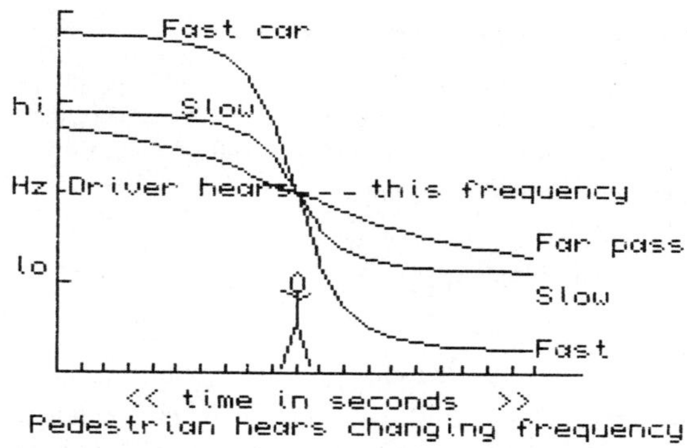

Fig 1.20: Graph showing changes in sound frequency experienced in the Doppler effect

The driver is not moving relative to the signal source, so he continues to hear the same original sound at a steady frequency.

The situation in Fig 1.19c shows that, at the exact moment of passing the pedestrian, the vehicle is no longer moving towards him. So the pedestrian hears the same frequency sound as the vehicle driver, because neither pedestrian nor driver has a velocity relative to the vehicle at that moment in time.

As Fig 1.19d shows, once the vehicle passes the pedestrian it is getting further away from him and so 'stretches' the sound, giving it a longer wavelength, and hence a lower frequency as heard by the pedestrian. Meanwhile the driver, still travelling at the same velocity as the sound generator, continues to hear the original frequency.

We can put all this information together onto Fig 1.20 and show that the frequency heard by the pedestrian alters in a peculiar way, whereby the slope of the changing curve of frequency is greatest as the vehicle passes. Before passing him the frequency is always higher than the actual sound the vehicle is producing. At the moment of passing, the pedestrian and the driver both hear the actual sound frequency the vehicle is producing; then after passing, the pedestrian hears a lower frequency than the driver.

If we make the vehicle do a second run at higher speed along the same course we see the same shape of frequency curve for what the pedestrian hears but it starts at a higher frequency and goes down to a lower frequency, producing the fast curve shown on Fig 1.20.

By contrast to the above, if we now alter the vehicle's route and make it pass further out from the pedestrian, the relative velocity of the vehicle with respect to the pedestrian is reduced, so we get a flatter Doppler curve. This effect is shown on Fig 1.20 as the far pass.

Satellite Dopplers – circular orbiters

Satellites sending radio signals can produce all these Doppler effects at the listening receiver. By monitoring Doppler changes we can get information about both the satellite's position from us, and the shape and timing of its orbit.

Practical satellite Doppler

To get an example of how Doppler shift affects the frequency of a signal from a satellite as it changes position and velocity, relative to your station, we can take an ordinary computer tracking program. This will normally tell us the latitude and longitude of the satellite's Earth sub-point. From this it is possible to calculate the slant range – ie the line-of sight-range from station to satellite.

If we have slant range at one minute intervals, the difference between each successive reading tells us how far the satellite has travelled towards or away from us in one minute. Dividing this dR range change by 60 seconds we can get the satellite's relative velocity in kilometres per second. Using equation 1.01 we can calculate the Doppler shift.

Please remember this Doppler shift is the average over one minute. So if you are going to graph plot it, say, for slant ranges taken at 0513 and 0514, the Doppler answer you get is for 0513:30.

Fig 1.21 shows a sequence of Uosat morning orbits coming in range of UK stations. Tables 1.01a, 1.01b and 1.01c list the times, azimuth bearings, elevation, slant range and range change per minute, satellite relative velocity and resulting Doppler shift in kilohertz, for each of the three orbits.

As shown by these tables, when an orbiting satellite is moving relative to a listening station that station hears the satellite signal at a different frequency from the one the satellite is actually transmitting. A receiver listening to a satellite moving towards it has to be tuned to a frequency higher than the transmitted original. Conversely, a receiver listening to a satellite moving away from it has to be tuned to a frequency below that of the transmitted original. The greater the relative velocity between satellite and station, the greater the Doppler shift of frequency.

The relationship between relative velocity and Doppler shift of frequency is given by the equation:

Doppler shift = Sat frequency * Rel velocity/speed of light [Eqn 1.01]

where Doppler shift is in kilohertz, satellite frequency is in kilohertz, relative velocity is in kilometres per second and

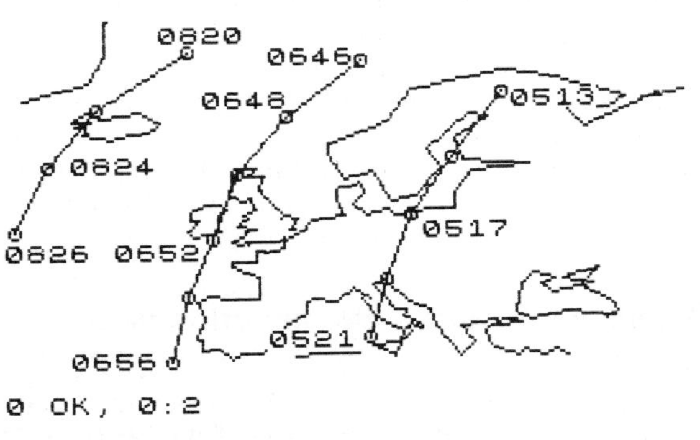

Fig 1.21: Sequence of Uosat morning orbits coming in range of UK stations

Table 1.01a-c: Uosat Doppler curves

Table 1.01a

UTC	Az (deg)	El (deg)	SlantR (km)	dR (km/min)	Velocity (km/s)	Shift (kHz)
0513	34	3	2,240	343	5.7	2.77
0514	43	6	1,928	312	5.2	2.52
0515	55	10	1,672	256	4.2	2.07
0516	70	13	1,497	175	2.9	1.41
0517	89	14	1,438	59	0.9	0.47
0518	107	12	1,507	–69	–1.2	–0.56
0519	122	9	1,688	–181	-3.1	–1.47
0520	134	6	1,951	–314	-5.3	-2.55
0521	142	2	2,265	–348	–5.8	–2.82

Table 1.01b

UTC	Az (deg)	El (deg)	SlantR (km)	dR (km/min)	Velocity (km/s)	Shift (kHz)
0646	12	3	2,174	428	7.1	3.46
0647	11	9	1,750	424	7.1	3.43
0648	10	16	1,334	416	6.9	3.37
0649	6	28	940	396	6.6	3.2
0650	354	51	619	321	5.4	2.6
0651	252	69	526	93	1.6	0.75
0652	212	38	752	226	–3.8	–1.84
0653	206	21	1,117	–365	–6.1	–2.96
0654	204	12	1,523	–406	–6.8	–3.29
0655	202	6	1,944	–421	–7	–3.42
0656	202	1	2,371	–427	–7.1	–3.46

Table 1.01c

UTC	Az (deg)	El (deg)	SlantR (km)	dR (km/min)	Velocity (km/s)	Shift (kHz)
0819	1	0	2,534	358	6	2.9
0820	353	3	2,206	328	5.5	2.65
0821	344	6	1,920	286	4.8	2.31
0822	331	9	1,703	217	3.6	1.75
0823	315	11	1,583	120	2	0.97
0824	298	11	1,583	0	0	0
0825	283	9	1,703	–120	–2	–0.98
0826	270	6	1,919	–216	–3.6	–1.75
0827	260	3	2,205	–286	–4.8	–2.32
0828	253	0	2,533	–328	–5.5	–2.66

the speed of light is taken as 300,000km per second. If the satellite is moving towards the station, the relative velocity has a positive value, if moving away from the station the relative velocity is given a negative value. The actual frequency heard by the receiver is satellite frequency plus Doppler shift.

This equation is used in the calculation of Tables 1.01a-c and this information is plotted as Fig 1.22. This set of orbit curves reveals several important points:

(i) In this simple circular orbit example, the Doppler shift is always causing the signal heard to decrease. This decrease is not steady. It changes most rapidly as the satellite is passing the station at the moment of zero relative velocity. This point of closest approach is taken as that at which the signal has zero Doppler shift, ie it equals the transmitted frequency. This assumption

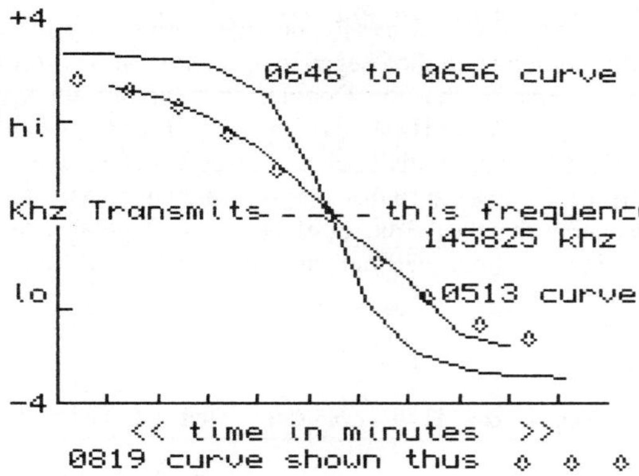

Fig 1.22: Uosat Doppler curves

is valid only in the simplest cases because it ignores the fact that the station is on a rotating Earth and therefore is itself moving relative to the satellite.

(ii) In practice, the continually decreasing received signal tells the operator that he is listening to a circular orbiter and, equally important, he is hearing it via the line-of-sight path (as opposed to anomalous propagation not by a line-of-sight path). Satellites in elliptical orbits have quite different Doppler curves.

(iii) Several authorities suggest that the operator can plot a Doppler curve and draw lines about its position of maximum slope by guessing the time at which the satellite made its closest approach. By calculating curve slope they then get a figure for slant range at closest approach. This procedure ignores several important practical considerations. In practice the slope of the Doppler curve cannot possibly be centrally balanced about time of closest approach; it simply is not symmetrically balanced with its top half reappearing as a mirror image in its bottom half. The curve is never symmetrical because Earth rotation can produce considerable modification and this modification is most unlikely to be balanced about point of closest approach. The examples in Fig 1.22 have been deliberately chosen because, although the 0819 orbit pass is almost a mirror image of the 0513 curve, it is not exactly so because Earth rotation contribution to the curves is quite different, as revealed by the fact that they do not overlap.

(iv) Experimenters wishing to use calculations of closest approach range are advised to use the Doppler rate method described later in this book, rather than the simple Doppler curves of the type used here.

(v) Experimenters should avoid, if possible, the temptation to tidy up and regularise or straighten Doppler curves. For example, any attempt to straighten up the centre section of the curve for the 0645 UTC pass would be ignoring the fact that, just before the point of closest approach, Earth rotation ceased to move the station towards the satellite and started to move it away from the latter.

(vi) It is most important that satellite users appreciate that when a satellite is moving towards a station with a relatively steady velocity, the Doppler shift is steady, so there is no apparent change of frequency. Examining Table 1.01b at 0645 to 0647, and again at 0655 to 0657, reveals this important but rarely mentioned feature of Doppler shift. At these two periods the satellite relative velocity was very steady so there was no shift of frequency. Only an observer who knew that the signal he was hearing was not the same as the one actually being transmitted by the satellite would be aware that it was moving. It had Doppler shift but this was temporarily steady so it had no Doppler rate. The Doppler frequency only changes when the satellite appears to accelerate or decelerate with respect to the ground station. This feature of Doppler becomes much more important when we go on to consider elliptical orbiters and deep space vehicles.

The elliptical orbit Doppler curve

The Doppler curve of an elliptical orbit satellite is much more complex than that of a circular orbiter. Elliptical orbiters do not go round their orbits at a steady speed. They go quickly near their perigee (orbit low point), then they slow down gradually so that they have almost no velocity relative to Earth by the time they reach their apogee (orbit high point). After a long period moving slowly around apogee, the elliptical orbiter builds up velocity, accelerating continuously as it falls back towards the Earth, so that at its perigee it is travelling at maximum velocity.

Fig 1.23: Satellite elliptical orbit. Satellites in elliptical orbits move quickly after perigee (lowest point of orbit), then gradually slow down as they rise toward apogee (highest point of orbit). They move very slowly through apogee then gradually speed up, so that by the time they have dropped back to perigee they are again moving quickly

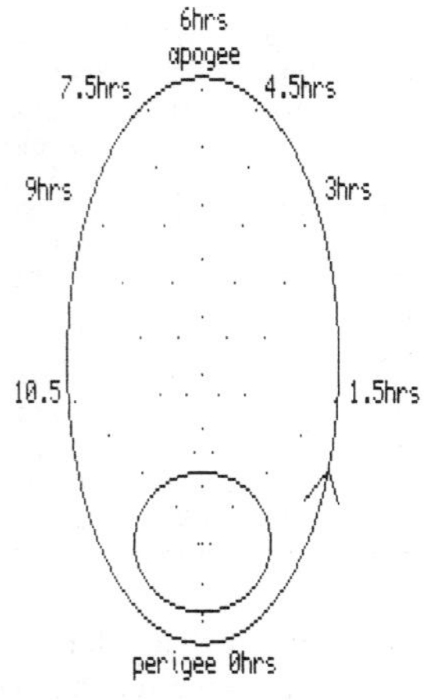

Satellite SRET 2 is in an elliptical orbit which takes it out to 40,000km above the Earth approximately once every twelve hours. Fig 1.23 illustrates the shape and scale of the orbit, and indicates the position of the satellite at one or two hourly intervals after perigee.

Table 1.02 gives a continuous track record of a typical SRET 2 orbit. This data is then plotted in Fig 1.24 to show a typical elliptical-orbit Doppler curve.

Table 1.02: Satellite Doppler – continuous record of a typical SRET 2 orbit.

UTC	Az	El	SlantR	dR	Vel	Shift
0930	227	−72	12,909	1,687	1.9	0.85
0945	209	−36	11,366	1,543	1.7	0.78
1000	206	−2	11,490	−124	−0.1	-7E−2
1015	206	22	13,113	−1,623	−1.8	−0.83
1030	208	38	15,401	−2,388	−2.7	−1.22
1045	211	48	17,862	−2,461	−2.7	−1.26
1100	215	56	20,289	−2,427	−2.7	−1.24
1115	221	61	22,599	−2,310	−2.6	−1.18
1130	227	65	24,766	−2,167	−2.4	−1.11
1145	234	68	26,777	−2,011	−2.2	−1.03
1200	241	70	28,633	−1,856	−2.1	−0.95
1215	249	71	30,339	−1,706	−1.9	−0.87
1230	257	72	31,901	−1,562	−1.7	−0.8
1245	264	72	33,323	−1,422	−1.6	−0.73
1300	271	72	34,610	−1,287	−1.4	−0.66
1315	277	72	35,767	−1,157	−1.3	−0.59
1330	282	72	36,799	−1,032	−1.1	−0.53
1345	287	72	37,708	−909	−1	−0.47
1400	291	71	38,498	−790	−0.9	−0.41
1415	294	71	39,172	−674	−0.7	−0.35
1430	297	71	39,731	−559	−0.6	−0.29
1445	300	70	40,176	−445	−0.5	−0.23
1500	302	70	40,511	−335	−0.4	−0.18
1515	304	70	40,735	−224	−0.2	−0.12
1530	305	69	40,848	−113	−0.1	-6E−2
1545	307	69	40,852	−4	0	−1E−2
1600	308	69	40,746	106	0.1	5E−2
1615	308	69	40,529	217	0.2	0.11
1630	309	69	40,200	329	0.4	0.16
1645	309	69	39,759	441	0.5	0.22
1700	309	69	39,204	555	0.6	0.28
1715	308	69	38,531	673	0.7	0.34
1730	307	69	37,740	791	0.9	0.4
1745	306	70	36,826	914	1	0.46
1800	304	70	35,787	1,039	1.2	0.52
1815	302	70	34,616	1,171	1.3	0.59
1830	298	70	33,311	1,305	1.5	0.66
1845	294	71	31,864	1,447	1.6	0.73
1900	289	71	30,268	1,596	1.8	0.81
1915	283	71	28,517	1,751	1.9	0.89
1930	275	70	26,600	1,917	2.1	0.97
1945	266	69	24,512	2,088	2.3	1.06
2000	256	67	22,244	2,268	2.5	1.15
2015	245	64	19,794	2,450	2.7	1.24
2030	234	59	17,177	2,617	2.9	1.33
2045	223	51	14,450	2,727	3	1.38
2100	212	36	11,807	2,643	2.9	1.34
2115	199	11	9,826	1,981	2.2	1
2130	184	−25	9,737	89	0.1	4E−2
2145	153	-62	12,004	-467	-0.5	-0.24

Consider the situation just after perigee at 0930 UTC. The satellite was reducing slant range to the station every 15 minutes, so relative velocity was towards our station, giving a positive Doppler shift. However, the slant range change was decreasing, hence the satellite was decelerating and the Doppler shift was reducing – becoming less positive. At the point of closest approach to the receiving station, between 0945 and 1000 UTC, the satellite had almost zero relative velocity, so there was no Doppler shift to its received signal at the station, ie the received signal was the same as the satellite transmitted signal of 137,532kHz.

From 1000 UTC onwards the satellite was moving away from the station but it then began to decelerate slowly from 1100 onwards, so that the Doppler shift having quickly dropped down −1.26kHz at 1045, the deceleration began to take effect, so that relative velocity away began to reduce and hence Doppler shift became less negative, with the consequence that the frequency of the received signal began to rise having 'bottomed out' at about 137,532 – 1.26 = 137,530.74kHz.

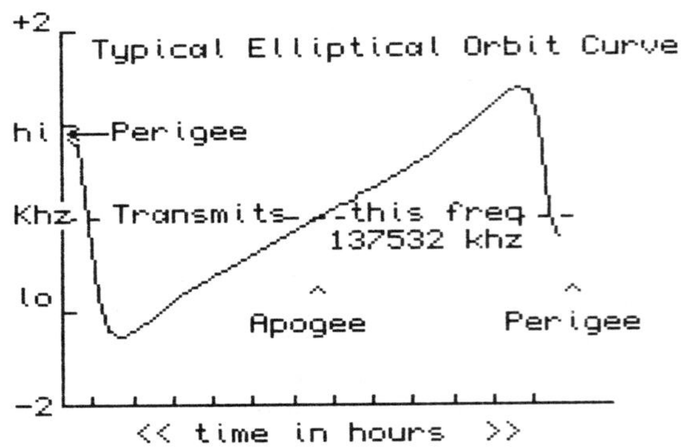

Fig 1.24: Satellite SRET 2 Doppler curve

All the way up to apogee at 1537 UTC, the satellite continued to move further away from the receiving station but at a decreasing range rate as it steadily decelerated, thereby making its Doppler shift progressively less negative and increasing the frequency of the received signal steadily.

At 1537, six hours and seven minutes after perigee, the satellite got to apogee. It was virtually stationary with respect to the Earth so it had no relative velocity and hence no Doppler shift. The received signal frequency at the ground station was therefore close to the transmitted signal frequency from the satellite: 137,532kHz.

The satellite slowly pulled away from apogee and began to fall back towards the Earth. It began to acquire a positive closing relative velocity against the ground station which gave its received signal a positive Doppler shift. Following Kepler's laws of elliptical motion, the satellite accelerated as it fell towards the Earth, so the relative velocity with respect to the station slowly built up, producing an increasing Doppler shift with the received signal frequency continuing to climb until at about 2045 UTC, nearly five hours eight minutes after apogee, the satellite was again close to the Earth.

This time the satellite made its closest approach to the station before perigee, because in the twelve hours since the last perigee the Earth had rotated 180 degrees, and as the satellite went round its orbit the Earth turned ahead of it. For this location successive perigee passages of SRET 2 never have quite the same positional arrangement as before.

Peak Doppler shift occurred at around 2045 UTC, and then the satellite's relative velocity decelerated fiercely as

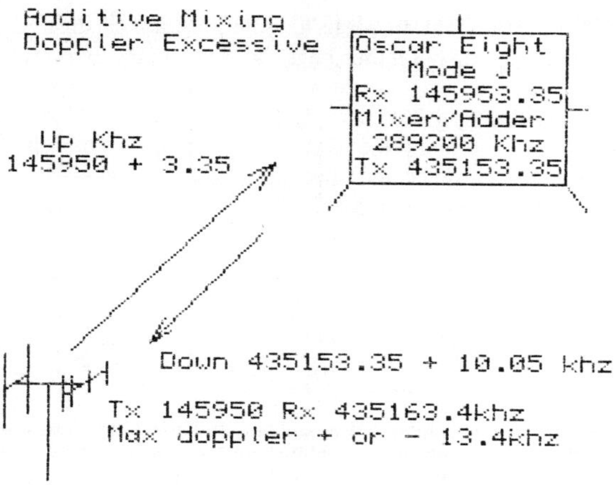

Fig 1.25: How additive mixing on a UHF satellite causes excessive Doppler shift.

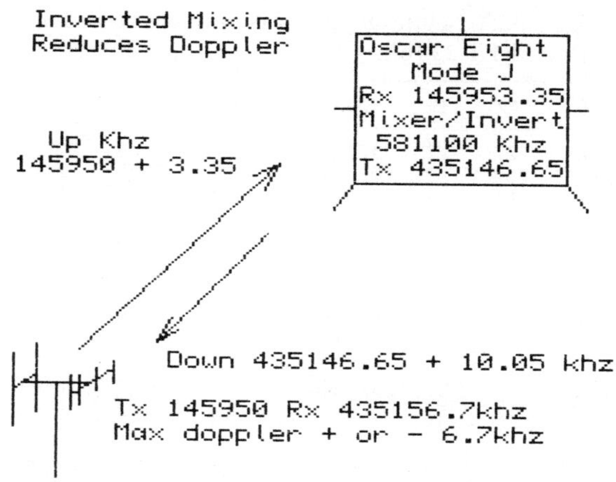

Fig 1.26: How subtractive mixing solves the problem of excessive Doppler shift on UHF satellites.

perigee approached, passing down through positive to negative near perigee.

It must be emphasised that the relative position of the station and the satellite near perigee markedly affects the Doppler curve at this time. If a different SRET 2 orbit had been chosen the overall shape of the Doppler curve would have been similar but instantaneous readings of actual Doppler shift at a particular time after perigee would not have been quite the same.

The Doppler curve shown in Fig 1.24 is the subject of a practical experiment in chapter 8. This experiment can be used to allow experimenters to gain an appreciation of how Kepler's laws of motion control elliptical orbits.

UHF satellite Doppler

In previous paragraphs Doppler shift has been considered as a positive source of useful information about distant satellites. However, there are times when Doppler shift can be a serious problem. The most obvious case of this occurs when frequencies being used for satellite communications are subject to large and rapid Doppler shifts.

In the early days of satellites this problem did not occur. The low-frequency 29MHz down link frequencies used produced small Doppler shifts, usually less than 1kHz. Even when VHF satellites came along using 145MHz, Doppler rarely exceeded ±3kHz in a 20 minute satellite pass, so good communication links could be maintained, provided the operators had some experience of keeping track of Doppler shift and staying on tune.

The advent of UHF satellites, in the shape of Oscar 7B in 1974, changed all that. Had Oscar 7 been designed in the normal way, operators would have had to deal with Doppler shifts starting 10kHz high, and going down to 10kHz low in less than 20 minutes of operating time.

Fig 1.25 uses the second UHF satellite as an example of the problem. With a Doppler on the up link of more than 3kHz, plus a Doppler on the down link of more than 10kHz, Oscar 8J users could have faced a total Doppler shift of 26kHz, with Doppler rates at the centre of the orbit pass reaching 3 or 4kHz shift per minute. Clearly the design shown in Fig 1.25 was not practical.

The solution turned out to be quite simple, and it has been used on every UHF satellite from Oscar 7B. Fig 1.26 shows the method used. Instead of adding the received up link signal to the mixer oscillator signal in the satellite, a high mixer frequency is used and the received up link signal is subtracted from it. This has the effect of making up link and down link Dopplers of opposite sense, so that they partially cancel one another. Instead of 27kHz Doppler shift, this design reduces Doppler shift to a maximum over the complete pass of about 13kHz. One side effect of this subtractive mixing is that the sidebands are inverted. It is therefore convention when using SSB to transmit lower sideband up and receive upper sideband down.

It is still necessary for operators to carefully correct Doppler shift about once every 30 seconds at the middle of the pass. This is usually done by tuning your own transmitter so that you hear yourself at the same frequency on the down link at all times. Even this solution is imperfect, because a station remote from you will be experiencing a quite different pattern of Doppler shift. So careful adjustment of your receiver to his signal may be necessary from time to time, in addition to regular tuning of your transmitter. Fig 1.27 refers.

Practical applications of Doppler measurement

It is not often appreciated that Doppler shift is almost the only tool we have for understanding what is happening to spacecraft and satellites. Doppler is being used:

(i) For accurate position fixing on the Earth's surface by systems such as the Transit and Cosnav navigation satellites.

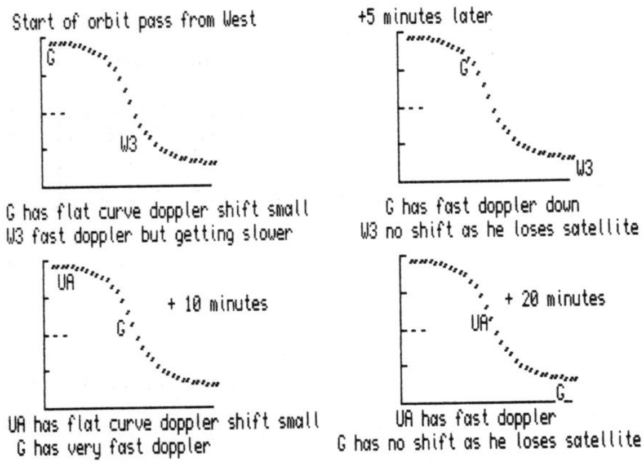

Fig 1.27: A satellite communications problem: different location = different Doppler.

(ii) For measuring from a satellite the position of a signal transmitter on the Earth's surface. In this case we reverse the action, the signal comes from the ground, say from a crashed aircraft, and its Doppler shift at the moving satellite is used to fix the location of the crash site. The satellite then transmits the location data to its Earth control station. Sarsat and Cospar sea air rescue systems use this technique.

(iii) To obtain accurate checks of Keplerian orbital elements.

(iv) To navigate deep space probes such as Voyager and Pioneer.

(v) To identify and classify the orbits of unknown satellites.

(vi) To probe the ionosphere from above using differential Doppler to locate ionospheric anomalies.

(vii) To establish whether satellite signals are coming to us by great circle line of sight routes, and hence test for non-great circle paths.

All these things and more can be discovered by examining Doppler shift. It is therefore important that space radio users understand Doppler and design their satellites so that Doppler measurement is easy, eg by transmitting unmodulated carrier.

Faraday rotation of signal polarisation

The mechanical alignment of a radio antenna determines the plane of polarisation of the transmitted signal. If, as in Fig 1.28, the antenna elements are vertical, that fixes the alternating electrical field of the transmitted signal in the vertical plane, ie a vertically polarised signal.

A vertically polarised signal is best received on a vertical antenna. As shown in Fig 1.28, the receiver using an antenna with its elements mounted horizontally gets poor results if the transmitted signal has vertical polarisation. If we had used a transmitter with horizontal antenna elements, it

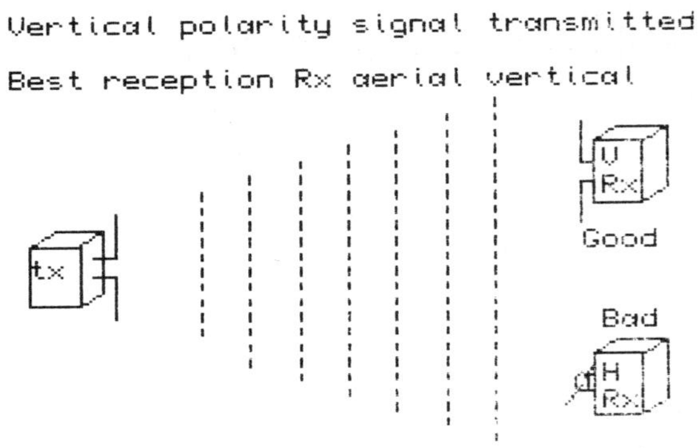

Fig 1.28: How alignment of transmitting antenna determines the plane of the signal and the importance of using the correct polarisation on the receiving antenna

would have given poor reception at receivers using vertical antenna elements. Best reception in that case would have been achieved by using a receiving antenna with horizontal elements.

In normal terrestrial groundwave use, signals transmitted with vertical polarisation are generally still vertically polarised when they reach a local receiver.

Signals at HF and above which are terrestrially propagated far beyond the line of sight often arrive at a distant receiver with changed polarisation. What starts out as a vertically polarised signal may not be vertically polarised when it arrives at its destination. It will probably not be exactly horizontally polarised either; it is much more likely to be some in-between polarisation. For signals going to and from space this change of polarisation can be quite severe and unpredictable.

Faraday rotation of polarisation

In the early days of electrical experiment the Englishman Michael Faraday discovered that the three phenomena of electric current, magnetic field and motion are connected. If any two were present, the third one always appeared.

This rule is the foundation of dynamo generation of electricity. We spin a conductor in a magnetic field and we get an electric current generated in it.

The rule also tells us how to build an electric motor. If we provide an electric current through a conductor in a magnetic field, that conductor will move. So it should come as no surprise that when we pass radio signals through the ionosphere and its associated magnetic fields, something has to move.

In fact the signal plane of polarisation can be turned not once but many times. Fig 1.29 shows why this is not always good news when the signal gets down to the ground station. Worse still, this can happen not only in near Earth space, but far out in space, if the path of the signal intersects a patch of plasma (ionised gas).

We call this rotation of the signal plane of polarisation the 'Faraday effect'.

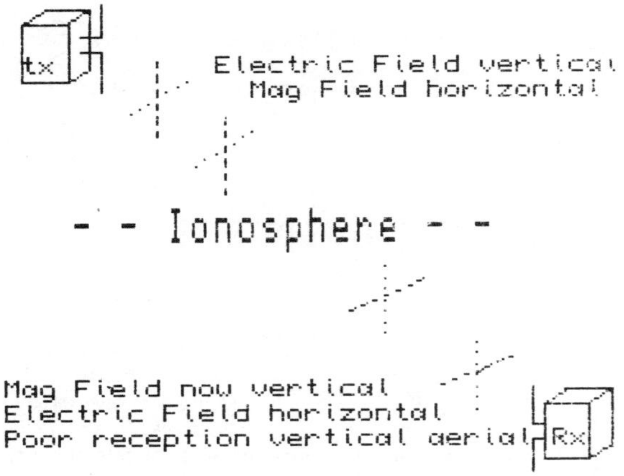

Fig 1.29: How the Faraday effect can change the polarity of radio signals

Faraday and satellites

Rotation of polarisation is least at high frequencies, worst at low frequencies. Fig 1.30 shows the problem which faces satellite users.

Even on the quietest, undisturbed day, a signal from a 29MHz satellite transmitter coming through the ionosphere at a shallow angle (satellite near station horizon), will have its plane of polarisation rotated about 80 times. A signal at 145MHz is less affected; it is turned perhaps four or five times, whilst a signal at 435MHz from a low-elevation satellite experiences about 0.75 rotations of polarisation.

As Fig 1.30 shows, when the satellite gets to the overhead position, there is a noticeable reduction in the number of rotations because it has a shorter path through the ionosphere – coming straight down through it as opposed to crossing at a shallow angle.

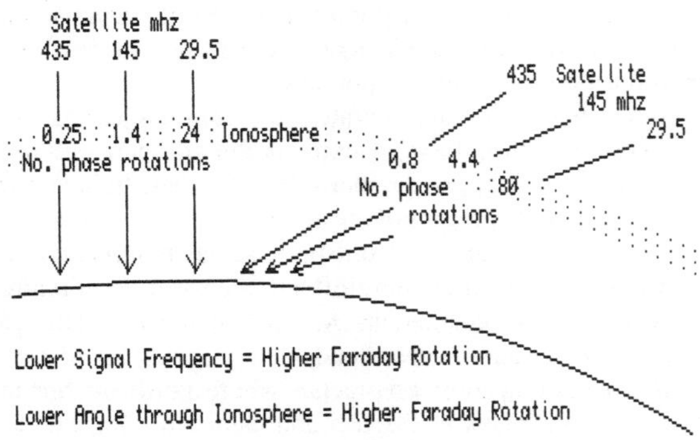

Fig 1.30: Faraday rotation of polarisation: effect of frequency and incident angle

Looking at this situation from the practical point of view, a ground station listener receiving 29MHz will not be aware that the signal started at his horizon with 80 rotations of polarisation. All the listener will notice is that between the horizon and overhead the signal he is receiving changed polarisation 56 times, ie 80 – 24.

The end result of this is that reception on a linear antenna will have meant that the ground station had a sequence of deep fades of the signal every 10 seconds or so as it transmitted from horizon to overhead. It is almost impossible to read a signal which fades at this sort of frequency. It does not matter which polarisation you use, vertical or horizontal, the effect is the same – you will be wrong half the time.

To combat the effects of Faraday rotation at HF, many stations employ pairs of crossed dipoles. A crossed-dipole antenna is less sensitive than an ordinary dipole but it compensates by being far less affected by the Faraday effect.

At first sight it might seem from Fig 1.30 that Faraday effect is hardly a problem at VHF. Certainly the receiving station does not suffer as many fades between horizon and overhead. But, unfortunately, what fades there are last longer. One revolution of polarisation is just as bad as 15. So most VHF satellite receiving stations have antennas designed to combat the Faraday effect, and the most popular of these is the crossed Yagi array. This is really two Yagi beams, one vertically mounted and hence vertically polarised, the other horizontally mounted and polarised. Both Yagis are usually mounted on the same centre boom. More expensive and elaborate circularly polarised Yagis or helixes can be used if the satellite is transmitting circular polarisation, eg a 145MHz signal being transmitted and simultaneously rotated at 145,000,000 times per second. This rotation is of course achieved electrically: the antenna itself does not spin at this speed!

Unfortunately both crossed Yagis and circularly polarised antennas (either crossed Yagis coupled to give circular polarisation, or special helical antennas with inbuilt circular polarisation) can have their problems. Separate crossed Yagis need manual switching every time the signal changes polarisation. Circular polarisation can also suffer, either because the transmitted signal is linearly polarised or because the circularity is in the wrong direction, ie a left-hand circularly polarised antenna is nearly useless for receiving right-hand circularly polarised signals. Whatever the operator does in respect of switchable or circularly polarised antennas it restricts the types of satellite polarisation he can receive effectively.

At UHF, Faraday problems are usually countered by using dedicated circular polarisation. Nearly all amateur radio UHF satellite links use circular polarisation. No attempt, however, has been made to standardise on either left- or right-hand circular. The reason is that when more than one satellite is in your sky, a difference in direction of polarisation of their signals gives a high degree of protection from mutual interference. Many commercial suppliers of antennas offer designs which can be used for both terrestrial connection as linear polarised antennas, or satellite communications using circular polarisation via phasing networks. It is not always simple to get useful results from these antennas. An antenna designed for terrestrial work with, say, element spacing for 432MHz, rarely adapts directly for circular polarisation at 435MHz, because the fixed elements are often the wrong separation for direct connection at 435MHz. In some cases some sort of phase adjustment is necessary in addition to the circular polarisation kit supplied with the antenna. Many radio amateurs, unaware of these stringent requirements, have found that incorrect phasing produces a hopeless situation where antenna pointing and polarisation are compromised.

Deep space signals and Faraday

Any spacecraft in deep space must eventually send its signal down through the ionosphere. So the rules for near- Earth satellites also apply to deep space probe signals. In addition, deep space probes have several additional problems of their own in regard to Faraday effect.

One special case in respect of Faraday is the geostationary satellite. Available on a fixed line of sight through the ionosphere, it might at first appear that the geostationary satellite would avoid Faraday problems.

This is not the case. While the line of sight between geosat and ground may not change, the ionosphere in between does move. In fact, on a quite normal day when the ionosphere is almost totally undisturbed, the polarisation of a VHF geosat down link will probably shift seven to 12 times as the ionosphere along the line of sight goes through its diurnal cycle of changes. When the ionosphere is disturbed the number of polarisation flips can get as high as 20 or more in a single day. It has therefore become common practice to make all geosat transmissions via circular polarisation. By 1990 most of the old geosats which disobey this rule have gone. All geosats since 1982 have obeyed this rule.

The simple geosat solution cannot be applied to true deep space craft. The spacecraft does not move quickly as seen from Earth but unfortunately the Earth rotates once a day so the ionosphere across the path is constantly changing. Worse still, out beyond the Earth there are other major sources of ionised plasma. Some relate to the two million mile long magnetotail of the Earth, but the majority are present in the solar wind as it moves through the solar system. Deep spacecraft simply do not use VHF or UHF. The lowest frequencies in use belong to the Soviet Venus exploration craft Venera and Vega, which use frequencies near 920MHz. Most deep space craft use even higher frequencies and virtually all use circular polarisation.

EME and Faraday

Fig 1.31 shows the problems faced by anyone who wishes to communicate over long distances by bouncing his signals off the Moon. He has double the problems faced by the ordinary artificial satellite user, because his signal must transit the ionosphere twice, without being amplified and having signal polarisation reasserted at the mid point.

The choice of frequency available to the moonbouncer is

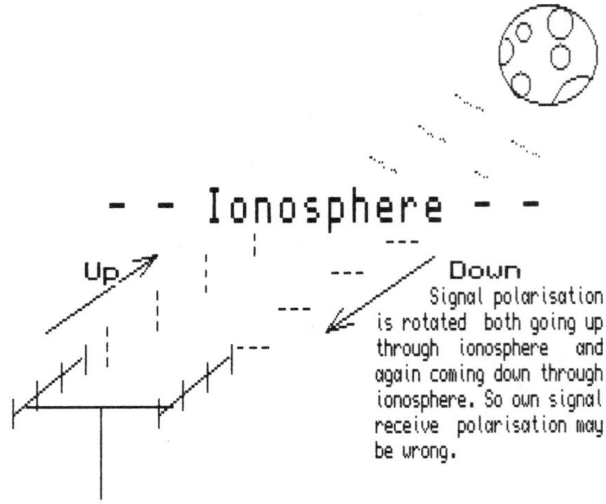

Fig 1.31: Effect of Faraday rotation on moonbounce propagation

not a simple one. Faraday and other ionospheric problems are very serious at 144MHz and are still serious at 432MHz. At higher frequencies the path loss on the half-million mile journey rises steeply. Equipment for higher frequencies is much more expensive and is mechanically demanding, particularly in important features such as servo control of narrow beam antennas. So, despite the obvious disadvantages at VHF, most moonbouncers opt for 144MHz, and this itself adds further reason to 'go to' the Moon on 144MHz, because you will have a better chance of finding someone to talk to.

So Faraday effect is a constant problem on 144MHz. As Fig 1.31 shows, whatever polarisation goes up, it is a lottery what kind comes back. Even the simple task of listening to the echoes of one's own transmissions is a game of chance rather than a serious test. You transmit up on vertical polarisation and it is most unlikely that you will get a strictly vertically polarised signal coming back. So, if you have not somehow switched your antenna polarisation in the brief wait for the echo, you will not hear it.

When two terrestrial operators are communicating via moonbounce, they face an extra problem. They are not using the same piece of the ionosphere for their signals and the two disparate patches of the ionosphere in use cannot be expected to vary in synchronism. Circular polarisation is rarely used to counter these effects, because the already large moonbounce antennas would become unwieldy if circular polarisation were added.

It is becoming common practice where a dish antenna is available, as in many 432MHz moonbounce installations, to make the antenna feed rotatable in polarisation. This is a positive step. If this method of combating Faraday effect is not available, the only recourse left to the moonbounce operator is to schedule his activities for those times when the ionosphere is likely to be least disturbed, eg late local mornings and early afternoons, and very late post-magnetic midnight to very early morning periods. More experiments concerned with the understanding of changes in ionospheric transparency and Faraday could help establish procedures for this type of scheduling.

Scintillation

Stars twinkle because their light is constantly being rerouted as it passes through the Earth's atmosphere. Ionised plasma in space and in the ionosphere have a similar effect on radio signals. All radio signals coming from space are subject to sudden arbitrary changes of phase and intensity. The phase scintillation changes the coherence of the signal wave form, dividing the signal up into random chunks of sine waves. The intensity scintillation affects the received signal strength by a process akin to multipath fading.

That scintillation was bad news on space signals did not really become obvious until designers of look-down satellite radars discovered that there was an awful gap between their theory and practice. Ocean survey radars launched in the early 1970s just did not work. Scintillation had affected ordinary satellites before, but it had not been taken seriously. The advent of high-powered satellite radars changed all that. Radars needed to get their signals down through the ionosphere to their targets and collect the very weak echoes after they had made the difficult trip back up through the ionosphere to the radarsat.

A great deal of attention was suddenly given to scintillation in the mid and late 1970s. The most successful experiment in this sudden flood of interest was satellite DNA P76. Launched in 1976, P76/5 was a much amended US Navy navigation satellite. Its payload was a family of phase-locked beacons, using harmonics of an 11.4729MHz fundamental, to radiate phase-coherent signals on frequencies of 137, 378, 390, 401, 413, 424, 435, 447, 1239 and 2,891MHz simultaneously.

The intention was to use the 2,891MHz signal to demodulate all the rest in a special receiver, thereby maintaining phase coherence. It nearly worked. Unfortunately even 2,891MHz was affected by scintillation, something which the designers had hoped would not be the case.

Despite this slight hitch, P76 worked superbly. Fig 1.32 shows the simple P76 signal received in Scotland at 435.9702MHz when scintillation simply destroyed the signal as the satellite line of sight crossed the polar auroral oval. Records taken in Ancon (Peru) and at Kwajelein in the Pacific demonstrated that at times scintillation over equatorial regions could be even fiercer. In middle latitudes, by contrast, eg from the UK south to the north coast of Africa, scintillation was rare and when it did occur it was weak.

Study over several years revealed that the equatorial scintillation is a local summer phenomenon. Middle latitude scintillation seems to be weak and non-seasonal, whereas sub-polar zone scintillation is a permanent feature present at the sub-polar front and polewards of this oval feature. This polar scintillation zone shifts latitude in step with the motion of the polar front, coming south in magnetically disturbed conditions.

System degradation by scintillation varies with the type of modulation used. Communications using high bit rates exceeding the scintillation rate are generally unaffected by phase scintillation. At lower bit rates, however, degradation is serious. By contrast, intensity fading via scintillation can affect even high bit rate modes although scintillation conditions need to be severe for this to happen. Signals which rely on phase information, eg some picture formats and radars (notably synthetic aperture radars) are badly affected even by moderate scintillation. There is some evidence that equatorial scintillation differs in its degradation effects. It may be the case that communications systems which work in polar zones will not work in an equatorial scintillation situation.

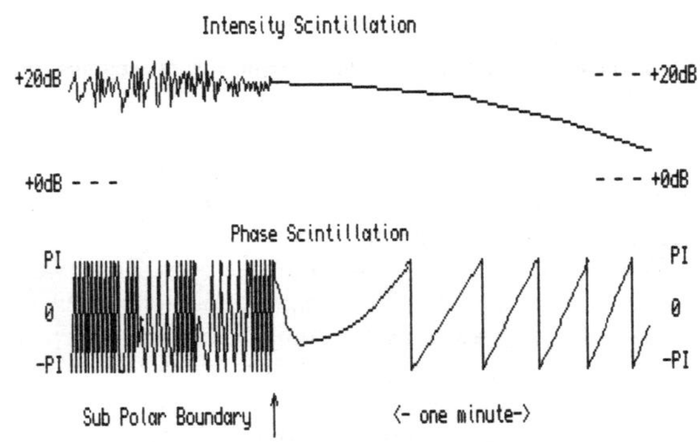

Fig 1.32: VHF satellite transit of sub-polar scintillation boundary

Beyond the ionosphere, scintillation is present in some degree on all signal paths which intercept ionised plasma. The solar wind is a particularly obvious and highly variable source of scintillation on interplanetary signal traffic. This apparent problem has been put to good use in one case at Cambridge University, where an 80MHz radio telescope carries out a daily survey of signals from quasi-stellar objects, active galaxies of enormous radio power. By studying the scintillation index of each quasar on a daily basis, a record of average quiet scintillation index can be arrived at for each quasar. Using this data as a 2,000 pixel sky survey, serious deviations from average scintillation on the part of any one quasar or a group of quasars can be used to locate enhanced patches of plasma across the lines of sight to those quasars. The solar wind is the most obvious source of these plasmas, and it is possible using this method to follow solar outbursts from the Sun to Earth.

Up to 1986 the problems posed by scintillation were evident on moonbounce signals and much more seriously on satellites transiting the polar zone. Seen from the UK, both Oscar 7 and Oscar 8 were particularly susceptible. At sunspot maximum, a time of severe magnetic storms and major auroras, Oscar 8 was unusable on two nights out of three from UK as it transited the polar oval, particularly on orbits where its ground track moved up between Greenland and Labrador.

It had been hoped that Fuji Oscar 12, with its lower orbital

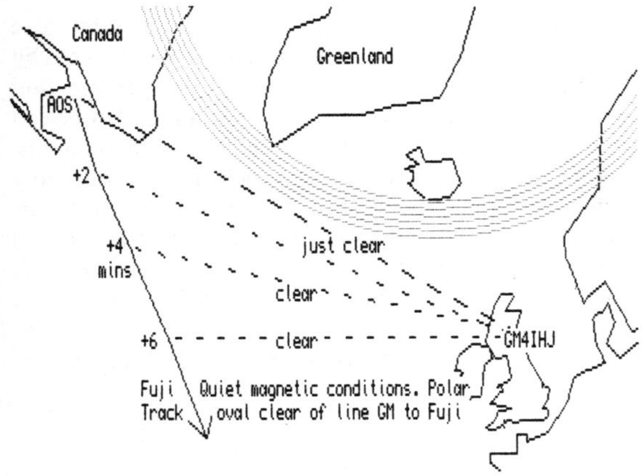

a: Fuji Oscar 12 signals pass below polar auroral scintillation zone kp0

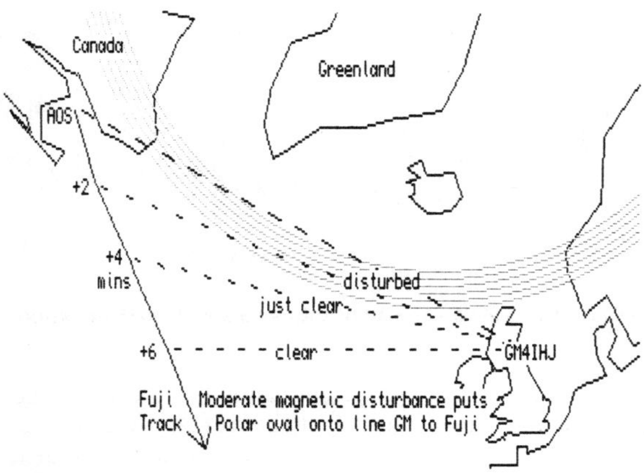

b: Fuji Oscar 12 signals hit polar auroral scintillation zone kp4

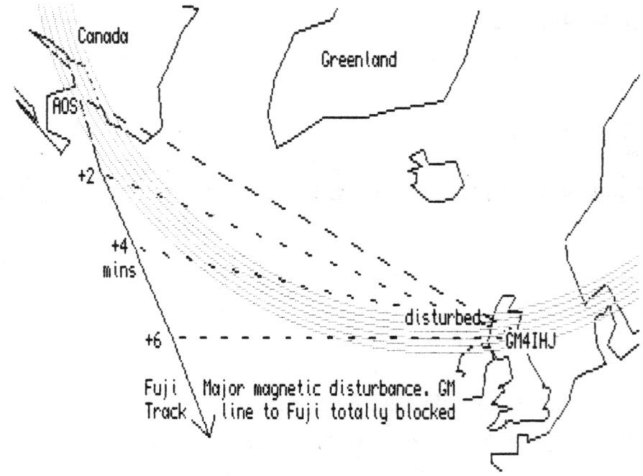

c: Fuji Oscar 12 signals are blocked by polar auroral scintillation zone kp8

Fig 1.33a-c: Effect on reception of Fuji Oscar 12 signals when the satellite nears the polar scintillation zone

inclination, might escape by passing south of these problem regions. Early tests on Fuji suggest that this is not the case. Severe scintillation disturbance of Fuji has already been noted on its passes from the Labrador Newfoundland area east towards the UK. What effect this will have on Fuji's digital mode is unclear at this time. Once the satellite is clear of this zone and started out across the Atlantic it is accessible. So this may prove only a brief inconvenience on digital orbits. In the case of the analogue system it is already clear that Fuji, like Oscar 8J, is often not accessible for transatlantic communications when its orbit high point is over the sub-auroral zone (see Figs 1.33a-c).

Fuji experiments, as we go toward solar maximum perhaps in 1991, will be interesting.

Chapter 2

Space radio physics II

VHF and the quiet ionosphere

It has been common practice in the past to ignore the effects of the ionosphere on VHF signals going through it. This view must be modified if we are to understand more about radio signals in space. Any signal coming from space or going to space must pass through the ionosphere and experiments soon reveal that this is not an easy passage. Fig 2.01 shows some of the problems.

In the normal quiet ionosphere, a passing VHF signal suffers only a small displacement from a straight path. Unlike the lower shortwave frequencies, VHF signals are not bent or refracted significantly. In fact, because the VHF signal traverses right through the ionosphere, the slight bending of its path in the first half (increasing ion-density gradient), is almost exactly corrected by a nearly equal and opposite bending, as the signal transits the second half (decreasing ion-density gradient) of its path. Fig 2.02 shows the sort of bending likely in daylight of a signal at 60MHz. Signals in the higher amateur radio band at 144MHz are hardly bent at all.

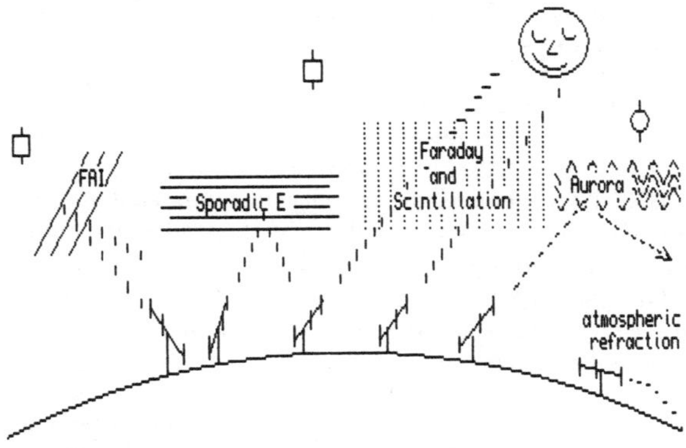

Fig 2.01: Some of the ionospheric problems affecting transmission of VHF signals into space

VHF and the disturbed ionosphere

Unfortunately for space radio users, the ionosphere is rarely if ever undisturbed. As Fig 2.01 shows, there are several kinds of anomaly which regularly disturb transiting VHF signals. Of these, sporadic E layer ionisation, radio auroras and field-aligned ionospheric anomalies are the most important.

At first examination, this disturbance of transmitting VHF signals is difficult to understand. With the exception of big auroras, the electron densities encountered in these anomalies are low, rarely exceeding 500,000 electrons per cubic centimetre. Calculating the natural plasma frequency of a cloud of electrons at this density we get:

$$fp = 9 * \text{square root (electron density/1,000,000)}$$

$$= 6.3\text{MHz approx}$$

We can expect to get refraction bending at oblique incidence to frequencies three times greater than fp, ie 19MHz, so we would clearly be wrong to expect anomalies at this density to refract or bend VHF signals. Since we know from rocket soundings that these density readings are correct, we cannot blame refraction for our problems at VHF (nor in fact can we blame it for terrestrial sporadic E and auroral propagation at VHF).

Fortunately the rocket data provide a strong clue to explain this dilemma. The electron density changes in SpE clouds and auroras are very sudden sharp changes of density gradient. These sudden changes in density along the signal

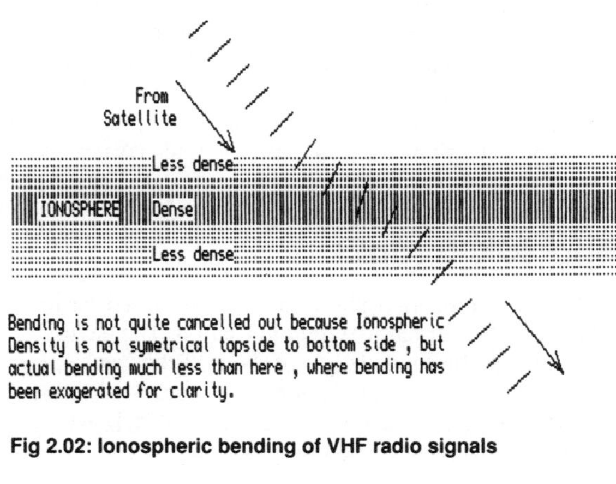

Fig 2.02: Ionospheric bending of VHF radio signals

path provide the source of our VHF space radio problems (and terrestrial SpE and auroras) via a process called 'partial reflection'.

Partial reflection is the effect you get when you look obliquely through a glass window. You see what is outside the window via transmitted light, but you also see what is inside the room via partial reflection from the surface of the glass where there is an abrupt change from air to glass. Because sporadic E, auroral and FAI events feature these sharp density gradients, they are a problem to VHF space radio users.

Solving VHF ionospheric transit problems

Surprisingly little has been written in radio literature about these problems. Professional satellite engineers soon realised how serious they were, and they tried at first using dual VHF-UHF systems, eg the Transit navigation satellites used 150MHz and 400MHz in the vain hope that the more expensive UHF signal would still be useful even when the VHF signal had been lost. Millions of pounds were spent by the United States and the Soviet Union on UHF satellite look-down radars before it became clear that ionospheric anomalies made them useless half of the time. So the superpowers built special test satellites such as the American DNA P76 specifically to explore solutions to their difficulties.

The professional studies of the problem revealed that the only solution for them was to go much higher in frequency, up to the microwaves. So in the late 1970s the expensive migration began. All weather satellites, navigation satellites, remote Earth sensing (Landsat, Spot) satellites, plus look-down ocean reconnaissance radars, built since 1979 have been provided with microwave up and down links.

Even for the professionals the microwaves were not always a possible option. Mobile communications and military satellites still use VHF and UHF, as do satellites covering the Earth's polar regions. In addition many scientists were anxious to use VHF satellites to study the ionosphere. Last, but by no means least, radio amateurs and space experimenters simply could not afford to build or purchase microwave equipment, and as a consequence are making heavy use of VHF space radio circuits. The following sections of this chapter will therefore describe the operating conditions one can expect to find at VHF.

Sporadic E (SpE)

The E layer of the ionosphere has been described earlier in relation to its 'normal' daylight ionisation. The daytime E layer is located around a height of about 110km, and it plays only a negative role (absorption), in regard to shortwave propagation, except at frequencies below 4MHz where it can provide some refraction propagation.

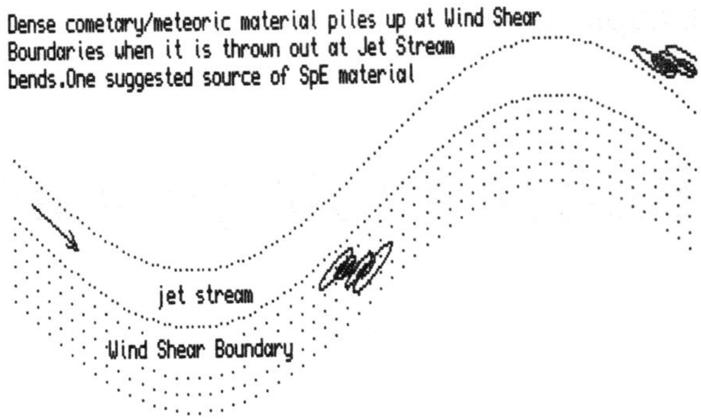

Fig 2.03: Jetstream boundaries and sporadic E

At VHF and UHF frequencies this normal daytime ionisation is of no great consequence. What matters at VHF and UHF is that at these frequencies local high levels of ionisation referred to as 'sporadic E' can have major effects. These localised zones of ionisation can have sharp density gradients where the normal E layer levels of around 30,000 electrons per cubic centimetre abruptly change to levels near 500,000 electrons per cubic centimetre.

The explanations for why these dense anomalies occur are at best sketchy and incomplete, but the underlying sequence of events can be described, recognised and used as a valuable predictor of SpE. The best clues to prediction of SpE are that it has a positive seasonal, local summer peak over temperate regions such as the UK. It is mostly a daylight phenomenon, so clearly solar illumination is a vital factor, producing the initial increase in ionisation. Less obvious is why this ionisation seems to collect in distinct clumps or platelets, and what mechanism restrains the normal tendency for charged particles to repel particles of similar polarity, whereby we would expect the platelets to break up as fast as they form.

Rocket experiments to investigate E platelets have revealed an excess of small pieces of meteoric dust in the plates. It is therefore possible that the upper atmosphere jetstreams act like vacuum cleaners, sweeping up this dust and then throwing it out at the outer edges of bends in the jetstream just as heavy gold ore is thrown out on the bends of mountain streams. What seems to be sure is that the dust then acts as a collector of charged particles. Fig 2.03 shows a sketch of how the upper atmosphere high-speed jetstreams may concentrate the meteor dust in clumps on their outside bends. It is perhaps no coincidence that there is a second minor sporadic E season in the local temperate zone winter, noting that the Earth on its slightly tilted orbit round the Sun crosses the comet/meteor debris-filled Sun-Jupiter plane in June and again in December.

Occurrence of sporadic E

SpE over temperate regions such as the UK occurs:

(a) In a major local summer peak lasting from May to August. Fig 2.04 shows this feature.

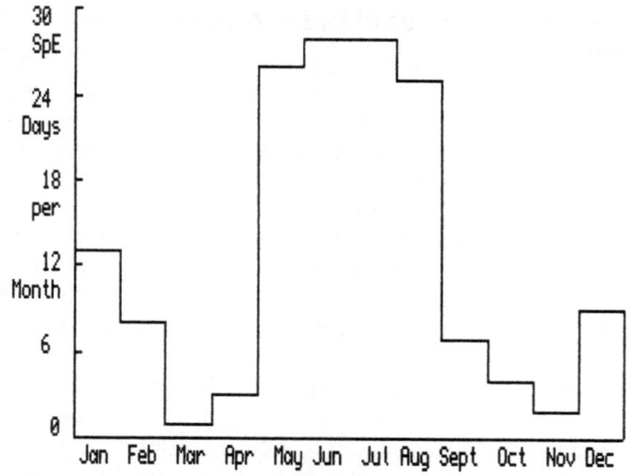

Fig 2.04: Graph showing days each month featuring sporadic E at 48MHz or above

(b) SpE occurs mostly in daylight as shown in the hourly chart of events: Fig 2.05.

(c) There is a minor winter SpE season from mid-December to late January for the northern hemisphere.

(d) SpE platelets can be quite small in extent, eg 10 to 20km horizontally. The platelets of SpE are very thin vertically, and it is sometimes the case that several platelets, each tens of kilometres long, are spaced 600 or 800km apart in a chain of platelets.

(e) SpE platelets provide enhanced terrestrial propagation at VHF out to about 2,400km range between stations using a single platelet. This same platelet can, however, simultaneously block communication to and from space, causing deep fluttery fading on VHF/UHF satellite and moonbounce paths.

Preferred locations of SpE platelets

The physics underlying the formation of sporadic E is not well understood; however, there are masses of empirical

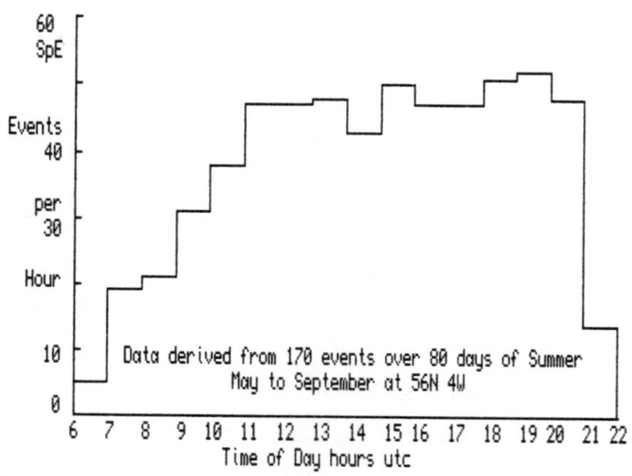

Fig 2.05: Graph showing events each hour featuring sporadic E at 48MHz or above

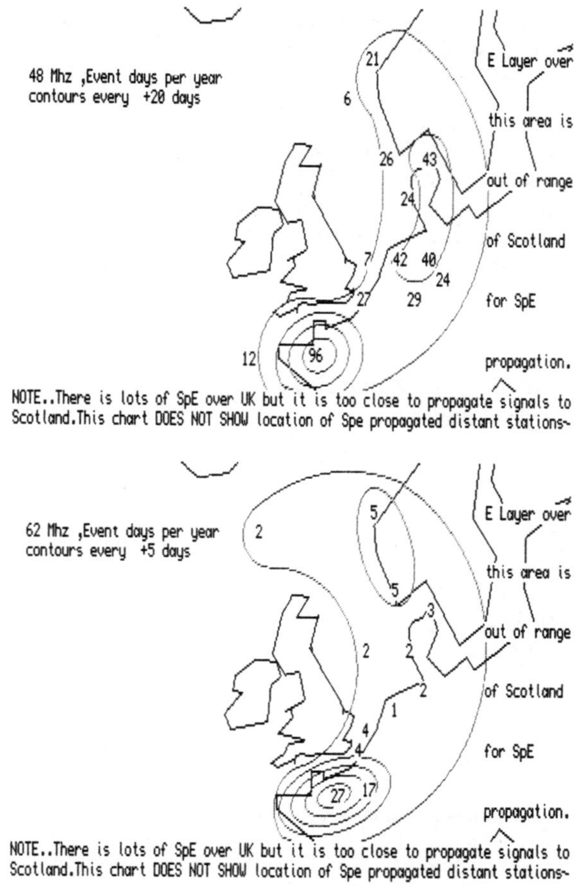

Figs 2.06 and 2.07: Locations in ionosphere of sporadic E propagation over Scotland

evidence collected over many years, useful for predicting the effect it may or may not have on an individual station's space communication capabilities.

Figs 2.06 and 2.07 show contour plots of the incidence of sporadic E over Europe as seen from a station in Scotland. The method is hopelessly incomplete, for it cannot show SpE within 400km or beyond 1,200km from one's station. Yet it does reveal a pronounced tendency for SpE to appear over northern France.

This French connection could be a consequence of the regularity of location of a jetstream eddy over that part of France. This is pure conjecture, because vertical ionosonde measurements from the London area reveal almost as much SpE over London (which the Scottish station cannot easily plot). None the less, contour plots for individual stations of this kind are useful for scheduling local satellite or moonbounce activity for times when the target is not being seen through a line of sight which transits the E layer over northern France.

The actual measurement of the size, shape and location of SpE platelets is in its infancy. Chapter 8 reports several advanced experiments in this field.

Frequency	Mapcode	Placename	Country	Channel
48.242	l	Saarland	Germany	E2
48.242	m	?	Sweden	E2
48.242	j	Oporto	Portugal	E2
48.249	d	Madrid	Spain	E2
48.249	e	Jauerling	Austria	
48.252	f		Switzerland	E2
48.252	g	Goteborg	Sweden	E2
48.257	b	Melhus	Norway	E2
48.258	h	Helsinki	Finland	E2
48.260	i	Gruten	S Germany	E2
48.261	a	Steigen	Norway	E2
48.264	k	Horsby	Sweden	E2
49.733	p	Prague	Czechoslovakia	R1
49.734	n	Budapest	Hungary	R1
49.742	q	Talinin	USSR	R1
49.745	r	Minsk	USSR	R1
49.749	s		Poland	R1
49.755	t	Bratislava	Czechoslovakia	R1
49.759	u		Poland	R1
62.253	v	Barcelona	Spain	E4
62.263	w		Italy	E4

Fig 2.08: High-power European VHF TV stations

Warning of sporadic E

Because it occurs mostly in daylight, and has a seasonal pattern, sporadic E should not catch the space radio user unaware. In addition several reliable methods of SpE early warning have been developed by radio amateurs in pursuit of long-distance terrestrial VHF propagation via SpE. These methods can be put to good use by space radio users who want to avoid SpE rather than use it.

The average British summer produces at least 110 days when SpE events propagate 50MHz signals; about five of these events are strong enough to propagate signals at 144MHz. By contrast the much shorter winter season features about 27 events propagating signals at 50MHz, but not much above this frequency.

This situation can be clarified for the space radio user if he uses the same early warning techniques as the terrestrial operator, monitoring the powerful broadcast FM and TV stations all around Europe as shown in Fig 2.08. By listening for these stations a clear picture of the location and intensity of the sporadic E can be obtained, and the space radio user can use this information to assess where and when his activities are likely to be interrupted. For those operators not equipped to monitor these broadcast TV and FM stations, the 28MHz beacons located in Europe offer a useful but less complete picture of SpE activity.

Technical procedures for reducing SpE problems

Very little work has been reported on this problem, but technical methods for reducing the effects of SpE on signals to and from space are possible. In the course of experiments described in the relevant chapter, the author discovered that space diversity reception could be effective in some circumstances. Two methods were found to be useful for reception of geostationary satellites in SpE conditions. The first method involved receiving antennas spaced 10 wavelengths apart horizontally; the second used two antennas on the same mast, one aimed at the geosat line-of-sight elevation of 28 degrees, the other aimed at the horizon (zero degrees elevation). Both these methods of diversity reception produced useful signals when the normal single antenna line-of-sight reception was zero, during the typical deep fading which SpE induces.

Recognising SpE effects on space signals

A typical effect associated with sporadic E is shown in Fig 2.09, where a NOAA weather satellite over Africa was being received in Scotland with poor signals, which were fading and scintillating so badly that the weather-map picture was periodically broken up. It was no coincidence that at this time terrestrial signals from Spanish TV, propagating via the same portion of the E layer as that being transited by the NOAA down link, were very strong in Scotland.

A second event involving sporadic E and space communications is shown in Fig 2.10. In this example the evening orbits of satellite Oscar 8J were not accessible via the 145MHz up link until the signal path had moved north of a big sporadic E centre, which was being reported as above Slough, near London, at that time. This incident allowed comparison of the simultaneous effects on the Oscar 8J up link on 145MHz and the down link beacon on 435MHz. The higher frequency was affected by deep fading but it was not completely lost. By contrast, the 145MHz up link at no time accessed the satellite until the signal path moved clear of the sporadic E.

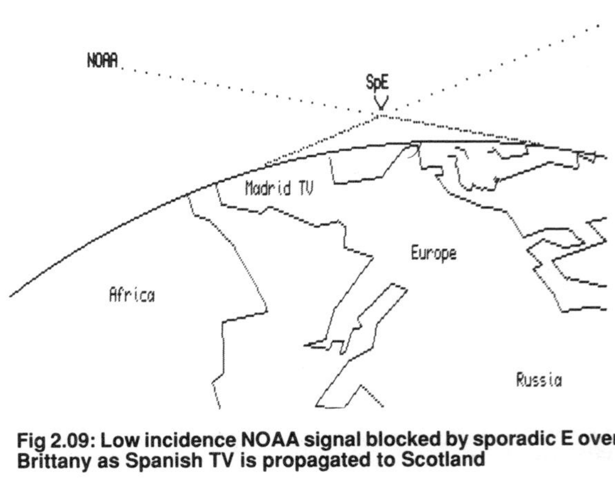

Fig 2.09: Low incidence NOAA signal blocked by sporadic E over Brittany as Spanish TV is propagated to Scotland

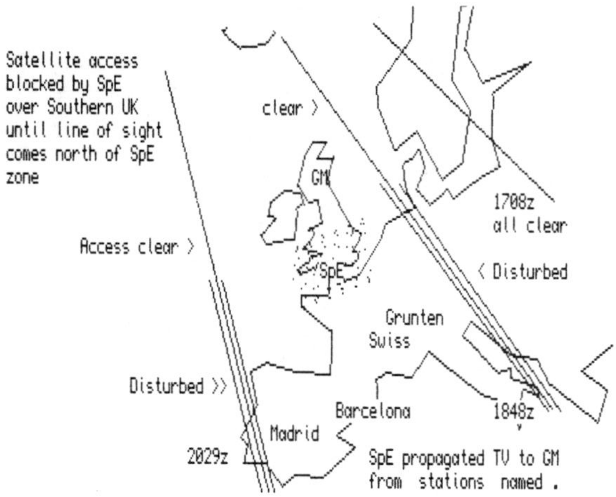

Fig 2.10: Sporadic E affects Oscar 8J access, June 1980

Sporadic E experiments

The experiments chapter of this book features several experiments which can help produce a better understanding of sporadic E. Differential Doppler described in chapter 8 can be used to delineate the boundaries of SpE features and record their shifting locations and shapes. Unfortunately very few satellite builders appreciate the possibilities of these relatively simple techniques, and in consequence the importance of providing uninterrupted continuous carrier wave beacons is passed over. Only relatively few military satellites and navigation satellites have continuous carrier signals and it is hoped that this technique will not be overlooked in future amateur radio satellites.

At the other end of the range of study methods available to SpE experimenters, no-one who wishes to appreciate the full extent of sporadic E and its effects on VHF communications should miss the annual VHF ionospheric activity reports, presented for the IARU by S Canivenc, F8SH. They are chock-full of useful information.

Auroras

As discussed earlier, the upper atmosphere of the Earth is the site of several zones or layers where the gas is ionised, whereby some of its constituent atoms and molecules are broken up, into free negatively charged electrons, or separate ions consisting of the remains of the original atoms or molecules minus some of their electrons, thereby making them positively charged.

One result of this ionisation is the formation of the D, E and F layers of the ionosphere. A second quite different consequence of the ionisation is the production of glowing bands of ionised gas, where the atmosphere acts like a huge fluorescent light tube, with colours depending on the types of atmospheric molecules and atoms involved.

These two effects, ionisation and fluorescence, have some points of similarity. However, they are best treated

Table 2.01 Visible auroras, air glows and dust clouds

Height (km)	Location	Colour	Source	Remarks
Emissions				
400-600	sub-tropical	red	atomic O_2	equatorial F2 aurora
100-400	sub-polar	green	O_2	low-altitude aurora
		yellow		weak auroral activity
		pearly-white		weak auroral activity
		red	$O_2 + N_2$	strong aurora
100	worldwide	green	O_2	night sky, thin band
95	temperate zone	yellow	OH hydroxyl	night sky, thin band
85	worldwide	orange-brown	sodium D	twilight emission
Scattering layers				
20-80	temperate zone	white	H_2O	noctilucent clouds
Interplanetary				dust reflecting sunlight
Absorption regions				
15-20	worldwide		dust	volcanic ash

separately when considering their effect on space radio or astronomy. The most obvious of the fluorescent 'airglows' is the Aurora Borealis, the Northern Lights, a splendid visual manifestation which has been known since early man. The Northern Lights are often contemporary or consecutive to 'auroral' events which seriously disturb space and terrestrial radio circuits, particularly over polar and sub-polar regions.

The highly visible Northern Lights take pride of place in any discussion of auroras. From satellites the visual glow of the polar auroral oval is clearly evident around the Earth's magnetic poles. Experimental satellites such as ISIS II, Dynamic Explorer, Viking and Polar Bear have all conducted auroral surveys from space, whilst on the ground specialised radars at Chatanika, Alaska; Sonderstrom, Greenland; Tromso, Norway; Uppsala, Sweden; and Wick, Scotland have probed auroras from below.

Auroras, air glows and dust bands

Despite all the radar and satellite activity, it was not until men became regular visitors in space via experiments like Salyut and Skylab that it was realised that near-Earth space was full of visual airglows. Table 2.01 shows the extent of the problem revealed by the astronauts and cosmonauts.

Other emitters

The space shuttle and other spacecraft create emission as they move through space. Much of this emission is thought to come from gas being slowly released from the metal

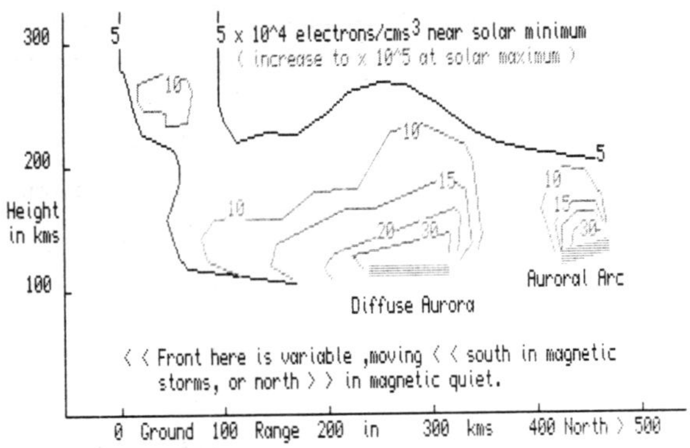

Fig 2.11: Side view through polar auroral front

surface of the spacecraft. This kind of emission is a great nuisance to observers and experimenters in low-altitude spacecraft.

For the most part, these visual emissions and dust bands are not themselves direct problems for space radio users. Never the less, they are often bad news, because they can be accompanied or preceded by effects which we cannot see, but which do seriously affect space radio circuits. We call these unseen effects 'radio auroras' and in the paragraphs which follow this radio aurora will be our chief concern.

Radio auroras

The source of all auroras, visual or radio, is the Sun and the ionised particle stream from the Sun, which we call the 'solar wind'.

Even when the Sun is relatively quiet, the bombardment from the solar wind compacts the Earth's shielding magnetosphere, forcing some of the solar wind particles into temporary storage in the Earth's Van Allen belts. From the poleward edges of the radiation belts there is a steady drizzle of charged particles down into the upper atmosphere of the polar regions. The resulting collisions with the upper atmosphere ionise it, creating the polar front, the outer edge of the permanent polar auroral oval.

Fig 2.11 shows a typical side view of the polar front compiled as a computer graphic from data derived by Leadabrand *et al*, using the auroral radar at Chatanika, Alaska. The overhead view of the quiet auroral oval is shown in Fig 2.12. Satellite pictures have shown very clearly that the complete ellipse (which causes radio problems) is a permanent feature, whereas the visual aurora which needs far higher levels of ionisation potential may sometimes be restricted to that part of the polar oval above the position of local magnetic midnight, ie beyond the magnetic pole on the other side of the oval away from the Sun.

The quiet auroral oval is visible from the UK only in its high-altitude sections. It usually lies slightly north of Iceland, stretching west towards Labrador at UK magnetic midnight. As can be seen from Fig 2.11, there are several regions of dense ionised plasma in the polar front, some high enough to be above the UK horizon. Many of these ionised plasmas are well to the southward of the regions of visual auroras. All these plasma concentrations produce radio effects. It is therefore not good practice to assume that radio auroral effects will occur where visual auroras are seen; in fact the two phenomena are rarely, if ever, collocated or contemporary.

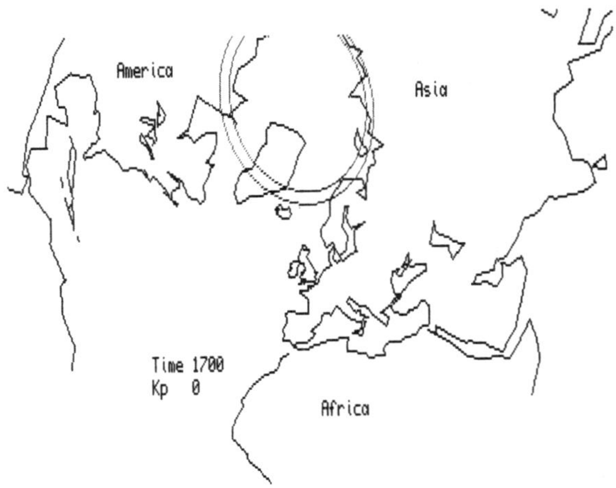

Fig 2.12: The location of the quiet polar auroral oval at 1700 UTC

Ionospheric circulation over polar regions

A different view of the polar auroral oval emerges when it is examined by radar. Fig 2.13 shows that we no longer have a simple oval structure. In fact the continuously circulating currents in the polar ionosphere follow two discrete semi-cylindrical tracks, flowing in opposite directions around the outside of the oval, then forming separate parallel streams to flow from nightside to dayside across the magnetic pole. Please note one important fact about this circulation pattern – it stays fixed in space – whilst the Earth with your station on it rotates underneath it.

This circulation pattern was first described in detail by

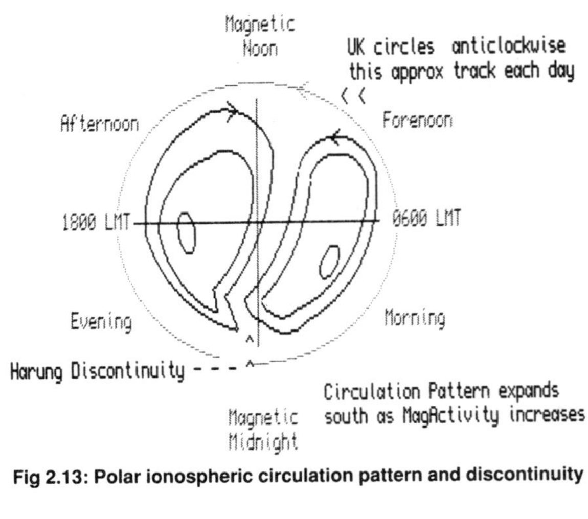

Fig 2.13: Polar ionospheric circulation pattern and discontinuity

Harung, who noted the sudden change in magnetic field as the discontinuity between the two halves of the pattern went over his station. Hence the split is often referred to as the 'Harung discontinuity'. It is very important in respect of the timings of the various phases of radio auroral events.

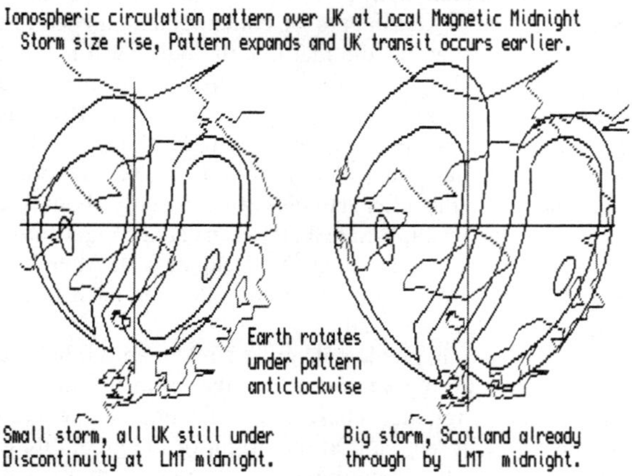

Fig 2.14: Storm size dependence of discontinuity passage time

If the solar wind is enhanced and a magnetic storm results, the ionospheric circulation patterns are enlarged and expand south. Fig 2.14 shows the effect this has on the position of the Harung discontinuity with respect to UK ground stations. Enlarging the circulation pattern brings the discontinuity further south and west. This has the result that an Earth station rotating counter-clockwise underneath the ionospheric circulation pattern passes under the discontinuity earlier than it would in quiet conditions. The bigger the magnetic storm, the bigger the pattern, which has important effects in that it 'fixes' the end of the first phase of radio aurora, because this phase usually ends as the Harung discontinuity passes north of the station. The end result of all this is that big auroras finish earlier.

When to expect radio auroras

The solar wind is highly variable in intensity. When the Sun is quiet, the reduced solar wind takes about 36 to 48 hours to reach the Earth. Its collision with the Earth's magnetosphere is relatively mild, and most of the solar wind is deflected over the poles and down the magnetotail. Some charged particles do get into the Van Allen belts, and then leak out from the belts' poleward edges, producing a steady drizzle of charged particles down into the upper atmosphere. This light rain of particles maintains the polar auroral oval in its quiet location, well to the north of the UK.

Fig 2.12 shows the position of the polar auroral oval in quiet conditions, at its 1700 UTC location. In a typical year this is the location of the oval on about 250 days.

When the solar wind is enhanced by coronal holes or minor solar flare activity, the increased bombardment of the Earth's magnetosphere can cause a magnetic storm. This increases the level of particle precipitation from the polar edges of the Van Allen belts, and it also provides another source of energetic particles coming into polar regions from the disturbed magnetotail. This increased activity and the magnetic field adjustments which accompany it cause the auroral oval to expand south out and away from the pole. At these times radio and visual auroras may be observed from the northern UK. Fig 2.15 shows the possible extent of visual and radio events in a magnetic storm of this modest type. Minor auroral storms are present for observers in the northern UK on about 40 to 70 days a year. Some years have more activity than others, a pattern generally in step with, but slightly offset from, the regular 11-year solar activity cycle.

On 20 or 30 days each year, the Sun is the site of medium to large flares and explosive break-up of solar filaments. At these times a major magnetic storm is triggered in the Earth's magnetosphere, about 36 to 48 hours after the solar burst. This major magnetic storm produces a very large

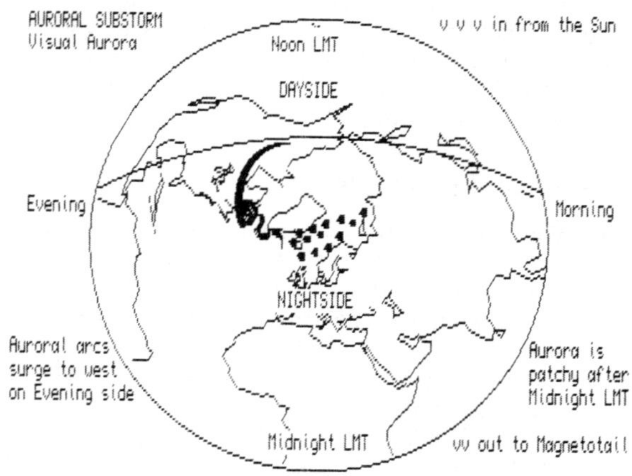

a: Visual aurora

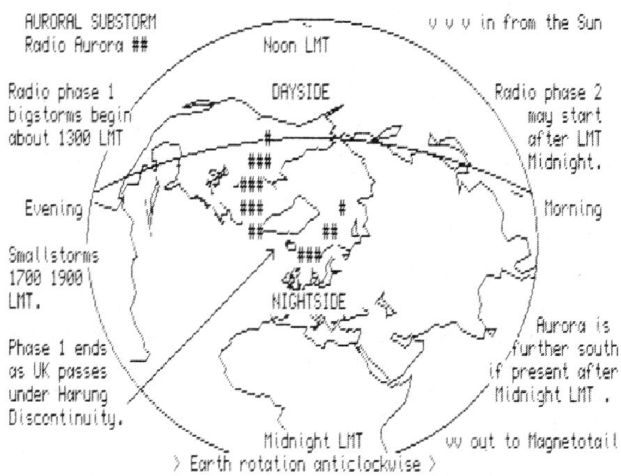

b: Radio aurora

Fig 2.15a,b: The possible extent of visual and radio events in a small magnetic storm

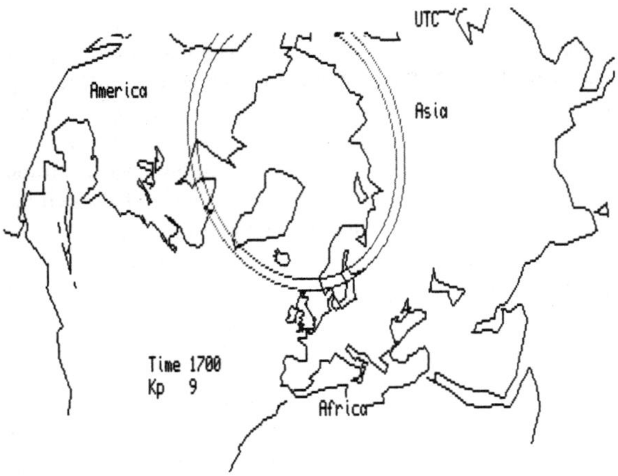

Fig 2.16: The very disturbed polar auroral oval at 1700 UTC during a major magnetic storm

southward expansion of the auroral oval, bringing radio auroral conditions overhead in the northern UK, with effects extending as far south as the Mediterranean Sea. Fig 2.16 shows the extent of the polar oval at 1700 UTC during a major magnetic storm.

The auroral timetable

The effect auroras have on satellite or terrestrial radio operating depends on the size of the associated magnetic storm and your station's position on the Earth's surface with respect to the alignment of the magnetosphere, which is the controller of the 'auroral timetable'. It is vital that space and terrestrial radio operators appreciate that auroras do not keep to universal time (UTC).

The reason for this is shown on Fig 2.17 which plots the straight line auroral/magnetosphere axis on top of a great circle map centred on the magnetic pole. The straight line diagonally across the map starts at the Sun and then goes through the magnetic pole and out down the magnetotail. Our station auroral time depends on the angle at the centre of the Earth between this line and a line to the Earth centre from our station. We say that the angle generated by this time frame is the 'local magnetic time'. LMT, as it is normally referred to, should be used in all auroral work.

Local magnetic time

The big snag with LMT is that it varies with the season of the year. Fig 2.17 shows why this happens. The problem is the tilt of the Earth with respect to the Sun orbit plane. In our northern summer the northern hemisphere tilts towards the Sun, so that the Sun appears to orbit around and above latitude 23.5°N, the Tropic of Cancer. By contrast, our northern winter finds our hemisphere tilted away from the Sun, such that the sub-solar point now tracks along the Tropic of Capricorn near latitude 23.5°S. In between, in March and again in October, the Sun rises directly above the Earth's equator.

The map in Fig 2.17 is a great circle plot centred on the magnetic pole, not the more normal rotation geographic pole. For the purposes of this simple time scale the magnetic pole is assumed to be 78.5°N 69°W, as if it were the pole of a simple dipole magnet. For the purposes of auroral timing this is accurate enough. If, however, more serious Earth/Space magnetic experiments are contemplated, it becomes necessary to allow for the fact that the real Earth is not a simple dipole. To get a realistic scale for serious magnetic measurements, the Earth is perhaps best considered as having an octopolar (eight-pole) system. The Earth is in fact a bit like an eight-pole electric motor, where two poles dominate, with the other six poles affecting only about five per cent of the result. Where factors can change logarithmically with respect to the magnetic field, eg Van Allen belt radiation dose rates, this more complex approach to the magnetic field is essential.

Fig 2.17 is a magnetic pole great circle map and has the geographic pole marked on it, together with the lines of geographic longitude. These longitude lines are curved because they do not start at the origin of the great circle. Using the diagonal line joining the subsolar point, the UK and the magnetic pole as reference, the winter Sun tracks around the curve from Nwin to Mwin. When the winter Sun is over Mwin the local magnetic time in the UK is LMT midnight. When the winter Sun is over Nwin, the LMT in the UK is noon LMT.

Checking with Fig 2.17, it can be seen that LMT UK noon occurs when the Sun is near geographic longitude 340°W. But if we shift up to N equinox we see that in March and October LMT UK noon occurs when the Sun is over geographic longitude 345°W, and by LMT UK noon in summer it is over about 350°W. We keep Greenwich time as UTC in the UK, which nearly, but not quite, fixes GMT noon as the time the Sun crosses longitude zero. So the UK LMT noon is about 1040 UTC in our winter and 1120 in our summer. (Note: this rough calculation must be corrected by the equation of time to allow for the fact that the Earth's orbit around the Sun is an ellipse, not a circle).

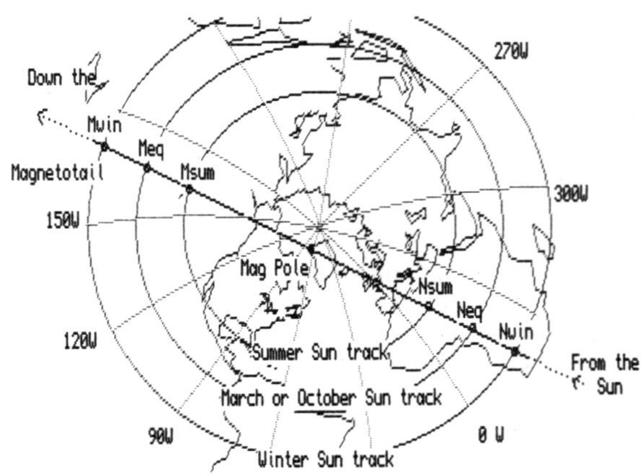

Fig 2.17: Seasonal change of UTC time of local magnetic noon and midnight

Table 2.02: Auroral timetable

LMT	UTC winter	UTC summer	Radio and visual
Noon	1040	1120	If major magnetic storm is present you get radio auroras from north east
1700	1540	1620	Smaller magnetic storms begin to produce radio auroras in UK
2000	1840	1830	Very small magnetic storms produce radio auroras in UK
2030	1910	1850	In big magnetic storms passage of the much extended Harung discontinuity over UK ends the first phase of radio auroras. At this time there is a strong possibility of auroral E*s* + FAIs. (Visual auroras often begin at about this LMT)
2300	2220	2140	In quiet magnetic conditions Harung discontinuity ends first radio phase small auroras. (Maximum visual auroral activity at this LMT)
0000	2320	2240	A second phase of radio aurora may now begin. A second phase is not guaranteed. (Magnetic midnight – visual auroral activity weakens)
0400	0320	0240	Even big magnetic storms cease producing radio auroras near UK but radio auroras may still be accessed far to west from UK. (Visual activity is rare at this LMT)
1000	0900	0940	There is a roughly twice-a-year chance of radio auroras at this LMT. It is the rare so-called 'proton event'

NOTE: Please treat all times and statements in this table as being for general guidance only. No two auroras are ever the same in all respects. Radio auroras can be accessed from the UK when they are 800km north of your station. So the 'end of radio phase 1' for small auroras occurs when the point 800km north of you goes under the Harung discontinuity. In bigger auroras the 'end of phase 1' to your north-east does not mean the end of auroral activity accessible from the UK. The aurora is still accessible to your far west. Now that 50MHz is available to UK operators, transatlantic auroral contacts are certain, probably around local magnetic midnight for UK. Operators in the southern UK should avoid answering northern stations who are trying for long-range contacts to their west, calling 'CQ W VE Aurora.'

From the point of view of timing radio auroras, we are more interested in the UTC of UK local magnetic midnight. According to Fig 2.17, this will occur when the summer Sun is at about longitude 160°W, when the equinoctial Sun of March and October is at about 166°W, and when the UK winter Sun is near 170°W. So LMT midnight in UK occurs at about 2320 UTC in winter, 2300 UTC in March and October, and 2240 UTC in the UK summer.

These local magnetic time sequences are important because large changes in radio auroral behaviour occur over the part of the world experiencing local magnetic midnight, whatever its actual time UTC.

Note: Readers will hear the terms 'geomagnetic latitude' and 'geomagnetic longitude' in some quarters. It is a mistake to use these terms when discussing auroras, visual or radio.

Fig 2.15 shows the different forms that visual and radio auroras take before and after local magnetic midnight. Now that we have defined the framework of local magnetic time, it becomes possible to define the timings of the various stages or phases of auroral events, as a typical 'auroral day timetable'. For convenience this timetable, Table 2.02, starts at local magnetic noon:

The late-night perseverance of radio auroras far to the west of the UK is a particular nuisance for users of satellites which are over Greenland and Labrador.

A big auroral storm

The progress of a large 'twice a year' magnetic storm is traced in Fig 2.18, which is taken from the viewpoint of a station located in central England at 51°N 1°W.

At 1200 UTC the LMT is post-magnetic noon. The auroral oval in a big storm often achieves altitudes above 480km, which puts it above the north-east horizon at this time with radio phase 1 already building up. Scatter/partial reflection propagation is available to VHF operators.

By 1600 UTC the active radio auroral zone stretches across the UK's northern horizon, from northwest to northeast, with VHF anomalous auroral propagation peaking on azimuths 30 to 60 degrees and 300 to 340 degrees.

Four hours later, as Fig 2.18c shows, the first radio phase of this big aurora is over. The UK is passing under the discontinuity in the ionospheric circulation pattern and VHF auroral propagation is only available by beaming far to the west at azimuths as low as 270 degrees. As this first phase ends it is often possible to hear signals losing their wideband auroral hiss, becoming clear tone for a few brief minutes of propagation using the dispersing auroral ionisation in the field-aligned irregularity mode (discussed in detail next in this chapter). Equally possible at this time is propagation at VHF through the dying radio aurora via auroral E*s*. In practice UK stations will hear FAI propagation to stations like themselves, south of the aurora, whilst the auroral E*s* will introduce new stations from far to the northeast of UK, typically northeast Sweden.

As we go towards 2400 UTC the UK LMT is already an hour or so past magnetic midnight. It is at this time that the second phase of radio aurora will occur, if indeed it is going to occur at all. Not all radio auroras have a second phase, but if they do it can be very interesting. In typical second phases the azimuth for useful propagation from the UK is much further south than it was in the first phase. Typical second-phase azimuths are 70 to 100 degrees, and propagation usually favours UK to eastern Europe and Baltic locations. Even if no second phase takes place, it should be remembered that far to the west of UK, the last of the first radio phase may still just be accessible over Greenland. American 47MHz paging stations are a good guide to possible 50MHz contacts at this time.

A small auroral storm

The progress of a small aurora is traced in Figs 2.19a-d. In this case the auroral oval does not extend very far south and auroral activity does not get above 250km altitude. So the

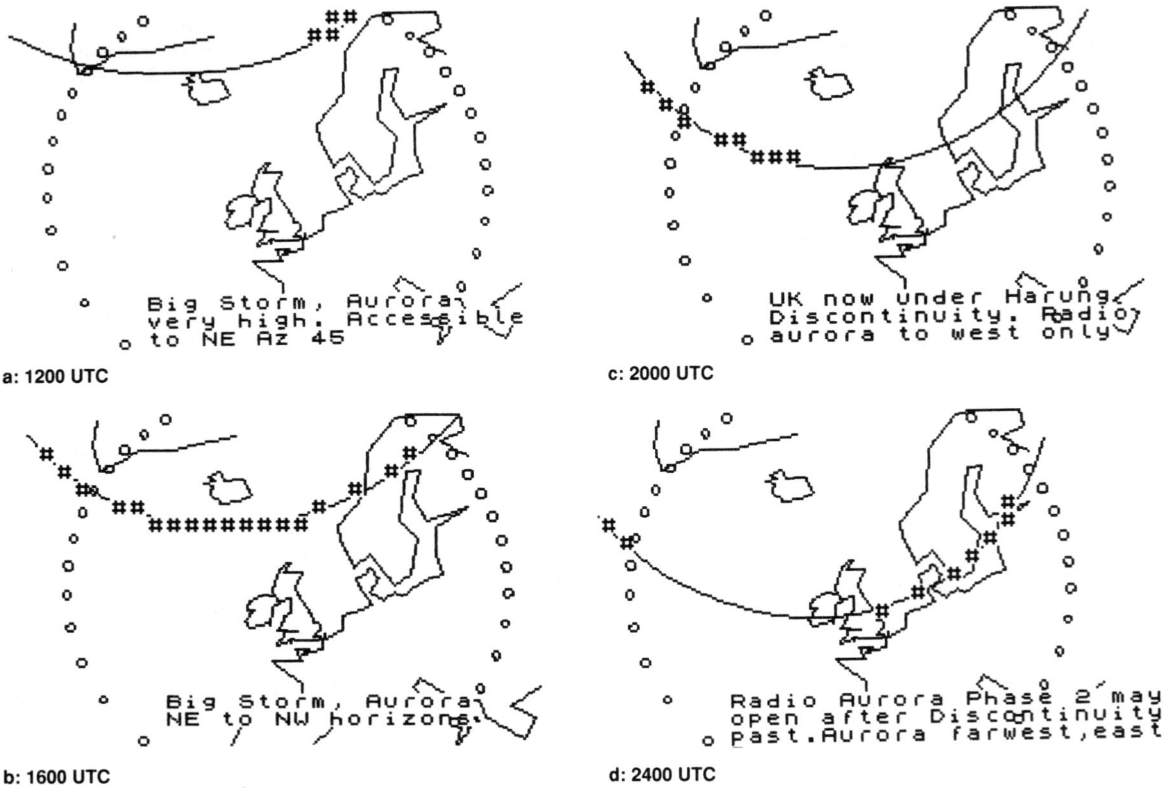

Fig 2.18a-d: Progress of a large aurora, strength kp8. Radio aurora is shown as #, central England station horizon shown as o

small aurora loses out in two ways. First, the oval itself is further north, and second the much reduced maximum altitude effectively pulls the UK horizon back to a smaller more southerly circle.

At 1200 UTC, Fig 2.19a, though there is probably a radio aurora active over north Cape Norway, it is far below the UK horizon.

By 1600 UTC, Fig 2.19b, the radio aurora is just getting above the UK horizon of northern stations only.

At 2000 UTC, the swing of the polar auroral oval has brought the section nearest the UK much further south, and there is radio auroral activity accessible to the north of the UK. However, the useful period of radio phase 1 aurora is nearly over, so UK operators should be anticipating 10 or at most 20 minutes of auroral E*s* propagation to Sweden and FAI propagation around the UK. These signals will be clear tone, and users should on no account train their antennas away from the aurora. Stay aimed at the aurora and do not turn your antenna towards the great circle path to the signal source, or you will lose it.

At 2400 UTC, Fig 2.19d shows that the aurora is probably over for UK operators. Second-phase radio auroras are rare during small magnetic storms. If the rare one does occur, it will peak on azimuths 60 to 90 degrees and favour contacts with Baltic states.

There is no record of activity west of the UK being possible in small auroras, but it should not be totally ruled out. Indeed, back scatter to Germany via azimuths near 330 degrees is common and at least one superb example of FAI propagation UK-Greenland followed a poor aurora.

Planetary magnetic index Kp

The term 'Kp' has been used in Figs 2.18 and 2.19. It is a measure of magnetic activity averaged and weighted to give a good general guide to changes in the Earth's magnetic field over several hours. Typically, Kp0 is magnetic quiet, Kp3 produces auroras accessible in Scotland, Kp4 auroras are accessible from central England, Kp6 are all-UK auroras and Kp8 auroras are accessible as far south as Switzerland and northern Italy.

The term 'magnetic A index' which is sometimes reported relates to a particular station and is not used for area auroral projections.

Magnetic storm fluctuations

The 'magnetic gun' in the Earth's magnetotail, which is triggered by large increases in the solar wind flux, takes about three or four hours to 'recharge' after firing. Big

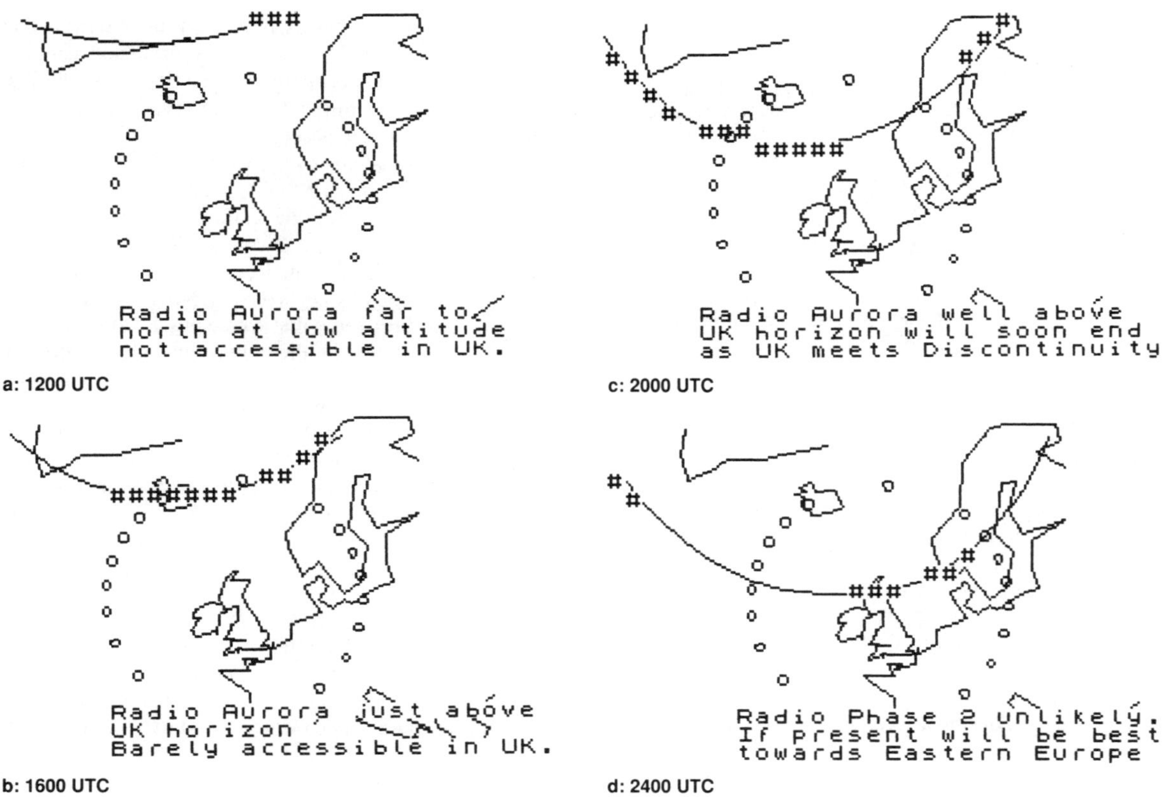

Fig 2.19a-d: Progress of a small aurora, strength kp4. Radio aurora is shown as #, central England station horizon shown as o

auroral storms are therefore subject to intense peaks every three or four hours, for as long as the enhanced solar activity continues.

Stop-start auroras

Please note that an auroral sequence starts when enhanced solar wind hits the magnetosphere. If this is LMT midnight at your station you can only get radio phase 2. If by contrast the solar wind decreases in phase 1, that ends the aurora.

Terrestrial auroral propagation

Both partial reflection and scatter propagation appear to be present in some degree in auroral conditions. Measured peak electron densities around 1 million electrons per cubic centimetre suggest plasma frequencies of about 9MHz maximum and hence possible oblique incidence refraction up to three times = 27MHz. So refraction does not appear to be a very likely mode unless the aurora is abnormally big. Radar measurements do show that the electron density gradients in auroras are often very sharp indeed, which makes partial reflection a likely propagation mode. In addition both forward and back scatter modes are encountered in auroras, with back scatter dominating most UK events.

One feature of auroras which makes them unique is the wideband Doppler shift imparted to the signal by the random motion of the auroral curtain. This has the effect of degrading frequency-modulated signals, usually beyond the point where the signal can be read at all. Single side-band voice signals can usually be understood if signal strength is high, but careful tuning is necessary. By contrast, CW morse signals are easily read and therefore feature strongly in the majority of long-distance auroral communication at VHF.

Aurora propagate signals in the frequency range 20 to 70MHz strongly. Frequencies up to 150MHz are propagated less strongly but still usefully, whilst signals up to 500MHz are sometimes propagated effectively in very strong auroras. So the motto of VHF aurora users is 'CW is best, at 50MHz or possibly 144MHz'.

Satellite auroral propagation

The satellite faces a lot of problems in auroras. It does not need the propagation out to several thousand kilometres, it already has it by virtue of its great height. All an aurora does for satellite users is produce problems and, because the satellite can see so far, virtually any radio aurora anywhere in the polar regions is a potential problem.

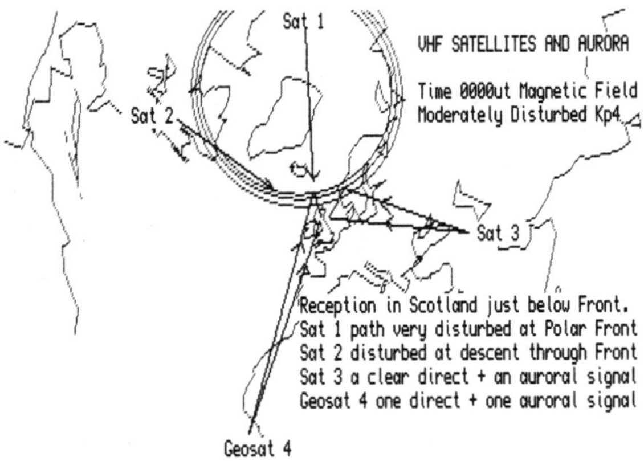

Fig 2.20: Examples of events involving several types of satellites in different orbits

Auroral enhancement of propagation of satellite signals can occur but it is an unnecessary nuisance. In a typical incident the author, accessing Oscar 8J (145MHz up), over Norway, found that his normal clear-tone down-link signal on 435MHz had a second auroral version of itself about 600Hz higher in frequency. The situation was further complicated when HG8CY answered GM4IHJ's CQ call, and they began to communicate using a quartet of signals, with the Hungarian signal received at GM4IHJ, both clear and auroral.

As is typical in this sort of situation, the doppelganger signals could be ignored by both stations using narrow-band CW, but communication in a wideband mode such as SSB would have been impossible. So, provided CW is used and the satellite is in between the user stations and the aurora, not much harm is done. The problems start when the aurora, as it often does, gets between the user station and the satellite. Fig 2.20 shows examples of events involving several types of satellites in different orbits.

The effect on satellite VHF signals as they pass over the polar auroral front has been reported in detail in chapter 1 which describes scintillation. Practical experience of these effects on mode J (145MHz up link/435MHz down link) satellites is considerable for both UK and North American operators. Seen from the UK, satellites over Labrador, Greenland or Newfoundland regularly display degradation of signals even on their 435MHz down links such that even the simple morse signals from the beacons of Fuji 12, Oscar 8J and Oscar 10 are unreadable or lost completely for several minutes at a time.

This situation is a very serious problem for professional satellite users. There are several large communities and military bases located above 75°N, permanently inside the polar oval. Normal geostationary satellites cannot see sites at 75°N properly, particularly when the severe 'Arctic mirages' cause severe bending and ducting of microwave signals at the obligatory low elevation reception angles appropriate at these high-latitude sites. Unfortunately VHF circular orbit satellites are no better, because scintillation during auroral zone transit totally degrades the complex signal modulation patterns used. At the time of writing the Americans are still trying, using an experimental satellite called Polar Bear. One day perhaps Polar Bear or something like it will bring real-time television to places like Thule, Greenland, but that day is some way off.

Several radio amateurs have done a great deal of exploratory work in this field. JW9DM, located at 77°N on the island of Svalbard, gave the author several interesting communication sessions via Oscar 8J. More recently, Gordon Wightman, VE5XU, in Regina, Canada, has been investigating Oscar 10 signals on high polar paths and, like the author, has discovered that where possible the satellite frequency used should be the highest available subject to Doppler shift constraints (Doppler shift on UHF satellites can be a serious operating problem).

To summarise, the satellite overhead the polar auroral oval poses special problems. VHF signals are scintillation degraded. UHF signals are partially degraded and microwave signals are subject to very fast Doppler shift when used in low earth circular orbits. The eventual answer to polar zone satellite communications could take one of two forms:

(a) Using elliptical orbit satellites, orbital inclination 60 degrees, giving 'same track, same time', every day, repeats. These molniya-type orbiters feature high apogee altitude and very low Doppler shifts, making them very effective as high-elevation microwave or UHF signal sources to polar ground stations. They have an additional advantage that they can 'see' the equatorial geostationary satellites and can relay signals received from them.

(b) A possible alternative system might use near-circular orbiters far out at long range from Earth. The latest versions of the Soviet and American navigation satellites feature this kind of orbit. It has relatively slow Doppler shift even at low microwave frequencies, but it is expensive to launch and needs powerful transmitters because of its long range. The proposed French satellite 'Arsene' may have some of these features and could therefore be a good guide to the future.

Worldwide auroras and satellites

In the early Soviet investigations of airglows and auroras, cosmonaut Valery Ryumin produced excellent photographic evidence for hydrogen-red auroras at a height of about 450km above the Earth's equatorial zones. Meanwhile, in a totally separate serious of experiments, radio amateur operators north and south of the equator produced clear evidence of transequatorial 7,000km propagation of VHF and UHF signals. These signals often exhibited marked auroral tone degradation.

At first sight this evidence might appear to be of no consequence to northern Europeans, noting that a site 450km above the equatorial regions is far below the UK horizon. It is, however, not below the horizon of many satellites accessible from the UK.

Fig 2.21: Salyut/Cosmos tracks during solar minimum from which auroral signals have been received in the UK

Fig 2.21 shows HF satellite tracks from which auroral signals have been received in the UK. These tracks appear to be of two types:

(a) The North American tracks, which are near enough to the polar regions for the satellite to see the polar auroral oval, whence signals might be scattered to the UK. But this apparently feasible mechanism overlooks the fact that these incidents take place at times when the magnetic field is quiet and hence the polar oval is well below the UK horizon. All of which probably explains why these events are apparently restricted to HF signals because they have the bonus that once they are scattered by the polar auroras, they may be propagated to the UK via the ionosphere.

(b) The west African tracks which are particularly notable in the UK morning, 0830 to 1200 UTC, in both summer and winter. Here there is no question of the polar auroras being involved, and there is as yet no suggestion from these events that they favour a particular level of magnetic activity. What is clear about them is that many of them exhibit anomalous high Doppler shift, consistent with the signal being received in the UK, not directly from the satellite via a great circle ionospheric path, but via the ionosphere and via a non-great circle path. The signal first goes south from the satellite, encounters an 'auroral scatterer' and is sent towards the UK where it arrives with the help of normal daytime ionospheric propagation.

This equatorial scatterer is not unknown to terrestrial HF users, being perhaps related to their 'route' to North America via an African back scatter zone.

This could be a rich area for satellite experimenters, noting that its equipment requirement, just a shortwave receiver, is easily satisfied.

Auroral absorption

Up to now this chapter has treated auroras solely as a propagation or scintillation source. However, the polar auroral zone is also the site of severe signal absorption at HF. Any signal path venturing above latitude 65°N, eg just north of Scotland, can be subject to this HF absorption. Care should be taken to distinguish this absorption, which severely reduces the signal strength, from the random Doppler bandshift which can turn a clear signal into an unreadable hiss.

Absorption of HF signals in the auroral zone is of two types:

(a) Polar cap absorption is an irregular phenomenon caused by a type of solar flare which emits a dense stream of protons (ionised hydrogen atoms). The polar cap absorption (PCA) event begins as the protons penetrate right down to the D layer of the polar ionosphere. The duration of a PCA event can be several hours, or in extreme cases several days, and its intensity is much reduced at night when free electrons produced by the proton bombardment disappear more rapidly. Fig 2.22 shows an idealised plot of a PCA event, with the day/night intensity modulation clearly evident. Strong PCAs can totally block HF satellite links which transit the polar auroral zone.

(b) Auroral absorption is by contrast a continuous phenomenon of varying intensity. It is caused by ionisation of the polar ionosphere induced by solar wind electrons accelerated in the Earth's magnetotail by field line reconnections, which are then guided back to Earth, entering the ionosphere above the polar regions. This is a continuous process, not a stop-go process as is the PCA event. What changes here is the scale. The bigger the solar wind input, the greater the spread away from the poles of the polar oval, thus bringing the absorption to signal paths crossing lower latitudes. Fig 2.23 shows a typical auroral absorption curve.

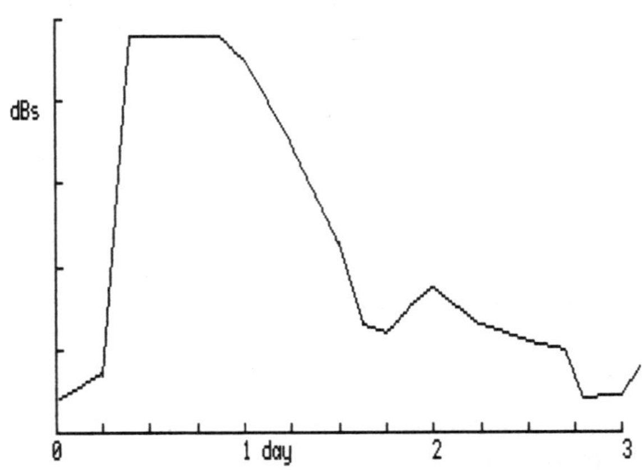

Fig 2.22: A plot of a polar cap absorption event. Note reduction in absorption at night

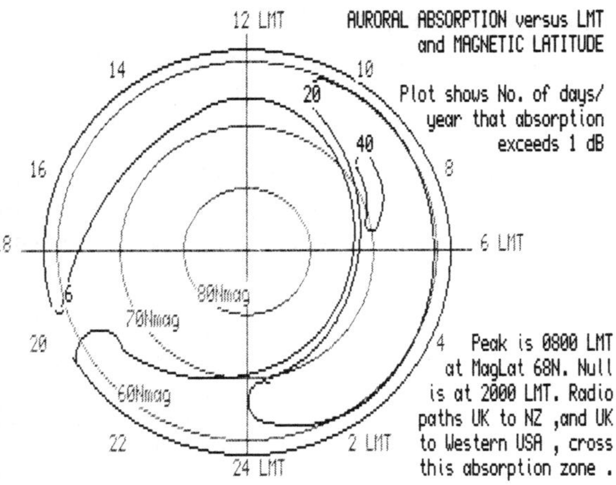

Fig 2.23: A typical auroral absorption curve

Up to the 1970s, the geographical extension southward of the absorption zone in magnetic storms was assumed to be in step with the movement of visual auroras. It is now appreciated that any association is a loose one at best. As a general rule, auroral absorption should be regarded as varying not only in accordance with geomagnetic conditions and the position of the auroral oval, but also, probably more importantly, varying with local magnetic time and the complexities of the far-from-simple octopolar Earth magnetic field. One serious effect of this is that auroral absorption in the southern hemisphere is not in step with auroral absorption in the northern hemisphere.

Because of the seasonal change of solar declination and hence the shape of the Earth's magnetosphere relative to a spot on its surface, there is a marked seasonal change in auroral absorption levels. Equally noteworthy there is superimposed on this a daily pattern of variation in auroral absorption which reaches its most extreme above geomagnetic latitude 68 degrees at around 1000 LMT. There is a secondary absorption peak around LMT midnight, and the absorption minima occur at about 1800 and 0500 LMT. Fig 2.24 shows absorption data for a Soviet station at 68°N magnetic. This data is derived from an instrument called a 'riometer'.

Many satellite orbits result in their down-link paths to the UK passing over the absorption zone. Even in quiet magnetic conditions HF satellites north of the UK experience severe absorption on their downlinks. Radiosport satellites are particularly at risk, passing north of the UK on five orbits out of 12 each day, and Oscar 6, 7 and 8 have all suffered severe absorption on their mode A HF down links whilst transiting polar regions.

As more riometer stations are set up, it may become possible to get enough empirical absorption data to allow the generation of suitable computer algorithms to predict absorption. In the satellite case the location at which absorption should be predicted is that where the signal path descends through the E and D layers of the ionosphere.

Predicting auroras

The standard chart for auroral prediction is a 27-day calendar synchronised to the solar equatorial rotation period.

The most likely time for an aurora is 27 days after a previous aurora. A simple 27-day chart soon reveals when this sequence is likely to repeat and it also has the merit of showing when three and four day clumps of consecutive aurora days have occurred and may repeat 27 days later. These clumps of auroras over several days are usually caused by coronal holes on the Sun. Each time the Sun rotates to bring a big hole round to face the Earth we can expect moderate auroras for the several days the hole is facing us. Then, 27 days and one solar rotation later, the process can repeat over again. In some cases five separate repeats of three or four days of auroras have spread over 108 days.

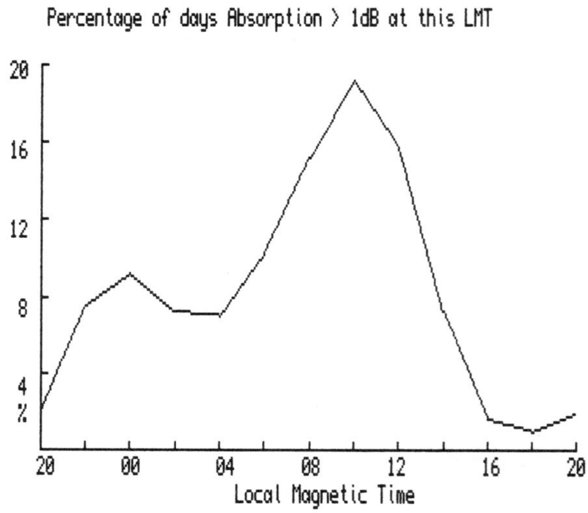

Fig 2.24: Plot of auroral absorption daily cycle at 68°N during solar minimum

Another useful source of auroral prediction is the RSGB news bulletins. Charlie Newton, G2FKZ, is responsible for this excellent service. He gets bulletins from several radio laboratories around the world who monitor solar activity. Each week he gives a steady stream of predictions for the next 10 days or so, including the likelihood of coronal holes or the other source of auroras, the solar flare. G2FKZ's predictions use measured solar parameters plus a lot of visual, radio and X-ray observation data. Given for example that a trained observer can spot a coronal hole as it comes round the edge of the Sun towards us, several days' warning is possible.

Personal early warning of auroras

Armed with G2FKZ's predictions and one's personal 27-day calendar of auroras, the satellite and terrestrial radio operator should know when to look. The next step is to decide on the best way to use the radio equipment you have to maximise your chances of hearing the aurora as soon as it starts. It is of course possible to listen to the radio amateur bands for auroral hiss on signals. A much stronger method used by many radio amateurs employs the high-powered European TV and FM stations. Fig 2.08 lists these stations. Equally useful, now that the 50MHz band is available to UK radio amateurs, are the excellent beacons appearing in that band. Experience with 50MHz in auroras is limited at the time of writing, but one group of frequencies worth monitoring in big auroras are the American and Canadian public service and paging frequencies around 47MHz. Many of these stations are callsign locatable, which gives an excellent hint as to just which part of North America you are getting auroral signals from.

Last but not least, early warning of auroras may be obtained by monitoring the 153.213MHz auroral radar at Wick. Using amplitude modulation reception for best results, this signal can be heard on azimuths near 10 degrees from all parts of the UK. The transmitter is one of a stereoscopic pair of scientific radars: the other is located at Uppsala in Sweden. Together these two SABRE radars aim at a patch of the E layer of the ionosphere west of Bergen, Norway. Even a weak Kp2 aurora, normally far below the UK station horizons, can produce strong reflections of the Wick SABRE signal for stations as far south as Lancashire. If you can monitor Wick, you should catch the start of every aurora likely to affect the UK, and it often gives evidence of weak auroras far from the UK which can affect satellite circuits. This radar is operated by Leicester University which has produced a wealth of papers reporting auroral ionospheric circulation patterns and their movements.

Auroral E*s*

This is the slightly confusing name given to a form of VHF anomalous propagation, which is neither auroral in tone, nor in any way connected with sporadic E. Auroral E*s* are zones of anomalous propagation in the E layer of the ionosphere, which sometimes precede or follow periods of radio auroral propagation at VHF. The characteristics of propagation via auroral E*s* are similar to those of sporadic E. The signals are received clear tone, un-degraded, with the two stations communicating via a roughly great circle path where the auroral E is located at the centre of the path. It is sometimes called 'through-the-aurora propagation', because after a standard radio aurora phase 1, auroral E*s* can sometimes provide a clear-tone propagation path to stations the other side of the recently terminated radio aurora. In a typical incident, as a small radio aurora phase 1 ended, a station in Northern Ireland had an auroral E*s* contact with a station in the far north east of Sweden at 144MHz.

Since this event, stations using moonbounce narrow-beam high-gain antennas and high transmitter powers have found that contacts seem to be possible on this path Scotland/Ireland to north Sweden, even when no obvious aurora is present. Auroral E*s* may prove to be very useful to terrestrial operators once the mechanism is better understood. There is no evidence of auroral E*s* affecting signals from space.

Operating in auroral conditions

Space radio operators should be aware of several special conditions which apply to operating in auroral conditions.

(a) The signal returned by the aurora comes back from a rapidly moving shimmering curtain. This imparts random Doppler shift to the elements of the signal, so that the receiver often has to cope with a signal coming by a direct path which is clear tone, overlaid by a signal resembling wideband noise, eg reducing the overall signal-to-noise ratio.

(b) Because of these Doppler effects, it may be necessary temporarily to use narrow-band communications such as CW. SSB voice signals need to be at least 6dB stronger than noise before they can be resolved properly. Frequency modulated speech or telegraphy using FM only succeeds when a very strong signal is present.

(c) Despite the wideband nature of a satellite CW signal read after passage through an aurora, weak auroral CW is often best copied on a narrow (about 200Hz) bandwidth filter. This technique seems to be useful for copying HF satellites in equatorial zone auroras.

(d) High-power, big antenna stations have a marked advantage in auroral conditions, always pre-supposing that the operator has accurate satellite tracking predictions and the signal follows the predicted great circle path.

Field-aligned irregularity propagation

Scatter propagation of radio frequency signals from 19 to 450MHz via magnetically aligned ionospheric irregularities has been observed but not well understood for 40 years. Generally referred to as 'FAIs' (field-aligned irregularities), they can take several forms and derive from several distinct sources. Work by radio amateurs, following up transequatorial contacts on 144 and 435MHz, was further supplemented by reports of reception of Oscar 7 at VHF when it was far below the receiving station horizon. Here in the UK, several radio amateurs noticed the brief propagation events which often preceded or followed auroras, and in central Europe radio amateurs began to explore what became known as 'transalpine VHF propagation'. This series of investigations was full of setbacks until operators began to appreciate the special rules which apply to FAI propagation. No one can use FAIs instinctively. If you treat them as a normal VHF anomalous propagation mode, you will fail to get results. Learn the FAI rules, and you will get plenty of excellent opportunities for communication and experiment.

How FAIs form

FAIs can have several different starting points, but all of those known so far can be grouped under a single broad description: FAIs most frequently occur when a major ionospheric anomaly such as sporadic E or an aurora begins to fade. In the case of sporadic E this usually happens after sunset. As the solar bombardment reduces as night approaches, it becomes too low to maintain the sporadic E. In the case of auroras, FAIs occur most often, just as the sub-polar ionospheric discontinuity comes past your station, terminating radio aurora phase 1. In both the SpE and auroral cases, the ionised plasma begins to disperse, but its direction of movement is constrained by the Earth's magnetic field. Ionised material/charged particles can easily move parallel to the magnetic field lines, but it cannot easily move across those same field lines.

In a typical situation over the UK, a sporadic E platelet goes into Earth shadow at sunset. Its constituent charged particles are free to disperse both up and down parallel to the steeply dipping magnetic field lines (about 65 degrees over the UK). In addition, the charged particles can disperse east-west between the magnetic field lines, but they cannot disperse north-south through the lines.

The charged particles behave rather like a herd of bulls in a meadow. If there is no barbed wire they can spread in every direction, but if they are in a lane between two lines of barbed wire, they cannot cross the wire and can spread only between the wire into a long thin line. Fig 2.25 shows what happens to the SpE platelet as it disperses to form a thin tilted plate of ionised material aligned with respect to the local magnetic field.

Eventually, of course, the material will disperse completely but there is a useful period during which the FAI will propagate VHF signals before complete dispersal ends useful propagation. In the case of SpE, extreme events can last for an hour but events of 10 or 20 minutes duration are much more common. In an FAI event following an auroral precursor, the useful period is rarely greater than 10 minutes.

VHF propagation occurs because the magnetically aligned sheet of charged particles forms a crude mirror capable of providing partial reflection or scatter. Only the south face of the FAI is useful, because the alignment of the magnetic field lines above Europe is such that they tilt downwards towards the south at an angle of 50 to 70 degrees to the horizontal. The north side of the FAI therefore tilts up into space, rendering it useless for terrestrial VHF propagation and a problem for signals coming from, or going up to, space.

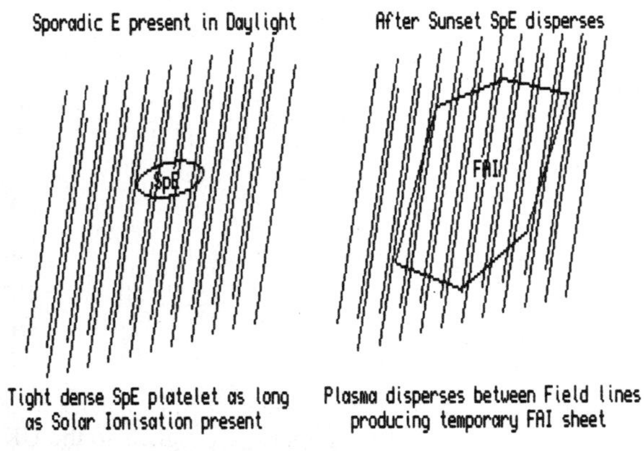

Fig 2.25: What happens to an SpE platelet as it disperses to form a thin tilted plate of ionised material

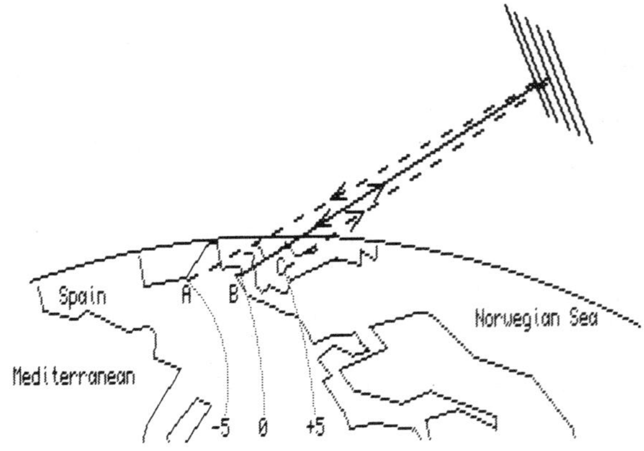

Fig 2.26: Typical geometry of magnetic field aligned irregularity propagation

Fig 2.26 shows the typical geometry of magnetic field-aligned irregularity propagation experienced over temperate latitudes.

History of FAI studies

Radio amateurs were among the first to recognise FAI propagation. The generally accepted first FAI event reported worldwide occurred when a station on the Caribbean island of Puerto Rico monitoring Oscar operation realised he was hearing a station far to his south below the equator in Argentina. The LU station was transmitting on 432MHz trying to access satellite Oscar 7, and it was this signal which was being propagated to Puerto Rico.

This was of course an equatorial FAI event, which employed the tangential alignment of the magnetic field lines across the equator as a propagation duct. FAI mirror scatter is only possible when the magnetic field alignment is near vertical. None the less, the field-aligned nature of the contact was soon appreciated, and several European and American stations began to wonder whether the European transalpine propagation and the American transcontinental propagation were field-aligned phenomena. Professional radar investigations in the USA soon settled the question in favour of FAIs.

Despite this good start, it was nearly 10 more years before the subject took off. The mathematics of FAIs are not simple, and it was not until microcomputers became commonplace in the early 1980s that FAIs became usable, due to the programs produced by amateur radio software specialists.

How and where FAIs propagate radio signals

A typical mid-latitude FAI 'spider plot' is shown at Fig 2.27. This reproduces 'in the flat' the situation shown in Fig 2.26. These two figures will be used to describe temperate latitude FAI propagation.

As Fig 2.25 shows, the FAI evolves as a tilted crude mirror facing south. Stations to the west, east and south can access this south face and scatter signals off it. There is no question of reflection or refraction; the electron density profile of the FAI is far too weak to support those modes of propagation. Signals scattered from the FAI return to Earth spread along discrete arcs.

A station at point B on Fig 2.26 is in the right position relative to the FAI to hit it absolutely normal at 90 degrees to its mirror surface plane. So a signal from B is back scattered by the FAI straight back, returning to Earth scattered along the 0 degree offset curve. This 0 degree curve is shown on both Fig 2.26 and Fig 2.27. The nature of the curve on the spider plot of Fig 2.27 becomes obvious when the signal is pictured as returning to the surface of the spherical Earth. Any station on this 'normal to the FAI' curve can communicate via the FAI with any other station located on this same curve. Please note the golden rule: both stations must point at the FAI – not at each other.

By contrast, a station in central England at point C hits the FAI at 95 degrees to its surface and its signal scatters back at 85 degrees to a –5 degree curve covering a wide arc from France to Yugoslavia. The English station is shown on Fig 2.27 on the +5 degree curve as befits its signal arrival angle at the FAI. The geometry of the FAI scatter dictates that he can only communicate with stations on the curve of equal offset angle and opposite sign. He can talk only to stations on the –5 degree curve; he cannot talk to stations on his own curve or any other curve except –5 degrees. Station A on the French Atlantic coast could communicate with the English Midlands, as could stations in Switzerland or anywhere else on the –5 degree curve.

For simplicity only three curves are shown in Fig 2.26. Fig 2.27 shows the much more practical set of curves.

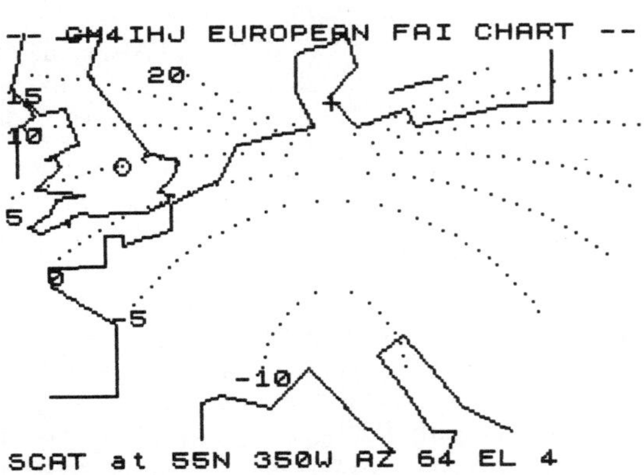

Fig 2.27: European FAI chart

Anyone on the –10 degree curve in southern France, Switzerland and Italy can exchange signals via the FAI with stations on the +10 degree curve covering northern England, north Germany, Poland and Russia.

GM4IHJ is located in Scotland just above the +15 degree curve but, as Fig 2.27 shows, the –15 degree curve does not touch the Earth in this event, so GM4IHJ and anyone else north of the +10 degree curve is out of luck.

Please note that you do not have to live exactly on a curve. A station in Bristol two-thirds of the way between the 0 and the +5 degree curves would find his signals coming down and replies coming from a curve two-thirds of the way down between the 0 degree curve and the -5 degree curve, ie Brittany, Calais, central Germany, south Poland and south west Russia.

Finding FAIs

The two best-known sources of northern temperate zone FAIs are sporadic E and auroras. Auroral FAI type propagation is sometimes present in the opening minutes of an aurora, but it is rapidly displaced by auroral tone signals as the radio aurora gets going. The best time for FAIs is as the aurora fades in the evening at the end of radio phase 1. As the aurora weakens you need do no more than keep your antenna pointed at it, at the azimuth which was previously giving you good auroral returns. You should listen for signals which get clearer in tone, gradually losing their auroral hiss. When you hear these signals do not under any circumstances move your antenna, keep it where it is and call the stations you hear. You probably have 10 minutes at most to get contacts and explore the FAI, so make the most of it.

There are three things to note about typical FAI signals. They can sound slightly auroral, they are fluttery, and they sometimes have quite large Doppler shift. This last property is very important on CW because the author has several times missed a contact because he stayed tuned on the other station. In fact tuning 1 or 2kHz down on your transmit frequency is often necessary to match the other stations actual transmit frequency – the frequency he is listening to. Note this shift applied to 144MHz signals.

Like auroras, sporadic E propagation is not hard to find. It has a big summer daylight season and a small winter season. As the Sun sets, the low-altitude E layer is soon in darkness and SpE starts to fade. As the SpE fades, the FAI propagation often starts. The clue to this change is the sudden absence of SpE great circle propagated signals from stations on the same azimuth as your antenna. Replacing them, the FAI signals come from places far from the great circle path and nowhere near where your antenna is pointing. Where the SpE signals were firm with deep slow fading, the FAI signals have fast flutter and sound slightly auroral in tone.

A typical event in 1986 involved a SpE platelet over Denmark, which had been propagating signals to the UK from east Poland. Suddenly, the Polish TV on 49.75MHz began to fade and fluttery 144MHz signals from Austria and

Yugoslavia appeared on a two-metre receiver tuned to the amateur radio band. These signals were present for about 10 minutes. But what is really interesting about this particular episode is that it is a clear example of the fact that FAIs can sometimes propagate signals at much higher frequencies than the relatively weak sporadic E they replace. If you identify the locations of SpE platelets during the day, assuming the platelet is in the E layer half-way between you and the stations you are hearing via SpE, you can run computer predictions to be ready for the FAIs which may follow. It must be remembered, however, that SpE platelets need to be east or slightly north of you for you to be able access the south face of any subsequent FAIs. SpE at a lower latitude than your station latitude is unlikely to produce useful FAIs.

FAIs and space communications

FAIs can be a brief but serious problem when they occur between your station and a satellite. Local sunset in the northern European summer is a time to be avoided by VHF and UHF space communicators. Unlike the terrestrial situation, where only the south face of the FAI is used for propagation, in space communications FAIs are bad news no matter whether they are north, south, east or west of your station.

There is clear evidence from radar experiments that FAIs are more frequently active propagators of HF signals 19 to 29MHz, than they are of, say, 50MHz signals or above. This radar evidence also confirms that mid-latitude FAIs are an E layer phenomenon. In spite of this, FAI propagation and other effects do not cease above 50MHz. FAIs can both propagate and degrade signals up to 250MHz and higher, but the clear message is that FAIs play a much greater part than formerly realised in propagation 19 to 29MHz.

Actual amateur radio operation does indeed show that sub-horizon reception of 20MHz and 29MHz satellite signals often has all the characteristics of FAI propagation. The signals are fluttery, slightly auroral in tone and carry anomalous Doppler shift, but they have one unusual feature: they occur in daylight. There is of course no reason why the FAI propagation has to occur at night. Its two chief sources are night-time events, but it is possible that there are other FAI sources available in daylight as yet unrecognised.

HF satellite events

At 1428 UTC Cosmos 1686 was overhead 51°N 116°W (western Canada), and its beacon on 19.955MHz was audible in the UK via sub-horizon ionospheric propagation. The signal had a Doppler shift 500Hz too high for its relative velocity with respect to the UK. The signal was fluttering and T4 slightly auroral, and was tracked until 1435:30 UTC when it suddenly became clear tone as it passed nearly overhead New York. It was then tracked for a further nine minutes during which period its Doppler shift was normally in accord with its relative velocity with respect to the UK. This event repeated again on the next day. Magnetic conditions were very quiet.

A second event, similar in many ways, involved the same spacecraft as it crossed Quebec, coming east at 1124 UTC. The signal had a high abnormal Doppler shift and, although the satellite aspect and relative velocity changed markedly as it continued east and south for the next nine minutes, the signal frequency stayed high with no tuning required, even though it was being read through a tight 200Hz filter. According to computer simulation, the received signal should have been 200Hz lower at first detection and another 400Hz lower when lost nine minutes later. This type of Doppler anomaly appears to point to a scatter zone ahead of the satellite, ie south of it, which does not sound like typical FAI propagation but points rather to a somewhat different source of scatter propagation.

This satellite evidence is more in accord with HF scatter propagation at sunspot maximum 1980 which provided UK to USA communication at 50MHz and 28MHz via west Africa, and or the Caribbean, when the direct great circle path to USA would not support these frequencies. A combination of satellite and terrestrial observation as we climb to the next sunspot maximum may produce more evidence in regard to these events.

Equatorial FAIs

Radio amateur studies, involving transequatorial terrestrial experiments and Oscar satellite sub-horizon experiments, have revealed a wealth of propagation features over the equator.

Above the magnetic equator the magnetic field lines are tangential – almost horizontal, with respect to the Earth below, a quite different alignment from that pertaining over Europe and other temperate regions. None the less, the equatorial version of FAIs seem to afford excellent propagation paths whereby the propagation appears to be ducted north-south, south-north along the flux tubes. Access to, and exit from, these tubes is clearly possible at related magnetic latitudes north and south of the equator.

It is therefore possible that satellite experiments from stations in northern Europe using, say, satellite Fuji Oscar 12, could be quite interesting as the next transequatorial VHF/UHF season approaches. All in all, FAIs, though at present one of the least understood of propagation modes, appear to offer some of the best opportunities for space radio experiments in the next decade.

Microwaves

Above a frequency of 1GHz we enter the microwave region of the radio spectrum. The first and most obvious indication that something has changed is the replacement of familiar circuit components such as coils, capacitors and coaxial cable, by strip lines, resonant cavities and waveguides. In many respects the bottom part of the microwaves – 1GHz to 2GHz – acts as a halfway house between these two totally different techniques, but above 2GHz microwave 'plumbing' takes over completely.

This new technology is expensive, but this is acceptable because we simply do not have enough bandwidth at VHF and UHF in which to cram all the satellite communications and TV facilities we now use. To summarise all the advantages and disadvantages of going up to the microwaves, we need to consider the following points:

Factor	**Microwave**	**VHF/UHF**
Propagation reliability	Good	Poor
Useful bandwidth	Good	Poor
Doppler	Problem LEO. Geostationary or deep space no problem	No problem
Costs	High	Low
Area coverage	Poor in polar areas	Good
Antennas	Good high gain	Poor low gain
Natural noise	Acceptable	No problems
Man-made noise	Some problems	Severe problems

No attempt has been made to weight these comparisons, but in fact some are so important that they cannot be ignored.

The enormous expansion of commercial and TV satellites simply would not have been possible in the VHF and UHF bands. In certain fields, such as deep space work, high antenna gain is essential at both the satellite and the ground terminals. Only at microwaves are mechanically practical high-gain antennas available. So it is no surprise that nearly all commercial and military space communication now uses microwave frequencies. Only mobile communications and radio amateurs remain on VHF and UHF for space radio work. Many services, eg weathersats and navigation sats, have up till now duplicated VHF/UHF and microwave facilities, but this changeover period is ending with all new satellites being exclusively microwave.

Mobile communications are likely to stay on UHF, because antenna constraints, eg guiding a beam antenna located on a pitching, rolling ship, are best satisfied by wide-beam antennas and robust hardware. Radio amateurs remain on VHF/UHF because microwave equipment is too expensive and is not easily available but, as more and more commercial microwave equipment is produced, the costs are falling rapidly and the number of readily available microwave components is rising exponentially. Take-off point is still a few years ahead, but by 1995 radio amateurs and space radio listeners will be able to exploit the microwaves without spending a fortune or having to make their own, often intricate, microwave components.

Propagation of microwave radio

The transparency of the atmosphere over the radio frequency spectrum from LF to microwaves is plotted in Fig 2.28. Below 3MHz the ionosphere is opaque, so no radio signals get through. From 3MHz to 50MHz the ionosphere is variable, nearly transparent at night, but far less so in daylight. Above 50MHz, all the way up to 30,000MHz (30GHz), the ionosphere is not a problem in its normal quiet state, whilst the neutral atmosphere can cause some problems but these are not insuperable. Above 30GHz the situation changes markedly as the wavelength of the signal decreases to the point where molecular attenuation can be very serious. At present few services use the microwaves above 30GHz but, by picking the gaps between the molecular absorption frequencies, it will eventually be possible to utilise frequencies up to 1,000GHz if required. Above this frequency we have left the microwaves and what are sometimes called the 'millimetric waves', and we have have entered the infra-red portion of the spectrum. Operation at infra-red is not practical from the Earth's surface, except on mountain tops.

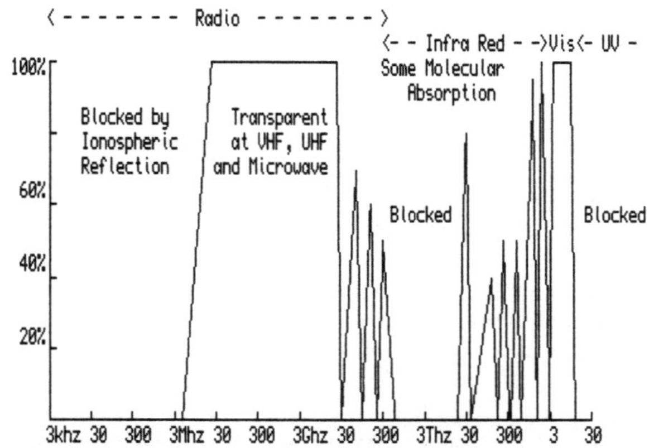

Fig 2.28: Radio transparent windows in space

The discussion which follows will therefore concentrate on the frequencies between 1GHz and 30GHz. In this region the degrading anomalous propagation present at VHF and UHF is mostly absent. Sporadic E, auroras, FAIs and special effects like Faraday rotation of polarisation are absent, but this does not mean that there are no microwave propagation problems.

Scintillation

One of the major shocks of the 1970s was the P76 experiment studying scintillation. Because scintillation was not anticipated at microwaves, the experiment used a 2.3GHz phase-locked reference signal for its family of UHF and VHF beacons.

It was anticipated that important scintillation measurements would be made using the clear, undegraded 2.3GHz signal as a reference for the other beacons. In fact this did not prove to be possible because scintillation was present at times on the 2.3GHz microwave reference. So scintillation is a problem even at microwaves, although not as serious a problem as it is at VHF. Scintillation can occur both in the ionosphere and the atmosphere, and in interplanetary space. In the latter case the solar wind is the premier source of plasma causing scintillation.

The atmosphere and microwaves

At microwave frequencies the atmosphere begins to have more effect on the signal than does the ionosphere. Attenuation/absorption increases with frequency, its principal sources being atmospheric oxygen, water vapour and rain.

Fig 2.29 shows typical attenuation curves for atmospheric oxygen and water vapour. Attenuation increases with frequency and it also increases if the path through the denser lower regions of the atmosphere is long, eg when path line of sight is low elevation.

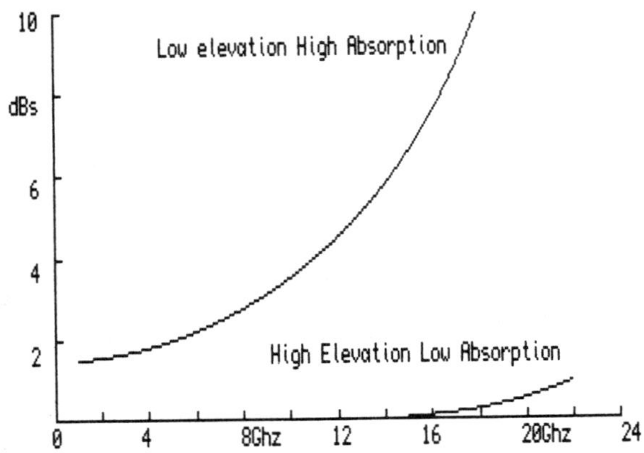

Fig 2.29: Microwave absorption by atmospheric oxygen and water vapour. Note reduction in absorption as elevation of line of sight increases

Fig 2.30 shows the attenuation produced by rain per kilometre of path length. Rainfall at 2.5cm per hour is heavy rain, rain at 5cm per hour is torrential rain. In each case the total attenuation must consider the length of the signal path affected by the rain, eg a high-elevation path getting quickly through the rain would be only slightly attenuated.

Atmospheric refraction bending

An observer watching the setting Sun sees an odd, enlarged shape as it nears the horizon. In similar circumstances the Moon is also distorted.

The problem is atmospheric refraction, the bending of any or all electromagnetic signals passing through a path of varying density and refractive index.

When the Sun is at 45 degrees elevation, refraction is slight at about +1 minute of arc. As the Sun descends to 10 degrees elevation refraction increases to +5 minutes of arc. By 5 degree elevation the Sun actually appears to be 10 minutes of arc, equal to one sixth of a degree higher than its true position, and by the time it gets half a degree below the horizon, refraction has risen to 34 minutes of arc, so it appears to be still above the horizon.

Assuming a pressure of 1010 millibars and a temperature of 10°C:

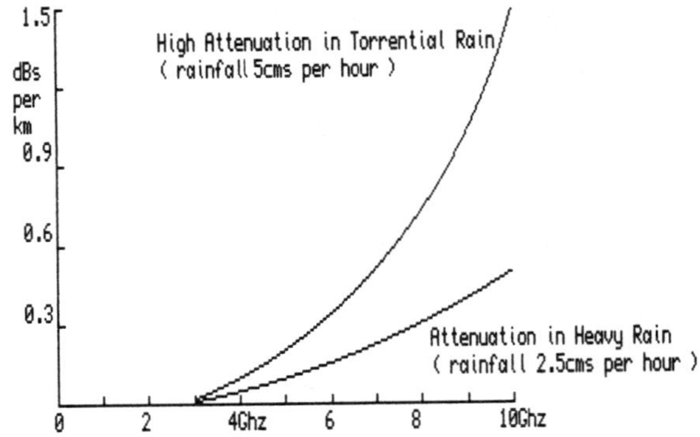

Fig 2.30: Microwave attenuation per kilometre in heavy rain

Refraction in mins =

$$(1.02/\tan(\text{true El} + 10.3 /(\text{true El} + 5.11)))$$

where elevation is in degrees.

This effect can have an important consequence, often missed by satellite users. Fig 2.31 shows the track of a low-elevation pass of Radiosport 7. Any attempt to relate the time the satellite is heard (usually called 'acquisition of satellite' or 'AOS') with true horizon crossing is likely to be 30 seconds to a full minute in error. A similar effect occurs as the satellite goes below the horizon, its radio signal being maintained by atmospheric refraction for a further 30 seconds or more.

Atmospheric refraction makes satellite position experiments of this type far too inaccurate for useful tracking. Doppler timing of closest point of approach is a much more accurate satellite position check.

Anomalous atmospheric bending

There are several different forms of atmospheric anomaly which can affect microwave propagation. Most familiar to VHF users is tropospheric bending, where sharp atmospheric pressure gradients can at times produce severe ray path bending of radio signals. There is, however, little evidence of the effect that tropospheric bending has on signals going to and from space. This is clearly an area where experiments would be desirable.

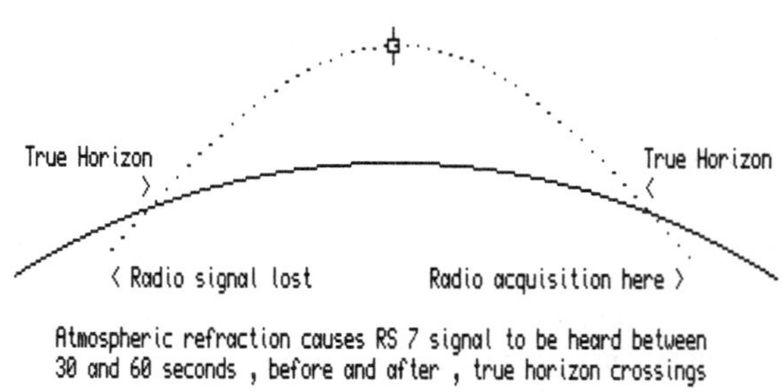

Fig 2.31: Atmospheric refraction makes Radiosport 7 early

Microwave propagation at low-altitude sites

Low-altitude sites have lots of problems at microwave. All signal paths transit the densest part of the atmosphere and all paths to and from space can be subject to anomalies in the atmosphere and thereby degraded.

Microwaves near the sea

Seaside sites or sea-borne platforms and ships have to contend with severe sea surface ducting at times. Sometimes the ducts are very thin, extending only a metre or so above the water, but in typical North Sea conditions equipment sited 30 metres above the water level can be affected quite frequently, with ducts extending up to 200 metres being rare, perhaps twice-a-year features.

Attenuation of microwave satellite signals reaching a site in the duct can be considerable, particularly at low satellite elevation angles. At times in areas bordering the North Sea, signal paths to and from geostationary satellites at typical elevations of 25 degrees max down to 10 degrees min are seriously degraded at low-altitude sites near or on the sea. The only practical solution is move the equipment higher or further from the sea.

In other temperate areas of the world, eg Puget Sound in Washington state in north west USA, this form of ducting can be very severe and frequent.

Microwaves in the Arctic

Severe surface ducting is a regular feature of arctic microwave operation in still air conditions. Microwave navigation satellite results should be treated with care in these conditions. However, the problem with geostationary microwave satellites does not occur in the Arctic, because geostationary satellites cannot effectively 'see' the polar regions.

Microwaves in the tropics

Surface ducting over sea paths is a regular feature of sea state 0 to 2 conditions in tropical waters. These events are most severe at night. Ducts can be thousands of kilometres long. Fortunately geostationary microwave satellites are at high elevation over the tropics and are quite unaffected by this form of anomalous microwave propagation.

High-altitude microwave sites

These have the double advantage of being above most microwave anomalous propagation events, suffering less atmospheric attenuation, so at first sight they might seem ideal for microwave reception of space signals. Unfortunately there can be other problems peculiar to high sites, as anyone who has had to clear the antenna dish of snow can attest. There are also the additional problems in regard to strength and construction of exposed hardware, such as antennas. Wind forces at high exposed sites should not be under estimated.

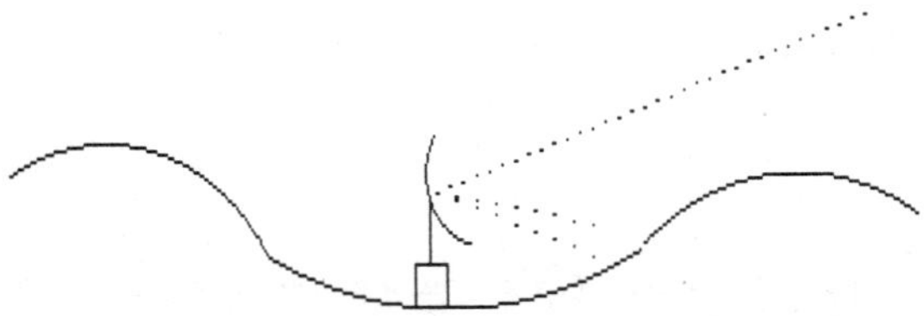

Fig 2.32: Getting a clean site for sensitive microwave reception. Sheltering low hills eliminate side lobe problems which could introduce man made electrical noise. Low elevation angles suffer propagation problems from anomalous atmospheric effects, so clear arcs at low elevation angles are not desirable. Sites under airline flight paths should be avoided

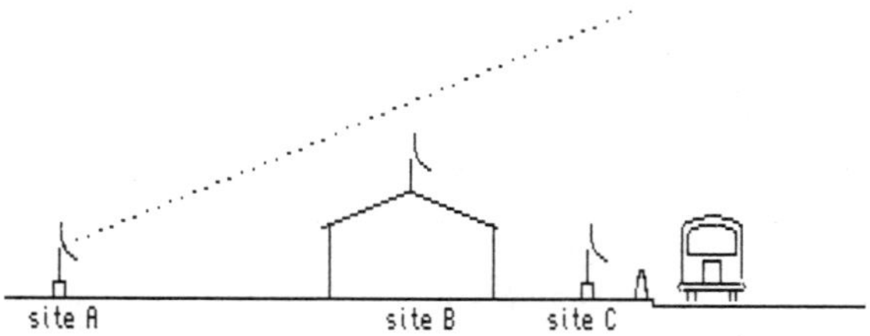

Fig 2.33: Siting of microwave antennas in urban areas. For space radio work a site sheltered from local noise and high winds, eg as at site A, is preferred

Siting of microwave stations

The lower the site, the greater the atmospheric attenuation and anomalous propagation effects. The higher the site, the greater the problems of exposed equipment structural strength and site accessibility. Even at low-altitude sites, microwave equipment such as antennas requires strong supports and fastenings. Never under estimate the wind. A visit by your microwave dish to a neighbour's garden could be very expensive!

Screening of microwave sites

As experimental and radio amateur facilities move up to the microwaves, reduction of man-made noise and elimination of side lobe and ground effects become vitally important. In the 1960s these rules were unknown. A typical problem occurred at a site in Alaska, when the side lobes of the dish antenna picked up so much reflected signal from the Alaskan mountain range 150km away, plus man-made signals from power lines and industrial sites, that sensitive main lobe reception was blanketed out. Fig 2.32 shows how the radio astronomers solved this problem. The microwave site does not need low-elevation reception (ducting will make it useless much of the time anyway). So low-angle reception is sacrificed and the antenna is located in a shallow bowl in the hills. These hills intercept the side lobe returns and all the man-made noise.

This screened site plan is now becoming standard for microwave sites, but does it apply to those of us who have to live in cities? Yes, it does. Fig 2.33 shows the microwave site options available at one Scottish urban site. Most people would probably plump for site B or C, but in fact site A is the preferred site.

Chapter 3

Types of satellites

Introduction

Detailed descriptions of amateur radio satellites, weather satellites and experimental satellites useful to space radio listeners and radio amateurs appear in other chapters of this book. They will therefore be mentioned here in this chapter, only in so far as they fit into the overall satellite picture.

The major portion of this chapter is in the form of a general review of all satellite types. While many of them are strange and indeed remote from the normal activities of the space radio listener and radio amateur, it is none the less clear that in several cases, types of satellites not yet used in the amateur radio or space experimenter field may one day be so used. Indeed, amateur radio co-operative ventures with other space science groups are most likely to venture into some of these less well-known areas of satellite activity. Hence their description here.

Communications satellites (comsats)

These are among the most important and numerous of near-Earth orbit satellites. With few exceptions they use the Clarke geostationary orbit at a height of 35,800km which causes them to circle the Earth's equator once every 24-hour day, and thereby appear to stay stationary when observed from an Earth ground station.

The apparent 'fixed' position in the sky of the geostationary satellites means they have no relative movement with respect to Earth stations in their view of the Earth or 'footprint' as it is called. This immediately solves two of the biggest problems of the communications satellite – Doppler shift tuning and antenna tracking are unnecessary. In addition the extremely high altitude of the geostationary orbit allows them to simultaneously 'see' a footprint area of about 80 degrees radius, eg a geosat stationed at 0°W should be able to see a footprint bounded by 80°W, 80°E (280°W), 80°N and 80°S. In practice, however, this footprint must be scaled down. The 10-degree edges of the footprint provide ground stations in that region with the triple problems of low elevation sighting angles (through buildings, hills etc), high ground-noise pick-up, and lots of atmospheric and ionospheric anomalies. For these reasons the geosat footprint radius is best considered as about 70 degrees, eg 70°W to 70°E, 70°N to 70°S of the equatorial location slot. A further point to remember with geostationary satellites is that the signal is receivable all over this footprint only if a broad-beam antenna is used at the satellite. This spreads and wastes lots of power over empty oceans, so spot beams are much more frequently encountered, and unless you are in

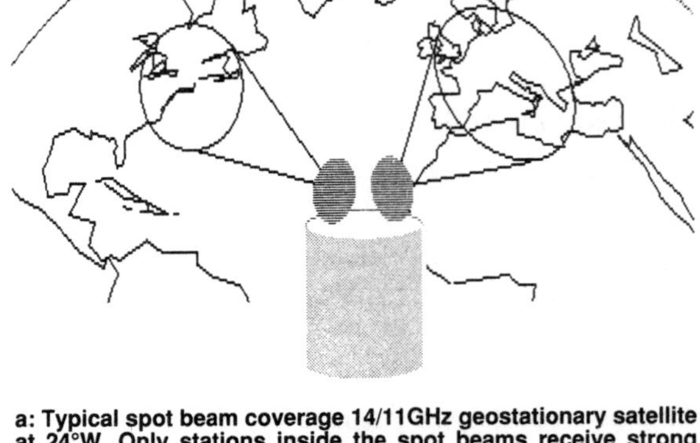

a: Typical spot beam coverage 14/11GHz geostationary satellite at 24°W. Only stations inside the spot beams receive strong signals

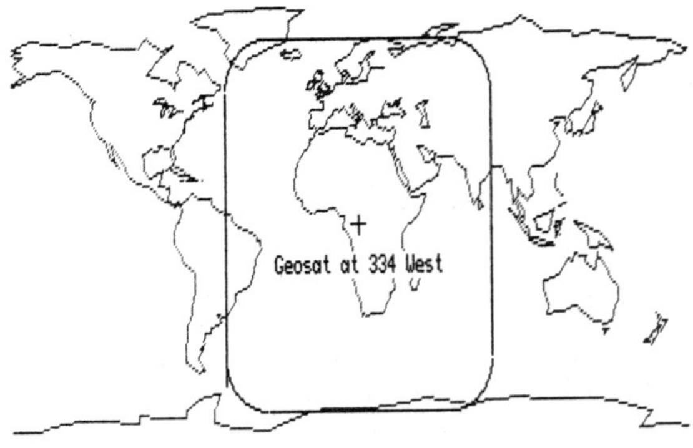

b: Typical coverage from a satellite not using spot beams. Practical coverage only is shown in the rectangle; the satellite sees 10 per cent more but loses this to horizon effects

Fig 3.01a,b: Geostationary communications satellite footprints the spot beam you may have difficulty hearing a particular satellite. Fig 3.01a shows a typical spot beam situation which concerns a satellite in view from the southern UK but not putting a strong signal into all parts of the UK. Fig 3.01b shows a 'non-spot' geosat coverage.

Geostationary satellites, a technological wonder 20 years ago, tend to be taken for granted these days. So heavy has public and commercial use of intercontinental communications become, that a standard comsat now routinely handles 36,000 simultaneous voice channels via 24 transponders. Each transponder uses 36MHz of bandwidth but they are staggered with 20MHz spacing, a reduction achievable by virtue of the use of alternate vertical and horizontal polarisation of transponder input/outputs. Typical transponder power is 5 watts each, provided by travelling-wave tube amplifiers, so individual signals are not strong. Operating frequencies are 3.7 to 4.2GHz.

Because of the low radiated power at the satellite, receiving antenna dishes must be large, with 6 metres diameter being typical even in the centre of the spot beam bore sight. Low-noise receivers are also obligatory.

In addition to the basic communications satellites in the geostationary orbit, there are also a large number of television relay satellites and business data relay satellites. These large numbers of geosats are beginning to fill the appropriate 3 to 4.2GHz, 5 to 7GHz and 10.95 to 15GHz down link bands, with experimental geostationary comsats already operating in the 19 to 30GHz regions.

As mentioned earlier almost all these geosats use narrow spot beam antennas. Not only is this tendency likely to increase but additional measures will soon have to be taken to sort out the rapidly increasing population of geosats. In early 1987 at least 100 operational communications satellites were in geostationary orbit, with a similar number of military geosats, weather geosats and other miscellaneous types all crowded together. By 1989 the number of geostationary comsats alone has doubled. Most satellites are now achieving eight to 10 years of useful life, so clearly the crowding will get worse and steps will have to be taken to correct it.

It is already clear that a general sorting out of geostationary satellites may be required when shuttles become available to take men up to the geostationary orbit. Once the transport is available it will probably be common practice to connect up groups of geostationary satellites in constellations, or perhaps more practically attach geostationary satellites to geosynchronous platforms with perhaps a dozen or more satellites per platform. The potential of these platforms for amateur radio satellites should not be overlooked.

UHF geostationary comsats

An increasing number of geostationary satellites act as relays and repeaters for ground mobile, marine and aeronautical communications. Typical of this group are the Marisats which relay ship/shore communications using frequency bands around 250MHz and 300MHz. Trials are proceeding with similar geosat relays for airline communication and air traffic control; initial frequencies are grouped near 810MHz. Fig 3.02 shows how Marisat links ships to shore.

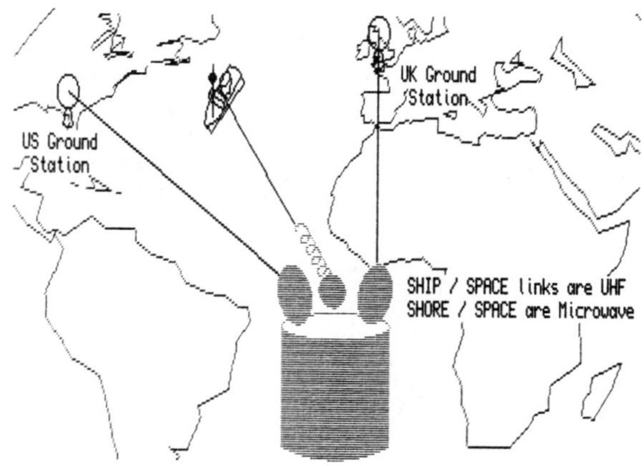

Fig 3.02: Marine ship-shore geostationary satellites (Marisat)

Non-geostationary comsats

As mentioned earlier the geostationary orbit is very useful, but it cannot serve some areas of the world. In particular, regions with major communications requirements such as Alaska, Greenland, northern Scandinavia and both European and Asiatic USSR cannot be served by the 'see below 70°N only' geosats.

The Soviets have solved their problems by using their famous molniya elliptical-orbit satellites. The molniya orbit takes 12 hours, and at least six of it is spent at high altitude above the Soviet Arctic. Twelve hours later the world has turned 180 degrees, so the next orbit rises high above the Canadian Arctic, but it is so high that it sees the Russian Arctic regions for at least four hours around its apogee. Given an orbital inclination which just eliminates Earth perturbation of the orbital plane, the molniya can repeat the same two orbits per day track for years. By using several molniyas separated 120 degrees in their orbital right ascensions, full 24-hour coverage of the USSR is possible for both voice and data traffic and, via another set of molniyas, television. Fig 3.03 illustrates the usefulness of the molniya concept.

By contrast the Americans did not until recently do much to enhance their Arctic communications. In 1987 a satellite called Polar Bear commenced operating in a 1,000km polar orbit. This satellite has been used for two separate communication trials. In the first of these it operates in tandem with an older satellite called HILAT, carrying out downward-looking probing of the Arctic ionosphere. In this mode Polar Bear transmits on at least three frequencies, one of which (435.974MHz) is in the UHF amateur radio shared section of the band.

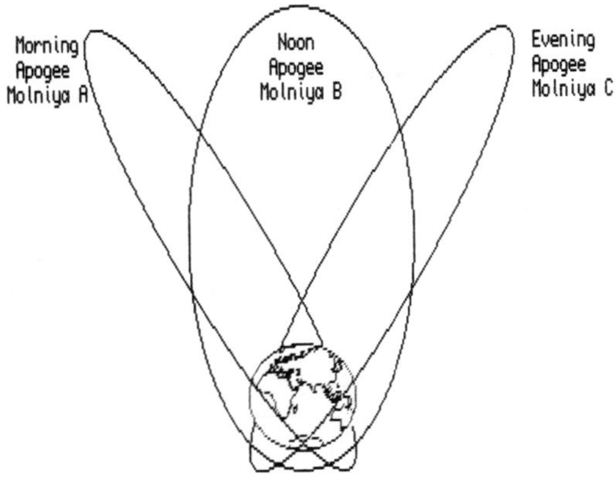

Fig 3.03: Three molniya orbiters provide Soviet polar coverage. Note: This diagram shows three separate satellites, the Earth rotates under them once a day, whilst the orbits are fixed in space

The second Polar Bear experiment is very different. As the satellite flies over the equator, it up loads, from a geostationary relay satellite, a TV programme which has been time compressed from one hour down to 10 minutes duration. It then down loads this compressed TV as it overflies Arctic ground stations, using the 12-minute window on each Polar Bear orbit.

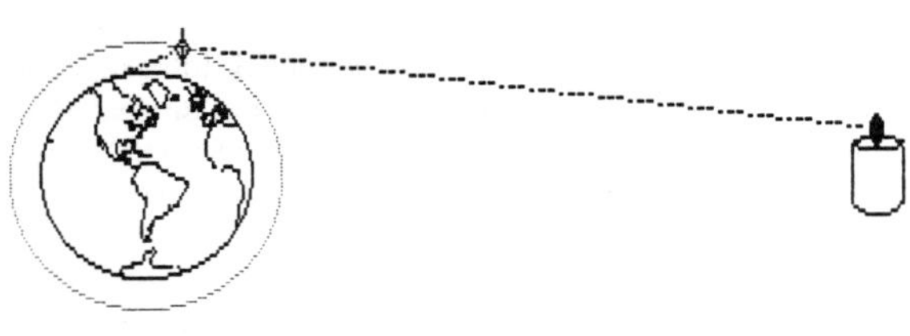

Fig 3.04: Low Earth orbiter used as polar relay for geosat. Geosat cannot see polar areas, so a low-altitude polar orbiter stores and relays for the 10 minutes of its orbit during which it sees polar stations

There are almost no other non-geostationary civilian communications satellites. Faraday rotation, scintillation Doppler shift and antenna tracking problems are the reasons for the abandonment of low Earth orbit for communications purposes.

Direct broadcast geostationary satellites (DBS)

These are a relatively new family of satellites made possible by the increasing power levels becoming available from satellite solar cells and satellite transponder final amplifier stages. In the past, geostationary comsats have used 5 watts power output from a single transponder carrying up to 1,500 two-way telephone channels. This weak signal, and the similarly weak television signal available from TV geosats, requires a ground station antenna dish of at least 6 metres diameter.

In 1984 the Japanese space agency launched Yuri, intended to be the first geosat capable of broadcasting strong TV signals receivable on a 1 metre dish. Yuri used three TV channels, each powered by a 50-watt travelling-wave tube. Unfortunately everything worked except the travelling-wave tubes. So it was not until Yuri's successor became operational in 1986 that direct (into your home) broadcast satellite TV became available.

By the end of 1990, there will be seven of these DB comsats beaming tight spot beam TV around Europe. Two of these spot beams will cover the UK, and this is leading to a flood of back garden and roof-top dishes around the country. While this in itself is unlikely to lead to any direct amateur radio use of the DBS concept, it will if successful lead to a feast of microwave dishes and components, hopefully at less than astronomical prices, and this could give a very interesting encouragement to amateur radio microwave activity.

Navigation satellites

Unlike communication satellites, navigation satellites have had a long and successful occupation of low Earth orbits. At the beginning of the 1960s scientists had demonstrated the feasibility of using reception of a satellite's Doppler signal at a ground station, in order to successfully compute the position of the ground station wherever it was on the Earth's surface. Pushed by imperatives such as the Polaris submarine programme, the Transit system of navigation satellites was born. In due course the Soviet Cosnav system followed, using the same frequencies and techniques, so that today any space radio listener can hear one or more of these satellites passing his station every half hour or so of the day or night.

The Transit and Cosnav satellites use near-circular polar orbits at an altitude of about 1,000km.

Frequency bands

Chan 1	2	3	4	5	6	7	8
149.91	149.94	149.97	149.978	149.982	149.988	150.00	150.03
399.76	399.84	399.92	399.941	399.952	399.968	400.00	400.08
MilSov	MilSov	MilSov	USN	USN	USN Op	CivSov	MilSov

The VHF signals carry both unmodulated carrier and an RTTY data signal, while the UHF signals transmit only unmodulated carrier, except for Channel 6 which has a very rough sawtooth modulation at about 600Hz. There is also a satellite of this general type which transmits on 150.01 and 400.034MHz, both frequencies unmodulated carrier. It orbits from an American launch but its exact purpose is not known.

Even in the 1970s it was obvious that all was not well with this VHF/UHF low Earth orbit system, and the author has vivid memories of fixes which were impossibly garbled by scintillation and non-line-of-sight Doppler, particularly on Arctic passes. So it was no surprise when the Americans began experiments to find a better system. Anywhere above the low Earth orbit had to abandon the Doppler shift method. The geostationary orbit could not see the polar areas so vital

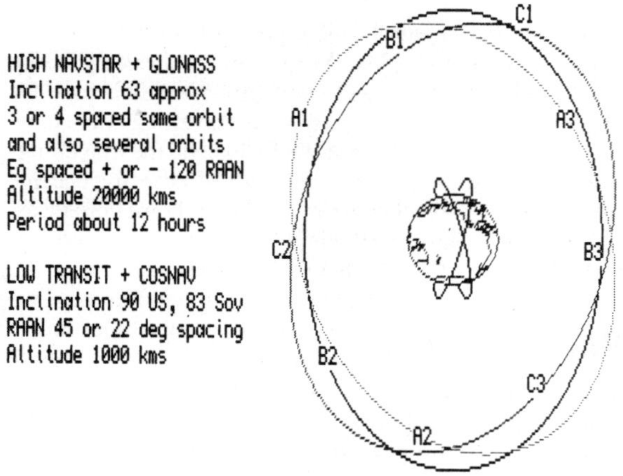

Fig 3.05: Orbital paths of navigational satellites showing LEO navsats and the later, higher-orbit Navstar and Glonass satellites

to military and airline navigators (longitude roulette plays havoc with polar navigation, so even when it did not work well Transit was a blessing). However, for really accurate within-100-metres navigation, it simply was not good enough, so the new Navstar GPS system was located in high inclination (circa 60 degrees), high altitude (20,000km) orbits to get it above the denser parts of the Van Allen belts. Instead of Doppler, it used accurate transit-time measurements of signal passage from satellite to ground receiver; given three or four such measurements, one from each of four widely spaced satellites it becomes possible to position fix on the Earth's surface to better than 20 metres accuracy. Coarse navigation data is provided to civilian users on 1,575.42MHz, and precision data is provided to military users on 1,227.6MHz. Fig 3.05 shows typical Navstar configurations. Once the American system was operating it was quickly followed by a Soviet system using the same techniques, orbits and frequency bands. The Soviet system is called Glonass and uses 1,250MHz and 1,603.5MHz down links.

Sarsat Cospar

One useful offshoot of the low Earth orbit navigation satellite programme has been the growing number of weather, Earth resources and other low-altitude satellites fitted with sea-air rescue capability. The small units operate on the principle (Fig 3.06) that a crashed aircraft down in some remote region can notify its position by transmitting a beacon signal at VHF or UHF. The satellite passing near the crash site hears the beacon as a descending Doppler frequency whose rate of change plots a curve unique to the satellite/crash site relationship. In this way the satellite can accurately pin-point the crash beacon location and then radio this data to its ground control station, which can alert the appropriate rescue organisations.

In one case, a newly launched NOAA weather satellite, less than six days old and not yet ready for Wefax service, used its sarsat to locate the survivors of an air crash in a remote part of Canada, and all were saved. Sarsat listens on 121.5, 243.0 and 406MHz, and it reports any detections via its down link on 1,544.5MHz.

Weather satellites

Like communications satellites, weather-reporting satellites come in several orbits and sizes. The original Tiros and Nimbus satellites took simple cloud cover pictures from low Earth near circular Sun synchronous orbits. Transmissions were and still are in the band 136 to 137.99MHz. As with other low Earth orbit satellites, however, the transionospheric propagation problems at these frequencies were serious, so most of the professional weather services have migrated to the low microwave frequencies between 1.64 and 1.75GHz, where the weather picture format FM signal is amenable to automatic frequency control at the ground receiver, so the very high Doppler shifts do not present a serious problem.

Weather patterns over polar regions are extremely important to forecasting meteorologists, so there is every likelihood that weather satellites will continue to use low altitude polar orbits. The American NOAA organisation keeps one or two LEO Wefax satellites in operation and the Soviet authorities keep a steady stream of their Meteor (equivalent of the NOAA) satellites operational.

Older versions of the weather geosats used down links in the 136MHz band but this practice has now ceased and almost all geosat weather down links are transmitted in the frequency band around 1.6GHz, with some secondary down links using UHF frequencies around 468MHz.

Earth resources satellites

A special LEO satellite called Landsat was launched into a near-circular 900km polar orbit in 1972. Its mission was to take pictures of the Earth in a number of narrow and wide spectral response bands. Today this successful service continues with Landsat 5 operational and Landsat 3 on standby. The original programme has widened to include

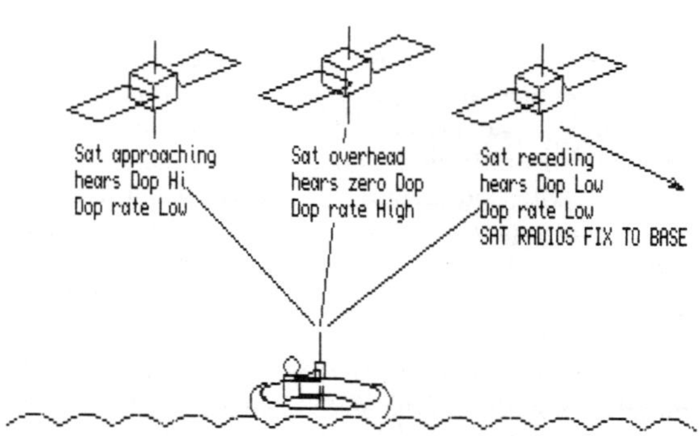

Fig 3.06: Sea-air rescue satellite (sarsat) using Doppler fixing

ground stations around the world, with each country handling its own territory. Since 1986 this service has been supplemented by Spot, a French satellite producing images of excellent quantity. Landsat down links are 2,265.5MHz video and 2,229.5MHz data.

Science experiment satellites

A detailed review of the satellites useful for radio amateur and space radio listener experiments is contained in chapter 8. In the broader field, experimental satellites have been launched at a rate of nearly one per month for the last 20 years. Some of the earliest of these broke totally new ground. The Explorer satellites found the Van Allen radiation belts, a Canadian satellite took the first overhead pictures of the Aurora Borealis, and a relatively simple X-ray satellite called Uhuru opened up a whole new range of the X-ray spectrum to investigation by astronomers. There have been some major successes and some notable flops. High hopes were entertained for a passive reflector satellite which would stay in low Earth orbit and strongly reflect radio signals back to Earth. This Echo satellite, as it was called, was successfully launched, and on command the metallised balloon which it would use as a reflector was inflated, to make it roughly as big as a house. It reflected signals beautifully but then it was noticed that it seemed to be changing orbit rather rapidly. Unfortunately no one knew very much about upper atmosphere drag in those days and it was simply not appreciated that something as big as a house but weighing very little, would rapidly drag out of orbit. The end came swiftly after a few weeks and needless to say the experiment has not been repeated.

Communications satellites have been a regular feature of experiments. Telstar was a short-lived low Earth orbit experiment which gave its designers heart failure when they got their antenna polarisations wrong and had a left-hand receiver listening to a right-handed satellite. Fortunately the error was correctable on the ground, but by 1965 a much better geostationary experiment called Early Bird paved the way to really useful satellite communications.

Moving closer to modern times, satellites have recently been used in the AMPTE experiment examining the interaction of the solar wind and the Earth's magnetosphere, producing a couple of rather dim imitation comets in the course of some special particle release experiments. Much better real comets have featured in other recent experiments: the ICE satellite passed through the tail of Comet Giacobini Zinner and no less than five spacecraft went to rendezvous with Comet Halley. However, the most important of recent experimental satellite was the Anglo-Dutch-American infra-red astronomical satellite (IRAS). In a scenario often seen in space activity, this small inexpensive specialised satellite was sent out to map the infra-red universe. This it did extremely successfully, but it far surpassed everyone's expectations by revealing a host of totally unsuspected solar system and galactic features which included maps of comet dust trails, old comet nuclei, new comets, dust bands in the asteroid belts, interstellar dust 'cirrus' like haze and, best of all, positive evidence of cold 'planetary building material' circling many of our nearest stellar neighbours.

Space science is perhaps the most exciting part of our present activities and space radio listeners can follow these missions at least some of the way if they develop reasonable microwave equipment. Almost all of this activity uses down link frequencies between 2.1 and 2.3GHz.

Space stations

The Soviets have had two space stations in low Earth orbit. Salyut 7, the older station, has been abandoned, and could re-enter the atmosphere before spring 1991. The newer Mir station is in an orbit at a mean altitude of about 350km. Mir is manned with down link communications on 143.625MHz voice. At times Mir cosmonauts have communicated via a geostationary relay satellite.

The proposed American space station may begin to be assembled in a 500km altitude circular orbit in the early 1990s. This station is expected to use tactical data relay geostationary satellites (TDRS) as its communications links, in which case all radio traffic will be on microwave frequencies. The orbital inclination of 28 degrees will place the station permanently below the UK horizon.

Space shuttles

The US space shuttle is back in service following the Challenger disaster. The Americans now have a ring of tactical data relay satellites in geostationary orbit, giving almost complete world coverage of shuttle communications. The Soviet space shuttle has had a successful unmanned flight. The Soviets have not yet completed their geosat data relay network, but their first shuttle flight was radio controlled throughout by geostationary comsats supplemented by high-altitude molniya comsats.

Manned space-support vehicles

This type of spacecraft has so far been employed almost exclusively by the Soviets. With the exception of the Skylab missions, the Americans have never made return visits, ferrying crews and stores to in-orbit spacecraft.

Soviet support vehicles come in four general categories: Soyuz, Soyuz T, and Soyuz TM personnel ferries; Progress automatically controlled stores capsules; Cosmos 1686, 1267 and 1443 space tugs; and science modules Kvant, Roentgen etc.

All these vehicles operate in low Earth orbit. The Soyuz ferries can take three persons up to a space station in a 330km orbit. They can carry equipment for fully automatic docking and their communications down link when automatic is 166.0MHz. When manned, communications are on 121.75MHz FM and 20.008MHz. Cockpit checks and comms checks of Soyuz docked to the space station give an excellent early warning of return to ground or space hopping between stations: Fig 3.07.

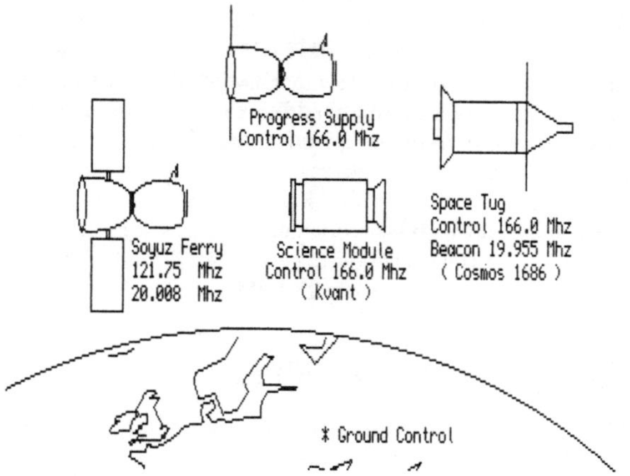

Fig 3.07: Soviet space station support craft: communications and control frequencies

The Progress automatic supply capsules use 166.0MHz for control down link. These are big craft and, when attached to the space station, their engines are often used to lift its orbit a little every time drag pulls it down.

The space tugs have been a feature of space station operations for nearly eight years. Salyut 7, particularly, had serious engine defects which have never been successfully repaired, so Cosmos 1686 has been used as Salyut's engine since October 1985. In addition to their use as tugs, these craft can also carry stores and separate re-entry recovery capsules for returning films to Earth. Cosmos 1686 is also reported to be fitted with astronomical experiments, noting that the unoccupied Salyut makes a very steady observing platform. Cosmos 1686 is fitted with a pulse duration modulation (PDM) beacon operating on 19.955MHz. At the interesting orbital height of 480km, this beacon was a most useful tool for ionospheric propagation experiments, several of which are described in chapter 8.

Fig 3.08: Soviet low Earth orbit military comsats using 'follow-my-leader' technique to remain in range of ground station. As one satellite goes out of range, its successor comes into range

The science modules beginning to be attached to the Mir station are a new feature. Like the Progress craft they can dock under automatic control. It is not yet clear how high-speed data telemetry from these experiments will be returned to ground. Clearly some of the experiments need real-time connection to a powerful computer. This can only be done via a microwave space/space/ground geostationary link of the TDRS, SDRN or Loutch type. At present these links do not seem to be available and a remarkable variety of high-speed data formats have been heard over the voice VHF link on 143.625MHz. This link is quite unsuitable because of its 10 minutes maximum in range time to any ground station, and our old friends Faraday rotation and scintillation.

It will be interesting to monitor how this particular space communications problem is progressed.

Military communications satellites

These satellites fall into two groups. The first group, employed by all the major powers (USA, NATO, Russia, and China), uses geostationary communications satellites which resemble their civilian counterparts except in their use of multi-channel UHF links. This usage of UHF is a feature required by the mobile element of military ground, sea and air activity, and it takes place between 240MHz and 320MHz.

Soviet military forces are so far the only ones to use the second communications option. For several years now the Soviets have launched increasing numbers of low Earth orbit satellites which fly, follow-my-leader fashion, in long chains with perhaps 800 to 1,600km separation between each satellite in the 'camel caravan', and up to six or eight satellites in each train.

Fig 3.08 shows the general pattern for one group; in fact, 1985 and 1986 launches saw three groups of eight and two groups of six satellites launch into this pattern. In this way Soviet military communicators have a choice of simple satellites, easily accessible, and using sheer numbers to overcome the 10 minute window problem of single satellites.

Soviet low Earth orbit comsats use a variety of frequencies around 153.6 and 204.8MHz. Satellites are often heard in the UK, one behind another.

There is also a unique set of Soviet satellites which seem to act as flying post boxes, taking up information over one country and dumping it as they pass over the USSR. These irregular, very short duration and quite strong data dump transmissions use a wide variety of covert modulation systems such as very wide-band, random noise modulated, spread spectrum.

According to US sources these satellites are used by foreign agents to transfer data out of the country. What is sure is that signals are heard from satellites passing down the Plesetsk-Moscow track, sending one-minute bursts of transmission and then going off, presumably having been commanded on by someone in the Soviet Union.

Photographic reconnaissance satellites

Both super powers make regular use of photographic reconnaissance from LEO satellites, although the Soviets outlaunch the Americans 20 to one in this field, with the interesting corollary that the American satellites seem to have, on average, 30 times longer useful lives. For several years now the American KH 11 (KeyHole 11) satellites have provided almost real-time observation and reporting, using photographic cameras of high quality which immediately process and print their films allowing them to be scanned digitally and transmitted back to the United States or to mission commanders in the field, via geostationary comsat relays.

These Keyhole 11 satellites are able to manoeuvre in orbit, in order to repeatedly overfly specific targets. Their orbital altitude is adjustable from a standard 530 by 250km to a short-term, close-look perigee, anywhere it is required. Orbital inclination is 97 degrees nominal and the operational life can be as long as two years; these satellites are mostly flying fuel tanks, able to successfully fight drag for a long time. These features ensure that the KH 11s are big, 20 metres long and 2 metres in diameter, so they provide a good Sun-reflecting visual target about one hour after local sunset. Film capsules can be released at any time for ground recovery.

The Soviet photo reconnaissance satellites are both more numerous than the American and more varied in their operational types. Several different categories have been identified, including non-manoeuvrable 251 by 90km orbiters, medium-resolution 350 by 415km orbiters, and high-resolution 210 by 290km orbiters. All these satellites have lives of only 13 or 14 days before they are commanded to destructive re-entry. By contrast two new types of Soviet photo reconnaissance satellites seem to be achieving lifetimes of 50 days, or in one or two cases, 200 days in orbit. In 1986 the Soviet Union launched 22 photo reconnaissance satellites. They are good visual targets, distinguishable from their American counterparts by the fact that the Soviet satellites track nearly west to east, or at most northwest to southeast or southwest to northeast. By contrast, the Americans track north-south or south-north.

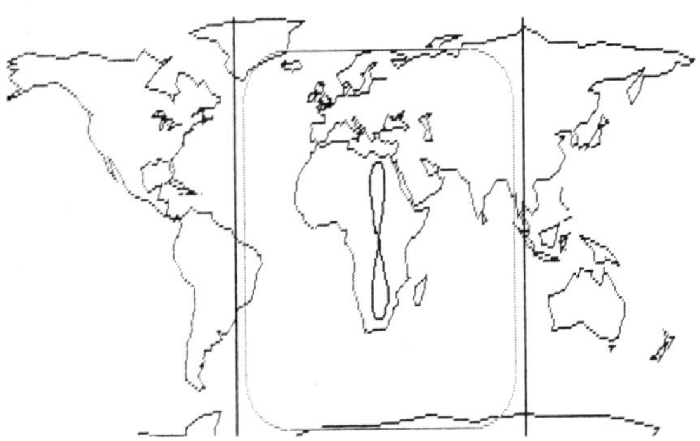

Fig 3.09: Geosynchronous satellite coverage with inclination of 30 degrees. The satellite describes a figure-of-eight every day, giving extended latitude coverage

Soviet photo reconnaissance missions use HF radio down links reporting their film use, and recovery/rendezvous of film drops at frequencies below 20MHz. The high resolution group seem to favour 19.989MHz, whilst recoveries of film drops seem to be on 19.995MHz when they are from the medium resolution group. In addition to these frequencies, some Soviet photo reconnaissance satellites are beginning to carry Earth resource observation packages. Data from these packages is transmitted on 39.978MHz. UHF frequencies used by photo reconnaissance missions are 232, 240 and 321.5MHz. The fourth generation 'long-life' photo reconnaissance satellites use 232.0MHz.

Early-warning satellites

The Soviets employ a family of nine satellites for warning of ballistic missile launches and nuclear burst detection. The nine satellites are spaced 40 degrees apart in right ascension, using molniya orbits, 600 by 40,000km, two orbits per day.

Originally the Americans used the Midas family of satellites in 3,200km altitude near-circular orbits, but these have been superseded by the DPS series of geostationary satellites, one parked at 69°E, one at 70°W and the other at 134°W. This series of satellites will eventually be replaced by detectors placed aboard standard Navstar GPS navigation satellites in their 20,000km circular orbits.

Soviet early-warning satellites use a frequency band centred on 2,292MHz for their down link reporting.

Elint and Ferret satellites

This class of satellites is used to fingerprint and analyse ground, air and space radars and communications channels. Small American Ferret packages are released by their photo reconnaissance satellites when specific targets are being checked. For long-term surveillance and analysis the Americans use satellites of the Rhyolite series in geostationary orbits, one of which is over the Horn of Africa monitoring European and western Asian targets, and another is located over south-east Asia to monitor eastern Asiatic Soviet and Chinese sites. Rhyolite systems are reported to use 1.8GHz down links. Fig 3.09 refers.

The main Soviet electronic intelligence gathering network consists of an average of six satellites in 635 by 665km orbits. These satellites use down links on 153.42, 204.56 and 153.48 and 204.64MHz.

Ocean reconnaissance satellites

The US Navy has for many years used trios of satellites launched together into near-circular 1,120km altitude, 63 degrees inclination orbits. These Project White Cloud satellites monitor and report radio and radar transmissions from Soviet ships and submarines. Their down link frequencies are grouped around 1,432 and 1,427MHz. In this programme, as in other Elint type operations, the grouped satellites provide data which can rapidly pin-point signal source locations. It has been suggested that this White Cloud network will be replaced, but this need not necessarily be the case, as it is clearly becoming the practice to attach Elint facilities of this sort to ordinary navigation, weather and communications satellites.

Unlike the Americans, the Soviets use active radar transmitting ocean reconnaissance satellites, as well as passive ones. The operation of radar looking down through the ionosphere and atmosphere, and then having to get its weak echoes back up through that same atmosphere and ionosphere, is not easy. It requires either very sophisticated microwave radar of the synthetic aperture variety, or high powered 'get through in spite of ionospheric problems' unsophisticated radar. The problem is that synthetic aperture needs very big antennas, and 'smash-bash' high-powered radar needs a power source totally out of the question with the capability of solar cells and batteries.

The Soviets have chosen the high-power approach, using a nuclear isotope generator to provide the power. This generator becomes inefficient (and highly radioactive) after a few months. The satellite therefore becomes both dangerous and useless. The Soviet solution is to fire the nuclear package into a higher long-life orbit where the highly active fuel can safely decay. Unfortunately this does not always work, and in 1978 Cosmos 954 failed to release its nuclear payload. Eventually Cosmos 954's orbit decayed and it re-entered, burning up over northern Canada, scattering radioactive waste over a path 40km wide and 1,000km long. It required an enormous clean-up operation by the Canadians and their American allies. Despite this incident the Soviets continue to use these satellites. Fig 3.10 shows the problems facing radar from space. Soviet active radars use 166.0MHz and 19.954MHz down links, but this can be a little confusing because passive Soviet Elint ocean reconnaissance satellites in 425 by 440km orbits also use 166.0MHz down links, although they can be sorted out by monitoring the

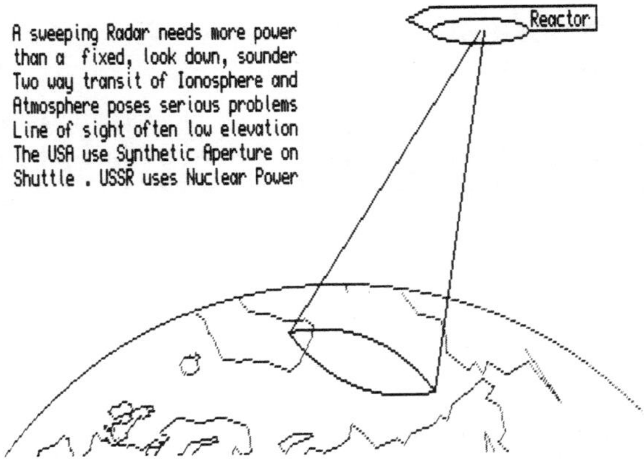

Fig 3.10: The problems of radar from space

higher Doppler rates and shorter in range windows of the active radars.

Several American satellites have been described as ocean survey radars. They are in fact vertical sounders using a narrow vertical incidence beam which do not require the high transmitter powers of the surface scanning radars.

Anti-satellite killers

In 1978 UK radio amateurs were surprised to hear a very wideband multiple carrier signal covering most of the bottom half of the two-metre radio amateur band. This signal was Dopplering and thereby revealing its satellite origins, and it also had the disconcerting habit of suddenly being 'switched off'. The signals were eventually identified as spread-spectrum, random-noise modulated telemetry from the target satellites in the Soviet killer satellite trials. More than 20 missions of this type were flown over the next four years with, in some cases, the transmission band shifting to the upper instead of the lower part of the two-metre band.

Chapter 4

Orbits and tracking

Getting into orbit

A big gun can fire a projectile a long way, and increasing the size of the gun still further could theoretically give the projectile so much speed that it would fall around the Earth, going into orbit where, provided nothing up there began to slow it down, it would stay for ever. Fig 4.02 shows how this might happen, and it also shows why the gun technique is unsatisfactory. Putting all the explosive thrust into an enormous gun is just not practical. Instead of a tremendous single thrust, the projectile needs a steady thrust over a sustained period of time, and this the rocket provides.

Firework rockets were known in China several thousands of years ago, but there is no mention of them being used for other purposes until 1232 AD, when they were used in war against the Mongols. Even then, rocket techniques evolved only very slowly, and it was not until the end of the 18th century that rockets became standard weapons in the armies of Europe, continuing in use but little changed until the 20th century when the V2 liquid-fuelled rocket burst on the scene.

The first orbit

The V2 rocket of the second world war was powered by a combination of liquid oxygen and alcohol, capable of lifting the 12 ton rocket and its 1 ton explosive payload about

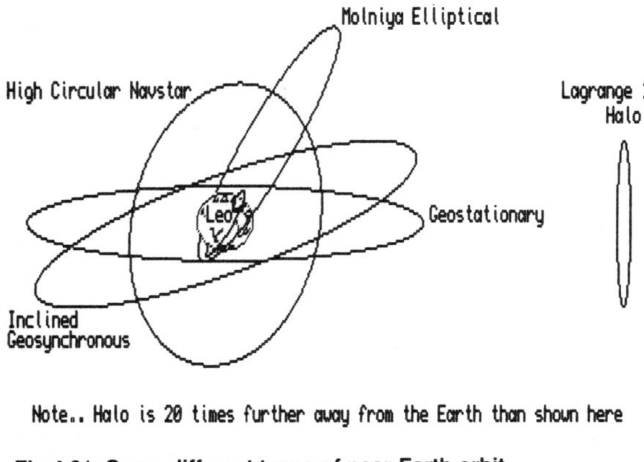

Fig 4.01: Some different types of near-Earth orbit

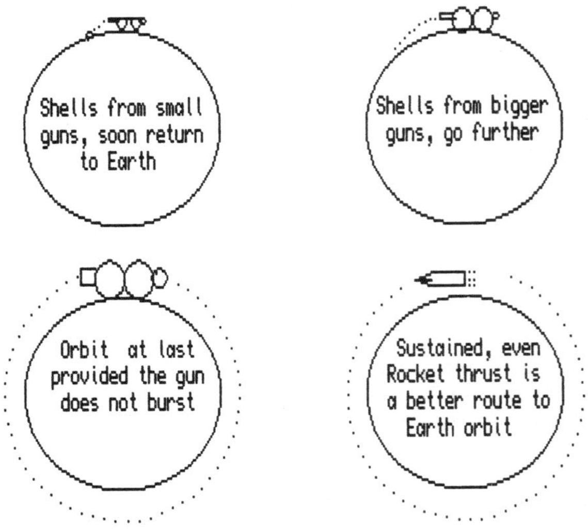

Fig 4.02: How to launch a projectile into orbit

240km. During the last year of the war, these rockets were used extensively against south east England and, as soon as the war ended, there was a rush by the victors to get hold of as much of this rocket technology as they could. In the years that followed, there was a slow programme of rocket firings in both the United States and the Soviet Union, but government money was scarce and it was not until 1954 that the first official public suggestions were made about a satellite launching rocket. The published data called for a US launch some time in 1957/58, but all this changed in October 1957 when the Soviets announced the successful launch of Sputnik 1.

Sputnik 1

The first satellite to be successfully orbited, circled the Earth for 92 days, sending strong shortwave beacon signals down to radio listeners all around the Earth.

Fig 4.03 shows a diagram of the Sputnik orbit. For clarity this diagram is not to scale; if it were, the orbit would be so close to the Earth it would hardly clear its surface. At its apogee of 939km, both the Sputnik beacon and its detached

Table 4.01: Sputnik data

Object	Life	Kg	Metre	Inc	Peri	Apogee	Ecc
Sputnik beacon	92 days	84	0.6	65	215	939	052
Carrier rocket	57 days	4,000	28	65	215	939	052

carrier rocket were well clear of the atmosphere, but at its perigee orbit low point, the two units came down to an altitude of only 215km above the Earth's surface. This low altitude meant that both units suffered a lot of drag friction in the atmosphere, which resulted in Sputnik getting down into the deep atmosphere and burning up after just 92 days in space.

By contrast the Sputnik carrier rocket re-entered and burnt up after just 57 days. The reason for this earlier re-entry was the sheer size of the rocket body. The drag forces acted on many more square metres of area on the rocket than they did on the Sputnik instrument package, so the rocket was rapidly dragged down into the lower, thicker atmosphere.

Atmospheric drag

A satellite in Earth orbit stays up in space only so long as it preserves its initial high orbit speed. If at any time in its orbit it encounters the upper atmosphere, particularly below 300km altitude, as Sputnik 1 did at its perigee, it begins to lose altitude as atmospheric drag pulls it down. As it gets even lower the drag increases, so that the decline in altitude gets faster and faster, until at about 70 to 90km height the drag friction is so great that all but the most solid satellites burn up. The few solid satellites (eg the heavy lead radiation safe from Skylab) which survive burn-up crash to Earth as hot debris.

All low Earth orbit (LEO) satellites (a term which describes satellites which come below 2,000km altitude at any time during their orbit) suffer drag to some degree but, as Fig 4.04 shows, a satellite above 1,500km will not re-enter for

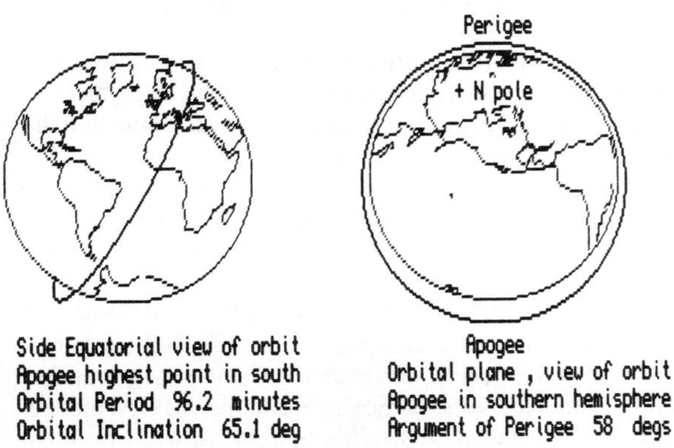

Fig 4.03: Orbit of Sputnik 1, the first artificial Earth satellite, launched 4 October 1957

thousands of years, whereas a satellite coming below 400km altitude will re-enter in 100 or at most 200 days.

Three factors modify the effects of atmospheric drag. The first two depend on the size and weight of the satellite; small heavy satellites last longer than big lightweight satellites; but whatever the size and weight there is a third less predictable feature of drag, caused by variation in both density and maximum height of the Earth's atmosphere.

The upper atmosphere variations are an upward expansion of the atmosphere in summer, and a quite separate change which results from a supplementing of the material in the upper atmosphere by the solar wind. This solar wind addition is a feature of the years around the solar cycle sunspot maximum. When solar flares and sunspot numbers are high, the enhanced solar wind supplements the upper atmosphere material density, with the result that satellite drag increases greatly even quite high up, eg around 1,500km altitude.

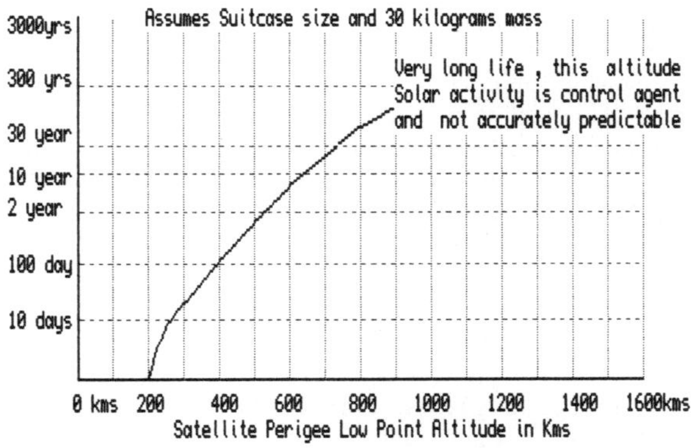

Fig 4.04: Graph showing that satellite life expectancy is governed by its altitude

This solar wind supplement was noticed most strongly in 1978 and 1979. Up to 1978 the author had used a satellite calendar which predicted equator crossing times and longitudes for Oscar 7 up to a year ahead. At the end of 1977, the calendar for that year was accurate to within about 1 minute, but in 1978 things started to go wrong. By September 1978 the calendar was eight minutes later than the satellite, ie Oscar 7 was suffering considerable drag for a satellite above 1,500km altitude. The drag had pulled it into a lower orbit, so its orbital circumference was reduced, and it therefore appeared to be going around the Earth faster than the calendar predicted: it seemed to be early, and indeed was early. The cumulative effect of this was that by the end of 1978 Oscar 7 was 14 minutes early; worse still, it was becoming obvious that these changes were not gradual. Sometimes there was no change for weeks, then suddenly the satellite would be very early, making month-to-month predictions almost impossible. Fortunately the first microcomputers were just arriving on the amateur radio scene and, though Oscar 7 and Oscar 8 calendars were published

Table 4.02: Drift of Sputnik's perigee

Date	Argument of perigee of Sputnik	Argument of perigee of rocket
4 Oct	58	58
26 Oct	49	–
4 Nov	–	45
24 Nov	–	36
25 Dec	23	–

and quickly got inaccurate, the author went over to computing his own orbit data.

Perturbation of orbits

During its 92 days of life, Sputnik beacon's perigee, and that of its carrier rocket, drifted slowly closer to the location of its ascending equator crossing. Fig 4.05 and Table 4.02 show how this affected the orientation of the orbit with respect to the Earth.

As these measurements of the arguments of perigee of the two separate units show, they were almost in step although the rocket quickly came lower and decayed earlier. This is normal because the agent pulling on the rocket body and the one pulling on the Sputnik beacon are one and the same. In fact this daily change of orbit argument of perigee is predictable by the equation:

Arg change = 4.97*(Earth rad/semi maj axis)^3.5
(5(COS(I))^2–1)

Argument of perigee varies in accordance with inclination angle of the orbit, and length of semi-major axis of the orbit. If inclination is 63.4 degrees the argument of perigee change is zero because 5*(COS(I))^2–1 = 0. As the inclination angle differs from 63.4 degrees, so daily change of argument of perigee increases.

This is an important feature which will be returned to again, but please remember the argument of perigee also changes, albeit much more slowly as semi-major axis is changed by drag. So unless inclination is exactly 63.4 degrees, argument of perigee change slowly but surely increases its rate of change.

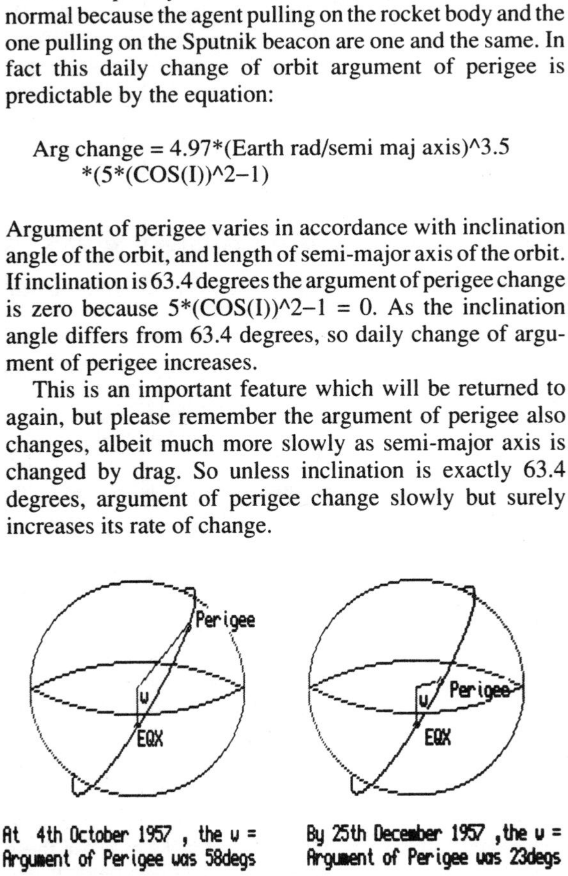

Fig 4.05: Sputnik 1 change of argument of perigee

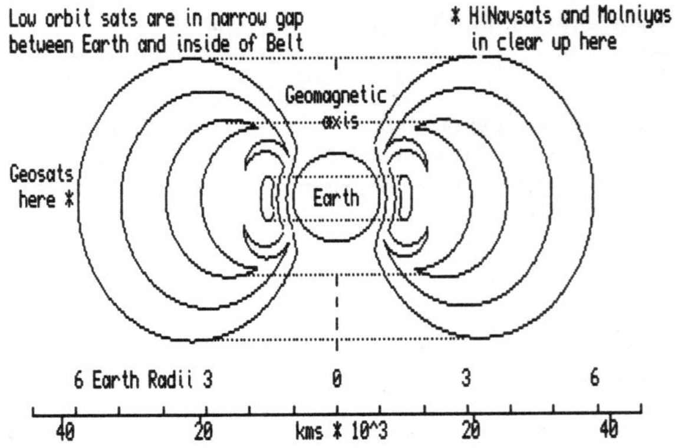

Fig 4.06: To-scale cross-section of the Van Allen radiation belts

This change is caused by the fact that the Earth is not a perfect sphere, but is fatter at the equator, and this not only affects the argument of perigee (just exactly which part of the world the orbit low point is over), it also affects the alignment of the orbital plane in relation to the stars and the universe. This shift in alignment in space changes the right ascension of the ascending node of the orbit, thereby shifting the position of the orbit relative to sidereal (star) time, and altering the equatorial longitude at which the satellite ascends over the equator. The equation describing this RAAN right ascension change is:

Omegadot RAAN dailychange =
9.95*(Earth rad/semi maj)^3.5*COS(I)

This daily change of RAAN is important because it can be used to arrange that the orbit keeps the satellite at the same angle to the Sun, day after day, for years in what is called a 'Sun synchronous' orbit. It also determines how often the satellite flies precisely overhead any ground location, a point which is important for reconnaissance, Earth resource prospecting and many other satellite studies.

The Van Allen radiation belts

Having got into low Earth orbit (LEO), the satellite is in a relatively safe environment unless it becomes subject to serious drag. The higher the orbit, the less the drag, but the more fuel it takes to get there. Up at 2,000km the satellite would be almost immune from drag and will stay up there for thousands of years, but unfortunately it will probably be dead after only a few years, because Van Allen belt radiation will destroy its electronics.

Electronic circuits, particularly modern transistors and microchips are easily damaged by radiation bombardment. Up at 2,000km the accumulated radiation dose soon becomes lethal for both microchips and human beings. Indeed, as Fig 4.06 shows, the Van Allen belts begin to be a problem at satellite altitudes as low as 1,600km, and they persist up to 36,000km, all around the Earth except over the polar regions. Fig 4.06 shows a scale drawing of a north-south section, through the Van Allen belts which are described in greater detail in chapter 1. What matters here as regards the choice of satellite orbit altitude is that circular-orbit satellites above 1,600km may stay up for thousands of years but, apart from the first 0.1% of that time, they will be electronic 'morons' whose 'brains' have been scrambled by Van Allen belt radiation.

Practical circular orbits

LEO below 300km altitude

Satellites in very low Earth orbits live short but hectic lives. Unless they carry onboard rocket engines and fuel to boost themselves higher every few weeks, they cannot survive much more than a hundred days. This short life span does have some compensations: the view they get of the Earth is superb, so it is no surprise that the majority of vehicles in this category are either reconnaissance satellites or manned spacecraft, both of which carry orbit booster engines.

LEO 300 to 600km altitude

This region of near-Earth space is subject to considerable drag effects, particularly at solar cycle sunspot maximum, but it has the advantage of being easy to get to, even for large payloads. Classes of spacecraft in this region are the manned space stations; 500km altitude is the maximum economically achievable altitude for a space station that needs regular supply of heavy materials, stores, food and personnel.

Scientific satellites are also found in this altitude band, taking advantage of being as near to Earth as possible without being so low as to quickly succumb to drag.

LEO 600 to 1,000km altitude

This is the home of most of the 'working' satellites. Drag is not a serious problem at this height, and radiation is only a problem under the south Atlantic anomaly where the Van Allen belts locally reach down to about 900km. As most satellites pass through the anomaly quickly, twice a day at most, this is not usually a serious problem. The extra height in this region is a considerable advantage: above 600km satellites are beginning to see large areas of the world at any one time, and in consequence of this are seen for longer each orbit and are seen on more orbits per day at a particular location. For example, Uosat is seen in the UK on eight orbits per day; by contrast, the Mir space station, which is at a much lower altitude, is only seen in the UK on five orbits per day.

LEO 1,000 to 1,700km altitude

If a satellite can be given reasonable radiation 'hardening' protection, via titanium shielding and/or hardened circuit components, this orbit altitude band is both practical and useful. Times in view of a particular ground station are longer (eg as much as 24 minutes at a time as opposed to Mir space station's eight minutes maximum), and the ground station sees the satellite on a higher percentage of orbits per day.

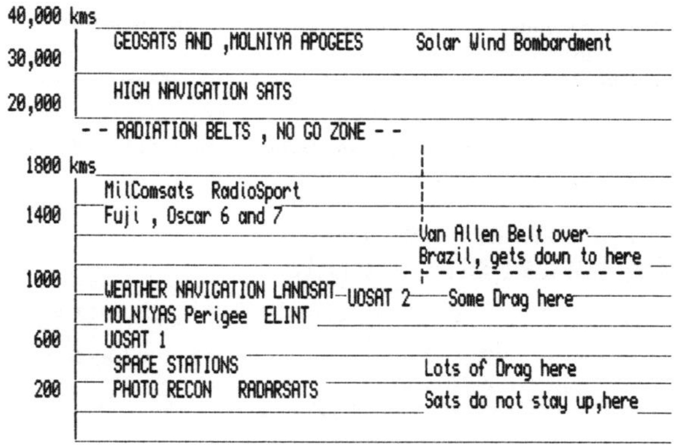

Fig 4.07: Satellite orbit height zones in near-Earth space

However, it does take a lot of fuel to reach this altitude and radiation hardening is expensive, and with several well-known satellites having their electronic brains radiation-scrambled (Oscar 8, Radiosport 1 and Radiosport 8), it is not surprising that launches to this altitude belt have become less popular of late, with the consequence that fewer amateur radio satellites are likely to hitch assisted passages to these altitudes than heretofore.

Medium-altitude 1,700 to 22,200km orbits

The Van Allen belts totally dominate this altitude zone, so almost no satellites use it, although some elliptical-orbit satellites pass through it quickly once or twice a day, usually above high-latitude polar zones to reduce radiation dosage if possible. Fig 4.07 shows the characteristics of the satellite altitude zones discussed in the previous paragraphs.

Special low-altitude orbits below 200km

Despite the reservations expressed earlier about excessive drag and the short practical life spans of satellites in very low orbits, there are enormous scientific benefits to be gained if a way to use these orbits can be found. One way which has been suggested is the tethered satellite towed on a long wire in an orbit 100km or more below the space shuttle orbiting conventionally at 300km.

With this type of flying satellite, it may be possible to explore the E layer at 110km, doing a whole series of ionospheric experiments. Space listeners and radio amateurs could perhaps expect to be able to monitor these studies which may commence with the space shuttle flying an Italian towed satellite in 1991.

Other features of circular LEOs

Height versus footprint

As a satellite increases orbital height, it sees more of the Earth at the same moment in time. Fig 4.08 shows the UK as seen from typical satellite heights. The great circle radial angle the satellite can see is described in the following equation:

Cosine GC Radial Angle =
6,378/(sat km over Earth centre)

Height versus orbital period

The time the circular orbit satellite takes to complete one orbit, its orbital period, is related to its height above the Earth by the equation:

Altitude + 6,378 = 6,378*((Period in mins/84.4)^(2/3) km

This relationship between altitude and orbit period in minutes is shown in Fig 4.24.

Total Earth coverage versus orbital inclination

How much of the Earth's surface is seen from a satellite each day depends on its orbital inclination and its altitude. Fig 4.09 shows how far a typical satellite at 300km could see at orbital inclinations of 30, 60 and 90 degrees, noting that the footprint horizon from a satellite at this altitude is 18 degrees either side of its orbital track.

Local time at which a satellite passes overhead

The time of day at which a satellite passes over your station is important. Although the satellite orbit is theoretically fixed in space, the Earth's equatorial bulge pulls it slowly or quickly depending on the inclination angle of the orbit. Looking at the equation for this change of orbital right ascension versus the universe and stars as quoted earlier, we have:

Omegadot = 9.95*(6378/semi major axis)^3.5*COS(I)

If cos (I) = 0 (I = 90 degrees), the orbit alignment in space is unaffected, but a typical space station like Mir has:

Omegadot = 9.95(6378/6728)^3.5*COS(51*PI/180)

= 6 degrees per day approximately

So Mir's orbital plane moves west 6 degrees each day, which brings its orbital window 24 minutes of time earlier each day. Please note, this does not mean orbits appear in range 24 minutes earlier each day.

The Kettering plot at Fig 4.10 shows more clearly what happens in practice. The pattern of times that orbits appear in range get roughly 26 minutes later each day, simply because Mir does 16 whole orbits in one day + 26 minutes

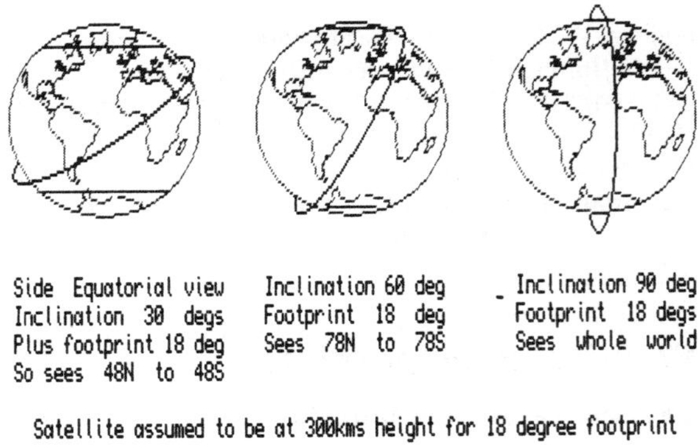

Fig 4.09: How orbital inclination affects satellite coverage

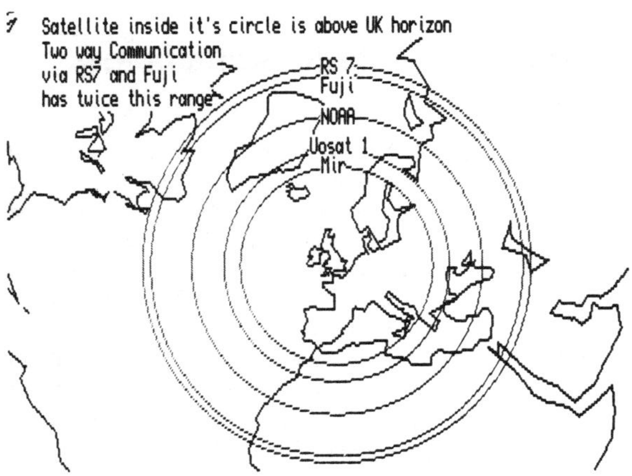

Fig 4.08: Satellite footprint range circles over UK

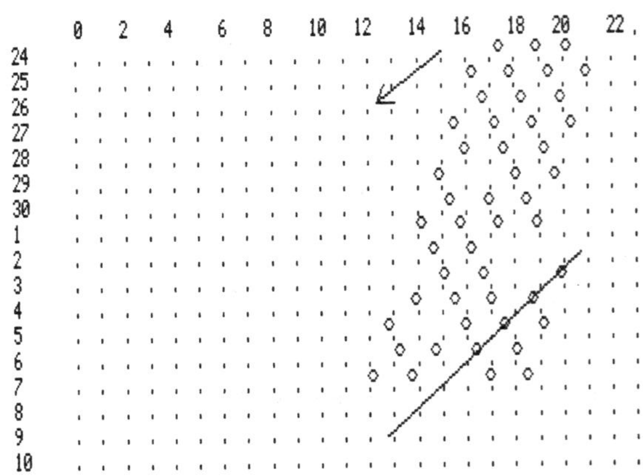

Fig 4.10: Kettering plot for space station window, April into May

Table 4.03: Typical local time orbit windows for different types of orbits

Satellite	Inclination	Ht	°W/day	Full 24hr shift
Fuji Oscar 12	50	1,497	3	118 days
Radiosport 7	83	1,660	0.5	663 days
Uosat Oscar 9	97.6	490	−1.0	352 days
Proposed US Station	28	500	6.75	53 days

or, as the diagonal line on the plot shows, 1 day – 66 minutes for 15 whole orbits. Coupled with the 24 minutes the in-range window moves each day, this results in the window appearing to move every second day down a leading edge which begins around 1715 on 24 April. By 7 May it has reached 1203 UTC, roughly 13 steps/days at 24 minutes each earlier. So clearly, at 6 degrees = 24 minutes of time per day, the orbits of Mir seen or heard over UK run through 24 hours in about 60 days. If you see them after sunset in late April, your next late evening viewing opportunities will be in late June, whilst your radio listening opportunities will occur late April evenings, early May afternoons, late May mornings, with early June having orbits in range late at night and in the early morning with little prospect of radio communications being heard.

Typical local time orbit window variations for other space radio listener targets are given in Table 4.03.

The pattern of orbits you see versus inclination angle

There are large differences in the patterns of orbits you see each day at your station from satellites of different orbital inclination angle. These patterns have a lot to do with the latitude north or south of your station. Let us take examples for UK stations, starting with Fuji Oscar 12. Fuji's orbital inclination is close to the same value as UK station latitude, so Fuji cannot pass north of the UK and it never goes above latitude 50°N. Fig 4.11 shows the daily orbit in range pattern it presents to a UK station.

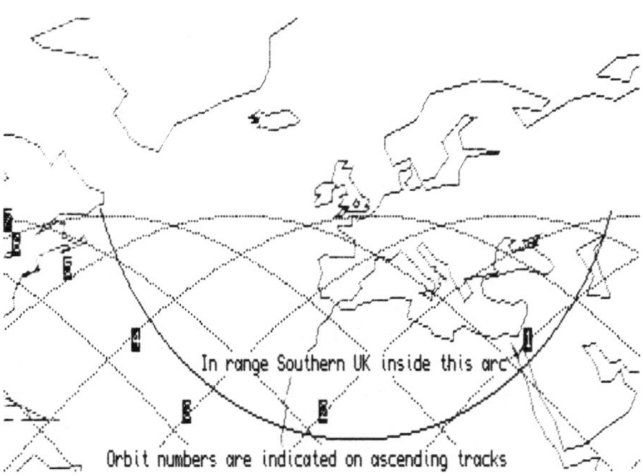

Fig 4.11: Fuji Oscar 12 orbital coverage near the UK each day

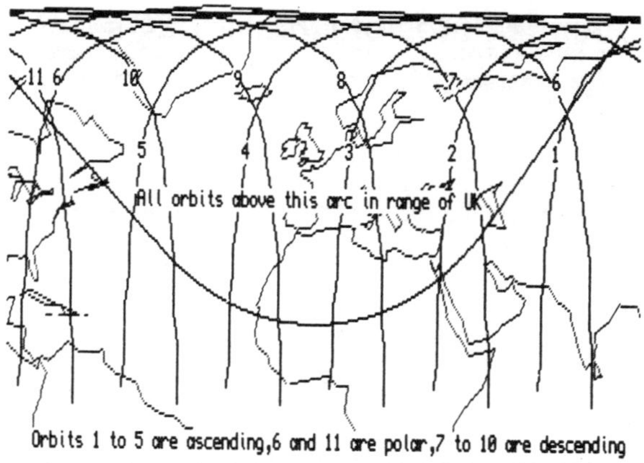

Fig 4.12: Radiosport RS7 orbital coverage near the UK each day

By contrast, Radiosport 7 has a high orbital inclination angle of 83 degrees versus a UK latitude of 51 to 60°N. So RS7 can go north, south east or west of UK stations, and is therefore in range of the UK for some part of nearly every one of its 12 orbits per day. Fig 4.12 shows the RS7 orbit tracks near UK over a Mercator map.

Not all high-inclination orbit satellites are at RS7's high altitude: Uosat Oscar 9 is much lower. So, although Uosat Oscar 9 has an even higher orbital inclination than RS7, some of its polar orbits north of the UK are not seen, producing the double pattern illustrated in Fig 4.13 (4 to 7, a gap, then 10 to 13).

Sun synchronous orbits

It follows from the previous paragraphs that the daily shift in right ascension of the orbit ascending node at the equator can, in the case of some satellites, bring them over your station one week in the dark, then a few weeks later in daylight. This would not be very useful if the satellite carried cameras and wanted to photograph you, or look at

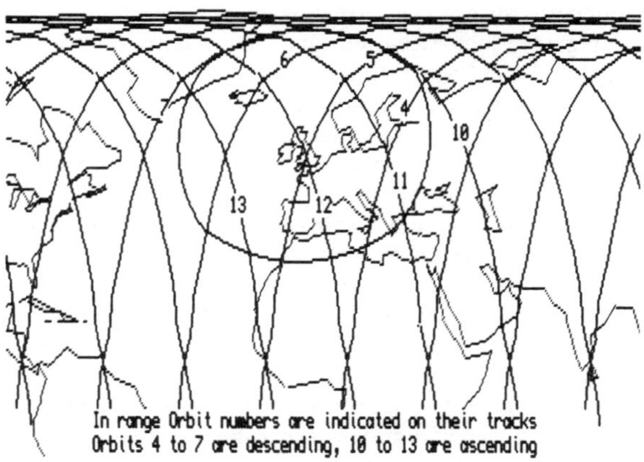

Fig 4.13: Uosat Oscar 9 orbital coverage near the UK each day

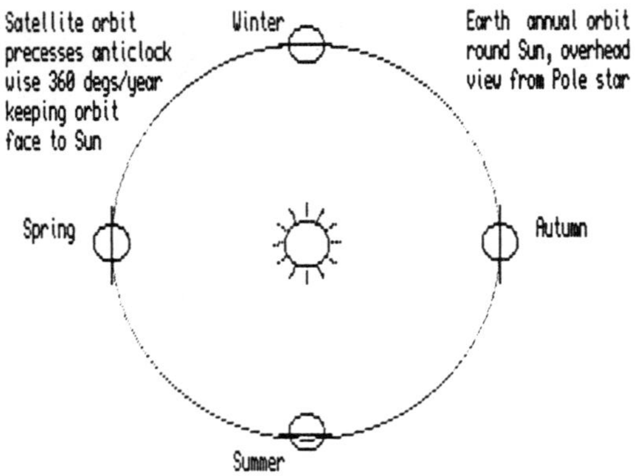

Fig 4.14: Sun synchronous 0600 up 1800 down, high-inclination orbit, always sunlit

your weather or cloud cover, and, where satellite operational requirements demand it, steps must be taken to change this.

The means to control just when, and how much, sunshine a satellite sees each day is present in the equation which describes the rate at which the Earth's equatorial bulge pulls the satellite orbit plane, altering its right ascension, ie its alignment against the stars. This equation:

Omegadot =
9.95*(6378/(6378+altitude))^3.5*COS(inclination)

allows us to put the satellite at a particular altitude and inclination angle, so that we can control the rate of change of right ascension and hence the alignment of the orbit relative to either the Sun or the stars. We can arrange that inclination is exactly 90 degrees, so that cos (I) is zero and the orbit plane is stationary with respect to the stars, but there is a more useful setting as shown in Fig 4.14.

In the so-called Sun synchronous orbit shown in Fig 4.14, we use an orbital inclination slightly greater than 90 degrees, making cos (I) in our equation a small negative number. This gives us a small negative Omegadot, rate of change of right ascension, and, if we have chosen our satellite height and inclination correctly, we get an orbit where Omegadot is just enough to correct for the difference between sidereal time and Sun time, which allows the orbit to keep a constant alignment with respect to the Sun, 24 hours a day, every day of the year.

The inclination angle for this Sun synchronous orbit must complement the satellite height, and this is its eventual undoing, because drag is always present in these low Earth orbits, and drag will eventually change satellite height, so that the satellite slowly becomes non-Sun synchronous. This process can take four or five years, so it does allow four years at least of Sun synchronism. Eventually the satellite begins to go out of Sun synchronisation into Earth shadow, very briefly at first, just as its four-year old batteries are becoming unable to withstand this dramatic 'Earth shadow' change in temperature and current loading. Drifting out of Sun synchronisation is often a critical time for ageing satellites.

As shown in Fig 4.14, the satellite has been launched at a moment in time which put it into a 6 am up, 6 pm local down, 24-hour-a-day orbit in sunshine. This is a useful Sun synchronous orbit for a communications satellite because it enjoys constant sunlight for its batteries and constant temperature for its electronics. Some satellites would not like this orbit at all. A typical reconnaissance satellite wants good shadow detail on its pictures, but shadows are long at 6 am and 6 pm. For reconnaissance, Earth resources and scientific satellites which do not want long shadows, constant daylight etc, it is common practice to fire them into an orbit with the same height and inclination as the all-Sun orbit shown in Fig 4.14, but to launch them at a time of day so that they do not follow the dawn, dusk track. Uosat Oscar 9 and Uosat Oscar 11 are in near-Sun synchronous orbits but their on-board science packages need to see the Earth at night as well as by day, so they ascend in the evenings and descend in the early mornings. By contrast, many weather satellites have to accept that, in order to get the right angle of solar illumination for their cameras, they ascend in daylight but descend at night.

It should be appreciated that these Sun synchronous orbits require inclination angles greater than 90 degrees. This means Earth spin does not assist the launch, and it places severe constraints on the launch sites which can be used. To get launch corridors to 90 degrees inclination the Americans built a special launch site at Vandenberg in California, because their main launch site in Florida has several major cities under any proposed launch corridors to the north. The Sun synchronous orbit has only been used by the Americans, and by the Europeans from Kourou. The Soviets could launch to this orbit from Plesetsk, but have not yet done so.

Earth shadow eclipse problems

Only a small number of LEO satellites are in 24-hour-a-day sunlit orbits; the rest have to suffer regular periods when they go out of sunlight into shadow behind the Earth. When in Earth shadow the satellite solar cells have no illumination, so the satellite battery gets no charge. In addition, the satellite going from sunlight to shadow experiences a very sharp drop in temperature and, unless it has good heat insulation and balance properties, vital parts can get very cold.

Eclipse in Earth shadow is therefore a problem for all satellites, but it is most serious for old satellites with failing batteries. It is therefore common practice in amateur radio to shut down older satellites just before they start a series of deep eclipses. For example, if a satellite has Omegadot change of right ascension of, say, three degrees per day, it goes through a 24-hour local time shift every 120 days, so every 60 days it is in the 6 am, 6 pm or the alternate 6 pm up, 6 am down orbit. If it has a low altitude it will still suffer short eclipses, but half way between these almost continuously sunlit orbits, ie at 30 days and 90 days, it will suffer long periods of eclipse every orbit for several weeks. In the case of the Radiosport satellites, their Omegadot is only about half a degree per day, so they take about 660 days for a full 24 hour local time cycle. This means that every 330 days they are subject to periods of deep eclipse every orbit, for several weeks, and some of these eclipses last nearly 40 minutes. It is therefore essential that, once their batteries start to decline, they are switched off during these eclipse seasons.

Very high circular orbits above 20,000km

In the past 15 years the problems associated with LEO navigation satellites have led to the use of a new class of satellites in high 63-degree inclination orbits with altitudes above 20,000km. For most of the orbit period of about 12 hours, these satellites with their high orbital inclination are above the Earth's polar regions, clear of the denser sections of the Van Allen radiation belts.

As yet there are no communications satellites in this orbit but, with launch opportunities (via geosat transfer orbits) from the European Ariane rocket, it is possible that French radio amateurs will be able to launch an amateur radio communications satellite into this orbit. This, and any other satellites like it, will clearly require radiation hardening, particularly of their electronics. This is because using geostationary transfer orbits implies low orbital inclination, so any satellite will go much deeper into the Van Allen belts than the successful American and Soviet near-polar very-high-altitude circular orbiters.

Elliptical orbits

The Earth's Van Allen radiation belts constitute a satellite 'no-go area', between 1,600 and 22,000km in altitude, for circular-orbit satellites. It is possible, however, to overcome this problem by using an elliptical orbit of the type shown in Fig 4.15, with the satellite spending most of its time high above the polar regions away from the radiation belts, and travelling through the radiation belts very quickly during the part of the orbit around its perigee.

The elliptical orbit has several features which assist this plan. The satellite following an elliptical track moves very quickly around perigee, then gradually slows down to take several hours to go through its apogee, well above the radiation belts.

In the orbit shown in Fig 4.15, the timing at various parts of the orbit is shown, and with its perigee being at about 1,500km, it does not suffer much drag. The orbit is therefore relatively stable, particularly if the inclination can be set near 63 degrees so that the argument of perigee remains relatively unchanged; and hence the apogee stays high in the northern polar regions for several years.

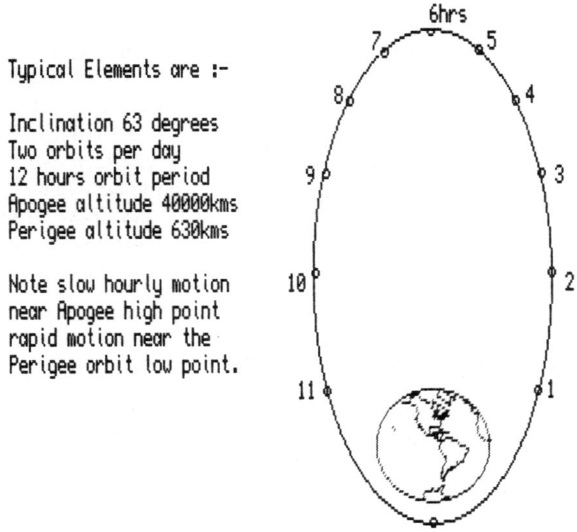

Fig 4.15: The elliptical orbit

The first use of this orbit was by the Soviets, and it is often referred to by their name for it – 'molniya'. They carefully launch to 63 degrees inclination to get a fixed apogee and perigee, then they adjust the orbit major axis slightly to give exact repeats over the same geographical locations every other 12 hour orbit. Fig 4.16 shows the standard molniya orbit pattern. This orbit gives regular TV and communications coverage to high-latitude Soviet territory which cannot be effectively covered by equatorial geostationary satellites.

These high-apogee molniya orbits have a period of about 12 hours, ie two orbits per day, so they make only two journeys down through perigee. If perigee is above 600km they suffer very little drag, so their orbits might be expected to be very stable. In practice, however, there are other factors which begin to affect these high-altitude orbits.

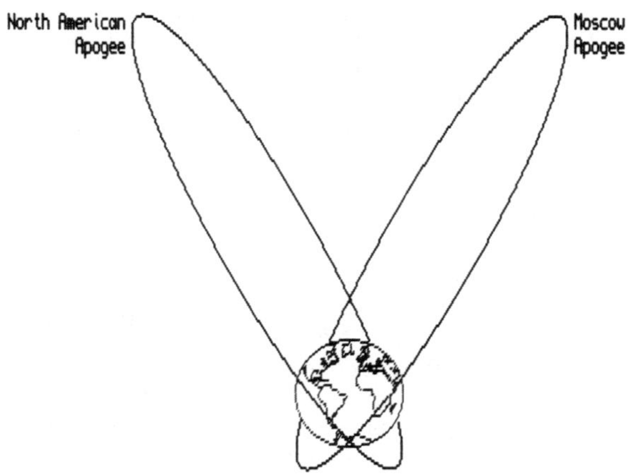

Fig 4.16: The molniya elliptical orbit. Note this diagram shows relative positions of consecutive orbits. In reality the Earth rotates once a day whilst the orbit is fixed in space

Going out to more than six Earth radii, these satellites are less affected by Earth gravity but now come under the gravitational influence of the Sun and the Moon. This can make perigees and apogees go higher or lower cyclically, depending on the relative alignment of the Sun and Moon versus the Earth and the satellite's apogee/perigee major axis. In some publications this effect is reported as negative or positive drag, but this should not be confused with atmospheric drag which hardly affects this type of orbit at all.

Geosynchronous orbits

The term 'geosynchronous' is used to describe any satellite which orbits at the same speed as the Earth rotates. In 1945 the science fiction author Arthur C Clarke pointed out that a satellite placed in an orbit of 0 degrees inclination and altitude about 36,000km would circle the Earth in 24 hours. Because this is the time the Earth takes to rotate once, this satellite will be geostationary, appearing to hover above the same spot on the Earth's equator. This is in fact the popular geostationary case of the geosynchronous orbit which has now been used for over 20 years. To be strictly correct, only an orbit with 0 degrees orbital inclination is geostationary. This is the popular orbit, but there can be good reasons for using an orbit which is geosynchronous but not geostationary; several of these useful geosynchronous non-geostationary orbits will be described later in this chapter.

The geostationary satellite orbit

As Arthur C Clarke suggested, the geostationary satellite (geosat), with its apparent fixed position in the sky, is perfectly placed for communication links and lots of other useful tasks. It can see nearly half the Earth and it is above the dense part of the outer Van Allen radiation belt. In addition its 'fixed' position allows it to be accessed via fixed ground station antennas.

There are some problems with this orbit. It is subject to the full fury of the solar wind, and therefore needs special protection against build-up of static electric charges on its surfaces; indeed, several early geosats literally electrocuted themselves. In addition the orbit is not completely stable and must be kept geostationary, for it will not remain so without help because the Earth's gravity field has some irregular features.

Unluckily for us, one of these irregularities is located above the equatorial Atlantic Ocean. This irregularity behaves like a gravity 'hill'. Nothing placed over the equatorial Atlantic stays there; it promptly begins to roll off the hill as soon as it is put up, moving east or west off-station. To counter this tendency, therefore, all Atlantic geosats carry position-keeping thruster rockets. In practice the geosat is allowed to fall just so far down the gravity hill, then it is gently pushed back up again by just enough thrust to get it to crawl slowly back to the top of the hill. Given a good 'pilot', the fuel carried by most geosats can be made to last for at least four years.

Sometimes things go wrong: thrusters stick open or the fuel catalyst fails. The geosat then becomes uncontrollable and usually drifts east to a point over the Indian Ocean where it runs into exactly the opposite of the gravity hill, the gravity 'hole'. Any geosat entering this hole slowly will be trapped there, and will stay for years.

This gravity hole situation has been exploited for years, by ensuring that when a main-circuit comsat which is geostationary over the Atlantic is running out of fuel, it is allowed to drift east and is replaced by a more-modern counterpart on the Atlantic station. Drifting east, the old geosat reaches the Indian Ocean gravity hole. It is stopped there and its remaining fuel is used to point it accurately so that it covers a useful but less intensely used communications circuit such as UK to Australia. In that position it may provide many more years of useful service.

Special geosynchronous orbits

Some scientific tasks are best performed by a satellite which 'tours' the same parts of the world using exactly the same time sequence and ground track, day after day. The satellite is not fixed above one spot, instead it moves in an ellipse, or a circle, or a figure-of-eight track, around a particular point.

This type of orbit is achieved by placing a satellite in a geosynchronous 36,000km altitude orbit, but with the orbit inclined to the equator by perhaps 20 or 30 degrees. One satellite which used this type of track was an ultra-violet astronomy satellite used jointly by the Europeans and the Americans. The satellite tracked in full view of the Europeans for the eight-hour period around their noon, then it was used by the west coast Americans as it moved in their view for eight hours around their noon, thus providing two full working days of experiments for both teams of users. In another version of this type of orbit, American signals intelligence specialists use a satellite in geosynchronous orbit over south east Asia. This satellite follows a figure-of-eight track, which allows wide views of both Russia and China.

Drifting near-geostationaries

The locations of geostationary satellites are protected and licensed by international law, with each country getting only a reasonable share. It has therefore become general practice to locate some less-important satellites in orbits with periods a little longer or a little shorter than the geostationary 24-hour period. By doing this it is possible to avoid using a geostationary slot, and stay about 1,000km clear of the geostationary orbit, whilst drifting no more than 10 degrees per day in longitude.

This type of drifting near-geostationary orbit presents few tracking problems, and it gives a superb relatively fixed line of sight for experiments like ionospheric transparency tests. The orbit is therefore favoured by organisations like

Nasa who need ionospheric transparency data as a vital ingredient in their navigation of their deep space exploration craft (Voyager, Pioneer, Mariner etc). Good Doppler navigation of Voyager 2 as it approached its encounter with Neptune relied greatly on a steady stream of ionospheric data.

This kind of orbit could be useful for amateur radio, but it does have one big disadvantage. In the case of, say, 10 degrees per day drift, it is in range of a particular ground station for periods of about 14 days; it then goes out of range for 22 days before returning back in range for another 14 days.

Halo orbits

Some of the best possible sites for space stations, industrial space activity and communications relays are the Lagrangian points. These are points in empty space where the gravity fields of two bodies are balanced. Perhaps the best example of a Lagrangian point is L1, which lies 1.5 million kilometres sunwards of Earth. At L1 the gravities of the Sun and the Earth balance, providing a location around which a satellite can be placed in a relatively stable long-term orbit. Fig 4.17 shows how Lagrangian point L1 can be used. It has already been used as the location for science satellite ISEE3, which was a dedicated Sun watcher which circled L1 for several years before being sent off to look at Comet Giacobini Zinner.

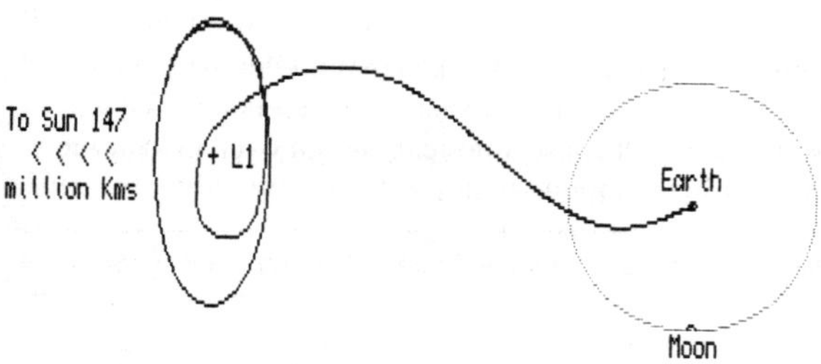

Fig 4.17: Launch track to Lagrangian point L1 halo orbit

These Lagrangian points appear wherever there is a balance between conflicting gravity fields. There is one between the Earth and the Moon, albeit very close to the Moon because of the Moon's low gravity. There is another Lagrangian point out beyond the Moon where there is another Earth/Moon balance point, and the big planets such as Jupiter have a rather different kind of Lagrangian point 60 degrees ahead and 60 degrees astern of the giant planet and following the same orbital track as it. These Jupiter parking places actually have material in them, having in the past captured asteroids into their gravity holes. The asteroids are observed today in these locations where they are given the collective name of the 'Trojans'. Given the relatively stable nature of these groups, they undoubtedly have a place in future space communications, exploration and science.

Lagrangian points such as L1 have the advantage of permanent 24-hour-a-day sunlight; by the time one gets out to Jupiter's Trojans the sunlight is becoming weak. So the near-Sun Lagrangian points will be more popular with the early colonists and space industrialists, and should make excellent sites for amateur radio recreational and scientific studies.

Deep space orbits

One of the big problems of mathematics is the three-body problem. We can easily work out how planet A affects spacecraft B, but if spacecraft B is halfway between planet A and planet C, we at present have no precise mathematical procedure for describing their interactions one with another.

For the last 30 years the problem has been side-stepped by postulating a sphere of unique influence around each planet or moon. Inside this sphere of influence a spacecraft orbit is described in terms of the effects of that controlling planet. To describe space flight from one planet to another, we can describe the beginning as being under one sphere of influence and produce an orbital conic section for that part of the orbit; similarly we can describe the end of the flight as a conic section whilst inside the sphere of influence of the target planet, but to join up beginning and end we must devise a 'best-fit joining track'

This rather rough method is appropriately named 'patched conics', and is at present something more of an art than a science. However, solutions may be on the way. A system of mathematical operations called 'restricted three body solutions', are being used with some success, and in the longer term it is possible that the problem may be more elegantly solvable using mathematical software designed to exploit parallel-processor computing.

As yet these problems do not affect space listeners or radio amateurs, but as manned flights to Mars and other planets begin, some elegant programming is going to be necessary if they are to be monitored on their way.

Tracking

Simple satellite orbit prediction

One of the more interesting aspects of space radio is the 'strange satellite'. No details are likely to be published about it, so it might seem at first to be a job for the experts. This is not in fact the case, for the physical laws governing satellite behaviour allow any satellite heard to be tracked and predicted using simple techniques developed by the Kettering (UK) Group of space watchers.

Fig 4.10 shows time in hours UTC along the horizontal axis, and days of the month down the vertical axis. By plotting when a satellite is heard, the pattern of the orbits quickly becomes apparent. Times at which the satellite is heard and plotted on this chart begin to go down the plot in diagonal lines. Clearly evident is the fact that the first orbit heard each day is getting gradually earlier. On the 25 April the first orbit heard was at 1610, but by 7 May the first orbit heard was much earlier at about 1207, a shift of about 243 minutes in 12 days, roughly 20 minutes earlier each day, which tells us that the satellite had a rate of change of right ascension of about 5 degrees per day.

The Kettering plot also shows what appears to be an in-range block of about five orbits per day, one after the other, except where the cosmonauts did not transmit. This single block of consecutive orbits, all with about the same time separation, suggests a satellite whose orbital inclination is the same, or less than, the latitude of our station. So we have enough information from rough Omegadot rate of change of right ascension, controlled by satellite altitude and orbit inclination, plus the fact that orbital inclination is near or less than our station latitude, to make a rough approximation at both these figures.

Less certain from this data is the actual orbital period, the time taken for each orbit. The records on this plot seem to be about 96 minutes apart; but be careful, this is not the orbit period. The problem is that the satellite is coming above our horizon from a point further west and usually higher in latitude each time it reappears. This means the gaps between our plots are going to be slightly larger than the true orbit period.

In spite of the above caution, it should be clear that by plotting on the diagonal lines joining one day's orbits and the next, we can get a fairly good assessment of when we will hear the satellite tomorrow or the day after. In this case the satellite orbits seem to be heard about 69 minutes earlier or 27 minutes later each day, with the whole window of five orbit sequence slipping earlier by about 20 minutes every day.

Your station location

In order to predict when we will see or hear a satellite, we need to know precisely where we are located on the Earth's surface. Any location on Earth can be described using its longitude and its latitude. Longitude is measured in degrees around the equator. Zero degrees longitude (or 360 degrees) is designated as that spot on the equator which lies on a line joining the north and south geographic poles of rotation, and passes through Greenwich, England. This Greenwich meridian is used as the zero reference for longitude, putting New York at longitude 74°W, San Francisco at longitude 122.5°W and Tokyo, Japan, at longitude 219.5°W.

In some astronomical references Tokyo would be reported as 140.5°E. Most computer software in professional and amateur radio use quotes longitude in degrees west, but please exercise caution and check your software uses this convention.

Latitude is measured from the equator to either pole, each in 90 equal steps of one degree. Greenwich, London, is at latitude 51.5°N. So the full location description for Greenwich is 0° west 51.5° north. Stations in the southern hemisphere report their latitude as either degrees south or as degrees negative. Sydney, Australia, is at latitude 33.83° or 33.83°S, longitude 208.83°W.

Table 4.04: Table of latitude and longitude of UK cities

City	Latitude	Longitude
Lerwick, Shetland	60.15	1.15
Inverness	57.5	4.25
Glasgow	55.9	4.25
Edinburgh	55.9	3.2
Belfast	54.55	6
Newcastle	55	1.6
Preston	53.75	2.7
Leeds	53.8	1.6
Birmingham	52.5	1.9
Norwich	52.7	358.75
Cardiff	51.5	3.2
London	51.5	0
Plymouth	50.4	4.2
Southampton	50.9	1.4
Dover	51.1	358.7
Jersey	49.2	2.1

A satellite track plotter

The ground track of a low earth circular-orbit satellite repeats the same incremental changes as it climbs from the equator through its highest latitude north and descends back down to the equator on the other side of the world.

Table 4.05 lists the ground track of the Soviet Salyut 7 space station on successive orbits. The table shows ground tracks for the northern hemisphere half of the orbit, commencing equator north-bound ascending crossing at 1513 UTC, and the succeeding orbit, ascending equator crossing (EQX) at 1647 UTC. In each case the two-minute latitude steps are exactly the same. The two-minute longitude steps

Table 4.05: The ground track of the Soviet Salyut 7 space station on successive orbits

Minute after EQX	Latitude	Long 1513 EQX	Long 1647 EQX
0	0	0	24
2	6	356	20
4	12	352	16
6	18	347	11
8	24	342	6
10	29	337	1
12	34	331	355
14	39	324	348
16	43	315	339
18	47	306	330
20	49	296	320
22	51	284	308
24	51	273	297
26	50	261	285
28	48	250	274
30	44	241	265
32	40	232	256
34	36	225	249
36	31	219	243
38	25	213	237
40	19	208	232
42	14	203	227
44	8	199	223
46	2	195	219

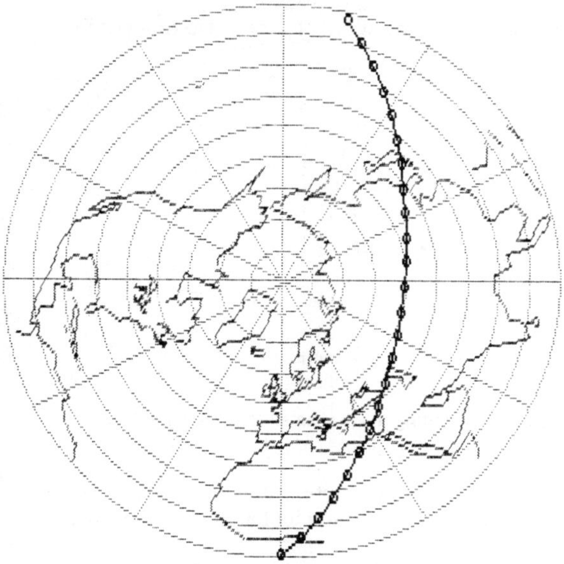

Fig 4.18: North polar great circle map with Salyut track overlay. Salyut track in two-minute steps from EQX 0°N 0°W

are also the same; they are in step but separated by 24 degrees of longitude at each step. This 24 degree step is called the 'orbital increment', ie the amount the Earth turns whilst the satellite makes one orbit plus the much smaller Earth oblateness pull on the right ascension of the satellite's orbit. In this case the Salyut 7 increment per orbit is about 94.078/4 minutes of time = 23.52 degrees plus about 4.79/15.3 degrees RAAN change per orbit = 0.31 degrees, which equates a total increment per orbit of 23.83 degrees.

It is clear therefore that if we know the time and longitude of an ascending equator crossing (EQX) on a given day, we can correct our standard 0° longitude EQX track to the longitude of this EQX and then use the track increments to plot that orbit across our map.

The next orbit that day will be the orbit period in minutes later at the longitude of the first EQX plus the orbital increment, eg EQX at 230°W at 0600 will be followed by an EQX at 0600 plus 94.078 minutes at longitude 230° plus 23.83 degrees, ie 0734.078 UTC at 253.83°W.

This regular pattern of orbit ground tracks also allows us to make a simple ground track plotter. First we produce a great circle map of the northern hemisphere centred on the north geographic pole. Then over this we place a transparent overlay pinned to the map through the north pole, and hence free to rotate around it. Taking a suitable indelible marking pen, we now mark onto the overlay the satellite track showing the two-minute steps, starting from 0°W 0°N and ending up at 195°W 2°N. Fig 4.18 shows the Salyut 7 track plotted over the great circle map. We now have a track plotter, by simply rotating the transparency above the map until the track starts at the actual longitude west of the equator crossing of the orbit we are going to follow. Thereafter we leave the track in place and follow the satellite as it makes the two-minute steps along the track.

Table 4.06: Typical presentation of orbital data

Date	EQX time	Bearing	Longitude increment	Period increment
4.2.87	1513	345	94.078	23.83
5.2.88	1444	342.4	94.078	23.83
6.2.87	1415	339.8	94.078	23.83

To use this EQX track plotter, we need to know EQX time and longitude. For subsequent orbits we also need satellite orbital period and orbital increment. A typical presentation of this data would be as shown in Table 4.06.

Please note the period and increment quoted apply to a single orbit. Between one day and the next the satellite does a little over 15 orbits, so the EQX steps day to day are 15 exact orbits, shifting the timing of EQX 15*94.078 = 1,411.17 minutes or 28.83 minutes earlier each successive day. Similarly the 15 steps of orbital increment amount to an EQX longitude shift of 15*23.83 = 357.4 degrees = –2.6 degrees less than the previous day's EQX.

This EQX data is published by some Amsat groups, but the only regular publication in the UK is *Practical Wireless* magazine. The same data can be obtained from computer software distributed for the Sinclair Spectrum microcomputer by SARUG, the address of which appears in appendix 1.

Near-circular low Earth orbit tracking

A typical low earth circular orbit is shown in Fig 4.19, which indicates the ascending equator crossing EQX, on a line drawn from the Earth centre through the equator to the orbit. From this line we measure back to another line joining the Earth's centre to the stellar position reference point in the constellation of Aries. We call this reference point the 'first point of Aries' and the angle it subtends at the Earth's centre with the line to the ascending EQX is called the 'RAAN', the right ascension of the ascending node of the orbit. This RAAN gives us the orientation of the orbit against the stars, provided we also know the orbit inclination angle, that angle the orbit makes with respect to the Earth's equator. Additional information on Fig 4.19 includes the perigee and the apogee of the orbit.

In the calculations which immediately follow we will

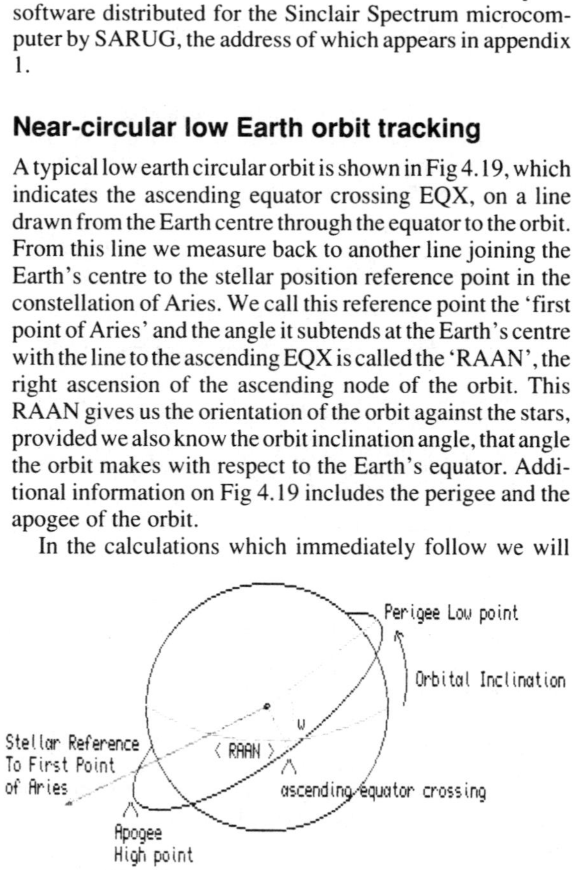

Fig 4.19: The near-circular orbit

assume the orbit is circular, with high and low points being the same, but later in this chapter we will consider the elliptical orbit and for that it is necessary to know the location of the perigee, ie just where it is around the orbit. As shown in Fig 4.19, perigee is about 90 degrees anti-clockwise from the ascending EQX. This angle is called the 'argument of perigee'. By definition for an ellipse, apogee is always 180 degrees from perigee, so a separate term for argument of apogee is not necessary.

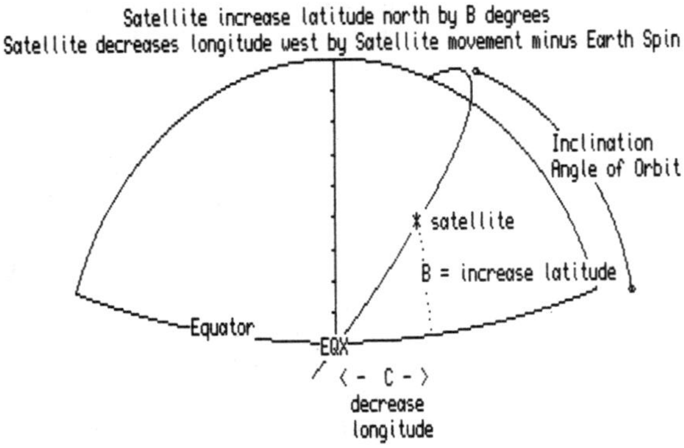

Fig 4.20: Ascending track of satellite in direct orbit

In order to track the satellite, its position at the time of equator crossing is defined by stating the time UTC of EQX and the bearing longitude degrees west of the EQX. This gives us our starting point. At time T minutes after EQX the satellite is at S. To describe this point we need to calculate the latitude and longitude of S.

As shown in Fig 4.20, in this example of a satellite going direct, ie in the same direction as Earth rotation,

Latitude B =
ASIN((SIN(inclination))*SIN(2*PI*T/Period))

where sine B is the product of the sine of the orbit inclination angle and the sine of an angle (in radians hence the 2*PI term) equal to time since EQX/orbital period, ie that part of the orbit which has elapsed since EQX.

The change in longitude in time T minutes is given by the equation:

Longitude change C = Earth rotation in T minutes/4 –
ACOS((COS(2*PI*T/Period)/COS(B)))

This expression requires careful handling. The Earth rotation is eastwards. So a point underneath the satellite rotates east under the satellite, giving the satellite a more westerly longitude. By contrast the satellite moves east in this direct (inclination less than 90 degrees orbit). So the term in the longitude expression due to satellite motion has a negative sign.

This leads to the point that in the case of a retrograde orbit satellite, such as Uosat Oscar 9, inclination angle 97.65

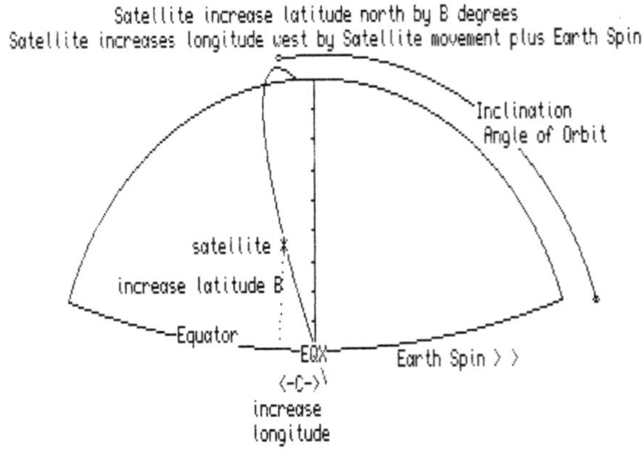

Fig 4.21: Ascending track of satellite in retrograde orbit

degrees, both satellite motion and Earth rotation are in the same sense, so the equation for longitude change becomes:

Long change C = Earth rotation in T minutes/4 +
ACOS((COS(2*PI*T/Period)/COS(B)))

Fig 4.21 shows this situation.

Worked example. Direct orbit Salyut 7, inclination 51 degrees, period 94 minutes, EQX at 0°W at 0000 UTC.

B in degs =
180/PI*(ASIN(SIN(51*PI/180)*SIN(2*PI*T/94)))

C in degs = T/4–180/PI*(ACOS((COS(2*PI*T/94))/
(COS(B*PI/180))))

EQX+ Tmins	Lat	Long	Corrected Long
2	5.945557	–4.33772	355.66228 west
4	11.84814	–8.781009	351.218991
6	17.6613	–13.44149	346.55851
8	23.3312	–18.44279	341.55721
10	28.79231	–23.92597	336.07403
12	33.96117	–30.05256	329.94744

By comparison, a worked example for a retrograde orbit satellite such as Uosat Oscar 9 produces a quite different track from EQX at 0°W at 0000 UTC. Period is 94.195 minutes and inclination is 97.6555 degrees.

B degs = 180/PI*(ASIN(SIN(97.6555*PI/180)*
SIN(2*PI*T/94.195)))

C degs = T/4+180/PI*(ACOS((COS(2*PI*
T/94.195))/(COS(B*PI/180))))

EQX+ Tmins	Lat	Long
2	7.575188	1.524245
4	15.1479	3.085361
6	22.71528	4.725675
8	30.27363	6.500197
10	37.81756	8.488484
12	45.33848	10.81715

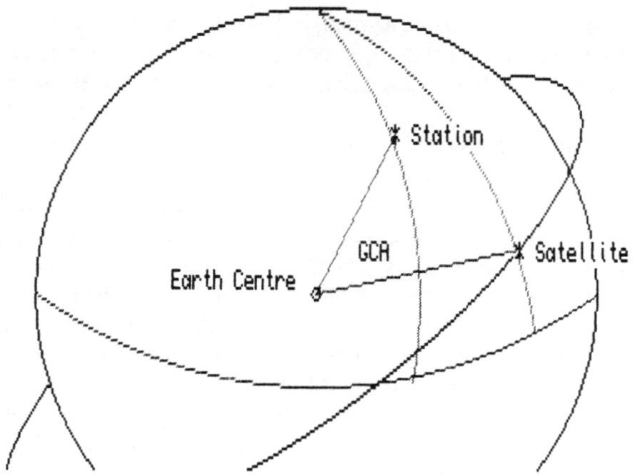

Fig 4.22: Great circle angle between station and satellite sub-point

Please note that in this retrograde example the satellite moves west, so the second part of the equation for longitude change is positive.

If the satellite started at EQX 24°W, it would have been longitude 24 + 1.524245°W at minute 2 after EQX, and 24 + 3.085361°W at minute 4 after EQX. Latitude change is unchanged whatever the EQX longitude.

In practice, numerical accuracy to five decimal places is meaningless. For practical use of this circular-orbit approximation formula, use nearest whole numbers for latitude and longitude.

Is the satellite in range?

Having calculated the latitude and longitude of the satellite sub-point at time T minutes after equator ascending crossing EQX, the next calculation examines how far the satellite is from your station, and then decides whether this separation means it is in range above your horizon, or out of range below it.

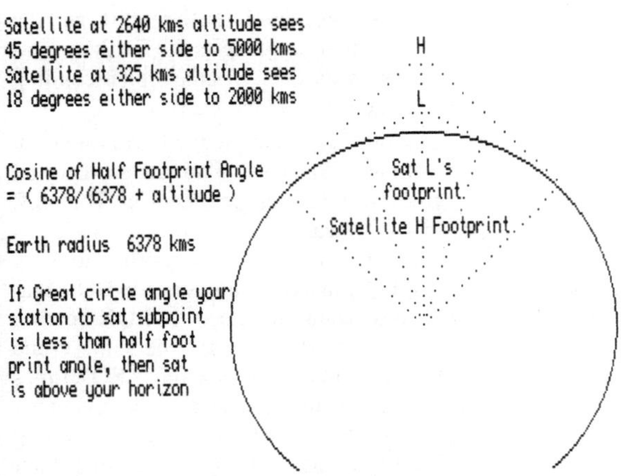

Fig 4.23: The area of the world the satellite sees is determined by its height above the Earth's surface

Fig 4.22 shows this situation. We know our own station latitude and longitude, and we know the instantaneous latitude and longitude of the satellite. From this data we can calculate the size of the great circle angle around the Earth's surface from our station to the satellite sub-point using the equation:

COS(great circle angle station to satellite) =
(SIN(station lat)*(SIN(satellite lat)))+
(COS(station lat)*COS(satellite lat)*
COS(longitude difference station to satellite))

Worked example. Station 56.125°N 3.6°W, satellite at 18°N and longitude 346°W, gives longitude difference of 17.6 degrees.

GCA = (ACOS(SIN(56.125*PI/180)*SIN(18*PI/180)
+COS(56.125*PI/180)*COS(18*PI/180)
*COS(17.6*PI/180))*180/PI

= 40.37316 degrees = 111.2*40.37316 = 4,489.49km

Now that we have this great circle separation angle, we need to discover if the satellite footprint angle, the radius of the area of the Earth's surface which it can see, is big enough to cover 40.37316 degrees separation.

Fig 4.23 shows that the area of the world the satellite can see in its footprint is determined by its height above the Earth's surface, and the great circle radius angle enclosing this area is described by the equation:

GCAngle =
ACOS(Earth radius/(Earth radius + sat altitude)

(Note: sat altitude = 6,378*(Period/84.4)^(2/3)–6,378)

Using Uosat Oscar 9 at period 94.195123, altitude is 484.3863. Fig 4.24 shows the relationship between period and altitude.

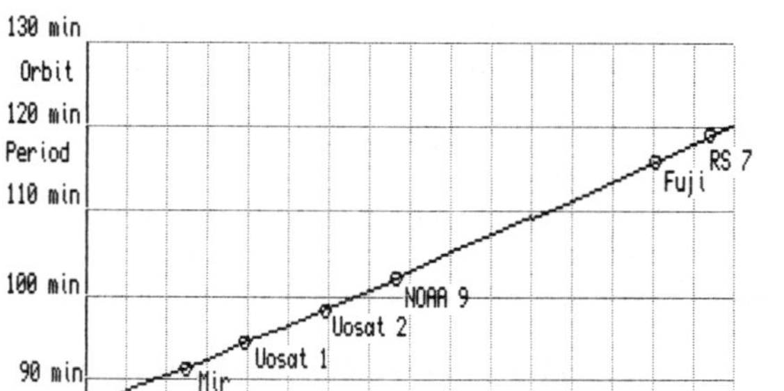

Fig 4.24: Low Earth circular-orbit satellite – orbital period against altitude

GCANGLE = 180/PI*(ACOS(6378/6378+484.3863))

= 21.6563

So our 40 degree plus separation of station and satellite in this example is well out of range below the station horizon.

Azimuth bearing and elevation – station to satellite

In the example just quoted the satellite is clearly outside the satellite footprint, so it would not normally be necessary to proceed to find azimuth and elevation.

If, however, the satellite were very much higher it could be in range, and the equation to find the azimuth bearing from the station to the satellite would be:

COS Azimuth = (SIN(sat lat)–SIN(station lat) *COS(GCangle))/(COS(station lat)*SIN(GCAngle))

The elevation angle can be calculated even when the satellite is below the station horizon, because it helps to know how quickly the satellite is coming in range, and is therefore useful in acquisition time calculations. The equation calculating elevation is:

EL = 90–(ATAN(Sat height above Earth centre *SIN(GCAngle)/(Sat height above Earth centre *COS(GCAngle)-6378)))*180/PI

Worked example. For our station at 56.125°N 3.6°W to a satellite at 18°N 346°W gave a GCAngle of 40.37316 which results in an azimuth:

AZ = 180/PI*(ACOS(SIN(18*PI/180)– SIN(56.125*PI/180)*COS(40.37316*PI/180)/ (COS(56.125*PI/180)*SIN(40.37316*PI/180))))

= 153.6437 degrees clockwise from north

EL = 180/PI*(PI/2–(ATAN((484.3863+6,378) *SIN(40.37316*PI/180)/((484.3863+6378) *COS (40.37316*PI/180)–6378))))

= 165.49 degrees which resolves as −14.51 degrees

These equations do not work out angles greater than 180 degrees, so it is often necessary to correct the sense of the angle. The example which follows shows how this is done.

Worked example. For station at 56.125°N 3.6°W to a satellite at 38°N 14°W, longitude difference = 10.4 degrees, great circle angle = 19.41007 degrees (well above Uosat horizon's 21.6563 great circle angle for zero elevation edge of footprint). Azimuth is reported as 154.6564 degrees but the satellite is south west of the ground station because its latitude is less and its longitude is more than that of the ground station. So true azimuth is 360 – 154.6564 = 205.3436. Elevation is 2.369254 degrees above station horizon, assuming satellite is Uosat Oscar 9 with altitude of 484.3863km.

The above paragraphs have developed all the calculations necessary to track and point your antennas at a circular low Earth orbit satellite. Essential prior knowledge was equator ascending crossing EQX, time UTC and the longitude west of that crossing. Also necessary were orbital period in minutes of time and orbital inclination angle. Generally speaking, these last two variables can be used for several months before they go out of date. So, provided you have an original record of period and inclination, all you need to track any low Earth circular orbiter is a regular supply of equator crossing times and longitudes. *Practical Wireless* publishes these every month.

Tracking successive circular orbits

Period and increment

Having mastered the tracking of one orbit, tracking successive orbits is not difficult. The extra information required consists of the time interval or orbital period between successive ascending equator crossings, and the bearing longitude interval or increment of longitude between one orbit EQX and the next.

The EQX time shift is easy, as it is equal to the satellite's orbital period. If a satellite has an EQX at 1237 UTC and its orbital period is 97.5 minutes, its next EQX will be at 1237 + 97.5 minutes = 1414.5 UTC and the orbit following that will have an EQX time of 1552 UTC.

To get the EQX time shift for a full day, the satellite orbit period of 97.5 minutes produces 15 orbits in 1,462.5 min, but a day is 1,440 minutes long, so our 15th orbit is 22.5 minutes later next day, which gives an EQX of 1237 + 22.5 = 1259.5 UTC. You can see this sort of daily shift pattern in the orbit in range times of the Kettering Plot at Fig 4.10.

To get the EQX bearing change between one orbit and the next, two factors must be considered: Earth rotation and the perturbation of the satellite orbit plane as the Earth's equatorial bulge 'pulls' the right ascension of the orbit ascending node, the RAAN change we call Omegadot.

Taking Earth rotation first, the angle the Earth rotates at is 1 degree every 4 minutes. So in a 97.5 minute orbit period it shifts 97.5/4 degrees = 24.375 degrees per orbit. This shift is always west, so EQX bearing west of Greenwich has 24.375 degrees of Earth rotation added every orbit. For very crude assessments of EQX this is all that is needed, Omegadot can be ignored, and orbital increment of EQX bearing can be taken as 24.375 in this case. By the same crude assessment, if 15 full orbits makes the next day's EQX times each 22.5 minutes later, then the EQX bearing increment per day is 22.5/4 degrees per day west = 5.625 degs/day. Using this crude method all EQX's next day are 22.5 minutes later in time and 5.625 degrees further west in longitude. The day after that they will be 45 minutes later (eg 1237 + 45 = 1322

UTC) and 11.25 degrees west increment. So if EQX bearing on the first day is 100°W, it will be 105.625°W one day later and 111.25°W two days later.

For accurate EQX bearing increments we must include

Omegadot = 9.95*(6,378/(6,378+sat altitude))^3.5 *COS(inclination)

Considering our 97.5 minute orbit at 82 degs inclination angle we get Omegadot per day = 0.9889, so

Omegadot per orbit = 0.9889*1,440/97.5

Note we have orbit every 97.5 minutes in 1,440 minute/day which means the number of orbits per day is not a whole number.

Omegadot per orbit = 0.066958 degrees/orbit

Accurate increment per orbit = 0.066958 + 24.375
= 24.441958°W/orbit

Accurate increment per day = 24.441958*15
= 366.62937
= 6.62937°W/day

Using the equations reviewed in the previous paragraphs, if we have an EQX time and bearing plus orbital period and inclination data we can calculate satellite tracks reasonably accurately over a period of several weeks. This data is not easily available, having fallen out of favour now that microcomputer users can solve Kepler's equations for elliptical orbits, but it does have advantages whereby many users seem to find it easier to employ.

The data required is published monthly in the satellite column of *Practical Wireless*. It is also available via computer software for the Sinclair microcomputers from SARUG: see appendix 1.

Elliptical orbits

Conic sections

A satellite in a perfectly circular orbit is fine in theory, but practically impossible. None the less, it is permissible for ordinary day-to-day calculation to treat near-circular orbits as if they were exactly circular. Not all satellites, however, have near-circular orbits; most commercial, military and radio amateur satellites have slightly elliptical orbits, with a considerable number having very elliptical orbits. In all these cases, if accurate tracking is required we must treat the orbit as an ellipse and use Kepler's methods to solve the tracking problems of elliptical motion.

The ellipse is a particular form of a conic section, the plane revealed when a cone is sawn in half by cutting across it at an angle, as shown in Fig 4.25. The ellipse is the plane generated when the saw cut avoids the base of the cone. When the cut is at a greater angle than the side angle of the cone we get a special form of the ellipse, the hyperbola, which never closes the loop. When the cut across the cone is parallel to the side and cuts the base of the cone we get a parabola, a conic section which closes only at infinity. All these conic sections can appear as satellite orbits and all are solvable using modern variations of Kepler's methods.

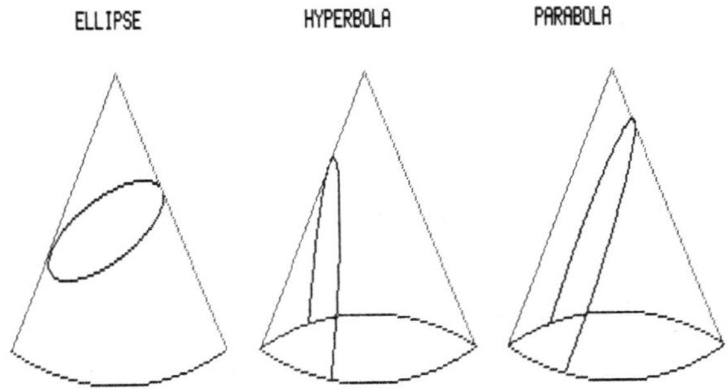

Fig 4.25: Conic sections

These three conic sections are important because the ellipse accurately describes the closed loop path of one body orbiting around another; the hyperbola describes a transit of one body swinging around another but going too fast to be captured by its gravity, the typical orbit of the new comet falling in past the Sun for the first and only time before it goes on an escape trajectory out of the solar system. The parabola looks like the special case of the body swinging in orbit around another and just failing to escape, but getting so close to escape that it does not return for millions of years. In fact, measuring positions of astronomical bodies such as comet and asteroids in orbit often leads to a near-parabolic solution, and it must be appreciated that our present inaccuracies of measurement often prevent us knowing whether these bodies are in hyperbolic escape orbits, or near-parabolic orbits due to return in 500 years.

In practice, near-Earth (within 1 million kilometre) orbits can generally be considered as ellipses, but from about 30,000 to 1 million kilometres apogee, the effects of the gravities of the Sun and the Moon must be considered in any long-term predictions.

Johannes Kepler

Until the 17th century the motions of the Sun and the planets were thought to be circles, revolving inside and outside other circles in complex nests of circles. By 1576, however, the Danish astronomer Tycho Brahe had begun to collect accurate night-to-night position sequences for the major planets, using a clock and simple visual surveying equipment. Astronomers at that time did not have telescopes. In 1597 Brahe left Denmark and settled in Prague in Bohemia.

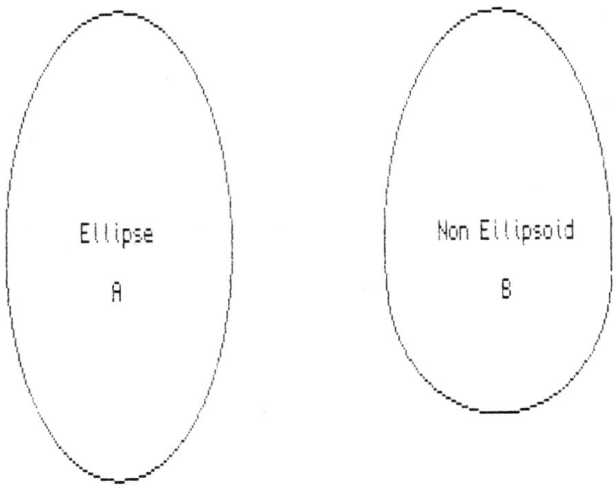

Fig 4.26: Ellipses and other figures

There he met the young mathematician Johannes Kepler and, on his death, Brahe bequeathed his by then nearly 20 years of records to Kepler.

Using Brahe's observations, Kepler was able to solve the mathematics necessary to descibe and predict the orbit of the planet Mars. He demonstrated that Mars followed an elliptical orbit around the Sun and in doing this he produced his three laws of elliptical motion which now provide the cornerstone to our understanding of its complex mathematics.

As Fig 4.26a shows, an ellipse is a regular figure. Cut it along its major or its minor axis and the resulting halves are the same, as are the resulting quarters, if these halves are cut again. It is a common mistake to say that Fig 4.26b is an ellipse: it is not.

Fig 4.27 shows an ellipse with its important features designated. Point C is the centre of the ellipse where the semi-minor, smaller axis, and the semi-major, longer axis intersect at right angles. The Earth is shown, positioned at one focus of the ellipse; the second focus F is empty. At point A the ellipse is nearest to its Earth focus; this nearest point to Earth is called the 'perigee', whilst at the far end of the major axis of the ellipse running from perigee through the Earth focus, the ellipse centre C, the second focus F, to the far end of the ellipse, the 'apogee' of the ellipse is found. The 'eccentricity' of the ellipse is a ratio which tells us whether it is fat and near-circular, or long and thin and far from circular. This eccentricity ratio is the ratio of the distance ellipse centre C to Earth, versus the distance centre C to perigee. If the Earth were at centre C, we would have the special case where the ratio was zero = eccentricity 0, which describes a perfect circle.

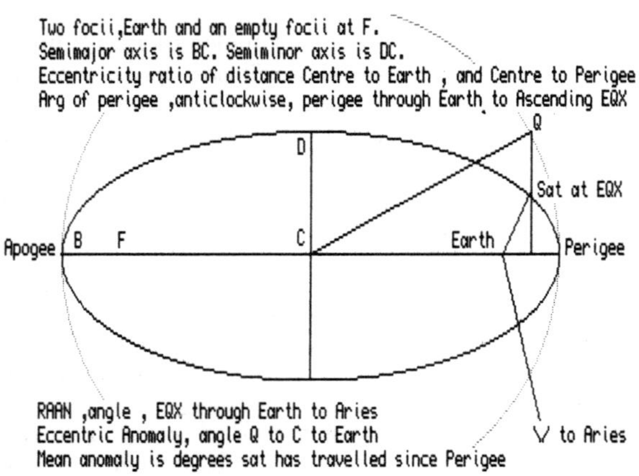

Fig 4.27: The major elements of an ellipse

Fig 4.15 shows the orbit of a typical high-apogee, low-perigee, elliptical-orbit satellite. Using Figs 4.27 and 4.15, the important features of this practical orbit are the designation of perigee position at an argument of perigee angle read anti-clockwise from the ascending equatorial crossing node, and two features which describe the alignment of the orbit in space, by designating the angle between the first point of Aries sky/stellar reference point and the ascending equatorial crossing. As with circular orbits we call this orbital element the right ascension of the ascending node, 'RAAN' for short. The second feature defining the orbit's position in space is the inclination angle of the orbit plane to the Earth's equatorial axis. This feature is not shown on Fig 4.15 but appears on Fig 4.28.

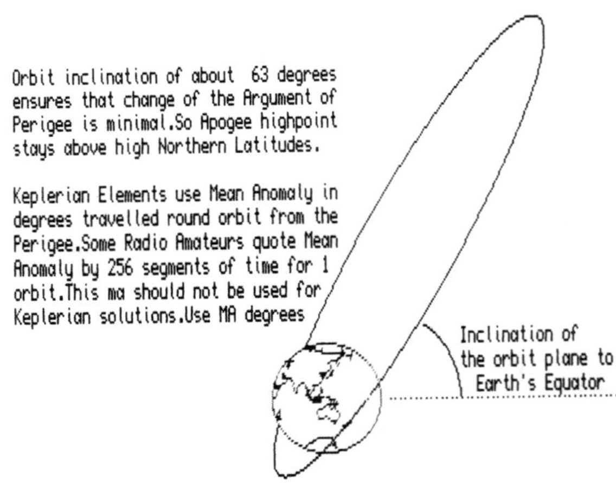

Fig 4.28: The practical elliptical orbit

Considering Fig 4.15, the satellite is clearly going very slowly around its apogee, and very fast around its perigee. The explanation for this lies in Kepler's second law, which states that the arc between the satellite and the Earth traces out equal areas in equal time. So, far out at apogee with long axis back to Earth, the satellite travels very slowly around the short axis of the near-triangular area it traces out. By contrast, when near perigee its axis length to Earth is much reduced (roughly six to one reduction in the practical case of a molniya elliptical orbit), so it has to go six times faster round the orbit to enclose the same area.

Kepler's success in solving elliptical motion depends

crucially on an equation which relates the eccentric anomaly shown in Fig 4.27, as the angle between the orbit major axis and a line joining the ellipse centre to an imaginary auxiliary circle, to the mean anomaly, the angle the satellite would bear if it were following the circular path (radius is the semi-major axis of the ellipse), at constant velocity.

Used in this manner, mean anomaly in degrees relates to the angle travelled from perigee, which is easily calculated as time since perigee/orbital period multiplied by 360 degrees.

The relationship between mean and eccentric anomalies is often called 'Kepler's equation', and is stated as:

Eccentric Anomaly = Mean Anomaly + Eccentricity * SIN(Eccentric Anom)

This equation is not directly solvable for eccentric anomaly. It is solved by either a repetitive iterative series of calculations or by binary search, a computer process which finds a binary series progressing from most- to least-significant binary digit for the eccentric anomaly. A third method of solution favoured when eccentricity is greater than 0.95 (nearly a parabola), is called the 'Gaussian' solution. An excellent summary of binary search and Gaussian solution is given in *Sky and Telescope*, August 1985, p159, by Sinnot.

In addition to solving Kepler's equation, would-be elliptical orbit trackers must be able to calculate Julian day and sidereal time and several other features. These calculations are not easy, so most satellite users employ specialist software and microcomputers. See appendix 1 for suppliers. For those who wish to write their own elliptical-orbit tracking software there are two good guides:

Amateur Radio Software by J Morris, GM4ANB, RSGB

'Basic Orbits' by T Clark, *Orbit*, March/April 1981

Data for elliptical-orbit calculations

In order to track elliptical satellites it is necessary to have an accurate statement of the satellite's position on the orbit at a given epoch time, and to have the Keplerian orbital elements which allow prediction of satellite position at a later time, by describing the exact shape and location in space of the orbit. Figs 4.27 and 4.28 show how these Keplerian elements relate to the actual orbit. A typical set of Keplerian elements are shown below:

Satellite: Oscar 10
Epoch year: 87
Epoch day of year: 023.13103915
(Sometimes combined as epoch 87023.13103915)
(Representing 23 January 1987 at 0308 UTC approx)
Inclination: 27.1040 degrees
Right ascension of ascending node: 38.6101 degrees
Eccentricity: 0.6022546 (dimensionless ratio)
Argument of perigee: 178.8941 degrees
Mean anomaly: 183.0539 degrees
Mean motion: 2.05877501 orbits per day

In some cases the semi-major axis of the orbit is given instead of the mean motion (each is calculable from the other, so only one is necessary).

Also sometimes quoted but not essential to the Keplerian elements are:

Drag factor: −8.7E−7
Revolution or orbit number since launch: 2717

Details are given in the computer chapter of this book of how often Keplerian elements should be updated in elliptical-orbit calculations.

Geostationary orbit tracking

The Clarke geostationary orbit is at present the most valuable satellite orbit, and it is rapidly filling up with individual satellites taking advantage of its special properties. If a satellite is given the correct west to east velocity as it enters a 0 degree inclination circular orbit at a height of about 35,800km above the Earth's equator, its orbital rotation will match that of the Earth, rotating beneath it, so that to an observer on the Earth the satellite will appear to be stationary.

From the point of view of any ground station inside its roughly 80 degree radius footprint, the azimuth and elevation of the geosat is fixed. So fixed pointing of the station antenna is all that is required and no tracking movements are necessary.

Because of the geosat's fixed position it is possible to show its azimuth and elevation from the ground on simple charts. Fig 4.29 shows a set of charts for UK latitudes 50, 52, 56 and 60°N. Choose the chart nearest your latitude then, having found the geostationary longitude of the geosat you want to point at, calculate the difference in longitude between your station and the geosat. Then select that longitude difference on the bottom line of the relevant latitude chart, read up from that longitude difference to the complete azimuth curve or the dotted elevation curve.

Worked example. Consider a station in Glasgow, Scotland, 56°N 4°W wanting to access a geosat at 40°E station (320°W). The longitude difference = 4 + 40 = −44 degrees apart; on Fig 4.29c this equates to azimuth 130.6 degrees, elevation 15.3 degrees.

Worked example. Station at Falmouth, Cornwall at 50°N 5°W wishes to access a satellite at 17°W (sometimes called 343°E) station. The longitude difference is +12 degrees; on Fig 4.29a this equates to azimuth 195.5 and elevation of 31.5 degrees.

Computer software for calculating antenna pointing data for

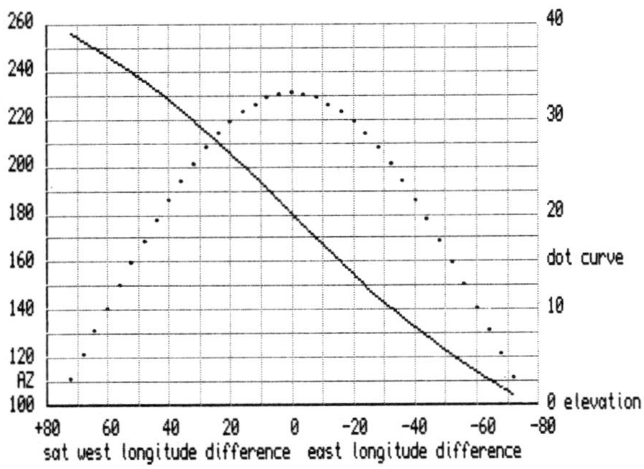

a: Latitude 50°N

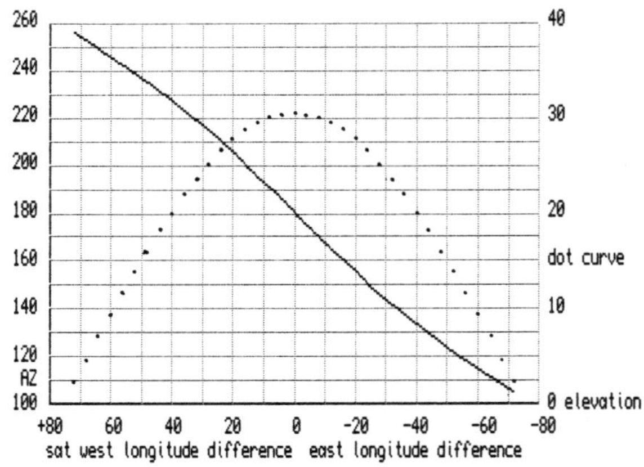

b: Latitude 52°N

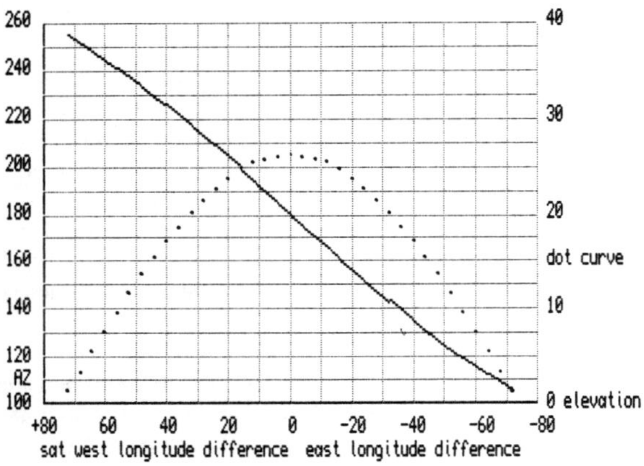

c: Latitude 56°N

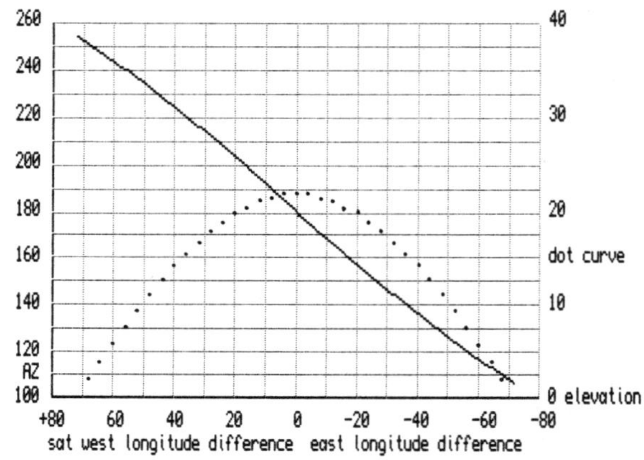

d: Latitude 60°N

Fig 4.29: Geostationary satellite finder charts.

access to geostationary satellites is available from SARUG, see appendix 1.

For those who wish to write their own software, the book *Amateur Radio Software* by John Morris, published by RSGB, is recommended.

Caution. There is a trap for the unwary in the geostationary satellite problem. Some geosats use narrow spot beam antennas – you can point at them, but they are not necessarily sending a signal in your direction.

Geosynchronous and near-geosynchronous orbits

These orbits should be treated as elliptical orbits. Software and calculations for elliptical orbits will predict the positions of these satellites and provide tracking data.

Chapter 5

Satellite radio reception

Introduction

Reception of signals from space is never a simple matter. The signal is highly susceptible to modification and attenuation in the last 500km or so of its path, as it comes down through the ionosphere and the atmosphere, where a wide range of different propagation anomalies can be present. These problems apply in some degree to virtually all radio signals but, from the point of view of ground station reception of radio signals from satellites and deep space craft, three general groups of factors apply. The first group affects HF signals (10 to 30MHz), the second affects VHF/UHF signals (30 to 1,000MHz), and the third and last affects microwave signals (above 1,000MHz). The paragraphs which follow describe these problems as they affect each of these three groups, subject to the proviso that some reception problems overlap from one group to another.

It is important, when considering reception of signals from space, to appreciate that exactly the same problems apply to signals travelling in the opposite direction from Earth. In the case of systems using both up link and down link paths, they may both have problems, and those problems may not be the same, particularly where the up and down link frequencies are markedly different one from another. Even more important and often less well appreciated, it is often the case that stations using a satellite as a communications link fail to appreciate that the paths to and from the satellite to the two stations are invariably different. One station may have almost no problems, whilst the other station experiences serious difficulties. Understanding the other station's propagation situation is almost as important as understanding your own.

Reception problems at HF

The ionosphere is only marginally transparent to frequencies in this group. At night a signal in this group will usually penetrate down from space to Earth without difficulty, particularly if it enters the ionosphere at a steep angle from nearly vertically overhead. Signals at the low-frequency end of this group may have difficulty making the transit if they enter at a shallow angle near the station horizon. In the day this situation is much more extreme. Fig 5.01 shows what happens.

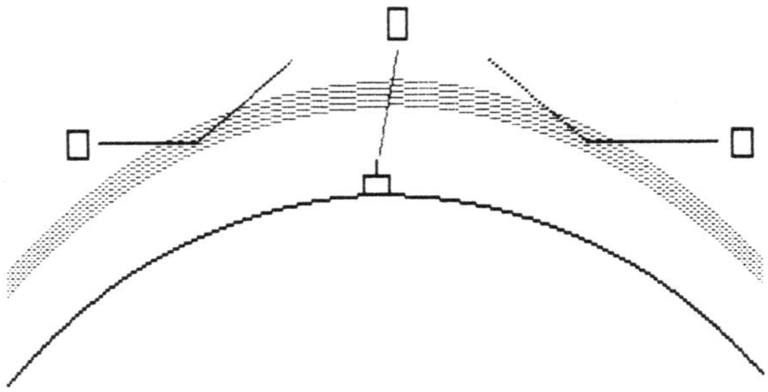

Fig 5.01: Loss of low-elevation signals from HF satellite (Earth and ionosphere not to scale). The ionosphere refracts low incident angle signals back into space when maximum usable frequency is greater than signal frequency

If the ionosphere were not there, the receiver would in theory get a signal whose strength varied as the inverse square of the ratio of its path lengths. Thus twice as far away means four times weaker, eg with a signal received from a satellite 1,500km overhead, losing 6dB (four times weaker), as it moved out towards the horizon to a range of 3,000km. The presence of the ionosphere changes all this, and if we try to listen to satellites within three or four hours of dawn or dusk we get a further complication. Fig 5.02 shows what happens when the satellite sees our station through a night-time ionosphere for the first half of the pass, and then encounters a dense daytime ionosphere for the second half of its pass in range of our station. It depends of course on the

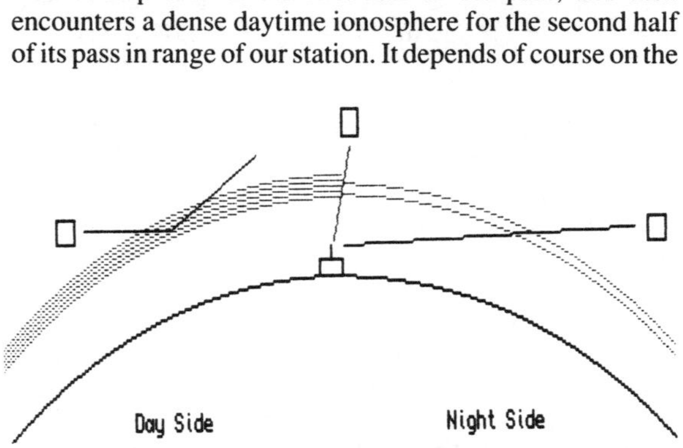

Fig 5.02: HF satellite reception problems due to day-night propagation variation (Earth and ionosphere not to scale). Day-side ionosphere refracts low incident angle signal back to space. Night-side ionosphere is transparent to satellite signals

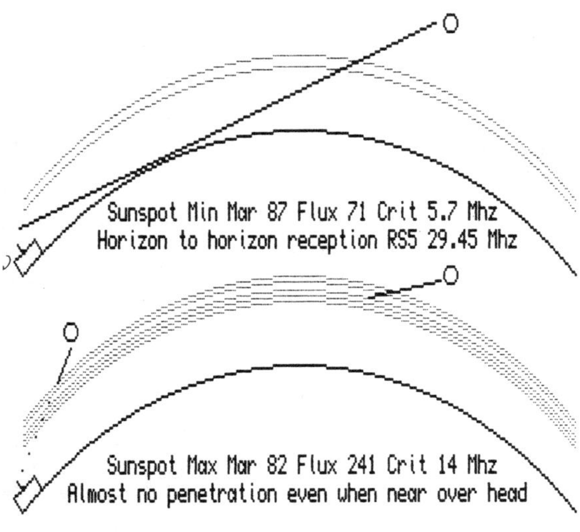

Fig 5.03: Effect of sunspot cycle on HF satellite reception during daylight

satellite signal frequency just how severe this situation is. The lower the frequency, the more severe the propagation problems.

Unfortunately the complications do not stop there. The solar sunspot cycle also has a marked effect on the density and location of the ionosphere. Fig 5.03 shows two contrasting views of satellite tracking at different parts of the 11-year solar cycle as applied in practice to Radiosport 5 transmitting on 29.45MHz. As Fig 5.03a shows, the situation in 1987 at the minimum of the solar cycle (March 1987 solar flux 71, critical frequency 5.7MHz, hence low oblique incidence MUF about 17.1MHz) was easy. Reception was possible from horizon to horizon, night and day, with only a little multipath fading (see Fig 5.05).

By contrast, five years before, just after solar cycle maximum, the situation was very different, with RS 5 passes over Scotland in daylight being almost hopeless. Only when RS 5 was nearly overhead Scotland did any signal get into the receiver, and even when the signal was heard it was subject to severe multipath fading (Fig 5.05 refers). Fig 5.03b shows the reception conditions experienced in Scotland at this time, March 1982, when the solar flux was 241 and the vertical incidence critical frequency was 14MHz, suggesting an oblique incidence maximum usable frequency of three times 14 = 42MHz. So it is not surprising that the 29.45MHz signal could not get down through the ionosphere at low elevation angles.

Would-be listeners to HF satellites must therefore check the propagation/ionospheric transparency predictions such as those published monthly in *Radio Communication* if they want to have some idea what is happening to their HF satellite signals. It is also appropriate to mention here that listening to a satellite regularly can be a superb guide to propagation conditions generally, and a considerable aid when considering likely terrestrial/ionospheric propagation possibilities.

Asymmetrical reception of HF satellites

As if the previous paragraphs had not included enough difficulties, there is a further less obvious propagation problem which has confused many would-be satellite communicators. Fig 5.04 illustrates the problem. Station UK is transmitting up to RS 10 on 145MHz and receiving both his own and other down link signals at 29.45 to 29.5MHz. So, too, is station USA on the other side of the Atlantic. They get in contact with one another but all is not well. Station USA cannot understand why station UK is so deaf.

The trouble is that the UK station is getting his down link via a thick daytime ionosphere, whereas station USA is receiving his down link via a thin pre-dawn ionosphere. The stations are 4,000km and five hours apart in time zones, but more importantly their ionospheric transit points are about three hours apart in solar time. Solar illumination is high for station UK at his mid-morning local time, and his ionosphere is almost opaque to the 29.5MHz down link, so station UK hears the down link badly or more likely with deep fading. By contrast, station USA under a thin ionosphere is getting strength nine signals and simply cannot understand why station UK cannot hear his 'perfect' down link. UK stations experience this same situation in reverse when talking to USA via HF satellites from the UK, near the midnight time period. Nine out of 10 operators simply do not allow for these conditions. When they hear the satellite clearly they talk fast, oblivious of the fact that the chap at the other end has reported poor reception. Indeed they conclude from his report that he is a poor operator. A sad but thoroughly understandable misconception.

Other HF satellite reception problems

There are two other problems which can plague the HF satellite user. The first, multipath fading, shown in Fig 5.05, is a consequence of variability between regions of the ionosphere, a condition which often occurs. The variations

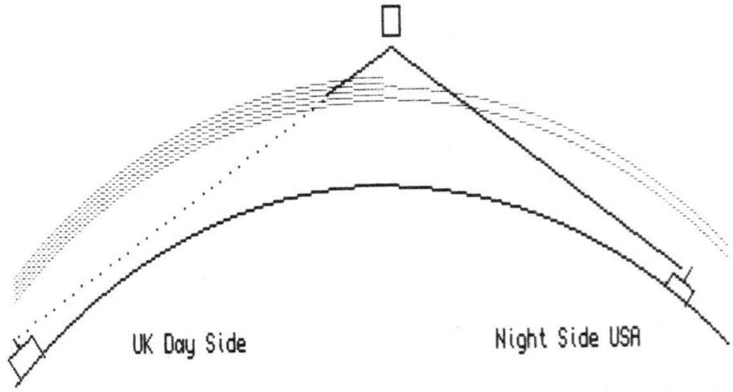

Fig 5.04: Asymmetrical down link reception for HF satellites (Earth and ionosphere not to scale). The day-side ionosphere attenuates satellite HF down link signal. Less dense night-side ionosphere is transparent to satellite signals

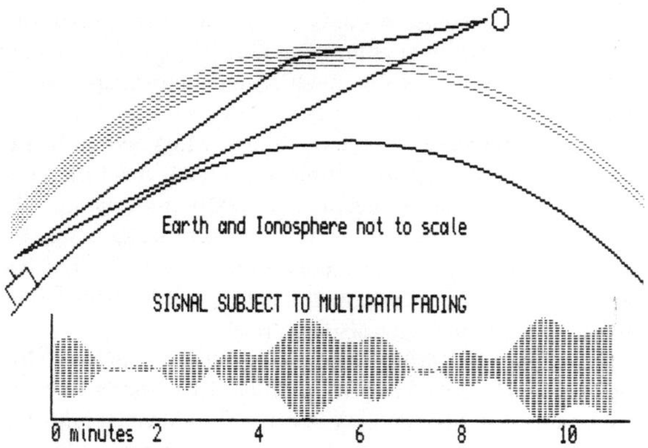

Fig 5.05: HF satellite multipath down link reception

in separate regions of the ionosphere impart different degrees of bending to the signal path, so that the signal can arrive at the ground station by several different paths of different lengths. The result when these disparate signals arrive at the receiver is that they add if they are in phase, but subtract if they are antiphase. Because the satellite is moving, this phase relationship is continuously changing; sometimes arrivals are in phase, sometimes antiphase.

The oscilloscope trace shows the effect this has on the signal amplitude over about half of a typical RS 7 satellite pass. Please note that in the typical case the RS signal is readable strength for perhaps as much as one or two minutes at a time, but these periods are separated by intervals of several minutes when the signal is poor or simply not detectable at all.

Another HF reception problem is Faraday rotation of polarisation which was described in chapter 1. Unless special antennas are used this produces an effect almost indistinguishable from multipath fading. Indeed the two effects occurring together are very difficult to cope with.

Solutions to HF satellite reception problems

Most HF satellite transmissions are strong, and it is therefore tempting to put up a simple long-wire antenna and make do with that. You will hear satellite signals now and then, but you will not receive them consistently and you will certainly not get much long-range satellite communications success.

As explained above, there are a lot of things which can go wrong. Some features like the transparency/opacity of the ionosphere are beyond operator control, but none the less it does help to ensure that your antennas are optimised to get you the strongest possible signal.

This strategy is often described by saying that your reception system has a 'good fade margin', meaning that it normally produces strong signals so that, even when deep fades occur, the signal is not totally lost. Getting a strong signal consistently can only be achieved if your antenna system has a degree of choice, with, say, switchable polarisation to overcome Faraday rotation and simple directional capability. Figs 5.06 and 5.07 show two systems in common use among HF satellite specialists. The circularly polarised cross dipole for 29.5MHz is made from an old TV Band 1 X antenna mounted horizontally with its elements extended to 2.5m length for each of the four legs. Placed on your chimney mast this is useful for all-round search, but it has no claim to be a weak-signal antenna.

To get a weak-signal antenna, the switchable sloped dipoles are probably the best answer. Again, this is a simple home-constructed antenna. The author's is made using old coaxial cable as the active elements of the dipoles. Each dipole has two of these active sections, each being about 2.5m long. The four dipoles are suspended from a pole mast about 8m high, and each dipole slopes down at an angle of about 30 degrees to the mast. Only one dipole is used at a time.

The dipoles are switched, listening first to one, then to another, and chasing the best signal as the satellite changes position relative to your station.

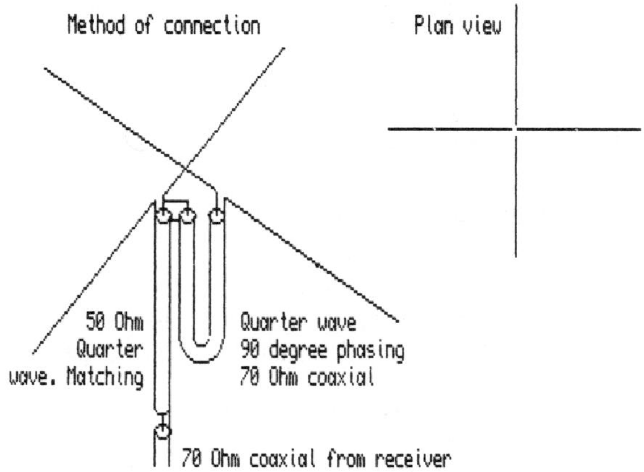

Fig 5.06: Crossed-dipole omnidirectional HF antenna

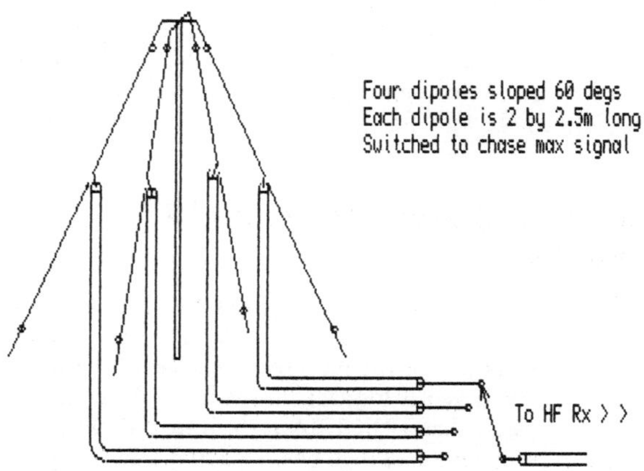

Fig 5.07: Switchable sloped dipoles for HF satellite reception

Another useful device for improving HF satellite reception is a preamplifier. Used properly these can be a great help. They can be switched out of circuit when conditions permit, because they do introduce the problem of reduced receiver dynamic range, whereby the high front-end gain receiver is swamped by strong local signals (power-line noise which often worsens in certain weather conditions is more often the problem, than a legitimate powerful adjacent radio signal). Another scheme which has worked well for the author is to change the front-end RF transistor in the station HF receiver for a more sensitive one. Again there is a loss of receiver dynamic range, but this is acceptable because the author lives in a small country village, well away from RF noisy industrial activity. This cure would be less acceptable in an urban environment.

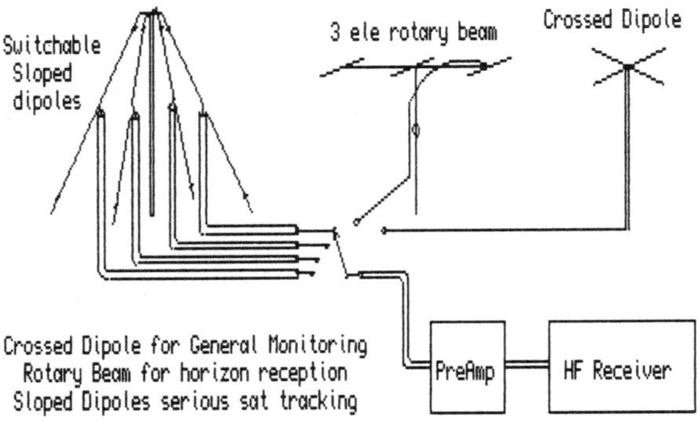

Fig 5.08: Deluxe station for HF satellite reception

Because of the continual Faraday rotation of signal polarisation, the use of HF Yagi beam antennas is not normally desirable. But like all rules this one has an exception, whereby a three-element 10m beam can at times be extremely useful when the satellite is at extreme range, right on the station horizon. Possible substitutes for an expensive beam are a ZL special or, in the author's case, a W8JK lazy H antenna made from old 300-ohm ribbon twin feeder. The *Radio Communication Handbook*, chapter 12, published by the RSGB, refers.

Fig 5.08 shows a deluxe HF satellite reception station. No-one should aim for this degree of sophistication at the start, but if real HF satellite performance is wanted this type of outfit can be built up slowly on a do-it-yourself basis.

Operating procedures on HF satellites

Whatever hardware you build for HF satellite reception, you can enhance your performance by sticking to some simple operating tactics. First you must prepare a useful operating schedule. If you want to log a lot of Americans, it is common sense to realise that a UK/USA path in total darkness is likely to be much easier than one in daylight. Even a path half in daylight is not a good bet.

Both the seasonal and sunspot cycle timing of operating activity is also critical. Summer is usually better than winter and sunspot minimum is much easier than sunspot maximum.

Please take note of sociable hours. Most people like to sleep 2300 to 0700 local time. So check the time zone differences for your target areas. Equally important, if you go on to transmit as well as listen, remember to assess the other station's propagation conditions. The author has lost count of the times that operators to his west fired back their replies despite his requests for repeats.

You may also find that a tape recorder helps. Most newcomers forget that it is their callsign the other man wants to know, not his own. A reply of 'GM4IHJ GM4IHJ GM4IHJ GM4IHJ GM4IHJ this is blurp bleep...' will endear you to no one, though even 'blurp bleep' may be amenable to massaging on a tape recorder loop replay. Please remember that HF satellite reception will never be perfect but, because HF satellites are accessible using relatively cheap equipment, that is where you will find the exciting stations, making all the effort worthwhile.

VHF satellite reception problems

Generally speaking, VHF satellites tend to be restricted to low earth orbits, because higher orbits suffer greater path losses which must be overcome by more power or more antenna gain. Higher satellite power is not easily achieved. The amount of sunlight seen by the satellite and the permissible size of the solar panels imposes a power limitation of 50 watts or less. In addition high-power amplifiers in satellites have not until recently been blessed with much reliability. Getting the gain at the satellite transmitting antenna is another non-starter, because VHF antennas soon get rather large and unwieldy. You cannot put a VHF moonbounce array onto an Oscar satellite the size of a suitcase.

In consequence of this, powerful satellites are not usually VHF satellites. Only satellites operating above the Van Allen belts can operate high-gain dish antennas and this operation has to be at microwave frequencies if practical dish sizes are to be used. Putting high-gain antennas on low-altitude satellites also poses problems of antenna pointing. Fortunately at low altitude, path losses are low, so VHF down links are practical.

Saying that VHF down links are practical does not mean they are free from problems. Indeed, most commercial operators have abandoned low Earth orbit simply because of the VHF propagation problems described in the following paragraphs.

Faraday rotation of polarisation is a constant problem on VHF satellite down links. Going from horizon to horizon, the signal from a VHF satellite can be expected to rotate its plane of polarisation perhaps six times, producing deep fading of the signal if linear polarised reception antennas are used.

Anomalous propagation is often present at VHF in the form of Sporadic E layer ionisation, aurora, or tropospheric bending. All of these can seriously affect VHF satellite operations from UK. Full details of these problems are given in chapters 1 and 2. The end result for VHF operators when one or other of these features is present is multipath fading or severe scintillation and, less often, complete loss of signal.

Doppler shift of the VHF satellite received signal can be a nuisance. At 145MHz, it usually requires four or five retunes of the signal in a 10-minute satellite pass. At 435MHz, the shift is three times faster and three times further and hence much more difficult to deal with, particularly for inexperienced operators.

VHF satellites – practical operating solutions

A simple VHF satellite reception facility is shown in Fig 5.09. The antenna used can be either a crossed dipole or individual switched dipoles. Using the crossed dipole shown in Fig 5.09, there is a slight loss of gain compared to a dipole, but the operator is free to ignore the antenna which copes with Faraday rotation. If the switched dipoles are used the operator has slightly more gain, but must be prepared to switch between them in an effort to chase the best signal. Because these antennas have low gain, a preamplifier is advisable, preferably placed on the antenna, although in the case of switched dipoles this may add complications. So, if switched dipoles are used, a preamplifier alongside the receiver is better than no preamplifier at all.

The choice of receivers is wide. There are many suitable commercial VHF receivers (although some are restricted to FM and AM modes – no CW or SSB operation, which does restrict the number of satellites which are available). Alternatively it is possible to use a convertor to a suitable shortwave receiver. Convertors are readily available for most satellite bands (136/137, 144/145 and 435/436MHz, all changing down to 28MHz). If a convertor is used and you decide to go on to transmitting as well as receiving, be careful you are not converting to your transmit frequency (eg 435 to 28MHz is fine, but 435 to 144MHz should be avoided).

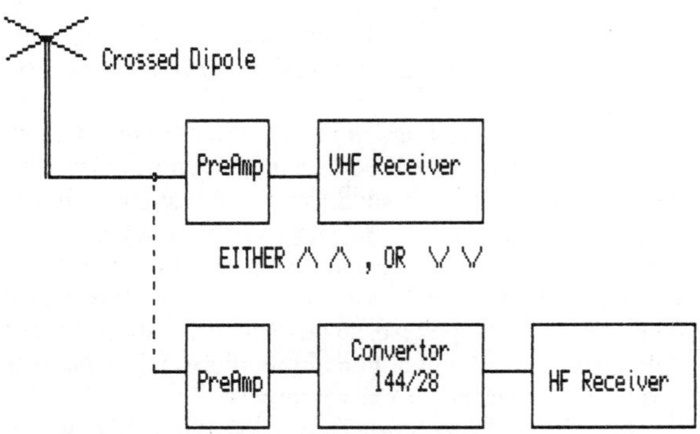

Fig 5.09: A simple station for VHF satellite reception

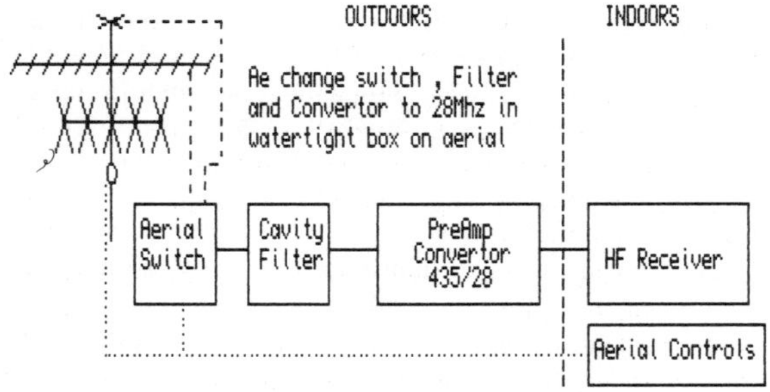

Fig 5.10: A station for UHF 435MHz satellite reception. A low-elevation 145MHz antenna is also shown

Equally important, even in this simple set-up, if any transmission is contemplated you may need a filter in the front end of your receiver. For example, listening to 435MHz satellites can be interfered with by the third harmonic of 144MHz transmissions nearby. The RSGB *VHF/UHF Manual*, fourth edition, has a suitable design of resonant cavity filter which can be scaled to 144 or 435MHz (p7.7, Fig 20). This type of filter is a 'must' if you are going to operate mode J (145MHz up, 435MHz down) satellites such as Fuji Oscar 20.

Improved VHF reception facilities

It might seem at first sight that VHF satellite reception could be improved by adding a narrow-beam antenna with appreciable gain. This antenna will of course need an azimuth rotator and it will need to be operated using predictions from a suitable computer program.

Used in this form, purely for Fuji Oscar 20 when it is at long range near the horizon, it will perform very well. Indeed most operators would not want to go further, because when Fuji is near UK, above and out of reach of this fixed-elevation system, it does not have much in the way of communications excitement. All the interesting communication is at low elevation and long range where tracking rates are slow and easy, and Faraday is slight.

If, however, the user wants to listen to Fuji as it goes nearly overhead, the linearly polarised, horizon-pointing Yagi antenna is hopeless. Fortunately Fuji has a powerful signal so the solution is easy: a pair of switched or crossed dipoles for short-range reception. Antennas can be changed over by remotely controlled switches so it is not necessary to bring all the antennas on long leads indoors. In fact, the antenna changeover switch, cavity filter and preamplifier convertor 435/28MHz can be mounted on the antenna. The signal making the journey indoors is then the low-loss 28MHz signal, not the high-loss 435MHz signal. Fig 5.10 shows this improved VHF/UHF facility.

By using a simple antenna layout which does not require constant repointing, the operator is able to concentrate on getting his tuning right in the constant battle to match the high-speed UHF Doppler shift. For communicators the tactic usually employed is to tune the transmitter to stay on the same spot on your receiver dial. This does require a transmitter which will transmit whilst tuning, a point worth looking for when buying a 145MHz transmitter – not all have this facility.

Users of an improved VHF/UHF rig of this type may still find anomalous propagation is a problem on some satellite orbits. Fuji Oscar 20 suffers badly at times when its evening orbits start over USA/Canada. From this position they often 'look' at the UK through the polar auroral front. With auroral quiet near solar cycle minimum, this is a problem on perhaps one orbit in 10 but, as solar maximum approaches, it could be a problem on one orbit in three from this location in the UK evening. It is in these conditions that a narrow-beam, high-gain Yagi works best. Faraday rotation is slow at the horizon so it is rarely a serious problem, and azimuth changes only very slowly so that is not a difficulty either, whereas the stronger signal from the high-gain antenna is a big advantage.

A first-class VHF reception facility

There are two reasons for building a sophisticated reception facility for satellite work. First, it gives a much better fade margin on weak signals and second, it permits optimum reception of the Phase III satellites which use VHF but are not in low earth orbit.

Fig 5.11 shows a station equipped for optimum VHF/UHF performance. This station was gradually constructed over a period of 18 months as a progressive experiment to receive better signals from Oscar 10 Phase IIIB. Oscar 10 goes out to 36,000km from the Earth with a consequent 30dB greater single-way path loss compared with an LEO satellite. Oscar 10 carries a VHF down link antenna with 6 to 8dB of gain and this antenna is connected for circular polarisation. Unfortunately, orbit insertion problems resulted in a less-than-optimum orbit and Oscar 10's antenna rarely points at the Earth. Indeed at certain times the antenna was pointed well away from the Earth, resulting in a very weak received signal and severe polarisation problems. Satisfactory reception of this signal requires a sophisticated station, which then has the additional merit of being useful for moonbounce and for terrestrial VHF work.

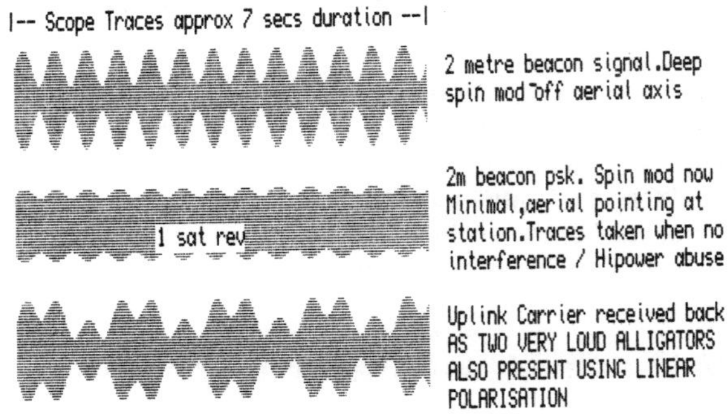

Fig 5.12: Spin modulation of Oscar 10 down link signal envelope

As Fig 5.11 shows, the receiving antenna is a 9 × 9 element XY Yagi for 145MHz. The X and Y sections have separate feeds to a polarisation switch, which permits a choice of right-hand or left-hand circular polarisation, or horizontal or vertical modes. The selection is made remotely at the control desk indoors. The polarisation switch is mounted on the antenna and feeds directly to a low-noise GaAsFET preamplifier before leaving the antenna mast on good-quality coaxial cable, leading to the operating bench and the 145MHz receiver. The up link is from a 435MHz transceiver feeding up to 8 watts to an array of four XY 19-element Yagis stacked two by two. All antennas are on a common minitower mast fitted with azimuth and elevation rotators.

Despite this elaborate and expensive hardware, reception of Oscar 10 is often marginal, because the system has no fade margin capable of dealing with some of the off-axis excursions of the Oscar 10 onboard antenna pointing. Fig 5.12 shows part of the problem, a pronounced amplitude modulation of the down link signal at three times the satellite spin frequency. This modulation gets deeper as the squint between line-of-sight station to satellite deviates markedly from satellite onboard antenna pointing. This problem is discussed in greater depth in the Oscar 10 section of chapter 6.

As this problem occurs at the satellite, ground stations simply have to make the best of it. Sometimes Oscar 10 points at Earth and its signals are reasonable strength; often, however, it does not do so and even this sophisticated reception system cannot produce something from nothing. When in use on Oscar 10 it is vital that the ground station pointing should be precise, so this antenna system is regularly checked on fixed alignment markers and extra-solar system radio astronomy marker targets.

This facility was rebuilt for use on Phase IIIC which became Oscar 13, and it continues to be used for Oscar 10.

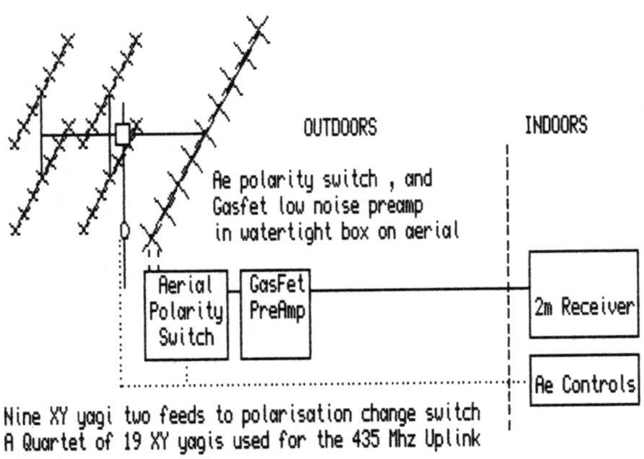

Fig 5.11: A station for distant VHF 145MHz Oscar 10 reception

In both cases its narrow-beam, high-gain antennas are the best answer to tracking these slow-moving satellites but, if antennas for tracking fast-moving LEO satellites such as Fuji JAS1-B and the new pacsats are required, the simpler rig shown in Fig 5.10 gives much better results.

VHF/UHF antennas – a general discussion

At VHF/UHF the antennas are all-important. So it pays to give them a lot of attention. Most of the 136/137MHz satellites are so strong in their LEOs that they can be effectively received on a crossed dipole. However, please look out for Faraday problems if you use linear antennas. It really does not matter if you use existing amateur radio 144MHz antennas to listen to 136/137MHz satellites as it makes no noticeable difference. So if you have 144MHz antennas try them and you will probably find they work well on 136MHz.

If you use a two metre 145MHz crossed dipole you can also use it for Fuji Oscar 20 up link with no standing wave ratio problems, whereas a 136MHz antenna would not be advisable for Fuji passes. Any crossed dipole or switched dipole can be improved by fitting it above a reflector. *Satellite Experimenters' Handbook* by Martin Davidoff (available from the RSGB) has the details, pp6-20.

If your station already has a two metre 144MHz Yagi beam or quad loop, this can be used for satellites on 136/137 and 144/154MHz. If it is fixed in azimuth, you will have a few problems when the satellite is outside its beam, so smaller three- or four-element beams are better in this respect than bigger ones. In fact, a big beam can be a nuisance and is difficult to keep trained accurately on a fast-moving LEO satellite.

Using ordinary terrestrial 144 and 432MHz antennas for satellite work makes sense, at least to start with. The purchase of specialist satellite antennas can be expensive and is not always the best answer. It cannot be over-stressed that all the best activity on amateur communications satellites takes place when they are at low elevation, and a long way from your station. Ordinary beams and quads perform well in this operating situation. When the satellite is close to your station, it has one advantage, strong signal, and three disadvantages – fast movement across the sky, fast Doppler shift, and a communications footprint which includes only local countries. So newcomers to a particular LEO satellite should always start on the easy-to-follow long-range parts of the in-range orbital passes, and they should find that their ordinary amateur radio equipment works quite well in this situation.

VHF polarising switches and controllers

Several VHF satellites (eg Oscar 10, SRET 2) are difficult to receive consistently because of non-circular polarisation at certain aspects or Faraday rotation of signals from linearly polarised antennas on the satellite.

The method used by radio amateurs to reduce these difficulties have varied. GM4DJS used switchable beam antennas of opposite polarisation to good effect. The author used twin feeders from a big XY crossed Yagi beam, feeding directly to a switch box, holding a variety of delay and matching options, which offered a choice of six polarisation modes (RSGB *VHF/UHF Manual*, 4th edition, chapter 8, Fig 71 refers). This box was on the antenna between the antenna and the subsequent GaAsFET preamplifier, and it was relay switched remotely from the operating bench. There is also a third option available commercially which can be used with XY Yagis to provide a continuous smooth rotation of polarisation. Though this latter may seem attractive, it cannot be remotely controlled, so it must be used on the operating bench, which means the preamplifier must also be on the operating bench. This requires a long 'lossy' feeder from antenna to operating bench, before the preamplifier, a far from satisfactory situation.

All the above solutions to Faraday and 'off-axis' squint polarisation problems are very frequency conscious. Their usable bandwidth does not exceed 4MHz at 144MHz, so used outside these frequency limits only the GM4DJS solution retains reasonable directivity. Both the polarisation modifiers produce serious directional squint misalignment when used outside the range 142 to 146MHz. None the less, despite these reservations, used at their design frequencies they are extremely useful. So useful in fact that the author tried to build a similar polarisation switch box for his up link 435MHz to Oscar 10. It did not work. The move to UHF is not a simple one, and the UHF polarisation switch produced some very serious squinting and standing wave ratio problems, as well as having a rather high insertion loss, attenuating the signal on its way up to the antenna.

This difficulty in applying techniques which work at 145MHz across to systems using 435MHz is covered in more detail in the next paragraph.

UHF antennas – precautions

Most would-be users of UHF satellite links buy antennas as kits, which they assemble themselves. This can lead to a lot of mistakes which are much more damaging in their effects at 435MHz than they would be at 145MHz. Bad practice at 145MHz is rarely critical: at 435MHz it is invariably disastrous. Points to be noted are:

(a) Most manufacturers optimise their antennas for terrestrial user frequencies, eg 144.3 and 432.5MHz. This situation sometimes applies when the antenna is described as a satellite antenna. In the specific case of antennas sold as satellite equipment, 432MHz used to be the operating frequency. This frequency has changed to 435MHz, but some antennas have not changed. This makes the task of anyone proposing to connect up an XY Yagi for circular polarisation extremely difficult because the X and Y active elements are not spaced a quarter wavelength at 435MHz. So any attempt to connect them for circular polarisation using feeders of the same length runs into serious trouble. At 145MHz antennas are rarely built with quarter-wave staggered X and Y elements, so this point rarely applies, but at 435MHz it can be vital. Before using the standard T junction coaxial cable supplied for circular polarisation, users must measure the active element spacing. If it is not a quarter wave they must modify the feeder connections to allow for this. For example, a difference of 2cm from a quarter wave requires 2 × velocity factor of cable (usually 0.6 or 0.7) = 1.4cm difference between the connection lengths on the two arms of the T junction. If in doubt, please consult the antenna manufacturers; you will find they are very helpful.

(b) Never run coaxial cable or metal tubing supports or masts through the near field of a UHF antenna, particularly not in front of the active elements to which the feeders connect. Always feed UHF antennas from the back, and use wooden or glass fibre support poles and masts. Failure to obey this rule can result in a radio beam squinting up to 6 or 8 degrees to one side of its mechanical axis. Several amateur radio magazines have carried photographs of these antennas with defects on them. A photo in a magazine does not mean it works.

Helical antennas

It is often desirable to use a dedicated circular polarisation antenna for a particular satellite, but please take care, for there is no one standard polarisation for either radio amateur satellites or commercial satellites. The reason for this is that satellite designers often use one direction of polarisation for one sub-system and the opposite direction of polarisation for another-sub system, in order to profit from the 9dB isolation this gives them between the two systems. For example, most commercial data and TV satellites use one polarisation for even-number channels and the opposite polarisation for odd-number channels. If you are unaware of this, scanning the TV down link channels can be very confusing. Amateur radio satellite designers use exactly the same tricks to separate down link signals and up link signals. So there is no preferred direction of circular polarisation, which tends to make helical antennas which are fixed polarisation less useful than XY Yagis which can be switched from one polarisation to another.

Despite this strong reservation, the author and many other radio amateurs have built a number of helical antennas and been successful with them. Helical antennas can be built from junk. The author has used old coaxial cable for the VHF helixes and central heating piping for the UHF and microwave helixes. These can be mounted on simple wooden frame supports and, if used indoors, need not be robust or waterproof. Impedance matching is important but not difficult (RSGB *VHF/UHF Manual*, 4th edition, page A.4, right-hand column refers).

Once built for, say, radio amateur work, the helical antenna has one important property – it retains its effectiveness over a wide band of frequencies. So space radio listeners who want a common antenna with some gain and a reasonably wide beam for, say, satellite monitoring of 121.75, 136, 145, 153, 166 and 199MHz will find that a helix is one of the few antennas that will support all these activities – the writer uses a 145MHz helical mounted under the roof tiles in his loft for VHF satellite monitoring. This antenna was built nine years earlier for Oscar 8 up link transmission, but has proved successful in a variety of other fields. The real luxury which this operator has yet to achieve is a pair of these helixes, one left-hand, the other right-hand, suitably switched to choose the one receiving the stronger signal.

Even at the lower microwaves the helical antenna should not be ignored by the space listener. It is a much more attractive solution to the microwave LEO satellite problem than any discone or other low-gain antenna. The helix built for 1,269MHz receives a quite strong signal from the 1,700MHz weather satellites.

A simple microwave satellite receiving station

The frequencies around 1,000MHz (1GHz) are used by several satellite families. Soviet spacecraft – Soyuz, Venera and Vega Venus probes – all use frequencies in the band 922 to 926MHz. Some navigation and radar satellites use frequencies just above 1GHz, and there is likely to be a continuing use of 1,269MHz for amateur satellite up links. All these services can be operated using Yagi beams or helical antennas but, whereas one helical antenna will suffice for this whole band, separate, tuned-to-one-frequency Yagis will be necessary for each sub-frequency band. At frequencies above 1.3GHz the helical can still be used but the Yagi antenna is difficult to build and is therefore rarely used.

Above 1.3GHz helical antennas compete with dish antennas and horn antennas, and are slowly being joined by a totally new class of antenna which uses a flat surface, steerable microwave beam. Horn antennas are simple to build. They have quite wide bandwidth, but they are ponderous, awkward beasts generally used only in simple, one-off, experimental rigs. The flat microwave antennas are not yet available in any numbers, but when available should be useful to radio amateurs and space listeners. This leaves the field to dish antennas which tend to predominate in most microwave applications at the moment.

Manufactured microwave dishes are at present expensive, but useful dishes can be 'home made' by following the procedure reported in the RSGB *VHF/UHF Manual*, 4th edition, from p9.63 onwards. At p9.71 the manual goes on to describe several useful types of linear and circular feed horns which are useful for those who will need to build one of these essential adjuncts to the dish.

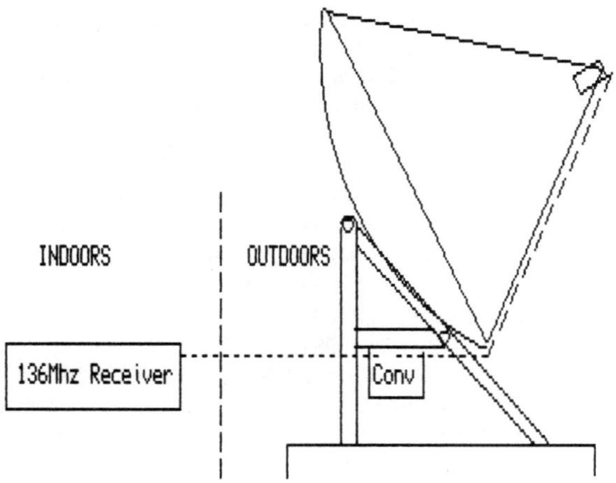

Fig 5.13: Microwave weather satellite 1.6GHz reception. The preamplifier is connected directly to the circular feedhorn. It uses Heliax cable to feed a 1,675/136MHz convertor, which is mounted in a watertight box near the dish

Fig 5.13 shows a simple microwave reception facility suitable for the weather satellites at 1,675MHz. The construction is robust, and the antenna is firmly fixed and aligned on its single geostationary satellite target. So this is not a system usable for, say, the LEO weather satellites which sweep across the UK sky roughly 16 times each day, transmitting on frequencies around 1,700MHz, nor is this system suitable for use with the 2.4GHz beacons of Oscars 9 and 11. The trouble with dishes is that they are easily pushed around by the wind. Hence a trainable dish needs a very stiff mounting and a precise motor drive system with high torque to drive it, if it is to follow LEO microwave satellites. Frankly, these requirements are outside the ability and bank balance of most radio amateurs and space listeners.

Considering Fig 5.13 in greater detail, several points are noteworthy. First, whilst the dish can be used over a wide range of frequencies, the feed horn can not. Feed horns of the type shown tend to have a bandwidth of about 2% of frequency, eg 24MHz at 1,269MHz, so operation is frequency limited. The second important point about Fig 5.13 is the care which has been taken to protect the weak received signal by mounting the preamplifier directly onto the feedhorn and then using the minimum length of high-quality Heliax cable to the 1,675 to 136MHz convertor located in a watertight box behind the dish. These precautions are not embellishments, they are absolutely necessary if good pictures are required.

There are commercially available preamplifiers for the weather satellite gigahertz down links, but for other frequencies users must be prepared to build their own. *VHF Magazine* has been a good source for construction details, and has also advertised some excellent kits for DIY builders. It cannot be over-emphasised that bringing microwave signals away on long feeders from this type of installation is a non-starter. When the author uses an R7000 receiver for microwave experiments he locates it within one metre of the antenna.

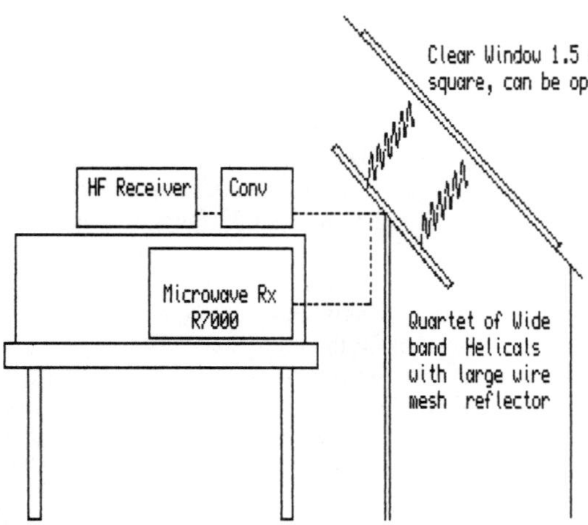

Fig 5.14: Indoor LEO microwave satellite monitoring station

An LEO microwave satellite receiving station

Fig 5.14 shows a typical layout for an experimental station tracking LEO satellites. The indoor location is dictated by weather conditions. The large window is hinged and can be swung open, but this is rarely necessary. Provided connecting cables are kept short, the simple wideband quadruple helix is a very useful antenna, producing strong signals from microwave LEO satellites at frequencies between 900 and 1,700MHz. Doppler shift is the biggest problem. Smooth tuning is the exception rather than the rule, with shifts of up to 80kHz being encountered in a typical pass. Despite these limitations, with two big windows, one facing north, the other south, the Clarke geostationary equatorial orbit can be monitored as well as LEO orbits in all directions, including those at very low elevation as the satellite passes between the UK and the North Pole.

Sheltered/weather-protected microwave operations

Most, but not all, grades of glass and some translucent plastics are relatively transparent at microwave frequencies. Indoor operating is possible with antennas looking through glass. Large windows allow freedom to follow quite a wide arc of tracking coverage, and custom-built radomes can be constructed to house microwave equipment for satellite monitoring.

Putting microwave equipment in unprotected exposed situations is acceptable for organisations like British Telecom, who go to enormous expense to strengthen and weatherproof their equipment, but for radio amateur and space listener projects this approach is rarely practicable. Under no circumstances should microwave dishes be attached to flimsy wooden roof locations. Microwave dishes which use mesh reflectors might at first seem safer and less likely to incur damage because of their lower wind resistance, but this suggestion can be rudely shattered in a January ice storm when the mesh acts as a collector for the ice to build on, sometimes turning a 25lb weight dish into a half-ton icicle.

Less damaging, but no less frustrating, the firmly mounted, solid-surface, professional-type dish is a marvellous 'natural' snow collector. If it is used regularly in winter it must have a safe adjacent, easily reached, platform which provides a firm operating position for the chap who has to go up and shovel out the snow. Snow clearance at positions some way above the ground can be very hazardous.

Microwave satellite propagation problems

Wind and weather difficulties so much outweigh all other operating problems that no excuses are offered for discussing them before going on to discuss propagation. Days when antennas cannot be turned in high winds far outnumber those featuring propagation difficulties. The plagues of VHF, notably Faraday effect, scintillation and sporadic E, have little or no effect at microwave frequencies.

Auroras, which might at first sight appear to offer problems for polar passes of microwave satellites, have not proved much of a problem in practice. Slight auroral effects have been observed when microwave satellites have been deliberately tracked through visible and VHF radio audible auroral storms, but no serious impediment has been noted, with auroral signal product being shifted so far by Doppler shift as to be outside the listening bandwidth.

Ducting and tropospheric bending of signal path from microwave satellites have been noticed by the author in the Arctic, but not so far been recognised whilst operating from the UK, although the deliberate choice of a seaside beach location during still, high-pressure conditions would not be recommended.

The only serious form of interference encountered in the UK has been a form of 'precipitation static', when charged rain drops or ice hitting the antenna produce a sound like thousands of ball bearings falling on a tin roof. This effect, which occurs mostly in the Scottish winter, completely submerges microwave satellite signals for the duration of the storm. It is usually accompanied by gale force winds, so the careful operator turns and parks his antenna in its least wind-affected position and leaves it there, suspending all operation until the storm is over.

Chapter 6

Amateur radio satellites

History

Amateur radio has participated in the space age from the first moment when Sputnik 1 bleeped its way around the Earth, with radio amateurs and shortwave listeners being one of the few groups with the knowledge, equipment and expertise to follow the event.

When cosmonaut Yuri Gagarin made the first manned spaceflight, he was already a well-known radio amateur and, just eight months later, he was followed by the first amateur radio satellite to be put safely into orbit. Since then a succession of increasingly complex amateur radio communications and experimental satellites have followed that first Oscar (Orbiting Satellite Carrying Amateur Radio) into orbit (see Tables 6.01 and 6.02).

In the paragraphs which follow, each of these operational satellites will be described in turn. In each case the general orbital characteristics will be reported first, with an appreciation of what these mean in terms of where and when the satellite will be seen and heard, and be available for communications.

Frequencies used by each satellite will be tabled, with, in the case of UHF satellites, a chart showing anticipated Doppler shift. Tracking of satellites in orbit will be reviewed by presenting a specimen northern hemisphere track for users of great circle hand plots (where applicable, ie not Oscars 10 and 13), and sources of equator crossing data will be listed. For users of computers, sources of tracking software will be listed, as will sources of Keplerian orbital elements for use with this software. In addition typical Keplerian orbital elements and a typical computer track prediction will be provided.

All the operational satellites listed above generate down link telemetry, reporting the satellite's state of health and its environmental conditions. In some cases the details of this telemetry are reported in the experiments chapter of this book. Where this is not so, the decode of a typical telemetry frame will be given in this chapter.

Table 6.01: Non-operational amateur satellites at the end of 1990

Satellite	Launched	Purpose
Oscar I	Dec 1961	Test beacon bleeper
Oscar II	Jun 1962	Test beacon bleeper
Oscar III	Mar 1965	Intercontinental communications
Oscar IV	Dec 1965	Communications relay
Oscar 5	Jan 1970	Computer command test
Oscar 6	Oct 1972	Communications relay
Oscar 7	Nov 1974	VHF communications relay
Oscar 8	Mar 1978	UHF communications relay
RS1 and RS2	Oct 1978	Communications relays
Uosat Oscar 9	Oct 1981	Scientific experiment package
RS3 to RS8	Dec 1981	Four comsats and two beacons
Iskra 2	May 1982	Ionospheric comsat relay
Iskra 3	Nov 1982	Ionospheric comsat relay
Fuji Oscar 12	Aug 1986	Comsat + digital store/forward

Table 6.02: Amateur satellites operational at the end of 1990

Satellite	Purpose	Freq up	Freq down	Modulation
Oscar 10	Comms	435	145	CW, SSB
Uosat 11	Experimental		145/435	FM, digital
RS10/11	Comms	21/145	145/29	CW, SSB
Oscar 13	Comms	145/435/ 1,268	145/435/ 2,400	CW, SSB
Uosat 14	Packet	145	435	9600 bps FSK
Pacsat 16	Packet	145	437	1200 bps PSK
Dove 17	Schools		145/ 2,401	Voice + AFSK
Weber 18	Packet	145	437	Video camera PSK
Lusat 19	Packet	145	437	1200 bps PSK
Fuji 20	Comms/packet	145	435	CW, SSB, 1200 bps PSK

Note: Uo14, Pacsat, Dove and Lusat are being set to work at the end of 1990.

Radiosport 10/11

Introduction

Launched from Plesetsk in the Soviet Arctic on 23 June 1987, these two Radiosport transponders (combined radio receivers and transmitters) are riding together on the same Soviet navigation satellite (Cosmos 1861) in a low Earth, near-circular orbit at a mean height of 1,000km. Cosmos 1861 is also carrying a full outfit of CosNav system beacons, transmitting on both the 149 and 400MHz bands in accord with normal navsat practice. The two amateur radio Radiosport transponders are identical twins. They both have receive and retransmit (transpond) facilities for mode K, 21MHz up, 29MHz down; for mode A, 145MHz up, 29MHz down; and for mode T, 21MHz up and 145MHz down. These transponder modes can be used singly or as two-at-a-time combinations of either mode K + T or mode K + A.

Never before have radio amateurs and space experimenters had such a wide choice of easily accessible and experimentally useful frequencies, but careful operation of these facilities is necessary if they are to be employed to maximum advantage. The problem is that because of their enormous flexibility these transponders have both good and not-so-good features. As experimental satellites they provide unique HF ionospheric propagation data, but by the same token they will also pick up, and inadvertently retransmit, lots of terrestrial signals not intended for space. Fortunately this will not seriously affect the terrestrial users as the signals returned by RS10/11 will all come down in bands set aside for radio amateur satellite down links. Satellite users may find that at times their favourite satellite link is seriously degraded by inadvertent terrestrial interference.

When RS10/11 was launched these problems loomed large, but with operating experience the problems have been seen to be far less serious than originally anticipated, and RS10/11 has emerged as a marvellous double package, whose experimental facilities and easy access for beginners and those with simple station equipment far outweigh the minor interference problems.

Where can RS10/11 be heard?

The orbital altitude of RS10/11 is lower than that of previous Soviet Radiosport satellites so, although it follows a similar inclination and path, it has to get closer to the UK before it is seen above our horizon. Fig 6.01 shows the 24 hour orbit family for this satellite, revealing that of the 13 or so orbits per day, orbit 1 is never in range of the UK, passing the North Pole on its Pacific Ocean side. Please note that orbit numbers given here do not imply that orbit 1 is the first orbit of the day: orbit 1 can occur at any time of day with its actual time shifting slowly from one day to the next.

Orbit 2, as shown on Fig 6.01, also tracks from Asia across the Pacific side of the North Pole then down into America, never coming in range of the UK. Even orbit 3 does not come in range of the UK, although it gets quite close to the circle edge which indicates the limit of the RS10/11 footprint (area which if entered brings the satellite above the UK horizon), as it crosses the Soviet Arctic coastline near the island of Novaya Zemlya, going towards Alaska.

As shown in Fig 6.01, orbit 4 is the first to cross the footprint circle, entering the UK footprint as it crosses north along the eastern edge of the Black Sea, to cross south to north just inside Asiatic Russia before it leaves above Novaya Zemlya.

The factor affecting the ground track of the satellite is the rotation of the Earth, and by orbit 5 the satellite is coming north across the equator in central Africa, entering the UK footprint as it overflies Libya, before travelling on to cross Italy, Poland and the Baltic Sea, prior to leaving the UK footprint over the Arctic Ocean to the north of Novaya Zemlya.

Orbit 6 comes much closer to the UK, and is shown on Fig 6.01 passing west of Gibraltar, before crossing Ireland and heading once again for the Arctic. Though RS10/11 will give strong signals on this orbital pass, it must be remembered that because it is close to the UK it will not see far beyond it to give communication to distant countries. By contrast, orbits which pass above the UK horizon but at long range, such as orbit 7, give communications possibilities down into USA at quite long range eg 3,500km from the UK. Indeed, as RS10/11 flies up the centre of the Atlantic in orbit 7 it can see both western Europe and North America at the same time.

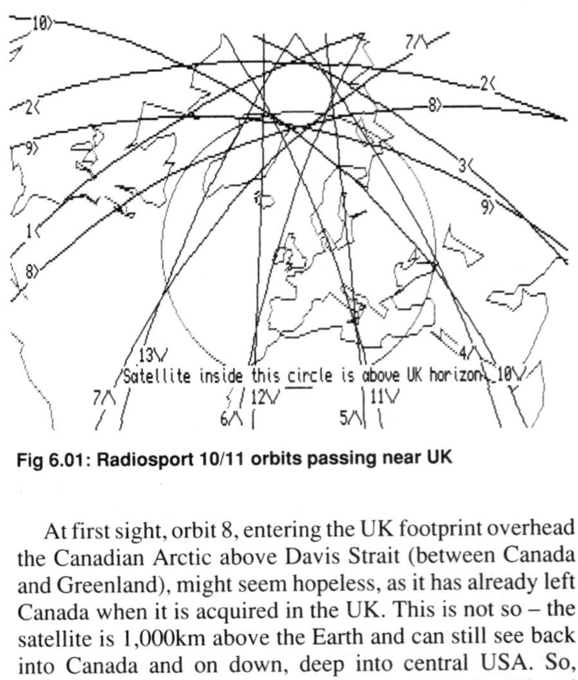

Fig 6.01: Radiosport 10/11 orbits passing near UK

At first sight, orbit 8, entering the UK footprint overhead the Canadian Arctic above Davis Strait (between Canada and Greenland), might seem hopeless, as it has already left Canada when it is acquired in the UK. This is not so – the satellite is 1,000km above the Earth and can still see back into Canada and on down, deep into central USA. So, provided this orbit occurs at a reasonable time for US and Canadian amateurs, there will be plenty of communications opportunities for the first five or six minutes before the satellite begins to lose sight of Canada as it crosses the Arctic Ocean and heads once again towards Novaya Zemlya. (Please remember most North American radio amateurs like to sleep from about 0400 to 1200 UK time, so you may feel bright and cheery after breakfast but the Americans will not be around to answer your calls.)

Orbit 9 is a typical Arctic pass, the kind of orbit which UK operators can access but which cynics suggest is unlikely to produce many replies, because very few polar bears have amateur radio licences. In fact this kind of track, which is a feature of almost all near-polar, high-inclination, circular-orbit satellites, covers the whole of the Arctic in the moving satellite footprint, and has given this operator lots of excellent contacts with Norwegian operators on Svalbard (Spitzbergen) and American servicemen at the Thule airbase in the north west of Greenland.

Orbit 10, by contrast, comes around to find the world has turned enough since the previous orbit to put its track well into range of UK, whilst overflying some good communications sites as it passes from Greenland to Sweden, then down the full length of the European USSR. Note that orbit 10 is nearly an exact reverse of orbit 4. RS10/11 orbits repeat in the opposite direction six orbits later. So, if you miss a good long distance contact on one orbit, you get another chance six orbits later, provided it is not then halfway through the night at the other station.

Orbit 11 is a curious orbit. When it crosses the UK horizon, it is over northern Greenland and able to see as far behind its track as Alaska, but in practice few Alaskan operators are heard. There are two reason for this. First, the Alaskans have their day during the UK night and their night during our day, so our activities are out of phase. Second, the polar route to Alaska is through one of the most seriously troubled propagation paths in the world, crossing the polar auroral front, sometimes twice. But, despite these problems, contacts with Alaska are possible, albeit infrequent. Also, if you miss out in Alaska, it is good to know that after orbit 11 has headed south east of UK it will start providing contacts deep into Africa for UK stations.

Orbit 12 by contrast, starts for UK operators in that same Greenland sector that may provide contacts with Alaska, but it then goes on to head south down the Atlantic, not quite far enough west to permit communications with USA, and with its eastward coverage limited to west Africa.

Orbit 13 is the last orbit of the sequence of RS10/11 orbits which come in range of the UK. It descends down the western Atlantic from north Greenland to South America, giving excellent communication opportunities (as did orbit 7), to the USA.

Let us summarise this series of RS10/11 orbits. The lower altitude of the satellite, as compared with its predecessors of the RS3 to 8 family, reduces the communication range slightly. RS10/11 needs to get closer to the UK to come above our horizon, so its orbital pass duration times in range of the UK are shorter than those for the previous RS series. RS10/11 polar orbits 8 and 9 are at very low elevation from the UK, which makes them difficult to use if polar auroral interference or absorption is present. None the less, RS10/11 is such a versatile combination that it is to be hoped that it will last as long as the successful RS5 and RS7. In this case it will give superb communications opportunities to many radio amateurs until the mid-1990s without the purchase of a lot of expensive equipment. Soviet sources say that RS12/13, a satellite flying a similar orbit but coming round with a daily pattern staggered in time from that of RS10/11, may be launched in late 1990.

When can RS10/11 be heard in the UK?

Fig 6.02 shows a typical annual calendar of RS10/11 orbits which come in range of the UK. At the middle date of each month the orbit numbers shown indicate when to expect a particular orbit going in a particular direction. Please note that this chart does not give exact orbit times, it simply indicates for example that on or around 15 January 1989 there was an orbit at about 0100 UTC which followed track 10 on Fig 6.01. A cross check with Fig 6.01 shows track 10 going from the American west coast, up across the Arctic Ocean and coming into the UK footprint circle when overhead the north east tip of Greenland. The UK operator should then be able to track this 10th orbit as it goes over Arctic Norway and down across European USSR, passing out of the UK footprint over the south east corner of the Black Sea. To get the exact time of this orbit the operator will either keep a daily log (RS10/11 orbits get roughly 29 or 30 minutes later each successive day), or use a computer to predict the orbit time as described in chapter 10.

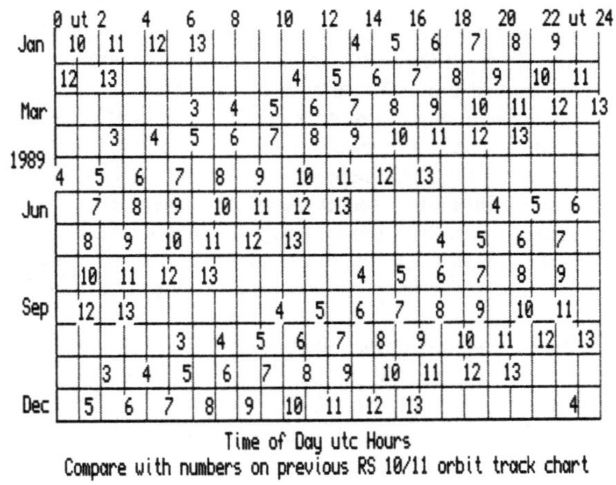

Fig 6.02: RS10/11 in range UK orbits versus date and time in 1989

The rest of 15 January 1989 saw orbits along tracks 11, 12 and 13 respectively up to about 0700 UTC, then there was a gap of about six hours when no RS10/11 orbit came in range of the UK.

Then at about 1300 UTC the first orbit of a new series, tracking along path 4 of Fig 6.01, gave the UK operator the chance to talk to RS10/11, as it followed a track in roughly the reverse direction to track path 10 of 0100 UTC. Further orbits then followed along paths 5 to 9 before midnight UTC.

By 14 February the situation had changed somewhat. Now the path of orbit 10 is occurring around 2100 or 2200 UTC and the gap when no orbits are heard has shifted earlier to 0300 to 1000 UTC.

It is important to note that had the operator wanted to check on orbits at the end of January, half way between the two printed sequences, he could have got a good idea of

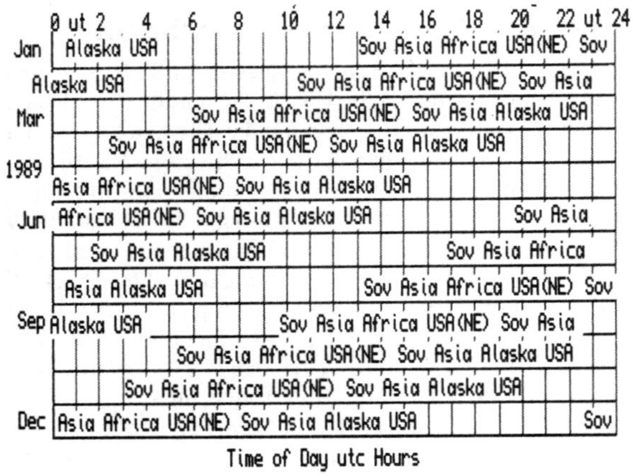

Fig 6.03: RS10/11 dates and times of world regions in range of UK in 1989

what to expect by noting that orbit path 6 changed from near 1700 UTC in mid January, to near 1400 in mid-February.

So, taking the halfway between these two times, orbits along path 6 at the end of January would have taken place within plus or minus 52 minutes of 1530 UTC.

Taking a quite different example, let us ask when an operator in the UK would expect to get good American communications in mid-September 1989. As Fig 6.01 shows, the good orbit paths when the satellite is between UK and USA are orbit paths 7 and 8, or path 13. So, switching to Fig 6.02, the operator will find that these orbit paths are at about 1500 to 1730 UTC for paths 7 and 8, and 2300 UTC for path 13.

Sharp-eyed operators will discover that the computer plotting Fig 6.02 has slipped in an orbit 3, and there is no number 3 track on Fig 6.01. This is not a mistake. On some days RS10/11 will squeeze in an extra orbit, but this orbit path 3 is one which just scrapes the UK horizon, making it

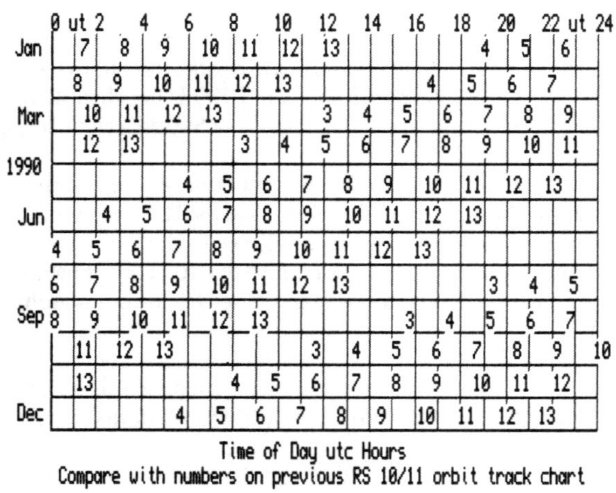

Fig 6.04: RS10/11 in range of UK orbits versus date and time in 1990

difficult to access unless you have a good site with a clear horizon (no buildings or hills), and a sensitive receiver.

RS10/11 is in a reasonably high orbit at an altitude of 1,000km, so it should not be slowed much by atmospheric drag, except at solar cycle maximum when the extra output from the Sun makes what little remains of the Earth's atmosphere at 1,000km much more dense for a year or so. Unfortunately, solar maximum is nearly with us again, and it is impossible to accurately predict RS10/11's orbit into 1991 and beyond.

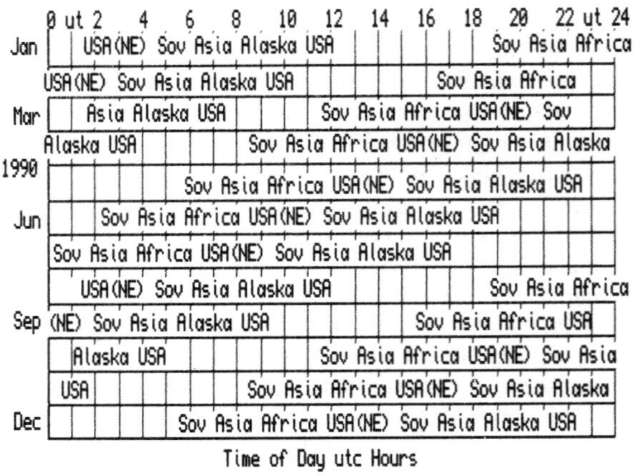

Fig 6.05: RS10/11 dates and times of world regions in range of UK in 1990

Fig 6.04 does carry the prediction of Fig 6.02 forward through 1990 but this should only be used with caution.

As can be seen from Fig 6.02, the gap in the day when no RS10/11 orbits come in range of the UK slips a full 24 hours in seven months. So in fact this RS10/11 orbit pattern repeats roughly every seven months. This of course means that RS10/11 is not Sun synchronous (always showing its orbit face to the Sun). Sometimes RS10/11 will go deeply into shadow behind the Earth and out of the sunlight, but this should not have any serious effects for a year or two yet. RS10/11 is still quite young so its batteries should easily stand the load placed on them when the satellite goes into shadow and loses the sunlight on its power-generating solar panels. Equally important is the fact that RS10/11 is part of a much bigger satellite, so it may have much tougher power supplies than its predecessors, the RS3 to RS8 family.

Who can you hear and talk to on RS10/11?

The footprint of RS10/11 is shown by the smaller inner circle on Fig 6.06a, eg from this position RS10/11 can connect UK stations to anywhere in western Europe, north Africa and most of Greenland. But a better idea of RS10/11's potential is shown in Figs 6.06b and c. In Fig 6.06b, the satellite is positioned at the centre of its footprint, overhead a point just east of Canadian Labrador. With RS10/11 at this location, stations in Minnesota, Chicago, Atlanta and New

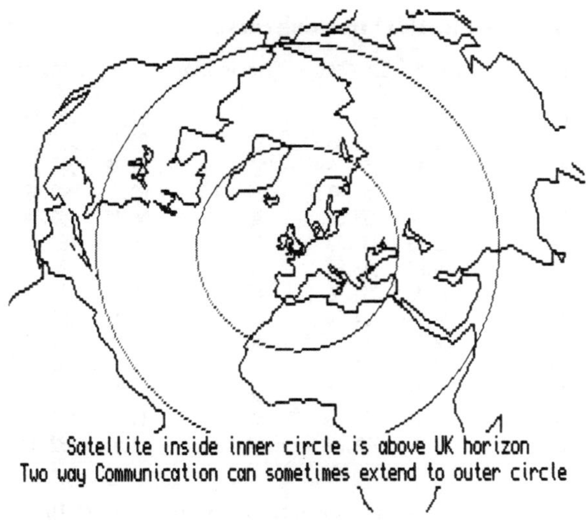

a: Over UK

b: West of UK

c: East of UK

Fig 6.06a-c: RS10/11 footprint range circles

York can all use its transponder repeater facility to talk to stations in the UK.

The second footprint, Fig 6.06c, positions RS10/11 far to the east of UK, overhead a point just north of the Caspian Sea in Soviet Asia. From this point RS10/11 can provide a communications link between stations in the eastern UK and the Persian Gulf, and almost all of Soviet Asia plus a part of northern Siberia.

The problem with diagrams like this is that they only refer to one specific example. By contrast, Figs 6.03 and 6.05 try to give a much broader view of who the UK operator could talk to at any time in 1989 and 1990. These diagrams are in fact a simple extension of Figs 6.02 and 6.04. Instead of nominating orbit path numbers, they show what the major part of the world under that particular orbit is. So, if your preference is to talk to stations in Africa, Figs 6.03 and 6.05 tell you that in January 1989 your best orbits would occur near the UK at about 1800 UTC, whereas in mid-January 1990, Africa is best placed for RS10/11 communications at about 2300 UTC.

Please note that Figs 6.02 to 6.05 are not intended to replace proper computer printouts of satellite footprint details in real time, but they are suggested as an aid to planning an operational schedule. They are also a useful tool for the operator who has no computer or orbit charts, who finds RS10/11 and wonders who he can talk to at that time of night.

Please remember, as you search for and use RS10/11, that the satellite can see to an extreme of 7,000km from your station. The zone time will be different from UK time and the propagation may be difficult at certain times of day.

The radio frequencies used by RS10/11

As Fig 6.07 shows, RS10/11 offers a wide choice of frequencies. All the RS11 frequencies are spaced just above the RS10 frequencies, and both RS10 and RS11 can operate in any of five different band patterns, although they are rarely if ever both on together:

Mode A	145MHz up link	to	29MHz down link
Mode K	21MHz up link	to	29MHz down link
Mode T	21MHz up link	to	145MHz down link

plus combined modes K and A or combined modes K and T

Full details of the frequencies for the transponders, beacons and robots carried in this combined package are given in Fig 6.07. Operating details are given later in this chapter.

Tracking RS10/11 by plotter or computer

For those who wish to make a tracking overlay for RS10/11 for use on a polar great circle projection, the details of the northern hemisphere track is given in Table 6.03. *Practical Wireless* prints equator crossing time data for use with this

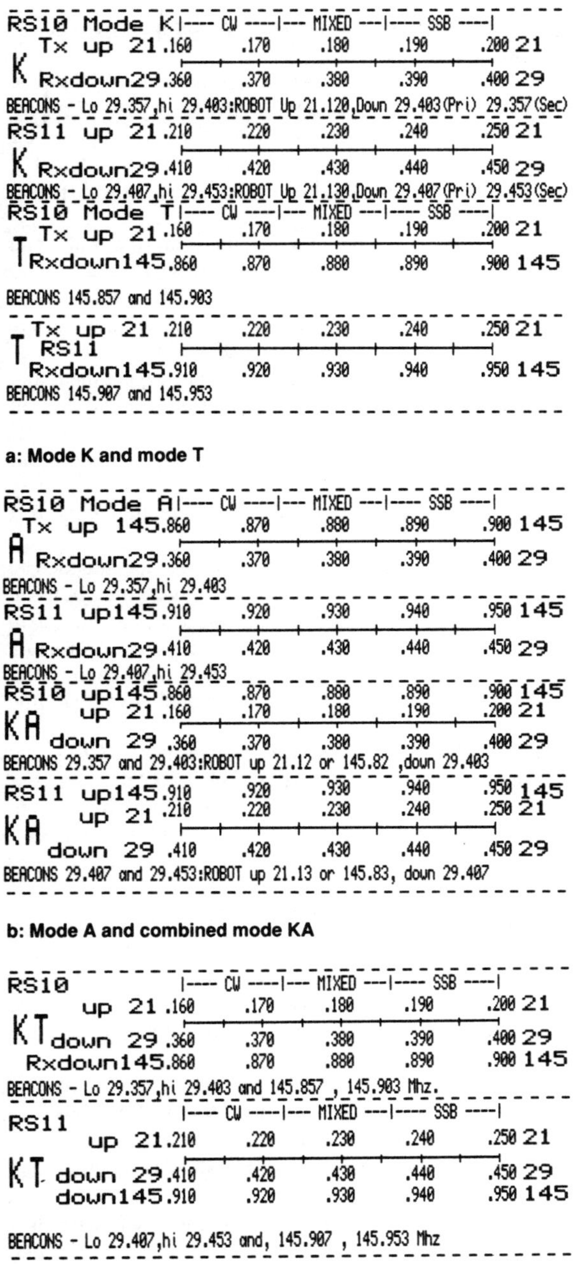

Fig 6.07: RS10/11 bandplans

type of track plotter every second month. A typical computer printout of an RS10/11 track is shown at Table 6.04. Computer software for tracking RS10/11 is available from SARUG and Amsat UK; see appendix 1 for addresses. This software needs to be kept up to date, as discussed in chapter 10, by the insertion of updates of the RS10/11 Keplerian

Table 6.03: RS10/11 tracking curve

Time in Mins	Lat N	LongWest	Time in Mins	Lat N	LongWest
0	0	0	28	80.91	237.58
2	6.82	359.65	30	75.56	216.26
4	13.6	359.29	32	69.33	207.2
6	20.39	358.87	34	62.8	202.49
8	27.16	358.36	36	56.15	199.69
10	33.93	357.73	38	49.44	197.87
12	40.69	356.89	40	42.69	196.61
14	47.43	355.76	42	35.92	195.7
16	54.14	354.14	44	29.13	195.01
18	60.8	351.71	46	22.33	194.47
20	67.36	347.74	48	15.53	194.03
22	73.71	340.45	50	8.72	193.64
24	79.44	324.46	52	1.9	193.29
26	82.88	285.09	54	-4.91	192.95

Table 6.04: A typical computer printout of an RS10/11 track

RadioSport 10/11 on 1/7/89

UTC	AZ	EL	Lat	Long	GndRange
1000	5	-31	51	192	8023kms
1002	4	-27	58	190	7291kms
1004	1	-23	64	187	6565kms
1006	359	-18	71	181	5848kms
1008	355	-14	77	170	5143kms
1010	351	-9	82	141	4458kms
1012	346	-4	82	89	3803kms
1014	338	1	77	59	3194kms
1016	327	7	71	47	2664kms
1018	312	11	65	41	2269kms
1020	292	14	58	38	2086kms
1022	271	13	51	36	2169kms
1024	254	9	45	34	2490kms
1026	241	3	38	33	2974kms
1028	232	-2	31	33	3552kms
1030	226	-7	24	32	4187kms

Press key twice access next option

orbital elements roughly every three months. A typical set of RS10/11 elements are:

Epoch day of year. Decimal day of year for 1989 11 January at 0204:35 UTC	89 011.08652120
Inclination	82.9267 degrees
Right ascension	354.1977 degrees
Eccentricity	0.0012862
Argument of perigee	122.7328 degrees
Mean anomaly	237.5078 degrees
Mean motion	13.71927738 revs per day

These figures give an orbital period of about 105 minutes and a longitude increment west per orbit of about 26.25 degrees shift of the crossing point at each successive ascending crossing of the Earth's equator. Keplerian orbital elements are provided by Nasa and are published by *Practical Wireless* at roughly two-monthly intervals, and are broadcast by Amsat UK, sometimes irregularly but always at G3RWL's monthly summary. UK packet radio bulletin boards also carry RS10/11 Keplerian orbital elements, as does Uosat Oscar 11's bulletins.

Operating on RS10/11

Telemetry

Telemetry is the method used by the satellite to tell users and its ground controllers what it is doing, what its operational state is, and whether it is in good health, ie are its batteries getting a good charge, is its temperature correct, are the operating transmitters and receivers of the various onboard transponders working at their correct voltage and power levels? This monitoring of the satellite's health is vital if it is to have a long and useful life. The satellite carries a set of sensors which record its temperatures, voltages and power levels and these are constantly transmitted back to Earth on the satellite telemetry beacons, so that users can tell what transponder bands are available, and ground controllers can monitor the satellite's operational state. This telemetry also acts as the down link part of a two-way loop whereby an up link signal from ground control can reset the satellite operating modes, and the down link telemetry then responds by reporting that the satellite has, or has not, obeyed the ground commands.

In normal circumstances this down link telemetry is sent in morse code at about 20 words per minute on the satellite beacons, but this situation can change temporarily when under certain forms of ground control: the 145MHz beacon down link sends high-speed ASCII automatic telegraphy AM (sounds like a computer tape loading signal) to the ground controllers.

Do not be put off reading the telemetry because you cannot read morse code; the morse telemetry always follows a very narrow set of characters and you can get all the information you need for successful operating by picking out and concentrating on just a few of these characters. If you cannot manage 20wpm morse, record the signal. Then you can either play it back repeatedly, concentrating on one telemetry box at a time or, if you have a suitable recorder, you can record at high speed and play back at slow speed, so that you have time to think between symbols. A brief table of the morse code symbols used is given at the end of these telemetry paragraphs. A typical telemetry frame sent at 20wpm is:

RS11		RS11					
ns 80	nr 13	nd 23	ng 45	iu 45	iw 00	ik 00	io 00
as 35	ar 37	ad 43	ag 32	mu 00	aw 45	ak 00	ao 88

This represents 16 telemetry boxes, eg 'ns 80' represents one box, and each half of the box tells you something. The letters give you one bit of information and the numbers give you another. The following decode file explains the meaning of each part of each box, in turn :

Channel	Purpose	First part decode	Second part decode
1	Telemetry sampling period	ns = 10min sample	Supply volts = n/4 = 80/4 = 20V

Note: had first part been 'is' instead of 'ns', that would have signified a 90 minute sampling period, but the second part would have stayed the same, eg 'is 80' would indicate 90 minute sample, 20 volts.

The full decode list for this full frame of telemetry taken box by box is shown in Table 6.05.

Note how the first pair of letters code for a particular piece of information, and the number pair after that specific letter pair give the number to insert into a small calculation to get a report of the size of a particular voltage or temperature etc.

The above sequence is the normal telemetry reporting state. When the command channel is in use this is indicated by the addition of an extra morse dot on the first letter of each information box if the 21MHz/15m command channel is active. This extra dot turns i into s, n into r, m into w, and a into u. So if the 15m command channel became active:

ns ..	nr ..	nd ..	ng ..	iu ..	iw ..	ik ..	io ..
as ..	ar ..	ad ..	ag ..	mu ..	aw ..	ak ..	ao ..

becomes

rs ..	rr ..	rd ..	rg ..	su ..	sw ..	sk ..	so ..
us ..	ur ..	ud ..	ug ..	wu ..	uw ..	uk ..	uo ..

Nothing else changes; the calculations in the numerical part of each box stay the same.

If the 2m/145MHz command channel is active, a morse dash is added to the front of the first letter, changing our frame example above into:

gs ..	gr ..	gd ..	gg ..	du ..	dw ..	dk ..	do ..
ks ..	kr ..	kd ..	kg ..	ou ..	kw ..	kk ..	ko ..

It sounds awfully complex, particularly if you do not read morse code, but remember that you do not have to read this telemetry if you do not want to. You can if you wish tune through the down link bands as described in Fig 6.07 and listen to find out which channels are in use.

For those prepared to put in a bit of effort, this telemetry can be quite rewarding. You soon learn to recognise:

dot dash dot	dot dot dot
dot dash dash dash dash	dash dash dash dash dash

as the callsign of RS10.

a is dot dash	d is dash dot dot	g is dash dash dot
i is dot dot	k is dash dot dash	m is dash dash

Table 6.05: RS10/11 telemetry decode list

Ch	Purpose	Designator	Decode	Number decode
1	Telemetry Sampling period	is ns	90min 10min	Supply volts = n/4
(So ns 80 = 10min sampling, supply volts 80/4 = 20V)				
2	2m + 15m 20dB attenuator	ir nr	IN OUT	2m TX power = n/10
(So nr 13 = 20dB attenuator OUT, 2m 145MHz transmitter power 13/10 = 1.3W)				
3	2m + 15m 10dB attenuator	id nd	IN OUT	10m TX out = n/10
(So nd 23 = 10dB attenuator out, 10m 29MHz transmitter power 23/10 = 2.3W)				
4	15m/21MHz up link status	ig ng	OFF ON	15m AutoGain volts = n/5
(So ng 45 = 15m/21MHz up link ON, 15m AutoGain = 45/5 = 9V)				
5	2m/145MHz RX status	iu nu	OFF ON	2m AutoGain volts = n/5
(So iu 45 = 2m/145MHz receiver is OFF, 2m AutoGain = 45/5 = 9V)				
6	Command Channel status	iw nw	OFF ON	Command AutoGain = n/5
(So iw 00 = Command channel OFF, Command AutoGain = 0/5 = 0V)				
7	10m/29MHz beacon output	ik nk	1W 300mW	Special command parameter
(So ik 00 = 10m/29MHz beacon output 1W, command parameter is 00)				
8	2m beacon output	io no	1W 300mW	Special command parameter
(So io 00 = 2m/145MHz beacon output 1W, command parameter is 00)				
9	No.1 memory status	as ms	OFF ON	10m TX temperature = n – 10°C
(So as 35 = No.1 memory OFF, 10m transmitter temperature = 35 – 10 = 25°C)				
10	No.2 memory status	ar mr	OFF ON	2m TX temperature = n – 10°C
(So ar 37 = No.2 memory OFF, 2m transmitter temperature = 37 – 10 = 27°C)				
11	Special service channel status	ad md	OPEN CLOSED	20V supply temperature = n – 10°C
(So ad 43 = Special service chan OPEN, 20V supply temperature 43 – 10 = 33°C)				
12	Code store memory status	ag mg	OPEN CLOSED	9V supply temperature = n – 10°C
(So ag 32 = Code store memory OPEN, 9V supply temperature 32 –10 = 22°C)				
13	Output information beacon in use	au mu	10m 2m	Backup 9V = n/5 volts
(So mu 00 = 2m beacon in use, backup 9V = 0/5 = 0V)				
14	Robot 15m attenuator	aw mw	–10dB 0dB	IF volts 15m RX = n/5
(So aw 45 = Robot attenuator for 15m is –10dB, IF volts 15m RX = 45/5 = 9V)				
15	Robot 2m attenuator	ak mk	–10dB 0dB	IF volts 2m RX = n/5
(So ak 00 = 2m Robot atten is –10dB, IF volts 2m RX = 0/5=0V)				
16	Command channel 2m power	ao mo	1W 300mW	Robot message count n=0 less than 33; count n 80 to 90 more than 32
(So ao 88 = 1W Command power 2m, robot message count more than 32)				

n is dash dot o is dash dash dash r is dot dash dot
s is dot dot dot u is dot dot dash w is dot dash dash

There you have all the letters used in this telemetry, and the numbers are:

1 is dot dash dash dash dash
2 is dot dot dash dash dash
3 is dot dot dot dash dash
4 is dot dot dot dot dash
5 is dot dot dot dot dot
6 is dash dot dot dot dot
7 is dash dash dot dot dot
8 is dash dash dash dot dot
9 is dash dash dash dash dot
0 is dash dash dash dash dash

The author uses the telemetry in a simple fashion. On 12 February 1989 the following was received at 1318 UTC:

rs 10 ss 82 rr 00 rd 10 sg 46 ru 55 sw 00 rk 00 ro 00
ws 35 ur 27 wd 37 ug 35 wu 00 ww 00 wk 46 uo 89

The extra dot to turn letter i to s and letter m to w signified that the 21MHz command channel was on, but all the author was interested in was that the figure in the second box, 'rr

00', indicated no 2m transmitter coming down, that the 'sg 46' indicated that the 15m up link was off, the 'ru' in the fifth box indicated the 2m receiver was on, and the number in the third box showed a 10m transmitter power output of one watt. All of which suggested mode A two metres 145MHz up, 29MHz down was available for communication on RS10.

Other people use this telemetry more effectively by comparing temperatures and voltages from one orbit to the next to build up a picture of the changes in the satellite, particularly if it is likely to be going deep into Earth shadow. So, all things considered, a careful study of RS10/11 telemetry can be very worthwhile.

Communications

In the previous telemetry example the operator found the satellite by listening for its beacon on 29.357MHz. He then established from the telemetry that it was operating mode A. Fig 6.07b gives the details of the RS10 mode A up and down link frequencies, and indicates that in mode A stations wishing to use morse code should transmit in the band 145.860 to 145.873MHz and listen for their own signal, and those of other people being repeated back, in the band 29.360 to 29.373MHz.

A quick tune across the 29MHz down link will soon establish whether anyone else is transmitting. If they are, note their down link frequency as, say, 29.370MHz. You will then see from Fig 6.07b that if your equipment and the satellite are perfect, you should aim to transmit up on 145.870MHz. But if, like this operator, you check your gear regularly, you know that you need to have a slight aim off, in this case about 2kHz high. So tune your transmitter to 145.870 plus or minus your personal aim off, then wait until the channel is clear before taping your morse key to transmit to make sure you are accessing the satellite correctly.

According to Fig 6.02, if this is mid-February 1989 at about 1300 UTC, the satellite is on Track 5 of Fig 6.01 which brings it up out of Africa then very close (ie at high elevation), past UK to the east. So you should have pointed your antenna to the east at 1318 UTC halfway through the orbital pass. In this case you should hear your own signal being returned and be able to fire off a quick CQ call to the other station. With the prospect of a good signal exchange, provided you remember that the satellite is tracking rapidly to your north east, so you must follow it with your 2m antenna. Fortunately the margin for error on RS10 is quite large, so you should find that your antenna tracking does not need to be perfect.

Almost exactly the same procedure is used if you want to have a voice contact. As Fig 6.10 shows, RS10 mode A voice is on SSB upper sideband both up and down. The up link is 145.887 to 145.900 MHz to come down between 29.387 and 29.400MHz. Again you may find, as this operator does, that you need a small fixed offset of, say, about 2 to 5kHz to put your down link exactly where you want it.

The most important rule is to listen before you transmit, to avoid transmitting on top of someone else and spoiling his communications. RS10/11 operators are recommended to keep their transmitters on the same frequency once they are in a clear spot on the down link, then adjust their down link tuning to follow any Doppler shift. This is relatively easy on mode A where your signal comes down in what should be a space band reserved for satellite traffic, but on mode K particularly, this may be difficult because, although you are coming down in the same 29MHz space section, the 21MHz up link has collected all sorts of 21MHz terrestrial conversations which can clog the 29MHz band. On mode T a similar problem can arise when the 145MHz down link is blocked by inadvertently up linked terrestrial 21MHz signals.

Robot operating

Both the RS10 and RS11 transponders for modes K and combined KA have robot communications facilities, whereby operators can call the robot in the satellite on morse, and get an acknowledgement. These robots are not left on continuously. To find out if one is on, listen on the robot down link frequencies shown in Figs 6.07a and b.

(a) You call on RS10 mode K on 21.120MHz and listen on 29.403MHz (primary) or 29.357MHz (secondary).

(b) You call on RS11 mode K on 21.130MHz and listen on 29.407MHz (primary) or 29.453MHz (secondary).

(c) You call on RS10 mode KA on 21.120MHz or 145.82MHz and listen on 29.403MHz down link.

(d) You call on RS11 mode KA on 21.13MHz or 145.83MHz and listen on 29.407Hz down link.

If the robot is free you will hear it sending :

CQ CQ CQ de RS10 QSU 29.403 (or 29.357 on secondary mode)

Robots only understand morse code. You can access them by waiting for a quiet period on the down link then keying your transmitter on or near the appropriate up link frequency plus your private offset. Be careful not to interfere with other stations. Key your transmitter as soon as it is quiet and as you hear yourself on or about the robot down link send:

RS10 de (your callsign) AR

For example, the author sends:

RS10 de GM4IHJ AR

Remember to leave a space after your call before you send the 'AR', and make sure you send 'AR' as one letter, ie dot dash dot dash dot, with no break between the 'A' and the 'R'. A successful call will get you a reply from RS10 quoting your callsign and a message reference number. If your call is unsuccessful, the satellite may ignore you or it may send 'QRZ' (who are you?), 'QRS' (send more slowly) or 'QRK' (send quicker). All successful calls are logged in the satellite memory, and this memory is regularly down loaded to Earth, where a QSL acknowledgement card is made out by the satellite controllers and sent off to you as confirmation of your success. Listening to these memory dumps, which occur on the beacon down link from time to time, is fascinating (and good morse practice).

Signal propagation features applicable to RS10/11

RS10/11 is the first long-duration radio amateur satellite to have up link frequencies in the shortwave, high-frequency part of the radio spectrum. In consequence of this, its performance, particularly on modes K and T, is highly dependent on the state of the ionosphere. RS10/11 takes us into what has until recently been unexplored territory, so the discussions which follow reflect actual use only as the Sun moved towards a new sunspot cycle peak as far as RS10/11 is concerned. Fortunately we do have quite a lot of knowledge gained by using previous Russian short-duration amateur satellites such as Iskra 2 and 3, and we have reception data-only studies from the non-amateur Cosmos 1686 and its predecessors. So what follows here describes only the first part of what is definitely an important experiment.

The first point to be made about RS10/11 mode K or T is that, as Fig 6.08 shows, it can perform poorly in certain circumstances when it is well above your station horizon. Indeed, experience with Iskra and RS10/11 indicates that as we approach the solar sunspot cycle maximum, it is very difficult to hear anything at all from RS10/11 in daylight on mode K or T, simply because the 21MHz up link cannot get through the ionosphere to access the satellite. Fortunately for experimenters the ionosphere is by no means homogeneous; it does have patches where the ionisation is thinner than at other places, so signals can get through now and again even in daylight. However, the occasions when this will happen are almost impossible to predict, except that as a general rule the higher the elevation of your signal path to the satellite, the nearer it gets to overhead your station, the greater your chance of getting your up link through the ionosphere to access the satellite.

Equally important and as yet unclear, it remains to be seen how effective the multiband coverage of mode KT will be. There is a chance that it could provide unique upwards and downwards scans of the ionosphere all across the sky, as the satellite's motion carries it from one horizon to the other. All this propagation interest is bad news for the operator who simply wants to communicate. Communication by modes K and T during 1991 is likely to continue to be difficult and sometimes impossible during daylight hours. In complete contrast, communications via RS10/11 at night should be good when the satellite is above your horizon, and most important not picking up ionospherically propagated interference. Do remember, however, that at 50°N in the UK we never really lose daylight from March to October at the ionosphere to our north, east, and west.

At longer ranges to RS10/11, beyond the UK horizon, the situation changes completely. Neither mode T or mode A will give sub-horizon propagation on a regular basis, although mode T will give space listeners interesting 145MHz signals, as in summer 1988 when, after a day of sporadic E producing lots of trans-Europe contacts for British radio amateurs, the late evening produced a flood of Argentinian and Brazilian stations all over the UK mode T down link on 145.86 to 145.90MHz. Needless to say, this was RS10/11 over the UK picking up ionospherically propagated 21MHz/15m signals from South America and rebroadcasting them on the UK 2m band. Lots of unsuspecting operators mistook them for a continuation of the genuine 2m sporadic E and called the Argentinians on 2m – they were quite unaware that the South Americas were transmitting and listening on 21MHz where they were enjoying some terrestrial-mode communications.

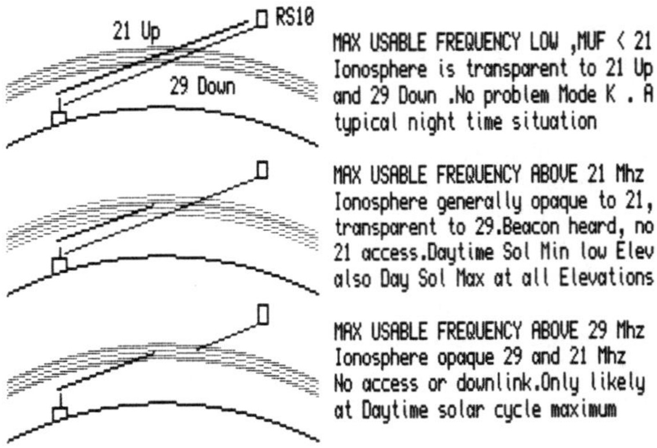

Fig 6.08: RS10/11 mode K ionospheric transit when above UK horizon

By contrast to modes A and T, mode K, being both HF up and down, can profit from ionospheric communication when the satellite can only see one of the stations involved but is picking up the other more-distant station via ionospheric propagation. As Fig 6.09 shows, these sub-horizon extensions on mode K will be rare at solar minimum, but may be quite frequent at solar cycle maximum. To communicate via a satellite far beyond your horizon, you must have a dense (daylight?) ionosphere above and out to near your station's horizon. This ionosphere underside must be capable of bending signals to and from your station at 21 and 29MHz back down again around the horizon, but in the vicinity of the satellite these signals must find a quite different ionosphere. Near the satellite the signal must easily penetrate up and down through the ionosphere to get to and from the satellite, so the ionosphere must be thin enough to be transparent to both 21 and 29MHz signals. This kind of sudden change is rare if all the ionosphere from above your station to underneath the satellite is in daylight, but if the ionosphere over your station is in daylight, you will get the sub-horizon propagation at times, allowing the

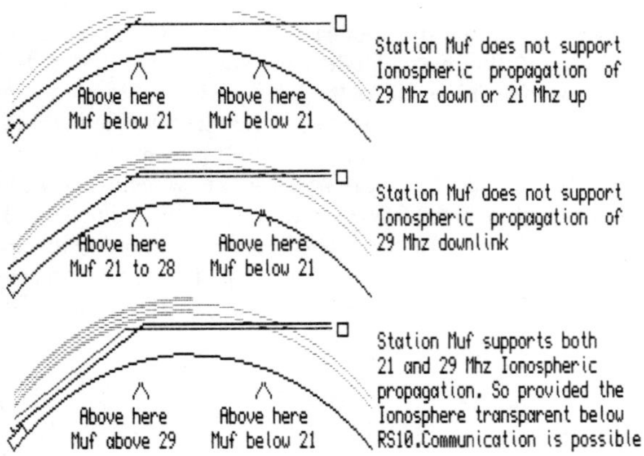

Fig 6.09: Conditions required for sub-horizon communications via RS10/11 mode K

signal to next hit the underside of the ionosphere over an area in darkness. These conditions may provide a 21/29MHz transparent ionosphere under the satellite allowing signal access for your 21MHz up link and then allowing the 29MHz down link reply down through the ionosphere and back to you.

We can therefore predict that these conditions will occur most often on any paths where the satellite is overhead the nightside of the Earth, as is one of the communicating stations, whilst the other station must be on the daylight side of the Earth.

Until 1986 we could not test this theory effectively, but in the summer of 1986 at solar minimum, one-way traffic to UK of this sort was certainly possible. Fig 6.11 shows the tracks of Cosmos 1686 transmitting on 19.955MHz (near 21MHz), when it could be heard in UK by sub-horizon propagation. One-way traffic of this sort was quite frequent when the satellite, far to the south of UK, made an evening pass over South Africa or the south Atlantic. The southern night-time ionosphere was thin, so the Cosmos 1686 signals got down through it almost unattenuated, and then travelled in a chordal hop mode, never quite touching the Earth until they re-encountered the underside of the ionosphere somewhere near the UK. Being the UK summer it was still daylight in this region so the ionosphere was quite thick, in

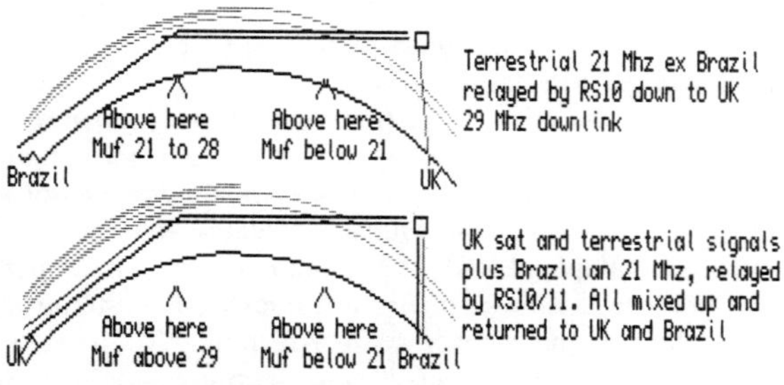

Fig 6.10: Possible conditions for terrestrial/satellite signal mix up on mode K. This situation may apply when day/night terminator is between UK and any DX station

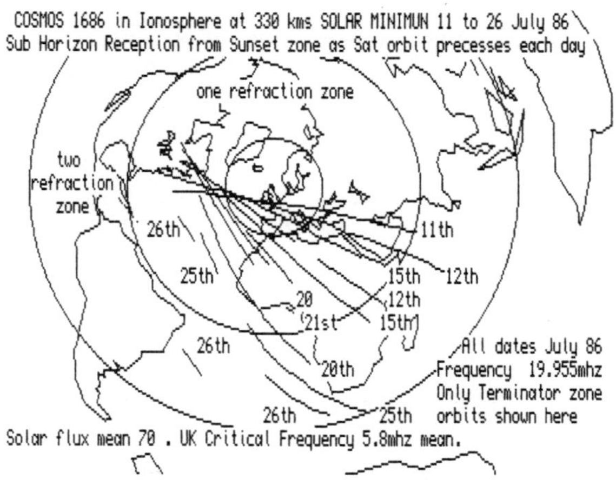

Fig 6.11: Where to expect sub-horizon HF satellite propagation to come from

fact it was experiencing the midnight Sun effect when its ionisation level stays relatively high for all the 24 hours of the day. So, even though it was solar cycle minimum, the ionisation was strong enough to refract/bend the signal down to Scotland.

The patterning and gradual movement of the track points from which the signals were heard shifted west at a rate of about 6 degrees per day because the oblate Earth pulls a satellite in this orbit that amount west each day. The double tracks on the same date indicate days when two successive orbits crossed the solar terminator, and demonstrated this form of sub-horizon propagation.

These sub-horizon satellite tracking experiments were applied to the whole world using Cosmos 1686 on 19.955MHz and Radiosport 7 on 29.501MHz, and the data collected is shown on Fig 6.12 which summarises signals received in Scotland by GM4IHJ during 1986 and 1987. RS10/11 is now developing a similar pattern and this shows

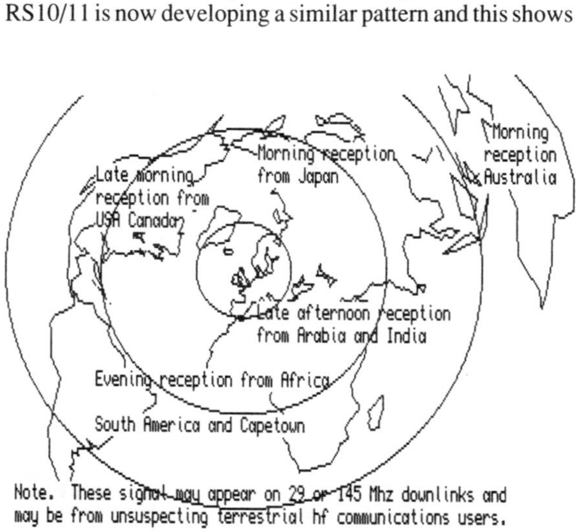

Fig 6.12: Possible sources of RS10/11 sub-horizon signals

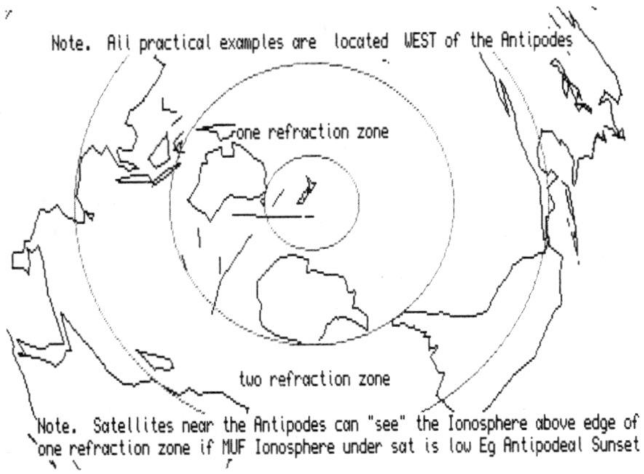

Fig 6.13. Tracks of HF satellites heard in the UK at solar minimum in 1986

much the same timing as that for the previous satellites. All these signals seem to come from locations where the satellite is overhead – the local evening or pre-dawn ionosphere. Note that the map circles, defining whether the signal needed one or two ionospheric refraction bends, applies only to satellite signals starting above the ionosphere. Terrestrial signal refraction zones have a quite different scale.

Antipodal propagation

The ultimate test of RS10/11 will be to find out whether it can support antipodal propagation, ie provide communication to and from the satellite to the UK, when the satellite is located at that point which is at exactly the other side of the Earth from the UK. This is the point where, contrary to fable, if you dig a hole straight down in your back garden through the Earth, you would not come out in Australia, but would emerge under the ocean south of New Zealand, at roughly 51°S 180°W.

The first Sputnik surprised many listeners by propagating its signal to the UK from near this point. Since then many

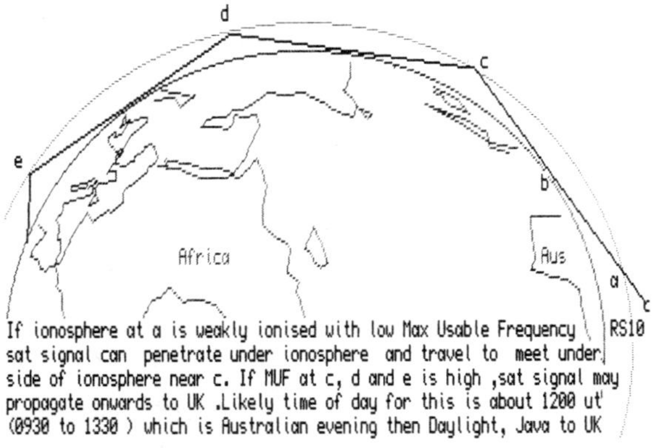

Fig 6.14: Possible mode K satellite Australia-UK path via ionosphere

other HF satellite beacons have repeated the feat. Even at solar cycle minimum, satellites tracking near the antipodes have been heard on HF in the UK (see Fig 6.13).

At the time of Sputnik it was suggested that something called 'antipodal focussing' was the mechanism responsible. Whether that is true or not, it does now seem, that with home computers to allow us to follow satellites much more accurately, we find that most of these near-antipodal signals originate from west of the actual antipodes, and they do so at times shortly after sunset in the F layer of the antipodal ionosphere.

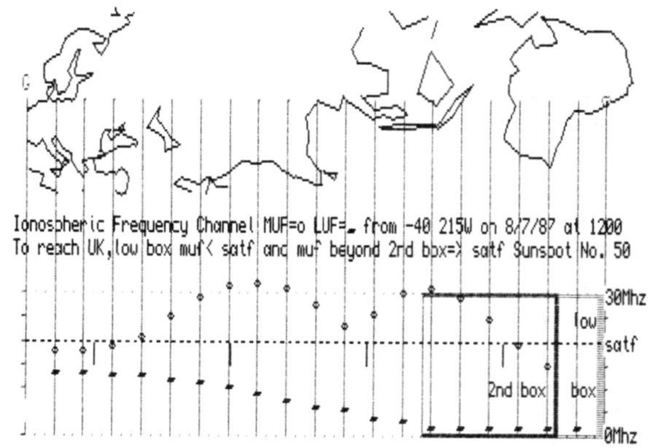

Fig 6.15: Short path from –40 215°W, azimuth great circle 75

It is therefore possible to explain this antipodal propagation as first consequent on the great height of the satellite, and second on the sort of day/night zone change path that Cosmos 1686 has demonstrated so well slightly nearer to the UK. Fig 6.14 suggests the night-to-day route a signal from near the antipodes might follow around the Earth via ionospheric propagation to the UK.

Experiments with Cosmos 1686 and RS7 at 20MHz and 29MHz respectively have clearly established the validity of this path one-way, antipodes to UK, along tracks which started far from the antipodes and ended near the antipodes as the satellite penetrated too far around the night side of the Earth. Fig 6.13 refers. However, it will take a much more selective process to make it two-way, 29MHz from the antipodes to UK, 21MHz from UK to the antipodes, in order to permit UK radio amateurs to talk via RS10/11 to radio amateurs in Australasia.

Fig 6.15 takes this suggestion a step further, showing a computer graphic produced by software used by the author to model the UK-Australia path, for comparing predictions by the computer model with actual dates and times of attempted antipodal RS10/11 communication. The upper half of Fig 6.15 shows a great circle track from Australia to UK. The satellite is over south Australia. The track is divided along its length into 20 equal sections, and for each of these sections the maximum usable ionospheric propagation frequency and the lowest usable absorption frequency are calculated and displayed graphically in the bottom half of Fig 6.15. Satellite beacon frequency (in this case Cosmos 1686 on 19.955MHz) is shown as a dotted line marked 'satf'. Alongside this label at the Australian end of the display is a short box delineating the satellite half great circle angle at the top of the ionosphere. This delineates the region where the signal from and to the satellite must penetrate through the ionosphere, ie the MUF must be low enough for transparency at the satellite frequencies.

The second box then defines the subsequent region where the signal must encounter its first ionospheric refraction/bending at the underside of a thick high MUF ionosphere, if it is to propagate further. Beyond the second box are short vertical marker lines descending from the satf dotted line. These short vertical markers indicate roughly where further underside ionosphere refractions must occur if the signal is to get to UK. The short vertical markers are roughly every 4.6 sections of the graphic apart, scaled to accord roughly with the extent of one refraction zone ie, ionosphere down to skim near Earth then rise to next encounter with the ionosphere.

In the example quoted in Fig 6.15, the author was just hearing faint signals from Cosmos 1686 getting to Scotland from above south Australia. The model prediction of Fig 6.15 shows that the right conditions existed almost all the way to UK. The end box under the satellite did have a very low MUF, then in the second box the signal did encounter a much denser ionosphere and hence higher MUF, rapidly exceeding 20MHz before the end of the box and therefore capable of sustaining oblique-incidence propagation. Thereafter the path to UK features MUF above 20MHz nearly all the way, although as the third section near UK shows, a refraction was needed quite close to UK, and the model suggested that this was doubtful at 21MHz. In fact the practical result on that occasion suggest the model was a little pessimistic. The signal did get to Scotland, but it has to be admitted that it was not of communications quality, being recognisable only because of the unique keying pattern of Cosmos 1686's pulse duration modulation with ripple reset.

For RS10/11 mode K we have to lift the satf line to 29.4MHz. This provides a much tougher situation. It is feasible to suggest that the signal might have got as far as the equator and, if luckily placed, might have straddled the dip in the ionospheric MUF curve at the equator, but it is then clear that the last section of the path to UK would not have supported 29.4MHz communication. However, this was only shortly after solar cycle minimum.

Whilst discussing the potential for antipodal communications via RS10/11 it must be mentioned that all the data available refers to the Australia-UK path or the Western Australia to eastern USA path. It should be possible to work the other way from a satellite near overhead UK to south Australia, or eastern USA to Perth. HF satellites above the UK should be audible from time to time in Australia. If a satellite over Australia at about 1100 UTC can propagate its signal to the UK, then a satellite over the UK at about 0500 UTC might get its signal eastwards into the daylight zone and onto Australia. It will be interesting to see what happens with RS10/11 in 1991.

Mode K and T interference problems

With all its exciting long-range communications possibilities, it should come as no surprise that there are also some problems which result from this exotic propagation boost to satellite operations.

Fig 6.10 explores two instances where problems can occur. As Fig 6.10 shows, it is possible for RS10/11 above the UK in the evening to have its 29.4MHz down link saturated with South America terrestrial signals.

These signals originate from local terrestrial communications in South America, where the stations concerned are quite unaware that they are accessing RS10/11 and that the satellite is transponding their signals to 29.4MHz and relaying these signals down into the UK satellite band. On 21MHz direct, UK stations cannot hear the South Americans, but the satellite 1,000km above UK can hear the 21MHz signals and proceeds to treat them as if they were genuine satellite signals. Worse still, as explained earlier, if mode T is active 21MHz up, 145MHz down, the UK 145MHz satellite band also gets its quota of South Americans via RS10/11.

As with the antipodal case, what can happen in one direction, can also happen in the opposite direction. When the satellite is over Brazil in the UK mornings, Brazil is still in the night zone. So 21MHz terrestrial signals from UK plus 21MHz UK satellite signals can get to Brazil, producing quite a mix-up unless the satellite operators specify as they call that they are CQ RS10/11.

As indicated above, this problem is not confined to mode K. Mode T is not usable to Brazil two-way via the ionosphere because its 145MHz signal will not be propagated by the ionosphere. None the less, if mode T picks up ionospherically propagated 21MHz signals on its up link, it promptly rebroadcasts them on 145MHz to all stations in its VHF footprint. The irony here is that these 145MHz signals come down in a part of the 2m band reserved for satellite traffic. So theoretically RS10/11 only interferes with satellite users in this mode, at least as far as the UK is concerned. In other parts of the world the situation is quite different. In the Far East particularly, the so-called satellite section is used by all and sundry, with the result that 21MHz signals ionospherically propagated to RS10/11 over, say, Japan could come down on top of FM or repeater traffic.

To reduce these difficulties, satellite users can resort to clear calling procedures, saying over the satellite who they are, what mode they are using, and clearly saying that they are operating through RS10/11. In this way other satellite users will be able to identify stations genuinely seeking satellite communications. The alternative proposed in some quarters – to restrict terrestrial operation in the RS10/11 up link – is far too harsh a measure to be practical or acceptable.

Summarising, it has to be said that RS10/11 operation need careful planning and lots of practice. Given a little bit of tolerance of terrestrial users there should be no serious problems and RS10/11 users should find the satellites almost continuously usable. The only exception to this comes from the high-power, over-the-horizon radars which have become such a regular nuisance to HF operators. If over-the-horizon radars come into the narrow RS10/11 frequency bands, the satellites are rendered almost completely useless. When, as it must, RS10/11 overflies one of these monsters, it gets an enormous signal overload. Fortunately, built-in protection ensures that the satellite can take these assaults, but the effect is to close the satellite down completely until it is well away from the radar. Unfortunately these radars chase the MUF, relying on optimum MUF, oblique-incidence propagation to achieve their over-the-horizon effects, and putting them directly in the frequency spectrum where RS10/11 is most useful. Fortunately, checks to date suggest that even these menaces have limited effect on RS10/11.

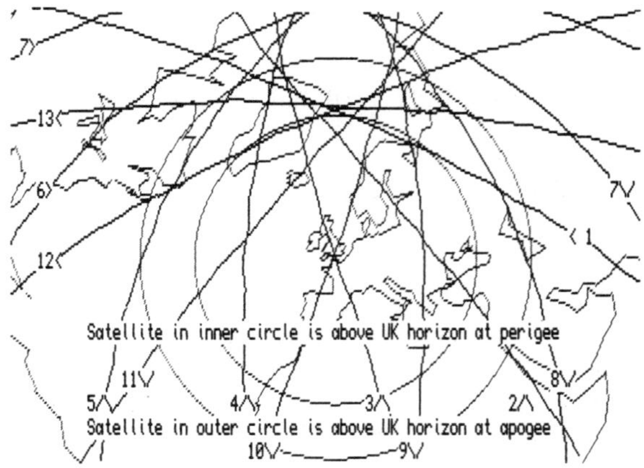

Fig 6.16: Fuji Oscar 20 orbits passing near UK

Fuji Oscar 20 (FO 20 JAS1-B) and associated packet radio satellites

This Japanese satellite was launched from southern Japan on 7 February 1990. It is a much improved successor to Fuji Oscar 12 (JAS1-A). Fuji Oscar 20 (FO 20) does not carry a simple mode A transponder; it uses the more complex mode J format of 145MHz up link and 435MHz down link. A further big difference from the Radiosport and other radio amateur satellites is that it has two completely separate operating modes. In the first mode it can operate as an analogue transponder, receiving up link signals in morse or SSB voice at 145MHz. In this mode the analogue signals are then routed through an amplifier and frequency change mixer, then they are retransmitted as a downlink on 435MHz providing communications out to more than 8,000km.

Completely separately, FO 20 can operate as a digital store-and-forward message carrier and distributor. In this digital mode FO 20 can receive digital packet signals sent up to it and store these signals in its onboard memory. It can then be interrogated by other stations on its up link, who can check whether it has messages addressed to them stored in its memory. If it has a message in store for an accessing station that station can then call for and receive a download of that message. In this way UK stations can up link messages for store until the satellite next flies over Japan, for example. As it overflies Japan, operators there can download any messages addressed to them.

Fuji Oscar 12 was very much an experimental satellite, operating principally as a test bed for digital message techniques and protocols. Its successor has profited from that experience and has been joined by four other packet radio store-and-forward satellites: Uosat D (UO 14), Pacsat (AO 16), Webersat (WO 18) and Lusat (LO 19). Because of their similarities it will be convenient to use the paragraphs which follow to record the main features of this whole group of satellites. But it should be appreciated that, by virtue of its unusual orbit, FO 20 will never actually be in step with the other packet radio carrying satellites and, because of its analogue transponder, FO 20 is of vital importance to a lot of radio amateurs who are not concerned with digital techniques or packet radio.

When can FO 20 be accessed from the UK?

The pattern of FO 20 orbits near the UK is shown in Fig 6.16. This pattern is quite different from that of its predecessor (FO 12) whose orbit was inclined with respect to the equator at only 50 degrees, not FO 20's 99 degrees). FO 12's ground track never rose above latitude 50°N, placing it always south of the UK. By contrast FO 20 passes near to both poles every orbit.

FO 20 orbits the Earth in about 112 minutes, so its orbit track appears to shift roughly 28 degrees west every time it returns to the northern hemisphere. As Fig 6.16 shows, FO 20 achieves just over 12 orbits per day, and the first of these is shown on Fig 6.16 (just the first of a complete series, not necessarily the first orbit of the day, which can be any orbit in the series depending on the gradual drift of the satellite's orbit plane in respect to the fixed stars). Orbit 1 just enters the inner circle on the map of Fig 6.16 in the top right-hand corner.

FO 20's orbit is eccentric. It goes far higher in one half of its orbit than it does in the other half. So just how much a UK station can hear of orbit 1 depends on whether FO 20 is up near its apogee or lower in altitude at its perigee as it follows this track. As will be demonstrated later, FO 20's orbit varies between apogee near the UK, through perigee near the UK, and back to apogee near the UK in a 160-day cyclic pattern. So FO 20 users must be aware of where it is on this cycle before they can tell whether FO 20 is in range on orbit 1 from east of the Caspian Sea to beyond Greenland, as it is when apogee is near the UK, or whether it is in range only from north Cape Norway nearly to Greenland, as it is when perigee occurs near the UK. Equally, when the situation of the orbit near the UK is intermediate between apogee and perigee, the in-range portion of the orbit is correspondingly intermediate between the two extremes quoted above.

For simplicity, the orbit descriptions which follow only the smaller shorter perigee track in-range of the UK will be described. Using this rule, orbit 2 is visible in the UK as it crosses southern Turkey, and until it crosses the north east coast of Greenland.

Orbit 3 comes into UK range south of Libya and is lost as it crosses the Greenland icecap. Orbit 4 is first heard off the North African coast and is trackable up to Greenland, whilst orbit 5 is never in range of the UK except on orbits where apogee occurs near UK.

Orbit 6 is always out of range of the UK, as is orbit 7, but orbit 8 is in range when the apogee is near the UK, but not otherwise.

Orbit 9 starts a sequence of orbits which are always in range of the UK. It comes in range on a perigee orbit over the north Cape of Norway and is lost as it descends over Egypt. Orbit 10 appears above the UK horizon when north of Norway and can be tracked until it goes below the UK horizon as it passes over North Africa. Then about 112 minutes later orbit 11 appears north and west of Norway and is trackable down the Atlantic until it is opposite Spain.

Orbit 12 may or may not be heard in the UK. Sometimes at perigee it will just be above the UK horizon whilst over Greenland, but the last orbit in the series, 13, is only seen in the UK on apogee orbits when it takes a high Arctic track from Siberia to Hudson's Bay.

Comparison with the pacsat orbits

Fig 6.17 shows the daily series of pacsat orbits. Superficially this figure resembles the FO 20 orbit, Fig 6.16, but on close examination there are two main points of interest. First, the pacsats (Pacsat, Uosat D, Webersat and Lusat) are in near-circular orbits, so there is little difference between a perigee pass and an apogee pass, and we only require one footprint circle to show where it comes in range of the UK. Second, this pacsat footprint in-range circle is almost the same as the FO 20 perigee footprint. So the pacsats have no obvious range advantage over FO 20.

Predicting the latitude sub-point of FO 20's apogee

Predicting when FO 20 is going to be near apogee and whether this will be near the UK is not difficult if the user has access to a microcomputer. Most tracking programs available to radio amateurs will print a mean anomaly by 256 list, whereby the orbit is divided into 256 equal periods of time from after perigee. So perigee is shown as mA 0 or 256, whilst apogee occurs at mA 128. To assist users who want longer term forecasting, Fig 6.18 charts the geographical latitude under the satellite's apogee sub-point for any date in 1990 or 1991. Using Fig 6.18a, a user of FO 20's analogue transponder can work out when the halfway point on the great circle between his station and a distant station is underneath the satellite's apogee. In 1990 the halfway point between the UK and western America, eg about latitude 60°N, was underneath apogee in early April, late

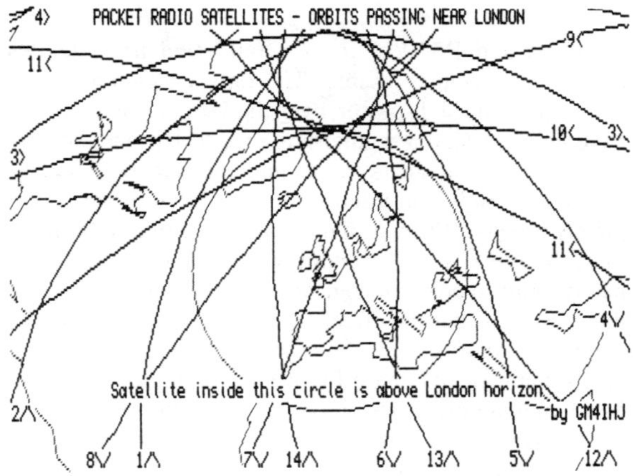

Fig 6.17: Packet radio satellites – orbits passing near the UK

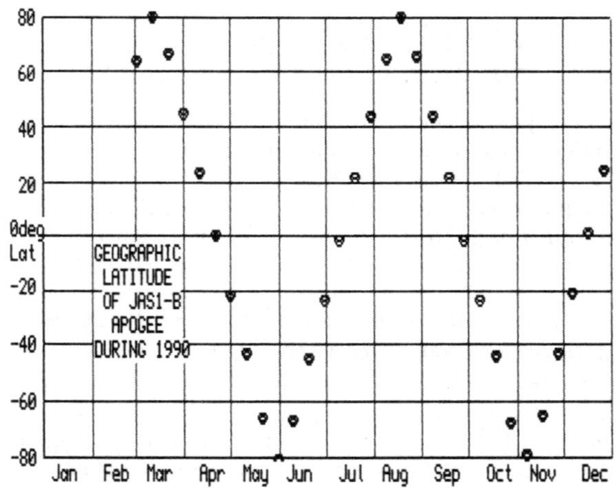

a: 1990

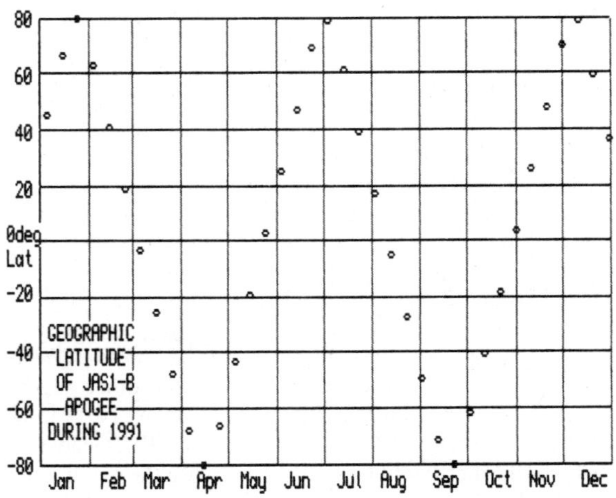

b: 1991

Fig 6.18: Geographic latitude of FO 20 apogee

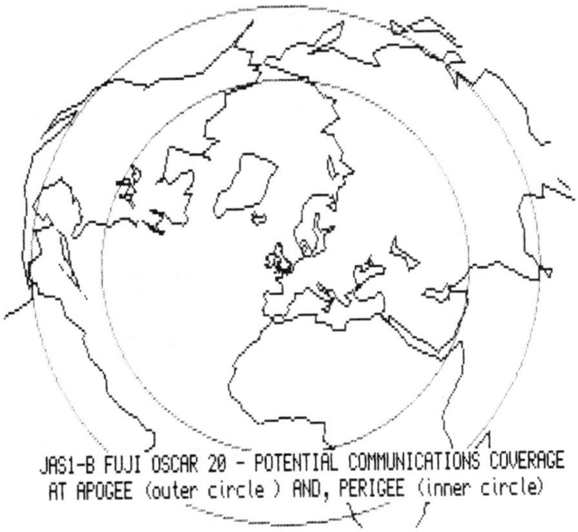

Fig 6.19: FO 20 potential communications coverage

July and late August. Fig 6.18b shows on its outer circle the approximate extent of the longest communications paths available from the UK when advantage is taken of the satellite apogee being directly above the halfway point on the great circle track.

Annual timing patterns of FO 20 and pacsat orbits in range of the UK

Fig 6.20a shows the approximate timing pattern of FO 20 orbits in range of the UK in 1990. In early March 1990 the FO 20 orbit sequence for a typical day started with an orbit near track 5 on Fig 6.16, at around 0045 UTC, and this was followed by a long break until an orbit along track 8 of Fig 6.16 started a long continuous sequence of orbits at roughly 112 minute intervals through to midnight. Please note the apogee of the satellite was near above the UK at this time.

By early May 1990, things are much more restricted and the in-range orbit sequence is reduced at either end. The sequence begins with an orbit along track 9 at approximately 0800 UTC and ends with an orbit along track 4 at around 2200 UTC. Not until July and August does the orbit 8 through 13 to orbit 5 sequence reveal that the UK is again nearly under the satellite's apogee. Note also that the in-range orbit timings are slowly drifting earlier each successive month, although this is partially hidden in the apogee-perigee cycle. Fig 6.20b shows the continuation of these trends into 1991.

The contrasting orbit timing situation for the pacsats is shown in Fig 6.21. In this case there is no apogee/perigee wobble and the orbit is in synchronism with the time of day. This means that a particular orbit on a particular track will be coming up at roughly the same time of day for the pacsats until 1992 or 1993, by which time solar wind drag may have pushed the satellites slightly off the Sun synchronous track.

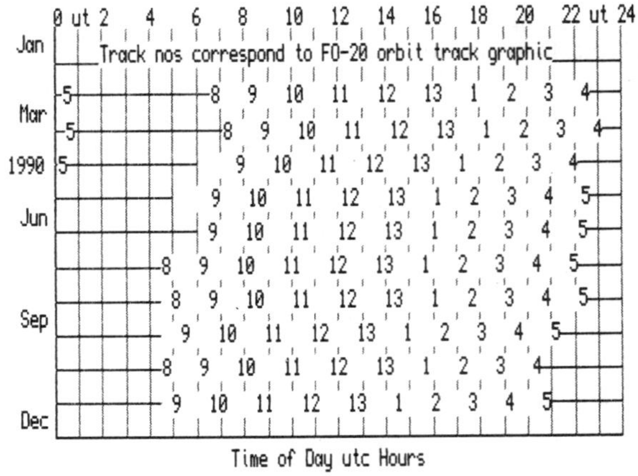

a: 1990

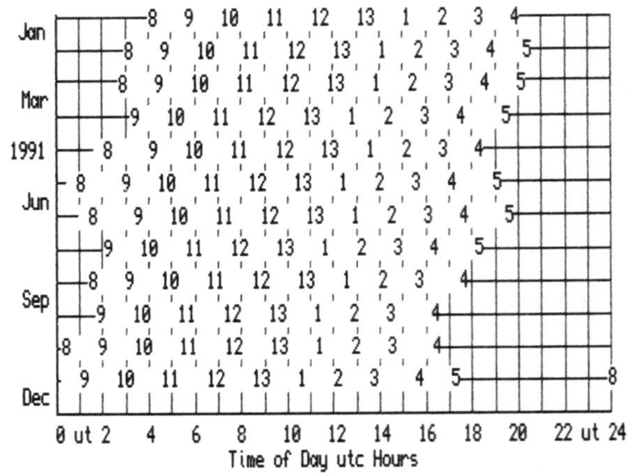

b: 1991

Fig 6.20: FO 20 tracks and times in UK range

For this reason it is possible to show the pacsats' orbit timing chart for both 1990 and 1991 together. It should be noted that these predictions only give the approximate track and

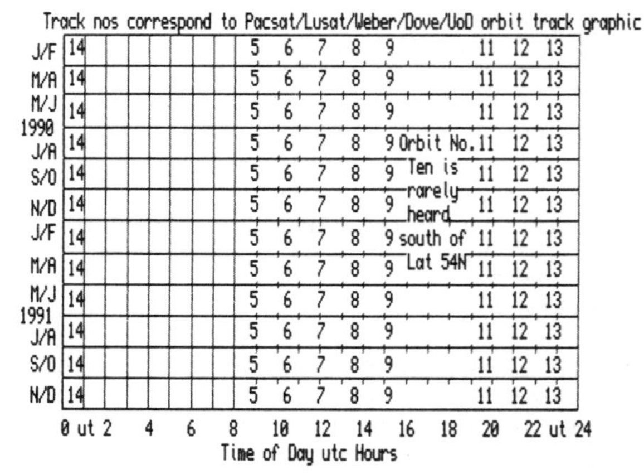

Fig 6.21: Pacsat tracks and approx times in UK range 1990/91

a: 55°N 68°W

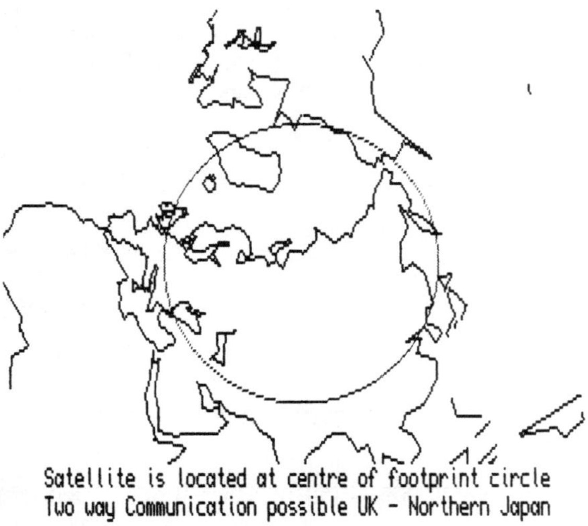

b: 70°N 290°W

Fig 6.22a,b: FO 20 footprints at apogee

timing of each satellite pass relative to the UK; they do not give the exact times of satellite passes.

Predicting who you can talk to via FO 20

Using typical footprint coverage, Fig 6.22, together with orbit apogee data from Fig 6.18 and orbit timing predictions from Fig 6.20, it is possible to predict where the best communication possibilities via FO 20 will occur during 1990 and 1991.

Fig 6.22 shows rough details of where and when the best long-distance communications opportunities will occur. Remember that in some cases these opportunities will arise

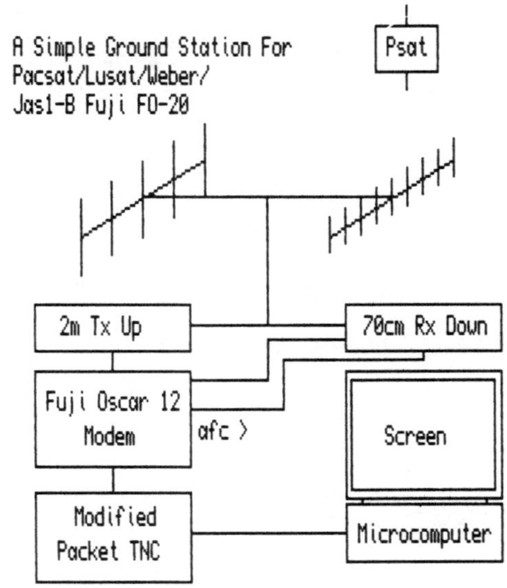

Fig 6.23: Simple ground station for pacsats and FO 20

as FO 20 comes above your horizon (eg western USA or Japan), and only if your procedure is very slick are you likely to get a contact before the other station slips out of the footprint. Thus forewarned, and provided the time of day is socially acceptable in the distant locations, good communications opportunities should follow.

To summarise, it can be expected that the FO 20 orbit will be generally predictable for several years with Figs 6.18 and 6.20, providing a useful quick reference for anyone planning a FO 20 operating schedule. In the case of the pacsats there is no real-time UHF communications facility so these problems do not arise.

Frequencies used by FO 20 and by the pacsats

The frequency band plans for both FO 20 and the pacsats are shown in Fig 6.24. As this plan shows, FO 20 analogue JA mode uses a frequency inverter, ie the up link at 145MHz is subtracted from a local oscillator in the satellite near 580MHz to produce a down link near 435.9MHz. Hence in analogue voice mode the up link on 145MHz should be modulated by a lower sideband voice signal, so that the inverted down link appears as the conventional upper sideband modulation in general use on satellite down links.

What the band plan does not show clearly is that the FO 20 and pacsat up links on 145MHz may, if they have any serious third harmonic content, interfere with reception around 3 x 145.9MHz = 437.7MHz, ie very close to where the station receiver at 435.9 or 437.15MHz is trying to tune the weak down link. So it is common practice with these mode J, 145MHz up, 435MHz down, signals to fit a filter in the receiver line from the antenna which is tightly tuned to 435.9MHz or 437MHz and strongly rejects both 145MHz and its third harmonic around 437.7MHz which may come from your station transmitter. Note this can happen on some azimuth bearings and not others, when the antenna points to the satellite and perhaps a building adjacent to the ground station whose flat wall reflects a lot of the 145MHz up link signal back into the 435/437MHz down link antenna. Present experience suggests that FO 20 is more likely to be disturbed by reception of harmonics of the 144.625MHz signal of terrestrial packet transmissions, but there may be some breakthrough onto the 437MHz pacsat reception from the pacsat 145.9MHz up link, which may need filtering.

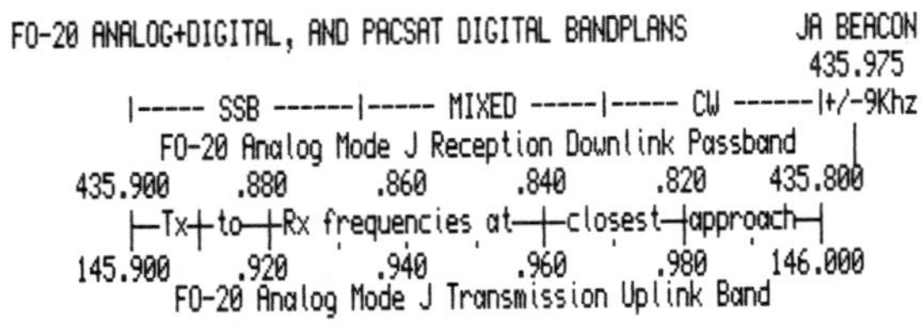

Satellite		Digital Down		Four Channel Digital Uplink
JAS1-B	FO20	435.91	1200 PSK	145.91 145.89 145.87 145.85 1200 FSK
Pacsat	AO16	437.05 437.025	1200 PSK	145.90 145.92 145.94 145.96 1200 FSK
Dove	DO17	145.825	1200 FSK	No uplink. Downlink Modem not needed
Lusat	LO19	437.15 437.125	1200 PSK	145.90 145.88 145.86 145.84 1200 FSK
Weber	WO18	437.1 437.075	1200 PSK	145.90 1200 FSK
UosatD	UO14	435.25 435.07	9600 FSK	145.90 145.975 9600 FSK
UosatE	UO15	435.12	9600 FSK	No packet uplink

Fig 6.24: FO 20 and pacsats band plans

Fig 6.20 in the *VHF/UHF Manual* (RSGB, fourth edition) can be scaled to 435.9 or 437.15MHz and built as an excellent filter to counter this problem.

Operating through FO 20

FO 20 operates either in analogue mode or digital mode on some days, then on other days both modes may be on together. Only after a lot more operating and some experience of how the FO 20's batteries cope with eclipse in Earth shadow will it be clear which operating schedule suits FO 20 and its users best.

If only the digital mode is on, there will be no beacon and the satellite may be idling waiting for someone to send a digital signal up to it. The satellite can be heard clearly when it is idling. So nothing on the screen does not mean it is off. Then, on receipt of a digital signal via any one of the up link channels, the satellite will be heard replying on the digital down link frequency. If the satellite is in use, its digital down link will be heard and seen on your screen. So there should be no doubt which modes of FO 20 are on, even if no one is using them.

In the event that the satellite is shut down/battery charging (mode C or mode JC, as this is called in some schedules), no signals will be heard and the satellite will not reply to a digital up link.

FO 20 Doppler shift

On a near-overhead pass of FO 20 in the analogue mode, the terrestrial operator has to cope with about 11kHz of Doppler shift, most of it occurring in the three-minute period around the time of satellite closest approach to his station. This serious Doppler problem remains in spite of the fact that the FO 20 transponder uses subtractive mixing of up link and transponder local oscillator frequency, so that Doppler change on the 145MHz up link partially nullifies the much bigger effect on the 435MHz down link. Few operators can stay tuned, keep a conversation going and train their antenna to track the fast-moving satellite. It takes a lot of practice to do it successfully and there are several important rules as to how this should be done.

The golden rule of FO 20 mode JA operating is to keep moving your transmitter up link frequency so that your down link signal stays in the same place on your receiver. This allows both you and the station you are communicating with to use your respective receivers as a firm reference for where you are. If you do not do this you will find that after you have been talking for a minute or so, the other station will appear to reply to you on a quite different frequency, noting that with 11kHz of Doppler shift you move through the 2.5kHz bandwidth of an SSB receiver more than four times in a FO 20 orbit passing near your station.

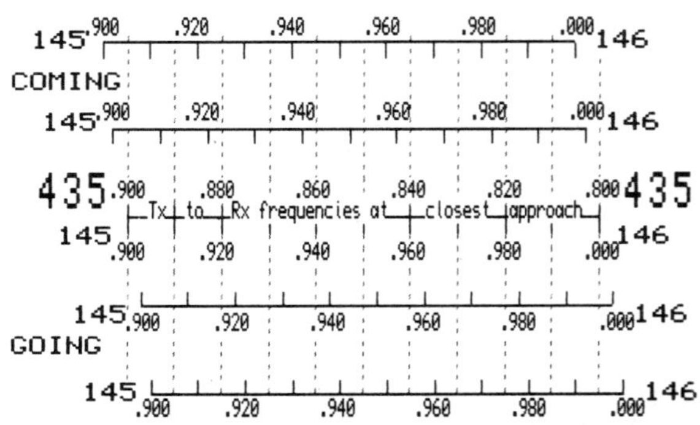

Use top to bottom for high elevation close passes,use 2nd to 4th for low elevation passes at a distance .Remember shift slow begin + end,fast mid.

Fig 6.25: FO 20 Doppler chart. Tune transmitter to remain on same receive frequency

Fig 6.25 is provided to assist FO 20 operators to prepare themselves for the effect of this Doppler shift. To use this chart it is necessary to decide which down link frequency you want to use or which down link frequency your target station is already on. Let us chose as an example a down link frequency of 435.890MHz. Next you must decide whether the FO 20 orbit you are using is going to pass near your station or not; tracks 3 and 10 on Fig 6.16 can be regarded as passing close to your UK station. Then, using the chart on Fig 6.25, you find 435.890MHz is on the middle scale of the chart, just in from the left-hand, high-frequency end. From this 435.890MHz point on the middle scale a line of dashes extends vertically upwards. Follow this dashed line up to the top scale on the chart and you arrive at a point on the top scale corresponding to an up link frequency of about 145.915MHz. Use this frequency for your up link as the satellite comes above your horizon prior to a close approach and you should find that your signal reappears on the FO 20 down link near to 435.890MHz. Note that individual receiver and transmitter calibrations may put you one or two kilohertz away from 435.890MHz but for this example please do not correct this slight mismatch.

As the satellite approaches, you should find that you need to bring your transmit frequency gradually lower, following the path through the horizontal frequency scales so that, halfway towards you, you cross the scale next to the top, transmitting on 145.913MHz to keep your down link on 435.890MHz. As the pass progresses further, so your transmit frequency descends with the dashed vertical line so that, as the satellite passes near your station, you are transmitting on about 145.910MHz. As it gets halfway out again to your horizon, you transmit on 145.907MHz until the time when the satellite begins to approach your far horizon, by which time the dashed line is indicating that your transmitter should be on a frequency near 145.904MHz.

A simpler procedure applies where the satellite is not going to come close to your home station, eg orbital passes using tracks 1, 2,4 ,5, 8, 9 and 11 and 12. In this case the overall Doppler shift will be only about half, or even less, of the shift experienced in a near-overhead pass. To follow a distant orbital pass, the second scale from the top of Fig 6.25 should be your starting point, then if you wish to talk to a station already on 435.810MHz as the satellite comes above your horizon, you should access with a frequency of about 145.992MHz (second scale down, where the dashed line rising from 435.810MHz on the central scale crosses the next scale line above it. As the orbit progresses you can expect to use an up link of about 145.990MHz as the satellite comes closest to your station halfway through the pass, dropping to the next scale down and an indicated frequency of 145.987MHz on your up link as the satellite drops towards your horizon at the end of the pass. Intermediate orbits passing closer to or further away from your station will have respectively more or less Doppler shift than this middle distance from your station example.

Using Fig 6.25 it should be possible to keep in your mind a rough idea of where you next need to tune your transmitter. Always remember that so long as the other station behaves sensibly you will always tune your up link steadily lower in frequency as the orbit progresses, with the speed of tuning being greatest in the middle of the orbit pass. Remember that Fig 6.25 is only a rough guide. If you wish to improve it, find out how close your measured up and down link frequencies are to the centre scale of Fig 6.25, and work out your standard personal equipment correction for Fig 6.25, to get your frequencies absolutely where you want them.

One last important point concerns your initial attempts to get contacts on FO 20. Use Fig 6.25 as a general guide, then

Table 6.06: Fuji Oscar 20 tracking curve

Min	LatN	LongW	Min	Lat N	LongW
0	0	0	32	80.36	118.34
2	5.90	1.44	34	77.05	144.65
4	11.75	2.89	36	72.26	159.13
6	17.56	4.38	38	66.85	167.62
8	23.33	5.94	40	61.13	173.21
10	29.05	7.57	42	55.21	177.25
12	34.75	9.34	44	49.14	180.39
14	40.42	11.29	46	42.95	182.97
16	46.05	13.51	48	36.66	185.19
18	51.64	16.12	50	30.27	187.16
20	57.19	19.30	52	23.79	188.97
22	62.67	23.46	54	17.21	190.67
24	68.03	29.25	56	10.56	192.30
26	73.14	38.19	58	3.82	193.89
28	77.64	53.63	60	-2.97	195.47
30	80.59	81.54			

you are much less likely to upset others by accidentally tuning on top of them when you have not found your own signal on the down link. You can usually find a quiet part of the FO 20 down link band and practise as much as you like. Learning how to ride with the Doppler is good manners, good sense and good fun.

Doppler on FO 20 and pacsat in the digital mode

The digital mode of these satellites has no transponder inversion, so the Doppler range on a near-overhead pass is 19 to 20kHz. This is too much for useful smooth manual operation. In consequence the G3RUH and TPR modems provide a signal automatic frequency control system, whereby DC levels from the modem tell your receiver up/down scanning circuits which way to track for 'hands off', smooth automatic Doppler correction. Full details of how to set up this AFC modem-to-receiver loop are given in G3RUH's excellent modem instruction book.

Tracking FO 20 and the pacsats on a hand plotter

Table 6.06 lists the standard FO 20 northern hemisphere track. These points can be inked onto an acrylic overlay and used over a northern hemisphere polar-centred great circle map. Using a plotter of this sort in conjunction with equator crossing times, you can easily follow FO 20 orbits near the UK. The suggestion made in some quarters that the eccentricity of the FO 20 orbit requires the use of two tracks, one for perigee and one for apogee, is not correct. Differences in the two tracks amount to no more than 0.04 of a degree of latitude or longitude. Table 6.07 shows the complementary pacsat northern hemisphere track. This track is suitable for Pacsat, Dove, Lusat, Weber, Uosat D + E.

Typical sets of Keplerian elements are shown in Table 6.08.

Table 6.07: Pacsat tracking curve

Min	LatN	LongW	Min	LatN	LongW
0	0	0	28	76.88	145.74
2	7.06	1.59	30	71.00	160.99
4	14.11	3.21	32	64.50	169.21
6	21.16	4.93	34	57.74	174.41
8	28.20	6.73	36	50.87	178.11
10	35.21	8.73	38	43.94	180.98
12	42.21	11.01	40	36.96	183.36
14	49.17	13.74	42	29.96	185.42
16	56.07	17.20	44	22.94	187.27
18	62.86	21.94	46	15.90	188.99
20	69.45	29.20	48	8.86	190.63
22	75.55	42.11	50	1.82	192.22
24	80.21	68.95	52	-5.23	193.80
26	80.86	113.77			

Track suitable for Uosat D, Uosat E, Pacsat, Lusat
Dove and Webersat . But not suitable Jas1-B Fuji FO-20

Because of FO 20's low perigee and the low mean height of all the pacsats, it is recommended that up to the end of 1991 Keplerian orbital elements in FO 20/pacsat software tracking programs should be updated every month if possible and every three months for certain. Thereafter, changes every three months should suffice. The best source for these orbital elements is the satellites' own bulletin boards. Failing that, your terrestrial packet BBS carries Nasa updates every two weeks.

Operating on FO 20

Telemetry

The complete range of telemetry from FO 12 is described in experiment 2.03 in chapter 8. This experiment illustrates the highest level at which manual telemetry decoding is practical. Both FO 20 and Lusat LO 19 send telemetry of this broad type but in addition they and the other pacsats send complex flexible patterns of digital telemetry. Would-be users of this digital telemetry are strongly recommended to obtain the download and decode software being offered by Amsat NA for use with digital telemetry. FO 20 and LO 19 telemetry is sent on both digital and analogue modes; the other pacsats are digital only.

Table 6.08: Typical sets of Keplerian elements for FO 20 and pacsat

Element	FO 20	Pacsat
Epoch year day of year. Decimal day of year	90 66.178202252	90 22.0786319
Inclination	99.0526	98.7376 degs
Right ascension of ascending node	131.8923 degs	102.95582
Eccentricity	0.0540615	0.001338
Argument of perigee	279.6136	110.95 degs
Mean anomaly	74.4312	297.18 degs
Mean motion	12.83116845	14.2853

Analogue operation

FO 20 provides excellent CW and SSB voice communications facilities in the analogue mode. SSB users should remember that the FO 20 transponder inverts the up link as it transcribes it to the down link. In order therefore to appear on the 435MHz FO 20 down link with upper sideband modulation, it is necessary to transmit lower sideband modulation on your up link transmission. Extreme care is necessary following the very fast Doppler shift on passes close to the UK but, on passes distant from the UK, FO 20 Doppler shift is low and the satellite frequently offers excellent long-range communication out to more than 8,000km.

Digital operation

FO 20 in the JD digital mode is basically a mail box. You put your messages in as it goes past you, and you check to see if anyone else has left messages for you, then the satellite carries on to other parts of the world where other users access it to see if there are messages for them and to deposit their messages to other stations.

In normal JD digital mode FO 20 is idling, sending occasional telemetry frames until it hears a genuine digital packet on one of its four up link frequencies. It operates a relatively extensive mail box facility with a capacity for 1,000 messages. Messages must be in AX.25 version 2 format. On receipt of a message on the up link FO 20 replies using phase shift keying on its 435.910MHz ±Doppler down link. Users should remember that the 435.910MHz down link has no partial Doppler reduction (as is the case with the FO 20 analogue channel). In the digital mode the FO 20 down link can have up to ±10kHz of Doppler shift. So, as Fig 6.23 shows, the ground station receiver uses a G3RUH FO 20 modem which has an automatic frequency control loop with the 70cm receiver.

Once the FO 20 mailbox holds 1,000 messages, transmission of further messages to it results in over writing and loss of the earliest messages in its memory. When mode JD is switched off all prior messages are lost.

FO 20 message packages should be tailored to a length (PACLEN) of not more than 199. FO 20 transmits PACLEN 128 and MAXFRAMES 1. Ordinary digipeater packets are not accepted by FO 20, in addition mode JD has no LOGOUT command, so users must disconnect themselves via the DISCONNECT command.

Typical commands for FO 20 JD are:

B List headers of messages addressed to ALL
F List 10 latest message headers and numbers.
F* List latest 50 message headers
R (number) Read message number ... contents to me
W Send a message. Where upon FO 20 asks you for: intended recipient TO? Message subject SUBJECT? Message TEXT?
You send carriage return. Carriage return to signify end of message.
K (number) Kill message number ... in your memory
H Help gets you details of FO 20 Commands

FO 20 terminal node controller requirements are:

Protocol	version 2 (or if TNC-1 additional WA8DED PROM may be necessary but recent reports say not for FO 20).		
	Commands are	TNC-2	Ax2512v2 ON
		TNC-1	V2
T1 timer	6 minutes minimum		
	Commands are	TNC-2	FRack 6
		TNC-1	F6
Max frames	2 or 3 is the suggested number		
	Commands are	TNC-2	MAX 2 or MAX 3
		TNC-1	02 or 03

The callsign by which you address FO 20 to connect is 8J1JBS. The special equipment required by the FO 20/pacsat ground station shown in Fig 6.23 is listed in paragraphs summarising all the FO 20/pacsat features. These paragraphs are located near the end of this chapter.

Signal propagation to and from FO 20 and the pacsats

When north of the UK, the FO 20/pacsat signal path to the UK often has to transit the polar auroral front. This has the effect that the signal suffers marked scintillation on the 435MHz down link, and worse still the satellite may be almost completely impossible to access on the 145MHz up link. The analogue mode of FO 20 is much more susceptible to these problems than the digital mode of either FO 20 or the pacsats.

At other times, particularly in the UK summer during daylight hours, the FO 20/pacsat up link on 145MHz may be poor when sporadic E is present along the line of sight to the satellite. This is not a problem peculiar only to FO 20. FO 12 and Oscar 8J and DNA P76 satellite suffered from both sporadic E problems and polar auroral zone scintillation.

FO 20 initial operating results, spring 1990

The operating schedule of FO 20 is a tremendous improvement over that of FO 12. It has much more powerful power supplies and a much bigger memory. But it still has a few problems, particularly on the onboard software. Most irritating of these are its occasional hang-ups, leaving an individual user in limbo and unable to proceed further or to disconnect. It also has a user list of 16 which rapidly fills up and, worse still, continues to hold user calls where the user failed to disconnect but has long since dropped out of the satellite footprint. These faults and several others are clearly amenable to software fixes and could well be removed by the time this appears in print.

FO 20 and the other packet satellites

As of October 1990, FO 20 is the only fully operational packet BBS in orbit. Uosat D UO 14, Pacsat PO 16 and Lusat LO 19 are in orbit being loaded up with their operational software. They can be expected to come on-line with a user protocol similar to that of FO 20, and with some innovations, including unsolicited downloading of bulletins for the benefit of the host of radio amateurs who just want down link copy of what is going on but do not want to initiate personal messages or bulletins.

The 1990s offer a marvellous feast of experimental and communications opportunities via this squadron of additions to the amateur satellite fleet.

Uosats – amateur radio science satellites

Introduction

Launched in October 1981 and March 1984 these two satellites have established a unique place in both amateur radio and professional space science history. Neither satellite carried real-time voice communication facilities – their mission was to measure and report their space environment and to act as space-borne test beds for hardware and software development. Particular emphasis was given to experiments involving digital communications and Uosat Oscar 11 (aka Uosat 2) provides a useful store-and-forward message relay facility for digital packets. Uosat Oscar 9 (aka Uosat 1) re-entered the atmosphere in October 1989, so the information given here refers only to UO 11.

When can Uosat be heard in the UK?

UO 11 is in a near Sun-synchronous orbit, ie it appears over the UK at approximately the same times each day, with its window of UK in-range orbits showing little change from one year to the next. Fig 6.26 shows the orbit tracks near the UK.

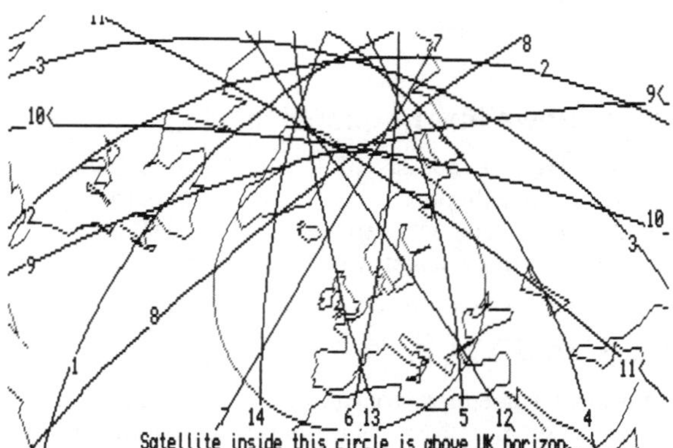

Fig 6.26: Uosat Oscar 11 orbits passing near the UK

UO 11 has suffered very little atmospheric drag, so it is still almost Sun synchronous. Fig 6.27 shows the effect of this with the straight-edged, UK in-range orbit window (orbits 5 to 14 inclusive) all in range of the UK, although polar orbits along tracks 9 and 10 of Fig 6.26 rarely give good signals in the UK, because they are both horizon scrapers here and they involve signal paths subject to the propagation problems of the polar auroral front.

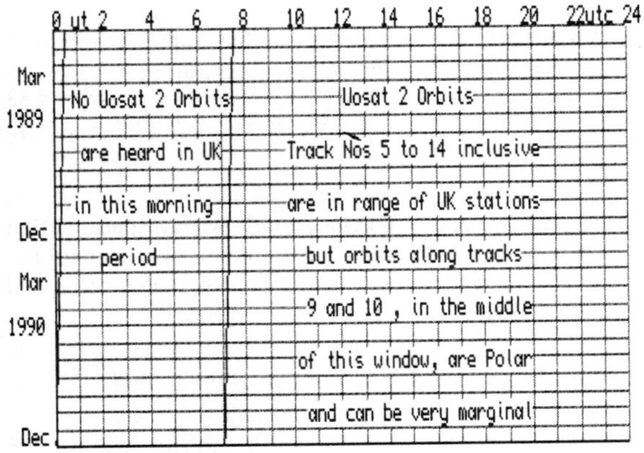

Fig 6.27: Uosat Oscar 11 windows of UK in-range orbits during 1989/90

Fig 6.28 shows the UK footprint circles of the now-defunct Uosat Oscar 9 and UO 11, with the higher-altitude UO 11 having the bigger footprint. The important thing to note about this map is that it reveals the area Uosat must enter for its signals to be heard in the UK. What must not be forgotten, however, is that UO 11 has a similar size footprint when near places of interest like Chernobyl and the polar zones, in either of which you might want to do experimental studies. UO 11 passes by each of these places 10 times a day. On these passes Uosat can collect radiation data and can down load it to you later as it passes the UK. So in fact, although UO 11 is not all that high, it can see every part of the world twice each day and can take records for you from wherever you need them.

UO 11 down link frequencies

145.825MHz: broadcasts of telemetry using computer generated voice digitalker, FM and PSK telemetry.
435.025MHz: same telemetry as on 145.825MHz.
2,401MHz: same telemetry as 145.825MHz.

Tracking UO 11

A northern hemisphere master track, which can be used on an acrylic overlay over a north polar-centred great circle map, is listed in Table 6.09. A plotter made in this way can be used with equator crossing times and bearings, available from *Practical Wireless* every second month or from ARRL satellite bulletins (put out on UK packet radio bulletin boards).

For microcomputer users, details of software suppliers are given in appendix 1. Table 6.10 shows typical computer tracking predictions for UO 11. As the computer track shows, it can be in range for 12 minutes or so and only needs to come within 2,800km of your station to be above your horizon.

Please note, the satellite does not follow these exact same tracks every day or every orbit. These specimen tracks are provided for the use of individuals who input new data into their computer, then find that its predictions do not line up with Uosat passes. The act of refreshing with new Keplerian elements is the single biggest problem in satellite tracking and is the time most mistakes are made. A short comparison of a typical orbit somewhere near the same track as the ones shown here should give the user a fair idea of whether the computation looks good or not.

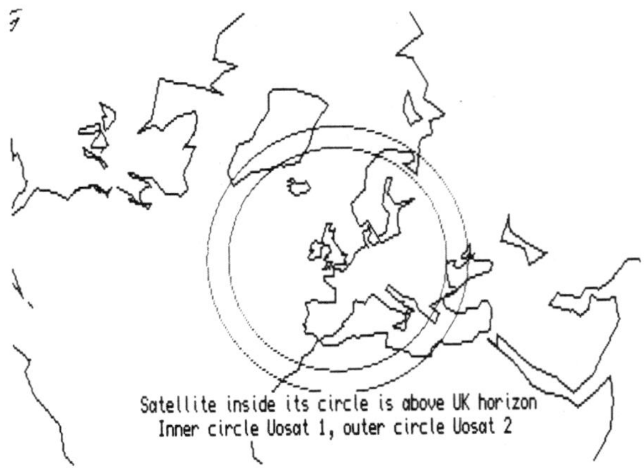

Fig 6.28: Uosat footprint circles over the UK

The same situation applies in respect of Keplerian elements. The elements quoted here will be out of date by the time this book is published, so do not put them in your computer, but do remember they are here. Then if you have occasion to suspect a new set of elements, compare them with those here. Elements like epoch time, right ascension argument of perigee and mean anomaly can change quite a lot between one element set and the next. But if mean motion, eccentricity or inclination have changed greatly, you can be pretty sure the new elements you have been given are wrong.

Specimen Keplerian elements for UO 11 are:

Table 6.09: Uosat Oscar 11 tracking curve

Time in Mins	Lat N	LongWest	Time in Mins	Lat N	LongWest
0	0	0	28	75.1	154.54
2	7.25	1.52	30	68.59	166.14
4	14.5	3.11	32	61.72	172.61
6	21.73	4.75	34	54.69	176.87
8	28.96	6.56	36	47.57	180.01
10	36.19	8.48	38	40.42	182.51
12	43.39	10.74	40	33.23	184.63
14	50.55	13.47	42	26.04	186.49
16	57.65	17.01	44	18.82	188.2
18	64.65	22.02	46	11.61	189.81
20	71.41	30.11	48	4.4	191.36
22	77.55	45.82	50	-2.82	192.89
24	81.59	81.3			
26	80.35	129.28			

Table 6.10: Uosat Oscar 11 track prediction

```
Uosat 2 on 1/7/89
UTC  AZ  EL  Lat  Long GndRange
0942 11  -16 76   220  5016kms
0944 13  -11 81   251  4211kms
0946 15  -5  80   301  3409kms
0948 19  2   76   329  2612kms
0950 25  11  69   342  1828kms
0952 39  26  62   349  1087kms
0954 86  46  55   354  588kms
0956 149 32  48   357  914kms
0958 169 15  41   359  1629kms
1000 176 4   34   2    2410kms
1002 180 -3  27   4    3208kms
1004 183 -9  20   5    4015kms
1006 185 -15 12   7    4825kms
1008 186 -20 5    8    5638kms
1010 188 -24 -2   10   6453kms
1012 189 -29 -9   11   7270kms

First letter or sector letter ?  P
```

Epoch year.day.decimal	89 5.22318128
Inclination in degrees	98.0281
RA of ascending node degs	68.6580
Eccentricity	0.0014021
Argument of perigee degs	109.7052
Mean anomaly degrees	250.5626
Mean motion revs per day	14.62747920
Epoch revolution number	25,871

Telemetry

Uosat telemetry reception and decoding is described in detail in chapter 8, experiments 2.01 and 2.04, later in this book.

The University of Surrey satellites provide an enormous range of experimental possibilities, going far beyond those described in chapter 8. The satellites were designed from the start as practical space research tools, they are in constant use, and there has been a tendency for increasingly intricate experiments to be added without detriment to the original wide portfolio of simple experiments available from day one. So there is enormous choice. You can do things at your own pace, at home, in school or in college, but you must keep track of the programme schedule the satellite operates on. Examples of typical programme schedules are:

UO 11 Schedules

Saturday	Diary and 2GHz beacon
Sunday	Diary WOD TLM STAT bull
Monday	Diary WOD TLM STAT bull
Tuesday	Diary WOD TLM STAT bull
Wednesday	Diary digital 70cm day
Thursday	Load new bull am, then diary
Friday	Diary

STAT reports onboard computer status (OBC). WOD refers to Whole Orbit Data where the satellite collects readings of a single telemetry parameter, eg radiation level, taken all around the world, then down loads them all to you. TLM refers to the standard telemetry frame reported in detail in chapter 8. On Wednesdays the 435MHz beacon broadcasts a mixture of diary at 1,200 bps and data store and readout (either science data, CCD, or particle wave experiment) at 4,800 bps. This 70cm 435MHz report has also been broadcast on Sunday mornings by UO 11, where data store and readout (DRS) is sent at 4,800 bps AFSK.

These data experiments are intended as a useful test signal for experimenters developing software and hardware decoding equipment.

One of the best features of the Uosat output is the digitalker computer-generated voice telemetry reports. These are popular because they can produce good results with simple ground station equipment.

A Uosat data booklet has been available for some time (see appendix 1) giving more details of all these varied possibilities and functions.

Operating Uosat

Typical operating patterns for UO 11 in 1989 featured the following whole orbit data channels:

Friday	1, 3, 20, 30
Saturday	0, 10, 20, 30
Sunday	10, 11, 19, 29
Monday	1, 2, 3, 63
Tuesday	19, 24
Wednesday	19

Points to consider when operating are that UO 11 has a big memory, allowing storage of excellent bulletins and whole orbit data packages, and it is extremely versatile and easily commanded from the ground. UO 11 can operate both 2m and 70cm at the same time but there is a penalty in that this makes the satellite rather deaf to ground commands. So in double beacon operation, 145 and 435 simultaneously, a lot of command up link power needs to be available. In addition, if the digital communications experiment (DCE) on UO 11 is operating, stations trying to up link DCE signals when both beacons are on will find they need to use a lot of power.

It has also to be remembered that although UO 11 started out in a Sun synchronous orbit, this was not the 24 hour sunlit type – 0600 local ascending, 1800 local time descending – orbits, used by some Oscars. UO 11 crosses the equator at about 1000 and 2200 local time. So, right from orbit number 1, the satellite has been experiencing periods in Earth shadow, with consequent sudden cooling and loss of solar power to the batteries. This is a tough environment, something that Oscars 6, 7 and 8 did not have to face until they were about four years old, and which rapidly resulted in their fatal demise. UO 9 had been in service for eight years, far longer than any other amateur radio satellite, when it decayed, a remarkable tribute to its builders.

Oscar 10 – Phase IIIB

Introduction

This satellite has been an outstanding success in spite of many problems. To tell its story coherently, the first part of this report describes its present working conditions in 1990, detailing how and when it can be used. Then the second part of this report takes the form of a history of all that has happened since Oscar 10 was launched.

Part 1 – Oscar 10 in 1990

Launched in June 1983, Oscar 10 was delivered to a geostationary transfer orbit and turned over to Amsat control. Partly because of a launch accident, and partly because of an onboard problem, Oscar 10 never got to its planned orbit, which was to have been a high-elevation elliptical orbit of the near-molniya type. Instead Oscar 10 stayed in a near-equatorial orbit.

As a result of this orbit, Oscar 10 had two difficulties. First, its very high 3,700km perigee and its near-equatorial trajectory placed it in the worst parts of the Van Allen belts. Second, because of its relatively low orbital inclination to the equator, the precession of the orbit's argument of perigee caused it to adopt a cyclic movement, which took it from apogee in the northern hemisphere to apogee in the southern hemisphere in only two years of operation. Fig 6.29 shows how the Oscar 10 orbit will continue to move its apogee back below the equator in 1989, then slowly return to better conditions with a northern hemisphere apogee again in 1991.

The end result of these problems has been that radiation damage has destroyed Oscar 10's onboard computer, so that it no longer obeys ground commands, leaving the satellite transponder stuck in mode B operation (435MHz up, 145MHz down) and, worse still, totally disabling the satellite's realignment facilities so that it can no longer be kept pointing at the Sun.

Oscar 10 is therefore quite uncontrollable but, most fortunately, it is not unusable. The mode B transponder is performing as well as ever, provided the satellite solar panels are getting enough sunshine to provide sufficient electric power.

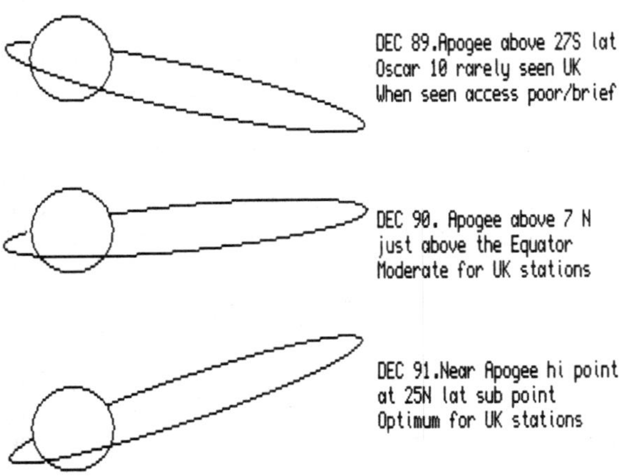

Fig 6.29: The wandering orbit of Oscar 10

Since Oscar 10's return from the southern hemisphere, usage of the satellite has gradually improved, as operators have learnt when to expect sunshine on the solar cells, and hence useful mode B capability. At times when the satellite orientation in space reduces the sunlight falling on the solar cells, Oscar 10 is dead, but it rapidly revives when it drifts back into more sunlight.

Operating Oscar 10 in its restricted single mode B 1989/1990

Because of its curious orbit, Oscar 10 is a wanderer, with conditions in 1989/1990 being dictated by its apogee occurring over southern latitudes. The effects of this are twofold. First, Oscar 10 will be heard in the UK most often when it is near its perigee, eg when it is moving quickly, and not necessarily pointing any of its antennas at the Earth. However, the problems this creates are slightly mitigated by the fact that because the satellite is much nearer to the Earth, its off-line-of-sight antennas cause few problems as the path to the satellite is very short, and little up link power is required to access on 435MHz. Equally important, although Oscar 10 is near to the Earth when above the UK horizon, its perigee height of 3,700km still gives it a very wide footprint, with stations as far away as India or the USA regularly being in range for UK stations.

The present situation, with the satellite apogee over the southern hemisphere, is very restricting. Seen from the UK, only orbits whose apogee occurs over the narrow (40 degree) band of longitude between 20 degrees east of Greenwich and 20 degrees west of Greenwich can see the UK at apogee. The result of this can be summarised by saying that during 1989 and 1990 only one orbital apogee in nine will be visible and usable in the UK. So during 1989 and 1990 Oscar 10 mode B users should concentrate on perigee operations. Fig 6.30a and b show examples of the best possible apogee conditions available on these southern orbits in 1989/1990 and again in 1993/1994, if we are lucky enough to have Oscar 10 survive that long.

Operating Oscar 10 in mode B in 1991/1992

By 1991, if Oscar 10 is still operational, it will be starting to have orbital apogee in the northern hemisphere. From the viewpoint of UK operators this will once again place nearly all the world except New Zealand back in the Oscar 10 footprint at some time or another. Figs 6.30c-e show the apogee situation which will prevail through 1991 and 1992. At these times UK operators should experience the best possible operating conditions with the satellite moving slowly at apogee, whilst it provides communications to nearly half the world at any one time.

Frequencies used by Oscar 10 from 1987 onwards

Oscar 10 cannot be controlled by ground command, so it is stuck in mode B. The frequencies for this mode are shown

a: Minimum footprint west of UK – southerly apogee Jan 1990

b: Minimum footprint east of UK – southerly apogee Jan 1990

c: Optimum footprint west of UK – northerly apogee Jan 1992

d: Optimum footprint when apogee is nearest to UK about Jan 1992

e: Optimum footprint east of UK – northerly apogee Jan 1992

Fig 6.30a-e: Oscar 10 footprints

in Fig 6.31. Please note that, although a beacon frequency is shown, you will only hear a CW carrier on this frequency. The dead computer is not providing any telemetry keying to the Oscar 10 beacon.

Operating techniques on Oscar 10 post 1987

The first requirement is to find out whether Oscar 10 is available for use. If it has not been getting enough sunshine, it will not be providing sufficient volts to power its beacon. So if you cannot hear the beacon, you should not expect to use the communications transponder. As sunlight returns to the solar cells the satellite comes out of hibernation only slowly, with the first sign usually being the appearance of a weak and watery beacon, usually unstable in frequency. Then quite rapidly this situation can change with the beacon becoming a firm note. At this point you may find the transponder available for communications.

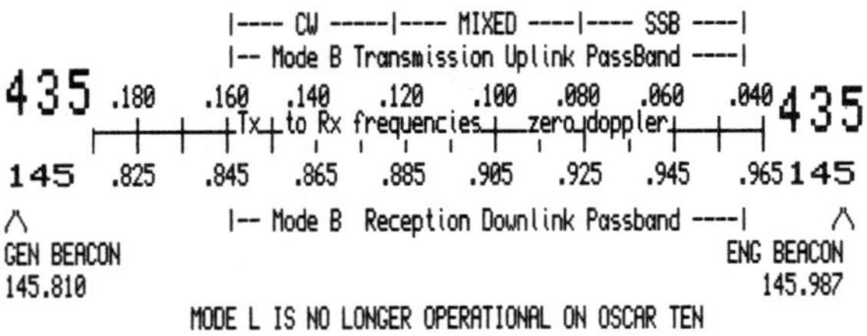

Fig 6.31: Oscar 10 Mode B bandplan

Always check the latest Amsat nets for up-to-date Oscar 10 information. Then, if you find Oscar 10 is on at a time reported to be a good time to use it, you can go ahead and enjoy its excellent communication facilities which remain almost totally unaffected by the damage to its computer. You should of course cease using the satellite immediately if the beacon begins to flutter or FM.

Tracking Oscar 10

The computer printout for an Oscar 10 track near the UK in July 1989 is shown in Table 6.11. This is a typical northern hemisphere pass just after perigee. Please note the rapid change in satellite azimuth bearing shortly after perigee. That this is just after perigee is revealed by the left-hand column Ma for orbital mean anomaly in units of 256, where Ma 0 or Ma 256 represents perigee, and Ma 128 would represent the apogee of the orbit. With an Ma of 10 at 0545, the satellite has just come through perigee, and it is starting to increase its altitude with respect to the Earth. Note also that the satellite sub-point latitude (Lat column) is heading rapidly south as the satellite disappears into the southern hemisphere. As this disappearance occurs at 0700 the satellite azimuth bearing is already steadying up and changing much more slowly as the satellite begins its slow climb up to apogee, by which time (about 1115 UTC) the satellite will be deep down in the southern hemisphere and well out of sight of the UK.

To get this tracking table the computer had to use software which contained relatively up-to-date Keplerian orbital elements:

Epoch time	89 7.83992758
Inclination	26.7859 degrees
RA of ascending node	286.2278 degrees
Eccentricity	0.6050471
Argument of perigee	7.3774 degrees
Mean anomaly	358.5347 degrees
Mean motion	2.051881846 revs per day

Please note that the mean anomaly in these Keplerian orbital elements is given in degrees. This must not be confused with the mean anomaly Ma reported in Table 6.11. The computer table is mean anomaly by 256 parts of time per orbit, a very different thing from Keplerian mean anomaly. Note also the eccentricity of 0.6, much higher for this elliptical orbit than the typical 0.002 of a near-circular low Earth orbiter such as Uosat.

Table 6.11: Oscar 10 computer track prediction

Oscar Ten on 1/7/89

UTC	AZ	EL	Lat	Long	Htkms	Sq	Ma
0545	155	32	24	348	6667		10
0600	133	23	18	330	9208		15
0615	125	16	12	320	11857		21
0630	121	11	8	314	14429		26
0645	119	7	4	310	16854		32
0700	119	5	1	307	19110		37
0715	119	3	-2	305	21194		43
0730	119	1	-4	305	23109		48
0745	120	0	-7	304	24861		54
0800	121	-1	-8	304	26460		59
0815	122	-2	-10	305	27910		65
0830	123	-3	-11	305	29218		70
0845	124	-3	-13	306	30391		76
0900	126	-3	-14	307	31433		81
0915	127	-4	-15	308	32348		87
0930	129	-4	-16	309	33140		92

First letter or sector letter ? P

The Keplerian parameters of Oscar 10 do not vary greatly in the long term, although there is a slight biannual variation due to lunar and solar gravitational attraction which causes short-term perturbation of the height of the satellite at apogee and perigee. Argument of perigee does change slowly but even this does not normally require renewal of the Keplerian orbital elements, because most computer programs can calculate how to allow for change in argument of perigee (which is highly predictable). So most Oscar 10 Keplerian orbital elements are useful for at least six months and perhaps up to one year.

Software for tracking Oscar 10 from the usual sources is listed in appendix 1.

Part 2 – history of Oscar 10

These historical notes are reported so that we may profit by our mistakes. In no way are they intended to criticise anyone. Indeed, these notes show how the builders and controllers of Oscar 10 have succeeded, in spite of appalling bad luck, and difficult and trying circumstances.

Oscar 10 was launched on 16 June 1983, and was delivered to a geostationary transfer orbit before separating successfully from its launch rocket. At the point of release the satellite was in an elliptical orbit with a perigee of 190km and an apogee high point of 36,000km.

Before Oscar 10 could get clear of the parent rocket, the rocket was told to jettison excess fuel, a procedure which promptly sent the rocket on a collision course with Oscar 10. As a result of this collision, Oscar 10 was flipped over on its back and spun in the wrong direction.

Unfortunately all systems in Oscar 10 were switched on in anticipation of ground commands, but the satellite was now on its back with no sunlight reaching its solar panels, and spinning in an uncontrolled fashion. At the same time the Oscar 10 battery was being rapidly discharged with no hope of any recharge until the satellite could be realigned to allow its solar panels to see the Sun. In fact Oscar 10 was within an hour or two of complete loss, noting that any further drain of its battery would have so depleted its receiver supply voltage that all chance of getting it to accept ground commands would have been lost.

Oscar 10 was rescued by the prompt action of the West German radio amateur control team, who immediately commanded it to switch off everything and use what little sunlight it was seeing to charge its batteries.

After several anxious days the battery voltage began to recover, and this was allowed to continue for several more days before the first attempts were made to turn and realign the satellite in space by energising the satellite's magnetic torquing system, whereby current is fed through coils in the satellite and the magnetic field thus created interacts with the Earth's magnetic field to produce a turning thrust on the satellite.

Each day thereafter, as the satellite slowly turned to face the Sun, it built up its battery charge which was then used for stronger and stronger magnetic torquing manoeuvres. Eventually the satellite was showing most of its solar panels to the Sun. Having thus solved the first problem, the next problem was the wrong-way spin imparted by the collision. Examination of the satellite spin characteristics suggested that it would be too dangerous to attempt to correct the direction of spin, because this would necessitate going through a no-spin condition, when the satellite could flop over on its back again, as it lost spin-generated stability. With this in mind, therefore, the magneto torquing was used to increase the existing spin, accepting that spin in the wrong direction caused few problems and involved least risk.

The spin-up was completely successful and so the controllers were then able to consider proceeding with the normal elliptical-orbit insertion programme. Oscar 10 was in an elliptical orbit, but it was one with a low inclination angle of about 11 degrees, and it had a perigee of only 190km, which meant that twice a day the satellite was being slowed up by atmospheric drag. The plan was to proceed in two stages. First, to fire the satellite kick motor for a very brief controlled burn aimed at bringing the perigee up near 1,500km then, once this was accomplished, the satellite would be reoriented in space so that a second firing of its kick motor could be used to lift the satellite orbital inclination to as near 60 degrees as was possible with the remaining kick motor fuel. This would have placed the satellite in a high-inclination, high-apogee elliptical orbit well clear of the Van Allen belt.

Unfortunately this did not happen. The satellite was placed in the correct orientation for the first perigee correction kick motor burn. The burn was started, but when the time came to terminate the burn, the satellite did not obey the terminate burn command.

Several explanations have been offered for this but the most likely one is that there was a wiring harness mistake in the 'stop firing' line. This is borne out by the fact that the one long burn drove the satellite up to 27 degrees of orbital inclination and a perigee height of 3,900km. This evidence alone discounts any suggestion about motor damage consequent on the earlier collision. The motor got it right and provided all the thrust that could be expected from the amount of onboard fuel. Unfortunately it was uncontrolled thrust in the wrong direction.

The end result of all this was that Oscar 10 was placed in an orbit which was satisfactory for communications in the short term but which had two important long-term defects. First, the high perigee and low orbital inclination meant that Oscar 10 would suffer fierce radiation problems as its orbit took it through the worst parts of the Van Allen belts twice each day. Second, the low inclination meant that the perturbation of the argument of perigee would be large, bringing with it the hidden extra that the satellite would become a wanderer with the apogee of its orbit flapping up and down across the equator in the north for two years then down in the south for two years, an uncomfortable prospect for northern hemisphere users (Fig 6.29 refers).

Time was to prove that the radiation belt problem was the more serious. The satellite performed superbly on its mode B communications transponder (although the mode L transponder was severely limited by a circuit failure early in the life of the satellite), but after two years of heavy use the satellite drifted further south, becoming of limited use to UK operators.

This is not to say that there were no other problems with Oscar 10, there were in fact several which will be of great importance if further satellites of this type are built. It is therefore proposed to review these problems first before following Oscar 10 into the southern hemisphere.

Oscar 10 operating problems

During 1984, discussions on Oscar 10 often included stations on three continents. As the satellite rode high in the northern sky, its sub-satellite track point coincided with its furthest north at 27°N latitude. Figs 6.30c-e show this situation. The diagrams are labelled for 1992 but this was also the situation that applied in 1984 when the satellite was working well.

Gradually the satellite's performance deteriorated. Oscar 10 has a power output of nearly 50 watts on mode B, nearly 1 watt for each of 50 consecutive conversations, but at apogee the satellite is 36,000km from the Earth, so some satellite antenna gain is necessary. To get this gain Oscar 10 antennas had to be directional, and they must point at Earth from the important apogee section of the orbit. However, closer to Earth in the orbit, the path length was much less, so less antenna gain was needed and the antennas need not point exactly at the Earth.

To maintain a stable pointing axis for its antennas, the Oscar 10 satellite had to spin like a top, at about 30 revolutions each minute, and this added a further complication to the antenna array, whereby with the antennas spread around the satellite body, any asymmetry was exaggerated by the spin. The solution used with Oscar 10 was to circular

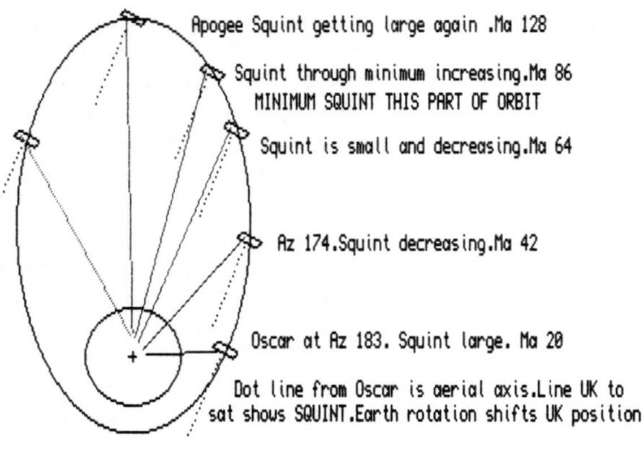

Fig 6.32: Oscar 10 station line-of-sight squint versus antenna pointing

polarise the antenna arrays so that in theory the signal was spun at a far higher rate than the antennas. Ground trials suggested that this compromise worked and smoothed out the worst excesses of spin modulation caused by less than ideally balanced antenna lobes.

This was a good idea provided Oscar 10 reached its designed orbit. With 50 degrees or so of inclination, the orbit would have kept the apogee over the northern hemisphere for several years, with a good Sun illumination angle for the solar panels, whilst the directional antennas on the spinning satellite pointed down at the Earth from apogee.

Unfortunately Oscar 10 did not achieve its designed orbit. Instead it languished near the equator at an inclination of only 27 degrees and even this began to change quickly as perturbation of the low-inclination orbit quickly drove apogee down into the southern hemisphere. At this point a conflict began, whereby in order to get a good Sun angle in order to keep the satellite's battery fully charged, the satellite antennas were being pointed further and further away from the Earth at apogee.

Fig 6.32 shows the effect this had, producing a situation whereby, for much of its orbit, there was a pronounced squint-angle difference between the satellite antenna pointing angle and the line of sight from the satellite down to the Earth. Some stations began using high power on their up link to offset this loss of performance, but this was exactly the wrong thing to do, because the real problem was in fact much more subtle than these amateurs appreciated.

Fig 6.33 shows one of the real roots of the original problem – namely that because the satellite antenna was no longer looking at the Earth, terrestrial stations were so far off the antenna axis that they no longer had the designed right-hand circular polarised signal. Oscar 10 uses three coplanar antennas spaced around the satellite body, which are mutually connected via a phasing loop, which, in step with their physical separation, adds up to produce a circular polarised signal along the line of sight of the antenna. If Oscar 10 is no longer pointing at the Earth, the apparent physical separation of the separate antenna elements with respect to the line of sight to the Earth is changed. So the phasing is no longer correct for circular polarisation, indeed the greater the squint becomes the more likely it is that the received signal on the ground will have exactly the opposite polarisation to that intended by the designers. Thirty degrees off-axis, the squint does in fact produce a reversal of polarisation, causing ground stations using the designed circular polarisation to lose another 9dB of signal gain due to the polarisation mismatch. When combined with a spin modulation effect due to antenna irregularities and a receiver gain kicking effect, generated every satellite revolution by amateurs using high-power linearly polarised antennas, the results are devastating.

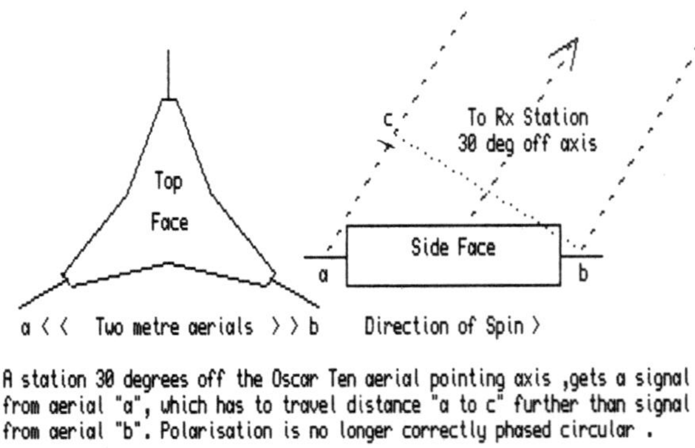

Fig 6.33: Oscar 10 off-axis, non-circular signal polarisation

Fortunately most operators behaved sensibly. Several stayed in touch with Oscar 10 by building antennas with switchable circular polarisation, so that the operator could match the vagaries caused by the satellite antenna design. The computer tracking program shown in the Oscar 13 section of this chapter also assisted in this antenna polarisation matching by calculating squint angle so that operator could become accustomed to which form of polarised switching worked best at which squint angle. But even this was not the complete answer because in addition to its polarisation irregularities the Oscar 10 antenna also produced a much weaker signal off-axis. Here again the radio amateur got the better of the situation by resorting to the use of sensitive low-noise GaAsFET preamplifiers up on their antenna masts, a trick which more or less succeeded in compensating for much of the antennas' design problem losses.

Throughout this period the 'alligators' (all mouth and no brain) refused to budge, using high power and paying no attention to low-noise preamplifiers or polarisation switching. These operators could hear their own signals, but they drove everyone else off the satellite whenever they appeared. Fig 6.34 shows some of the oscilloscope traces recorded by the author during this period. The top trace corresponds to reception of Oscar 10 145.810MHz beacon sending PSK from a position corresponding to mean anomaly Ma 30 on the orbit chart shown in Fig 6.32 (mean anomaly 30 is about halfway between Ma 20 and Ma 42 as shown on this diagram).

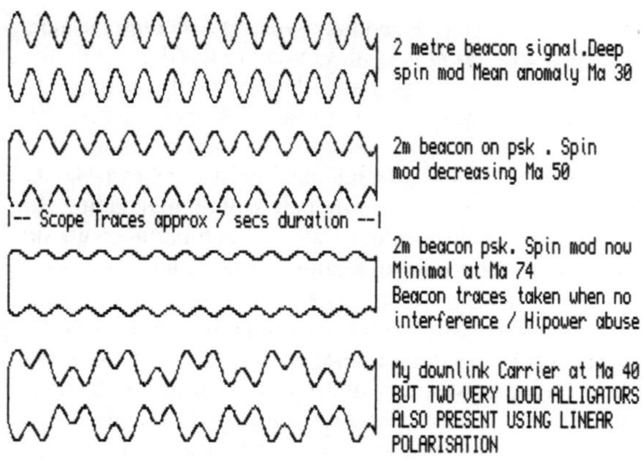

Fig 6.34: Oscar 10 spin modulation varying with squint angle/mean anomaly

As the top record of Fig 6.34 shows, the 145.810MHz antenna on Oscar 10 produced amplitude modulation of the beacon signal which had three peaks for each spin revolution of the satellite (one peak for each element of the antenna as shown in Fig 6.33. There are 13 peaks on this record in just seven seconds of recorded time, so the satellite spin at the time was about 37 revs per minute. The next record on Fig 6.34 shows the spin modulation to be much reduced, and by the third record, the spin modulation has almost disappeared. Indeed, at the part of the orbit where the third record was taken the satellite's antenna was briefly pointing almost directly at the Earth. Thereafter, as the satellite climbed towards apogee, the oscilloscope records of spin modulation showed a gradual return to the deep spin modulation shown in the top recording.

Trying to communicate with Oscar 10 at these times was more difficult than the simple beacon oscilloscope records suggest. The bottom record of Fig 6.34 shows what happened when the author put a simple constant carrier signal into Oscar 10 via the 435MHz up link. The result is far worse than anything heard on the beacon, because the carrier had first to access the satellite from a position off the axis of its 435MHz receiving antenna, before putting the up linked carrier on to the satellite transponder, which then fed the 145MHz satellite antenna to send the signal back to Earth via a path off the axis of the satellite's 145MHz down link antenna. To make matters worse, it was not possible to find a moment when the satellite was not being abused by high-powered 'alligators'. In one case, an 'alligator' was using linearly polarised antennas which put a signal into the satellite which varied with satellite spin, alternately depressing the auto gain control on the satellite receiver one half second, then allowing it to recover the next half second. This produced a sort of pumping effect which can be seen on the bottom record of Fig 6.47, whereby what should have been a flat-topped RF signal was turned into a distorted jumble. Readers will appreciate that if it did this to a simple carrier-only signal, the effect on a modulated speech signal was an absolute disaster.

As Oscar 10's orbit slipped south in 1985 these effects were multiplied by the increasingly poor path to the UK from the satellite. So the author and a lot of other Oscar 10 users decided to give it a rest, in the hope that when it returned from the southern hemisphere in 1987 it would be in good working order. Unfortunately this did not happen. Long before Oscar 10 returned north it became clear that the memory of the onboard computer was rapidly being destroyed.

The new problem was of course due to radiation damage. The low inclination of the Oscar 10 orbit, coupled with its high altitude perigee, had meant that during its trip south, then back north again, Oscar 10 had orbited for long periods in the most intensely active parts of the Van Allen belts. Unprotected computer microchips have a susceptibility to radiation damage close to that of human flesh and blood. At a minimal estimate Oscar 10 had been subject to more than four times the fatal human dose.

This radiation damage was almost critical. Oscar 10 did not die, but it lost control of all its vital functions, as a human being may do when he or she suffers a serious stroke. From that moment, ground control of Oscar 10 ceased to be effective, and the satellite can no longer be controlled to align itself so that it sees a lot of sunshine and gets a good battery charge. Indeed, as the sunlight on its solar panels gradually reduced in the autumn of 1986, it became obvious that Oscar 10 would not have the necessary basic voltage to keep any of its systems alive. Many observers assumed this would be fatal.

In fact Oscar 10 did go into hibernation but, as the eclipse period ended, it began to collect more and more sunlight each day. It slowly recharged its battery, and its transponder and beacon came back to life, such that by May 1987 Amsat was able to announce that Oscar 10 was open for limited low-power use, subject to the observation of some strict rules. These rules are:

The satellite is mindless. It cannot be controlled. So if its antennas are pointing at the Earth, we are lucky. If they are not, there is nothing we can do about it. It is at present stuck in mode B 435MHz up, 145MHz down, and it is unlikely to change from that mode. It is uncertain which of the satellite's antennas are connected. It may be using directional antennas. It may have reverted to one or both (145MHz and/or 435MHz) of its perigee omnidirectional antennas.

There is no way to point the satellite's solar panels at the Sun. Seasonal changes of solar azimuth and elevation plus Oscar 10 orbit changes will probably put it into Earth shadow for long periods each orbit, every day for several weeks, with this cycle repeating twice or three times each year. At these times it will be non-operational. The satellite can no longer tell us where it is pointing. So tests such as those shown in Fig 6.34 have to be used to find when spin modulation and other effects are least, indicating that it is pointing roughly towards your station. Because Oscar 10 cannot be switched on or off, you may hear it when its battery/solar cell output volts are low, and it would be dangerous to its health to strain its supplies by using it.

Amsat NA, Amsat UK and RSGB bulletins and packet bulletins issue regular guidance to would-be Oscar 10 users. They will tell you whether the satellite is available for use or not. Because you hear someone else using it, does not mean it is safe to use it. Please check the news and bulletin sources first. Last, but not least, never use high power to access Oscar 10. Please discourage high-power users by ignoring them.

Obey these rules and Oscar 10 may last for a long time, but whatever happens this writer will remember it with affection and be grateful to those who built it, and have controlled and cosseted it through all these vicissitudes. Old soldiers never die. Hopefully Oscar 10 may yet survive to be a very old soldier, but it has to be said that the state of its batteries is giving cause for concern.

Oscar 13 – a high-altitude elliptical orbiter

Introduction

Those who listened to the broadcast commentary of the launch of Phase IIIC Oscar 13, on 15 June 1988, could be excused for being slightly worried. Oscar 13 was the third attempt by amateur radio to orbit a Phase III-type elliptical orbiter. Attempt number one had failed when the Phase IIIA launcher, complete with its satellite cargo, plunged into the south Atlantic in May 1980. Attempt number two put the Phase IIIB satellite Oscar 10 into orbit, but left it stranded in a less-than-perfect equatorial ellipse. Now it was the turn of Phase IIIC.

Fortunately Phase IIIC did much better than its predecessors. The delivery to a geostationary transfer orbit was flawless, and the Amsat DL controllers were able to use the magneto torquing to spin the satellite up to about 30rpm, which made it safe and stable, and allowed it to be aligned for its first kick motor burn. This first step from the transfer orbit was designed to lift the satellite's perigee clear of the thick atmosphere around 225km, increasing it by perhaps 1,000km.

This manoeuvre was slightly uncertain because it was not possible until then to test the fuel flow of the motor, and the rate of flow was a little uncertain.

On 22 June 1988 this first burn was successfully completed, although the efficiency of fuel supply was unexpectedly high, and the burn was 115% effective. Then the satellite was carefully checked for several days before being spun up to nearly 60rpm, to get good fuel flow for the second motor firing. This second firing of the kick motor took place on 6 July 1988 and it placed Oscar 13 in a useful orbit with an inclination of about 57 degrees and a perigee height of 2,459km. All things considered this was an excellent result for, although the high perigee will mean that the satellite could receive a higher radiation dose rate, the 57 degree inclination means that for several years the perigee will occur over or near latitude 57°S, where the Van Allen belt radiation is much reduced as compared with regions nearer the equator.

Oscar 13's orbit

When Oscar 13 was launched, several writers described it as having a molniya-type orbit. This is very misleading. Fig 6.35 shows the true state of affairs, comparing both side views and face views of a molniya orbit and Oscar 13's orbit.

A molniya orbit has a precise orbital inclination of 62.99 degrees, and perigee and apogee heights of 586 and 39,759km respectively, producing a high elliptical orbit which repeats the same track day after day, keeping its apogee always above latitude 62.99 degrees north because its argument of perigee is tailored to be exactly 270 degrees. In this true molniya orbit a great deal of time, trouble and fuel is used to achieve this precise orbit. This is good news if your satellite is intended for use by stations at high northern latitudes, but is quite bad news if communications with southern hemisphere stations are part of your plan.

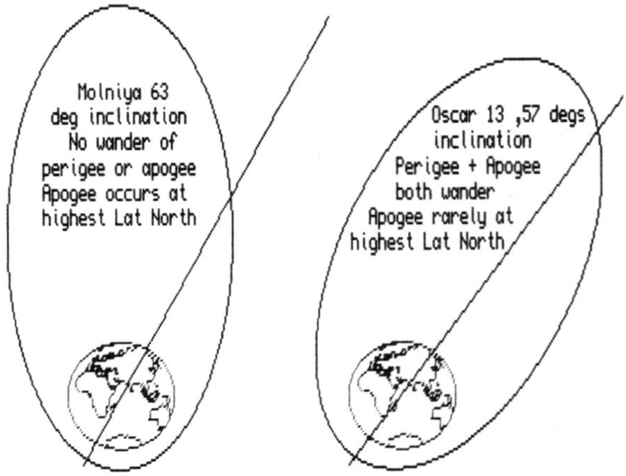

Fig 6.35: Differences between Oscar 13's orbit and a molniya orbit

Oscar 13 is not in a pure molniya orbit for two reasons. First, as mentioned, Oscar users want opportunities for communications to and from southern hemisphere stations. Second, getting argument of perigee at exactly 270 degrees takes fuel which simply was not available in the small launch package. So Oscar 13 entered its final orbit with an inclination of 57 degrees and an argument of perigee of 187 degrees, which results in slow perturbation of the satellite's argument of perigee and hence its apogee sub-point latitude as shown in Fig 6.36. In this orbit Oscar 13 will favour northern hemisphere stations in the period 1991-93 but thereafter it will gradually improve its apogee performance and availability with respect to southern hemisphere stations.

As Fig 6.36 shows, Oscar 13's apogee does not occur at a constant northern sub-point latitude. It drifts from around

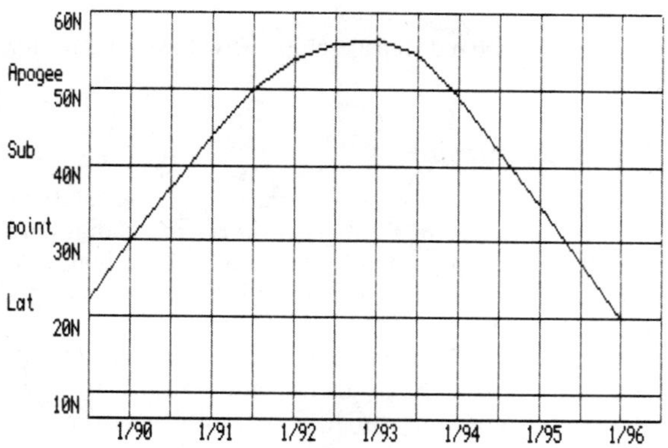

Fig 6.36: Plot of Oscar 13 change of apogee sub-latitude against time

22°N in July 1989 to near 57°N from July 1992 to July 1993, then by January 1996 it will have dropped down again to 20°N, carrying on further south each year thereafter for several more years.

Who can be heard on Oscar 13?

Almost all the world except New Zealand was accessible from the UK during 1989 and 1990, but by 1991 southern hemisphere stations on the other side of the world from the UK will rarely be accessible from it. None the less, southern stations in the Atlantic hemisphere (South America and South Africa) will continue to be accessible from the UK in 1991 to 1994, albeit not at apogee but at times before and after apogee, as the satellite rises from, or falls back to, its southern hemisphere perigee.

Figs 6.37a and b show footprint snapshots of typical Oscar 13 situations in 1990, and Figs 6.37c and d show the changes which will have occurred by 1992/99, due to the more northerly apogee sub-point. By 1994 the situation will revert to that shown in Figs 6.37a and b as the satellite apogee starts to become less northerly, and this situation will apply until about 1996, when the southerly progression of the apogee subpoint can be expected to sharply affect the number of hours per day that Oscar 13 is available to UK operators.

Where and when can Oscar 13 be used for communications?

Because of its relatively high northern latitude at apogee in 1990, Oscar 13 can see the UK on the orbit when it is above the Atlantic hemisphere, and roughly 11 hours later it can see the UK again whilst the satellite is high above the Pacific hemisphere. Above the Pacific, on the other side of the world, Oscar 13 sees the UK over the North Pole, an effect which becomes even more marked as we approach the maximum northern apogees of 1992 and 1993.

As shown in Fig 6.37a, Oscar 13 could not quite see the UK from its Pacific apogee in 1989/90 but, shortly after apogee on Pacific orbits in those years, its satellite sub-point climbed high enough in latitude whilst its orbital height only decreased a few hundred kilometres below its apogee maximum, and it then saw the UK over the Pole. By 1992 this situation changes with the apogee sub-point being high enough in Pacific latitude to see the UK on every Pacific side orbit.

So, from 1989 onwards, UK operators saw some parts of both of Oscar 13's two orbits per day. In July 1989 the UK had Oscar 13 above its horizon twice per day, giving a typical 3 hours 30 minutes plus 9 hours for a 12 hours 30 minutes total of Oscar 13 opportunities. By July 1993 this double window of Oscar 13 use will have increased in duration to a typical 7 hours 30 minutes plus 9 hours 45 minutes for a total in one day of 17 hours 15 minutes when Oscar 13 is in range of the UK. Then, as can be expected by January 1996, the Oscar 13 viewing time has dropped back to a total of about 12 hours per day and shortly thereafter UK operators will begin to find that they can only access one of the two Oscar 13 orbits in each day, with orbits on the Pacific side of the world never coming above the UK horizon.

It is therefore clear that, if Oscar 13 continues to operate effectively, UK operators can expect excellent near-worldwide communications coverage until at least 1996.

Oscar 13 radio frequencies

Fig 6.38a shows the bandplan for Oscar 13 mode B and mode L. These two modes are never used concurrently. Usually, as mode B goes off, mode L comes on, stays on for a few hours, then mode L goes off and mode B comes back on again. Periods when the satellite is near apogee are preferred for mode L.

Fig 6.38b shows the bandplan for Oscar 13 mode J. This mode is licensed for use in the UK, but care is necessary, particularly if you live in the south of England near a big city. You must listen before transmitting on the 144MHz up link, to make sure you are not going to interfere with meteor scatter stations and other specialist users. The rule is that mode J operators move to keep clear of terrestrial users. Outside of the south of England, the mode J up link part of the 144MHz band is almost totally empty at all times, so operating can be more relaxed, although a good listen around before you transmit is a common courtesy. Mode J is usually on when mode L is on, ie around apogee.

Fig 6.38c shows the bandplans for Oscar 13 mode S and for the Oscar 13 Rudak message system. Mode S is usually activated when the satellite is near its apogee. Rudak has unfortunately had a number of problems and it is by no means certain that it will ever be operational.

Tracking Oscar 13

A specimen computer track printout for Oscar 13 is shown in Table 6.12. Note particularly the next-to-last column, reporting squint angle. Much of the software available for microcomputer prediction of Oscar 10 tracking works extremely well if used with Oscar 13. One exception to this has

a: After apogee 34°N 246°W 1300 UTC 1 July 1989

b: Apogee 22°N 43°W July 1989 at 2245 UTC

c: Apogee 57°N 125°W 1 Jan 1993 at 1045 UTC

d: Apogee 56°N 297°W 1 Jan 1993 at 2215 UTC

Fig 6.37a-d: Oscar 13 footprints

been Amsat NA software where attempts to use it on Oscar 13 hang up on the calculation of eccentric anomaly. This problem has been corrected in all new Amsat NA software since late 1988. Software for Oscar 13 is available from the addresses given in appendix 1.

A typical set of Keplerian orbital elements for Oscar 13 is:

Epoch time	89 001.64745422
Inclination	57.3549 degrees
RA of node	225.5808 degrees
Eccentricity	0.6633630
Arg of perigee	196.4008 degrees
Mean anomaly	122.2160 degrees
Mean motion	2.09689954 revs per day

Details of up-to-date Keplerian elements are available from the usual sources. See appendix 1. In addition the Amsat North America Sunday net relays Keplerian elements off Oscar 13 itself using mode B or mode L.

Table 6.12: Oscar 13 track predictions

Oscar 13 on 1/7/89

UTC	AZ	EL	Lat	Long	Htkms	Sq	Ma
1200	45	-4	27	236	35454		148
1215	46	-2	29	238	34958		154
1230	47	1	30	240	34340	12	160
1245	47	3	32	242	33597	15	165
1300	48	5	34	244	32728	17	171
1315	48	7	36	245	31726	19	176
1330	48	9	38	247	30589	23	182
1345	47	11	41	248	29309	26	187
1400	46	13	43	248	27881	29	193
1415	45	15	45	248	26296	33	199
1430	43	16	48	248	24545	38	204
1445	40	16	50	246	22618	43	210
1500	37	16	53	243	20502	49	215
1515	32	15	55	237	18184	57	221
1530	26	13	57	228	15654	66	227
1545	18	7	57	214	12905	78	232

First letter or sector letter ? P

Operating Oscar 13 – telemetry

The Oscar 13 beacons on 145.812 and 435.650MHz carry continuous telemetry in several formats.

On the hour and the half hour there is a simple CW morse code bulletin giving up to date news, eg on 21 February 1989 it was saying 'please do not use Oscar 10'.

On the quarter hour and the three-quarter hour, Oscar 13 sends RTTY telemetry. USB is the correct reception mode.

In between the CW and the RTTY, Oscar 13 sends 400 baud BPSK telemetry. Suitable PCBs and advice for building modems to allow this telemetry to be decoded by your computer are available from Amsat UK.

Oscar 13 automatic telegraphy BPSK features both bulletins and a complete block of satellite system and environment status checks. The decoding table for this telemetry is shown in Table 6.13.

Operating on Oscar 13 – mode B

It was originally hoped that it would be possible to operate on Oscar 13 mode B using about 50 watts of transmitter power output on 435MHz, feeding a cable with about 2dB of loss which was attached to an antenna with about 16dB of gain versus a dipole, eg a right-hand circular-polarised helix or a 12 by 12 element XY crossed-Yagi connected for right-hand circular polarisation. For reception a right-hand circular helix (or more practical at 145MHz – a 10 or 12 element XY crossed-Yagi antenna connected RHC) with a gain of about 13dB would feed a Mutek low-noise GaAsFET preamplifier connected directly to the antenna, from which a feeder would run in to the station 145MHz receiver. In fact neither of these combinations has proved completely effective.

There are two main reasons for this lack of mode B performance on Oscar 13. First, the mode B option is never

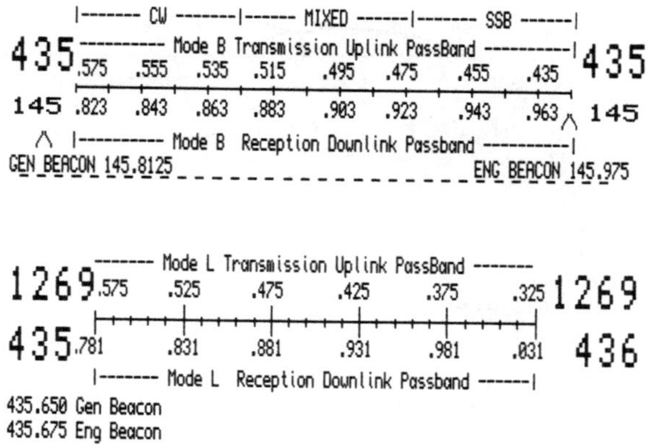

a: Modes B and L

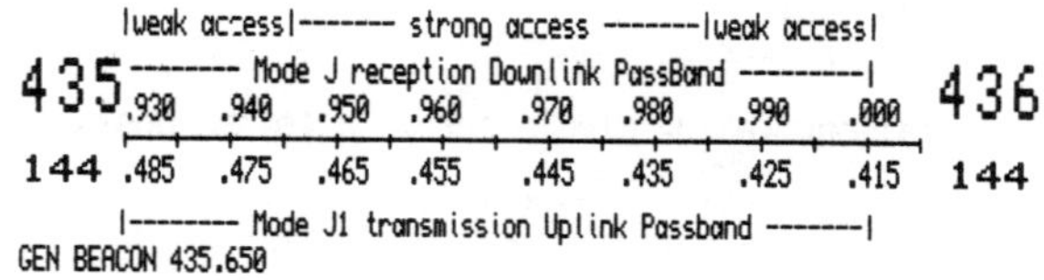

b: Mode J1

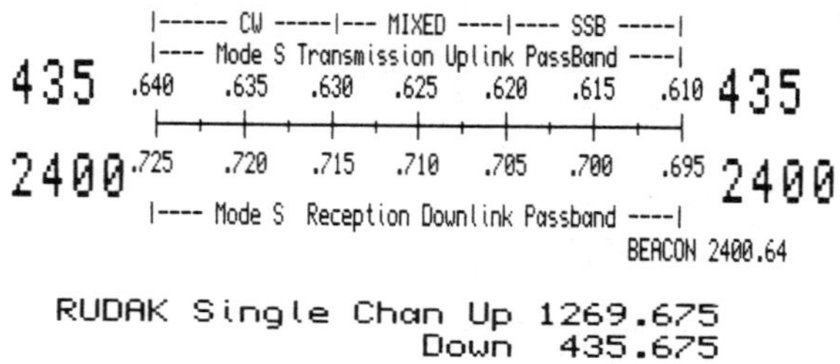

c: 13S and Rudak

Figs 6.38a-c: Oscar 13 band plans

on at apogee or when the antennas of Oscar 13 are pointing directly at the Earth. Mode B has taken second place in this respect because mode L is even more insensitive at large squint angles than mode B. So mode L is usually the mode on at apogee, with mode B on at the less favourable parts of the orbit, away from apogee.

The second reason is that the mode B down link is noisy and suffers badly from spin modulation. This means that the listener hears the down link noise and signals going up and down about 90 times per minute as the satellite spins at about 30rpm, producing a 90-element spin modulation pattern from its asymmetrical three-element 145MHz down link antenna.

Some of the blame for this spin modulation and asymmetry has been laid on the designer who added an S band antenna in the RF field of the two metre down link antenna shortly before the satellite was launched. However, like Oscar 10, Oscar 13 seems to suffer most from the fact that the three-element 145MHz down link antenna has a less

Table 6.13: Decoding table for Oscar 13 telemetry

Ch	Function	Decode	eg n =	result units
00	Solar panel out BCR in	(n–10)*167	245	39,245mV
01	70cm TX mean power	(261–n)/1724	7	36W
02	70cm receiver temp	(n–120)/1.71	147	15.8C
03	Reserved			
04	BCR out and main battery volts	(n–10)*79.5	192	14,469mV
05	Special purpose			
06	2m TX power amp temp	(n–120)/1.71	138	10.5C
07	+14V rail amps to transp	(n–15)*24.27	48	800.9mA
08	+10V regulator	(n–10)*53.2	200	10,108mV
09	Helium tank hi pressure	(n–14)*6.56	126	734.7bar
0A	IHU temperature	(n–120)/1.71	137	9.9°C
0B	+14V amps to magtorque etc	(n–15)*4.854	15	0mA
0C	BCR oscillator #1 status	0=OFF, n>10=ON	96	ON
0D	He tank lo side pressure v	(n–15)*117	134	13.923bar
0E	BCR temperature	(n–120)/1.71	143	13.4°C
0F	+10V regulator amps	(n–15)*4.854	47	155.33mA
10	BCR oscillator #2 status	0=OFF, n>10=ON	7	OFF
11	N2O2 tank pressure	(n–106)*0.733	143	7.12bar
12	SEU temperature	(n–120)/1.71	138	10.5°C
13	Battery charge current	(n–15)*12.135	7	0mA
14	Top +Z Sun sensor	(n–10)*8.53	14	34.12mV
15	Motor valve status	102=Closed, 118=Open	99	Closed
16	Aux Battery #1 temp	(n–120)/1.71	136	9.4°C
17	Active BCR output amps	(n–15)*24.27	56	995.07mA
18	Bottom –Z Sun sensor	(n–10)*8.53	7	0mA
19	not allocated			
1A	Battery #2 temperature	(n–120)/1.71	135	8.8°C
1B	Active BCR 28V bus input amps	(n–15)*12.135	7	0mA
1C	Spin rate	n<139 (131–n)*0.85+20 n>=139 479/(n–109)–2	116	32.75
1D	Mode L receiver AGC	((n–75)^2)/–1125	7	0dB
1E	Main battery temperature	(n–120)/1.71	137	9.9°C
1F	Solar panel #6 current	(n–15)*4.854	7	0mA
20	2m TX mean power out	((287–n)^2)/1796	206	3.653W
21	He tank temperature	(n–120)/1.71	136	9.4°C
22	Solar panel #1 temp	(n–120)/1.71	134	8.2°C
23	Solar panel #5 current	(n–15)*4.854	7	0mA
24	70cm receiver AGC	((n–71)^2)/2465	69	0dB
25	70cm TX PA temp	(n–120)/1.71	131	6.4°C
26	Solar panel #3 temp	(n–120)/1.71	138	10.5°C
27	Solar panel #4 current	(n–15)*4.854	35	97.08mA
28	Special purpose			
29	24cm receiver temp	(n–120)/1.71	140	11.7°C
2A	Solar panel #5 temp	(n–120)/1.71	138	10.5°C
2B	Solar panel #3 current	(n–15)*4.854	7	0mA
2C	+14V regulator	(n–10)*66.8	226	14,429mV
2D	Rudak temp	(n–120)/1.71	137	9.9°C
2E	Top +Z skin temp arm #1	(n–120)/1.71	129	5.3°C
2F	Solar panel #2 current	(n–15)*4.854	7	0mA
30	Mode B transp 9V supply	(n–10)*54	178	9,072mV
31	Wall temp arm #2	(n–120)/1.71	134	8.2°C
32	Bottom –Z skin temp arm #1	(n–120)/1.71	122	1.2°C
33	Solar panel #1 current	(n–15)*4.854	7	0mA
34	Special purpose			
35	Wall temp arm #1	(n–120)/1.71	133	7.6°C
36	N2O4 tank temp	(n–120)/1.71	137	9.9°C
37	Reserved			
38	Auxiliary battery voltage	(n–10)*78.5	15	392.5mV
39	Mode S transp temp	(n–120)/1.71	122	1.2°C

than perfectly matched lobe pattern, and also suffers from loss of circularity of polarisation which becomes serious at squint angles greater than 15 degrees.

The end result of these mode B antenna problems is that users find that sometimes Oscar 13 is accessible with only about 1,500 watts eirp, but more often than not it needs at least twice this signal level, and sometimes it needs even more than that. Users of Oscar 13 have noted that it pays to try to use it when the squint angle between your line of sight to the satellite, versus the satellite's antenna pointing axis, is small. It is also clear that accessing Oscar 13 when it is east or south of your station is much easier than accessing it when it is west of your station. Several computer programs calculate squint angle for you, and this can be a good guide to Oscar 13 performance, in that the lower the squint angle the better the performance.

Despite these power and access problems Oscar 13B is the preferred mode for most users, because the combination of VHF/UHF antennas and transceivers is easy to assemble, although it must be said that getting 50 watts on 435MHz requires some expensive equipment. Mode B is open for users of morse code CW, RTTY, SSTV and upper sideband voice (you transmit lower sideband on your up link to get upper sideband on your down link).

Mode B is generally on before and after, but not during, apogee and it uses its high-gain directional antennas at these times. It is also sometimes on near perigee and at these times it may be commanded to switch to its omnidirectional antennas. In this omnidirectional antenna mode B format, whilst near the Earth at perigee, it is readily accessible by relatively low-power up links and it does not show the problems associated with use of the directional antennas discussed earlier.

A typical Oscar 13 schedule of mode switching is:

Mode B from mean anomaly by 256 Ma 3 until Ma 100

Mode JL from mean anomaly by 256 Ma 100 until Ma 150 (apogee Ma 128)

Mode B from mean anomaly by 256 Ma 150 until Ma 240

OFF from mean anomaly by 256 Ma 240 until Ma 3 (perigee Ma 0/256)

This was the operating schedule from February 1989 to 15 March 1989. Please note that in this instance the omnidirectional antennas were not indicated and the satellite was OFF around its orbital perigee.

Operating Oscar 13 – mode J

Oscar 13J is a delight to use. It is sensitive and gains enormously over mode B by being on around apogee. It can frequently be accessed by using 8 to 10 watts transmitter power feeding an 8 by 8 element 145MHz XY crossed Yagi connected for circular polarisation. Reception in the UK, using a 48-element multibeam with a Jamsat 435/28MHz converter connected directly to the antenna, produces a strong 28MHz signal from this low-noise convertor which is fed into the station receiver (a Yaesu FT 101E HF transceiver).

Stringent tests have been carried out to reveal whether breakthrough of the third harmonic of the 145MHz up link would desensitise the 435MHz down link, but no trace of desensitising has been found unless the antennas are deliberately pointed at the wall of an adjacent building. So it has not proved necessary to fit a tight 435MHz filter as protection for the convertor/receiver.

There is one problem which has nothing to do with electronics. The mode J up link band in the UK is licensed for satellite use, indeed it is licensed for miscellaneous use and is open to all licensed modes, but it has for some time been used by meteor scatter operators and operators of other specialised propagation modes. There is therefore a chance that if you live in the south of England in or near a big city you may find that you can hear meteor scatter or other signals in the Oscar 13J up link band. It is most unlikely that these signals will occupy all the up link band, and by careful listening before you transmit, you should find that you can easily keep clear of these other signals and ignore the effect they have on the satellite. The rule is: always move clear if you believe there is the least chance of causing interference. Any situation of this sort needs careful operating but with a modicum of care and attention from all users, there should be no problems. Outside the big cities these problems should not exist at all, and in preparing this chapter by operating on mode J for several months, this village-dwelling, Scottish farming-community type did not have one single incident where he heard terrestrial or meteor scatter signals in this band.

Fig 6.38b shows the mode J bandplan frequencies. Mode J is usually operated at the same time as mode L and, because mode L only works well near apogee at small squint angles, mode J, which is far less particular about squint angles, is available at the best possible time in the orbit. In addition to this reason for mode J's popularity, potential users need look no further than their bank account before picking mode J. The ordinary radio amateur usually starts with a shortwave receiver and a 2m transmitter/receiver, plus antennas. To get on mode J he or she need only add a 435MHz antenna and a 435/28MHz converter and suitable coaxial cables. By contrast, to get on mode B the operator needs to have access to 50 watts of 435MHz power which will leave little change from £800, plus the cost of a 435MHz antenna and cable, and a low-noise preamplifier for his 2m receiver. Mode L is even more expensive.

Because mode J and mode L are on at the same time and use the same down link frequency, mode J operators can talk to mode L operators at anytime using the same or adjacent down link frequencies, and mode J users can also listen to the full mode L band and monitor the 435MHz telemetry. An operating package which makes a modest investment in mode J equipment is one of the best bargains available in present-day amateur radio.

Operating on Oscar 13 – mode L

Fig 6.38a shows the frequency bandplan for Oscar 13 mode L. Mode L is usually the operational mode when the satellite is at or near its apogee. It provides a wide band of communications possibilities and is at present only sparsely used, although operator numbers show a slow but steady increase. Like mode B, mode L has a rather variable access threshold. At times it can be accessed on CW using only 800 watts eirp (about 15 watts minus feeder loss to a 20dB antenna), but for consistent access eirps of at least 5,000 watts are more often required. At fortunately much rarer intervals, signals as high as 6,000 watts eirp may be required for a reasonable signal-to-noise ratio when squint angles become large, eg 30 degrees or more.

To produce 5,000 watts of eirp the user needs 50 watts of RF energy to an antenna of at least 23dB gain. Producing this sort of combination at 1,269MHz is not cheap. Commercial equipment to generate 50 watts will cost nearly £1,000 and even if, as many mode L users do, you build your own power amplifiers to amplify the 2 or 10 watts from your 1,269MHz transceiver, the cost of components for a home-built power amplifier are high (particularly for the thermionic valve power amplifiers). Antennas can be expensive but most users seem to be trying and succeeding with pairs of matched home-made helical antennas. At 1,269MHz, Yagi antennas need precise element sizes and separations and helical antennas are by contrast amenable to far less stringent building specifications.

For the future it will be interesting to see how mode L use of Oscar 13 proceeds, and it could be that mode L will finish up being the preferred band for most serious users.

Operating Oscar 13 – mode S

Mode S operation is available on a regular basis, at times when the satellite is near apogee with its high-gain antennas pointing at the Earth. Several good convertor kits are available for mode S reception and a 2m dish is about the minimum useful size for respectable reception. Feedhorns and polarisers can be made by scaling the models shown in the RSGB *VHF/UHF Manual* (4th edition), pp9.73 to 9.83. The frequency bandplan is shown in Fig 6.38c. Activity on mode S was slow to start, but is now going ahead well, so there are always signals there to test your equipment on as you construct it. For details of mode S operating times, the bulletins broadcast by Oscar 13 beacons on mode L and mode B are the best up-to-date source of information. The experimental potential of mode S should prove to be an attractive feature for any microwave enthusiast.

Operating Oscar 13 – Rudak

The frequency band plan for Rudak is shown in Fig 6.38c. Rudak worked well on terrestrial tests, but once in space it has proved impossible to get its PROM to boot up. All attempts so far have failed after a few seconds when the processor latched and refused to accept any more signals. This may be a fault caused by the low temperature in which Oscar 13 at present finds itself. Attempts are being made to warm up the Rudak electronics to see if this will persuade it to load from PROM, but hopes that this will work are not high. So there is at present no indication of whether, or when, Rudak will ever be operational in Oscar 13.

Mode switching of Oscar 13

Mode switching schedules for Oscar 13 appear on:

Amsat Oscar 13 beacon bulletins
Uosat DCE bulletins
Amsat UK packet radio bulletins
Amsat NA nets Sunday 1900 UTC 14.282 and 21.280MHz

Knowing where Oscar 13 antennas are pointing

In order to keep Oscar 13's batteries fully charged, it is necessary to ensure that the spin axis of the satellite is as near as possible, at 90 degrees to the line from the satellite to the Sun. This alignment ensures maximum sunlight on the satellite's solar power panels.

At some seasons of the year, and some apogee/Earth alignments, it becomes impossible to maintain the spin axis of Oscar 13, and hence its antennas, pointed at the Earth at apogee because this would cause a poor Sun angle on the solar power panels. So a compromise has to be made whereby antenna pointing accuracy has to be traded for Sun angle, and about five or six times a year the alignment of Oscar 13 in space is altered to meet the changing orientations of satellite apogee versus the Sun-Earth line and solar declination.

The Oscar 13 operator needs to know how Oscar 13 is aligned, so that he can work out at what part of the orbit the satellite's antennas will point nearest to his station. So Amsat controllers publish advance notice of these satellite alignment changes, reporting the satellite's Bahn numbers (sometimes referred to as 'ALAT' for apogee latitude pointing, and 'ALONG' for apogee longitude pointing).

If Oscar 13's antennas are pointing in the orbit plane the ALAT is reported as 0 degrees. If the antennas point above the orbit plane ALAT is positive, eg 'ALAT 10' means 10 degrees above the orbit plane. If the antennas point below the orbit plane ALAT is reported as negative. The second Bahn number, ALONG, refers to an imaginary line from the Earth's centre through the satellite at apogee. If Oscar 13 antennas point directly along this line, away from the Earth, ALONG is reported as 0 degrees. If the satellite's antennas point directly back at the Earth from apogee, ALONG is said to be 180 degrees.

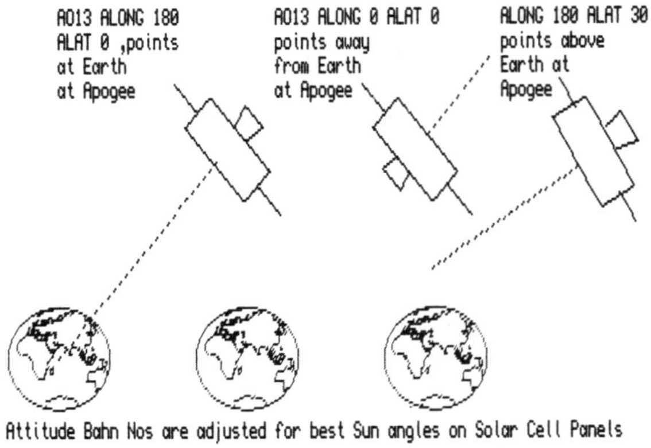

Fig 6.39: Oscar 13 attitude pointing Bahn numbers ALONG and ALAT

Fig 6.39 shows three different situations. In the first situation the satellite is at apogee with its antenna pointing in the orbit plane and directly back at the centre of the Earth. So ALAT = 0 and ALONG = 180 degrees. In the middle example the satellite's antennas point in the orbit plane, but directly away from the Earth. So ALAT is still 0, but ALONG is now also 0. In the last example the satellite's antennas point out above the orbit plane and parallel to the line back to the Earth's centre. So ALAT is now 30 degrees positive, and ALONG is 180 degrees.

Several Oscar 13 tracking programs, including the one from SARUG shown in Table 6.12, ask the operator to input ALAT and ALONG, and then the program calculates the squint angle between the line from the satellite to your station, and the line along which the satellite's antennas are pointing. In this way operators can experiment to see which squint angles give best access, and thereafter can plan to use those periods when the useful squint angles are present. Amsat bulletins publish Bahn number alignment changes at least 14 days before they occur. These bulletins are transmitted by Oscar 13, and are relayed by most packet radio bulletin board systems including Uosat.

Operating Oscar 13 – experiments

Oscar 13 is a first-class vehicle for space experiments of all types, including:

(a) Using its telemetry to check its solar power supplies and temperatures, to get a picture of its general operating environment.

(b) Checking the spin modulation at different parts of the orbit, using the techniques described in the Oscar 10 section above.
(c) Listening for Oscar 13 in the role of satellite-to-satellite-to-Earth relay. Checking situation where the high-flying Oscar 13 can hear other satellite's down links on its up link, and then rebroadcast these signals so that they can be heard in areas where the originating satellite is far below the local horizon.
(d) Using Oscar 13 to relay space shuttle Get Away Special (GAS) experiments, as described in chapter 8.
(e) Joining in the Amsat NA sponsored ZRO contest programme, a series of special experiments conducted through Oscar 13 at regular intervals to test your station equipment in competition with that at other stations. It involves the transmission of messages at progressively lower power levels. You can join in as a competitor, submitting your results, or you can try your luck in a simple but revealing personal private test. This experiment really sorts out those who can and cannot operate sensitive equipment.

All the above and many many more experiments are available through Oscar 13 for both listeners and transmitter users.

Oscar 13 handbook

A handbook compiled by Amsat DL is available. Enquiries to Amsat UK with an SASE or IRCs will get you details.

New amateur radio satellites being built in 1990

In the autumn of 1990 the following amateur radio satellite projects are underway:

Radiosport 12/13

These will be clones of RS10/11. They have been built at the Tsiolkovskiy Museum for the History of Cosmonautics in Kaluga, 180km southwest of Moscow. Leaders of the project were Aleksandr Papkov and Victor Samkov. RS 12/13 will ride on a standard CosNav LEO navigation satellite as does RS10/11. RS12/13 will follow the same orbit tracks as its predecessor but at a different time of day. The orbit will be near polar, 83 degrees inclination with a mean height of 1,000km and an orbital period of about 105 minutes. The provisional bandplan is shown in Table 6.14.

RS12/13 will radiate about 8 watts on each transponder, with beacons and robots transmitting 0.45 watts or 1.2 watts.

Table 6.14: Provisional bandplan for RS12/13

		RS 12	RS 13
Mode A	up link	145.910-145.950	145.960-146.000
	down link	29.410-29.450	29.460-29.500
	beacon	29.4081 or 29.4534	29.4582 or 29.5043
Mode K	up link	21.210-21.250	21.260-21.300
	down link	29.410-29.450	29.460-29.500
	beacon	29.4081 or 29.4543	29.4582 or 29.5043
Mode T	up link	21.210-21.250	21.260-21.300
	down link	145.910-145.950	145.960-146.000
	beacon	145.9125 or 145.9587	145.8622 or 145.9083
Mode KA	up link	21.210-21.250	21.260-21.300
	up link	145.910-145.950	145.960-146.000
	down link	29.410-29.450	29.460-29.500
	beacon	29.4081 or 29.4543	29.4582 or 29.5043
Mode KT	up link	21.210-21.250	21.260-21.300
	down link	29.410-29.450	29.460-29.500
	down link	145.910-145.950	145.960-146.000
	beacon	29.4081 or 29.4543	29.4582 or 29.5043
	beacon	145.9125 or 145.9587	145.8622 or 145.9083
Robot	modes	A, K, T, KA, KT	A, K, T, KA, KT
	up link	21.1291 and/or 145.8308	21.1385 and/or 145.8403
	down link	29.4543 and/or 145.9587	29.5043 and/or 145.9083

Packet radio satellites

By January 1991 the pacsats launched in 1990 should have their operational outfits of software, and be providing full bulletin board facilities. Additionally, a Russo-German package RM-1 (Rudak 2, formerly referred to as 'RS14', not the same vehicle as RS12/13) should have been launched. This will have a 435MHz up link and 145MHz down link and feature 1,200 bps and 4,800 bps FSK and PSK modes.

The simplest packet satellite ground station will need:

(i) 2m and 70cm antennas.
(ii) A 2m FM transmitter providing about 25 watts output.
(iii) A 70cm SSB receiver system capable of tuning 437MHz (not all do), and providing up/down frequency control facilities to utilise the modem AFC.
(iv) A terminal node controller using AX.25 protocol packet software.
(v) An RFI-quiet microcomputer with packet control software (eg Packcom, Procomm, Yapp etc).

The 9,600 bps system aboard Uosat 3 requires special care, noting that the high keying speed has wide flat bandwidth requirements. Hence, whereas 1,200 bps modems can be coupled direct to microphone sockets and direct from audio outputs, the 9,600 bps modem output and input must go directly to the transmitter varactor diode and come directly from the output of the receiver discriminator. On most equipments this means going inside with soldering iron and cutters.

Note. A 1,200 bps modem PCB, FSK up, PSK down, designed by G3RUH, is available from Amsat UK for use on NA Pacsat, Lusat, JAS1-B and RUDAK 2.

For the 9,600 bps signals of Uosat D a PCB or made-up modem is available from G3RUH, 3 Benny's Way, Coton, CB3 7PS, England.

Old satellites

Some satellites are working one minute, dead the next, struck down in their prime by a sudden battery short circuit or the demise of some other vital component. Other satellites can suffer near-fatal disasters and then go on for many more years. Sometimes they spend long periods in hibernation, like Oscar 10, but return regularly to useful status as the change of season and, with it, the change of Sun angle, brings light to solar cells after a long absence, providing the electrical power to run a transmitter or recharge a flat battery.

Perhaps the most stubborn of these 'old soldiers' is Radiosport 1. RS1 was launched in October 1978, and was active for only a short time before its batteries failed completely. Fortunately, at least one of the batteries failed 'open circuit', unlike most satellite batteries which fail short circuit and leave a short across all the satellite's power supplies, putting them completely out of action.

In the case of RS1, this open-circuit battery meant that the rest of the satellite's power supplies were unaffected. So when the solar cells on the outside of the satellite were sunlit, the satellite got electric power, but if the satellite tumbled in space to point its solar cells away from the Sun, or went into the shadow zone behind the Earth, the supply of solar power temporarily ceased. It soon become obvious that RS1 was alternating between active periods when it saw the Sun and inactive periods when it did not. As it came back into sunlight, its transmitter beacon would slowly come to life, at first sending odd blips and bleeps of telemetry but gradually, as it got more sunlight, beginning to send readable morse telemetry.

Unfortunately RS1 is not completely *compos mentis*. It never has quite enough volts to cross the threshold where it would behave correctly, becoming 'sane'. It tries to carry out the orders in its actuating circuits (RS1 was too early for full computer control), but its low voltage keeps it in a sort of dream state. It knows it has to look in its memory, it looks and finds it is at memory box 5, so it transmits a morse 5, then it reads the contents of memory box 5 and sometimes manages to transmit that as 11 or 51, but then it gets stuck. It does not go on to read all the memory boxes in order as it should. Instead it goes back and starts reading box 5 again. The result is that whenever RS1 appears, all the listener hears is a broken-up morse transmission which now and then resolves as 511 511 551 511 551, or something like that.

RS1 has now been doing this for nearly 10 years. Its signal can be tracked and predicted and it is interesting to compute when it will go into Earth shadow according to your computer and when it will come out again. This process can then be followed in real time, to see what actually happens.

Given its history and its location (its orbit takes it into the lower edges of the Van Allen belts), it must be suffering considerable radiation damage to its solar cells. Indeed, its present dream state indicates a solar-powered supply voltage well below half of what it had the day it was launched. Eventually this cumulative damage will so reduce solar cell output volts that it will cease to be able to power-up its transmitter beacon, but for the present it may well continue on, like a gramophone record stuck in a groove, sending its repetitive meaningless message. Its operating frequency is 29.401MHz.

Chapter 7

Weather and experimental satellites

Weather satellites

Introduction

Tiros 1, the first satellite devoted to Earth weather reporting from orbit, was launched on 1 April 1960. By taking photographs of the Earth and its cloud cover directly below the satellite, Tiros 1 provided two months of excellent service.

None the less, the photographic technique was cumbersome and it was superseded in December 1963, when the eighth member of the Tiros series was launched, carrying the first of the automatic picture transmitters (APTs). The APT could relay its picture data back to any suitably equipped Earth station, and from that moment weather satellite observing became possible for all.

All the early Tiros family flew in low Earth orbit, and it was not until 1966 that the ATS 1 satellite sent the first APT-type pictures from geostationary orbit. Since then a steady stream of low Earth orbiters and geostationaries have provided continuous weather pictures from space. The first of the now-familiar NOAA low Earth orbiters flew in December 1970, and it was followed in 1975 by the first of the present GOES (Geostationary Operational Environmental Satellite) series.

In each case these satellites carried much improved visual and cloud cover sensors, plus infra-red sensors and temperature and water vapour content measuring devices. Up to 1980, the United States launched 46 weather satellites, of which eight geostationary and 35 low Earth orbiters gave excellent service.

Weather satellites in the 1990s

Space radio listeners and radio amateurs have access to at least two NOAA and five Meteor (Soviet) low Earth orbiters and at least one or two of the five operational geostationary weather satellites.

Fig 7.01 shows the present situation, with Soviet, Japanese, Indian and European satellites having joined the original American orbiters. In Europe access is available to the third-generation Metsat geostationary located near 0°W, and polar weather coverage is available from two NOAA LEO satellites in Sun synchronous orbits (one morning up, the other afternoon up).

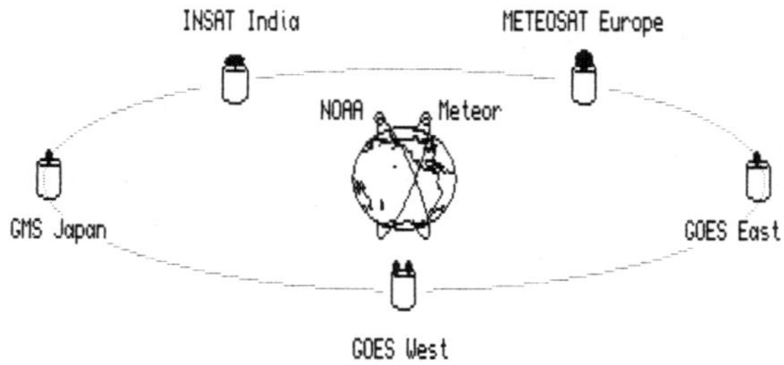

Fig 7.01: Weather satellites observe from geostationary and low Earth orbits

In addition there are a group of Soviet Meteor LEO satellites in near-polar orbits, inclined at about 82.6 degrees. These Soviet satellites are not Sun synchronous but they are numerous and hence frequently available. At this time, satellites numbers 16 to 19 inclusive of the Meteor 2 series are sending useful signals. At least two satellites of the Meteor 3 series have been launched and are sending signals. Table 7.01 lists the operational satellites together with their

Table 7.01: Operational weather satellites at the end of 1990

Satellite	Orbit type	Transmit frequencies (MHz)
GOES East	75°W Geo	468.85, 1,681.6, 1,682.5, 1,684
GOES West	135°W Geo	468.825, 1,687.1, 1,688.2, 1,690.2, 1,691, 1,694, 1,696 GOES also retransmits polar pix
Metsat 3	near 0°W Geo	468.925, 468.875, 1,691 Wefax
Met 4 (presently off)		1,694.5, 1,675.929, 1,675.281
INSAT	74°E Geo	not known
NOAA 9	99 deg LEO	136.77, 137.62, APT 1,707.2
NOAA 10	99 deg LEO	137.50 APT
NOAA 11	99 deg LEO	137.62
OKEAN 2	83 deg LEO	137.4
Meteor 2/16	83 deg LEO	137.4
Meteor 2/17	83 deg LEO	137.3
Meteor 2/18	83 deg LEO	137.3
Meteor 2/19	83 deg LEO	137.85
Meteor 3/02	83 deg LEO	137.3
Meteor 3/03	83 deg LEO	137.85
Feng Yun 1A	98 deg LEO	137.8 (Chinese Wefax)

Other Soviet weather satellites use 464, 461.5, 466.5, 468.5, and 461.15

Table 7.02: Automatic picture transmission format

Receiver FM detector
Audio out with 2,400Hz sub carrier
Amplitude modulated, 5% black, 80% white
Square sync pulses start every line
120 lines per minute
Russian pix require 2,280 to 2,520Hz local osc

operating frequencies. Table 7.02 gives the specification for the APT format.

Accessibility of LEO weather satellites from UK

The pattern of in-range orbits of a NOAA LEO weather satellite seen from the UK is shown in Fig 7.02. The particular pattern shown here is described as 'afternoon ascending', ie south to north ascending equatorial crossings occur around 1400 local time. There is usually a second NOAA satellite which has an orbit which is 'morning ascending', ie it comes around at about 0730 local time for its ascending equator crossings. Fig 7.03 shows the relationship between these two orbits, both of which are Sun synchronous and stay steady for years.

As Fig 7.03 shows, one of the NOAA orbiters is synchronised to an 0730 local time up, and a 1930 local time down, pattern of equator crossings. The other NOAA is in a 1400 local time up, 0200 local time down, pattern of EQXs. This latter satellite used to be in a 1500 up, 0300 down, orbit but this was changed in winter 1986/87, to 1400 up, 0200 down, because of poor lighting conditions in the northern hemisphere, high-latitude zone of interest. The change was achieved by using the NOAA attitude thrusters to shift the NOAA orbit right ascension.

As can be seen from Fig 7.02a, the 0200 descending orbits of NOAA 9 are of little value to UK operators. Only the most dedicated will be alert at that time of night, and it is possible to catch the later orbits just before noon when NOAA tracks across to the north of the UK and despite its low elevation can be heard with quite a strong signal. The best pictures of the day from this satellite are on the afternoon ascending orbits, as shown in Fig 7.02c.

By contrast, the NOAA 10 morning ascending orbits can give good pictures in the UK around breakfast time. In all cases operators must allow for seasonal changes of solar elevation. Do not expect good pictures in winter in the UK on 0730 ascending or 1930 descending orbits. Only the 1400 ascending orbit has good lighting in winter.

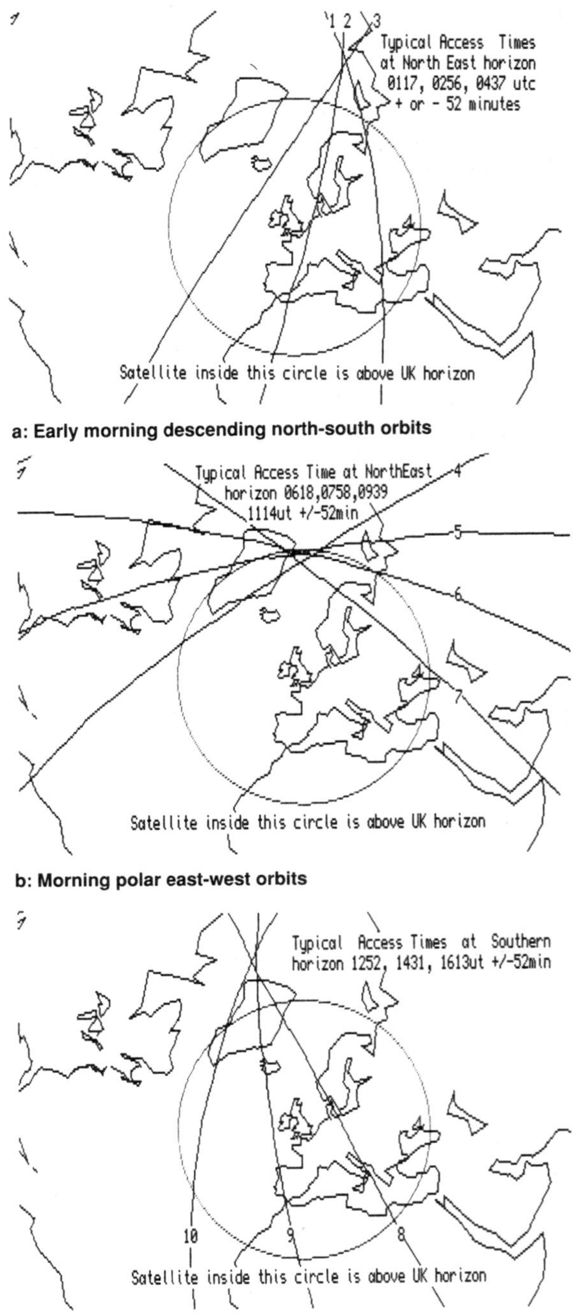

a: Early morning descending north-south orbits

b: Morning polar east-west orbits

c: Afternoon south-north orbits

Fig 7.02a-c: NOAA satellite orbits in range of the UK

Accessing Soviet Meteor weather satellites

The Meteor 2 series of Soviet weather satellites are in 82.5 degree inclination orbits at a mean altitude of about 940km. From this information we can calculate that the right ascension of the orbital plane of their orbits will precess about 0.8 degrees per day.

Because of this non-Sun-synchronous behaviour, the orbital planes will shift in space, gradually changing from, say, morning ascending to evening ascending orbits in about seven months. Apart from this small departure from Sun synchronism the Meteor orbits are similar to the NOAA orbits, except they ascend east past the North Pole in contrast to NOAA's west ascent past the North Pole.

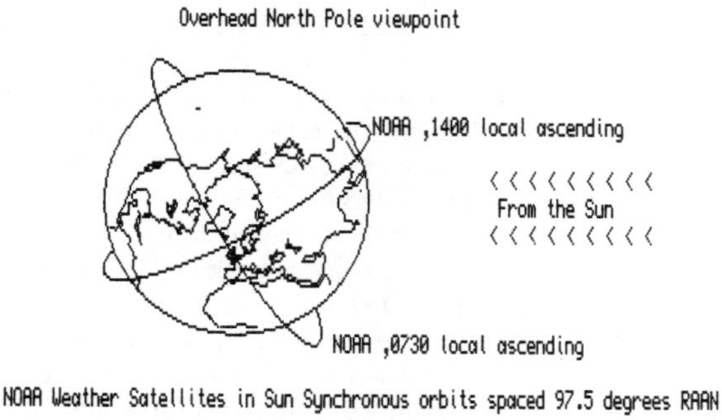

Fig 7.03: NOAA orbits are positioned to give different local time equator crossings

Receiving LEO weather satellite VHF signals

As discussed above, the average complement of two NOAAs and three or four Meteors gives the UK radio listener lots of suitable targets for weather picture reception. All of these satellites use the 136 to 137.99MHz satellite band, so a common receiver will tune them all. Several possible choices are available in respect of just what form this receiver should take.

If you already have a good shortwave receiver with FM detection, you can add 136 to 137.99MHz by buying one of the readily available simple 136 to 28MHz convertors. Many popular shortwave receivers are fitted to detect FM signals and they can tune 28 to 29.9MHz. Please make sure your receiver can do this before you buy a convertor. Fig 7.04 shows how the convertor/shortwave receiver combination can be fed by a simple dipole antenna.

In practice, antennas for the 144MHz radio amateur band are quite satisfactory for weather satellite 136/137MHz reception, so you can use an antenna of this type if you have one. Do not waste money on dedicated 137MHz antennas until you are sure you need one. Some authorities recommend preamplifiers at the antenna operating at 137MHz but the weather satellite signal is so strong that this is an unnecessary luxury. When you are satisfied that you can

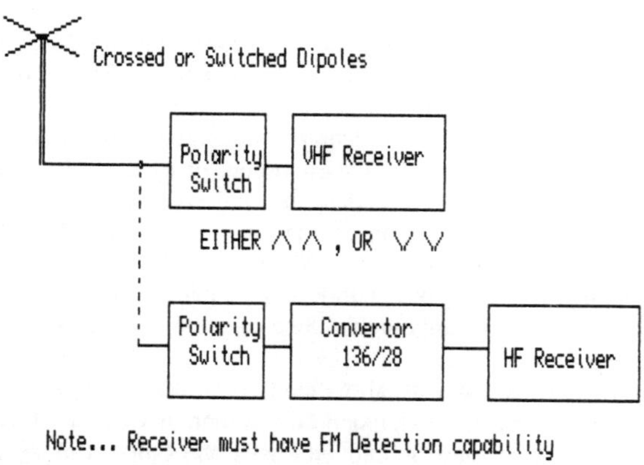

Fig 7.04: A simple station for VHF weather satellite reception

receive weather satellites properly then, and only then, should you consider spending money on picture display equipment, special antennas and expensive receivers.

Fig 7.05 shows a more sophisticated station for receiving signals from LEO weather satellites. The antenna is a Yagi beam fitted to receive variable polarisation of signal to overcome Faraday effect. Being directional, the antenna needs a rotator to point it in azimuth. By using a relatively small Yagi beam, it should not be necessary to have variable control of antenna elevation, so an elevation rotator is not required. It is simply not good sense to fit a narrow-beam, big, multi-element Yagi beam, for not only will it need an elevation rotor, that rotor and the azimuth rotor will need constant positional adjustment, making the operator tracking task very difficult. Stick to a three- or four-element XY crossed Yagi beam: it is much easier to operate when tracking a satellite which moves quickly across your sky.

Again, a preamplifier is quite unnecessary. Faraday rotation of signal polarisation is the big problem when receiving VHF weather satellites, so a small XY adjustable polarisation Yagi is the best practical solution.

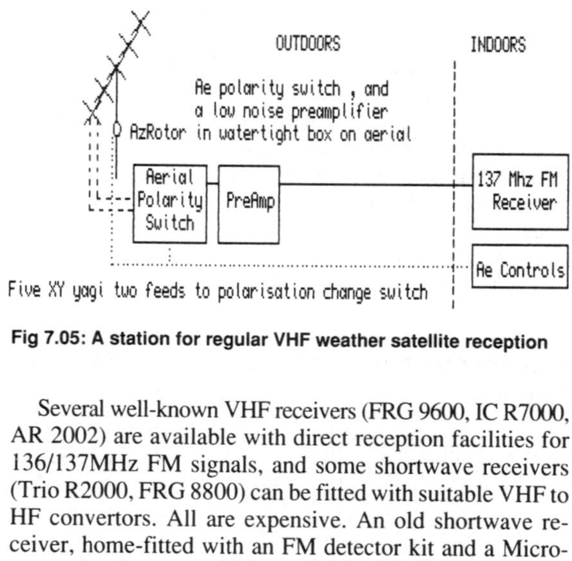

Fig 7.05: A station for regular VHF weather satellite reception

Several well-known VHF receivers (FRG 9600, IC R7000, AR 2002) are available with direct reception facilities for 136/137MHz FM signals, and some shortwave receivers (Trio R2000, FRG 8800) can be fitted with suitable VHF to HF convertors. All are expensive. An old shortwave receiver, home-fitted with an FM detector kit and a Microwave Modules 136/28MHz convertor, is a lot cheaper and just as sensitive as the Far East 'black boxes'.

Receiving LEO weather satellites on microwaves

The NOAA satellite family transmit excellent down link signals on 1.7GHz, in addition to their transmissions on 137MHz. Present American plans suggest that both these frequency bands will continue to be used for these low earth orbiters for some years to come. So weather satellite users can expect to continue using 137MHz for some time yet. If, however, they want to try a much more difficult target, they can try monitoring the 1.7GHz signals. Before anyone rushes out to buy or build the expensive 1.7GHz equipment, please check the following advantages and disadvantages of Wefax reception on 137MHz versus 1.7GHz.

Advantages: 1.7GHz is free from Faraday effect, so polarisation rotation as the satellite crosses your sky is not a problem. Equally encouraging, the scintillation effects which plague European Wefax LEO operation at 137MHz are virtually absent at 1.7GHz.

Disadvantages: 1.7GHz reception equipment is expensive. There are no ready-made antennas. The Doppler shift is monstrous, about 60kHz or more, and antenna tracking of a fast-moving satellite on the obligatory narrow-beam antenna is fiendishly difficult at 1.7GHz.

The author built a 1.7GHz helical antenna (*Radio Communication Handbook*, 5th edition, RSGB, Table 13.13 refers). On this antenna reception is excellent, but smooth antenna tracking by hand or by auto control is almost impossible with available primitive amateur radio antenna rotators. When the concurrent requirement to tune the receiver to follow the high-speed Doppler shift is added to the antenna pointing task, the whole thing becomes impossible. The Doppler rate is 12 times faster at 1.7GHz than it is at 137MHz, so installing automatic frequency control is an expensive 'must'.

The equipment layout used by the author is shown in chapter 5, Fig 5.14, with the warning that he discovered he needed to be an octopus to operate this manual tune-and-track system effectively. Would-be purchasers of weather satellite microwave convertors should note that several do not tune 1,700MHz; they only tune the Meteosat/GOES frequencies at about 1,694MHz.

Reception of geostationary weather satellite signals

For radio weather watchers in western Europe the geostationary satellite of interest is Met 3 (Met 4 presently u/s), stationed at longitude 0°W. This location puts the satellite almost exactly due south at azimuth 180 and elevation 34 degrees for users in southern England. Users in Scotland will find the satellite near azimuth 174 degrees, elevation 28 degrees.

Only a high-gain antenna directly connected to a good low-noise preamplifier will lift the 1,691 and 1,694.5MHz signals above noise. The author has used a 2 metre diameter dish, which should be at least 2 metres above the ground, to reduce ground noise and side-lobe pick-up. Various dish feeds have been tried, starting with a simple dipole, which produced noisy signals permitting a check of the rest of the equipment, before then proceeding to improve the antenna feed using a circular horn similar to the one described in the *VHF/UHF Manual*, 4th edition, RSGB, p9.76. A GaAsFET preamplifier gave best results mounted directly to the feed horn, with high-quality coaxial cable then feeding the signal to the nearby 1,691 to 137MHz convertor. In these initial experiments (before computers), the signals were displayed on a wet-paper recorder.

If you have never tried moonbounce or any other form of weak signal work, you may be surprised by the problems you have getting respectable signals from a geostationary weather satellite. Antenna alignment is critical. Meteosat 2 was allowed to wander about 1 degree either side of its designated slot because it had little attitude control fuel left. This satellite wandering should not have serious effects if your antenna is centrally aligned on the Metsat's designated location, but it can give trouble if you inadvertently line up to it when it is at one of the extreme ends of its wandering pattern.

Please remember also that dish antennas are easily moved by the wind, and unless firmly mounted you will find they can be pushed out of alignment. Flimsy garage rooftops are not recommended as sites for 2 metre dishes. A suitable Metsat reception dish is shown in chapter 5, Fig 5.13.

Picture reception and display

Until the early 1980s, would-be users of weather satellite images had a problem. Several picture handling and display methods were available and all were expensive to purchase and run.

The four quite different methods for printing the weather picture used either a wet-paper recorder, a dry paper recorder, a photographic printer or a facsimile printer. These methods are still available. All have their problems, and the equipment for them can be expensive and, perhaps worst of all, do not always produce results with good picture contrast. The photographic method is complex but generally superior to the rest. It was described in detail in *QST* in April 1981 by Emilani and, in June 1978, by Winkler. By 1983 the home computer had appeared on the operating bench, with the best storage and scan convertor of the time being described in *VHF Communications* for winter 1982 and spring 1983 by its builder, M Vidmar.

Weather picture software and hardware

The weather satellite user can spend a great deal of time and money on equipment, and it must be stressed at the outset that if your requirements are for weather pictures, rather than developing the techniques to get them direct from satellites, you will find it much cheaper to ignore the satellite route entirely and simply take the outputs of processed satellite data, broadcast regularly by a worldwide chain of LF and HF broadcasting stations. If your interest really is the weather, or say the effects of the weather on tropospheric propagation of VHF radio signals, then the satellite route for your pictures is an expensive detour. You can get all you want much more easily and at better quality on HF.

Having sounded the above caution, if your interests lie in direct satellite observation of the weather, then by all means read on. The construction and operation of picture display equipment can be fascinating, not least because you will not find it easy to duplicate the received signal quality of the professional station. This will stretch and enhance your competence, and as regards software development, the field is wide open for new ideas. After several years of home computer processing of weather pictures, the computers are just becoming big enough in terms of memory, sharp enough in terms of screen definition (eg 512 by 512 pixels minimum), and fast enough in their central processor chips to permit sophisticated software to be designed and run.

This increased sophistication is most evident in picture quality. No longer is it necessary to stick with low-contrast black and white. It is now possible to display in false colours, to add two pictures, say, one visual-light and the other infra-red, to get improved definition and to provide a wide range of contrast control, eg to emphasise an important minor contrast boundary like land versus sea. These improved features can be purchased, but it is much more fun to do it yourself, and in this regard a steady improvement in the software produced by, and available to, radio amateurs is already evident. This software does of course require powerful computers, and it will therefore be necessary for users to eventually forsake their faithful Spectrums and 'Beebs' for something bigger and faster.

When this point in time arrives, do be careful. If you intend to write your own software, make sure your prospective micro purchase has good read only memory (ROM) with simple access to machine code (many modern IBM clones do not have this facility). If you do not contemplate writing your own advanced software, you absolutely must first ensure you locate and trial-run the sort of high-quality software you want, then buy the machine that software runs on.

It is also important to exercise the same care if you contemplate buying weather-satellite picture-interface software (some micros simply cannot handle direct input of analogue picture data). Hardware interfaces are made to work on one type of computer only. So take care you purchase the right interface for your micro, and be clear in your mind that even when you have done this you will still need to purchase the usually separate software for it. Very few companies bundle the interfaces, their software, and the micro picture format software as one package. Software on plug in ROM is the most convenient if your micro has EPROM or ROM inputs. Software on tape or disc is much less convenient, though it does have the merit of being amendable.

The weather pictures

NOAA LEO weather satellites send two types of pictures in real time; one picture is taken using a visual-light sensor and the other is taken using an infra-red sensor. At night (whenever the visible-light sensor has a low input), the NOAAs switch off the visible-light sensor and bring in a second infra-red sensor.

Night, as imaged by an orbiting NOAA, depends on where it is and, most important, the season of the year. In the UK, winter has long nights and, indeed, even whilst the NOAA is accessible from the UK it goes above the Arctic Circle. In winter months this means 24 hours of night.

In the UK summer there is, by contrast, no night to the north at any time in the 24 hour day. So NOAA satellite polar orbits passing between UK and the Pole give visible-light pictures all summer. This contrast, whereby a NOAA satellite north of the UK in winter has no visible light to see by after 1400 or 1500 local time, has forced the NOAA operators to change the Sun-synchronous alignment of their formerly 1500 local time ascending satellite, so that it now has a 1400 local time ascending orbit. Even so, users of both NOAA and Meteor LEO weather satellites will find that their visible-light pictures often suffer from marked lack of contrast on the evening (easterly side of the picture of an afternoon ascending orbit) or the morning (westerly side of the picture of a breakfast time, ascending orbit).

Users of NOAA satellites who have a picture frame store can regularly enjoy alternate viewing of the separate visible-light and infra-red pictures. In some cases they can also mix these two pictures. Some of the Arctic infra-red pictures are very good indeed for Earth resource and geologist hobby viewing.

Because the two sides of the same visible-light picture can differ markedly in contrast, and because of the advantages which can sometimes be gained by picture mixing or overlaying, a whole range of active software is coming into use to allow the weather satellite user to set his own standards for gain/contrast across the picture, computer enhancement of minute contrast changes, and vivid display of these picture variables using 'false' colours. These techniques are still in their infancy, and there is lots of scope in this field for the amateur software writer. Users of these software techniques will find that it is quite often the case that the Meteor weather pictures offer more scope for this kind of data enhancement, and are capable of being contrast 'stretched' much more than the NOAA pictures.

For experimenters interested in using weather satellite pictures for special 'non-weather' experiments (as opposed to simply using weather satellites to find out if it is raining in Reykjavik), the variations in contrast and lighting on the picture are a useful guide to the satellite's track, even when the shape of the land masses is not discernible. When the land masses are discernible on the picture, the experimenter has a unique tool for all sorts of experiments. Foremost amongst these are propagation experiments. By monitoring the signal characteristics and observing propagation-induced changes, whilst simultaneously viewing the satellite picture, the experimenter is able to exactly pin-point the satellite's position in respect to any sequence of propagation anomalies. The satellite is directly overhead whatever is appearing in the centre of your picture as you observe the screen in real time, or as you check old weather pictures. So if you see signs on the picture of the characteristic signal flutter as the weather-satellite signal path down to you crosses sporadic ionisation in the E layer, you know from the picture where the satellite was at that moment. Hence by simple trigonometry the location where the signal path to your station passed down through the E layer can be deduced. For example, signal dropouts with the satellite over north Africa indicate E layer transits to Scotland via a E layer location over Nantes in north west France.

This trick does not work with geostationary satellites, at least not in the same way. The geosat signal path is relatively fixed in regard to your station location, so the signal would appear to be transiting the same part of the E layer all day. In spite of this reservation, the signals from geosats are useful for propagation experiments because they show how the state of the ionosphere along a fixed path changes with time.

In fact, the situation with geostationary satellite weather pictures is somewhat more complicated than the above paragraph suggests because, strange as it may seem to newcomers, geostationary weather satellites often transmit pictures they have not taken themselves. Very early in the life of weather geosats it was appreciated that, because they see the same view of the Earth all the time, they give an excellent report of the gradual changes but, when taken on a short term basis, this can be very boring viewing. In addition the pictures from geosats suffer from the same variable lighting problems experienced by LEO weather satellites, but worse. Using mainframe computers at the receiving station, this situation can be overcome by sophisticated software providing contrast enhancement and filling in the important land/sea boundaries that are often almost invisible on the raw pictures.

It has therefore become the practice to combine two aspects of weather geosat operation, first by sending back up to the satellite enhanced pictures of its original raw images and using the satellite as a rebroadcaster of these improved images. Second, the fact that it is unnecessary to keep broadcasting the only slowly changing enhanced picture allows the operators to use it to retransmit pictures captured from other satellites, and/or enlarged segments of pictures from the original satellite or other satellites. In this way users of European Metsat get a regular flow of:

- Enhanced Metsat pictures
- Sectional Metsat pictures
- Sectional or hemisphere pics from GOES East or West
- NOAA LEO pictures
- Metsat operating schedules

How the geosat takes its pictures

There are two sensors in use simultaneously, one sensitive to visible light, the other sensitive to infra-red light. The satellite sees an area slightly less than a hemisphere. Its footprint is about 80 degrees, imaging 80 degrees west to 80 degrees east longitudinally of its equatorial sub-satellite longitude, and 80 north to 80 degrees of latitude south of the equator. In practice, because it is viewing a spherical Earth, not a flat plate, the edges of the footprint are cramped up, and in addition are viewed at low elevation through a dense, long atmospheric path. So only the inner 65 degrees of the footprint produce a really useful picture.

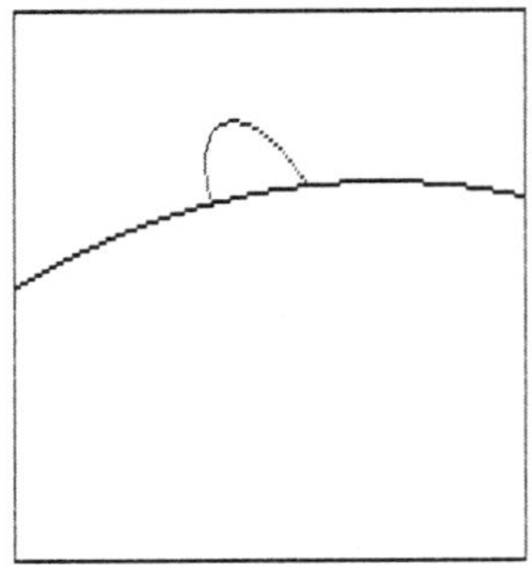

Lunar motion as Wefax scans produces elliptical Moon with fretted edges

Fig 7.06: Weather satellite astronomy: moonset from geostationary orbit

The satellite is spin-stabilised by rotating it at 100 revolutions per minute, and it is this spin which allows its sensors to be swept across the Earth beneath in a narrow strip about 8km north/south. The sensors, usually referred to as the VISRR (Visible/Infra Red Spin Scan Radiometer), have their point of aim shifted upwards 26 seconds of arc between each spin/scan. So each of the 100 scans per minute takes images from a strip 8km higher than the previous strip, gradually building up a picture of the Earth in about 2,500 strips, taken over a 25 minute single picture time scan. Picture elements are recorded simultaneously from both visible and infra-red sensors, building up two separate pictures, each 2,500 pixel elements per line by 2,500 individual lines. In addition it is possible, if required, to use a pair of sensors for the visual image, thereby doubling the picture resolution to 5,000 × 2,500 pixels. Every 30 minutes the VISSR begins a new picture scan.

Weather satellite astronomy

It is sometimes possible to see other astronomical objects in the pictures from geostationary weather satellites. Users of these satellites should be alert therefore for these events, particularly where something as obvious as the Moon is concerned. Fig 7.06 shows a representation of the sort of target you may get as the Moon sets behind the upper limb of the Earth, as seen by the geosat. Actual photographs of an event of this type are shown in *Sky and Telescope*, February 1987, p225.

Two things to note about this type of event, and the pictures which result, are that the Earth and the Moon are scanned in thin strips by the VISSR. Between these scans the Earth is stationary with respect to the geosat and the Moon is moving. This has the effect of giving a reasonable representation of the Earth, but the Moon is portrayed in a series of strips with a staggered staircase-stepped edge and elliptical proportions, rather than circular, with the major axis along the lunar line of motion.

One useful clue to the likelihood of this Wefax astronomy is that it was noticeable in some parts of the world (ie on certain geosats) during a recent lunar eclipse. Unfortunately not all weather satellite operators keep their satellites operating during these interesting events, which is sad because whilst they may have no weather content, they do give a vivid illustration of how the scanning system of the VISSR works, and they are a good test of computer prediction capabilities.

The Moon is of course the best and most obvious astronomical target, but it may also be possible to image the bright planets (Venus, Jupiter, Mercury, Saturn, Mars), and it should be possible to image the brighter stars (Sirius, Canopus, Capella, Vega etc). Whether it would be possible to image other satellites, eg polar shuttle flights, is not so certain, but perhaps some of the big, low-altitude, photo-reconnaissance satellites will show up briefly. We will never know unless we try.

Experimental satellites

Introduction

A historical study of experimental satellites would involve a lot of jumping about from one field of scientific research to another, with potential loss of continuity. In order to avoid this danger, the paragraphs which follow will describe experimental satellites in terms of their target zones, starting with satellites which examine the Earth's surface, and then gradually moving outwards and upwards, to finish this review with the experimental satellites in deep space. Along the way, emphasis will be given to the most important satellite experiments in each zone, concentrating on those which could be duplicated, and further progress made, by home experimenters, or science-oriented clubs or societies.

Satellite experiments looking at the Earth's surface

A wide range of satellites have focussed their sensors on the Earth's surface. Amongst these, the Landsats 1 to 5 and the French Spot satellite have been outstanding, focussing a sophisticated battery of sensors to produce images over a wide range of the visible and infra-red parts of the spectrum, in both wide- and narrow-band investigations. However, Landsat technology is far too sophisticated and expensive for it to be of direct use in secondary or undergraduate studies of geology and geography, and therefore a large gap exists in these fields which could be filled by simple amateur science surface imaging satellites. Uosat Oscar 11 has already made a start in this field, and other opportunities will undoubtedly occur for direct or sub-contracted amateur radio involvement.

In respect of amateur experimental use of existing satellites, the Landsat series are probably inappropriate, noting that a whole range of less-expensive experiments in Earth surface studies is available via the LEO weather satellites. The images and the software to enhance their pictures are improving all the time, and all kinds of science surveys are possible using Wefax, including Arctic and mountain snow cover records, glacier advance or retreat, volcanic activity etc, and it should not be overlooked that the infra-red Wefax images are an excellent source of data on major forest fires, oil field petrol flaring and accidents, and volcanic activity.

As regards building an amateur satellite for use in this field, there is a clear need for what might be described as a simple geography satellite. Using a standard image format such as SSTV, pictures could be received directly in schools and classrooms, via amateur radio. Indeed radio amateurs could also help provide the ground station equipment to assist other countries to develop these studies.

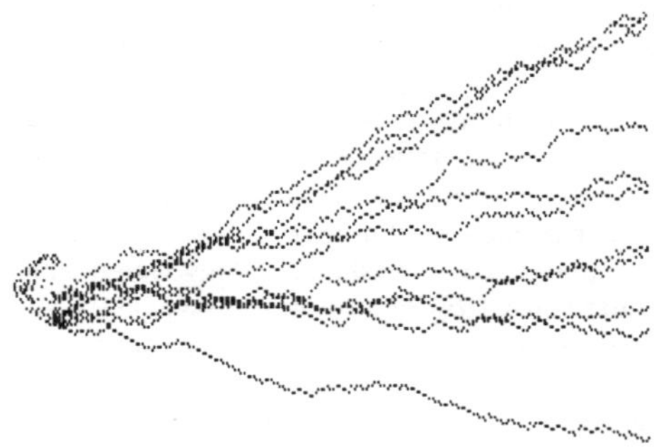

Fig 7.07: Looking at the Earth from space – strange events. Ocean currents spreading phytoplankton, causing a possible fisheries problem. Observed by NOAA

In a related area of Earth surface studies, the oceans and seas of the world provide an endless series of experimental opportunities via satellite remote imaging. Fig 7.07 shows an unusual natural event captured by a NOAA satellite over the Great Barrier Reef of Australia. The curious pattern was created by a sudden massive bloom of phytoplankton, but it could just as easily have been a man-made oil slick. Studies of this type are readily available to amateur experimenters with relatively modest equipment.

Satellite studies of the atmosphere

It might appear at first consideration that the atmosphere was 'out of bounds' to satellite studies, because, of course, satellites cannot operate in that region. This is, however, not the case: though satellites cannot orbit in the atmosphere, they can examine it both from above and off to one side.

This latter sideways viewing technique has been used successfully by satellites like Solar Mesosphere Explorer (SME). As Fig 7.08 shows, SME views the Sun through the atmosphere, using the atmosphere as a diffraction grating whose properties depend on its highly variable constituents. Examining what happens to sunlight as it passes through the upper atmosphere is an excellent way to study the important ozone density, and in a slightly different experiment it is possible to monitor the effects of atmospheric carbon dioxide, the suggested culprit for the 'greenhouse effect' heating of the Earth. In addition it is useful to use microwave

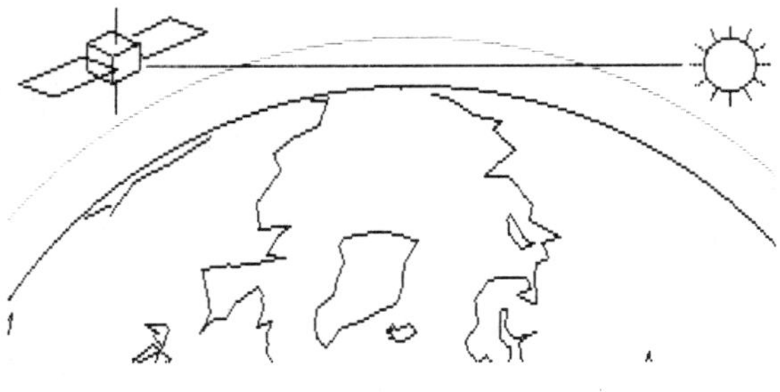

Fig 7.08: Satellite using sunlight to examine the Earth's atmosphere (not to scale)

satellites for tropospheric bending studies. Regular monitoring of a selection of geostationary microwave transmissions is very revealing in regard to atmospheric density anomalies. If a satellite transmits on several frequencies at the same, it can be a useful probe of the atmosphere and ionosphere. One famous satellite of this type was SIRIO, an Italian experimental satellite. SIRIO was a geostationary drifter; it came in range for about 10 days each month, and was regularly used by organisations such as Nasa as a pointer to the locations of atmospheric or ionospheric anomalies.

Amateur radio VHF, UHF and microwave beacons placed onboard geostationary platforms could provide valuable services to students of the atmosphere and ionosphere, and it may be possible to devise experiments to measure atmospheric pollution, although it must be said that the natural wide-band radio sources out in the universe may prove to be more useful in this respect.

Satellite studies of the lower ionosphere

This is a field which continues to be well served by experimental satellites. There were many superb auroral and E layer satellite studies in the 1960s and 1970s, culminating in satellite P76 with its 10 phased-locked beacons covering VHF to microwaves. Fig 7.09 shows the characteristics of P76.

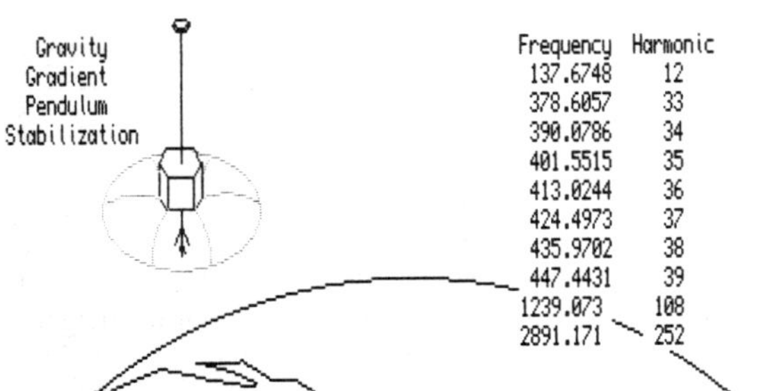

Fig 7.09: DNA P76 – a multiple beacon experiment using 10 phase-locked signals. This experiment helped explain why satellite radars are so poor and why satellite polar communications at VHF and UHF are difficult

Fig 7.10: Dynamic Explorer discovers the theta auroral circulation pattern. Circulations cross the pole together then split to opposite ways round the edge

Following P76, the trend in lower ionospheric satellite studies has been to put the satellite into a high elliptical orbit and 'look down' on the lower ionosphere. The satellites of the Dynamic Explorer experiment were of this type. They could hover almost stationary above the Earth's poles and transmit both visual and infra-red images of ionospheric activity. Dynamic Explorer was the first experiment to clearly reveal the 'theta aurora', the pattern shown in Fig 7.10 which reveals the ionospheric circulation above the northern hemisphere. That the circulation pattern in the southern hemisphere would be quite different was not expected. The pictures from the Explorer satellites told a story which could be explained in terms of the much greater distance separating the south rotation pole from the south magnetic pole, as compared with the situation in the north where the separation is far less, suggesting that in the south, the magnetic effects and the solar effects are decoupled. These studies of the polar regions will undoubtedly be a rich field for students of the lower ionosphere and its plasma physics.

There are two amateur radio satellites which make good auroral probes – Uosat Oscar 11 and Fuji Oscar 20. These satellites can be accessed from the UK whilst their signals are transiting the disturbed lower ionosphere.

In a totally unrelated field, the lower ionosphere can be studied from above by Uosat, using its whole-orbit data dumps. This is particularly useful for comparisons of drag on satellites in decaying orbits, eg Iskra drag versus the radiation levels and solar-wind-induced magnetic levels reported by Uosat.

Satellites in the upper ionosphere

There is a rich vein of experiments waiting to be exploited in this region. Satellites and spacecraft in this zone, or just above it, are numerous, and frequent use of them is made by space radio experimenters and radio amateurs. Indeed the first papers on the subject date right back to Sputnik 1.

Sputnik 1 introduced radio experimenters to antipodal radio reception from satellites. Fig 7.11 shows the situation in respect of the UK during sunspot cycle minimum. Since early days, this antipodal propagation has been reported

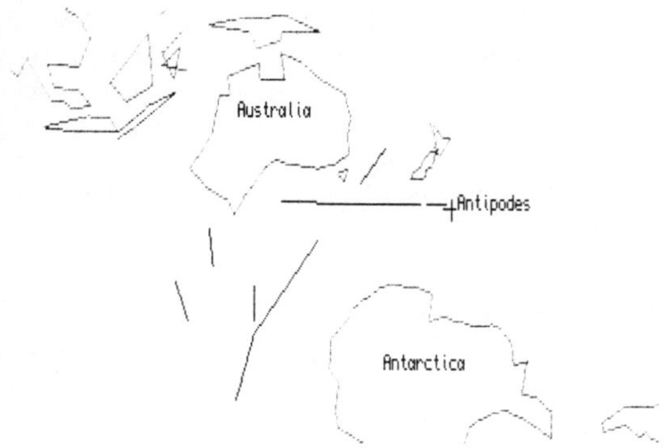

Fig 7.11: Antipodal satellites tracked in the UK at solar minimum. Frequencies: 19.955MHz (six tracks) and 29.502MHz (two tracks)

many times but has never been effectively explained. Recently, satellites Cosmos 1686 (19.955MHz) and Radio-sport 7 (29.502MHz) have added a lot of fresh information. Fig 7.11 shows reception tracks for these satellites near the time of sunspot minimum (1986), a pattern which suggests that at least part of the explanation is propagation via the route shown in Fig 7.12. Certainly these newer reports of antipodal reception favour the 'one side of the antipodes only' path, which can be explained in simple daylight propagation terms.

Nearer to home, as explained in chapter 8, satellites like RS10/11 and the star module (Cosmos 1686) type beacons can all be used for detailed HF propagation studies. Hopefully, the Soviets will launch another of their Iskra ionospheric probes to add to the list of useful satellites and to fill the gap at very low altitude for studies in this zone as we drop away from sunspot cycle maximum 1990. Experimenters should be alert for both standard satellite launches and simple launches such as Iskra, where the satellite is simply pushed out of the space station air lock.

All space radio reception is modified as the signals transit down through the Earth's ionosphere. In the past Nasa have used drifting geostationary orbiters in order to monitor these

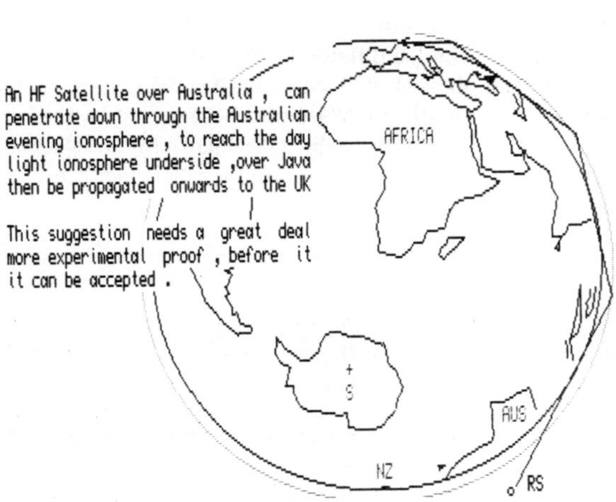

Fig 7.12: Antipodal satellite signal propagation

important variations in ionospheric transparency, in order to apply the results to their navigation of deep space craft such as the Voyagers, Vikings and Pioneers. The Italian wandering geosat was particularly useful in this respect as was the old Meteosat 1 signal on 136MHz. Unfortunately both these satellites have ceased operating, so this experimental field is at present untenanted and could be a logical recipient of amateur radio beacons on geosynchronous platforms, if suitable opportunities occur. Fig 7.13 refers.

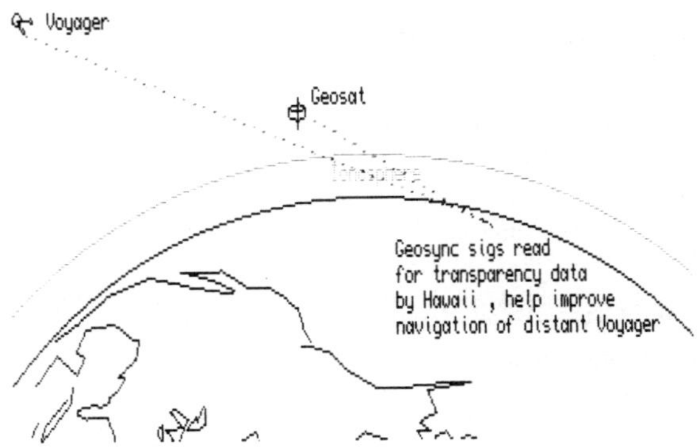

Fig 7.13: A geosynchronous satellite reports ionospheric radio transparency. To navigate deep space craft, ionospheric transparency must be known. Diagram not to scale

The Van Allen belts

James Van Allen was the leader of the Explorer satellite team, whose radiation counters were driven off-scale high by the unexpected levels of radiation which the satellite encountered a mere 2,000km above the Earth. There still remains a great deal we do not know about this region and it could be a rich, albeit highly specialised, zone for amateur satellite experiments.

Experiments in the Earth's magnetosphere

Several families of satellites have explored this region, where the magnetic field of the Earth meets, and is modified by, the solar wind.

The classic satellite experiment in this field was AMPTE – the Active MagnetoSpheric Particle Tracer Experiment. AMPTE used three satellites orbiting in the zone shown on Fig 7.14. One satellite carried cans of lithium or barium, which it could release into the solar wind either side of, or at, the magnetosphere bow shock. A second smaller satellite orbited nearby to record local effects of the release, whilst the third satellite was deep down inside the Earth's magnetosphere, ready to report any of the easily recognised barium or lithium products which got through to it. Several discharge experiments were carried out, producing minor comet-like trails, but the subsequent tracing of the lithium and barium inside the magnetosphere did not go as expected, and it is clear that new experiments in this field are called for. Whilst this type of experiment may not directly

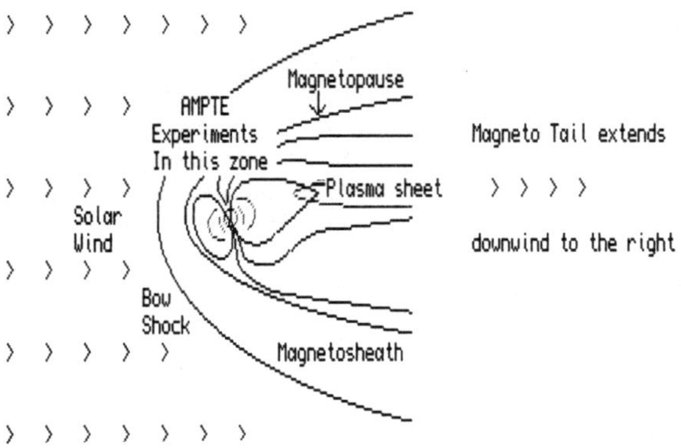

Fig 7.14: Experiments on the edge of the Earth's magnetosphere

concern radio amateurs, they could provide hardware for telemetry and satellite up and down links.

Experiments along the Earth's magnetotail

The Earth's magnetotail extends outwards away down the solar wind, for at least a million kilometres. The magnetotail is known to be the source for much of the Earth's magnetic storm activity, and in consequence of this activity it often contains very dense, high-speed patches of plasma. The magnetotail was first explored by the ISEE 3 satellite. ISEE 3 was originally located as solar watchdog at Lagrange 1. This location, with its intense gravitational potential (eg it could be made to fall all the million miles back to Earth), made ISEE 3 the logical candidate for an American comet probe. Note that, in order to intercept the comet, ISEE 3 could achieve a free gravity boost by dropping it from Lagrange 1 and then winding it up slingshot fashion, by several close orbits around the Earth-Moon loop. In this way, when enough speed had been achieved, ISEE 3 could be released from the loop and fired on a course to intercept Comet Giacobini Zinner. This complex menu of orbital ballistics was in fact highly successful, and a very useful encounter with the comet resulted.

By happy chance the looping slingshot wind-up manoeuvre between Earth and Moon sent ISEE 3 on a sequence of high-speed runs down the magnetotail. Even more important, ISEE 3's original solar watchdog mission meant that it was instrumented with just the right kind of detectors to monitor magnetotail plasma. The third equally important bonus was that its unusually high speed was just what was needed to keep track of the high-speed plasma.

The result was that when nature duly obliged with some excellent magnetic storms whilst ISEE 3 was in the magnetotail, the satellite responded by producing a fully documented record of these events. Fig 7.15 shows the rough track of ISEE 3 down the magnetotail, in disturbed conditions similar to those it actually encountered.

Whilst radio experimenters may have no direct interest in these phenomena, there will doubtless be many opportunities in the future, where long lunar missions and lunar orbital missions could carry equipment capable of monitoring the conditions in the magnetotail. Radio amateurs could provide software and hardware to telemeter this information back to Earth. Once lunar manned stations are established, they will be in a position to directly monitor and report these conditions whenever the Moon is in the magnetotail. Indeed, they may have to monitor them closely to safeguard their own health.

Lunar experimental satellites

The present lull in lunar exploration will shortly end, and be followed by a slow steady build-up of lunar surface activity and facilities. Niches for amateur radio experiments will undoubtedly be forthcoming, with the emphasis likely to be on inter-lunar communication, and Earth-Moon communications. These two features may in fact be interconnected, with 'Earth relay' offering a relatively straightforward solution to the problem of communication between scattered nearside lunar sites. In addition there will be ample opportunity for recreational communications and secondary/emergency communications by amateur radio, to and from the Moon.

The Earth is of course a 'lunar stationary satellite', albeit one whose spin axis we cannot conveniently aim at the Moon. So the possibilities for long-term communications experiments are enormous. The author has not yet investigated the possibility of Earth orbits synchronous with the Moon, ie moonwatcher satellites in Earth orbit (in the same way as some Earth orbits can be made 24 hour Sun synchronous), but orbits of this type may be possible and might afford some excellent experimental features.

Solar observation satellites

Observation of the Sun has featured in many experimental satellite programmes. Deep space probe Pioneer 9 orbited the Sun for many years, sending back early warning of solar flares and other disturbances which could have affected the Apollo programme. More recently the Solar Maximum Mission (SMM) was launched into low Earth orbit in order to monitor solar activity in the peak period after the 1979 maximum. Eventually, however, SMM developed faults on its passive three-axis stabilising wheels, and most of its experiments ceased to operate optimally. Then in 1985 a space shuttle recaptured SMM, repaired it, and put it back to

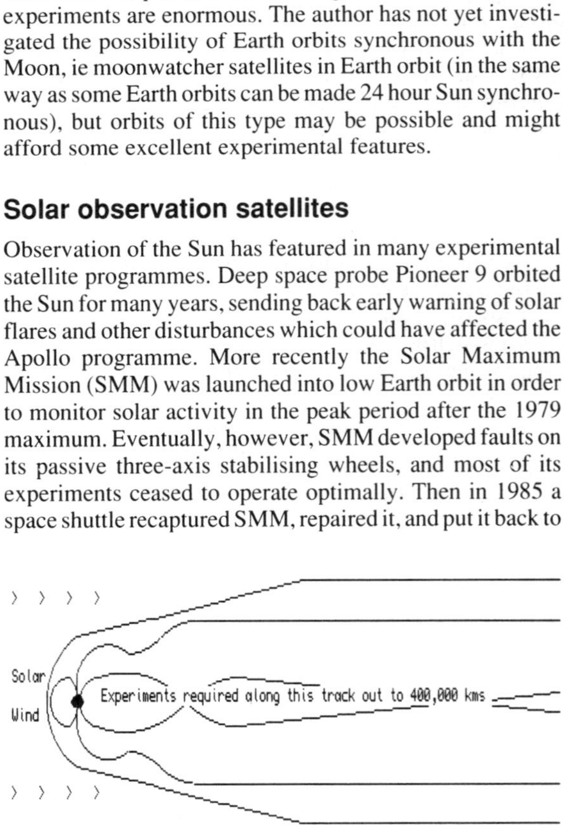

Fig 7.15: Experiments along the Earth's magnetotail. This track was followed by satellite ISEE 3 / ICE 3

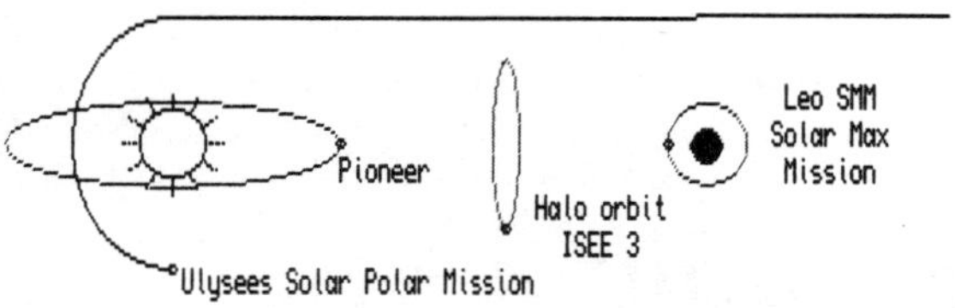

Fig 7.16: Sun watching experimental satellites (not to scale)

work, where it continued to give excellent service. Solar Maximum Mission provided years of solar observation, but it is perhaps best known for the way it has revealed the 152-day flare cycle periodicity around solar maximum.

As yet amateur radio has not felt the full benefit of these experiments. RSGB news bulletins carry excellent solar reports, some of whose material comes from these satellite studies, but few radio amateurs are as yet familiar enough with the new data to use it effectively. This situation is however ripe for change.

The situation in respect to amateur radio use of complex solar data is improving rapidly. The RSGB has pioneered the way with its detailed weekly reports, and this is now bearing fruit as useful propagation software dependent on this accurate solar data begins to appear in amateur radio. As more radio amateurs and space experimenters become aware of the value of these solar studies, it may one day be possible to launch dedicated amateur radio satellites as Sun watchers. Meanwhile, with the Ulysses solar polar mission on its way to the Sun, there is a promise of further interesting solar study material available to all. Fig 7.16 shows a group view of solar watching satellites.

Deep space probes

The stars of the TV space spectaculars have been the interplanetary probes. The innermost planet Mercury has been photographed by a Mariner probe, and cloud-covered Venus has been the target of several successful Soviet Venera and Vega missions, plus the American Pioneer and Magellan. Mars has also been the target for several Soviet missions, but pride of place at the red planet must go to the Mariner fly-by probes and the Viking landers. Jupiter and

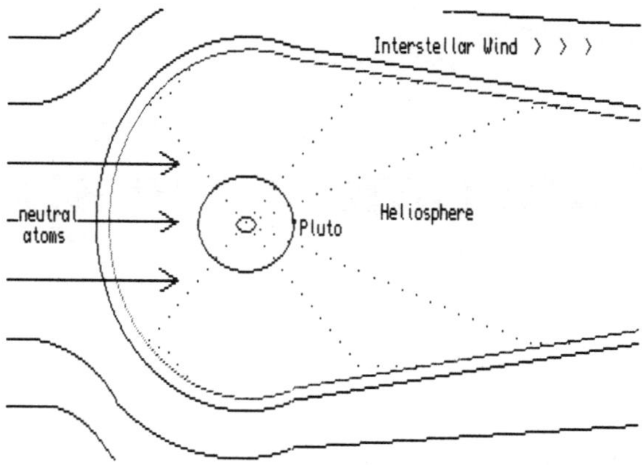

Fig 7.17: Exploring out to the heliosphere collision of interstellar and solar winds

Saturn with their host of Moons have been visited by two Pioneers and two Voyagers, and one Voyager has carried on to Uranus and Neptune, thus completing, less than 40 years after the space age began, a series of visits to all the known major planets in our solar system. Most of these probes are destined never to return to Earth, and some are already out beyond the range of the known planets.

Fig 7.17 shows the orbit of Pluto which, because of its highly eccentric orbit, shares with Neptune the honour of being the furthest known planet. Two Pioneer craft and one Voyager are just at or beyond this Pluto orbit which, as the diagram shows, is less than half way to what is believed to be the next important milestone. This is the junction of the solar wind from our Sun and the galactic stellar wind, the general movement of gas in this part of our Milky Way galaxy. One day, the first of the Pioneers or Voyagers will reach this zone, which we call the 'heliopause', and being curious creatures there is no reason to suppose that men and their probes will stop there. It may seem impertinent to suggest that amateur radio will be involved, but historic parallels suggest there is a good chance that it will be. Marconi could never have predicted amateur radio moonbounce would follow less than 50 years after his initial experiments. Who knows what awaits us!

Chapter 8

Experiments in space radio

Amateur radio is all about experiments. Satellites and space vehicles provide a wealth of experimental opportunity, making it possible to learn radio physics, as you progress in easy stages from simple tests, all the way up to complex investigations at the frontiers of modern science. Many spacecraft actually help by sending down experimental data, so that you can if you wish directly participate in space experiments as they happen. Indeed, many radio amateurs and space radio listeners already contribute directly to a number of interesting space projects.

The experiments described in this chapter are grouped in five sections. In each section the experiments start simply and gradually get more complex as you work through the section.

Section 1. Passive experiments using satellite radio characteristics, needing no co-operation from the satellite.

8.1.01 Simple orbit data collection (Classify and track any satellite)

8.1.02 Doppler shift of HF satellite signals (A simple Doppler experiment)

8.1.03 A better method of Doppler investigation (A more accurate Doppler measurement)

8.1.04 Doppler at very high frequency (The message in the Doppler curve)

8.1.05 Double Doppler (Using Doppler to probe the ionosphere)

8.1.06 Elliptical orbit Doppler (Using Doppler on deep space orbits)

8.1.07 Doppler rate curves (A tougher test of Doppler data)

8.1.08 Differential Doppler (Charting the ionosphere by computer)

8.1.09 Faraday rotation of polarisation (When signals spin in space)

Section 2. Active experiments using measurements and pictures taken by the satellite, or employing equipment in the satellite such as a radio repeater transponder or a telemetry transmitter.

8.2.01 Digitalker Uosat telemetry (Uosat computer talks from space)

8.2.02 Telemetry from Soviet satellites (Monitor standard Soviet telemetry)

8.2.03 Fuji Oscar 12 telemetry and status (Try yourself as a satellite controller)

8.2.04 Uosat whole orbit data (Uosat reports the world)

8.2.05 Death of a satellite (How and why satellites die)

Section 3. Manned space vehicles carrying or deploying experimental packages which actively co-operate with ground experimenters by sending details of experiments and results.

8.3.01 Listening to the cosmonauts (How to monitor manned spacecraft)

8.3.02 Talking to the astronauts (Take your first radio trip in space)

8.3.03 Monitoring space shuttle experiments (Join in shuttle experiments)

8.3.04 Shuttle experiments via satellite relay (Amsat relay of shuttle experiments)

Section 4. Radio propagation studies, using passive and active satellite observations for study of the ionosphere, near Earth space and the magnetosphere.

8.4.01 Ionospheric transparency at VHF (Explore ionospheric problems at VHF)

8.4.02 Concurrent ionospheric studies at VHF (Locate/identify ionospheric anomalies)

8.4.03 Satellites and anomalous VHF propagation (Scan the ionosphere with satellites)

8.4.04 Weather satellite propagation studies (Weather sats and ionospheric anomalies)

8.4.05 Sub-horizon HF satellite propagation (HF propagation tests by satellite)

8.4.06 Identify non-great circle propagation (Satellites reveal non-linear paths)

Section 5. A general class of miscellaneous experiments, both visual and radio, in near-Earth, translunar and deep space, including meteors, EME communications and solar radio astronomy.

8.5.01 Monitoring the radio Sun (Keep watch on our unstable star)

8.5.02 Listening to moonbounce (Half a million miles of real DX)

8.5.03 Meteor scatter monitoring (Millions of mini satellites)

8.5.04 Satellite visual tracking and photography (Satellite 'candid camera')

Experiments – presentation format

Each separate experiment will be introduced by a brief description of its aims. The equipment required will be described, where possible with several alternatives being given especially in regard to the target satellite. A description of the method of execution of the experiment will then follow, after which tables and reports of actual results obtained will be listed in detail. Each experiment report will be closed by a concluding summary.

Where possible, it is suggested that experimenters record at least the minimum of data shown here in each experiment. All too often, extremely useful work is spoilt by a failure to keep precise records. Too much reporting of results is infinitely preferable to under-reporting. Equally important, all times should be rationalised to UTC and full dates should be given, noting that many of the space experiments have marked seasonal variations.

Amateur status is no barrier to the presentation of experimental data in the highest professional forums. Some of the experiments described here have already been presented by radio amateurs at professional symposiums and reported in papers in professional journals. The typical radio amateur, backed by home computers and micro-electronics, is in a strong position to make major contributions to science. Used effectively and reported properly, amateur radio experiments in the forefront of modern science are increasingly enhancing the reputation of amateur radio.

Why experiment?

It is reasonable to ask 'Why take valuable operating time to do these experiments when others have done it all before?' First, very little of this work has been done before and second, if you listen to FO 20, a superb satellite, you will hear half Europe at present getting themselves in a hopeless tangle as one Fuji conversation Dopplers into another, punctuated by the shouts and whistles of those who find the satellite and access on high power one minute, only to disappear back into space the next minute. Few of these operators have the least idea how to follow a satellite signal Dopplering at 4kHz per minute.

Proficient space radio operating is an acquired characteristic. No one is born with the talent already perfected. All the operator has to guide him is the signal-to-noise ratio and its Doppler shift. There are no other clues except experience of just how this sort of orbit performs as regards Doppler or Faraday, and that sort of knowledge is not acquired from text books. Try out these experiments and you will gradually acquire the ability to think ahead to what the signal will do next. You will know that a slowly dropping Doppler at the start of a pass is a sign that it will drop very fast in the middle of the pass, whereas a modest Doppler at the start will probably stay that way throughout the pass.

You will doubtless know some operators who talk about satellites all day, but rarely if ever appear on them. If you plan to get a little further than that group, you should find the earlier experiments in each section will help you. Use the experiments to pick up tracking and tuning fundamentals at your own pace. Then, when you are ready, try the Radiosport satellites.

The Soviet Radiosport satellites are first class for beginners and old timers. They are easy to access, have low Doppler rates and use simple wide-coverage antennas. This said, their long-distance communications potential is excellent.

But Fuji has lots more facilities. So when you are happy with your RS performance, shift over to Fuji using the low-elevation, slow-Doppler orbits down near your horizon. You lose nothing by doing this because all the best long-distance communication is on these low-elevation orbits. Tracking Fuji on a high overhead pass is a bit like riding wild horses. It does not make much sense when you could have a smoother ride and get long-range communication on a horizon-scraping orbit. On the high overhead orbits Doppler is fierce and antenna tracking must be continuous and, just to rub salt in the wound, you can only talk to locals on overhead orbits. So like bronco busting – why bother, you can get more challenge trying the weak-signal techniques necessary to follow the Phase III satellites. Experiment 8.1.06 is good training for weak-signal work.

Finally, when you have mastered all the satellite types, you can really get down to it and try some of the experiments at the end of each section. Here you will be on brand-new territory. We really must learn more about HF propagation and the use of computer techniques like differential Doppler to get better ionospheric data.

There are lots more questions here waiting for answers. Can you help find some of these answers, and help enhance the good name of amateur radio?

Experiment 8.1.01: Simple orbit data collection

Purpose

To make sure you can always find the satellite you want. No experiment can succeed unless the satellite can be located easily and repeatedly. This is not a problem if the satellite is a well-known one in a stable orbit. NORAD/Nasa two-line Keplerian orbital elements are usually readily available.

All too often, data is either not available or is out of date. Manned spacecraft frequently change their orbits without prior notice. Many of the most interesting satellites from the point of view of the radio amateur space watcher are interesting because they are unreported, and perhaps doing something unusual. Some satellites change their orbits so fast, that not even a steady supply of NORAD data can keep up with them. NORAD often cease reporting rogue satellites, or old satellites which although still transmitting have long since totally exceeded their design life and ground station tracking budget.

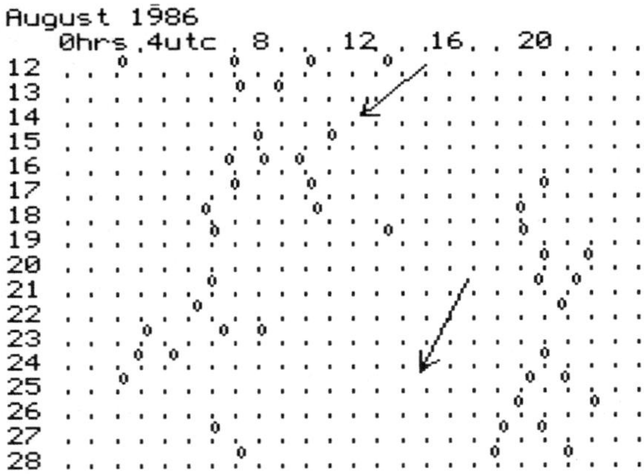

Fig 8.1.01: Kettering plot for 19.995MHz satellites

There are therefore many occasions when the satellite experimenter is anxious to track an unreported satellite. This experiment seeks to show a simple procedure for getting approximate orbit data of sufficient quality to allow useful tracking of totally unreported or unknown spacecraft.

Method

This procedure is applicable to any satellite in Earth orbit. It requires that the satellite be received by radio or observed visually. The simple example quoted here uses an HF shortwave radio receiver listening via a wire antenna to the 19.955MHz CW keyed beacon on a Soviet space station. Although NORAD publish regular data on Salyut 7, the station regularly adjusts its orbit, and sometimes, as in this case, makes big alterations, such that if this method of keeping track of it was not available, it could be lost for days. (Mir on 143.625MHz is also a good target.)

Every time the beacon is heard the operator records time and date in Universal/Greenwich time co-ordinates (UTC). These times and dates are then plotted in a form first reported to the author by the well-known group of satellite watchers and listeners based on Kettering, England. Each horizontal line of the plot relates to a specific day, and it is graduated for 24 hours. Every time the satellite is heard or seen on that day is marked on the plot at the appropriate time column UTC. Next day the procedure is repeated on the next line down, gradually developing a plot as shown in Fig 8.1.01.

Table 8.1.01

Date	Times heard (UTC)
16 Aug 1986	0643, 0813, 0947
17	0702, 1010, 2002
18	0547, 1903, 2027
19	0610, 1329, 1909
20	2000, 2152
21	0600, 1944, 2118
22	0527, 2043
23	0320, 0634, 0810
24	0258, 0428, 1956
25	0221, 1919, 2054
26	1851, 2207
27	0610, 1817, 1952
28	0715, 1751, 2102

Results

These are shown in Table 8.1.01. Note that it is not possible for a single observer to hear every orbit in range, every day for weeks. Nor was it possible to listen exactly at those moments when the spacecraft came above the station horizon. Equally important, some of the orbits recorded here were clearly detections of the spacecraft beacon received from a sub-horizon location via ionospheric propagation. The table, as the method suggests, simply reports when the spacecraft was heard.

Conclusions

As tabulated in Table 8.1.01 the signals seem almost random in timing and distribution. Plotted in the manner used by the Kettering group, several features begin to appear in the data.

In particular there seem to be two distinct patterns. The arrow at the top of Fig 8.1.01 aligns with the general trend of all reports up to the afternoon on 19 August. Then at 1909 there is a signal which does not fit at all.

From 20 August a new pattern gradually emerges. Whereas the plot up to 19 August showed the satellite appearing roughly 71 minutes earlier each successive day, thereafter the slope of consecutive days orbits is about 32 minutes earlier each day.

These facts give direct clues as to what has happened and when it happened. Prior to 19 August the satellite completed a little over 15 orbits per day, obtained by simply filling in the missing spaces at roughly the right steps in time. In fact 15 orbits took one day – 71 minutes = 1440 – 71 for 15 orbits, ie about 91.26 minutes period each orbit. After 19 August, 15 orbits take longer = 1440 – 32, ie about 93.87 minutes per orbit. On 5 September NORAD reported the Salyut was in a new orbit of 94.04 minutes, so this simple plot was only about 10 seconds low.

At any time whilst this plot is being used it is easy to plot on to estimate when that day's orbital passes will be heard. So even when NORAD/Nasa elements are not available this method allows the operator to keep track of when he can next expect his satellite to appear. In situations where several satellites use the same frequency this method is invaluable for sorting out which is which, and in this particular instance it was possible to say by 21 August that the beacon orbiting on Salyut at about 340km altitude had suddenly either gone to 480km altitude, or been switched off and replaced by a new beacon/vehicle at 480km. In fact no visual check was possible because of poor visibility until 3 September. On that date the sunlit Salyut space station was clearly tracked over Scotland coincident with the beacon orbiting at 480km putting in a strong signal. It was obvious Salyut had moved with the beacon. The Soviet space agency made its first announcement confirming this on 5 September.

Experiment 8.1.02: Doppler shift on HF satellite signals

Purpose

To examine why satellite velocity with respect to your receiving station turns the constant frequency signal emitted by the satellite into a variable frequency at your receiver.

Method

A shortwave receiver capable of receiving any of the following target signals is attached to a simple wire antenna, say, 30ft long, and switched on. An accurate watch is needed for timing the taking of the measurements. Possible target satellites are:

- 19.955MHz Soviet beacons (now rare)
- 20.008MHz Mir Space station and Soyuz ferry craft (rare)
- 29.357MHz Radiosport 10 (regular)
- 29.503MHz Radiosport 11 (rare)

This method is applicable to any HF receiver with a calibrated tuning dial. The receiver is connected to the antenna, switched on and allowed to warm up until stable. Having previously consulted a computer-generated track prediction or worked out when the next orbit will arrive using the method outlined in the previous experiment, start tuning around for the satellite beacon signal a little before you expect it above your horizon.

When the satellite beacon is heard, start your watch or note start time, then adjust the receiver tuning so that the signal tone in the CW or sideband mode gets lower and lower, more and more bassy. Continue tuning until the signal tone is just too low to be heard.

Quickly write down the dial frequency and a note of the time at which this reading was taken in hours, minutes and seconds of time UTC.

Table 8.1.02: Satellite RS7 Doppler shift, starts 1859 UTC

Time (min)	Frequency (MHz)	Time (min)	Frequency (MHz)
0	29.50100	9	signal faded
1	29.50100	10	29.50045
2	29.50100	11	29.50035
3	29.50090	12	29.50020
4	29.50090	13	29.50020
5	29.50080	14	29.50015
6	29.50075	15	29.50010
7	29.50070	16	signal lost
8	29.50070		

Try to get a new reading every half minute. Logging the zero beat reading and the time it was taken ('zero beat' is the phrase used for this technique where a signal frequency is measured by tuning your receiver in the USB, LSB or CW mode to lose the note at too low a frequency to hear). Remember to tune for zero beat by turning the frequency dial slowly until the signal becomes too low a note to be heard. What you are doing is rather crudely measuring the signal carrier frequency with its Doppler shift at that moment.

Results

This method is crude. Table 8.1.02 shows a typical set of readings produced by following the Doppler shift of satellite RS7 on 14 July 1986 at 1859 UTC. One-minute steps were used in this example.

Fig 8.1.02 shows this information plotted as a graph of frequency versus time.

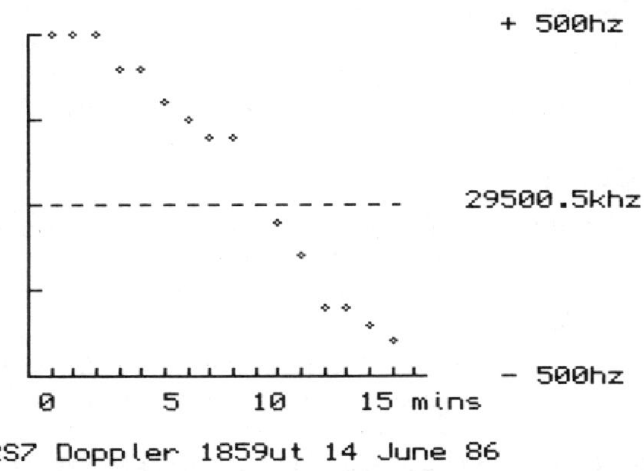

Fig 8.1.02: Radiosport 7 Doppler graph

Conclusion

After remaining steady for several minutes the frequency reading began to fall quite quickly from minute 3 onwards, but at minute 12 it began to slow up again, so that when lost completely at minute 16, it was changing only slowly. Another point to note from this example of the Doppler curve from a circular-orbit satellite is that the Doppler is always going down in frequency.

This set of results is not really very good. If we want better information from Doppler the experimental method must be improved. The next experiment, 8.1.03, uses a slightly better method.

Experiment 8.1.03: A better method of Doppler investigation

Purpose

To obtain Doppler curves giving useful information, such as time of closest approach of satellite to your station.

Method

Using either a dial frequency analogue display receiver or a digital frequency readout receiver with step tuning, connect the receiver to a simple antenna and power supply.

Check your computer track print-out or use experiment 8.1.01 to find out when the next orbit of your target satellite is due above your station horizon. Targets listed in experiment 8.1.02 are all suitable.

When the target satellite is heard, tune the signal to find the lowest note you can just hear in the CW or SSB position. Then set the receiver to the next lower 100Hz tuning step. Wait and listen as the signal Dopplers down to a lower and lower note, then carefully note the exact time at the moment when the note disappears at zero beat (as described in experiment 8.1.02).

Having written down both the time and the frequency, quickly shift the receiver tuning down exactly 100Hz and time the next zero beat. Repeat this procedure, timing and recording all the zero-beat crossings until the signal is lost as it goes below your far horizon. What you should now have is a list of times as the signal passed through a regular series of equal frequency steps, as shown in Table 8.1.03.

Results

These, listed in Table 8.1.03, are shown in Fig 8.1.03a, plotted as a graph of frequency versus time.

Conclusion

A clear (almost too perfect) Doppler curve, which starts slowly then rapidly descends in the middle section as the

Table 8.1.03: Cosmos 1686, 18 June 1986 at 19.955MHz

Time (UTC)	Frequency (MHz)	Time (UTC)	Frequency (MHz)
0644:01	19.9555	0648:48	19.9550
0645:50	19.9554	0649:31	19.9549
0646:52	19.9553	0650:40	19.9548
0647:26	19.9552	0652:12	19.9547
0648:05	19.9551	0654:39	faded above 19.9546

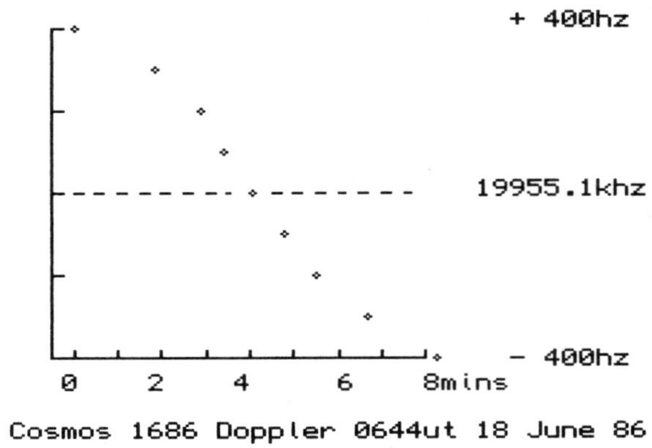

Fig 8.1.03a: Cosmos 1686 Doppler graph

satellite passes the closest point of approach to station (CPA). This point of maximum slope on the Doppler curve appears to have occurred at about 0647:30, indicating CPA at about this time. From the actual slope of the curve it is possible to make a rough calculation of satellite slant range from the station at CPA, but this HF experiment is too crude to give a really reliable answer. Please note that the bottom half of the Doppler curve is not a mirror image of the top half. This is because other factors such as the movement of your station on the spinning Earth can take it towards or away from the satellite at different parts of this overhead pass.

A simple way to examine your Doppler curve's asymmetry is possible if you fold the graph paper first along the vertical axis through the assumed CPA point of maximum slope of the curve, then fold it again, this time horizontally through the point of maximum slope. Hold the graph paper up to the light to see how closely the two halves of the curve overlay one another. They should be quite different if your experiment has been done properly. This kind of data can be most important. Amongst other things the asymmetry of the curve is a good check of whether the satellite spent more time to your east or your west, and whether at some time during the pass your station changed from approaching the satellite, to receding from it, or vice versa. This sort of information becomes more important when satellite Doppler is being used for navigation position fixing, as in the Transit and Cosnav systems.

Fig 8.1.03b shows you how to fold the paper for this check.

Experiment 8.1.04: Doppler at VHF

Purpose

To accurately measure and examine Doppler shift at VHF and UHF.

Method

A VHF or a UHF receiver is required which can receive and tune either CW continuous carrier signals or SSB single

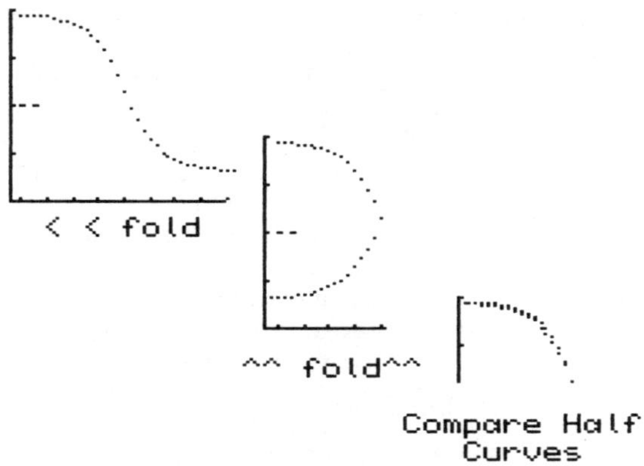

Fig 8.1.03b: How to fold a Doppler chart to check asymmetry

sideband signals. Please note that with this kind of receiver it is perfectly in order to read Doppler shift on a frequency-modulated signal using CW or SSB reception. What is not possible is to measure Doppler on a receiver which can only receive at FM or AM. Therefore Uosat is a good target but you must use CW or SSB reception even though it is an FM signal. The receiver should be connected to a relatively simple VHF or UHF antenna as appropriate. Most of the satellites of interest put out strong signals. Potential target satellites are:

137.3MHz	Meteor weather satellites
137.5MHz	NOAA weather satellite
137.6MHz	NOAA weather satellite

Or navigation satellites simultaneously on VHF and UHF:

Ch1	**Ch2**	**Ch3**	**Ch4**	**Ch5**
149.91	149.94	149.97	150.00	150.03
399.762	399.842	399.922	400.02	400.082

Or Uosat Oscar 11 on 145.825MHz.

Note that if you use a navigation satellite, you will find more of them on channel 4 than the other channels, and you should avoid the satellites on 399.968MHz ±10kHz of

Table 8.1.04a: Navsat, 400.0MHz, 16 June 1986 at 1316 UTC

Time	Freq	Time	Freq	Time	Freq	Time	Freq
0	400.0094	5	400.0078	10	399.9965	15	399.9933
0.5	400.0094	5.5	400.0073	10.5	399.9957	15.5	399.9932
1	400.0093	6	400.0066	11	399.9950	16	399.9931
1.5	400.0092	6.5	400.0057	11.5	399.9946	16.5	399.9931
2	400.0092	7	400.0045	12	399.9943	faded1332:40	
2.5	400.0091	7.5	400.0031	12.5	399.994		
3	400.0089	8	400.0014	13	399.9937		
3.5	400.0088	8.5	399.9995	13.5	399.9936		
4	400.0085	9	399.9983	14	399.9935		
4.5	400.0082	9.5	399.9973	14.5	399.9934		

Table 8.1.04b: Navsat, 400.00MHz, 16 June 1986 at 1351 UTC

Time	Freq	Time	Freq	Time	Freq	Time	Freq
0	400.0082	4	400.0051	8	399.9980	12	399.9948
0.5	400.0079	4.5	400.0044	8.5	399.9974	12.5	399.9946
1	400.0076	5	400.0035	9	399.9969	13	399.9944
1.5	400.0073	5.5	400.0025	9.5	399.9964	faded1404:20	
2	400.0070	6	400.0015	10	399.9960		
2.5	400.0066	6.5	400.0005	10.5	399.9956		
3	400.0062	7	399.9994	11	399.9953		
3.5	400.0057	7.5	399.9987	11.5	399.9950		

Table 8.1.04c: Navsat, 400.00MHz, 16 June 1986 at 1503 UTC

Time	Freq	Time	Freq	Time	Freq	Time	Freq
0	400.0068	4	400.0027	7	399.9983	faded1513:05	
0.5	400.0065	4.5	400.0019	7.5	399.9979		
1	400.0061	5	400.0012	8	399.9975		
1.5	400.0058	5.5	400.0004	5	399.9971		
2	400.0053	6	399.9995	9	399.9967		
2.5	400.0047	6.5	399.9989	9.5	399.9963		
3	400.0041						
3.5	400.0034						

Doppler because their note is too rough for accurate measurement.

Acquire the signal as it comes above your horizon. Tune it for zero beat every half minute thereafter, recording the frequency and the time UTC at each measurement. Plot the results on graph paper. Repeat the experiment once or twice more on other orbits.

Results

These are shown in Tables 8.1.04a-c.

Conclusion

Figs 8.1.04a-c show the results of an experiment which is still crude, but none the less accurate enough to tell a great deal about the satellites concerned. The first two curves were obtained in too short an interval to be the same satellite. Navigation satellites complete an orbit in about 107 minutes, so results from a shorter time interval cannot be the same satellite. Two satellites are involved and it is clear from both the shapes of the first two curves and the slopes of their central portions that these two satellites were on dissimilar tracks. The 1316 UTC satellite displays almost no Dopplering of frequency at the start, which indicates that it was coming almost directly towards the receiving station. Then in the middle of the curve it had an extremely steep slope, suggesting that it passed nearly overhead. By contrast the 1351 satellite was not coming directly towards our station at the start. Its Doppler curve has a marked slope even at the start, none the less it had quite a steep slope as it made its CPA. Perhaps less obvious, please note also that the

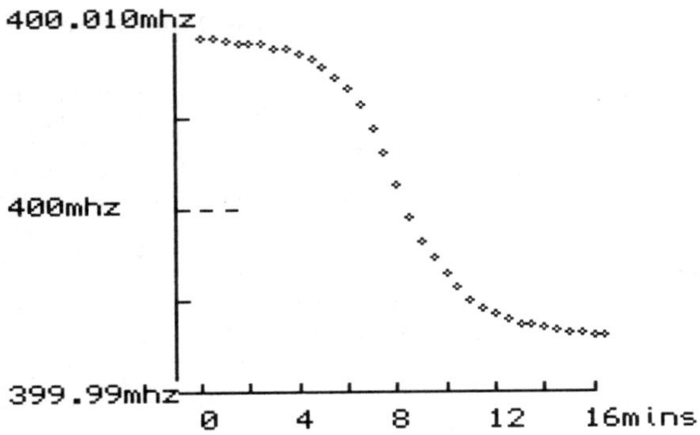

a: 1316 UTC

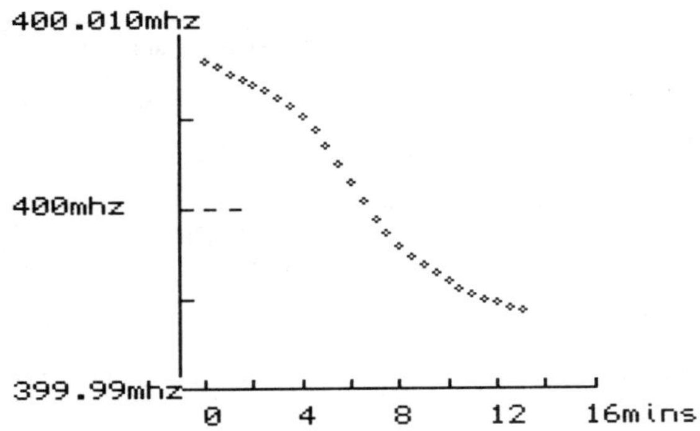

b: 1351 UTC

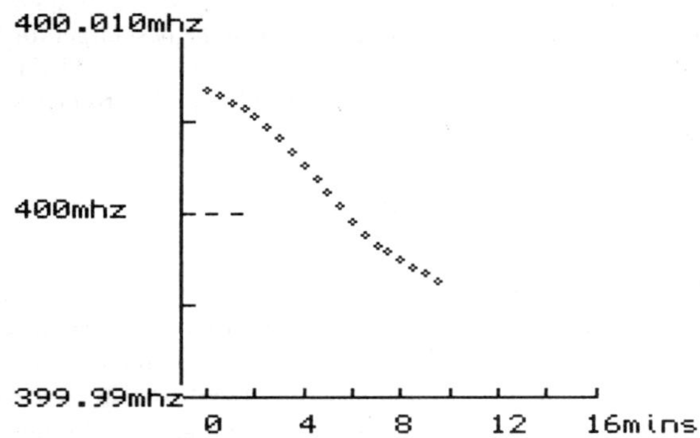

c: 1503 UTC

Fig 8.1.04a-c: Navsat UHF Doppler curves, 16 June 1986

1351 pass was shorter than its predecessor and that at the end its Doppler curve still had considerable slope, whereas the previous pass had almost no Doppler curve slope as it went towards the horizon.

More of the same sort of study of the data reveals that the pass at 1503 (note the roughly 107 minute spacing) was probably a return of the satellite which produced the 1316 UTC curve, but on this return its CPA was a long way out from the receiving station. Its Doppler curve covers even less change of frequency than the 1351 curve, it has a relatively gentle slope, and even at CPA the frequency received is changing only slowly. Add to this the fact of its short duration, and it is clear that all these clues complement one another to tell us that, although none of these satellites was seen, we are able to tell from their Doppler curves just where they passed in relation to the receiving station.

Please look critically at these curves. There are obvious anomalies in the record for the first pass at 1316. In particular the curve between the fourth and fifth readings, and again the curve between the seventh and eighth readings, is irregular. Then the curve is again regular until the 27th and 28th points, where it is again irregular. By contrast, the record for 1351 UTC shows none of these obvious bumps, but a close look at its slope at the start suggests it is steeper than it is shortly thereafter around the fifth, sixth and seventh readings entered. Last but not least, the pass at 1503 may have produced what looks like a smooth curve, but it certainly is not. On close inspection it looks more like a collection of disparate straight lines which are added end to end.

All this study of the curves is not nit-picking. Some of these anomalies are certainly due to experimental error, but some are not. These latter are due to irregularities in the ionosphere plus asymmetry due to Earth rotation. Both these features contain a wealth of information if we know how to tap the Doppler curve, but to do this more effectively we must again change our method, as some of the following experiments show.

Experiment 8.1.05: Double Doppler

Purpose

Before going on to more serious Doppler experiments, there is one simple experiment which is well worth doing. This experiment measures Doppler shift simultaneously on two frequencies from the same satellite. Sometimes special experimental beacon satellites carry five or six phased-locked beacons. The famous P76 had beacons on 136, 376, 436, 496, 1,238 and 2,476MHz, all phase-locked. Today P76 is silent, so we have to make do with the two-frequency navigation satellites, though multi-beacon satellites will undoubtedly be launched in the future. This multi-frequency technique makes the Doppler anomalies more obvious, and it reveals how the ionosphere treats the individual frequencies quite differently, one from another.

Method

Two receivers, one covering 150MHz and the other covering 400MHz, are required. Both are used in the CW/SSB reception mode. Suitable targets are:

Ch1	Ch2	Ch3	Ch4	Ch5
149.910	149.940	149.970	150.000	150.030
399.762	399.842	399.922	400.002	400.082

Table 8.1.05: Navsat double Doppler, 16 June 1986, 1721 UTC

Time	Freq1	Freq 2	Time	Freq1	Freq 2
0		150.0040	7		150.0015
	400.0085			400.0009	
1		150.0039	8		150.0008
	400.0082			399.9990	
2		150.0037	9		150.0002
	400.0077			399.9976	
3		150.0035	10		149.9996
	400.0070			399.9965	
4		150.0032	11		149.9992
	400.0060			399.9956	
5		150.0027	12		149.9989
	400.0048			399.9950	
6		150.0022	13		149.9987
	400.0029			399.9945	
			14		149.9985
				399.9941	faded

More satellites use Channel 4 than any other. Ignore the beacons with the rough notes on 399.968MHz. All 400MHz signals start up to 10kHz above and finish up well below the channel centre frequencies shown above.

The signals are quite strong, so simple three- or four-element beam antennas are more than adequate. Amateur radio antennas for 144 and 432MHz work quite well.

Using these two receivers and one fast (or two slow) operators, acquire a suitable navsat as it comes above your horizon. Tune in both the 149MHz and the 399MHz signals, then at one-minute intervals measure the zero beat frequency, taking the 149MHz signal on the minute, and the 399MHz signal on the half-minute if only one operator is available.

Results

These are shown in Table 8.1.05. In Fig 8.1.05 the scale of the 150MHz curve has been changed to allow it to align with the 400MHz curve as closely as possible.

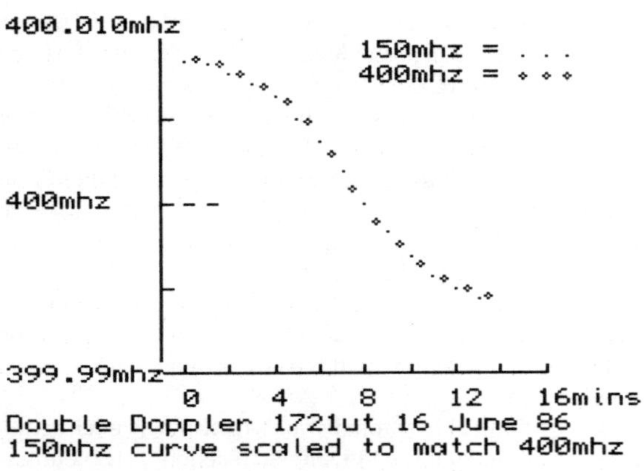

Fig 8.1.05: Double Doppler

Conclusions

The two curves are almost the same shape but, when laid close together with appropriate scaling, the anomalies in the 150MHz curve begin to be more obvious. Note for example how the third dot and the sixth dot are out of line, and also note that the end of the 150MHz curve has a different slope from the 400MHz curve. This method is still rather crude and is prone to experimental errors, but it can reveal some interesting features, particularly when curves taken in quiet ionospheric conditions are compared with those taken when the ionosphere is disturbed. Double curves repeated at different times of day can show marked diurnal variation, with curves taken just after local sunset being most irregular.

Experiment 8.1.06: Elliptical-orbit Doppler

Purpose

Previous experiments in this series have concerned themselves with satellites in circular orbits. These are special cases, and to obtain a broader view of Doppler experiments it is necessary to examine the very different elliptical orbit. Unfortunately good targets for this experiment are rare. The main series of elliptical orbiters are the Russian molniya type, but they use either higher UHF or microwave frequencies not normally covered by amateur radio receivers. Oscar 10 is a good target on 145.812MHz provided it is not 'FMing' (warbling). Oscar 13 changes frequency regularly, so it is not a good target. For the moment the best target for this experiment is the rather ancient French satellite SRET 2. Using this satellite, this experiment explores Kepler's laws of satellite/planetary motion.

Method

A sensitive VHF receiver for 137.53MHz used in the CW or SSB mode is fed by a Yagi beam antenna of at least 10dB gain versus a dipole. A low-noise preamplifier at the antenna is desirable but not essential. Keplerian elements ceased to be published for this satellite many years ago, long after it had far surpassed its design life. So the first task is to find it. It has good positive signal classification features so this is not difficult, but it will take time. Leave your receiver tuned around 137.53MHz, with your antenna pointing south at the horizon. Every 12 hours or so SRET 2 sweeps down to, or up from, the horizon quickly with a strong signal because it is quite near the Earth at its perigee. When heard near perigee the signal should consist of three carriers, relatively fixed notes, spaced about 4kHz apart, eg 137.5258, 137.5301 and 137.5339MHz. You may quickly lose SRET 2 as it goes behind the Earth at perigee, in which case you will catch it ascending between 30 and 90 minutes later. You may catch it ascending, climbing away from the Earth, having been through perigee.

Track it as it ascends towards its apogee at about 40,000km

Table 8.1.06: SRET2, 24 June 1986, 0631 UTC

Time	Carrier 1	Carrier 2	Carrier 3
0631 UTC	137.5275	137.5316	not heard
0730	All signals lost as satellite passes perigee		
0957	137.5252	137.5296	137.5333
1039	137.5256	137.5300	137.5339
1125	137.5260	137.5302	too weak
1300	too weak	137.5304	too weak
1325	137.5266	137.5307	137.5346
1400	137.5267	137.5308	too weak
1456	too weak	137.5309	too weak
1552	137.5272	137.5312	too weak
1615	too weak	137.5315	too weak
1700	too weak	137.5317	too weak
1735	too weak	137.5318	too weak
1815	137.5279	137.5319	137.5358
1826	137.5280	137.5320	lost
1835	137.5280	137.5321	137.5359
1845	137.5282	137.5322	137.5359
1900	137.5283	137.5323	lost
1915	137.5283	137.5323	137.5364
1938	137.5283	137.5323	lost
1946	137.5281	137.5322	137.5363
1954	137.5280	137.5321	137.5361
(From this point only the strong central carrier was followed because the Doppler shift was too great to allow complete recording of all three carriers)			
1956		137.5320	
1958		137.5319	
1959		137.5318	
2000		137.5317	
2001		137.5316	
2002		137.5315	
2004		137.5313	
2007		137.5310	
2008	Lost the satellite completely		

above the 60°N parallel of latitude, ie it will go very high in elevation somewhere north of the UK. As it climbs you will hear something distinctive – the signal has positive Doppler and is rising in frequency, something circular orbiters simply do not do. As it rises in altitude and frequency you will notice that its position in the sky changes only slowly. You should record its frequency, if possible for each of the three carriers, every 15 minutes. You can expect the centre carrier of the three to be stronger than the two outer carriers, and it may be the only one you can hear as SRET 2 climbs to apogee; if this is the case keep recording its frequency every 15 minutes.

If you lose it for 15 minutes, do not stop the experiment. Keep looking for it and you will probably find it again. The signal output of SRET 2 is only 250 milliwatts, so it is a tough low-power test of your receiving and operating capabilities. SRET 2 takes about 12 hours to go once around its ellipse, so you have two orbits per day which you can check. Both orbits will be high in your sky at apogee, but only the orbit with perigee on your side of the world will be heard during its early post-perigee phase.

Please note that SRET 2 does not have exclusive use of this frequency. You must expect to hear other satellites

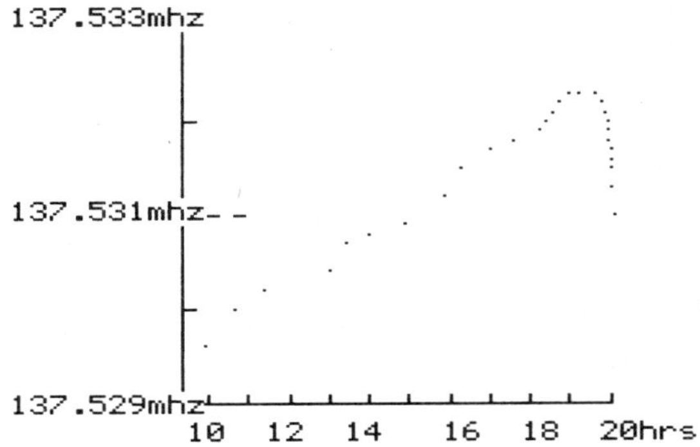

Fig 8.1.06a: Elliptical-orbit Doppler graph, 0957 UTC, 24 June 1986

Dopplering across the frequency from time to time. Once you find you can locate SRET 2, try following it for a few practice orbits, then when you have roughly mastered this part of the experiment, start taking frequency readings on all three carriers if you can hear them. Be careful at the end of the orbit; the slow steady rise over eight or nine hours, from perigee through to apogee and then back towards the Earth, is a complete contrast to the sudden dramatic drop in frequency which occurs literally in minutes near perigee. At this part of the orbit you will need to take records every minute and it may be too fast for you to follow all three carriers, so concentrate on the middle one.

Results

These are shown in Table 8.1.06. For insurance, an attempt was made to log the frequencies of the two weaker outer carriers. These were often lost, but the centre carrier remained audible just above the noise threshold throughout the experiment. This data is plotted as Fig 8.1.06a.

Conclusions

This experiment is a difficult operational task. It may be necessary to practise for several days before an orbit is tracked throughout.

The first point of interest about the Doppler curve shown in Fig 8.1.06a is that throughout the whole period from 0957 to 1938 UTC the received frequency rose steadily. This is in total contrast to the more familiar circular-orbit Doppler curve. Satellites in circular orbits are received with a continuously descending frequency for the period of their orbit when they are above your station horizon. Only elliptical orbiters display increasing received frequency for most of the time they are above your horizon.

The reason for this steady increase in received frequency lies in Kepler's laws governing elliptical motion. Fig 8.1.06b illustrates the way in which the law of 'equal areas, equal time', operates.

It is difficult at first for anyone to grasp why a retreating satellite produces a rising Doppler. The main problem lies with our misconception of Doppler.

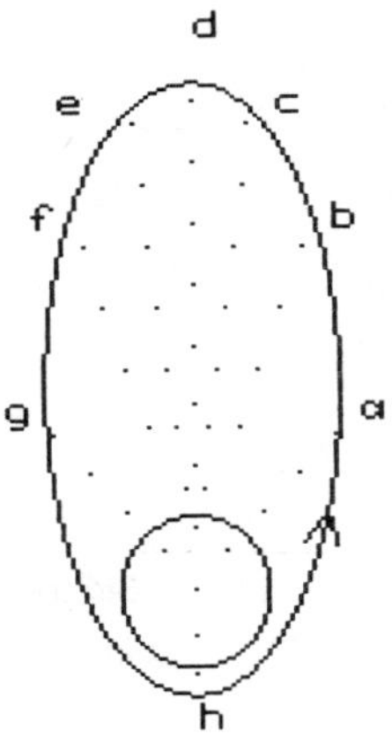

Fig 8.1.06b: Kepler's laws of motion. The lines of dots divide the orbital ellipse into sectors. If each of these has the same area, then a body in that orbit will take the same time to go round the edge of each sector. But the distance between points ab is greater than the distance between bc, and bc is greater than cd. Therefore a satellite would slow when climbing to apogee at d. From d to h, however, the satellite would speed up = Doppler positive up and down

Consider a satellite which has just gone through its perigee. It comes up out of the Southern Hemisphere past your station, then quickly recedes. As you tune the signal you find (only if you know the actual satellite transmitter frequency) that the frequency has Dopplered well below the transmitted frequency. But most of the time you do not know the actual transmitted frequency, so all you are aware of is that once the satellite has gone past you, the received frequency begins to climb. You could say it has positive Doppler, but a more appropriate description is that its Doppler shift is getting less negative, and the reason for this is that the satellite is slowing up. It is still going away from you, so its Doppler shift is negative below the satellite transmitted frequency, and because of Kepler's law of equal areas, equal time, it does not need to go so fast to sweep out the same area. Each kilometre of its track is therefore taking longer to cover. This situation applies all the way up to apogee. At apogee the satellite is hardly moving at all with respect to your station, so it has no relative velocity (no Doppler shift), and reception of the satellite signal is at roughly the satellite transmitter frequency.

After apogee the pattern is reversed, but the result is the same. The satellite begins to drop slowly back to Earth, achieving relative velocity towards your station, so the Doppler shifts to a higher frequency. If the satellite kept the same speed towards your station its received frequency would stay the same, but in addition to coming towards you the satellite has to obey Kepler's laws: as it gets nearer Earth it must travel faster to cover 'equal area, in equal time'. So the satellite accelerates as it drops towards the Earth. This produces a gradual rise in its relative velocity towards your station, and so the signal you receive has a higher Doppler shift and its received frequency after apogee, all the long way back to Earth, continues to climb.

Eventually it flashes past your station and dives towards perigee in the southern hemisphere. As it does so the Doppler situation changes dramatically as in Fig 8.1.06a from 1946 onwards. Having taken readings at 30 minute or 15 minute intervals for several hours, the experimenter will find that he must change the tempo. The sudden shift back to a falling frequency happens quickly and should be monitored minute by minute, as the satellite is soon lost as it disappears under the Earth as it swings round perigee at latitude 60°S.

If time permits the experimenter may care to look for the Russian molniya elliptical orbiters. They use the same type of orbit as SRET 2, but they transmit on frequencies between 800 and 1,000MHz.

Once the experimenter has familiarised himself with the important Doppler characteristics of each orbit type, it is not a big step to progress towards classifying and tracking orbits where only a brief portion of each ellipse is heard, eg lunar and deep space orbits. Most lunar and interplanetary probes use orbits called 'patched conics', which are quite simply derived from an ellipse around the Earth being, for example, patched (connected to an ellipse around the Moon or a planet). If you can follow the Doppler behaviour of a spacecraft, you can do quite a good job of navigating it and predicting its future track – all by simply listening to its Doppler.

Experiment 8.1.07: Doppler rate curves

Purpose

To maximise the potential of Doppler information it is often best to plot change of frequency with time (Doppler rate of change), rather than frequency. This experiment uses exactly the same procedure as experiment 8.1.04 but instead of simply plotting the curve of changing frequency, it takes another step and uses the frequency data to calculate change of frequency. This change of frequency is scaled in kilohertz change per minute of time, and this value is graph plotted.

Method

This experiment can be performed using any transmitting satellite. The equipment needed is exactly the same as that for experiment 8.1.04 and uses exactly the same procedure as that experiment to get frequency versus time data at a fixed interval of time. When the satellite pass is over, the frequency data recorded is converted to change of frequency versus time data. For example, if the frequency at time 0 is 400.004MHz and half a minute later it is 400.0038, then frequency change = 0.2kHz in half a minute = 0.4kHz/min negative (down in frequency). This frequency change figure is then graph plotted at the appropriate centre time of this measurement, ie time 0.25.

Results

Figs 8.1.07a to 8.1.07c show the plotted Doppler rate curves derived from the data in Table 8.1.07.

Conclusions

The Doppler rate curves derived by this method provide a positive way of identifying the time of CPA. The CPA is the

Table 8.1.07: Navsat, 16 June 1986

Run 1 at 1316 UTC Time	Freq	kHz/min	Run 2 at 1351 UTC Time	Freq	kHz/min	Run 3 at 1503 UTC Time	Freq	kHz/min
0	400.0094	–	0	400.0082	–	0	400.0068	–
0.5	400.0094	0	0.5	400.0079	0.6	0.5	400.0065	0.6
1	400.0093	0.2	1	400.0076	0.6	1	400.0061	0.8
1.5	400.0092	0.2	1.5	400.0073	0.6	1.5	400.0058	0.6
2	400.0092	0	2	400.0070	0.6	2	400.0053	1.0
2.5	400.0091	0.2	2.5	400.0066	0.8	2.5	400.0047	1.2
3	400.0089	0.4	3	400.0062	0.8	3	400.0041	1.2
3.5	400.0088	0.2	3.5	400.0057	1.0	3.5	400.0034	1.4
4	400.0085	0.6	4	400.0051	1.2	4	400.0027	1.4
4.5	400.0082	0.6	4.5	400.0044	1.4	4.5	400.0019	1.6
5	400.0078	0.8	5	400.0035	1.8	5	400.0012	1.4
5.5	400.0073	1.0	5.5	400.0025	2.0	5.5	400.0004	1.6
6	400.0066	1.4	6	400.0015	2.0	6	399.9995	1.8
6.5	400.0057	1.8	6.5	400.0005	2.0	6.5	399.9989	1.2
7	400.0045	2.4	7	399.9994	2.2	7	399.9983	1.2
7.5	400.0031	2.8	7.5	399.9987	1.4	7.5	399.9979	0.8
8	400.0014	3.4	8	399.9980	1.4	8	399.9975	0.8
8.5	399.9995	3.8	8.5	399.9974	1.2	8.5	399.9971	0.8
9	399.9983	2.4	9	399.9969	1.0	9	399.9967	0.8
9.5	399.9973	2.0	9.5	399.9964	1.0	9.5	399.9963	0.8
10	399.9965	1.6	10	399.9960	0.8	Run 3 faded		
10.5	399.9957	1.6	10.5	399.9956	0.8			
11	399.9950	1.4	11	399.9953	0.6			
11.5	399.9946	0.8	11.5	399.9950	0.6			
12	399.9943	0.6	12	399.9948	0.4			
12.5	399.9940	0.6	12.5	399.9946	0.4			
13	399.9937	0.6	13	399.9944	0.4			
13.5	399.9936	0.2	Run 2 faded					
14	399.9935	0.2						
14.5	399.9934	0.2						
15	399.9933	0.2						
15.5	399.9932	0.2						
16	399.9931	0.2						
16.5	399.9931	0						

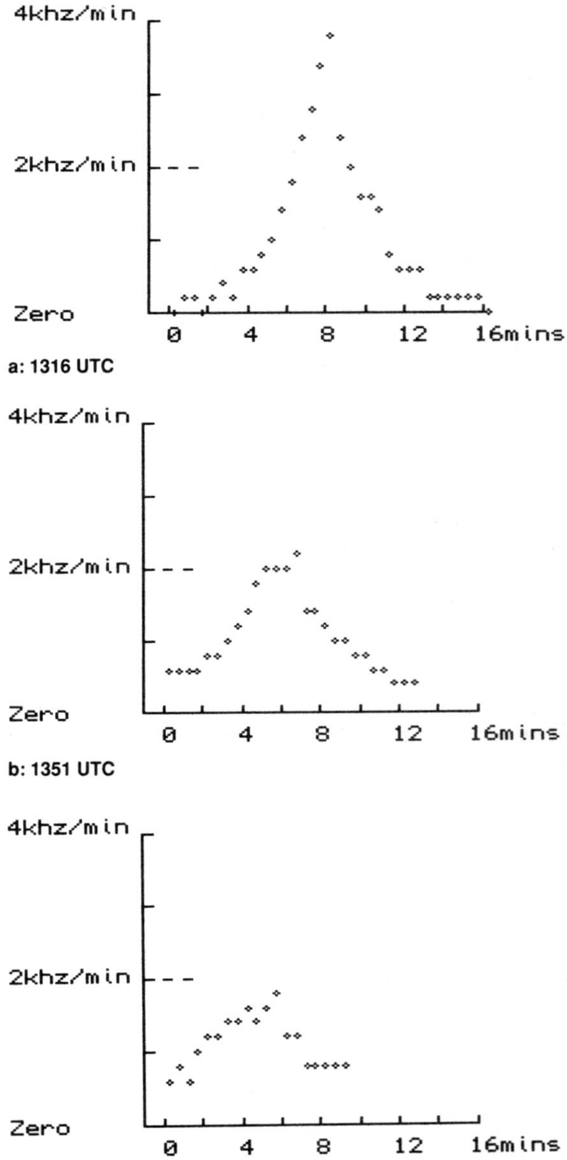

c: 1503 UTC

Fig 8.1.07a-c: Plotted Doppler rate curve graphs, 16 June 1986

time of the curve maxima, insofar as the accuracy of this data permits. Whereas an ordinary Doppler curve may purport to show the time of CPA, after the operator has guessed the location of the point of maximum slope, the Doppler rate curve shows just how blurred that point can be. This blurring is in part due to the experimental crudeness of the technique, eg the method is incapable of recognising Doppler rate changes of less than 0.2kHz/min, but some of the irregularities in the curve are due to the ionosphere. Only Doppler rate plotting gives the operator a clear chance to decide which anomalies are experimental artifacts, and which are real. The plotting of simple Doppler curves does not reveal any of these flaws and is therefore misleading.

Armed with these specimen Doppler rate curves, the experimenter can begin to explore the interesting changes which occur in the ionosphere, by day and by night, between magnetically quiet days and magnetically disturbed days, and between days when anomalies such as auroras or sporadic E are present or not. If Doppler rate curves are examined in detail all kinds of useful data begins to emerge. Satellites which are going to pass close to your station advertise this fact by having almost no Doppler rate at all as they come up from the horizon. The lower the initial Doppler rate, the closer the satellite passes overhead. The higher the initial horizon Doppler rate, the greater will be the distance from your station of the satellite at CPA. These are coarse rules which can provide a lot of information.

With an experimental method whereby the minimum discernible frequency rate change is 0.2kHz/min, there is no point in investigating areas where flats or hang-ups occur on the rate curve. When the satellite is Dopplering at a rate of 1.6kHz/min and this is decelerating at about 0.2kHz/min/min, as in the minutes 10 to 11 record of Run 1, it is difficult to see how this sort of result can be achieved by experimental error. This particular minor bump therefore suggests a far-from-homogeneous ionosphere under that part of the satellite's track. Given a regular sequence of satellites like NOAA, Meteor, CosNav, Transit or Uosat Oscar 11, it is not difficult to find another one whose signal is going to traverse that same patch of the ionosphere, thereby positively confirming the anomaly if the second record shows the same hang-ups, in the same part of the sky.

To check the asymmetry of Doppler curves either side of CPA, examination of Figs 8.1.07a to 8.1.07c should leave no one in any doubt about their asymmetry. This applies in particular where the curve has a low Doppler rate with Earth rotation, therefore playing a more prominent role as in the horizon skimming path of Run 3, where the overall result of the effects of Earth rotation experimental error and ionospheric anomalies can produce an awful jumble. So the experimenter has at least the satisfaction that, unlike a Doppler frequency curve, a Doppler rate curve does show in no uncertain manner when its data content is poor.

Experiment 8.1.08: Differential Doppler

Purpose

Lest any reader imagine that the previous experiments have exhausted the subject of Doppler shift, this last Doppler experiment should dispel that illusion. There is so much information contained in the Doppler signal (and so little information anywhere else), that we should try to develop experiments which exploit the Doppler phenomenon fully. The recent arrival on the space experimenter/radio amateur's bench of frequency counters and powerful home computers allows us to do just this. So, whilst the experiment which follows requires a complex build-up of equipment, this effort involved will be many times repaid by the results.

If we consider the signal travelling to us from the satellite to be passing through an imaginary vacuum (Fig 8.1.08a), we can say the following things about it.

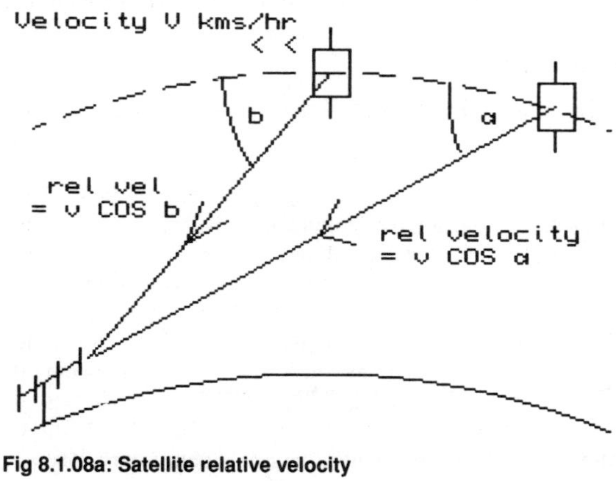

Fig 8.1.08a: Satellite relative velocity

Given that we know the Keplerian elements which describe the satellite's orbit, we can calculate its velocity and direction of motion. We can then calculate its velocity relative to our station and, knowing this relative velocity and the satellite transmit frequency, we can calculate the instantaneous Doppler shift.

However, nature does not understand vacuums. Given a hole, it will fill it with something. So in reality, wherever our satellite is, near Earth or far out in deep space, the line of sight from it to us is never empty, nor is it an homogeneous, well-mixed and even conglomeration of material. It is lumpy and diverse, and can be electrically charged in one place and electrically neutral in another. Fig 8.1.08b shows the situation.

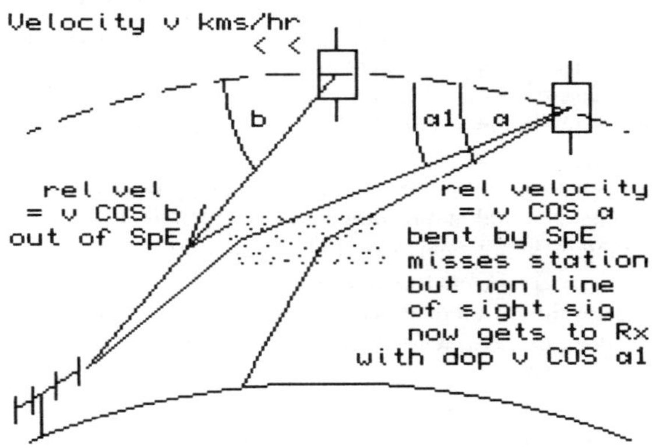

Fig 8.1.08b: Non-line-of-sight Doppler

Consider what happens in an extreme case where the E layer ionosphere is locally, temporarily, heavily ionised, with the line of sight from the satellite to the ground station crossing this disturbed area. As Fig 8.1.08b shows, this E layer ionisation is not strong enough to partially reflect terrestrial signals back to Earth, it just redirects them to odd places in outer space. Signals coming the other way get down through the ionosphere to Earth but suffer a slight dog-leg diversion from the direct line of sight. So a signal from a satellite, which up to then has been getting a clear line-of-sight path to the ground station receiver, suddenly encounters a slight change of direction. The signal coming via the original line of sight no longer gets to the receiver, so we lose its familiar consistent smooth Doppler, and in its place we either get no signal at all or we get a signal which was not aimed at the ground station when it started out from the satellite. This second signal starts from the satellite at a different angle to its track than the original line-of-sight signal; it therefore has a different velocity relative to the ground station, and the latter hears a step change in Doppler shift.

What we have, if we can measure the signal Doppler shift accurately and consistently, is an account of just what the satellite encountered in the ionosphere over an arc from horizon to horizon. To extract this data we need the best possible Doppler monitoring facilities, ie automatic or semi-automatic recording of frequency versus time.

This experiment outlines a simple way to start exploring the subject of 'differential Doppler', the name given to this powerful technique.

Method

Any satellite transmitting a constant carrier is satisfactory as a target. It is recommended that initial experiments are carried out on the 150 or 400MHz Navsat frequencies, because of the simplicity of their signal spectrum. When some expertise has been obtained, differential Doppler can be used on satellites such as Uosat or SRET 2 using their FM carrier. It is not recommended that this experiment be carried out initially on HF satellites, because their signal path is so irregular. Nor is it possible to carry out this simple version of the experiment on satellites using PSK and keyed CW signals because the automatic frequency measurement is unable to cope with these classes of interrupted carrier signal.

In its simplest form differential Doppler can use an ordinary digital audio frequency counter. Most frequency counters do not easily match the audio output terminals of radio receivers, but this can easily be overcome by using an old-fashioned loudspeaker transformer (from thermionic valve equipment) wired in reverse – low impedance in, high impedance out.

As a simple alternative, a home computer can be programmed to automatically read the audio frequency output and log its value in memory, and screen plot it. The method outlined here will stick to the simplest possible. Users will improve on it as their equipment and facilities permit.

The satellite signal is acquired aurally as it rises above the station horizon. The signal is tuned to produce an audio frequency of about 2kHz, and this audio frequency is measured on the frequency meter every one or two seconds as set by the frequency meter scan. A continuous record of frequency is tape recorded by voice. Every time the signal Dopplers down to about 200Hz it is reset up to 2kHz and the recording continued. After the satellite pass the recording is examined in detail for anomalies.

Results

Table 8.1.08 shows these, one count every second, count continuous through record.

Conclusions

This is a simple introduction to a large subject. In the example quoted in Table 8.1.08, the Navsat signal frequency received was fluctuating cyclically until the audio tone Dopplered to 1,220Hz. At that point and for the next five seconds the Dopplering signal was highly disturbed. This irregularity corresponded to about 20km of satellite travel along its track, then the smooth sequence resumed and continued to the end of the record.

Table 8.1.08: Partial record of Navsat, 18 June 1986

Frequency	D rate (Hz/s)		Frequency	D rate (Hz/s)
1,355	–		1,142	13
1,344	11		1,129	13
1,331	13		1,115	14
1,320	11		1,102	13
1,307	13		1,088	14
1,296	11		1,074	14
1,283	13		1,061	13
1,270	13		1,047	14
1,258	12		1,033	14
1,246	12		1,019	14
1,232	14		1,005	14
1,220	12		991	14
1,220	0	Anomaly	977	14
1,208	12	start	964	14
1,194	14			
1,192	2			
1,168	24	Anomaly		
1,155	13	end		

Explanations of what the various differential Doppler effects observed can mean, in practical terms relating to the ionosphere, must be left to a more specialised report than this one, but if the experimenter is prepared to try a few experiments of this kind, in varied ionospheric conditions, the full power of the experiment will slowly be revealed. Up until now, it has been used for professional studies to determine the size, distribution and electron density of sporadic E platelets. It has been used to chart the effects of heavyweight rocket boosters which continued to fire their engines as they passed through the ionosphere (most rockets cease firing before they get to the ionosphere), showing that their exhaust rapidly neutralised the ionosphere, forming a large hole which remained for some considerable time. This experiment only scratches the surface of what is possible, but radio amateurs can clearly build much more sophisticated automatic differential Doppler plotters via their microcomputers and suitable software. Fig 8.1.08c shows a plot of the simple frequency counter method used for the data in Table 8.1.08.

Fig 8.1.08d shows a much more sophisticated computer record acquired by the author with professional computing

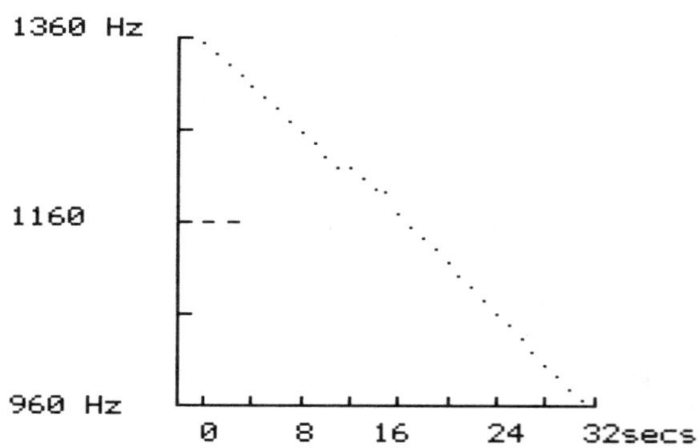

Fig 8.1.08c: Plot of differential Doppler anomaly, June 1986

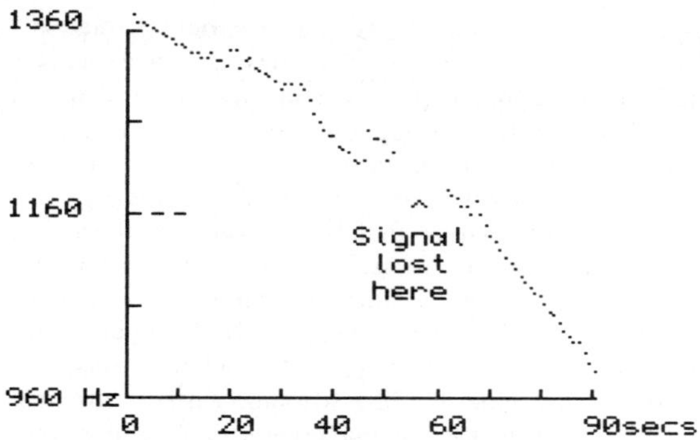

Fig 8.1.08d: Plot of differential Doppler anomaly, 30 November 1980

equipment, during an orbit when the ionosphere was markedly disturbed.

Experiment 8.1.09: Faraday rotation of polarisation

Purpose

Radio signals can be described as having two components, an electric field and a magnetic field. These components are orientated at 90 degrees to one another in space. Where the electric field is aligned in the vertical plane, the radio signal is said to be vertically polarised. Similarly a horizontally polarised signal has its electric field aligned in the horizontal plane. To send or receive a vertically polarised signal the active elements of the antenna should be aligned in the vertical plane. In all linearly polarised radio systems the antenna elements should be aligned in the plane required for the signal's electric field. The magnetic field of the signal will align at 90 degrees to the antenna elements.

As radio signals from space come down through the ionosphere, the plane of signal polarisation can be rotated. This experiment examines a signal from space and tries to follow its rotation of polarisation.

Method

Two separate antennas for reception of signals at 145MHz are mounted, one with its elements in the vertical plane, the other with its elements in the horizontal plane. Both antennas are pointed to track the test satellite. The antennas feed a two-way switch, so that either one or the other is connected to the receiver as determined by the switch position. The receiver is set to receive either SSB or CW. The audio output of the receiver is fed to a high-impedance meter or an oscilloscope.

Suitable satellite targets are Uosat Oscar 11 on 145.825MHz, or one of the navigation satellites on 150MHz (exact frequencies are listed in the earlier Doppler experiments in this section of this chapter).

Check the satellite orbital predictions and acquire its signal as soon as it comes above your horizon, then tune the

Table 8.1.09: Faraday rotation

Time	H (cm)	V (cm)	Time	H (cm)	V (cm)
0855 UTC	1.75	1.8	6	4.5	4
+0.5	-	-	6.5	2	3
1	1	2	7	1.2	1.3
1.5	2.2	1	7.5	1.2	3.2
2	1.2	2	8	2.2	4.5
2.5	2.5	1.8	8.5	1.2	3.3
3	1.9	1.7	9	1	1.5
3.5	4	1	9.5	1.2	1.2
4	2.2	2.2	10	2.5	1.2
4.5	3.6	2.4	10.5	2.6	1.2
5	4	1.5	11	1.2	0
5.5	6	1	faded		

signal for maximum vertical deflection on the meter or the oscilloscope (useful scope settings are 0.5 seconds per centimetre horizontal, 100 to 500 millivolts per centimetre vertical). Quickly measure the amplitude of the signal via the horizontal antenna, then repeat the measurement using the vertical antenna. Keep a written or tape recorder record of time, vertical signal amplitude and horizontal signal amplitude.

Try to repeat these readings every half minute, moving your antenna to track the satellite in between readings. Tune for maximum signal every second or third pair of readings so that you stay on tune despite Doppler shift.

Results

These are given in Table 8.1.09.

Conclusions

This is not an easy experiment. It rarely produces a clean, clear result, and this example is no exception – it does not give clear-cut answers. There are five obvious changes of dominant polarisation, plus two near-misses when the signal nearly changes polarisation, but please note that there are some features which tell us a lot more. All the rapid changes of polarisation occurred at the beginning when the

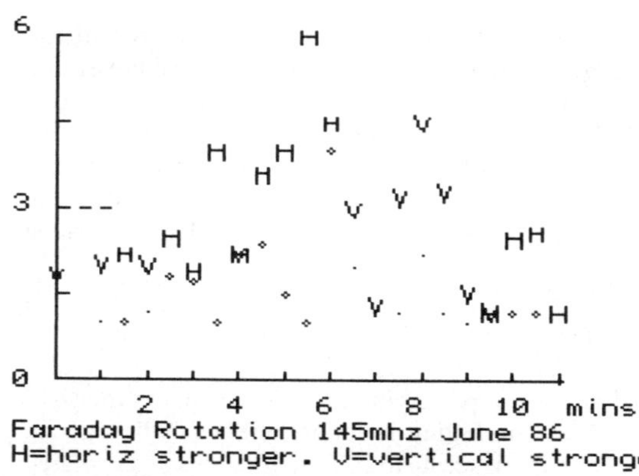

Fig 8.1.09: Plot of Faraday rotations, June 1986

satellite signal was coming through the ionosphere obliquely at a shallow angle. When the signal path is short and straight down through the ionosphere, as it is in the middle of the pass, there is no change in polarisation over quite a long period of time. This is clear evidence that the angle at which the signal hits the ionosphere is important, because the shallower the incident angle the longer the time the signal spends in the ionosphere.

Please note that this crude experiment does nothing except reveal the changes in polarisation between different ionospheric transit points in the orbital pass. We do not get an exact reading of polarisation changes. What we can say is limited to the statement that at the start there were X unknown polarisation rotations as the signal came through the ionosphere. By minute +1.5 this had changed to either X + 1 (or any other odd number), or X – 1(or any other odd number). All we really know is that at the start the vertical component is stronger, then, 1.5 minutes later, the horizontal component is stronger, then half a minute later it has changed back to vertical being strongest. Please also take care to note that only once in the experiment do we appear to have a true horizontal signal (at minute 11); we never have a true vertical signal. Throughout the experiment the polarisation was never truly linear, vertical or horizontal (except at minute 11). What we usually got was a signal of some intermediate polarisation.

It will be clear to those who might wish to take this kind of experiment further that we really need vector addition of the received vertical and horizontal components to establish the true polarisation received. As should be evident from this simple experiment the true polarisation is only rarely a linear vertical or horizontal, which makes sense when you consider two things:

(i) As the satellite comes towards you pointing its antenna at the Earth's centre, that is not aligned with your vertical but is at least 20 degrees different.

(ii) As the satellite passes near overhead its aspect from you places its antenna in a quite different plane to that which it occupied at the start of the pass.

This last point is particularly important with geostationary satellites, for example Meteosat, with vertical polarisation pointing at Earth centre through the equator, was 50 degrees off the UK vertical. So please be careful: the satellite's idea of what is vertical depends on where it is, and in addition the quite separate action of Faraday rotation then adds further confusion as the signal comes down through the ionosphere to your receiver.

It is important to understand why this experiment only reveals the change in polarisation between one ionospheric transit and another half a minute later. It does not reveal the actual number of polarisation rotations at either transit. At 145MHz a signal hitting the ionosphere at a shallow grazing angle can experience up to 20 or so rotations of its polarisation whilst transiting that ionosphere. Next moment, at a slightly steeper entry angle, it experiences only 19 rotations. We record only that this one change has taken place, and we need a much more complex experiment to tell us it was in fact 20 changes to 19 changes which actually occurred.

This is a difficult experiment to get clear results because so many other factors intervene to affect signal propagation. Despite this it is well worth doing several times in varying ionospheric conditions, because its very confusion does make clear why most commercial satellite operators have opted to use circular polarisation, whereby the signal rotates at the transmitted frequency, ie 145,000,000 times per second, against which the 20 or so rotation in the ionosphere are of no consequence. Circular polarisation requires complex expensive antennas, but with Faraday rotation present on all signals it fully repays the extra cost in improved performance.

If time permits operators should try to repeat this experiment on UHF and HF satellite signals. Experiments on satellite signals below 28MHz become difficult because of antenna complications, so for HF studies 29MHz satellites are preferred.

Experiment 8.2.01: Digitalker Uosat Oscar telemetry

Purpose

A satellite which sends its information in plain English is the obvious starting point for active experiments. The University of Surrey satellites do just that. They transmit regularly scheduled bulletins of scientific information via digitalker, a computer-driven voice chip.

This experiment describes the reception, decoding and practical use of the science data from Uosat Oscar 9.

In 1991 Dove Oscar 17 is scheduled to have voice telemetry on 145.825MHz.

Method

The Uosats transmit on a frequency of 145.825MHz, sending out a frequency-modulated signal which carries either the digitalker voice or a variety of phase-shift keyed, automatic telemetry. Here the digitalker is reported and decoded. The decode system used is also applicable to the data sent via PSK.

To copy digitalker, you need a good 145MHz Yagi beam antenna which is kept trained on the satellite in azimuth and if possible elevation. The antenna should feed a standard 145MHz FM receiver and if possible it is best to tape record the digitalker transmissions.

Uosat Oscar 11 takes about 98 minutes to circle the Earth. In practice its polar, high-inclination orbits bring it over the UK about eight times a day. As shown in the radio amateur satellite chapter of this book, these in-range orbital passes consist of a group of three or four consecutive orbits in the morning going north to south, and another group of three or four consecutive orbits going south to north in the afternoon

Table 8.2.01a: Digitalker frame, 12 December 1982 at 1354

00110	01150	02769	03002	04407	05745	06307
07207	08468	09458	10100	11090	12000	13000
14316	15642	16716	17284	18467	19403	20160
21030	22677	23000	24007	25416	26424	27262
28471	29426	30190	31020	32667	33218	34012
35267	36376	37400	38480	39402	40100	41090
42742	43300	44040	45000	46002	47490	48510
49520	50000	51090	52270	53200	54900	55318
56010	57500	58510	59480			

and evening. In between there are two or three orbits which pass east to west between the UK and the North Pole. The Uosat Oscar 11 orbits in this category can be heard in the UK.

Experimenters should concentrate on getting a good recording or transcript of a frame of digitalker data. Please note the satellite simply goes to digitalker from PSK, then straight back to PSK after one frame of digitalker. So you must be all prepared before it starts. Take copies of digitalker on several orbits if possible.

Results

These are given in Table 8.2.01a. Digitalker simply calls out this series of numbers at quite high speed. The first two numbers identify the frame section, and the last three numbers give the data for that specific section. So we need to know what each section represents and how we translate the data reported in that section into volts, amps, decibels or whatever is appropriate.

A complete decode of the whole frame is given in Table 8.2.01b. As an example of how it works, consider the first number. The identifier is 00, which the decode table tells us is current being taken by the spacecraft's secondary computer. To find how much current we use the formula given in the decode table:

Secondary Computer mA = 1.2 times N

where N is data in frame 00, which is 110. So:

Computer mA = 110*1.2 = 132mA

At first glance this list of data looks formidable, but if you take a close look you will find that the data you want for a report on temperature of all the different faces of the satellite is listed in the sections which are all end in nine. To do a satellite surface temperature experiment, you therefore need to work out all the nines, ie 09, 19, 29, 39, 49 and 59.

Anything concerned with magnetism is last section number five, six or seven, ie 05, 06, 07, 15, 16, 17, 25, 26. Navigation magnetic readings are grouped separately at 53, 54 and 55. Solar panels are all the ones, ie 01, 11, 21 and 31.

So in fact there is considerable order in this data reporting frame, and many experiments can be done using this data.

Table 8.2.01b: Decode table

Sect	Data	Device reported	Decode formula	Result
00	110	Secondary computer	1.2*N mA	132mA
01	150	Solar Array +X	200+1.12*N mA	368mA
02	769	Battery half volts	N/100*1.01 volts	7.76V
03	002	Radiation Detec A	40*N*1.04 counts	83
04	407	Radiation Detec B	40*N*1.04 counts	16,931
05	745	Mag Field HX coarse	129*N–64,824	+31,296
06	307	Mag Field HY coarse	129*N–64,433	24,830
07	207	Mag Field Hz coarse	129*N–64,072	–37,369
08	468	Battery Pack Temp	(474–N)*0.202	1.2°C
09	458	Craft Facet +X Temp	(474–N)*0.202	3.2°C
10	100	CCD Camera current	1.2*(N–30)	84mA
11	090	Solar array +Y	200+1.12*N	301mA
12	000	2.4GHz beacon power	(N–145)*0.45	0mW
13	000	Radiation Det EHT	N volts	0V
14	316	Radiation Det mA	(N+20)*0.1225	41mA
15	642	Mag Field HX fine	18.05*(N–511)	2,364nt
16	716	Mag Field HY fine	17.97*(N–510)	3,794nt
17	284	Mag Field HZ fine	17.76*(N–510)	–4,014nt
18	467	Battery B Temp	(474–N)*0.202	1.4°C
19	403	Craft Facet –X Temp	(474–N)*0.202	14.3°C
20	160	Main Computer	1.2*(N–25)	162mA
21	030	Solar Array –X	200+1.12*N	234mA
22	677	Battery 14 volts	N*0.0211	14.2V
23	000	Sun Sensor +Z	N*0.00505	0
24	007	10.4GHz beacon	(N–40)*0.2425	–8
25	416	Mag Temp	(474–N)*0.202	11.7°C
26	424	Mag Current	N*0.1243	53mA
27	262	Tele RX mA	(N–16)*0.119	30mA
28	471	Radiation Exp Temp	(474–N)*0.202	0.6°C
29	426	Craft Facet +Y Temp	(474–N)*0.202	9.7°C
30	190	Battery Charge mA	2.9*N	551mA
31	020	Solar Array –Y	200+1.12*N	222mA
32	667	Power Condition 10V	N*0.0155	10.3V
33	218	Telemetry Sys mA	(N–16)*0.0361	7.3mA
34	012	2.4GHz beacon mA	(N–11)*0.4288	0.43mA
35	267	145MHz beacon power	1.67*(N-82)	309mW
36	376	145MHz beacon mA	0.2535*(N–7)	93mA
37	400	145MHz beacon Temp	(474–N)*0.202	14.9°C
38	480	Pri Sc –X1 Temp	(474–N)*0.202	–1.2°C
39	402	Craft Facet –Y Temp	(474–N)*0.202	14.5°C
40	100	–14V Supply mA	N*2.86	286mA
41	090	–5V Supply mA	(N–50)*1.28	51.2mA
42	742	+5V Supply mA	N*0.00747	4.27mA
43	300	Sun Sensor –Z	N*0.0056	16.8mA
44	040	HF beacon mA	(N–36)*0.346	1.384mA
45	000	435MHz beacon power	(N–102)*1.792	0mW
46	002	435MHz beacon mA	(N–34)*0.351	–11.7mA
47	490	435MHz beacon TempA	(474–N)*0.202	-3.2°C
48	510	Sec Sc Temp +Y1	(474–N)*0.202	–7.27°C
49	520	Craft Facet +Z Temp	(474–N)*0.202	–9.3°C
50	000	+10V current mA	3*N	0mA
51	090	–10V current mA	(N–60)*1.3	39mA
52	270	Power Condition –10V	0.0158*N–0.0224 *ref 50	0
53	200	Nav Mag Y	(N–663.44) *183.486	–84,729
54	900	Nav Mag Z	(N–336.55)*189.54	106,596
55	318	Nav Mag X	(N–496.5)*194.55	–34,532
56	010	Digitalker Current	(N–16)*0.1009	–0.6mA
57	500	CCD Temperature	(474–N)*0.202	–5.2°C
58	510	Tele –Y1 Temp	(474–N)*0.202	–7.2°C
59	480	Craft Facet –Z Temp	(474–N)*0.202	–1.2°C

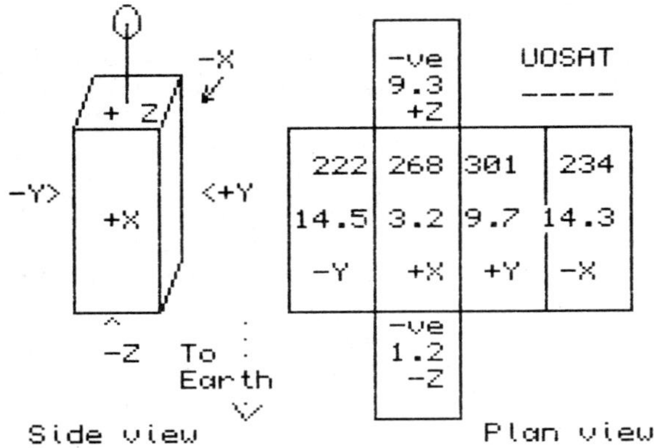

Fig 8.2.01: Uosat face temperatures and solar currents obtained from telemetry

The example quoted here uses the spacecraft's outside facet or face temperatures (all the nines), plus solar panel currents (all the ones) to generate Fig 8.2.01, a statement of the effect of sunlight plus internal heat sources at the time this digitalker frame was received.

As mentioned earlier, this data frame is also sent by phase-shift keyed telemetry and uses exactly the same decode pattern. So when digitalker is off, you can read PSK telemetry over several orbits and take satellite temperature measurements over a wide range of conditions. It is possible to watch Uosat go into and emerge from Earth shadow whilst taking the readings. Uosat goes into Earth shadow on part of most orbits, but the crossing of the shadow zone does not always take place in range of the UK.

Conclusion

Once experimenters get to know the digitalker schedule, it opens the door to a simple-to-operate and receive, but powerful, set of experiments. Digitalker is a winner and it is to be hoped that it will be copied and used on all future amateur radio space science satellites.

Experiment 8.2.02: Telemetry from Radiosport 5 and 7

Purpose

For sheer numbers of satellites and suitable overhead orbits, the Soviet satellites of the Radiosport series are far ahead of the rest in terms of usefulness and experimental potential. This experiment examines a typical set of scientific telemetry from RS5/7 which is no longer operational. The reason that it is included here is that a number of countries are planning to launch amateur radio satellites in the 1990s and indications already given suggest that simple telemetry of the RS5/7 type will be used. Please note that the newest Radiosport satellite, RS10/11, has a rather different telemetry format from the one reviewed here. The details of the RS10/11 telemetry format and decode are given in chapter 6.

Method

The signals from Radiosport satellites 5 and 7 both come down on 29MHz. At present, in 1987, RS5 uses 29.452MHz and RS7 uses 29.502MHz. Soviet Iskra satellites have used 29.577MHz to send the same sort of telemetry as that described here, but none of them are at present operational.

The signals from RS5 and RS7 are quite strong and they can be received on a simple wire antenna feeding a standard shortwave communications receiver. The satellite receiving chapter of this book describes more elaborate reception antennas which could be used for RS5 and RS7 if experimenters want to ensure getting data on the difficult orbits between UK and the North Pole. The sloped switchable dipoles shown in the chapter referred to are suitable for this task.

Radiosport 5 and 7 orbit the Earth every 120 minutes at an altitude of more than 1,600km, which puts them just in the interesting lower edges of the Van Allen radiation belts. In addition they regularly cross the polar regions whilst in range of the UK. They also have the advantage, from the experimenter's point of view, that they are not in Sun-synchronous orbits. This is useful in propagation research because the slow perturbation of the satellite orbit allows it to see the world under a slightly different Sun angle each day, thereby allowing an overview of signal propagation against a gradually varying time of day.

Telemetry data from Radiosport 5 and 7 is sent at 22wpm morse code. Do not be put off by this as more than a third of each frame section is redundant letters – all the important data is in the two numbers which follow each pair of section letters. It is recommended that experimenters tape record the telemetry frames, then little is missed and the recording can be replayed at slow speed if required.

Results

Taking Table 8.2.02 as a typical RS7 telemetry frame, we must now decode each of the frame sections.

Fig 8.2.02a is a grid for the complete telemetry frame. Using a grid of this type you can listen for the particular frame section you want, ignoring the rest, or, if you cover the grid with clear acetate, you can write in each section the figures transmitted, ignoring the frame section letters because they are already on the grid and do not change. This all helps if your morse is shaky or you cannot write fast.

Fig 8.2.02b shows what the author's grid looks like when it is filled in with the data from the telemetry frame in Table 8.2.02a. These two figures are a worked example of each of the decode formulae shown in the respective sections on the

Table 8.2.02: RS7 telemetry frame, 19 June 1986, 1451 UTC

RS7	K 88	D 78	O 70	G 01	U 23	S 19	W 20
RS7	IK84	ID06	IO99	IG01	IU11	IS14	IW01
RS7	AK99	AD91	AO77	AG91	AU77	AS93	AW76
RS7	MK98	MD01	MO02	MG10	MU12	MS11	MW11

Radio Sport Telemetry Decode Grid

K transpond output power mW 0.2*N^2	IK < same	AK < same	MK < same
D battery volt 0.2*N	ID zero level check	AD 9v transpond 0.1*N	MD Robot message No.
O batry I 20*(100-N)	IO beacon W 0.2*N^2	AO 7.5v transp 0.1*N	MO Therm heater 0.1*N
G calibrate marker	IG trnspdr sensitivty	AG 9v reg 0.1*N	MG input power 20*N
U not used	IU trnsp S .1*(N-10)	AU 7.5v reg 0.1*N	MU Command power 20*N
S Main Reg Temp = N	IS Robot S .1*(N-10)	AS 9v transp 0.1*N	MS Robot Atten NdBs
W 10m Tx Temp = N	IW Comd Rx .1*(N-10)	AW 7.5v reg 0.1*N	MW Input Atten NdBs

Fig 8.2.02a: Radiosport telemetry decode grid

Radio Sport Telemetry Decode Grid with Worked Examples

N = 88 K =1550mW transpond output power mW 0.2*N^2	N = 84 IK =1410mW < same	N = 99 AK =1960mW < same	N = 98 MK =1920mW < same
N = 80 D = 16v battery volt 0.2*N	N = 01 ID = 1 zero level check	N = 91 AD = 9.1v 9v transpond 0.1*N	N = 01 MD = 1 Robot message No.
N = 70 O = 600mA batry I 20*(100-N)	N = 99 IO =1960mW beacon W 0.2*N^2	N = 77 AO = 7.7v 7.5v transp 0.1*N	N = 02 MO = .2w Therm heater 0.1*N
N = 01 G = 1 calibrate marker	N = 01 IG = 1 trnspdr sensitivty	N = 91 AG = 9.1v 9v reg 0.1*N	N = 10 MG = 200mW input power 20*N
U not used	N = 11 IU = 0.1 trnsp S .1*(N-10)	N = 77 AU = 7.7v 7.5v reg 0.1*N	N = 12 MU = 240mW Command power 20*N
N = 19 S = 19C Main Reg Temp = N	N = 14 IS = 0.4 Robot S .1*(N-10)	N = 93 AS = 9.3v 9v transp 0.1*N	N = 11 MS = 11dB Robot Atten NdBs
N = 20 W = 20C 10m Tx Temp = N	N = 01 IW = -0.9 Comd Rx .1*(N-10)	N = 76 AW = 7.6v 7.5v reg 0.1*N	N = 11 MW = 11dB Input Atten NdBs

Fig 8.2.02b: Radiosport telemetry decode grid with worked examples

grid, eg we received K88 for the first section. The decode formula shows this section to be for transponder power output. The decode conversion takes the number N, in this case 88, and calculates the value of one fifth of N squared = (88*88)/5 = 1,548.8 milliwatts. Sections IK, AK and MK report the same parameter but some half a minute later in time in each case. The value of N varies from 88 to 84 to 99 to 98 as stations communicating through the satellite alternately transmit and listen – so during this frame the transponder output power varies through 1,548 to 1,410 to 1,960 to 1,920 milliwatts.

At telemetry windows D and O we can check the all-important satellite battery. D80 and O70 report to us that the satellite battery voltage is 16V and that it is taking a 600mA charge. Following this pair of readings through an eclipse of the satellite in the Earth's shadow can be interesting.

At sections AD, AO, AG, AU, AS and AW we can check the various voltages supplying the satellite equipment. All voltages seem to be within a nominal 5 per cent of design figure even after many years in service. Equally satisfactory, as reported by sections S and W, the temperatures of the main regulator and the 29MHz transmitter are a comfortable 19 and 20°C respectively. This is very good indeed for a satellite which can be basking in warm sunlight one minute and plunged into total darkness the next minute as it goes into Earth shadow and loses the Sun. Management of the satellite twice a year or so, when it sees these deep eclipses every orbit, is a tricky job. The Radiosport ground controllers keep a careful watch on these temperature sections of the telemetry and the equally important battery section reports. When a series of deep eclipses is likely to take the battery to the point where its reduced periods in sunlight do not give it time to recover between one eclipse and the next one, the controllers switch the satellite off, to stop any drain on the battery until after perhaps a fortnight it gets through the deep eclipse period and emerges on an orbit on which its battery can get a full charge. Once they are satisfied from the telemetry figures that the satellite is safe, the controllers switch it back on again.

Conclusion

Using the telemetry data transmitted by the satellite, it is possible to monitor its state of health and keep an eye on several interesting features of its space environment. RS7 was clearly in good health when these readings were taken on 19 June 1986. At that time it had completed more than 21,000 orbits which reflects great credit on its radio amateur builders and its flight controllers.

Experiment 8.2.03: Fuji Oscar 12 telemetry and status

Purpose

Despite enormous advances in computer control, satellites left to themselves and their onboard computers would soon be useless. This experiment puts the experimenter in the position of the flight controller for Fuji.

Fuji is not much bigger than a suitcase. None the less it is packed with sophisticated transponders, and store-and-forward message handling equipment. To keep all this equipment working on schedule, the satellite must be controlled. If everything is on at once there is a negative power budget, even in full sunlight. So provision must be made to monitor the battery and if necessary switch sections of the satellite off, if battery charge gets too low. This cannot be done to a fixed timetable because things like the number of transponder users cannot be predicted, and will doubtless vary from hour to hour.

The experimenter's task in this experiment is to monitor the status of the satellite and decide when to take action. As the satellite is monitored from day to day, you will become aware that controllers in Japan and at the University of Surrey, are switching things on and off. The test is to see if you can predict any of these control operations and thereby qualify to become a satellite controller yourself.

Method

The Fuji telemetry channel uses morse code at about 20 words per minute on a frequency near 435.797MHz, plus or minus about 10kHz of Doppler shift. So you need good tracking information from your computer so that you can keep a Yagi antenna, of about 8dB gain versus a dipole, trained on the satellite.

Table 8.2.03a: Fuji Oscar 12 analogue telemetry channel

Channel	Parameter	Decode equation
1A	Total solar array current	20*(N+4) mA
1B	Battery charge/discharge	40*(N–46) mA
1C	Battery voltage	(N+4)*0.22 volts
1D	Half battery voltage	(N+4)*0.098 volts
2A	Bus voltage	(N+4)*0.2 volts
2B	+5V regulated	(N+4)*0.06 volts
2C	JTA power output	2*((N+4)^1.618) mW
2D	Calibration voltage *1	(N+4)/50 volts
3A	Battery temperature	1.5*(62–N) °C
3B	Baseplate temp 1	1.5*(62–N) °C
3C	Baseplate temp 2	1.5*(62–N) °C
3D	Baseplate temp 3	1.5*(62–N) °C

Table 8.2.03b: Fuji telemetry status points

Chan	MSB bit4	bit3	bit2	bit1	bit0 LSB
4A	JTA beacon	Eng2	Eng1	JTD power	JTA power
1	PSK	...	...	On	On
0	CW	...	...	Off	Off
4B	Main Relay	Batlogic	Batstatus	UVClevel	UVCstatus
1	On	Tric	Tric	1	On
0	Off	Full	Full	2	Off
4C	Eng 3	Eng 4	PCUcontrol	PCUstatus	PCUstatus
1	...	...	Manual	Bit 2 MSB	Bit 1 LSB
0	...	...	Auto		
4D	Computer Power	Mem 3	Mem 2	Mem 1	Mem 0
1	On	On	On	On	On
0	Off	Off	Off	Off	Off
5A	Eng 7	Eng 6	Eng 5	Memselect	Memselect
1	...	...	...	Bit 2 MSB	Bit 1 LSB
0	...	...	...		
5B	Solar Pan5	Solar Pan4	Solar Pan3	Solar Pan2	Solar Pan1
1	lit	lit	lit	lit	lit
0	dark	dark	dark	dark	dark
5C	Eng 11	Eng 10	Eng 9	Eng 8	CWbeacon-feed
1	...	...	...	...	CPU
0	...	...	...	...	Telemetry
5D	Eng 16	Eng 15	Eng 14	Eng 13	Eng 12
1	...	...	...	...	...
0	...	...	...	...	...

Table 8.2.03c: Fuji telemetry frame 1300UTC on 4 October 1986

HI	HI	122	146	163	164	269	279	220	257	344	345
		345	345	401	423	400	400	500	536	500	500

Fuji can be received on a simple antenna but if you are to keep track of its health all day, every day, every time it orbits into range, you need a good antenna. You may also find a low-noise preamplifier connected at the antenna is a big help. The antenna should be connected to a suitable radio amateur band receiver for 435MHz, via high-quality coaxial cable to minimise losses. Fuji comes over the UK about 10 times each day.

In 1990 Fuji Oscar 20 succeeded Oscar 12. Telemetry is almost identical, allowing this experiment to be repeated by other users.

Results

A typical telemetry frame for Fuji is shown in Table 8.2.03c.

The decode of the first 12 sections of analogue data from the first frame 1 to the last frame 3 is given in Table 8.2.03d.

The decode of the remaining telemetry uses a quite different procedure to examine the condition of each of the status points. Using Table 8.2.03b we find the decimal number in each section window. We convert this number to octal and we use each separate bit of the binary number that results as a status point check (Table 8.2.03e).

The decode of the telemetry frame for Fuji provides a wealth of information. Section 5B, the second section in the 500 numbers, shows 536, sometimes 537, a moment later as solar panel 1 is alternately in shadow or in sunshine as the satellite spins in space. This gives a good record of satellite spin rate and spin axis at this time. Being early in the flight, the Fuji passive magnetotorque dampers had not had time to completely dampen out the satellite's spin imparted at launch.

Table 8.2.03d: Fuji Oscar 12 decode analogue telemetry channels

Channel		Parameter	Decode equation	Result
1A	122	Total solar array current	20*(N+4) mA	520mA
1B	146	Battery charge/ discharge	40*(N–46) mA	0mA
1C	163	Battery voltage	(N+4)*0.22 volts	14.74V
1D	164	Half battery voltage	(N+4)*0.098 volts	6.664V
2A	269	Bus voltage	(N+4)*0.2 volts	14.6V
2B	279	+5V regulated	(N+4)*0.06 volts	4.98V
2C	220	JTA power output	2*((N+4)^1.618) mW	342mW
2D	257	Calibration voltage*1	(N+4)/50 volts	1.22V
3A	344	Battery temperature	1.5*(62–N) °C	27.0°C
3B	345	Baseplate temp 1	1.5*(62–N) °C	25.5°C
3C	345	Baseplate temp 2	1.5*(62–N) °C	25.5°C
3D	345	Baseplate temp 3	1.5*(62–N) °C	25.5°C

Table 8.2.03e: Telemetry decode results

4A	401	00001	MSB = 0	JTA beacon is sending CW
			= 0	empty engineering data
			= 0	empty engineering data
			= 0	JTD power is Off
			LSB = 1	JTA power is On, Fuji in analogue mode
4B	423	10011	MSB = 1	Main relay is On
			= 0	Battery logic is Full
			= 0	Battery status is Full
			= 1	UVC level is 1
			LSB = 1	UVC status is On
4C	400	00000	MSB = 0	empty eng data
			= 0	empty eng data
			= 0	PCU control is Auto
			= 0	PCU status MSB
			LSB = 0	PCU status LSB, ie PCU status is 00
4D	400	00000	MSB = 0	Computer power is Off
			= 0	Memory unit 3 Off
			= 0	Memory unit 2 is Off
			= 0	Memory unit 1 is Off
			LSB = 0	Memory unit 0 is Off
5A	500	00000	MSB = 0	empty eng data
			= 0	empty eng data
			= 0	empty eng data
			= 0	Memory select MSB
			LSB = 0	Memory select LSB, ie memory bin 00
5B	536	11110	MSB = 1	Solar panel 5 sunlit
			= 1	Solar panel 4 sunlit
			= 1	Solar panel 3 sunlit
			= 1	Solar panel 2 sunlit
			LSB = 0	Solar panel 1 is in darkness
5C	500	00000	MSB = 0	empty eng data
			= 0	empty eng data
			= 0	empty eng data
			= 0	empty eng data
			LSB = 0	CW beacon data source is telemetry
5D	500	00000	MSB = 0	empty eng data
			= 0	empty eng data
			= 0	empty eng data
			= 0	empty eng data
			LSB = 0	empty eng data

The status point check in the first 400 window, labelled 4A on the table, tells us the satellite is in the analogue mode, so we can expect to find radio amateur communications through the satellite in the band 435.8 to 435.9MHz. Fuji only runs one mode at a time so status point 4a, bit4, reports the JTD digital mode as off, and as expected all memory for message store-and-forward associated with the digital mode is shown as off in status section window 4D.

Satellite performance is read in the analogue part of the telemetry (numbers 100 through 399). Solar cell current is a healthy 520mA and battery voltage a respectable 14.74V, but there are signs that these original telemetry calibration decode equations are slightly wrong because the main bus supply bar can be at a higher voltage than the battery, which takes a little explaining. In fact, this is early days in the satellite's life, so no doubt several of the telemetry decode equations will need revision once the satellite has been despun and has settled down in its space environment.

Conclusion

Equipped with this analogue and digital telemetry from Fuji, there is no reason why experimenters should not become proficient at practising what they would do if they were in the hot seat trying to keep the satellite healthy and ensuring it has a long life.

Experiment 8.2.04: Uosat Oscar whole orbit data

Purpose

To examine some of the powerful whole orbit data from the University of Surrey satellites. Uosat Oscar 9 took us into a new age with its highly technical but simple digitalker. For those who get together a slightly more sophisticated receiving station, Uosat also offers the extremely powerful whole orbit data (WOD) facility. Sitting up in Scotland the author can receive measurements taken by Uosat all over the world.

Do you want to know the levels of radiation over the South Pole? No need to do a Captain Scott – Uosat will bring them right to your station wherever you are.

Method

The equipment required must be capable of receiving 145.825MHz FM signal from Uosat, producing a strong noise-free audio signal from the satellite's phase-shift keyed down link. A microcomputer is required which can demodulate and decode the telemetry and then display its information on the computer screen. A regular radio amateur receiver for FM 145.825 reception is connected to a good trainable and elevatable Yagi beam antenna of at least 8dB gain versus a dipole; the received PSK signal audio is tape recorded. Then, after the Uosat pass has finished, the tape is played to suitable hardware/software microcomputer equipment using one of the several excellent Uosat decode software packages (some microcomputers can both demodulate and decode via software, some must have additional hardware to demodulate the signal). Having got the whole orbit data frames the experimenter is free to either plot the data by hand, or get the microcomputer to do it for him.

Results

Fig 8.2.04a shows a graph plotted from Uosat WOD readings of solar array Xs current output. What the graph reports is a minute by minute record of just what current the solar array produced, and therefore how much sunlight it saw, minute by minute as it completed one orbit of the world.

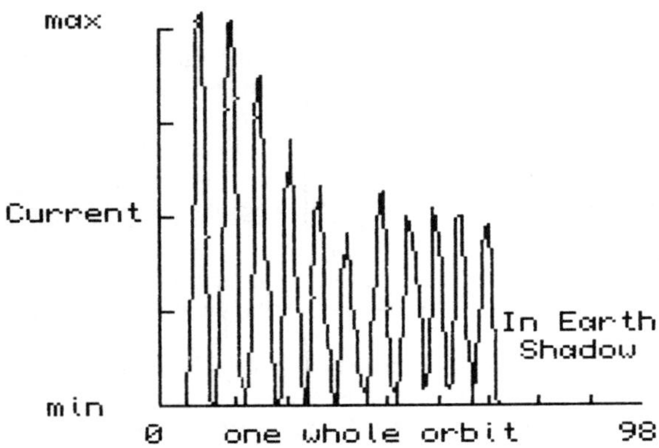

Fig 8.2.04a: Status graph of Uosat Oscar 11 solar array on 8 June 1986

The first point to notice is that the current is varying cyclically. Every 5.5 minutes or so the panel sees no sunshine, then 2.7 minutes or so later it is seeing lots of Sun and producing a high output. This data reveals how fast the satellite is spinning.

As the orbit progresses the peak solar current at each 5.5 minute spin decreases noticeably. Clearly the satellite is showing more of its X panel to the Sun at the start of the orbit than it is halfway through the orbit. Remember Uosat is not fully gravity stabilised but it does alter its alignment to the Sun as it goes round its orbit. Equally important, though Uosat is in a near-Sun-synchronous orbit, it is not following the peak sunlight (0600 up, 1800 local time down) version of that orbit, so it does go into Earth shadow and, as the WOD record shows, this occurred for the last 20 minutes of this record.

The next graph at Fig 8.2.04b shows the WOD report for the important battery which of course depends on the solar cell current from the previous report. These two figures have been arranged so that they show the synchronism between solar panel supply of charge to the battery, and what the battery did with this supply. As the records could not be obtained at exactly the same orbit the eclipse time is

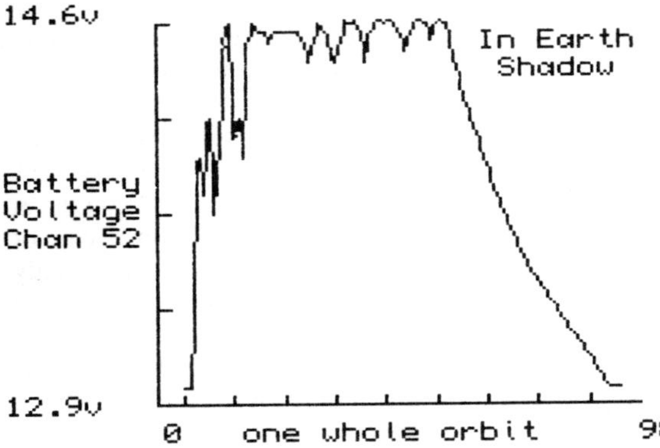

Fig 8.2.04b: Status graph of Uosat Oscar 11 battery voltage on 9 June 1986

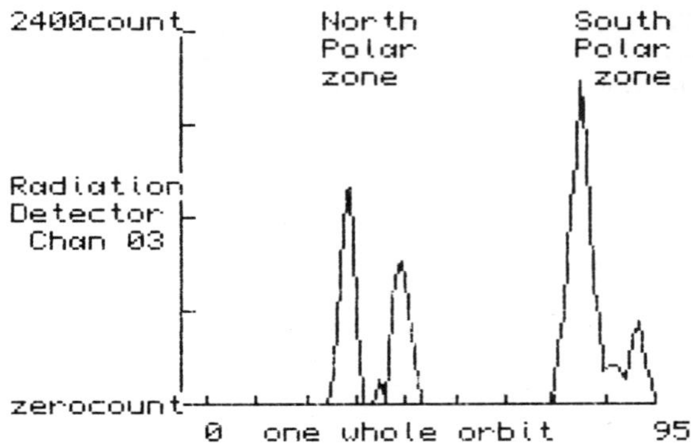

Fig 8.2.04c: Uosat Oscar 9 radiation detector graph on 10 May 1986

slightly different, but in all other respects the battery faithfully follows the solar panel output.

Battery voltage is quite low as the satellite comes out of Earth shadow at the start of the WOD record in Fig 8.2.04b. The battery quickly acquires a more healthy looking voltage, albeit in a slightly bumpy fashion as a consequence of the satellite's spin-modulated uneven current supply from the solar panels. When back in full sunlight the battery voltage hovers easily around full charge, but as the end of this WOD report approaches a new eclipse is starting. The battery gets no support from the solar cells but it is still feeding the satellite so its charge begins to drop quite rapidly under this loading, as it carries the full drain of the satellite electronics, until the satellite re-emerges in sunlight.

A very different WOD graph is shown at Fig 8.2.04c. Here the satellite is not reporting on itself, it is reporting on its space environment. Specifically it is reporting the levels of radiation it found as it journeyed around the Earth. The patterns here are clear. Twice in the orbit, once near the South Pole and once near the North Pole, the satellite measured hard radiation. Even more interesting the patterns at the two poles were nearly the same. In each case there was a sudden encounter with hard radiation as it approached the pole, then a drop, followed by another peak as it departed from the pole. At each pole it saw two radiation peaks which occurred as it crossed the polar auroral oval around each magnetic pole (the space radio physics chapters of this book describe the polar auroral zones in detail). In fact Uosat was measuring the charged-particle precipitation from under the polar edges of the Van Allen belts, as they dropped down towards the ionosphere where they produced the polar auroral oval. It is also of interest that this record was made during the nuclear power accident at Chernobyl in the USSR.

Conclusions

A whole book can and should be written about the use of Uosat WOD. This method of using the satellite to take a continuous record, which can be read thereafter by stations far removed from where the measurements took place, allows experimenters to explore the whole of near-Earth space. So far this technique is unique to the two University of Surrey satellites. It is to be hoped that all future satellite builders will take note of what has been achieved by Uosat and build on this experience. Uosats have given us digitalker and WOD, clear pointers to successful space experiments for all. A whole sub-culture of software writers and experiment developers has slowly emerged, so that even now we are only slowly beginning to utilise the sheer experimental power of these satellites. This sort of experimental climate could not develop overnight but, now it has happened, all future satellite builders should capitalise on its achievements.

Experiment 8.2.05: The death of a satellite

Purpose

This experiment records the dying moments of satellite Oscar 8. It reveals the typical progressive pattern of failure which can be monitored for some time before the satellite actually expires.

Method

A simple receiver appropriate to the satellite down link frequency fed by a modest antenna, is all that is necessary. In this case a dipole antenna and a shortwave receiver were used to read the telemetry on 29.402MHz.

Results

There were few alarms during Oscar 8's early years and the telemetry record shown below was fairly typical of the situation until 1983. Then in early 1983 Oscar 8 telemetry began to reveal problems, when it became impossible to continue running both its mode J and mode A transponders simultaneously. In January 1983 the telemetry frame was:

28 Jan 1983: 186 250 377 435 536 601

Please note the block 377, indicating 0.1*77+8.25 = 15.95V from the battery. Not much below the previously regular 16.35 but quite enough to cause alarm.

Then six months later there was a more significant change. On 2 June 1983 block 3 read 350, indicating battery volts of 0.1*50+8.25 = 13.25V. This seemed to indicate that the previously weak cell had failed completely, deleting 1.5V or more from the battery output and, worse still, the rest of the cells were clearly struggling.

This situation could not last. The Oscar 8 onboard computer needed at least 13V to stay 'sane', and on 8 June 1983 the telemetry indicated that this threshold had indeed been crossed.

8 June 1983: 180 252 324 496 568 696

This was hopeless. The battery at report 324 suggested only 10.65V, but whether this was correct was doubtful because the readings in blocks 496 and 696 were completely off the scale, so the satellite was no longer competent to report its own state of health.

In fact Oscar 8 had reached the point where its computer no longer obeyed ground commands sent up to it. In the jargon of the trade, Oscar 8's computer had 'latched', and ground stations gave up trying to command it. For 16 more days the Oscar 8 beacon continued to send corrupt telemetry, then on 24 June 1983 it ceased transmitting and has not been heard from since.

Table 8.2.05: Typical Oscar 8 telemetry on 29.402MHz, March 1978

Chan	Data	Decode	Parameter	Result
1	61	7.15*(101–N)	SolarArray mA	286mA
2	48	57*(N–50)	Battery Current	–114mA
3	81	(0.1*N+8.25)	Battery Volts	16.35V
4	52	(95.8–1.48*N)	Baseplate Temp	18.84°C
5	47	(95.8–1.48*N)	Battery Temp	26.24°C
6	26	N*23	J power	598mW

Conclusions

Simple monitoring of telemetry is a good guide to satellite health. In this instance the demise of Oscar 8 was inevitable. The satellite had been in daily use for five years, and battery failure at this age is common.

Sometimes satellite users are lucky and the battery fails open-circuit. It is no longer useful thereafter when out of sunlight, but if the solar cells continue to supply power and the battery does not short out this supply, the satellite will work when in sunlight and have periods of silence when in Earth shadow. This is disconcerting, but better than nothing. Oscar 7 failed battery open-circuit and gave several useful years of service in sunlight thereafter. Radiosport 1 also failed battery open-circuit, and it still transmits from time to time when in sunlight. Unfortunately the RS1 solar panels cannot supply enough voltage to raise its command functions to an operational 'sane' level, so it sends meaningless corrupt telemetry.

Oscar 8 had no such luck. Death was stalking it from 28 January 1983 onwards, and complete failure was just a few months away.

Less spectacular failure modes have occurred on other satellites. Radiosport 8 is typical of the group, which has a good battery but dies at the hands of a 'mad' computer, in this case killed off by radiation from its many years of orbiting close to the Van Allen belts. RS8 got increasingly 'deaf' to ground commands, and finally stopped obeying any commands at all. Oscar 10 is also a Van Allen belt victim, having lost its computer 'mind' in October 1986, although it continues to operate from time to time, albeit totally deaf to ground commands.

Satellites can therefore provide real experiments in control and failure prediction. Reading the telemetry regularly is well worth the time and the effort.

Experiment 8.3.01: Listening to the cosmonauts

Purpose

Do you want to know when the cosmonauts are likely to return to Earth? Do you want to listen as they go space walking, or when they are hopping from one space station to another? These activities and many more, have characteristic radio signatures. By listening for these tell-tale signs, you can be forewarned and ready to listen at interesting times.

Method

The technique involved requires a modest tracking antenna, say a five-element 144MHz Yagi plus a good wire antenna or dipole for HF listening. Two receivers are required for complete coverage, a shortwave receiver for 20.008MHz voice and a VHF receiver on 143.625MHz FM for Mir, 142.42MHz FM for Salyut 7 and 121.75MHz FM for the Soyuz personnel ferries.

The first requirement is that the experimenter listen to the VHF down link from the manned station (either Salyut or Mir), recording transmissions heard on VHF, particularly when no one is talking. On checking these tapes it should be possible to hear quite a few bangs, bumps and buzzing noises plus a great many other things far removed from cosmonaut speech. Many of these noises will come from space station machinery and will include ventilation, air conditioning, air purification, servo systems and hydraulics, power supply hum, and scientific instruments such as pen recorders and scanners. Additional sounds will come from space station loudspeakers, giving you rebroadcasts of the ground control up link and many other radio circuits which the cosmonauts monitor. You will also hear cosmonauts working, and entertaining themselves when they are not at work, and some of these sounds will have quite distinctive qualities imparted to them by space station hull and piping resonances. So even if you do not understand one word of Russian, there is a lot to listen to.

Keep listening regularly, and you will find one day that all the noises are gone, or are subtly changed. At this point you will need to go back to your old tapes to compare, and discover just what has changed.

If you have access to an audio spectrum analyser, you can examine your tapes in detail, and classify much of the machinery. But it is not necessary to go this far; you can get useful results simply by using your ears.

When background noises change, you may well find that you also hear a change in the communication procedures being used. Voice procedures invariably sharpen up when things start to happen, and you will probably get more clues when the standard 143.625 or 142.42 link is supplemented by simultaneous use of either or both 121.75MHz and HF 20.008MHz. Listen carefully to these comchecks. If the speech is bassy and perhaps reverberates a little, with the sound of breathing and ventilation in the background, it is pretty certain the cosmonauts are in spacesuits, either on a spacewalk, or getting ready for one.

Listen to anything and everything, and replay your recordings, and you may be surprised how much these noises off are telling you.

Results

There have been several noteworthy events since 1985:

(i) In June 1985, Salyut 7 was saved by a special rescue mission. Instead of using Salyut communications, the cosmonauts continued to use the communications in their Soyuz ferry, and to live in the Soyuz ferry for several days after successfully docking with the space station. The reason for this became clear only when they got enough electric power in Salyut to start using Salyut's 142.42MHz communications. It was so cold inside Salyut that their breath was freezing as they spoke, rattling the microphones, and every time they spoke their voices soon got croaky as the cold air got down through their mouths to freeze their vocal cords. It was a week before communications from Salyut sounded normal. Later the cosmonauts reported that the inside of the space station had been covered in ice.

(ii) On 18 November 1985, the long-stay crew in Salyut had a rather excited conversation with Zarya (Soviet ground station callsign meaning 'dawn' in English), after which they ceased transmitting, although firmly over Russia. Next day they were quiet and on 20 November signals from the space station had lost a lot of machinery background noise. On 21 November they did not transmit at all, but it was not until late on the 22nd that the Soviet TASS news agency reported that the cosmonauts had shut down the space Station and returned to Earth on the 21st because the mission commander was seriously ill.

(iii) On 5 May 1986 there were no signals from the resident crew in the new Mir space station. Next day, still with no signals from Mir, the Salyut 7 station went overhead with its 19.955MHz beacon very loud, and less than two minutes later a Soyuz ferry craft transmission was heard on 121.75MHz. A quick tape comparison of voices showed that this was not a new crew going to Salyut, but the resident crew of Mir now changing over to Salyut 7. Ninety minutes later, as the next Salyut orbit came around, this was confirmed at 2002 UTC when the former Mir cosmonauts Kizim and Solovyev both spoke on the Salyut 142.42 down link. They said Salyut was cold, and they returned to spend the night in the warmth of their Soyuz ferry, transmitting from there at 2140 on 121.75MHz. It seemed reasonable to assume they had switched on the heaters in Salyut to let it warm up, whilst they slept in Soyuz. This in fact proved to be the case. So this historic first-ever transfer from one space station to another was heard in its entirety from the UK.

(iv) On 31 May 1986 at 0645 UTC, Salyut was far to the east of the UK, well below the horizon, when the 20.008MHz cosmonaut HF link came alive with cosmonaut Russian. This frequency and the very bassy tones of their speech suggested that the cosmonauts were in space suits working outside Salyut. At 0824 UTC Salyut came above the UK horizon for the first time that day, and sure enough the cosmonauts were working outside building a pylon onto the end of Salyut. They were transmitting simultaneously on 20.008MHz, 121.75MHz and 142.42MHz, a standard space walk safety feature, and their voice tones were pure 'goldfish bowl' as their speech reverberated inside their helmets. On the next return at 0956 the cosmonauts were using VHF only, though the speech quality suggested they were employing space suit microphones. There was no goldfish bowl quality to the speech so they were presumably back inside Salyut, still in their space suits but with their helmets off.

Conclusion

A space station is like a house. When it is empty, it makes quite different sounds from those it makes when it is full of active humans. These simple examples show how careful listening can give a good picture of just what is going on in the space houses that orbit 360km above our heads.

Experiment 8.3.02: Talking to the astronauts

Purpose

To describe the first two-way communications experiments between astronaut radio amateurs in the space shuttle, and ground-based radio amateurs around the world.

Method

The frequency band used for all communication experiments up to 1986 was the two-metre (145MHz) radio amateur band. Transmissions, both up and down link, used frequency modulated speech at frequencies around 145.555MHz. Ground-based radio amateurs used their standard station equipment to communicate with W5LFL in shuttle *Columbia* and W0ORE in shuttle *Challenger*. Shuttle tracking data was transmitted by RSGB Headquarters station GB2RS. These transmissions on 3,650 and 7,048kHz were heard around the UK. Home counties amateurs were also able to copy GB2RS data bulletins on 145.525MHz FM. In this way UK radio amateurs received orbit tracking data directly relevant to passes over the UK.

Results

During the first flight in December 1983, W5LFL in *Columbia* used a simple window antenna and a portable 2m rig. He carried out several tests of communications with single radio amateur stations around the world, but in general he concentrated on being heard by as many individual radio amateurs as possible, and then tape recording their individual callsigns. The trial was limited by the relatively poor performance of the temporary antenna which was used in the shuttle.

A typical exchange in this W5LFL test occurred over the UK at 1525 UTC on 4 December. The message clearly logged in Scotland was: 'This is W5LFL, I hear G6E and lots of others.' W5LFL reported that he was taping all signals he heard, and would listen for the next 90 seconds. At least 60 individual GM stations were heard sending their callsigns. So it was clear that over the UK as a whole this level of interest would result in W5LFL hearing thousands of simultaneous calls. Indeed this proved to be the case and, as is typical with FM reception when many signals are present, only the strongest one at any instant was clearly recorded and logged by W5LFL.

On 19 July 1985 *Challenger* launched with astronaut radio amateur W0ORE aboard. His equipment was much better than that of the first flight and included a good outside antenna. As expected the first few days of the flight were taken up with shuttle operational tasks. The first break for UK radio amateurs came at 2030 on 1 August as *Challenger* passed low across the southwest horizon of the RSGB Headquarters station. Good slow-scan television pictures were copied from *Challenger* by GB3RS.

Next day scheduled contacts were made with radio amateurs in Wales, and on the following day, 3 August, GB3RS had two-way voice and SSTV contacts with *Challenger*. On the final day Sunday 4 August even better pictures were received. Amateurs all around the UK found that for much of the time the excellent signals from *Challenger* were full-quieting copy on hand-held portables using simple antennas.

Conclusions

In two short flights W5LFL and W0ORE succeeded in putting amateur radio space communications on a firm footing. This would not have been possible without a lot of intelligent planning and data dissemination by amateur radio organisations.

On 12 November 1988 Musa Manarov became the first Soviet cosmonaut to use amateur radio from space. Since then, 2m FM operations from Mir have featured several cosmonaut radio amateurs. In 1991 it is hoped to start packet transmissions from Mir.

Operating to and from space with standard amateur radio equipment has been shown to be relatively straightforward. However, the disciplined, well-mannered operating required of all concerned in future activity of this kind will call for careful study, planning and control, if we are to capitalise on these excellent beginnings. 'Don't call us, we'll call you' looks like being the rule from space and it may be best to limit terrestrial responses to specified command (club or headquarters) stations.

It is hoped that amateur radio facilities will be available in the near future in both the Soviet and American space stations. Planning and building of these facilities is already in hand, though the US station will be out of UK range.

Experiment 8.3.03: Monitoring space shuttle experiments

Purpose

To describe how a major space experiment was relayed to radio amateurs, enabling them to participate in the experiment in real time.

Shuttle flight 51F released into space a plasma receiver. Plasma (ionised gas) makes natural radio signals. Any cloud of ionised gas transmits a radio signal whose frequency is dependent on the charged particle density. Dense plasma makes high-frequency transmissions, low-density plasma makes low-frequency transmissions. Given the tremendous variety of plasma clouds in the universe, near-Earth space is full of radio signals from these natural sources. The great planet Jupiter transmits strongly over a band from 16 to 20MHz in the shortwave region. Nearer Earth the frequencies are much lower: in the 1 to 20kHz band. So there is a lot to listen to, and every transmission tells us something about its source. Given that the universe is 99 per cent plasma, some authors have even suggested that we will one day encounter giant creatures made of the stuff, and naturally they will communicate by radio.

Shuttle Flight 51F in July/August 1985 was not concerned to find mythical space beasts, but it was carrying a free-flight package which would be released from the shuttle and would listen to the plasma radio signals from near-Earth plasma in the band 1kHz to 20kHz. Normally we on the ground cannot hear these signals because the ionosphere blocks them off, but the plasma receiver was designed to relay what it heard back to the ground on 400.655MHz.

The problems and the results obtained by one radio amateur station in this experiment are reported here as a typical example of what may be possible, many times in the years ahead.

Method

The plasma receiver package was scheduled to be tested in three different locations as shown in Fig 8.3.03. Firstly it would be released to fly free, away from the shuttle. The shuttle would circle it at a distance then fly close to it. This would enable listeners to hear the plasma signals as they occurred naturally, and then to test whether the shuttle itself was contributing any signals.

For the second part of the experiment the plasma receiver would be recaptured by the shuttle remote arm and then held by the arm over various parts of the shuttle's outer surface, the receiver would test for plasma radiation and then be used to test the effect of firing discharges from a plasma gun past the package.

Finally the plasma receiver would be brought back into the open shuttle cargo bay and left there for some time for further tests. At all times the receiver would feed a broadband signal to modulate the 400.655MHz FM down link transmitter.

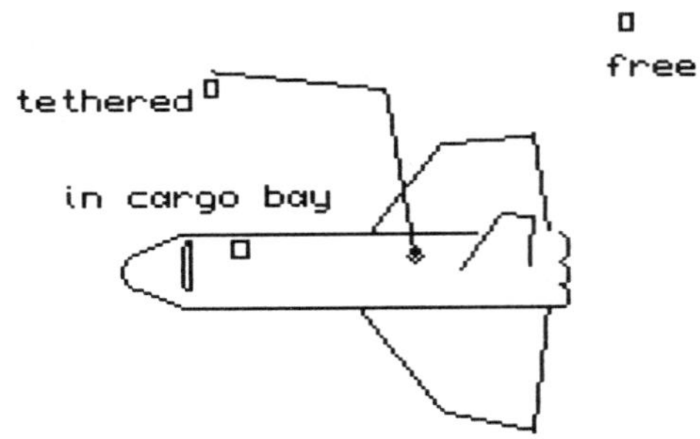

Fig 8.3.03: Shuttle plasma receiver experiment 31 July to 2 August 1985

Arrangements were made in the ground station to listen for the first pass of the shuttle. Radio amateur W0ORE was aboard *Challenger* and was planning to use amateur radio on 145.55MHz FM voice and SSTV. Receivers used on the ground were a Yaesu FT 221R for the 145MHz FM, and a Yaesu FRG 9600 for the 400MHz experiment. The 145MHz antenna was a five-element XY crossed Yagi and the 400MHz antenna was in fact a standard 432MHz radio amateur 21-element long Yagi. Both antennas were trainable in azimuth but not elevation, so they were tilted up 10 degrees in elevation to be able to follow the shuttle's relatively low elevation track south of Scotland.

The signal coming down from the plasma experiment was expected to be complex, so a tape recorder was run from beginning to end of every shuttle pass. The tape was fed from the recorder socket of the FRG 9600 and was therefore unaffected by any change in receiver audio settings.

Table 8.3.03: Plasma receiver reception, 31 July to 3 August 1985

Date	Time UTC	Report
31 July	1831 to 1837	Signal heard but unable to get full quieting. Tape unsatisfactory
	2003 to 2011	Recorded full quieting with wide range of plasma whistles/chirps
1 Aug	1536 to 1541	3 deg max elevation never got full quieting
	1708 to 1716	Good recording
	1842 to 1848	Moderate record lost at times
	2016 to 2018	Poor record
2 Aug	1548 to 1555	Two operators, one tuning, one moving antenna. Excellent record
	1721 to 1729	Good recording
	1855 to 1903	Poor record perhaps shielded in cargo bay
	2029 to 2037	Poor copy suddenly came good in last minute
3 Aug	1735 to 1743	No signal
	1908	W0ORE reports plasma experiment has ended

Results

At 1831 UTC on 31 July 1985, *Challenger* was heard on 400.655MHz down link from the plasma experiment. The log for the next three days showed a gradual improvement in the quality of the recordings obtained. Table 8.3.03 gives details from this reception record.

Several weeks after the mission ended, *Spaceflight*, the magazine of the British Interplanetary Society, published a Nasa report to the effect that the plasma experiment had run for three days. The first day the package was flying free well clear of the shuttle. The second day the package had been recaptured by the remote arm and had been operated whilst held by the arm at various locations around the shuttle. On the third day the package had been parked in the shuttle cargo bay, still transmitting. Fig 8.3.03 shows these test locations.

The full set of tape recordings were replayed, and reviewed in light of this later information. No obvious differences in the records were noted despite the changes of location. In all cases the plasma receiver seems to have heard a lot of typical space plasma signals rather than signals or noise from the shuttle itself.

For future experiments of this nature a concurrent whole orbit radiation data log from Uosat would be most desirable.

A full catalogue of natural radio chirps, whistles and sliders was recorded. There were brief periods of silence, but these were rare, and the overall impression was one of chaotic unco-ordinated signals, sounding like an aviary full of parrots. Positively no star beasts were encountered.

Conclusions

This first glimpse of natural radio signals was all too brief. There is a clear need for amateur radio research in this field, by way of remote-reporting orbiting plasma receivers returning their data on amateur radio down links. The ionosphere will always block our direct access to these signals but, given simple amateur radio orbiting plasma repeaters, who knows what we would find.

From the practical standpoint this experiment was extremely useful. Aside from indicating the way in which a simple electronic package can open a completely new window in the radio spectrum, this experiment also gave clear pointers as to how we might better organise our personnel and resources prior to events of this type, and how there is an urgent need for better, more timely dissemination of information, both before and after the event. Far more people could have taken part had this event been effectively publicised.

Experiment 8.3.04: Shuttle experiments via satellite relay

Purpose

This experiment reports a test where a radio amateur far beyond the shuttle's horizon took part in an experiment by

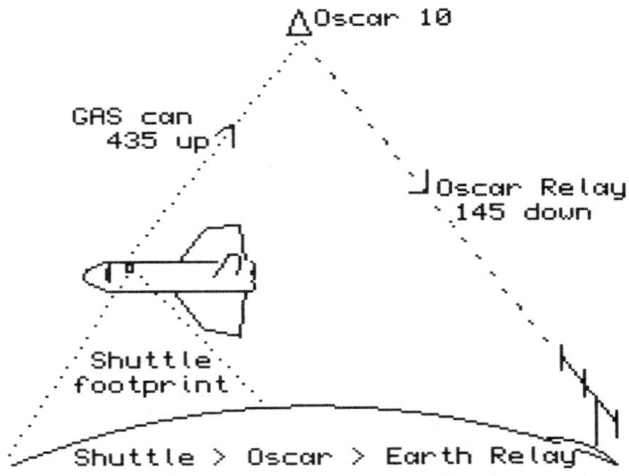

Fig 8.3.04: Shuttle satellite relay experiment

using a relay from high-flying Oscar 10. This was not a stunt. The method used here may be commonplace in five or 10 years time, enabling northern European radio amateurs far beyond the range of the American space station in its near-equatorial orbit to participate in space science studies planned from the station.

Method

On 12 January 1986 the shuttle *Columbia* launched from Florida into a low-inclination equatorial orbit. Onboard *Columbia* was an experimental package called MARECS.

Built by members of the radio club at the Marshall Space Facility, this 'get-away special' experiment comprised a computer which generated speech telemetry. The computer speech modulated an FM transmitter, operating on a frequency in the 435MHz amateur radio band, which fed a small antenna on the can which housed the experiment. The experiment was stowed in the shuttle cargo bay and operated from there, when the bay was opened up, once the shuttle got into space.

Many stations within a belt from latitude 35°N down to latitude 35°S clearly heard the experiment direct from *Columbia* as it flew over their stations.

What was of great interest to radio amateurs outside this direct reception zone was the fact that it appeared possible that the shuttle experiment transmission might be strong enough to access amateur radio satellite Oscar 10.

Oscar 10 is in a highly elliptical orbit but there were clearly times when at closest approach of the two spacecraft transfer of the signal might be possible, albeit with Oscar 10 at a minimum of 4,000km above and beyond the shuttle, ie further out from Earth, where its greater height gave it coverage of nearly half the world. Amateurs distant from the shuttle track were therefore asked to listen for any possible relay by Oscar 10.

Results

As shown in Fig 8.3.04, the shuttle flew far below Oscar 10 even when the latter was at its perigee, but signals from the experiment can were about 6W nominal to a simple antenna, so reception appeared possible but not certain. In fact the 435MHz experiment signal did get up to Oscar 10 and it was rebroadcast on 145MHz on the Oscar 10 down link.

One operator on the Pacific island of Guam, KG6DX, was ready and listening. He tuned across the Oscar 10 down link and found the experiment signal, he got full quieting and he was able to tape record it.

Conclusion

This experiment relied on a lot of luck. The satellite used for relay was the fast-moving Oscar 10, even so the experiment was successful, demonstrating that perhaps with simpler acquisition and signal relay via a Phase IV geostationary relay satellite which radio amateurs hope to have aloft concurrent with the US space station, it should be possible to participate from nearly any part of the Earth in the proposed space station science studies programme.

Experiment 8.4.01: Ionospheric transparency at VHF

Purpose

A satellite sweeping across the skies as it orbits above the ionosphere might appear at first sight to be a perfect tool for ionospheric experiments. Unfortunately this is not so, for its motion can add an irregular source of confusion because its signal path down to a ground station is constantly shifting its ionospheric transit point. We see it through a different piece of the ionosphere in each succeeding element of time.

This need not always be the case. Geostationary orbits provide satellites which have a fixed line of sight to our station. Signals from geosats are therefore unique, in that the only motion with respect to the line of sight is that of the ionosphere. Using a geosat signal at VHF, it is therefore possible to follow variations of the ionosphere, relative to a fixed line of sight, over a time scale of years.

Method

Signals from geostationary satellites are weak. So high-gain dual or switchable polarisation antennas are essential. In the author's case, the antenna used was an XY 10-element Yagi with one set of elements aligned vertically, and the other aligned horizontally, together on the same central boom. The antenna was fixed at the required elevation and azimuth for the satellite line of sight. Separate feeds were taken from the horizontal and the vertical sections of the antenna to a change over switch, which fed the chosen antenna to a low-noise preamplifier and then to the receiver. The audio output of the receiver was fed to an oscilloscope for signal-to-noise measurements.

The original experiment used Meteosat on 137.080MHz as its target. Unfortunately this satellite has now ceased transmitting and its successor does not transmit on VHF. As of 1987 the two best VHF signals available from the UK were:

137.160MHz positioned near 15°W, az 210, el 15
137.0483MHz positioned near 3°W, az 180, el 28

Stations in other parts of the UK must expect their bearings to differ slightly.

The important point is to position the antenna for maximum signal strength and leave it fixed. You need only one target, so the antenna mounting can be substantial and windproof. Only when a great deal of expertise has been achieved, will it be desirable to monitor both satellites at once, eg to examine the transits of ionospheric anomalies from one line of sight to another.

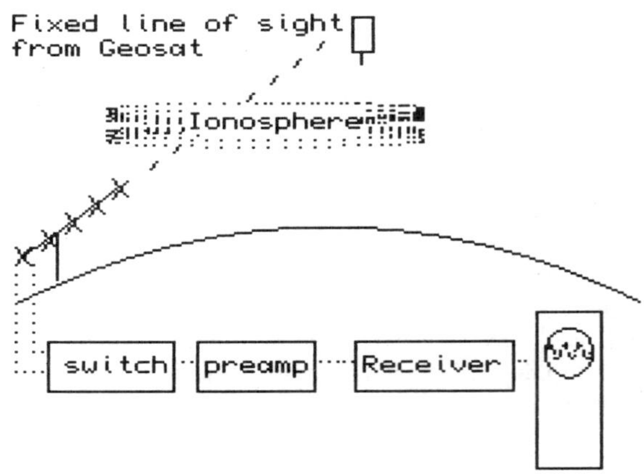

Fig 8.4.01a: Ionospheric transparency test

The received signal is selected by the antenna switch, fed to the preamplifier and thence to the receiver, whose audio output is monitored on the oscilloscope. The scope was usually set to 100mV/cm vertical deflection but was easily switched for big signals. The horizontal trace was locked to the signal waveform.

To set up the system the receiver was tuned off the signal to an adjacent quiet frequency, and receiver gain was adjusted to give 1cm vertical amplitude of peak noise. The receiver was then tuned back onto the signal and its amplitude was read off the scope. These values and time were recorded. The switch was then changed to the other antenna and the process was repeated. The signal was never received exactly horizontally or vertically polarised versus the station, so to get a proper appreciation of its amplitude the vector sum of the two received signals was calculated and recorded.

Vector sum = Square root of (horizontal squared plus vertical squared)

This value was graph-plotted versus time UTC, and measurements were repeated at 60 minute intervals, or smaller intervals if interesting things were happening.

Table 8.4.01: One day's observations, Meteosat 137.08MHz on 31 August 1985

Time (UTC)	H (cm)	V (cm)	Vector sum	20 log Vsig/ Vnoise (dB)	Remarks
0640	3.3	2.8	4.3	12.66	
0733	2.9	2	3.5	10.88	
0801	2.1	3	3.6	11.12	
0820	1	3.4	3.5	10.88	
0928	3	1.1	3.2	10.1	
1028	1.3	3.2	3.5	10.88	
1208	1.1	3.1	3.3	10.36	
1242	1.3	3.7	3.9	11.82	
1405	2.8	2	3.4	10.6	
1503	3.1	1.6	3.5	10.88	
1615	3.8	1.3	4.1	12.25	aurora began
1648	2.8	1.9	3.4	10.63	
1725	in noise	3.5	3.5	10.88	
1826	1.4	3.8	4	12.04	aurora ends
1945	1	3.8	4	12.04	deep fading
2017	in noise	4	4	12.04	deep fading
2039	3.1	in noise	3.1	9.82	deep fading
2122	2.9	2.2	3.6	11.12	fading decrease

Results

Table 8.4.01 and Fig 8.4.01b show the results for 31 August 1985. Please note the detailed information on this computer graphic daily summary. The aurora produced quite strong reflections of the Meteosat signal into the back of the antenna, but it was wide-band auroral, 'multiple Doppler' noise and it did not cause multipath fading or indeed even affect the signal-to-noise ratio at all seriously. By contrast, the local sunset selective fading did appear on the Meteosat signal, presumably via multipath effects in the ionosphere. This fading made the signal useless for communicating data until the fading ceased at 2122.

At the bottom of this daily record an account is kept of dominant signal polarisation. There were six occasions during the day when the plane of polarisation changed. This is typical of a relatively undisturbed day. On disturbed days 14 to 20 changes are typical. Both the overall 1 or 2dB variation in signal to noise during daylight, and the deep fades after sunset, are regular features of these daily charts.

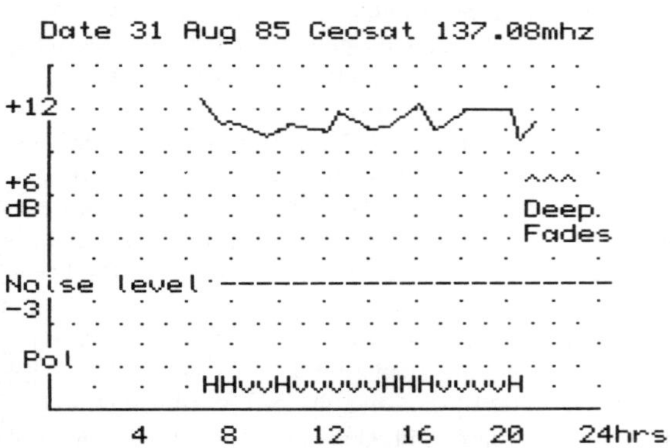

Fig 8.4.01b: Plot of results for ionospheric transparency, 31 August 1985

On some days there is also a considerable disturbance coincident with the passage of the Harung discontinuity in the ionospheric polar circulation pattern before local magnetic midnight.

Conclusions

A few days of operating this experiment should rid anyone of the common but totally erroneous belief that the ionosphere is bland and innocuous for signals above 30MHz. Trying to cope with the random changes of polarisation is bad enough, but deep cyclic fading due to multipathing can be a far worse problem.

Unfortunately this experiment signs its own death warrant. It demonstrates quite clearly why satellite links at VHF and UHF have been less than successful. The result is that soon there will be no VHF geosats left on which to do this experiment. Meteosat 1 ceased transmissions in September 1985 when it began to drift off-station, having run out of attitude-adjustment fuel. Meteosat 2 has not operated at this frequency. Indeed all new weather geosats are UHF and microwave only.

For even deeper studies of ionospheric transparency, it is possible simultaneously to monitor two separate geosats in different parts of the sky, and to watch the travel of ionospheric anomalies between them. Equally interesting, VHF geosat studies can be combined with simultaneous studies of their microwave signals. Many of the serious interruptions of the VHF signal are visible on the microwave signal, albeit much reduced.

Experiment 8.4.02: Concurrent ionospheric studies at VHF

Purpose

The previous experiment showed that the path from a geostationary satellite can often be interrupted as it transits the ionosphere. This experiment shows how the happy coincidence of a terrestrial beacon propagating to the experimenter via partial reflection in the E layer (sporadic E propagation), using almost the same spot in the E layer as the descending geosat signal, can be used to demonstrate a direct connection between sporadic E and disturbance of the geosat signal.

Method

The geostationary satellite chosen formerly transmitted at 137.08MHz from a location great circle azimuth 176 and elevation 26 degrees from the ground station in Scotland. Located close to the same azimuth, approximately 700km from the station, was amateur radio beacon GB3SX on 28.215MHz. This station pair were suitable for this experiment because the line of sight from the geosat, and any sporadic E layer ionisation propagating the beacon signal to the ground station, must use approximately the same patch of the E layer ionosphere. Fig 8.4.02a shows the relative geometry.

Reception of the satellite signal was made simultaneously on both the horizontal and the vertical elements of a 10-element crossed Yagi antenna mounted on a common-centre boom. Separate antenna feeders fed a switch, and the signal chosen at the switch went through a preamplifier to a Yaesu FRG 9600 receiver, with the receiver audio output being connected to an oscilloscope for signal-to-noise measurements.

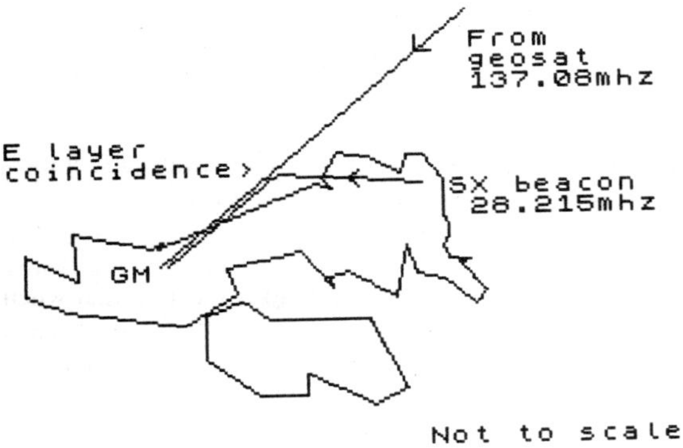

Fig 8.4.02a: Beacon and geosat signals E layer co-passage

In addition to the above, a full European SpE situation report was available roughly every two minutes, using computer controlled receivers to check two groups each of 30 remote transmitters. These were so disposed that their signal acknowledgement of SpE could be plotted as a 30 pixel grid of real-time European SpE conditions, thereby permitting monitoring of SpE movement and relationship to deep space line of sight such as that from the Moon or a geosat. A close watch was kept for disturbance of the geosat signal on the oscilloscope, and any concurrent appearance of sporadic E propagation near the geosat line of sight, with particular emphasis being given to the GB3SX beacon because of its use of the same patch of the E layer as the geosat down link.

Please note the close agreement between columns 3 and 4, showing strong evidence for both being the result of the same agency. In fact the relationship is much closer than shown here, noting that columns 3 and 4 were almost always closely synchronised in time.

Column 6 above reports the overall pattern of geosat signal during the day, considering all propagation effects, not just the sporadic E.

Results

Table 8.4.02 records details of 35 days of monitoring during the peak of the summer sporadic E season. SpE was observed on 28 days but it had no direct effect on the propagation of the geosat VHF signal. On 15 days SpE was observed propagating the GB3SX beacon signal to Scotland on 28.215MHz, using the same general region of the ionosphere as that transited by the geostationary satellite signal. On each of the 15 days the geostationary satellite signal was

Table 8.4.02: Effect of SpE on geostationary signals

1 Date	2 SpE during day	3 Disturbance on geosat path	4 GB3SX via SpE	5 Faraday Pl/2/day	6 Remarks overall propagation effects
15 Jun	yes	yes	yes	6	Disturbed day
16 Jun	yes	yes	yes	4	Repeat SpE on geo
17 Jun	yes	no	very faint	6	Too weak to block
18 Jun	yes	yes	yes	3	Disturbed day
19 Jun	yes	no	no	4	Disturbed day
20 Jun	yes	no	no	8	Disturbed day
21 Jun	yes	yes	yes	8	Disturbed day
22 Jun	yes	no	very faint	6	Very disturbed day
23 Jun	yes	yes	yes	5	Very disturbed day
24 Jun	yes	yes	moderate	1	Disturbed day
25 Jun	faint	no	no	6	Disturbed day
26 Jun	yes	yes	yes	5	Disturbed day
27 Jun	yes	yes	yes	5	Disturbed day
28 Jun	yes	yes	twice briefly	3	Only 1 geosat fade
29 Jun	yes	yes	yes	3	Calm day
30 Jun	yes	yes	yes	4	Slightly disturbed
01 Jul	no	no	no	3	Slightly disturbed
02 Jul	yes	yes	yes	2	Slightly disturbed
03 Jul	no	no	no	6	Disturbed day
04 Jul	no	no	no	6	Disturbed aurora
20 Jul	yes	no	no	6	Calm day
21 Jul	yes	no	no	3	Calm day
22 Jul	no	no	no	4	Calm day
23 Jul	yes	yes	yes	7	Disturbed day
24 Jul	yes	no	no	2	Calm day
25 Jul	yes	no	no	6	Disturbed day
26 Jul	yes	no	no	5	Calm day
27 Jul	no	no	no	3	Calm day
28 Jul	yes	no	no	3	Calm day
29 Jul	yes	yes	yes	6	Calm day
30 Jul	yes	no	no	4	Calm day
31 Jul	severe	yes	yes	14	Very disturbed day
01 Aug	faint	no	no	6	Calm day
02 Aug	no	no	no	8	Calm day
03 Aug	no	no	no	3	Calm day

disturbed concurrent with hearing GB3SX. In all 22 separate incidents, each lasting between 30 minutes and 3 hours, were recorded. In these incidents the presence of the SpE propagated beacon was concurrent (±2min or less) with severe fading of the geosat signal, such that the latter faded from +9dB down into noise roughly once every one or two minutes.

Four other events were noted when the SpE-propagated GB3SX signal was barely audible in Scotland. On one incident this had no effect on the geosat signal. In the other three cases the geosat signal was disturbed, but the concurrence of beacon signal and disturbance were less well synchronised.

In 35 days, each of about 15 hours of observation (a total of about 525 hours), about 23 hours total of geostationary satellite reception was ruined by SpE on this one line of sight. Brief checks with a second geostationary satellite suggested a roughly similar but not necessarily concurrent situation there.

Conclusions

When these results are extrapolated from a single path, one way only, to a continuously varying two-way path typical of a communications satellite or moonbounce operation (often with the two stations in quite different SpE-related time zones and/or seasons), it is clear that operators of space circuits must be prepared to allow for the effects of sporadic E when using VHF.

It is possible to some extent to forecast the possibility of sporadic E. It is highly seasonal in temperate latitudes. The northern-hemisphere main season commences in May, peaks in late June, and fades in late August. There is also a minor winter, northern-hemisphere, temperate-latitude season from mid-December to mid-January. SpE is generally a daylight phenomenon. So, collating all these features, some scheduling to avoid SpE on both a daily and a seasonal basis is possible.

In real-time operations the 'test for SpE' situation varies around the world. In Europe, a wealth of radio amateur beacons, and language-identifiable, commercial VHF stations can be used to obtain real-time checks over the azimuth arc 030 to 240. A modest computer program can be compiled for western Europe which gives real-time SpE assessment based on automatic examination of up to 50 VHF stations variously located to form the basis of a useful 50 pixel grid, or the program can display a bullseye centred on the azimuth elevation of interest (eg the Moon or a spacecraft). As shown in Fig 8.4.02b, the lunar bullseye shows adjacent beacons at 1800 on 24 August 1985, pointing up areas of likely SpE in the ionosphere.

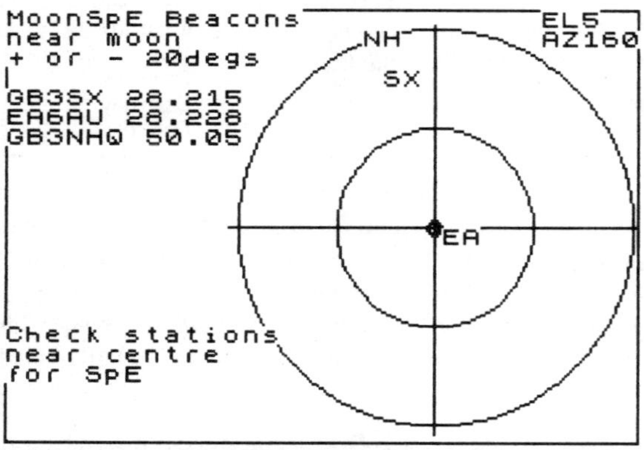

Fig 8.4.02b: Moontrack bullseye sporadic E test

This short experiment can be modified in a hundred different ways to look at propagation phenomena other than SpE, and to equate their effects on geosat signal paths at VHF or indeed at any other frequency. Experiment 8.4.01 reveals a repetitive disturbance around 2030 UTC and a less frequently encountered disturbance around 2230 UTC. Hopefully this situation will eventually be clarified in regard to causes and effects, by using a variation or variations of this experiment. This is no easy task. No one pretends that moonbounce will oblige by exactly imitating shorter geosat paths, but we have to start from the point that they do have quite a lot of things in common. So geosat paths should provide a happy hunting ground for experimenters for a long time to come, sitting as they do beyond the Van Allen belts, subject to the full blast of the solar wind, and having to take regular trips through the magnetotail.

Experiment 8.4.03: Satellites and anomalous VHF propagation

Purpose

From time to time amateur radio stations are able to communicate with stations far beyond the line of sight, via any one of several forms of anomalous propagation, eg sporadic E, auroras, tropospheric bending, field-aligned ionospheric irregularities etc. It is reasonable to conjecture that when ionospheric anomalies return terrestrial VHF signals back to Earth, signals from space trying to transit down through these same regions will be disturbed.

This experiment shows how VHF observations of terrestrial and satellite signals can be used to examine what happens when ionospheric anomalies are present.

Method

This experiment requires facilities for detecting and monitoring VHF anomalous propagation, whilst simultaneously monitoring satellite up and down link performance.

Sporadic E, FAIs and auroras can be readily detected by monitoring the 28MHz beacon band for European beacons giving evidence of these phenomena. They can also be detected by using a VHF TV set covering European Ch E2 (48.25MHz) and E4 (62.25MHz), or eastern European R1 on 49.75MHz. In addition all these phenomena can be detected using amateur radio 50MHz equipment, and stations able to monitor 153.213MHz can get excellent warning of auroras from the Wick auroral radar.

In parallel with the watch on terrestrial propagation, the experimenter must keep a regular watch on the chosen satellite or satellites. The choice of satellite is important. It might seem at first that Uosat down links on 145.825MHz would be useful targets, or that dual-frequency monitoring via the navigation satellites would be most useful. In the author's experience the amateur radio communications satellites such as Fuji Oscar 12 are a much better proposition, noting that they allow the experimenter to add his own up link signal to the test, thereby checking the path two ways if the Fuji beacon is also monitored as a yardstick of the one-way path.

Not every station will have the facilities to utilise all these features, but there are enough suggestions here to allow a station to be used for useful experiments even if it is restricted to monitoring a single 145 or 435MHz satellite down link.

It is vital that the experimenter start by getting lots of records of satellite signal strength when absolutely nothing is happening in the ionosphere. Only if a full appreciation of normal conditions is acquired first, will the experimenter be able to recognise all aspects of anomalous conditions when they eventually occur. Care is necessary even when anomalous propagation is clearly present. SpE and FAIs are patchy. SpE to the east is quite unlikely to effect a satellite passing west of the station, and it is vitally important to remember that the place of interest is not the satellite position or its sub-point, but that point in the ionosphere that the satellite signal is transiting.

For example, if you live in southern England and you see Italian TV via SpE, you know the SpE is located on roughly the Italian bearing but it is 100km above the Earth, half way between you and Italy. Does your satellite line of sight cross this 'half way to Italy' region as it comes down through the E layer? Please remember that this is a much more complex situation than experiment 8.4.02. There the path was fixed; here the path, and more important its transit point in the E layer, is moving quite rapidly as the satellite sweeps across your sky.

Stations who wish to investigate auroral effects on satellites should note that most of the northern UK can observe the almost daily effect of auroras. The polar auroral oval in its magnetic quiet configuration reaches as far south as Newfoundland (because the magnetic pole is in North America). So even in magnetic quiet conditions a satellite over or beyond Newfoundland being received in UK has actually sent its down link through the upper regions of the auroral oval. Fuji Oscar 12 showed these effects even in its first days after launch as it came towards the UK from the direction of Newfoundland. Be alert to look for clear signals on the down link plus auroral versions of the same signals from 500Hz to 2kHz higher in frequency.

Results

It is impossible to summarise all likely eventualities in an experiment as varied as this one. These results therefore report a set of incidents on one single evening as seen from Scotland during the operational life of FO 12's illustrious predecessor Oscar 8J (also built in Japan). Fig 8.4.03 shows three orbital passes by Oscar 8J across northern Europe on the evening of 28 June 1980. Strong sporadic E signals were being received from locations shown, at Madrid, Barcelona, Switzerland, and Grunten in south Germany. This indicated an intense patch of SpE in the ionosphere above southern England and northern France. In addition, the ionosonde at the Rutherford Appleton Laboratory located at Slough, just west of London, was showing blanket sporadic E directly overhead.

At 1708 UTC Oscar 8J was heard in Scotland as it came above the horizon low in the east, the line of sight did not intercept the sporadic E zone and the pass was accessed satisfactorily.

At 1848 UTC the next orbit of Oscar 8J appeared above the Scottish horizon, but for the next seven minutes the up link signal from Scotland failed to access. Some 435MHz down link was heard, as was the 8J beacon, but neither were at normal strength. At 1855 UTC the satellite line of sight to Scotland cleared the SpE and normal 145MHz access was obtained and established for the rest of the above-horizon pass.

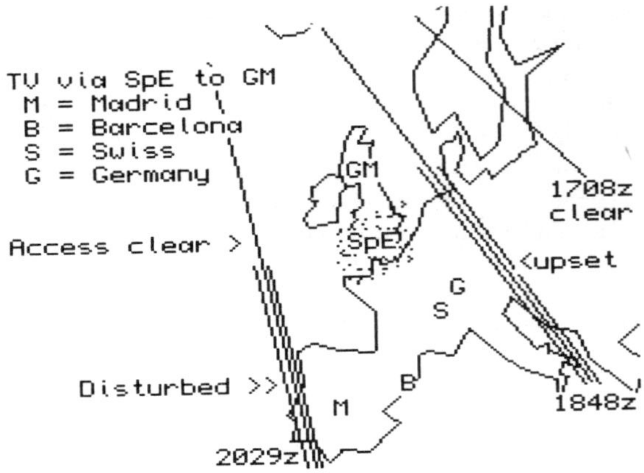

Fig 8.4.03: SpE blocks Oscar 8J access 28 June 1980

At 2029 UTC Oscar 8J appeared again but until 2037 UTC no signal from Scotland could access its transponder and its down link and beacon signals were very poor indeed. At 2037 UTC the satellite line of sight came north of the SpE area, and again access was quickly achieved and several useful conversations took place with other radio amateurs via the satellite transponder.

Clearly one short experiment of this sort proves nothing. So this experiment was repeated several times, always with the same result when blanket sporadic E was present.

Conclusion

This type of experiment can be set up as part of normal amateur radio operations. It can provide a wealth of data provided the operator keeps a useful record of what happened. It provides data on many different aspects of VHF propagation, and gives a good introduction to radio propagation science.

Experiment 8.4.04: Weather satellite propagation studies

Purpose

This experiment uses pictures from circular-orbit, near-Earth weather satellites to investigate ionospheric propagation anomalies. Fig 8.4.04a shows a half-frame picture from a weather satellite. The picture is marred by horizontal bands of interference. These bands of interference give clues in regard to the exact location of the satellite at the moment that an ionospheric propagation anomaly interfered on its down link signal path to Earth.

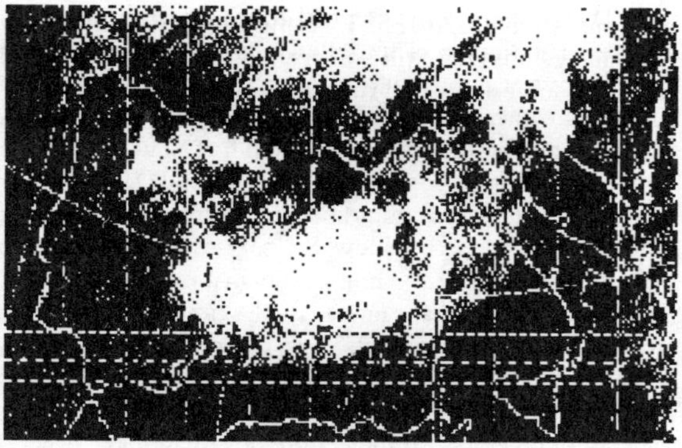

Fig 8.4.04a: A simple low-contrast weather satellite chart showing a weather system over Spain. The dotted lines on the picture are interference caused by an ionospheric anomaly

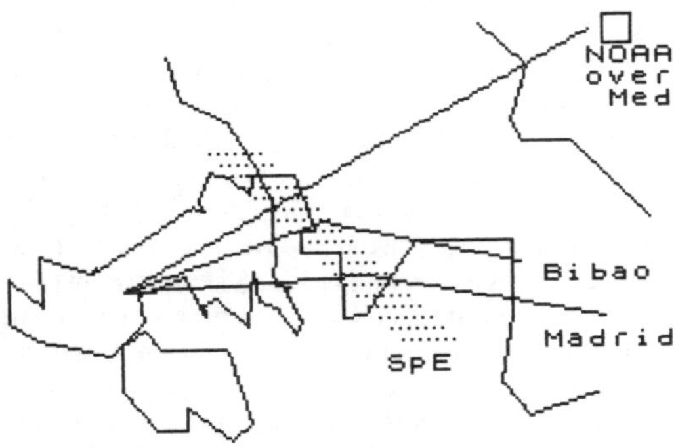

Fig 8.4.04b: TV and weather satellite signals, E layer co-passage

Method

Using any available circular-orbit, near-Earth weather satellite of the US NOAA or Soviet Meteor classes, make a record of its picture transmission using the 137MHz down link and a suitable facsimile receiver attached to a wet or dry fax printer, or a microcomputer and printer as illustrated here in Fig 8.4.04a.

Watch closely as the picture is produced, looking particularly for brief periods of picture break-up. Listen to the receiver audio so that you can discount any periods of local interference. Identify those occasions where the picture is broken, when there was no obvious local interference. Note the times UTC and picture locations of these breaks. Where picture break-up is present, carry out a listening survey of the terrestrial VHF bands to identify any signs of the presence of anomalous propagation. Fig 8.4.04b shows a side view of the picture and signal path geometry likely to be encountered.

Results

Given a picture with transmission breaks as shown over Spain, it is possible to extrapolate to identify the sub-satellite point at the moment when the transmission signal path was disturbed. In the example shown, the satellite was directly above an east/west line extending from the north part of the island of Sicily to Gibraltar. The actual satellite position was the centre point of this line which equates to an approximately 37.7°N 5°E sub-satellite point. We know the satellite altitude above this point from our computer-tracking data, or Nasa/NORAD elements, is about 940km. We can therefore calculate the position where a signal from a satellite in this location would penetrate through the E layer of the ionosphere on its way to Scotland, thereby delineating the place where the propagation anomaly is most likely to be.

Conclusion

Used in conjunction with terrestrial monitoring of VHF anomalous propagation, interference to LEO weather satellite signals can provide good clues to the location of anomalies in the ionosphere. The example in Fig 8.4.04a shows three periods of interruption of signal quite close together. This is quite typical, with the anomaly being in the form of several spaced 'platelets'.

This method does not work with geostationary satellite pictures. If it is possible to simultaneously monitor the weather satellite 1,700MHz down link, an interesting comparison of the effect of the anomaly on 137 and 1,700MHz can be obtained.

Experiment 8.4.05: Sub-horizon HF satellite propagation study

Purpose

Despite all sorts of predictions that long-distance terrestrial HF communications via ionospheric propagation would be replaced by satellites, this has not happened. Indeed the diversity of types and usage of HF ionospheric links has increased, thus rendering the need for a proper understanding of the ionosphere more important today than it has ever been.

Most professional ionospheric studies use ionosondes transmitting pulsed HF vertically upwards. This is a good way of exploring your local ionosphere. Unfortunately the HF communicator is uninterested in his local ionosphere. What he needs are real-time data regarding the ionosphere en route to his target.

Some advances have been made in this respect by using oblique-incidence ionosonde transmitters pulsating towards the local horizon, but this method requires careful interpretation of a reflected or back-scattered signal, which is really somewhat different from the forward propagation signal data the practical user requires.

Satellites can provide this one-way forward propagation data quite readily, particularly where the satellite is flying somewhere in the ionosphere and is transmitting at a frequency near the maximum usable forward propagating frequency expected.

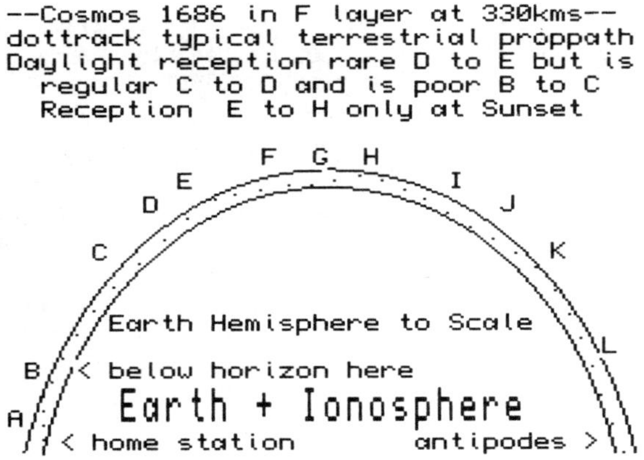

Fig 8.4.05a: Scale drawing of the Earth hemisphere surrounded by ionosphere at roughly 330km above the Earth's surface

This experiment reports how a varied group of satellites transmitting from different heights, at different HF frequencies, could be used to explore HF propagation, at different seasons and at different parts of the solar sunspot cycle. This experiment is not easy to perfect, but any station equipped with standard HF communications reception capability can participate and build up expertise in this important study.

Method

Satellites which circle the Earth at the same height as major HF propagation zones are rare. In October 1985 Cosmos 1686, a Soviet space tug, was docked on the Salyut 7 space station to replace the station's defunct engines. The station was orbiting at about 330km height, ie in the F layer of the ionosphere. Cosmos 1686 transmitted a beacon signal continuously on a beacon frequency of 19.955MHz.

This Cosmos 1686 frequency was by chance close to the anticipated daylight MUF to the south of the UK at this sunspot minimum.

A scale drawing of this situation is reproduced here as Fig 8.4.05a. Please note that this chart may differ markedly from drawings of the Earth and the ionosphere in some handbooks. It is most important that experimenters appreciate that the ionosphere, in its true scale relationship to the Earth, is very thin. Too often handbooks use the wrong scale and produce impossible 'bouncing propagation paths'. The true geometry is as shown here. Any signal going out to a long-distance path must literally skim the Earth and graze the ionosphere at the shallowest angle possible.

Fig 8.4.05a shows a scale drawing of the Earth hemisphere surrounded by an ionosphere at roughly 330km height above the Earth's surface. This figure should be used in conjunction with examination of great circle signals paths from Cosmos 1686 to the UK. It is not a chart of the spacecraft track. It is intended to indicate the conditions at any instant on the great circle path from the spacecraft to your station.

The chart is marked around the ionosphere with letters A to L. These letters denote typical zones where propagation features can change. The dotted line between Earth and ionosphere traces a signal from a terrestrial station at the antipodes (other side of the Earth from the UK) to UK. Starting from this mythical station south of New Zealand the signal transits up through the absorbing E and D layers, near zone L. It is refracted and propagated forwards for the first time in the ionosphere somewhere near zone K. From there it continues northward, skimming down through the absorbing E and D layers at zone J, then skimming above the ground (no ground reflection is desirable or required), before going straight on and upwards (because Earth is curving away from it), to another absorbing D and E layer transit around zone I. It then continues to another forward refraction in the ionosphere somewhere near zone H, and thence downwards and north again to another E and D layer transit at zone G followed by a skim over the Earth and a climb back through the D and E layers somewhere around zone F.

Its next ionospheric refraction occurs at zone E and from there it has two more E and D layer transits at zones E and D, separated by another skim close to the Earth, before it meets the ionosphere at its last refraction point at zone B. From there it has to get down through the E and D layers yet again before it arrives at your station. It will if it survives have experienced at least eight E and D layer transits and four ionospheric refractions, all requiring rather exacting conditions for useful propagation. It is understandable why signals from this area are extremely rare but, given absence of any E and D layer absorption, ie at night, and given a low enough frequency to propagate via the ionosphere at night, it is possible, as 1.8MHz sunset/sunrise terminator chasers will verify.

From the point of view of a spacecraft flying in the ionosphere the position is rather different. Exploring Fig 8.4.05a from the Cosmos 1686 point of view, the signals from its beacon were very loud in the overhead zone near the UK, but as the satellite receded towards zone B its signal was transiting the E and D layers with lower and lower incident angles. So in daylight there was lots of absorption and hence signals got quite weak as Cosmos 1686 went out to the UK horizon.

In zone B the signal was often lost, never to be heard again that orbit, but at times the break in reception ended and the spacecraft was heard as it receded to zone C. This is explained by the fact that it is difficult for a satellite in the ionosphere transiting zones B to C to get a useful path to the ionosphere overhead the station and be refracted down through a large angle to the ground station. Sometimes conditions allow this, but such conditions are infrequent. More often the spacecraft signal is lost after zone B and not heard again until it gets into the zone between C and D. In this latter zone it has a good straight line path to the ionosphere nearly above the home station, with a simple refraction angle down to the station.

Beyond zone D the spacecraft signals encounter a new problem. Before it can illuminate the ionosphere above your station horizon it must make two low-incidence skimming transits of the D and E layer absorption zones at C and D. Signals from this situation/region are rare, perhaps no more than once or twice, even on days of undisturbed ionosphere.

From zone E onwards we meet the most interesting conditions. The spacecraft beyond zone E must propagate its signal to the home station via ionospheric refractions in region E to B, and, again, overhead the home station. In addition, the signal must survive E and D layer absorbing transits twice somewhere in region E to B and again in the home station overhead zone. At times when the Sun is above the horizon all along this track, propagation along it is impossible because the E and D layers are ionised and capable of considerable absorption, particularly where four separate transits are involved. But there are periods when the absorption disappears at E and D layer height, whilst much higher in the F layer the Sun is shining. This is the greyline, the solar terminator zone of sunset and sunrise. When the Sun has risen high enough to ionise the F layer but not the E and D layers, or when the Sun has set below the horizon as seen from the Earth and the D and E layers, but not the much higher F layer, greyline conditions apply. It is then possible to get signals from the spacecraft from as far away as 10,000km, ie Cape Town or China.

Beyond zone H, a third ionospheric refraction and more E and D layer transits are necessary. Signals to the UK from satellites in this region are rare except in special conditions applying around solar cycle maximum, and therefore not applicable to the Cosmos 1686 case.

Still further out from the UK, we begin to go around the far side of the Earth and approach the UK again so chances of signal propagation start to improve again as the path shortens albeit on the reciprocal azimuth.

This long appraisal of the obstacles a signal from a satellite or a terrestrial station must overcome to get to your station is necessary if the experimenter is to be clear what is happening. Using a computer print-out of satellite or spacecraft position, the experimenter can tell at any time he hears the spacecraft signal just what sort of obstacles it is overcoming to get to his station.

The computer data can be checked against actual measurement (via Doppler shift) of the spacecraft's time of closest approach and in this way the experimenter can keep a check on what is going on, perhaps aided by a home-made Kettering plot (experiment 8.1.01) to ensure he is not taken unawares by unannounced engine firings and orbit modifications of his target spacecraft.

For convenience the author plotted all Cosmos 1686 signal reports on a great circle computer-generated plot. This allows day-to-day comparison of records and is a convenient way to store the results of observations.

Results

The results of some typical Cosmos 1686 observations are shown in computer map format, illustrating the spacecraft's track only in those places from which it was heard. Fig

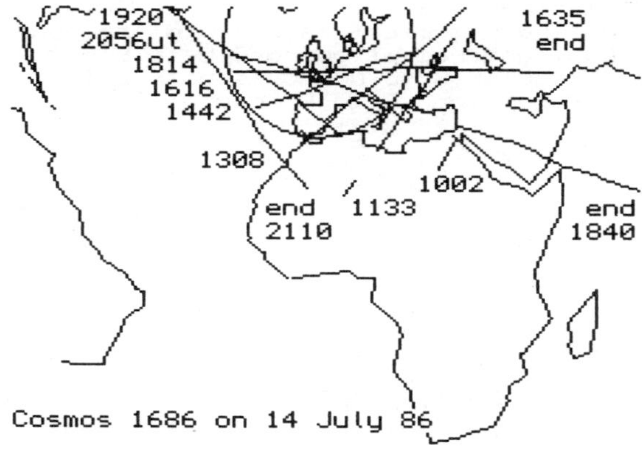

Fig 8.4.05b: Cosmos 1686 reception tracks, 14 July 1986

8.4.05b shows the results of 14 July 1986. This was an above-average day for reception in Scotland of the 19.955MHz signal.

On 14 July 1986 Cosmos 1686 was first heard on an orbit which never came above the UK horizon, as the spacecraft tracked from 1002 to 1004 UTC over a short track starting over south east Egypt and ending over the Gulf of Suez. This type of reception from the sub-horizon at the time of sub-horizon closest approach is common. The oval around the UK shows the horizon for Cosmos 1686, so it was far to the south east beyond this horizon.

The next orbit was heard in two sections, first over Chad and southern Libya, at 1133 UTC. Then it was lost for several minutes, before being re-acquired as it crossed the Mediterranean coast of Libya from whence it was tracked over Greece and beyond the Black Sea on a sub-horizon or horizon-scraping path. Once more the path was balanced either side of the sub-horizon closest approach.

The third orbit of the day was detected at 1308 UTC as it crossed the Atlantic coast of north Africa, and shortly thereafter it rose above the UK horizon for the first time that day as it passed overhead Gibraltar. It then proceeded across Europe, going below the UK horizon over the Ukraine, but still clearly audible until deep in Soviet Asia, north and east of the Caspian Sea.

At 1442 UTC there occurred the first orbit which was never heard sub-horizon at all, but was tracked from the UK horizon west of Finisterre in northern Spain to Kiev in the Soviet Union at the UK eastern horizon.

Somewhat in contrast, the orbit which followed was detected at 1616 UTC as it came above the UK horizon west of Ireland and was then tracked without a break to the UK horizon near the north west corner of the Black Sea. Unlike the previous orbit the signal then continued to propagate to the UK until the spacecraft had crossed the south east tip of the Caspian Sea and travelled on to Pakistan where it was lost at 1635 UTC, ie the spacecraft had begun to exploit the sunset path.

The next orbit at 1814 UTC did even better. Tracked from the UK western horizon down across Europe and Greece it

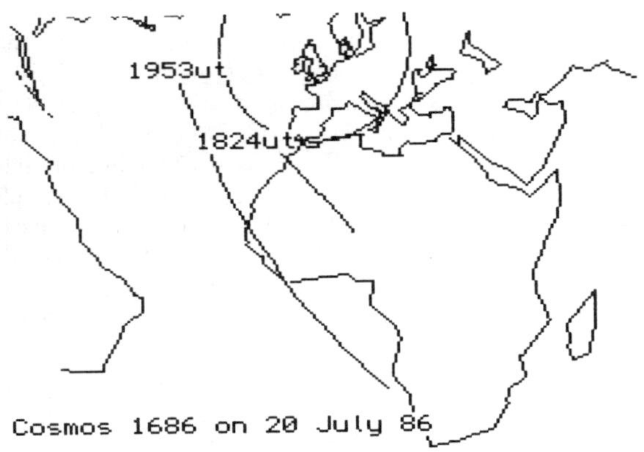

Fig 8.4.05c: Cosmos 1686 sunset zone, 20 July 1986

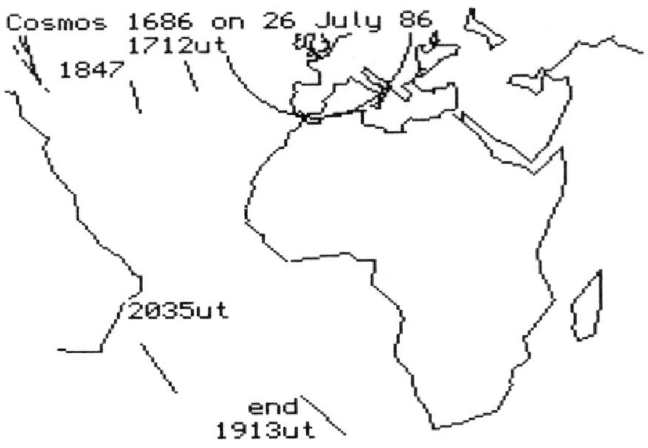

Fig 8.4.05d: Cosmos 1686 sunset zone, 26 July 1986

was then briefly lost, only to reappear strongly over a track from Israel down over Arabia and on down across the Indian Ocean where it was lost at 1840 UTC. This was a long sunset-zone, sub-horizon track.

The next orbit, detected early at 1920 UTC, produced a quite different effect. It was detected sub-horizon over Newfoundland, then tracked to the UK horizon west of Ireland and on down to north Africa where it was lost as it crossed the UK southern horizon.

The last recorded orbit of the day was never above the UK horizon. It was picked up over Newfoundland at 2056 UTC, and produced an interesting track balanced about its sub-horizon closest point of approach, ending deep in west Africa.

At first sight this may look like a nasty conflicting mess, but it does show several interesting features:

(i) Three of the sub-horizon tracks balance nicely about their sub-horizon closest point of approach.
(ii) Although at different times of day and hence different propagation conditions, most orbits received sub-horizon seem to start and/or end about 3,000km from Scotland, ie in zone C on Fig 8.4.05a.
(iii) Only the 1616 UTC and the 1751 UTC orbits were heard beyond 3,000km zone C. The 1616 orbit extended to 5,600km from UK, ie zone E, and the 1751 orbit extended to 8,200km from UK, well into zone F to G on Fig 8.4.05a. The two orbits which gave long-range, sub-horizon results were clearly travelling along the local sunset terminator zone.

These observations of Cosmos 1686 were repeated over many days and provided many more examples of the propagation patterns mentioned in the above paragraphs. The spacecraft orbit is gradually pulled west by perturbation in a manner which results in it flying overhead a particular longitude at a slightly earlier time each day. Putting this another way, the spacecraft encountered the sunset zone later, further west each day. Fig 8.4.05c for 20 July 1986 shows only the sunset orbits for reasons of clarity. They are no longer over Pakistan and the Indian Ocean, but are much further west over west Africa and the eastern south Atlantic. By 26 July the pattern of sunset tracks heard in Scotland is even further west and becoming broken up, as shown in Fig 8.4.05d. Please note how they end with sharp clarity at region H of Fig 8.4.05a just where they would need another refraction to get to the UK, if they were slightly further away.

Conclusion

This experiment is simple to set up, but extremely difficult to interpret unless the data is clearly presented. Despite being difficult to analyse, it clearly is a superb way to see propagation in action. Here the description has been kept simple but experimenters who wish to take this method further will already have seen how it could be enhanced by adding signal strength data, eg to assist with questions in the 'how much absorption resulted at that E and D layer passage?' category. The next experiment discusses another useful addition to this type of propagation exploration by spacecraft.

Experiment 8.4.06: Identifying non-great circle propagation

Purpose

Everyone knows that radio signals always travel in straight lines along great circle paths, but everyone is wrong, and so are most radio handbooks! Radio signals can be reflected, refracted, partially reflected and scattered by ionised plasmas, but why should this be confined to the vertical plane? In the normal world signals can be propagated along paths bent at any plane, vertical, horizontal or intermediate.

Much of the time these deviations from great circle paths are small, but major deviations can occur, more frequently in some parts of the world than in others, eg west Africa, the Caribbean and the equatorial central Pacific.

This experiment requires a clear understanding of satellite tracking, and Doppler measurement and theory. So please ensure you have done the previous experiment in this

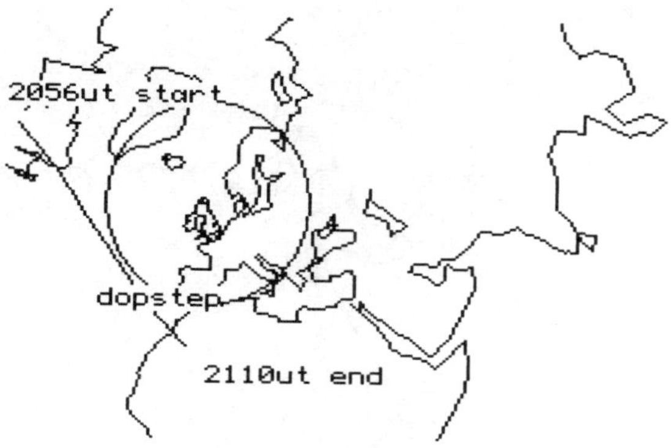

Fig 8.4.06a: Cosmos 1686 sub-horizon, non-great circle propagation, 14 July 1986

chapter and the Doppler experiments at the beginning of this chapter before you tackle this experiment. It is not easy. It is unexplored territory. There are lots of areas in the world where these effects might be expected but have not been reported, eg the southern hemisphere. Any reports should therefore be carefully and thoroughly compiled, this being state-of-the-art experimentation in a field where the professionals are clearly lagging behind the amateurs. Accurate reporting is essential; this is not a simple laboratory exercise, it has serious practical implications.

Method

This experiment uses the same equipment as the previous experiment, ie a shortwave receiver and a good antenna. The difference here is that the received frequency of the signal is carefully logged at frequent intervals and used as a guide to whether the signal is arriving at the receiver via a line-of-sight great circle path, in which case we can anticipate its Doppler from our knowledge of its track and velocity relative to the line of sight. If, however, the signal frequency is not what would be expected, the signal must be leaving the satellite in a direction different from that of the receiver, and being subsequently redirected towards the latter.

On most orbits the received frequency is in accord with a line-of-sight path, but in about one case in 50 it is not. In this event it becomes possible to use the received frequency to determine which path the signal was following when it left the satellite and, to facilitate this, a record is kept of the frequency every half-minute of the time over which it is heard.

Where anomalous Doppler shift is heard it is possible to calculate the angle relative to the satellite track at which it departed the satellite and, although this could be anywhere in a cone around the satellite track, it is usually possible to estimate the actual track from its possible, as opposed to impossible, geometry with respect to the receiving station. For example, for Cosmos 1686 its signal straight ahead corresponds to a closing velocity of about 7km/s versus a stationary receiver dead ahead, producing a Doppler shift about 600Hz high. Directly astern of the moving spacecraft the Doppler shift will be about 600Hz low. Signals received 30 degrees on the spacecraft's bow have a signal shifted about 520Hz high. So by measuring Doppler shift, we can estimate the divergence of the signal from the line-of-sight pass. This method is necessarily crude with the simple equipment used here. As previously stated, there is no way of knowing whether the signal is being bent, left or right, up or down or in between, but the possible geometries for a received signal limit these options considerably.

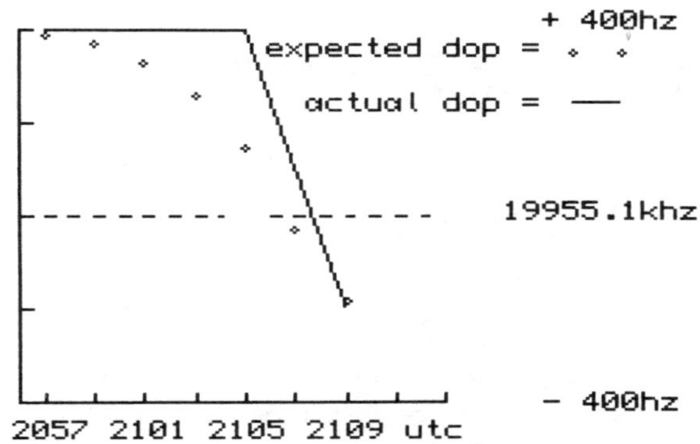

Fig 8.4.06b: Cosmos 1686 non-great circle Doppler plot, 14 July 1986

Satellites sending continuous-carrier (CW) signals are best for this experiment but the choice of useful satellites is so small that any modulation type is acceptable if necessary.

Results

Fig 8.4.06a shows the track of Cosmos 1686 on 14 July 1986. Fig 8.4.06b shows the Doppler curve anticipated for this track. As expected, with the spacecraft not coming directly towards the UK the anticipated Doppler at first detection is slightly high but not anywhere near maximum and, as the spacecraft passes down the Atlantic, its line of sight to UK is at an increasing angle to its track. Hence the anticipated frequency drops steadily towards a zero positive Doppler at sub-horizon closest approach, a little over half-way along the track.

The actual signal frequency measured is shown as the full line on Fig 8.4.06b. The Doppler is roughly correct at the first detection of the signal, but its frequency stays steady until 2105 by which time the signal should have had negative Doppler shift. It is still a high positive shift, however, which suddenly falls precipitously over the next three minutes during which time signal reception is confused. Fig 8.4.06c tries to show one possible explanation of what may have happened. From 2105 to 2109 the signal was disturbed and it quickly reverted to the correct anticipated Doppler via a great circle path. Whether there is a scatterer/reflector over Africa and the Atlantic in the position shown is not absolutely clear. Some subsequent experiments placed

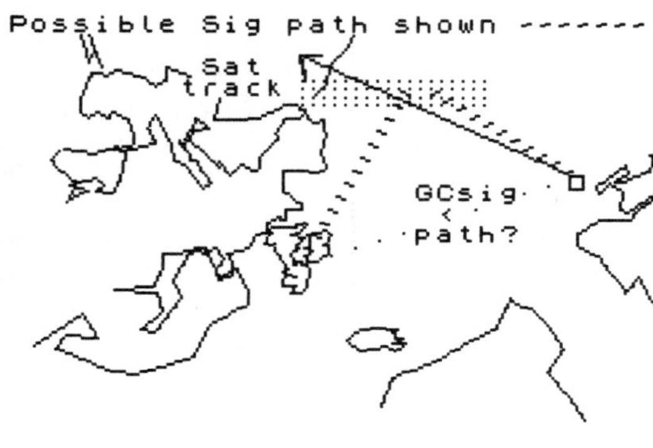

Fig 8.4.06c: Possible path of Cosmos 1686 signal to explain Doppler anomaly, 14 July 1986

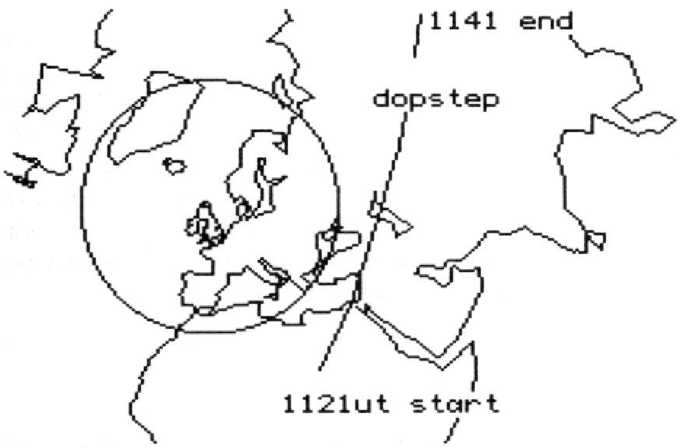

Fig 8.4.06d: Cosmos 1686 sub-horizon, non-great circle propagation, 10 September 1986

it further south than shown here, but the Doppler anomaly produced was of much the same form.

In August 1986 Salyut 7/Cosmos 1686 changed orbit to fly above the ionosphere at 480km height, but none the less this experimenter kept watching it for sub-horizon propagation, particularly when over this potential African scatterer. On 10 September 1986 Cosmos 1686 came north over Africa on the track shown on Fig 8.4.06d and it told a different Doppler story, as shown in Fig 8.4.06e. The next

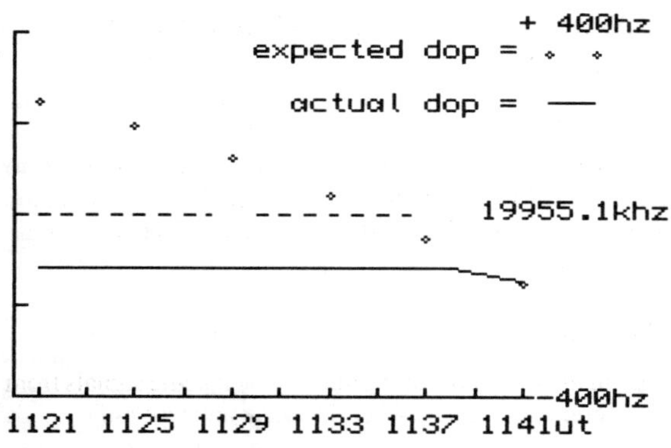

Fig 8.4.06e: Cosmos 1686 non-great circle Doppler plot, 10 September 1986

Fig 8.4.06f: Cosmos 1686 sub-horizon, non-great circle propagation, 11 September 1986

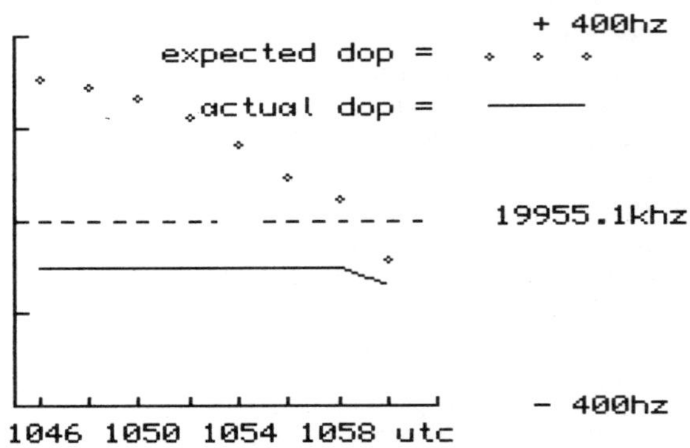

Fig 8.4.06g: Cosmos 1686 non-great circle Doppler plot, 11 September 1986

day there was a repeat performance as shown in the track chart at Fig 8.4.06f and the Doppler curve of Fig 8.4.06g for 11 September 1986.

Close examination of these Doppler tracks for September shows that the situation appears to be almost a mirror image of the earlier 14 July event. In September the spacecraft was acquired over Africa heading north east. In both cases the Doppler started abnormally low, although the spacecraft was coming towards the UK albeit at a low relative velocity. The signal should have had slight Doppler high, but in fact it had a marked Doppler low. A possible reason for this was that the signal heard in the UK was not coming by the short line-of-sight route, but was coming via a longer route off the back of the spacecraft via a scatterer/reflector south of the satellite over Africa.

Conclusion

No claim is made here that the tentative explanations given above are correct, though the presence of the anomaly over Africa is strengthened by the two sets of disparate but complementary results. This experiment is typical of a kind now open to radio amateurs and space radio listeners equipped with modern receivers and computers. Used properly and fully reported, it should enable radio amateurs to thoroughly analyse and document this non-great circle propagation. Non-great circle propagation is not yet in the handbooks but it undoubtedly will be one day. Meanwhile the African anomaly is not the only northern hemisphere candidate. Other similar effects have been observed over the Caribbean and the equatorial central Pacific, both on satellite and terrestrial signals, and there is less firm evidence for a similar anomaly over Indo-China. Do we actually have separate anomalies, or is this a belt around the Earth? Is there one belt or two separate belts, one in each hemisphere? Used carefully, this experiment could tell us.

Experiment 8.5.01: Monitoring the radio Sun

Purpose

Our Sun is a variable star. It has enormous changes of mood, and it could be a potential killer if unprotected astronauts were to be caught by one of the outbursts we call solar flares.

Here on Earth our atmosphere protects us from most of the deadly radiation, but we are still aware of it, not least from the way it disturbs radio propagation.

The majority of big solar outbursts take place around the 11-year peaks of the solar activity cycle – the 'sunspot cycle'. The radio experimenter can use quite simple equipment to monitor these outbursts and, over a period of time, this can generate a set of records of solar activity, affording a view of long-term trends, and giving warning by a day or two of many of the extreme propagation features which result from these solar bursts, ie auroras.

Method

Solar activity produces huge outbursts of radio frequency energy. From the standpoint of simple experiments the energy produced in the VHF is the easiest to monitor. This means we can use antennas and receivers for the 136MHz satellite band or the 145MHz radio amateur band. All that is necessary is to pick a quiet, normally unoccupied frequency and mount a three-element Yagi antenna pointing south and elevated about 20 degrees, tune the chosen receiver, and then leave it. Solar bursts can be heard simply by leaving the loudspeaker on. Alternatively the output of the receiver audio can be fed to an oscilloscope or high-impedance meter, but by far the best records are made using a pen recorder if one is available.

Results

A profile of a typical solar radio burst is shown in Fig 8.5.01. The actual radio noise was very loud, for about five minutes. There had been several bursts like this one on previous days, and the activity continued for a few more days. After that, the sunspot area from which most of the flares were coming went out of sight of Earth, as the Sun revolved the active part of its face away from us.

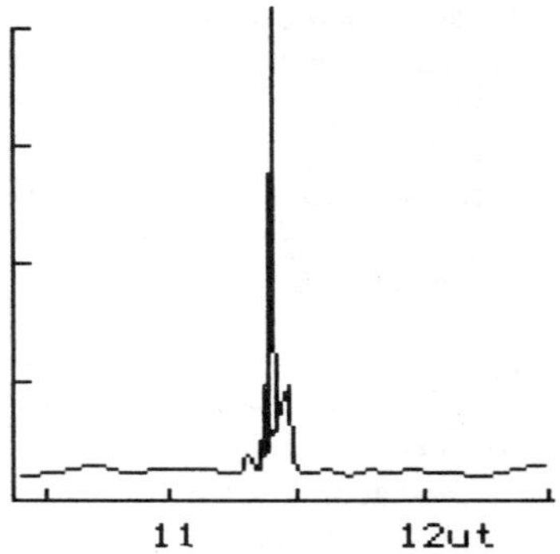

Fig 8.5.01: Plot of solar radio noise burst on 144MHz, 8 November 1979

About 30 hours after this burst, there was a small aurora over Scotland. However, this was upstaged completely on 13 November when a much bigger aurora occurred.

Solar flux, the measure of solar output reaching the ionosphere, was high at this time. Indeed, though it was not known at the time, that month and the next were to be nominated as the cycle peak.

Conclusion

Radio frequency monitoring of the Sun is one of the best ways to keep a check on the source of all our terrestrial radio propagation and its disturbance.It requires no unusual equipment. Indeed the average radio amateur already has most of the bits required. Over the years 1989 to 1992 and again, 2000 to 2003, the Sun may again give us good strong cycle peaks, as it did in 1979/1980. Indeed cycle 22 has already shown some spectacular activity in spring 1989. Radio frequency monitoring is the best way to keep appraised of what is happening, if you want to catch the exciting 50MHz F2 transatlantic openings, the really big auroras, and those super days when 28MHz contacts with Australia are as easy as talking to locals.

Experiment 8.5.02: Listening to moonbounce

Purpose

To describe a simple experiment which should allow you to hear amateur radio signals being reflected by the Moon, the first step to trying Earth-Moon-Earth (EME) communications for yourself.

Method

The smallest possible outfit likely to hear some signals from the Moon will use the 144 or 432MHz amateur radio bands because path loss is minimal at those frequencies. In addition, the 144MHz band has the most powerful and the most numerous group of EME operators. So there is a far better chance that you will hear someone than you would, say, on the higher frequencies.

To hear even the strong signals, you will need a big antenna. The minimum requirement is a 12-element, long-boom, high-gain Yagi beam antenna which can be pointed precisely at the Moon in both azimuth and elevation. You will also require a low-noise GaAsFET preamplifier mounted directly on the antenna to minimise signal loss. There are two ways of approaching the receiving problem. You can use a standard 144MHz amateur band receiver, but you must add to it a good audio filter so that you can listen in a narrow bandwidth to maximise your chances of hearing what will be the weakest signals you have ever heard. The alternative method of reception is to use a convertor to change the signal down from 144 to 28MHz. You need a convertor which has quiet mixing. You then take the signal from the convertor to a good-quality shortwave receiver which should have a narrow-band CW filter. It will also probably have the advantage of smooth slow-motion tuning, which helps a lot as you slowly search for Doppler-shifted EME signals hidden in noise.

Before you can listen to signals from the Moon, you must first know where it is. You can get accurate azimuth and elevation data from a microcomputer program. But you must also know just exactly where north and south are with respect to your station because if you are using a large antenna, you have to point its narrow beam quite accurately. So check one night on the exact location of the Pole Star, and put two big stakes in the ground either side of your antenna, lined up so that looking along the tops of the stakes through the centre of your antenna mount you get a straight line to the Pole Star. You can come back in daylight and either mark the north/south line on the ground in bricks, decorative stakes, or paint marks on nearby buildings. Then, rain or shine, whether you can see the Moon or not, you can always work out the correct azimuth to point at it. Elevation is much easier; you can make a scale using a Perspex degree scale and use a weighted string to show the line of the vertical against the degree scale fixed to the antenna.

Having made sure the Moon is above your horizon, you can check everything is correct by using your computer data to set your antenna on its azimuth and elevation scales, then, when and if the Moon is visible, you can see how closely your antenna actually points at the Moon.

Another good trick is to listen when the Moon is not there. Try tuning the EME band from 144.001 to 144.020MHz and find out what you can hear. Beware of home computer and TV set artifacts, which often completely block parts of the band. If you can, switch off the offending TVs or computers. Listen to get the feel for what the band sounds like in wide-band mode, then try it through your filter.

With no Moon present you should hear the noise level rise as you bring your antenna down from an elevation of, say, 30 degrees. As your antenna begins to point near the ground, you should be able to detect a rise in noise in your receiver. This signal is generated by the ground. Having satisfied yourself that your equipment is sensitive enough to hear ground noise, you can think about listening to the Moon. The best place to find out when and where EMErs will be using the Moon is to listen to them making their schedules on their 14MHz SSB liaison net, usually on Saturdays. An even better plan for beginners is to find out the dates and times of the annual ARRL moonbounce contests. They will have chosen dates covering a weekend or consecutive weekends when the Moon is at its perigee, ie nearest Earth (in order to minimise path losses). In moonbounce every little thing you can do to increase your chances is vital.

Having made sure your antenna is accurately pointed at the Moon at the appropriate time, you can start listening. Do not expect to hear anything at all at first. You can search methodically, tuning up and down the moonbounce band or, like the author, you may find that slowly moving the tuning back and forwards over 300 or 400Hz of the band will enable you to pick the signals out of the noise. Do not expect to hear signal notes; all you will hear on a simple rig as you tune back and forth is what appears at first to be changes in the noise as you rock the tuning back and forth. With luck you may finally pick up a faint signal. If you do it will only be a station running high power to a monster antenna. Do not be put off by this. These stations run these monster rigs specifically to get minnows like you who are using minimal antennas.

Listening to these 'big guns', you will gradually become familiar with the one-letter shorthand that moonbouncers use in their signal reports. Remember, most moonbounce contacts never rise above the noise. You will have to be able to read morse CW whilst it is 3 or 4dB in noise, and whilst it is fading and disappearing as it is afflicted by Faraday rotation of polarisation and other problems as it makes its up and down transits of the ionosphere.

Do not expect to hear other stations using minimal rigs like yourself. To begin to hear the 'medium guns', you need about 6dB more antenna gain, ie four Yagis, each 12 elements on long booms, or better still eight of these Yagis or another antenna outfit of similar high gain. With the high-gain antenna you will of course have to point at the Moon much more accurately than before. So this is not the way to start. Learn on something easier to point before you then spend a fortune on antennas. Erecting a moonbounce antenna in Scotland, where winds up to 100km/h plus are regular visitors, is expensive. A good push from the wind and your expensive elevation drive can be reduced to scrap in seconds.

If your minimal antenna rig produces nothing, do not give up. Find out if you have an active EMEr in your area, and if possible arrange with him when it would be convenient for you to listen on his rig. Then later you can find out when he will be operating and you can try to hitch a ride on his QSOs, listening to what he is listening to. You should hear him direct, and you will then be able to listen for echoes of his signal and any replies he gets, knowing from his responses just exactly how he is getting on. Remember, moonbouncers use separate receive and transmit cycles to avoid the problem of both trying to talk at once. So you can listen directly and for echoes when your local EMEr transmits, and then listen for replies.

Results

The best time to get results is the ARRL contest weekends. Listening to QSOs, you will get used to the fading and complete loss of signal, and you will also become familiar with the one-letter reporting code (described in the meteors and moonbounce chapter of this book).

Conclusion

Moonbounce is difficult even when you have enough money for the equipment and a big enough house and grounds to put it in, but if you want to be at the sharp end of amateur radio, this is the way to go. New signal detection techniques and other aids are beginning to appear, and moonbounce is the logical place to test them. Indeed, one enterprising enthusiast is already sending some packet radio transmissions via moonbounce!

Experiment 8.5.03: Meteor scatter

Purpose

To provide a simple guide, so that anyone wishing to try this excellent sport may do so. It combines state-of-the-art astronomy, comet orbital dynamics and good radio operating techniques. None the less, immediate results should be available to anyone, even with the simplest equipment.

Every moment of the day the Earth in its orbit around the Sun is colliding with thousands of pieces of space debris. Most of them are extremely small, but even those no bigger than a grain of sand have several millions of atoms to contribute to the short-lived ionised plasma cloud they make as they are vaporised on entering the top of the Earth's atmosphere. In milliseconds they are superheated by friction and vaporise, forming a cloud of charged particles. It is this cloud trail of ionised gas that for a brief moment makes a perfect reflector or scatterer of radio signals at low VHF frequencies. Reflected or scattered radio signals can be relayed from one terrestrial location to another, more than 2,000km distant, all by the last dying flourish of this grain of rock or dust.

As discussed in the meteors and moons chapter of this book, many of these meteors are members of streams, debris cast off from comets perhaps thousands of years ago, forced by their inherent velocity to follow the comet's track century after century. After a thousand years or so the debris can become an almost continuous stream all around the comet's orbital track. Every year the Earth, on its orbit around the Sun, must cross near this old comet track twice. So even when the parent comet is far away, some of its faithful followers are captured by the Earth.

Because the positions of many of these meteor streams are well known, the dates and times of their Earth crossing can be calculated from year to year. Thus informed, operators specialising in high-speed communications can be ready, and can use the meteor trails to get their signals to and from distant stations.

This simple experiment will not concern itself with two-way meteor-scatter communications, as that is covered in the specific chapter on meteors. Here the experiment will chart a method for anyone who wishes to learn from practical study of these fascinating space wanderers.

Table 8.5.03: Meteor scatter observation frequencies

Frequency	Service	Schedule
28.205	DL0IGI beacon Germany	24 hour
28.215	GB3RAL beacon London	24
28.237	LA5TEN beacon Norway	24
28.257	DK0TE beacon Germany	24
28.277	DF0AAB beacon Germany	24
48.25	European E2 TV	07 to 23
49.75	East Europe R1 TV	06 to 22
50.02	GB3SIX beacon Wales	24
50.035	ZB2VHF beacon Gibraltar	24
50.05	GB3NHQ beacon London	24
62.25	European E4 TV	07 to 23
70.031	FM Gdansk Poland	07 to 23
144.91	DL0PR beacon Germany	24
144.925	GB3VHF beacon England	24
144.975	GB3ANG beacon Scotland	24

Method

A wide variety of equipment can be used for meteor-scatter observations, but it helps to use either frequencies at the top of the HF shortwave band, eg 28MHz at the lowest, or, at the high end, frequencies in the 144MHz band. If equipment is available the best results will be obtained either on the powerful European TV transmitters around 48.25MHz (European E2 channel) or 50MHz amateur radio using the UK amateur radio beacons, or 70MHz eastern European FM broadcast stations. For maximum sensitivity, whether you listen to TV or FM radio, you should listen using the CW or SSB detection mode.

For antennas, a simple dipole or loop is quite adequate. One regular observer of 48.25MHz TV meteor scatter uses a simple bamboo-and-wire loop antenna facing east, standing upright in the roof space of his house. So whatever equipment you have, some of it should allow you to get into meteor watching. The following are specific frequencies used by many observers. Please remember that TV and FM stations rarely come on before 0700 local time and most close down at local midnight. Therefore, whilst their high power gives marvellous meteor scatter during the day, you should be prepared to shift to the 24-hour-a-day 50MHz amateur radio beacons if you want a full picture around the clock.

The TV transmitters are powerful and there are lots of them. So an antenna aimed east at central Europe will always pick them up. Gdansk FM is also powerful but it should not be used for serious studies because the FM signal can produce a complex result and several other transmitters are on exactly the same frequency as Gdansk.

As has been mentioned earlier, most meteors come in streams arriving on specific dates. A full calendar of these dates is given in the meteor chapter of this book.

It is quite unnecessary to wait for one of these dates, particularly if you can listen to the big TV transmitters. There are lots of random meteors, not officially allocated to any particular stream – although most are thought to have once belonged to streams which have perhaps broken up over a million years or so, usually because of perturbation from too close a passage to one of the big planets (Jupiter or Saturn).

The best time to catch these random meteors is on the front of the Earth as it orbits the Sun. Every station is on the front of the Earth at about 0600 local time daily. So from 0600 to 0900 local time you can usually find lots of random meteors as the Earth runs into them. Please remember, if you listen for them, that TV stations will not be on at 0600. So use amateur radio beacons until 0700, then switch to a TV station to listen to the full 'dawn chorus' at 0700.

Results

From 0700 to late evening a receiver tuned to 48.25 or 62.25MHz will pick up a succession of bleeps and chirps, and a few rare long pings which last several seconds, often fading in and out several times before they finally disappear. Many of the signals will have a Doppler shift of frequency as you listen.

Some observers use automatic counters to count pings, and these studies have suggested that there are more random meteors in January and again in June than there are at other times. This is not really surprising. The Earth's orbit is inclined a few degrees with respect to the orbits of the gas giant planets, Jupiter and Saturn. Each year in January and in June the Earth goes through the orbital plane of these planets. As the majority of comets were captured by these big planets, most of the comet debris which becomes meteors is trapped in their orbital plane, hence the excess of random meteors when the Earth passes through that plane.

Just counting random meteors will soon get boring. So a good meteor shower is always welcome. The tables and figures in the meteor chapter of this book list the dates and timings of these showers. Some, like the January Quadrantids, are compact, going through an intense maximum in just a few hours: see Fig 8.5.03a.

By contrast, as Fig 8.5.03b shows, the Draconids meteor shower is quite different. The Draconids last for several days and only come above the UK horizon in the morning hours. This spread of the Draconids over several days indicates that the meteor stream is a wide one. Its double peak suggests we are looking at two streams, one laid down long ago, the other more recent, following a slight shift in the parent comet's orbit, probably as a result of a close encounter with either Jupiter or Saturn. What this chart of the Draconids does not show is that some years it hardly appears at all. In normal years it is very weak. But in 1985 the parent comet, Giacobini Zinner, passed near the Earth which may or may not account for the bigger-than-usual display.

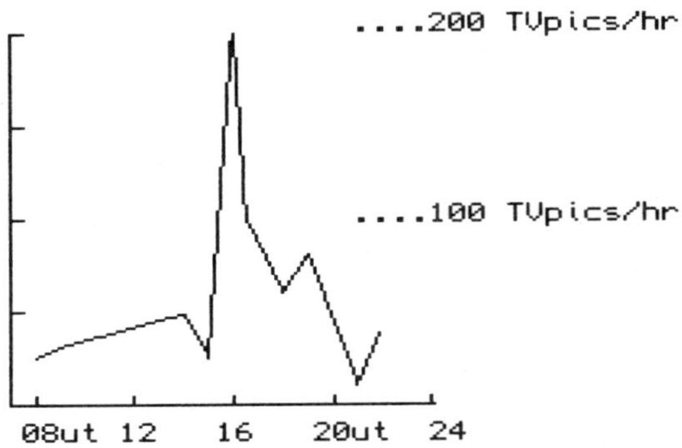

Fig 8.5.03a: Plot of TV pics during Quadrantids meteor shower, 3 June 1981. Audible pings continuous 0900 to 2000

When these big meteor showers occur, the reception of audible pings can become quite deafening and impossible to separate and count. One tactic used by some meteor shower experimenters is to use two reception systems of different sensitivity. One system uses audible reception. The other system uses visual reception of actual meteor-scattered TV pictures, literally counting the number of pictures which flash up on the screen per minute. As TV uses about 100 times the bandwidth of voice, it is about 30dB less sensitive. At shower peak the Quadrantids may be audibly continuous and uncountable for an hour or more, but a TV will count three pictures a minute for 15 minutes at the actual shower peak.

Conclusions

Meteor scatter can provide a great deal of simple experiment or serious study. It is full of interesting astronomical detail and sometimes there are some real surprises in the shape of

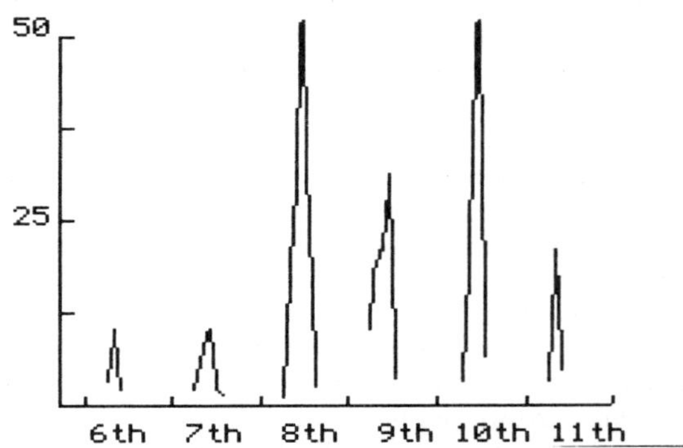

Fig 8.5.03b: Plot of audible pings during Draconids meteor shower, October 1985 (abnormal hi). Audible pings/minute, 62.259MHz E4 TV

a major storm, the most famous of which was reported in the song 'Stars fell on Alabama'. That was the famous Leonids storm of 13 to 15 December. Poor in most years, once every 33 years or so it puts on a magnificent performance. The next time is due in 1998 or 1999.

For those who wish to progress from meteor-scatter observer to meteor-scatter communicator, there is now a firmly established group of serious experimenters whose activities and methods are described in the meteor chapter of this book.

Experiment 8.5.04: Satellite visual tracking and photography

Purpose

Under certain conditions satellites can be seen quite clearly in the night sky. Tracking them visually can help the observer to a better understanding of orbital motion and, combined with photography, it can produce accurate position versus time fixes for determination or checking of orbital elements.

As sunlit satellites pass over ground stations in darkness after sunset, or just before dawn, they shine by reflected sunlight, resembling moving stars. Quite often the satellite goes into Earth shadow as it crosses the observer's sky. At these times the reflected light from the satellite often sputters for a few seconds before finally going out. This variation of light at extinction can tell observers a great deal about the atmosphere at the satellite's sunlit horizon.

Method

Few, if any, satellites carry powerful lights. Even the cabin lights of the space shuttle are difficult to see from the Earth. But as the satellite passes over the post-sunset or pre-dawn portions of the Earth, it can still see the Sun from its high altitude and reflect the sunlight incident on it. At these times observers see the space shuttle or the Russian space station as a bright magnitude 0 or 1 star.

Observers with normal eyesight can see much dimmer objects than this, usually down to at least magnitude 4 (the bigger the magnitude the dimmer the object). With binoculars, it is possible to see targets magnitude 6 to 8 on clear haze-free nights. Even tiny satellites such as Uosat Oscar 11, not much bigger than a suitcase and 900km up, can be seen easily by anyone.

This clear viewing of Uosat is all the more remarkable when you consider that it is the equivalent of a Scotsman in Glasgow following the flight of a suitcase as it flies above Paris. Uosat is magnitude 5 to 6 as is FO 12, so binoculars are useful if you are looking for them in hazy skies.

Some satellites such as Ajisai, launched with Fuji, sparkle and flash as they reflect sunlight. This effect comes from their being constructed of several hundred small mirrors deliberately designed to reflect light. Other satellites appear to go on and off as they cross the sky. This is because they are tumbling or spinning in space, first showing a bright side to the Sun, then showing a dull side. Old rocket cases give this effect as they spin end-over-end, before their vast size and small weight conspire with the atmosphere to pull them down to an early burn-up.

Not every flashing light crossing the sky is a satellite. Aeroplanes use powerful flashing lights, but they quite often also show coloured lights, something few satellites do.

So the time to look for your satellite is just after dusk or before dawn. The higher the satellite, the longer after-dusk or pre-dawn you can see it. In winter in the UK the shuttle and the Mir station are visible up to about two hours after sunset or from two hours before dawn, whereas the higher-flying navsats are visible four hours after or before. In summer the midnight-Sun effect complicates things. Summer nights are short but even low fliers like the shuttle and Mir can see the Sun every time they come over the UK on a summer night. Northern UK stations see this effect much more pronounced.

Finding satellites, even when you have their az/el tracks, is not easy. So the best way to improve this situation is to use a microcomputer. There are several programs which tell you which satellites are sunlit over a darkened Earth, and when they go into Earth shadow. Some programs even show the satellite's track against the star background, with the satellite colour coded to show when it is sunlit and when it is in shadow.

Photographic methods

Viewing satellites is fine but to get accurate orbital data, a permanent record is necessary. To get a photographic record, a good clear viewpoint, well clear of street lights, is necessary. The camera must be mounted on a sturdy tripod and be fitted with a fast wide-aperture lens, at least F2.8 or, better still, F2 if available. Film should be fast speed, rated at a minimum of 400 ASA 27 DIN. Useful films are:

- Polaroid Polagraph slide positive, ASA 400, 35mm B/W. You can process the slides straight away in a dry processor.
- Ilford HP5 negative film, ASA 400, B/W, all sizes. Super-quality negatives, then home or trade prints. Can be used as negatives for orbit data studies.
- Kodak Kodacolor VR colour negative, 1000 ASA. Super colour, but needs trade processing.

Set up the camera with the shutter in the bulb position. Focus on infinity and set aperture to widest possible, F2 or wider. Use a cable release to open the shutter and hold it open for about 20 seconds as the satellite crosses in the viewfinder, then close the shutter and wind on the film.

With practice you can get at least three 20-second exposures of a typical Mir pass. Remember you have to realign the camera between each shot. If you want accurate timing of the position of the satellite versus the stars, you can open the shutter at a specific recorded time and close it, say, exactly 10 seconds later. Then it is simple to measure on your slide or negative exactly when the satellite passed a particular star. Knowing the stellar positions in terms of right ascension and declination, it is then only a matter of calculating the satellite's right ascension and declination from its displacement from the stars.

Results

In the summer sky there are several bright star groups used for centuries by the old Arab navigators. Amongst the best for satellite orbit checking are the stars Yed Prior and Yed Posterior (Delta and Epsilon Ophiuchi), which act as an excellent pair of goalposts for Mir orbit photographs. In the winter sky the constellation of Orion provides a host of bright stars along the Mir track, while Castor and Pollux in Gemini are useful for high-inclination satellites like Uosat.

Conclusion

Satellite observation and photography can be a useful supplement to radio observations.

Chapter 9

Man in space

This chapter tells the history of manned spaceflight, with particular emphasis on those flights which have involved direct radio amateur participation. The chapter then goes on to review how and why launch and mission features affect where manned spaceflights can be seen and heard, and where and when radio amateurs will be able to communicate with them.

History

Yuri Gagarin – the first man in space

Manned spaceflight began on 12 April 1961, when Yuri Gagarin became the first person to orbit the Earth. It is significant that he had so much to do on this first flight that he had no time to relax and use amateur radio, although he was in fact a well-known radio amateur whose callsign (UA1LO) was already familiar all over the world. Please note that this callsign was reassigned after Gagarin's death in 1968 so please don't think you are contacting a ghost if you hear it!

Owen Garriot, W5LFL

By 1983, operating conditions in space had relaxed to the point where astronaut Owen Garriot was able to propose an amateur-radio element for his flight in the space shuttle STS 9 mission, planned for autumn 1983. His proposal was accepted by Nasa, and he arranged a simple equipment package for this scientific shuttle mission in *Columbia*. By good fortune the orbital inclination was high (circa 57 degrees), so the mission flew almost overhead Glasgow, Scotland, giving excellent coverage over the whole of northern Europe.

The equipment W5LFL used had of necessity to be simple. So he chose to use a simple handheld 2 metre FM transceiver connected to a metal strip antenna taped onto the inside of a shuttle cabin window. He proposed to make standard calls on 145.55MHz FM at roughly two-minute intervals, listening in between calls for replies on a separate up link frequency, and simultaneously tape recording all stations heard. He wanted to talk to someone on every continent, and he was only able to operate during rest periods between his official duties as a mission specialist. In consequence he was only able to operate on one or two orbits over each continent.

This first flight was a mixture of triumph in space and near farce on the ground, with W5LFL's simple call: 'This is W5LFL in space shuttle *Columbia* listening for next two minutes' being answered by anything up to 10,000 radio amateurs all talking at once. Despite this maximum noise equals minimum communications situation, W5LFL was able to take callsigns and messages all around the world. In the UK the best reception undoubtedly occurred at 1525 UTC on 4 December 1983. As received in Scotland his signals were readability 5 strength 9, as he reported hearing stations in Ireland and England.

Tony England, W0ORE

In July 1985 Tony England launched aboard the space shuttle *Challenger* for science mission 51F. Orbital inclination was about 48 degrees so that there were five good orbital passes in range of the UK each day. Even more important perhaps, a permanent external antenna was wired to W0ORE's amateur radio equipment, and his transceiver had facilities for FM voice and SSTV transmissions.

One of *Challenger's* special science packages was a very-low-frequency plasma wave receiver, which was rebroadcasting its signals on wideband FM at 400.66MHz, and it was this signal which was heard first at 1831 and again at 2003 UTC on 31 July.

Next day W0ORE was not available for amateur radio operating over the UK, but the VLF plasma broadcast was again successfully monitored here at 1536, 1708, 1842 and 2016 UTC. Then on 2 August at 1721 UTC, W0ORE was heard on amateur radio at 145.55MHz in firm contact with UK stations. He had arranged schedules with club and headquarters stations in the UK, and was clearly having excellent communications with them. In addition the plasma experiment continued to be monitored on all that day's orbits in range of the UK.

By 3 August W0ORE had got his SSTV running, and at 1735 UTC he was heard sending pictures and communicating with RSGB headquarters. He also reported at 1908 UTC that the plasma experiment had been successfully completed. Next day, 4 August, produced further excellent SSTV orbits at 1442 and 1616 UTC.

This was an outstanding performance by W0ORE. Both his organisation and that of RSGB HQ were very good indeed, and it is now clear that, building on W5LFL's first efforts of 1983, W0ORE and the ground organisations associated with him had provided a model performance, setting the pattern for all future missions of this type.

DP0SL/PE1LFO

The European Space Lab mission of October 1985 included several radio amateurs in its crew. On the first two days of the mission, 30/31 October, there was no amateur radio activity, but thereafter, on 1 to 4 November inclusive, there were amateur radio operations every day.

As before the amateur radio activity was concentrated into scheduled contacts with club/headquarters stations, and with experimental work. Reception was generally good, although there was a tendency to call stations which were still at least two minutes outside the shuttle radio footprint. So all too often the astronauts were talking to themselves – a point which suggests a need for better planning detail on future flights. However, this minor point aside, the real message of this flight was reflected by the way it followed that of W0ORE in demonstrating that careful pre-mission scheduling of communications opportunities is the best way to ensure good circuit discipline.

Cosmonaut radio amateurs

The *Challenger* accident of January 1986 put a temporary stop to amateur radio operation in space. This hiatus came to an end when amateur transmission started from the Mir space station. A number of cosmonauts are active radio amateurs, but prior to 1988 there was no Soviet cosmonaut amateur radio operation from space. The first sign of this Russian activity was an announcement in October 1988 that the cosmonauts had fitted a 145MHz amateur radio antenna onto the outside of Mir, and that the cosmonauts then in space were studying for the radio amateur examination. Then suddenly on 12 November 1988, cosmonaut Musa Manarov began the first of a series of amateur radio transmissions using callsign U2MIR. In the weeks which followed he operated regularly during his normal 0500 to 2000 UTC day, making contact with radio amateurs in the UK, USA, Finland, Austria and Czechoslovakia. Most of these contacts took place with Mir transmitting on 145.4MHz FM and listening for replies on 145.55MHz FM.

After Manarov left Mir in December 1988, the resident doctor cosmonaut Valeri Poliakov transmitted using the callsign U3MIR and occasionally the other resident cosmonauts were reported to be using callsigns U4MIR and U5MIR. As with the Americans, actual transmission times depend on workload and the availability of cosmonaut radio amateurs.

Hopefully, now that the shuttle is operational again we may see a resumption in astronaut activity. Along with the commencement of cosmonaut operation there is clearly a good chance that many more Earth-bound radio amateurs

Fig 9.01: Major space launch sites around the world

will get the opportunity to talk to the spacemen over the next few years and, who knows, maybe the first US astronaut to USSR cosmonaut amateur radio contact. The paragraphs which follow report the shape and form these missions are likely to take.

Major space launch sites

In order to be able to listen to cosmonauts or astronauts as they talk to the ground, or to progress further and talk to cosmonaut or astronaut radio amateurs when they are in space, it is essential to know how to follow their spacecraft when they are above your horizon. This is not difficult, but it does require a simple understanding of spacecraft orbits and just where they can go and, equally important, where they cannot go. The most important of the rules governing spacecraft orbital tracks are determined by where they launch from. The paragraphs which follow describe each of the world's major launch sites in turn, and report the individual limits on the orbits which are set by the locations and geography of these sites. Explanations are also given as to why these orbital, launch corridor and landing area restrictions apply, and, why a great deal of attention must be paid to astronaut safety.

If you know where a spacecraft was launched and what its mission tasks are, you can have a good idea of where and when it will come near your station, even if you get no further information. Once you find it, you can then collect more information and produce your own rough but useful predictions as to when you will next see it. So whilst launch and orbit data may be a little dull, it is vital information.

Plesetsk, at 320°W 62.5°N in the Arctic zone of European Russia, is the launch site for the majority of unmanned Soviet flights into orbits inclined at 70 to 82 degrees. The launch corridor goes out over the Arctic Ocean, so it is not suitable for manned flights, where any sort of abort would result in a crash in very inhospitable territory. Fig 9.02 shows the Plesetsk site.

Kapustin Yar, at 314°W 48°N, is on the border between

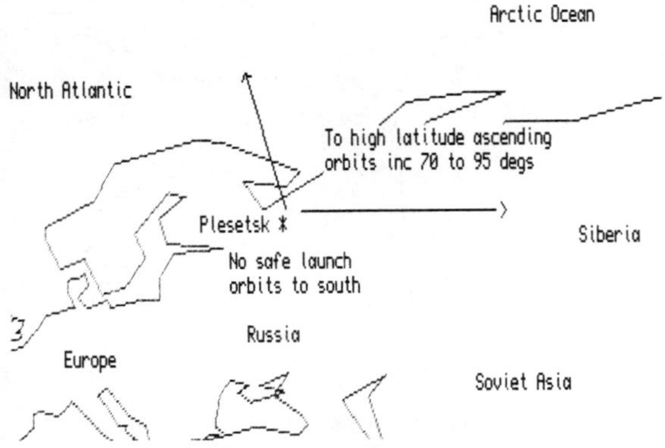

Fig 9.02: Plesetsk, Arctic Russia, launch corridors to high-latitude orbits

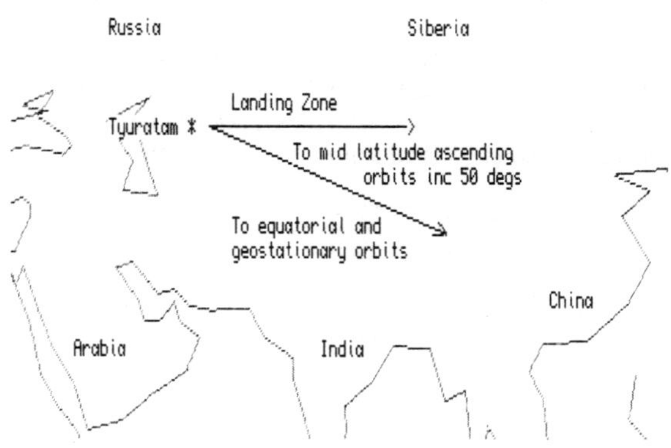

Fig 9.04: Tyuratam, launch corridors to mid-latitude and equatorial orbits

Europe and Asia, southeast of Volgograd (formerly Stalingrad). Once the regular launch centre, it has not been used much in recent years. It can support launches inclined from 50 to 80 degrees but not all launch corridors are safe. The site is also easily overlooked by electronic monitors from other countries. Fig 9.03 shows the Kapustin Yar site.

Tyuratam, at 297°W 45°N, is in Soviet Asia on the Syr Dara, 100km east of where the river flows into the Aral Sea. This site is often referred to as the 'Baikonur Cosmodrome', although this does not appear to be the Russian name for it. All manned Soviet flights at present launch from this site. Launch corridors to orbital inclinations from 50 to 80 degrees are usable, extending for thousands of kilometres over Soviet territory to the east. Manned spacecraft landings are usually targeted for the 800km stretch of steppes extending north east from Tyuratam towards Karaganda. Fig 9.04 shows the Tyuratam site.

Soviet manned launches from Tyuratam climb east along the 50th parallel of latitude. This has the effect of putting them over the UK on their fourth orbit, about six hours after launch. Launches used to be timed for the local noon or early afternoon, but since 1987 they have been occurring at all times of day.

Zhongdian, at 260°W 28°N, is a relatively new Chinese launch site (the old site at Jiuquan, or Shuang Cheng Tzu in old-style nomenclature, has not been used for some time). Zhongdian is an isolated site near the old town of Chung Tien in Xichang province. It began operating with the first Chinese launch to geostationary orbit, and is being used for orbits between 30 and 68 degrees inclination. It is anticipated that China could commence manned launches from this site in the early 1990s. Fig 9.05 shows the site configuration.

Kourou, in French Guyana at 5°N 52.6°W, is probably the best of the world's launch sites, noting that it is near the equator and can make full use of Earth spin to assist launches to low-inclination and geostationary orbits. Equally important, it has good clear launch corridors to a variety of high-inclination orbits. It is probable that launches of Hermes, the manned mini shuttle, will fly from Kourou. Fig 9.06 shows the site plan.

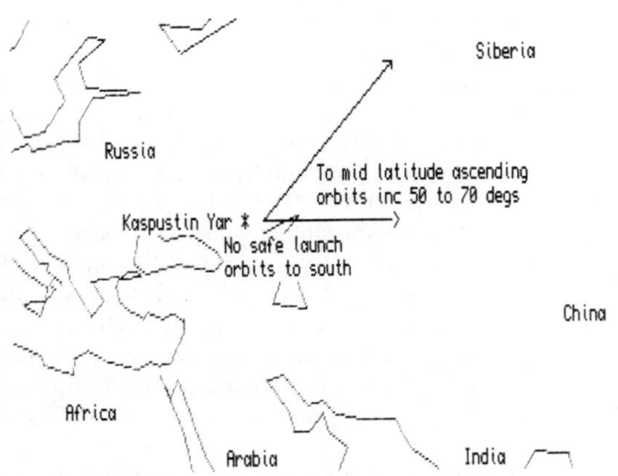

Fig 9.03: Kapustin Yar, launch corridors to mid-latitude orbits

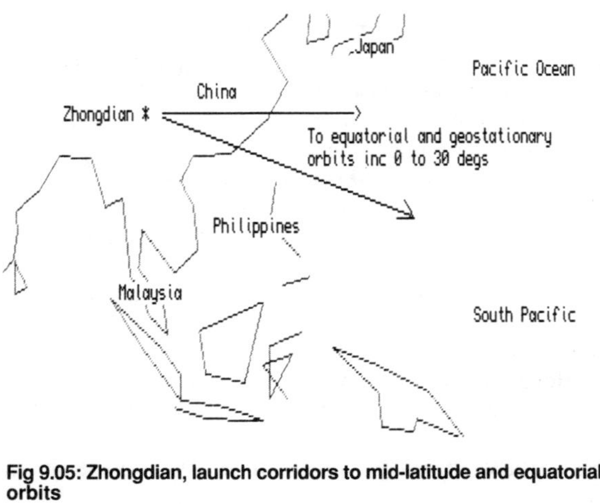

Fig 9.05: Zhongdian, launch corridors to mid-latitude and equatorial orbits

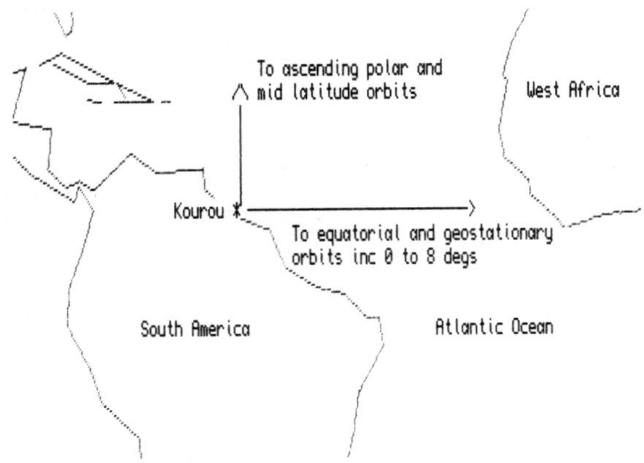

Fig 9.06: Kourou, launch corridors to polar, mid-latitude and equatorial orbits

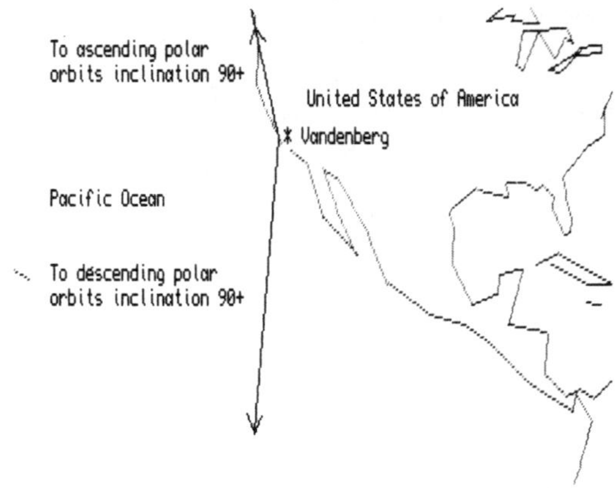

Fig 9.08: Vandenberg, launch corridors to polar orbits

Kennedy Space Centre, at Cape Canaveral in Florida, USA, is located at 80.5°W and 28.5°N, placing it as far south as possible in the continental USA to provide economical launch corridors to low-inclination and equatorial orbits. Kennedy has good launch corridors to low-fuel-budget orbits at 28 degrees inclination, and it can launch reduced payloads into orbits up to 60 degrees inclination. It cannot safely launch into polar orbits, noting that several big cities, including New York and Washington DC, lie under the potential polar corridor. Kennedy launches the majority of its manned missions into low-inclination 28 degree orbits which never come in range of the UK. Some few special scientific missions have launched from Kennedy into 48 or 56 degree inclination orbits. They achieve orbit as they climb up across the north Atlantic before flying over or near the UK about 20 minutes after launch. Fig 9.07 shows the Kennedy site plan.

Vandenberg is located in California on the Pacific coast at 120.6°W 34.8°N. It has been specially equipped to launch manned and unmanned spacecraft into high-inclination polar orbits. Launch corridors are either down across the south Pacific, or up outside the American northwest coastline. Space shuttle flights from California were planned for 1988/1989 but were cancelled. No shuttle launches are planned from Vandenburg in 1991 or 1992, and this facility may be abandoned. Fig 9.08 shows the Vandenberg site.

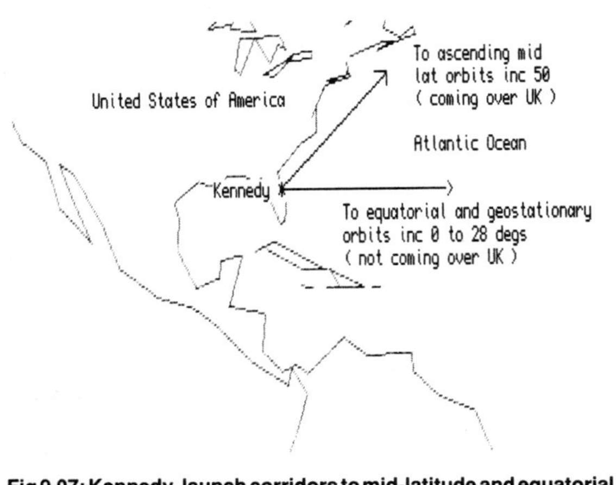

Fig 9.07: Kennedy, launch corridors to mid-latitude and equatorial orbits

Tanegashima is located on an island 1,000km south west of Tokyo, Japan. Clear launch corridors exist to the south east and to the east, providing launch routes to geostationary and equatorial orbits, and to descending paths to mid-latitude orbits. Routes to polar orbits, launching on southerly bearings are possible and safe. On launch, satellites climb up above the central and south Pacific Ocean. Launches to mid-latitude circa 50 degree inclination orbits swing down the south Pacific then ascend over South America, coming in range of the UK by 80 to 90 minutes after launch. Fig 9.09 shows the site plan.

Safe orbits

When spacecraft are manned, special precautions must be taken to ensure that the orbit is safe.

Orbital height

Below 150km altitude any orbit decays quickly because of the intense drag in the dense atmosphere. So satellites and spacecraft cannot remain in orbit below 150km altitude. Conversely above 900km altitude spacecraft begin to encounter the bottom edges of the Van Allen belts, particularly in those parts of the world where the radiation belts are abnormally low, such as the area over the south Atlantic. Above 1,600km spacecraft are in the Van Allen belts for most of each orbit. So manned spacecraft do not linger in this region – if they did by some mischance, it would soon be fatal for the crew.

The Van Allen belts extend upwards to nearly 36,000km above the equator, but once above that height the trapped radiation becomes less of a problem. Unfortunately, however, there is still the problem above 36,000km of the solar wind, but this is an occasional, not a permanent problem, being serious only when large solar flares enhance the wind. Astronauts must be well shielded when solar flares occur, and they usually achieve this by turning the spacecraft to put the maximum of protection, such as heavy machinery, between them and the flare.

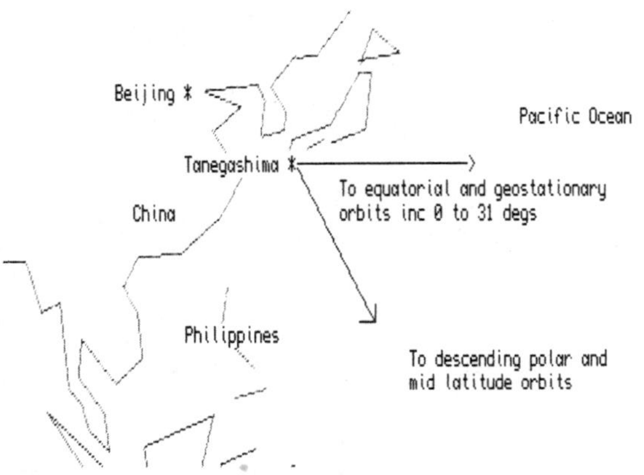

Fig 9.09: Tanegashima, launch corridors to polar, mid-latitude and equatorial orbits

Last, but by no means least, in the list of things that determine the operating altitude of manned spacecraft is how much fuel it takes to get there. The shuttle is restricted to 500km maximum altitude by this consideration, and the Soviet ferry craft Soyuz can only take three men and stores up to 350km. So paradoxically the space station usually drops to 350km to collect Soyuz passengers, then goes back up to about 380km once they are aboard. A cross-section of the Van Allen belts is shown in chapter 1, Fig 1.04.

So, summarising these conditions, manned spacecraft occupy the altitude zone 350 to 500km, except when transiting to the Moon or somewhere further out.

Orbital inclination

Manned spacecraft can have a wide variety of orbital inclinations but, in practice, considerations of safety, mission objectives, and launch and landing sites, reduce the choice considerably. High-inclination polar orbits allow study of the whole world but they use a lot of launch fuel. By contrast, low-inclination orbits can see only a narrow belt round the Earth's equator, but they get lots of Earth spin assistance on launch so their fuel bill is light (or they can carry more payload). It might appear that the best gambit would be to launch to a low-inclination, spin-assisted eastern orbit, then shift to a high-inclination orbit whilst in space. This is an absolute non-starter because the relevant Murphy's law says 'If you insist on changing the inclination of a spacecraft orbit, the cheapest way to do it is to come back to Earth and get a fresh launch'.

So in theory you might expect all launch sites to be on the equator, busily putting spacecraft into low-inclination orbits. One look at the map soon demolishes this idea. The USSR and USA have no land near the equator. All Soviet manned launches to date have used roughly 50 degree inclination orbits, consistent with the need to launch from secure homeland bases and, even more important, return there to land. Equally important, the main manned launch site in Soviet Asia has no major cities in the critical first 1,000km of the launch corridor. Fig 9.01 shows the location of the major launch sites around the world. Figs 9.02 to 9.09 show their launch corridors

Inhospitable environments

An important feature of all manned spaceflight is the need for emergency landing and rescue facilities. Very few facilities of this kind are located above latitude 55°N or 55°S, so only missions with a specific imperative to explore higher-latitude and polar regions will have orbital inclinations greater than 55 degrees. Indeed, to date (1990) no manned flights have ventured above 60°N.

Summary of manned launch constraints

1. Most manned craft fly in the altitude zone between 300 and 500km.
2. Where suitable launch sites and launch corridors exist, manned mission planners prefer orbital inclinations below 30 degrees.
3. As a second best, orbits between 30 and 55 degrees inclination have to be used, either because the available launch sites preclude other possibilities or because mission tasks require high-latitude studies, eg auroras.
4. Manned orbits have never been flown above 60 degrees as of 1990. The polar launches planned were for the American shuttle, launching from Vandenberg in California. These launches to polar orbit use a lot of fuel and therefore restrict the amount of payload carried. So polar orbits need expensive high-priority reasons, and it is no coincidence that most of them concern shuttle 'whole Earth viewing military missions'.

Please note that only launches in categories 3 and 4 above overfly the UK.

Observers in the UK can only expect to contact manned flights when their orbital inclination is greater than 30 degrees. In practice this means that virtually all Soviet manned flights have several orbits per day in range of the UK. By contrast, the majority of American shuttle missions use inclinations of 28 degrees and are therefore too far south to be seen or heard here. Only special shuttle scientific missions use higher inclinations when they launch from Florida. So shuttle flights over the UK have been rare. If ever shuttle launches commence from Vandenberg in California they will overfly the UK, but they are not expected to be numerous.

Spacecraft tracking

Considered on a day-to-day basis, a typical manned spacecraft orbit is fixed with respect to the stars and the rest of the universe. Inside the spacecraft orbit the Earth is turning one full revolution every day. If, for example, the sunlit part of the orbit is that part which is over the northern hemisphere of the world, stations north of the equator will have a series of orbits passing in range during their local daylight, wherever the station is located on the northern hemisphere. Conversely stations in the southern hemisphere will be overflown during their hours of darkness.

Figs 9.10 and 9.11 explore this situation for a station in the UK Midlands at latitude 52°N, on an imaginary shuttle orbit inclined at 50 degrees, crossing the northern hemisphere in daylight, from an equator crossing south to north at 0600 local time.

At 0600 UK time the shuttle climbing up from the southern hemisphere crosses the equator at 0°W, but then passes well east of the UK without coming above the UK horizon: see Fig 9.11a.

At 0730 approx the shuttle makes its next equator crossing, to find the world has turned about 22.5 degrees eastwards. So this time the shuttle is just seen on the southeast horizon by stations in the southern UK at about 0744: see Fig 9.11b.

At 0900 approx the third orbit starts with an equator crossing near longitude 45°W. This time the shuttle comes well above the UK horizon from about 0912 to 0921: see Fig 9.11c.

At 1030 the fourth orbit starts with Earth spin having carried the equator crossing point to about 67.5°W. From 1044 to 1054 the shuttle comes above the UK horizon, travelling from south west to east, going almost overhead southern UK stations: see Fig 9.11d.

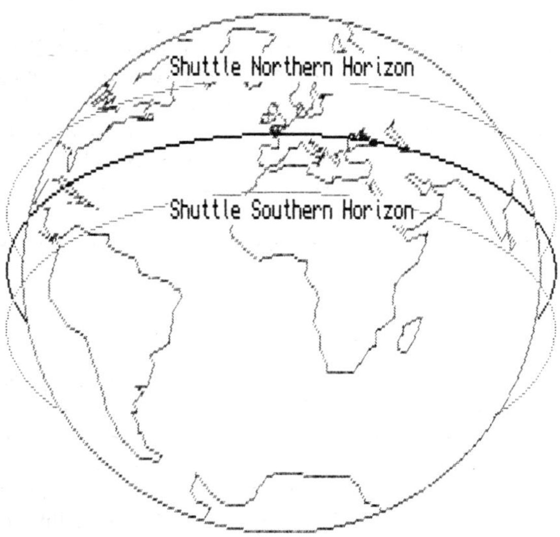

Fig 9.10: Imaginary shuttle orbit inclined at 50 degrees. The shuttle orbit is fixed in space, the Earth turns at 15 degrees per hour inside it

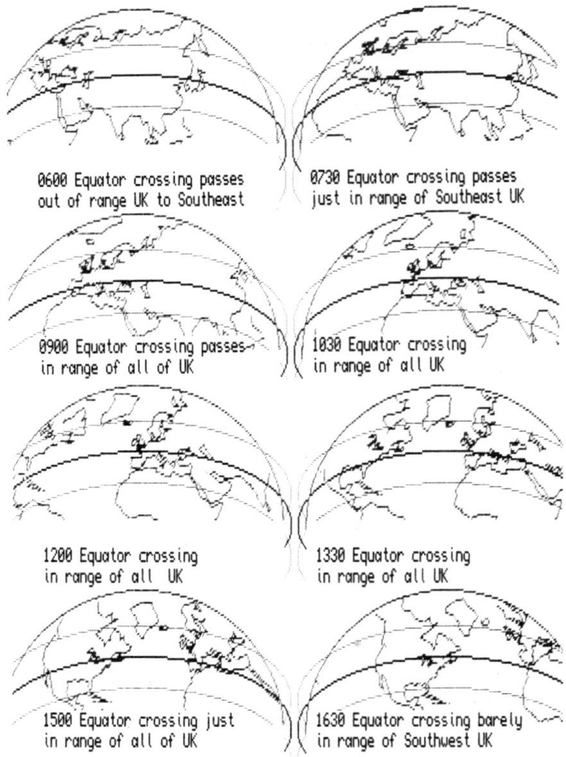

Figs 9.11a-h: Imaginary shuttle 50-degree inclination orbits, crossing equator every 90 minutes

By 1200 the fifth orbit finds the equator crossing has moved to near 90°W. From approx 1218 to 1227 the shuttle crosses from west to east above the English Channel: see Fig 9.11e.

At 1330 the sixth orbit crosses the equator near 112.5°W. From 1351 to 1400 the shuttle crosses southwest of the UK, well above the horizon: see Fig 9.11f.

By 1500 the start of the seventh orbit finds the shuttle crossing the equator at 135°W. English stations get a short look at the shuttle as it passes low in their west and south west from 1525 to 1532: see Fig 9.11g.

At 1630 the equator crossing is near 157.5 degrees west. The shuttle passes southwest of the UK, well below the horizon of all but stations in the far south west of England and Ireland: see Fig 9.11h.

All subsequent orbits that day are out of range of the UK.

The above example arbitrarily selected a set of shuttle orbits crossing the UK in daylight. If, by contrast, the north-going equator crossings had occurred at 1800 local time (12 hours later than shown here), the succession of six orbits in range of the UK would have occurred in the evening twilight and darkness. Please note that this sequence of five or six orbits in range of the UK and passing at about this distance is also typical of the Soviet space stations Salyut and Mir. They follow an almost identical track to the one shown here.

The majority of shuttle missions use a lower orbital

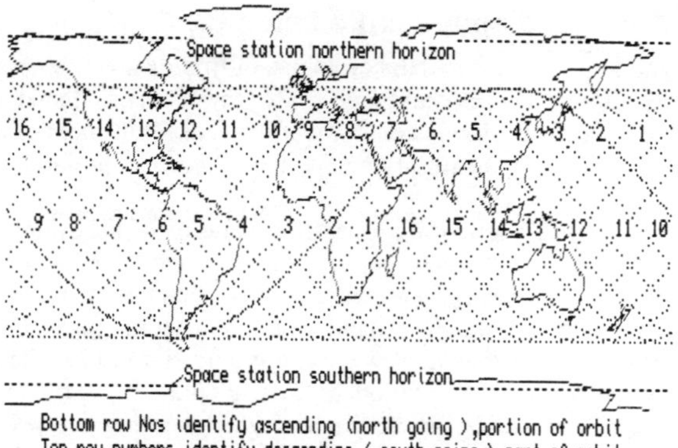

Fig 9.12: Daily orbit pattern of Mir space station

inclination than the example given. Always check the orbital inclination, using as a rough guide the fact that a spacecraft at 320km can see or be seen for a great circle angle of about 18 degrees. So, given for example a spacecraft in a 28 degree inclination orbit at 320km, it can see north to latitude 28 + 18 degrees at the top of its orbit and, in the course of a day, sees all the world in the latitude band 46°S to 46°N, ie not the UK.

Please note that stations outside the latitude band 45 to 68 degrees see a quite different pattern of orbits from that shown in Fig 9.11. Fig 9.12 shows the daily orbit pattern for the Soviet Mir space station, and Fig 9.13 shows which of these orbits comes in range of the UK.

Manned spacecraft radio beacons

Soviet manned spacecraft and their support craft carry HF radio beacons which provide excellent tracking information and practice.

The American space shuttle does not have these useful beacons, nor does it operate over Europe daily. By contrast there is usually a signal on 19.955MHz every day of the year, often heard from all over the world via ionospheric

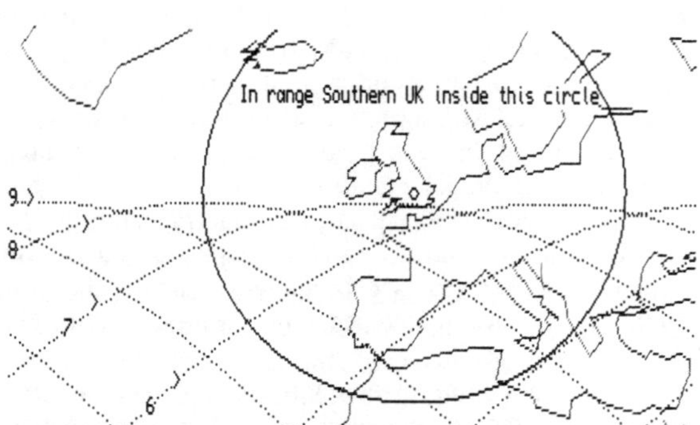

Fig 9.13: Mir space station orbital coverage near the UK each day

Table 9.01: HF beacons

Frequency	Keying	Schedule	Notes
19.955MHz	Two tone slow dots dashes + ripples	Continuous	This form of signal is called pulse duration modulation
20.008	as above plus AM	Spasmodic usually	Either pulse duration modulation or voice
may	voice	only when	be used.

propagation. Please note that the US Space Control Network Station at Ascension Island in the south Atlantic uses SSB on 19.955MHz, so you may also hear Americans reporting space launches on this frequency, as well as Dopplering Soviet beacons. The 20.008 frequency is used during the launch and landing phase of Soviet manned flights, and is also used when the cosmonauts are outside the space station performing extra vehicular activity (EVA). Again ionospheric propagation often propagates the signal to the UK, particularly during Russian morning-time launches or EVAs. Some of the 19.955MHz beacons are located on the space tugs of the Cosmos 1686 series, which whilst not manned themselves, are used to push the manned space station around. Much of this activity takes place in range of the UK. By contrast, the proposed American space station will never come in range of here.

Space radio operating

The equipment required for listening to spacecraft and for communicating with radio amateur astronauts or cosmonauts need not be complex. None the less, would-be listeners and radio amateurs will not find it easy to adapt to the special techniques required to talk to someone who is in a vehicle flying over their station at a speed of 25,000km per hour.

The problem is not solved by going out and buying a lot of expensive equipment. Experience in space operating must be acquired gradually, with the wise man sticking to simple, cheap equipment until he has mastered all the problems, and in so doing built up enough experience to know what is best for himself.

Simple space radio listening

Ordinary shortwave listeners and radio amateurs can start space radio listening using their standard radio receivers and terrestrial antennas. Equipped with a standard shortwave receiver, there is a lot of space radio waiting to be heard, including the Soviet radio amateur satellites of the Radiosport family on 29MHz and lots of Soviet satellite and spacecraft beacons on 19 and 20MHz. See Figs 9.14 and 9.15.

Stations equipped with two-metre VHF receivers or

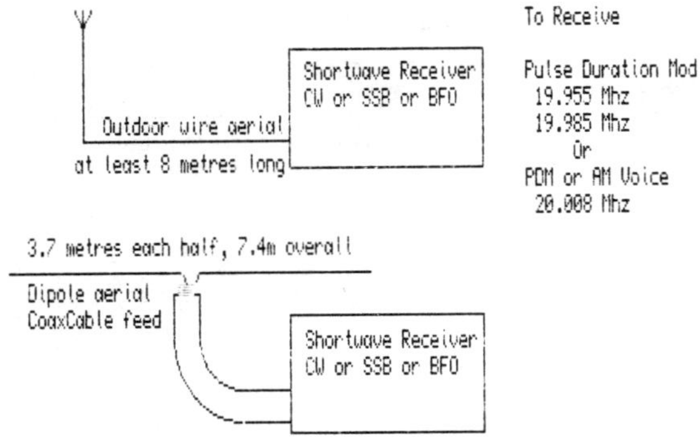

Fig 9.14: Simple reception of shortwave space radio

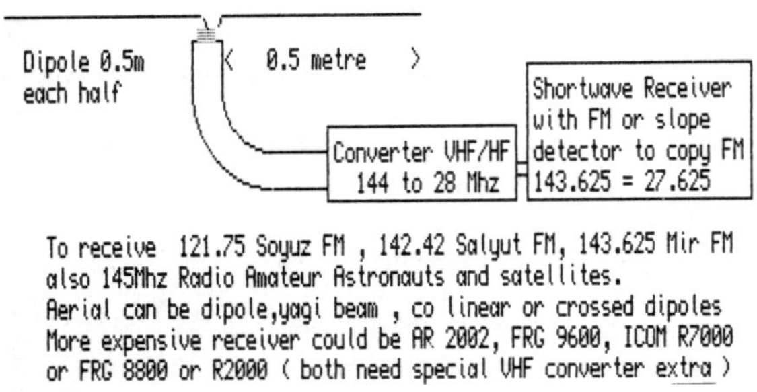

Fig 9.15: Reception of VHF space radio

transceivers can listen to astronaut and cosmonaut radio amateurs if they have an antenna with some gain, but, generally speaking, a simple antenna will suffice for most satellite monitoring at HF or VHF. It is not necessary to buy expensive antennas before you start to do some space radio listening.

Antennas for space radio reception can be quite simple, for most spacecraft put out reasonably strong signals. For shortwave HF space reception a long wire or a dipole antenna is adequate to start with (the author uses an old television X antenna extended to cover the longer wavelengths, and wired as a crossed dipole). At 144MHz, any of the standard smaller amateur radio antennas (dipoles, crossed dipoles, two- or three-element Yagi beams or collinear arrays) will suffice. It is simply not wise to rush out and buy expensive monster beams and rotators, at least at the start. Nor should you be tempted to buy the complex circularly polarised antennas in your early days as a space radio user. More satellites have been lost through incorrect circularity (eg the notorious Telstar incident with the BBC in the 1960s) than have ever been improved as regards reception. So please avoid these complications until you are absolutely sure you know what you are doing. It is cheaper, easier and surer to progress via, say, a single horizontal Yagi to a pair of Yagis, one horizontally and one vertically polarised, switchable to whichever is momentarily giving the better signal, than it is to cover your house with massive circularly polarised arrays.

Advanced space radio listening

Having first mastered the problems of finding and tracking the simpler satellites and spacecraft, the space radio listener then has to decide what equipment he needs for the next step – regular monitoring of manned spacecraft communications.

The totally dissimilar operating patterns of the Americans and the Soviets leave the shortwave and VHF listener little choice. Except on rare occasions when radio amateur astronauts use amateur band equipment from space, the Americans stick to microwave communications links when in range of their geostationary tactical data relay satellites (TDRS), which in practice means whenever they are over Europe or America. When out of range of TDRS, the Americans use UHF frequencies of 259.7 and 296.8MHz FM. These same frequencies are also used during launch and landing phases, and during EVAs. Little or none of this type of activity takes place in range of the UK. So there is little point in buying expensive commercial equipment to receive these frequencies here.

The consequence of little or no American VHF/UHF radio activity over Europe is that European listeners have had to rely on Soviet spacecraft for VHF space radio, except on those rare occasions when the shuttle has come over Europe carrying radio amateurs using VHF. Fortunately the Russian cosmonauts have been available five orbits in range almost every day, with the spacecraft manned continuously for half a year or more at a time.

The Soviet cosmonauts use 143.625MHz from Mir and 142.425MHz from the Salyut station. When in transit up or down aboard the Soyuz Troika 'Taxi' craft they use 121.75MHz and are often simultaneously present on 20.008MHz in the shortwave band. So there is no excuse for not being able to hear the Soviet activity. The VHF frequencies are in use every day the cosmonauts are aloft, and if you have an old shortwave receiver you can add VHF by purchasing one of the amateur radio converters made by Microwave Modules. These relatively inexpensive convertors take a 144MHz signal and transform it down to a 28MHz signal. So the Cosmonaut 143.625MHz from Mir becomes 27.625MHz to the shortwave receiver from one of these convertors (the 142.425MHz from Salyut becomes 26.425MHz). Do be careful, you still have to detect the frequency-modulated speech, and not all new shortwave receivers will do this. Most old shortwave receivers have 'slope detectors' which can detect FM signals, but if you have a newer receiver which uses a product detector for CW demodulation, you may need an FM adapter. If you can use one, VHF to HF 144 to 28MHz convertors are the cheapest and most efficient way to listen to the cosmonauts. See Fig 9.15.

There are of course a whole range of commercial VHF receivers and transceivers available for the radio amateur 144MHz band. These are good for the radio amateur satellites including the cosmonaut/astronaut amateur radio activity, but at present this activity is rare. If you want to listen to the cosmonaut VHF transmissions just below the amateur band you will need a receiver that covers those frequencies and is capable of receiving FM signals. The following commercial receivers are suitable in most cases, but they are expensive.

- AR 2002 – good VHF/UHF, FM/AM reception, but not CW or SSB
- Yaesu FRG 9600 – VHF/UHF, FM/AM/CW/SSB
- Yaesu FRG 8800 with VHF convertor – FM/AM/CW/SSB (not UHF)
- Trio R2000 with VHF convertor – FM/AM/CW/SSB (not UHF)
- ICOM R7000 – VHF to microwave, FM/AM/CW/SSB, but expensive

Please note two of these receivers cannot receive space shuttle UHF signals on 250 to 280MHz, and other types of receivers – usually called 'airband receivers' – cannot receive any cosmonaut or shuttle signals at all. So please make sure your purchase covers the right FM frequencies.

Cosmonaut operating

Spacecraft VHF down links are operated in plain language. Callsigns are rarely used, but when they are the European ground control uses the callsign 'Dawn', pronounced in Russian as 'Zarya'. Teams of cosmonauts have callsigns chosen by team leaders: the crew led by Dzanibekov used the callsign 'Pamir', Kizim and his crew used callsign 'Mayaks', and the Vasyutin crew used callsign 'Chegets'.

Soviet spacecraft come into range of their VHF control stations over the eastern British Isles, therefore cosmonauts usually begin calling the Kaliningrad Control as they pass south of London. Initial calls vary from 'Dawn this is Pamir', to 'Nez Spatzia' (ground or underneath this is space), or 'ras ras tri dva adyem' (calling calling three two one).

Types of communciation

Procedures used from space can vary enormously and thereby give a useful impression of what is going on.

The Mir space station is fitted with area microphones. These are often left on all the time, broadcasting all noises inside the space station (work tasks, machinery, surveillance systems, and even video or musical entertainment tapes or broadcasts).

Whenever area microphones are in use, it is possible to hear rebroadcast of the audio from loudspeakers tuned to the ground control up link signals, thereby permitting both sides of the duplex conversation to be monitored.

From time to time, however, the cosmonauts revert to more secure procedures. Press-to-talk is often used when they are busy. At other times the communications procedures used are very short with transmissions only occurring when something important has to be said. In these 'zip lip' periods the exchanges are very brief indeed.

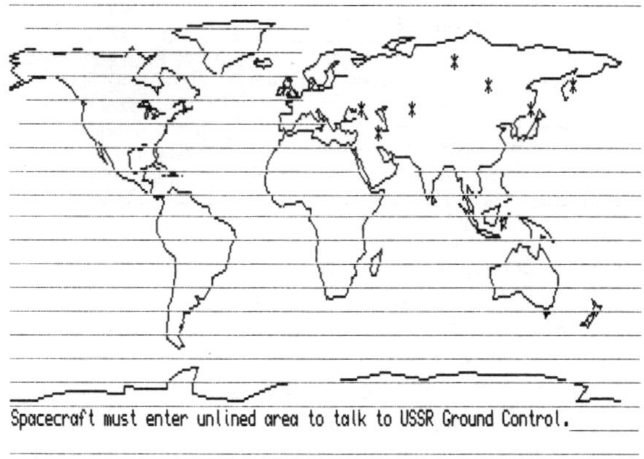

Fig 9.16: Coverage of Soviet VHF ground control network

At weekends the cosmonauts often talk to their families. Messages exchanged with wives and friends are often heard duplex, both sides of the conversation via the area microphones, and the rebroadcast up link.

Special transmissions

A frequent addition to the rebroadcast VHF traffic is a burst of RTTY packet type transmission lasting six to eight seconds, transmitted from the ground as the space station comes clearly inside the ground control footprint, for the first time each orbit.

Soviet VHF down links

General use of VHF by spacecraft is at present a feature of Soviet but not American spacecraft. The would-be space radio listener has therefore only one choice. Luckily for Europeans living on the edge of Soviet-controlled air space, transmissions are three to five times a day for months at a stretch. The map at Fig 9.16 indicates, in the portion which is not shaded by horizontal lines, the general limits of coverage of Soviet VHF down links from manned spacecraft. Listeners in the unshaded portion of the world map should hear up to five periods of transmission each day. These periods are of maximum duration about eight minutes, spaced about 93 minutes between transmission periods.

In the past the small size and limited accommodation available in Soviet space stations and Soyuz ferries has restricted cosmonaut crews to one working watch each day, usually from 0800 to 2100 Moscow time. There are exceptions to this when (roughly every 60 days) the orbits over the Soviet Union occur at night. Generally it is reasonable to expect transmissions over western Europe only when the spacecraft is overhead between the hours 0500 to 2100 UTC.

With the advent of the enlarged space station Mir, it is anticipated that two or three watch 24 hour operation may be possible.

This increased use of VHF by the cosmonauts may only

Table 9.02: Soviet VHF down links

User	Frequency	Mode	Remarks
Mir station	143.625	FM	Voice and PSK
Salyut 7	142.42	FM	Voice
Soyuz ferry	121.75	FM	Voice

be temporary. Soviet authorities have indicated that, like the Americans, they to intend to launch geostationary microwave relay satellites. The Soviet system is scheduled to have three geosats roughly 120 degrees apart. Until this geostationary chain of microwave relays becomes operational the VHF frequencies listed in Table 9.02 are likely to continue in use.

Until the Russian space station has a permanent complement of four to six cosmonauts, it is unlikely that communications will be manned on a 24-hour basis. As described earlier, the pairs of cosmonauts normally occupying the space station today work a 'Moscow daytime' routine. Although they see 15 dawns and 15 sunsets a day in space, they work in step with their Russian ground controllers, ignoring the fact that space outside the station may be dark or daylight.

The effect this has on their communications schedule is shown in Fig 9.17, a Kettering plot of the Mir VHF down link from 9 to 25 April 1987. Date is plotted vertically, and the time of any VHF activity heard in the UK is noted by the computer drawing a circle centred on the appropriate horizontal time scale UTC. As shown, the level of VHF activity heard dropped to zero between 9 and 14 April. On 9 April the last two orbits in the UK window were heard, then there were four blank days as the window slipped roughly 24 minutes earlier each day. On the 14th the window had slipped two hours earlier, just enough to put the space station over the UK before the cosmonauts went to bed. As the plot shows, Mir was seen passing over the UK at 0330 UTC on 12 April but no VHF was heard as it was right in the middle of the cosmonauts' sleep period.

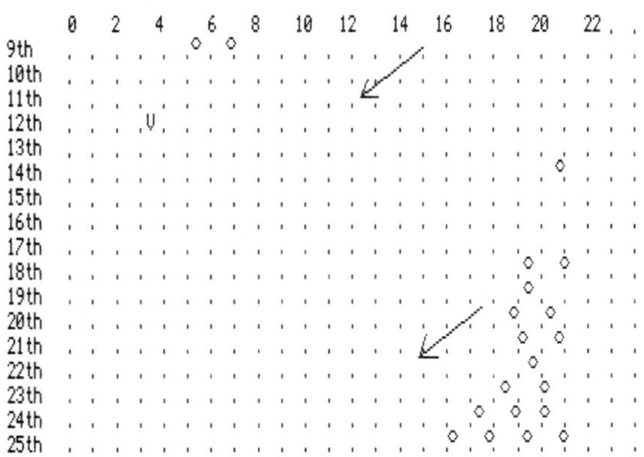

Fig 9.17: Kettering plot for Mir – changing from early am to late pm window, April 1987. Time UTC. Note: no radio signals from 2100 to 0500 UTC. (V = visual)

After 14 April the orbit window over the UK continued to get earlier each day, so that by 25 April it was possible to hear orbits with VHF radio traffic before the cosmonauts went to bed. As the orbit window comes earlier there is less pressure on the cosmonauts to make the – for them – late 2000 to 2100 UTC calls, so these calls are frequently dropped, with last call of the day usually being about 1900 UTC if the orbit window permits. With bigger crews planned for Mir, this operating schedule could well expand to cover most if not all of the 24 hours, in which case, irrespective of when the seven-hour/five-orbit UK window occurred, transmissions would probably be heard.

Transmission aids to tracking

As the Soviet cosmonauts do not transmit continuously on VHF, the listener looking for tracking assistance can often use the HF beacons or non-voice VHF signal transmissions to check that the space station is in range but is silent on VHF voice, perhaps because it has not yet entered Soviet airspace. Data transmissions on 166.122MHz are often heard from Mir, even when the cosmonauts are asleep; these are frequently made to Soviet communications ships all around the world, thereby affording a useful aid to Mir tracking at all times of day and night, almost anywhere in the world.

Communications ships and geostationary communications relays

Throughout the first 25 years of Soviet spaceflight, Soviet controllers had to accept that they would be out of touch with their cosmonauts except when they were over or near the Soviet Union. To reduce this problem, large, expensive communications ships (comships) were deployed to strategic spots along the spacecraft track. Sites chosen included the Straits of Gibraltar, the Atlantic coast of north Africa, and a point east of the coast of Brazil. All these locations were chosen because of their proximity to the last stages of any flight coming in on a re-entry and landing track. A completely different reason was necessary for the selection of Sable Island off the east coast of Nova Scotia, Canada. Here the choice of site was determined by the fact that this location could cover parts of several orbits which would otherwise never contact the Soviet Union. These ascending orbits over the USA descend into the southern hemisphere as they cross Soviet home longitudes, so without a comship at Sable Island, there would have been a communications gap of several hours. Fig 9.18 shows these comship locations.

Despite filling in some gaps, there simply were not enough comships to cover the world, so at times the Soviets resorted to using HF radio communications via ionospheric propagation. This was a most unreliable method, particularly because Mir and Salyut orbit near the top of the ionosphere, but better than nothing.

This situation has recently changed in two ways. First, the Soviets have announced a plan to launch Satellite Data

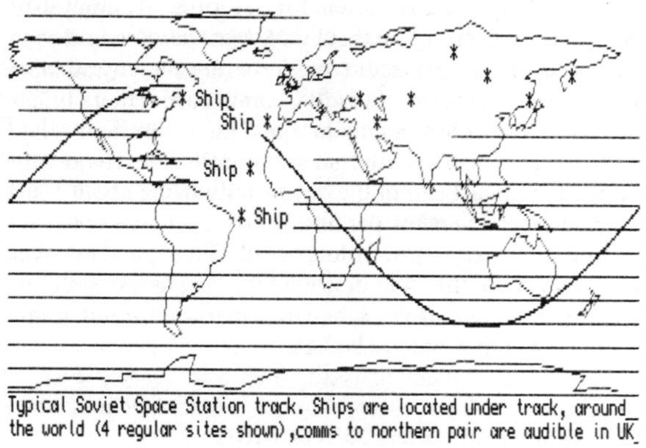

Fig 9.18: Extension of Soviet VHF radio control network using communication ships

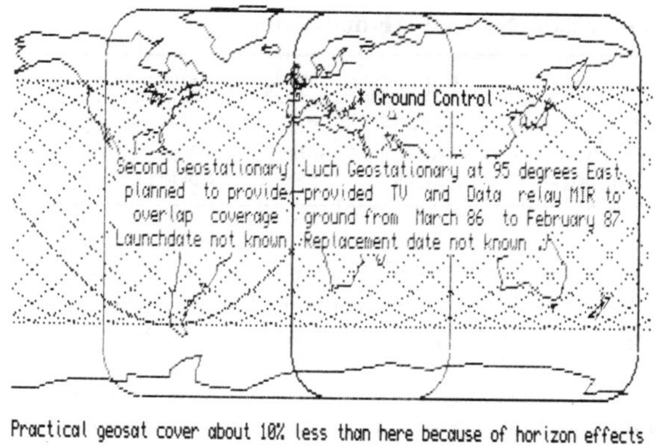

Fig 9.20: Soviet space station-geostationary satellite telemetry and communications links

Relay Network (SDRN) geostationary satellites, similar to the already active American Tactical Data Relay Satellites (TDRS). Figs 9.19 and 9.20 show the disposition of the first Soviet satellites of this general type. These microwave relay satellites will relay communications directly from the Mir space station to the Soviet Flight Control Centre (FCC) near Moscow. In addition to these direct relays, the second Soviet deployment takes the form of letting Mir use a VHF two-way link to a comship, with the comship then directly connecting these Mir signals to and from the FCC via suitable microwave geostationary relays.

An early precursor of the SDRN type link was signalled in 1986 when the Soviets placed a Louch-type microwave comsat package in geostationary orbit at about 95 degrees east. This Ku band (11GHz) microwave link was used by cosmonauts Kizim and Solovyev from Mir in 1986. But by 1987 it was clear that this link was no longer available to the new Mir crew, and it has not appeared in regular use even in 1988. Some TV broadcasts have taken place from Mir in

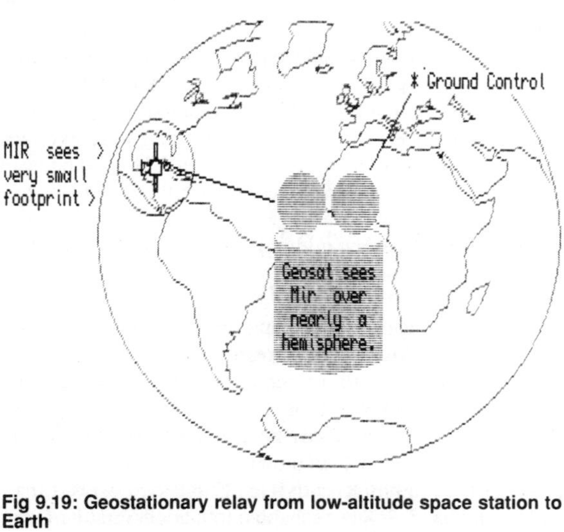

Fig 9.19: Geostationary relay from low-altitude space station to Earth

1988, but these do not appear to have used dedicated space-ground relay geosats.

At the time of writing in 1990, it does not appear that the Soviets have successfully deployed any elements of the SDRN, but as American experience with TDRS shows, this is no easy task. The Americans had to launch three TDRS satellites before they got one which worked to design specification. So space listeners should not expect things to happen quickly, and it must be stressed that even when the Soviet SDRN network is deployed it will not be easy to monitor it from the ground. The trouble is that when the space station is using a direct connection to a geostationary satellite, its microwave dish is looking away from Earth, out into space towards the geosat 36,000km above it. So the signal from Mir is unlikely to be heard by Earth stations. However, given that the signal coming down from the geosat will also illuminate the ground underneath the Mir track, listeners may well hear the geosat down link as Mir overflies their station and, somewhat less likely, ground stations near the Soviet Union may be able to intercept the down link from the geosat going to the FCC near Moscow.

So whilst the future for direct interception of Mir microwave relays by geosat to the USSR is uncertain, it is interesting to report that an obvious but unannounced use of Soviet microwave geosats by Mir is perhaps going to be audible to terrestrial listening stations. This second type of relay link utilises a duplex VHF voice or data link from Mir to a comship. The comship then acts as a simple through way exchange to a microwave geostationary satellite relay and onwards to the Soviet FCC. Any suitable geosat can be used for this link, thereby allowing the Mir cosmonauts excellent long-duration communications as their signals are relayed, first via one comship then by another, onwards until they come into VHF line-of-sight range of Soviet ground stations.

This VHF to microwave geosat link needs to be carefully controlled if feedback loop problems are to be avoided. The cosmonauts usually operate with headsets and shielded boom microphones, using a strict 'push-to-talk' procedure, ie switching their microphones off when they stop speaking so that they do not pick up any feedback or echoes from Mir loudspeakers broadcasting the up link returning to Mir. None the less, despite the normally excellent communications procedure, things do go wrong and at these times the careful listener can hear the effects of the long-distance link. Sometimes the only clue the listener gets is that the cosmonauts are talking to the same person without a break for more than four or five minutes, but now and again someone breaks the rules, as when the third crew member joins in the conversation using a handheld microphone with no shielding. When this happens the signal starts to echo.

The echo mechanism is quite simple and distinct. The cosmonaut transmits on VHF to the comship which retransmits his signal on microwave up to the geosat relay and onwards to the FCC. In the FCC the duty operator has the cosmonaut voice on loudspeaker, so some of this voice leaks into his microphone and starts the return journey up to the geosat and down to the comship, where it is retransmitted once again on VHF up to Mir, appearing on the Mir loudspeaker whose audio output promptly links to the unshielded cosmonaut microphone to be retransmitted yet again.

This long relay path goes up to the geosat, down to the FCC, then back up and down again to the comship and on to Mir – a journey of about 160,000km which even at the speed of light takes a little over half a second. The result is a clear half-second delay echo on everything the cosmonaut says. Any station listening to his VHF can hear this echo, and stations equipped for C band (3GHz) or Ku band (11GHz) reception should start searching to see which of the various Gorizonts, Radugas or Cosmos geosats visible from his station is relaying this signal.

Launch and landing patterns

It is not often realise how restricted manned spaceflight operators are in regard to what they can do. Flight safety must be emphasised at all times, so launches and landings usually take place in daylight, although the Soviets are beginning to relax this rule, with several recent launches having been at night.

During docking with the space station it is necessary for the Sun to be behind the Soyuz taxi to help the pilot see his docking target ahead of him. It takes roughly 26 hours to launch and rendezvous for docking, using the quick, uneconomic approach, whereas the slow, economic approach takes about 50 hours. Either way, the pilot comes in to dock with the space station one or two days plus two hours after launch. So this sets his docking viewpoint and illumination conditions, as he overflies the Soviet Union whilst attempting to dock. Hence, if he has launched in daylight, he should have relatively easy, clearly illuminated, landing conditions if he has to abort the docking and quickly return to Earth.

Spacecraft can be thought of as flying along invisible grooves. To intercept a space station, you must launch to exactly the same track as the overhead space station, leaving the ground a few minutes before the space station overflies the launch site. Until 1987 this meant that all launches and landings had to fit the 56 to 60-day orbit window drift caused by Earth perturbation of the space station orbit plane, ie every 56 days the space station flew an exact repeat of its launch orbit. There was some five or six days leeway in this intercept manoeuvre. So if you launched on day A, that had to be a day on which the target space station overflew your launch site, and the launch had to be timed to match the space station's overhead timing.

Since February 1987, this has all changed. First, it is inconvenient for the Mir station to have to turn to point its docking port towards the Sun in order to meet the upcoming Soyuz ferry craft. Since 1987 Soyuz pilots must be able to dock with Mir whatever its alignment. In consequence of this, the only rule which now applies is that launches can go any day of the 56/60-day cycle, but they must launch as the space station goes overhead the launch site even if this is at night. So, using a knowledge of the times of day when the space station overflies the launch site, listeners can get a good idea of likely launch times.

This launch and land when the space station is passing over the launch site applies to both the present Soviet space stations and the proposed American space station. In practice the American station, with its 28 degree inclination and 500km orbital height, should have a 53-day cycle of repeat orbits over the same ground track, but with the choice of several landing sites the Americans will be much more flexible than the Soviets.

Extra vehicular activity (EVA)

When working outside the space station in spacesuits, the cosmonauts continuously broadcast what they are doing. Soviet EVAs up to 1987 were accompanied by simultaneous broadcasts on 20.008MHz and 121.75, and 143.625 or 142.42MHz VHF, but since 1987 the HF link has apparently been dropped and the 121.75MHz link is rarely used. EVA activity often occurs when the space station is in range of western Europe and the signals are clearly recognisable because of the ventilation noises inside the spacesuits. Old (pre-1988) Soviet spacesuits were noisy and the speech had a bass characteristic like men talking into a 'goldfish bowl'. Recent improvements in Soviet spacesuits have eliminated this characteristic, but spacesuit ventilation noise and distinct cosmonaut breathing are still clearly audible, even on the latest spacesuits.

Astronaut operating

Radio communications

The American space shuttle crews employ microwave voice links almost exclusively when operating over Europe or the Americas. All space-to-ground and ground-to-space communication is routed via the geostationary Tactical Data Relay Satellite (TDRS) located over the equator at longitude 41°W. A second TDRS relay is at 171°W. The TDRS relay has facilities for Ku band (15.25 to 17.25GHz) up links and S band (circa 2GHz), C band (circa 5GHz) and Ku band

(13.7GHz) down links. Signals from TDRS are beamed at the ground station located at White Sands in New Mexico. From White Sands shuttle traffic is passed to the Johnston Space Centre in Houston Texas via commercial geostationary satellite links. See Fig 9.21.

Types of communications

American shuttle spacecraft use a wide range of signal frequencies and modulation types. The S band circuits use:

- 2,250MHz FM primary and 2,205MHz FM data traffic
- 2,287.5MHz phase-modulated primary
- 2,217.5MHz phase-modulated secondary

FM voice communication is used continuously whilst in orbit, being relayed to TDRS 1 on the 2,250MHz frequency, with telemetry data being sent on the FM 2,205MHz frequency via the same route. The phase-modulated frequencies carry high data rate telemetry, plus digital voice channels and a special round-trip Doppler carrier signal used for shuttle navigation. This sophisticated communications system is accessed via an equivalent onboard distribution system with facilities from all parts of the shuttle including the payload bay.

Due to its ability to carry higher data rates, the wider-band Ku frequencies of 13,766 and 13,775MHz are brought into service as soon as the TDRS locks into the S band transmissions on each orbit. Capture by TDRS via the wide-beam S band antennas is much more effective than would be the case with the narrow-beam Ku antennas. So, with 60+ minutes or so of locked TDRS link per orbit, it is apparently common practice to leave the S band and Ku band links on in parallel.

Another microwave frequency which may be heard from the shuttle is 1,280MHz. This is the shuttle SIR B radar. It is not carried on all flights, but it can be a good beacon when in use.

UHF down links

Because of problems with the TDRSs, shuttle flights up to 1986 continued to use UHF frequencies for down link traffic when out of range of TDRS 1 (ie roughly from 300°W eastwards to 130°W the Caspian Sea to California). The UHF frequencies are:

- 296.8MHz primary, 259.7MHz secondary
- 279.0MHz low-power spacesuit reserve

One of the first payloads planned for renewed shuttle flights in 1988 was a second TDRS geosat, with a third following within a year. It is therefore likely that nearly all space/ground communications will hence forward be via TDRS geosat relay with no regular use of UHF frequencies during the normal orbit phases of the flight.

At the critical post-atmospheric re-entry (landing phase), communications will revert from TDRS to direct UHF down links. UHF use may also feature in some mission launches. Both the landing and launch phases are below the UK horizon, so no UHF traffic is likely to be heard in the UK unless the shuttle does an emergency landing in Spain or the Azores.

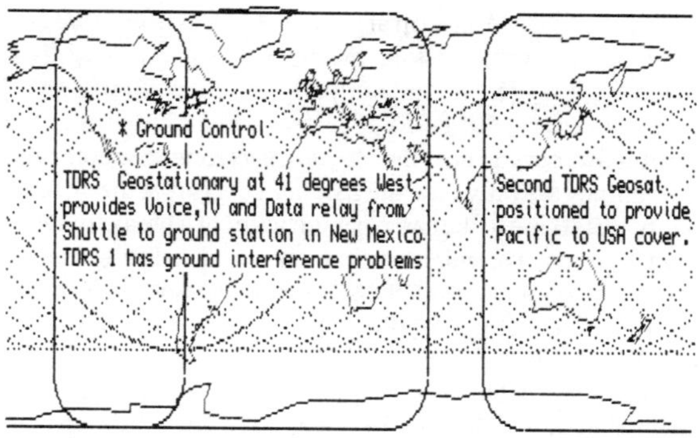

Practical geosat cover about 10% less than here because of horizon effects

Fig 9.21: High-inclination shuttle mission with TDRS relay link

Geosat relays

As discussed in the two previous paragraphs, geostationary TDRSs are expected to handle almost all future shuttle communications.

Fig 9.21 shows the coverage the TDRSs can provide to an orbiting shuttle. Any part of a shuttle orbit shown in the almost square geosat footprint will enjoy TDRS relay facilities. As shown in Fig 9.21 the TDRS relays can cover the shuttle over almost half of every high polar orbit, and with two TDRS geosats operational there is only a five-minute communication gap in each orbit. This long-duration (80 to 90 per cent) orbital cover by TDRS is vital if complex scientific data is to be fed down from the shuttle at high data speeds in near-real time. Neither the shuttle nor Mir or Salyut can carry the computer power necessary to support these experiments, so in both cases microwave wideband relay via geosats is essential.

Because this high data rate, traffic uses tight antenna beams; ground listeners are unlikely ever to hear it.

Astronaut EVA procedures

UHF shuttle communications are used exclusively during extra-vehicular activity. Whenever astronauts are in spacesuits the UHF frequencies of 296.8 and 259.7MHz are used continuously in the duplex voice mode.

A third frequency of 279.0MHz is also available as a spacesuit low-power spare. Both cabin crew and space-walking astronauts use these frequencies to talk to one another during EVAs. Unfortunately most EVA activity takes place out of range of northern Europe and, whilst the author has heard hours of Soviet EVA traffic, he has yet to hear anything from the Americans in this mode. The reason

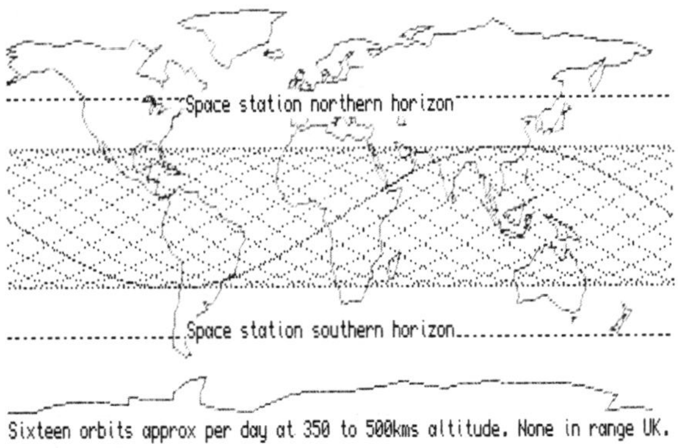

Fig 9.22: USA space station daily orbital coverage

for this is quite simple – most American EVA work has concerned satellite recovery, repair and relaunch, usually directly over the equator and far out of range of the UK.

Astronaut experiments

Up to 1986 there was almost no opportunity for ground listeners to eavesdrop on shuttle experiments. The problem was that whilst opportunities did occur, they were not always publicised early enough to allow would-be listeners to prepare to receive them. This situation could be improved by a slightly better dissemination of this type of pre-mission information.

What is principally required is frequency and modulation data, given that most listeners will be able to listen and perhaps learn a little. The one exception to this blanket no-go situation was the plasma experiment flown by shuttle 51F. The author got data on frequency and mode for this experiment four hours before the shuttle launched, and an excellent three to four days of operating produced an superb series of 'VLF from space' signal tapes.

'Get-away special' experiments

'Get-away specials' (GAS) are self-contained experimental packages built by students, amateur radio and amateur science groups which are flown in the space shuttle payload bay. Some, but not all, carry radio beacons and/or voice/digitalker/telemetry transmitters. By common consent, most GAS packages use the radio amateur satellite band at 435 to 437MHz and employ frequency-modulated digitised voice and phase-shift keyed, high-speed telemetry.

This excellent series of schools/civilian participation experiments is expected to resume in 1991. Listeners using ordinary radio amateur receivers should have no difficulty monitoring these flights and participating in these experiments – *Amateur Satellite Report* is the source of pre-mission data reports on these experiments. In some special cases the GAS down link has been deliberately placed in the up link band of an amateur radio satellite. The experiments chapter of this book reports a GAS experiment which used this technique to relay the experiment to ground stations far below the space shuttle horizon.

Soviet activity in this field has progressed since 1979, when the first of the Iskra series of free-flying experimental packages was released from the Salyut space station. These Soviet Iskra experiments are continuing with experiments planned for 1991. The particular emphasis of the Soviet experiments has been on ionospheric physics and signal propagation, with the experiments usually being of much longer duration than the shuttle get-away packages, eg seven weeks as opposed to seven days.

Stations

Space station orbits

The existing Soviet and the proposed American space stations will use typical low-altitude Earth orbits (LEO), so their orbital tracks and communications opportunities are no different from those already experienced by Salyut and space shuttle monitors. It cannot be emphasised too often that the space stations are not geostationary, so they have only a maximum of 10 minutes at a time above any particular ground station and, in the case of the American station, will not be directly accessible from the UK, never coming above our horizon.

Figs 9.20 and 9.22 show daily orbit patterns for the existing Soviet Salyut and Mir space stations, and for the proposed American station. From these stations it is possible to see a horizon no more than 2,000km away. The north and south viewing horizons are shown on Figs 9.12 and 9.22.

Station operating procedures

The two clear differences between the space stations and previous manned craft are:

(a) Probable 24-hour round-the-clock shift manning.
(b) Almost total reliance on geosat relay communications.

These two features will result in increased communication to ground, but this communication will be almost totally restricted to tight-beam microwave relay links. Exceptions to this rule are likely to be visiting shuttle and Soyuz supply craft and personnel taxis, and increased spacesuit activity around the space station, both using VHF and UHF frequencies.

Station-to-geosat-to-ground relays

These will be a permanent feature of space station communications. At present these relay geosats have been amongst the most fragile and failure-prone of satellite types, and it is possible this situation could continue for some time, with recourse to back-up UHF and VHF links being required from time to time. So space radio listeners may hear some VHF/UHF communications at times.

Eventually those who wish to monitor space station communications will be forced to install sensitive microwave reception equipment in order to try to copy the weak sidelobe signals from the tight-beam microwave relay links. The rapidly improving situation in regard to supply of microwave equipment at other than astronomical prices as heretofore will assist this change. In respect of the American space station, we can already say that it will most probably use the same TDRS links as the space shuttle, employing S band for general work and Ku band for the passage of high-speed data and wide-band multiplexed systems.

With regard to Soviet geostationary relays of LEO space station communications, the picture is much less clear. In 1986 the Soviets were making daily use of a Louch geostationary satellite to relay signals from Mir. Soviet VHF signals from Mir continued and in fact rebroadcast some of the Louch signals (eg time pips for experimental equipment, warning signals such as a six-pip sequence to indicate Mir had entered Soviet airspace, plus some high-speed data traffic). In addition Soviet TV began to broadcast regular colour coverage of the cosmonauts in Mir. See Fig 9.19.

At no time was it clear whether the Louch geosat was being used as a temporary relay until the promised SDRN relay network was in place, or whether the Louch satellites were the SDRN by another name.

In February 1987, when the cosmonauts returned to Mir, it quickly became obvious that the geostationary signals were disappearing from the VHF rebroadcast. At the same time the Soviets introduced a communications ship, the *Yuri Gagarin*, moored in international waters off Sable Island, someway out from the Canadian Nova Scotia mainland. The communications ship would have been quite superfluous if the Louch geosat had still been available. Since then heavy use of VHF, including attempts to pass long blocks of PSK scientific telemetry, appear to confirm the demise of the Louch relay.

Published Soviet plans call for a trio of relay satellites of the SDRN series spaced roughly 120 degrees apart above the equator. The Louch satellites used 11GHz channels but it is not clear whether this practice will continue when replacement geosat relays appear.

Space station amateur radio

This is an area which may see the biggest opportunities in the next few years. The Soviets began amateur radio operation from the Mir space station in late 1988. In the United States planning is underway for an amateur radio facility aboard the proposed American space station.

The most obvious feature of any planning of space station amateur radio is that it cannot follow the free and easy style of terrestrial operating. Fig 9.23 shows a view of the W5LFL operation of 1983 as seen from Scotland. It is an inescapable truth that the presence of a space station signal on an amateur band can produce chaos. The reason is perhaps not at first sight obvious, but it stems from the fact that radio

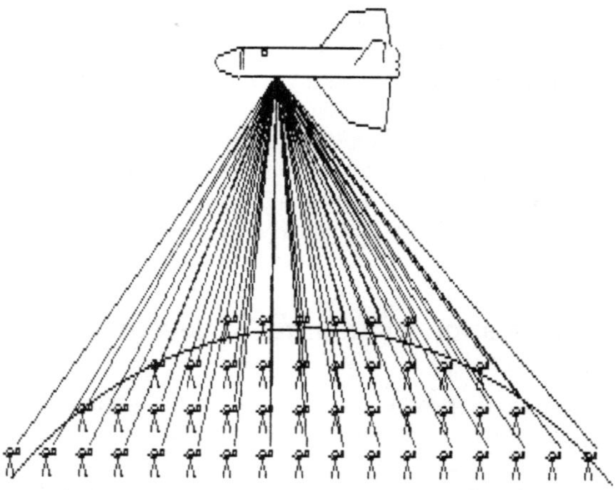

Fig 9.23: The problems of VHF amateur radio operation from space. Normally Earth-bound VHF operators are limited in range by propagation conditions, but the appearance of a spacecraft encourages an enormous response. The operator in the spacecraft is overwhelmed but the operators on the ground are mostly unaware of each other

amateur VHF operators are used to being isolated by limited propagation into small geographic units. The presence of a space signal able to reach and encourage responses from half a continent is a totally new situation. Thousands of individual ground-based operators can respond, and being isolated one from another they can be quite unaware of the vast numbers of other people in other places doing exactly the same thing. The result is the arrival at the space station of all these signals on top of one another in a quite awful noisy heap.

Casual operating from space stations is therefore not to be recommended. W0ORE demonstrated in 1985 how to get round the problem effectively, with his well-organised operation from *Challenger* 51F. Following W0ORE's example, it makes sense to assume that space station amateur radio communications will be to specifically nominated ground stations only. These ground stations will be club or headquarters stations where local authority can preside as large numbers of individuals take their turn to talk to the space operator.

There are also other important groups to whom amateur radio should open its facilities to allow them to talk to the space operators. These groups include school science classes, undergraduate groups, youth groups and amateur science and astronomy groups. Indeed it is possible to see this form of amateur radio facility being offered to a wide audience in respect not just of simple conversation but also in regard to direct association in scientific discussion and experiment. This would also appear to be a field in which the richer amateur radio countries could sponsor ground facilities in poorer communities.

It should be obvious of course that the time that space station astronauts and cosmonauts can give to these activities will be strictly limited. This problem can, however, be offset by ensuring that the space station amateur radio facility can offer features such as: broadcasts of regular space science bulletins, SSTV pictures of space station activity and of the 'fly over my school variety', plus robot conversations with the space station's computers.

All in all, the space station amateur radio facilities would seem to require organised amateur radio to prepare to design and produce these facilities, making them as automatic as possible, with perhaps full emergency facilities as a useful extra.

Space station amateur radio geosat or molniya relay

As seen from a particular ground station, the orbiting space stations provide communications opportunities of no more than 10 minutes maximum duration. In addition to this 10-minute barrier for stations in range of the space station, there are many parts of the Earth which will never be in direct contact range of the American space station.

It may be possible to relay space station amateur radio via suitable amateur radio geostationary Phase IV or molniya Phase III elliptical-orbit comsats. This relay facility could increase contact duration to, say, 30 minutes and provide coverage to those parts of the world out of range of the station. This sort of facility might provide access to the American space station for northern Europeans, Soviets and Canadians. Fortunately this is not necessary with the higher-orbital-inclination Soviet space stations which can 'see' to the Arctic and Antarctic regions unassisted.

Geostationary space stations

The next logical step, following the establishment of LEO space stations, is the construction of space stations in the Clarke geostationary orbit. If amateur radio facilities could be included in these geosat stations, they would provide much improved coverage for the dissemination of amateur radio science and recreational features. Given the relative isolation of these facilities, amateur radio could provide both recreational and emergency features of considerable value. Beyond Earth orbit, the Moon beckons as a site of enormous potential. A positive foothold should be established there by the end of this century, providing opportunities which are discussed in chapter 13.

Chapter 10

Space radio computing

Introduction

Space rockets and digital computers were children of the second world war, and in the years since then they have both expanded enormously in scope. This should surprise no one, because spacecraft would not have got far without the careful control and monitoring of their onboard computers, and no one would have attempted the expensive research and development of computers if the money to do so had not been available because of the space race.

Every day more and more evidence of the windfalls from this research appears in our homes and factories, and nowhere is this more obvious than in amateur space radio listening and communicating. When a home computer is provided with space-related programming software, every home can become a miniature control station. In six seconds or so, computations which 100 years ago took six months can be processed and displayed, allowing the radio amateur or listener access to experiments and communications power undreamed of in the past.

It is not proposed here to describe how computers work or how they are programmed. The intention in this chapter will be to describe just what computers can do when used by anyone, whether they have an understanding of what goes on inside them or not. The computer is the 'tool of the 20th century'; like any good tool it provides enormous extension of power, so whether you treat it as a 'black box' or not is not really of consequence, as long as you put it to good use. Few of us know what goes on under the bonnet of a motor car, but none the less most of us make lots of use of them. So please make full use of any computer you have, and thereby enjoy its power to enormously enhance your understanding and accomplishments in amateur radio.

Satellite tracking

In order to use a satellite or spacecraft for experimental or communications purposes, it is essential to know exactly where it is in space so that you can keep your antenna accurately trained on it. The best way to do this involves big computers and radars which get precise position data, say, once a fortnight or once a month. This data can be put into a simple home computer which will, if suitably programmed, provide reasonably accurate data for minute-by-minute tracking.

It is important to be clear that even the best of today's home computers is not really good enough for original satellite tracking, unless it is provided with these accurate 'fixes' of position data at regular intervals. The interval is about once a fortnight for a low-altitude satellite, eg 300km high, to about six months for a relatively high circular orbiter, eg 1,700km high.

Types of satellite tracking data

Accurate position and tracking data for satellites can come in several different forms. Please make sure you get the form used by your computer software.

1. Keplerian elements

These are sometimes called 'two-line elements' because they are issued by Nasa in a two-line format. They list satellite orbital parameters in a form which can be input directly into the majority of home computer programs. The computer uses these inputs to solve the Keplerian equations of elliptical motion which describe the satellite orbit. Keplerian elements work for circular-orbit satellites, elliptical-orbit satellites and geostationary-orbit satellites in Earth orbit. A typical example of Keplerian elements is given below:

Satellite name	Amsat Oscar 10
Epoch time	year 87 epoch day 1.0000 (0000 UTC 1 Jan 1987)
Inclination	27.00 degrees
Right ascension	42.54 degrees
Eccentricity	0.603
Argument of perigee	172.91 degrees
Mean anomaly	340.98 degrees
Mean motion	2.0587846 orbits per day
Epoch orbit	2,670 orbits

Some programs use semi-major axis of the orbit as an alternative to mean motion, eg:

Semi-major axis	26,105.3km

This term is not directly interchangeable. It should be used only if your program calls for it because it has the calculations necessary to handle it.

Given up-to-date Keplerian elements as above, most computers will perform happily for weeks. Several modern programs allow menu choice of 'change Keplerian elements', a service which allows you to input new elements without the need to list and edit the program. Look for this facility in any program you think about buying.

2. Equator crossing data

This form of presenting satellite data derives from an original tracking method which used polar projection chart maps of the northern hemisphere, over which a transparent orbital track overlay was rotated. The method is simple and flexible but has gradually fallen out of use as more and more people started using computers for satellite tracking. None the less, several pre-1982 computer programs used this method for circular-orbit satellites (it does not work so well for elliptical orbiters).

A typical program using equator crossing data asks for input of the time in UTC of any ascending south-to-north equator crossing. It then asks for input of the bearing in longitude of that equator crossing in degrees west of the Greenwich meridian. A typical presentation of 'EQX data', as it is called, would look something like:

Equator crossing times and bearing west
Salyut Seven space station on 3 February 1987

Time (UTC)	0119	0253	0428	0602	0736	0910	1044	
Bearing (°W)	330	354	18	42	66	90	114	
Time (UTC)	1218	1352	1526	1700	1834	2008	2143	2317
Bearing (°W)	137	161	185	209	233	257	281	305

This method of inputting data is simple and effective but has fallen out of favour. Recently, however, several computer programs have appeared which call for Keplerian data to run them, but then offer the option to print out, for months ahead if necessary, equator crossing data. Users of these programs can therefore still continue to use older programs which feature this form of data input. These printouts of EQX are also useful for those still using maps and transparent orbit track overlays.

3. Launch data

This method of inputting data to satellite tracking computer programs has been totally superseded. It may still be found in American computer programs written in the 1970s, but nobody now gives launch timing data, site data, azimuth and injection timings which this method requires. Do not buy programs which use this sort of basic orbit data.

Keeping orbit data up to date

Having got your Nasa Keplerian elements, or your equator crossing timings and bearings, how long will your computer provide accurate tracking data before it needs refreshed data? All satellites and spacecraft are subject to gradual change of their orbits' shape, dimensions and location in space.

The Earth is not a perfect sphere. So its gravitational pull on the satellite varies, gradually altering the alignment of the orbit in space. Satellites coming near the Earth suffer drag in the tenuous upper atmosphere. The lower they are, the worse the drag. The bigger their volume-to-weight ratio, the bigger the drag.

We can, however, predict the effects due to the oblateness of the Earth (but only prediction programs based on Keplerian elements can be expected to have the built-in mathematics to do this). By contrast, drag is totally unpredictable, being highly variable and mostly consequent on the strength of the solar wind and the nearness to solar cycle sunspot maximum.

Satellites like Oscar 7 went for years on minimal drag correction, then suddenly, as solar maximum approached in 1979, all the tracking calendars started to slip badly as the satellite gradually got tens of minutes early on predictions which had previously been good for years. Satellites in very high orbits like Oscar 10 (perigee nearly 3,900km, apogee near 42,000km), are not seriously bothered by drag, but they get so far out from Earth (thereby diminishing Earth gravitational effects) that they come under the gravitational influence of the Sun and Moon. So whilst all low circular-orbit satellites gradually drag down into lower, shorter-period orbits, high-altitude elliptical orbiters sometimes go further out from the Earth, leading to what some programs insist, incorrectly, is negative drag.

Manned spacecraft are even more unpredictable, because they often use their engines to correct drag and push themselves up to a higher orbit. Salyut 7 used to make about eight to 10 powered engine burns each year, to maintain its orbital height between 280 and 360km. Needless to say, the first intimation a space radio user has of this is that his target spacecraft is heard later than expected.

In these circumstances, therefore, there are several categories of orbits, each with its own desirable time interval for supply of refreshed orbit data. Here is a summary.

Weekly. LEO satellites, eg Salyut and Mir, orbiting below 400km altitude, suffer severe atmospheric drag and require weekly orbit data updates for accurate tracking.

Monthly. Drag is still quite severe for satellites orbiting between 400 and 1,000km altitude, particularly in years around solar cycle maximum. Many of these satellites are used regularly by radio amateurs and space radio listeners, eg Uosat Oscar 11, NOAA and Meteor weather sats, Transit and Cosnav navigation satellites. All need a monthly data update.

Three-monthly. Most medium-altitude circular orbiters operate at heights between 1,000 and 1,700km, where they suffer far less drag than low-orbit satellites. Because drag at high altitude increases near solar sunspot maximum, these medium-altitude satellites do require some correction of orbital parameters at this time. Refreshment of orbital data every three months at sunspot maximum will give reasonably accurate tracking predictions for most users. At solar minimum this refreshing of data can be extended to six-monthly intervals.

Six-monthly. Satellites rarely orbit in the altitude zone 1,600 to 22,000km because Van Allen belt radiation would be fatal for their electronics (particularly the onboard housekeeping computers). Many elliptical orbiters do, however, go above 22,000km at apogee, then descend to about 1,700km at perigee. Provided their perigee is not below 1,600km they are unlikely to suffer serious orbit perturbation from drag effects and, provided their perigee passage is fast and repeats only two or three times each day, Van Allen belt radiation dosage cumulative effects will not affect them for two or three years. All satellites which venture beyond 36,000km from Earth during any part of their orbit are subject to the gravitational attraction of the Sun and the Moon, with these effects being most pronounced when satellite apogee, Sun or Moon and Earth centre, are on a straight line. Refreshment of orbital data every six months will take care of any changes that this extra-terrestrial attraction may produce.

Special cases of orbit data correction

Certain types of satellites, such as geostationary orbiters, require to stay in roughly the same location year after year. To achieve this, they are fitted with attitude adjustment and orbit adjustment low-powered thrusters. Small thrusts from these devices are used to keep these satellites oscillating slowly either side of a mean position. After a few years the fuel for these thrusters is exhausted and the satellite begins to drift round the equator. This drift continues until it reaches one of the gravity 'holes' over the Indian and Pacific Oceans. Once in either of these holes, the satellite stays where it is and can continue to be employed on any useful circuits in its footprint. These locations have strong possibilities for amateur radio geostationary satellite locations.

Methods of updating computer data elements

Very few home computer programs have menu-driven methods allowing simple updating of Keplerian orbital elements. If menu provision for data updating is not provided, extreme care is necessary when listing and editing to change data fixed in a program. The Sinclair Amateur Radio User Group (SARUG) can supply software with menu-updating facilities.

Station location data needed by a computer

It is essential that your computer program contains your correct station location data. As this data rarely changes, it normally needs inputting when you buy the program, then rarely thereafter. Standard practice in most program software is to ask for your station latitude in degrees (decimal degrees, eg 35.5 degrees not 35 degrees 30 minutes). For southern latitudes, enter a negative sign before the latitude figure. Longitude of your station is normally given in degrees decimal west of the Greenwich meridian. Station height above sea level can also be input in metres. Typical examples of station data are:

Norwich, England	52.7	358.5	10 metres
West London	51.5	0.1	20 metres
Cardiff, Wales	51.48	3.3	20 metres
Glasgow, Scotland	55.9	4.25	50 metres
Sydney, Australia	−33.5	208.9	30 metres

Many professional astronomy programs quote longitude the other way round the world, east from Greenwich. Be sure you get it right for your computer program. Again only a few programs contain menu access to alter station data; buy this kind of program if it is available.

Always remember when you refresh or alter data in a program, you must save a copy of the new version!

Display of tracking information

Fig 10.01 shows a typical computer display of satellite tracking information. Time is always given as UTC which is Greenwich mean time and British winter time. So care must be taken in summer in the UK where, for example, clock time 1300 British Summer Time is actually 1200 UTC.

The next column in the table of Fig 10.01 gives the azimuth great circle bearing to the satellite from your station. Azimuth is measured clockwise from north. For example, azimuth 190 is bearing 10 degrees west of south.

Satellite elevation in degrees is given in the next column. A negative figure in this column indicates that the satellite is below your horizon. A positive elevation angle signifies the angle through which you need to raise your antenna elevation to point at the satellite. You should be careful when you use this elevation term, for it applies to a perfect zero-degree horizon, something which few of us have. Hills and buildings raise the actual horizon around most ground station sites. So if you wish to use this information accurately, make sure you have a rough idea of the actual horizon elevations in the directions of interest from your station.

Also displayed in the computer table shown in Fig 10.01 is the latitude and the longitude west of the point on the Earth's surface immediately below the satellite. This information can be a valuable guide to propagation likely to be found on the radio path to the satellite, eg does the path go near polar regions with likelihood of auroras? Equally useful is ground range between your station and this sub-satellite point given in kilometres. Be sure you distinguish between ground range to satellite sub-point and slant range to satellite. This slant range term and the term for satellite

Uosat 2 Tracking on 19/6/86

UTC	AZ	EL	Lat	Long	GndRange
1901	92	0	47	324	2834kms
1903	78	5	54	327	2277kms
1905	57	10	61	331	1922kms
1907	32	10	68	337	1886kms
1909	10	6	75	349	2187kms
1911	355	1	80	14	2716kms
1913	345	-5	81	61	3366kms
1915	339	-10	77	97	4080kms
1917	334	-15	71	113	4830kms
1919	330	-19	64	121	5602kms
1921	328	-24	57	127	6388kms
1923	326	-28	50	130	7183kms
1925	324	-32	43	133	7984kms
1927	322	-36	36	135	8790kms
1929	321	-40	29	137	9598kms
1931	319	-44	21	139	10408kms

Fig 10.01: Typical computer tracking prediction (Uosat Oscar 11)

altitude above the Earth are shown in Fig 10.02. Please note that satellite height or altitude must be given with respect to the Earth's surface. Some computer programs give a term which is actually satellite distance from Earth centre. This can be confusing, but if you remember that this distance to Earth centre is a bigger value, eg satellite altitude plus Earth radius (radius is usually given as 6,378km), you will soon appreciate that the distance to Earth centre is so big that it is obvious.

Footprint maps

The satellite footprint is that area of the Earth's surface the satellite can see at any given time. Low Earth circular-orbit satellites keep nearly constant height above the Earth. So the size of their footprint is relatively constant. By contrast, satellites in elliptical orbits are altering their height above the Earth all the time. So the footprint they see when high up at apogee is much larger than the one they see at perigee.

Fig 10.03 shows an example of how computers can show

Uosat 2 Tracking on 19/6/86

UTC	AZ	EL	Lat	Long	SlantR	Ht kms
1901	92	0	47	324	3037	701
1903	78	5	54	327	2486	702
1905	57	10	61	331	2141	702
1907	32	10	68	337	2112	703
1909	10	6	75	349	2411	703
1911	355	1	80	14	2936	704
1913	345	-5	81	61	3583	703
1915	339	-10	77	97	4290	703
1917	334	-15	71	113	5021	702
1919	330	-19	64	121	5758	701
1921	328	-24	57	127	6487	700
1923	326	-28	50	130	7202	699
1925	324	-32	43	133	7895	697
1927	322	-36	36	135	8561	695
1929	321	-40	29	137	9196	693
1931	319	-44	21	139	9796	691
1933	318	-48	14	141	10357	689
1935	316	-52	7	142	10877	687

Fig 10.02: Typical slant range and height prediction (Uosat Oscar 11)

the extent of the footprint on a map. The satellite's position is marked on a mercator map of the world by a cross over north west USSR. The shield-shaped figure around the cross, made up of arrows, defines the limits of the footprint, the area of ground the satellite can see. Because a mercator map is a non-linear projection, this area has the rather curious shield shape but in the real situation, looking down onto the curved surface of the Earth sphere, the footprint is really circular.

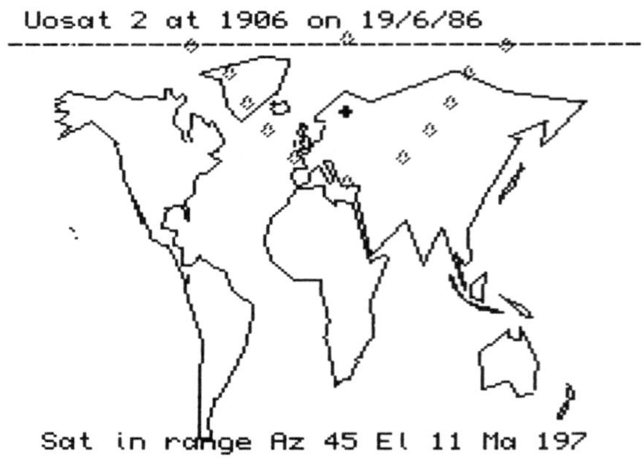

Fig 10.03: World map showing satellite footprint

If the satellite has a broad-beam antenna pointing at the Earth, or an omnidirectional antenna, all stations inside the footprint can see the satellite and can hear its signals. If the satellite has a transponder, any station in the footprint can communicate with any other station in the footprint. So this kind of display tells you who you can talk to or listen to, and it warns you when a wanted station is entering or leaving the footprint area.

Supplementary data below the map gives the azimuth bearing clockwise from north of the line of sight between your station and the satellite. Another term given in some radio amateur programs is 'mean anomaly', usually printed as 'MA' or 'Ma'.

This is not the same term as Keplerian element mean anomaly. In professional programs mean anomaly is measured in degrees from perigee. By contrast, the somewhat misleading amateur radio term is a counting system where the satellite orbit is divided into 256 equal intervals of time. In this system perigee is still 0 (or 256), but apogee is 128. Because the 256 bits are of equal time, they are not equal divisions of the orbital path. So a satellite in a non-circular orbit can move a large distance going between mean anomaly by 256, from 0 to 10, but move only a short distance relative to your station between mean anomaly by 256, from 120 to 130. This rather confusing situation must be treated with great care.

Given the high-speed performance of many home microcomputers, it is quite practical to drive displays of the type shown in Fig 10.03 so that they change every minute or so, keeping in real-time step with the satellite.

Auto tracking

A small number of satellite programs have the facility to drive specially modified antenna azimuth and elevation rotators. Programs of this type need special hardware to connect to the antennas and they only work on antenna rotators equipped to be driven digitally. G4GPQ has produced an excellent program of this type.

Satellite acquisition timetables

When a satellite is circling the Earth 12 or 15 times each day, it is important that users can refer to tables of times when the satellite will come in range of their station. Fig 10.04 shows a typical acquisition timetable from a SARUG program. The initials 'AOS' stand for 'Acquisition of Satellite' time. As the list shows, the Scottish station running this program could expect to hear Uosat Oscar 11 above his horizon 11 times on the day in question.

The table in Fig 10.04 also shows the azimuth bearing at which the operator should point his antenna in order to hear the satellite as it comes above his horizon, eg at 0750 the azimuth to aim at would be 56 degrees clockwise from north. This type of display is popular with regular satellite users because it allows them to plan their day's operating. They can decide which orbits they will be free to watch. If they want long-range, low-elevation orbits, they can work out from the table that there is a long period between midnight and 0750 when no orbits are in range, which tells the operator that the orbits either side of this period, eg 0750, 0925 and 2214, 2355, will be the long-range, low-elevation ones. By contrast, in an 11-orbit pattern of 0750 to 2355, the polar orbits will be the ones in the middle at 1240, 1417 and 1555. Used effectively, this display can help the knowledgeable experimenter find auroral polar orbits or orbits far to his east or west.

```
Acquisition Times
Uosat 2
Date 19.6.86
            AOS at 0750 Az 56
            AOS at 0925 Az 24
            AOS at 1102 Az 15
            AOS at 1240 Az 10
            AOS at 1417 Az 7
            AOS at 1554 Az 11
            AOS at 1728 Az 47
            AOS at 1901 Az 94
            AOS at 2035 Az 141
            AOS at 2213 Az 189
            AOS at 2355 Az 246
```

Fig 10.04: Acquisition times of Uosat 2, 19 June 1986

Unfortunately the mathematics of acquisition calculations are not simple. In consequence not all satellite tracking software has acquisition data. Would-be purchasers of software are advised to check the availability of these sorts of features in any program they may consider buying.

Doppler calculations

Computer calculation of satellite signal Doppler rate is shown in Fig 10.05. This is the more advanced form of Doppler rate calculation appropriate to an experimental satellite like Uosat Oscar 11. Doppler rate is predicted for the satellite beacon operating frequency of 145.825MHz during the period whilst the satellite is above the station horizon. Further details of how to use Doppler rate tables are given in chapter 8.

```
   Uosat 2 Tracking on 19/6/86
 UTC    AZ   EL   Lat   Long DRate Hz/sec
1901.0 93   0    47    324   -3.58
1902.0 87   3    50    325   -5.07
1903.0 79   6    54    327   -7.01
1904.0 69   8    57    329   -9.27
1905.0 58   10   61    331   -11.35
1906.0 46   11   64    334   -12.46
1907.0 33   11   68    337   -12.01
1908.0 21   9    71    342   -10.25
1909.0 11   7    74    349   -7.99
1910.0 3    4    77    358   -5.88
1911.0 356  1    80    13    -4.19
1912.0 350  -1   81    35
1913.0 346  -4   81    61
1914.0 342  -7   80    82
1915.0 339  -9   77    97
1916.0 337  -12  74    107
```

Fig 10.05: Doppler rate prediction

Less complex, but very useful, several satellite programs list the actual instantaneous, Doppler-shifted, down link frequency an operator can expect to hear from a satellite's beacon or, better still, his own signal down link coming back from the satellite.

This latter facility of predicting down link frequency avoids the considerable nuisance of operators who put their signal onto a satellite but cannot find it without disturbing everyone else on the satellite. Knowing where your own signal will come up for a certain transmitted up link frequency is a very valuable aid.

Special software facilities

The facilities described in this section are all available on computer software for amateur radio operators and space listeners. However, only a few people supply them. Most software sold lacks these facilities. A supplier who does provide these facilities is SARUG; the address is in appendix 1.

Visual tracking facilities

Fig 10.06 shows a display from a visual tracking program available from SARUG. The spacecraft concerned is Salyut 7 which is large and can shine like a bright star provided it is still in sunlight and the observer on the ground is in darkness. This program works out just when these rules are met, displaying the spacecraft in yellow if it is above the horizon but not sunlit, white if it is sunlit and red if it is below the horizon.

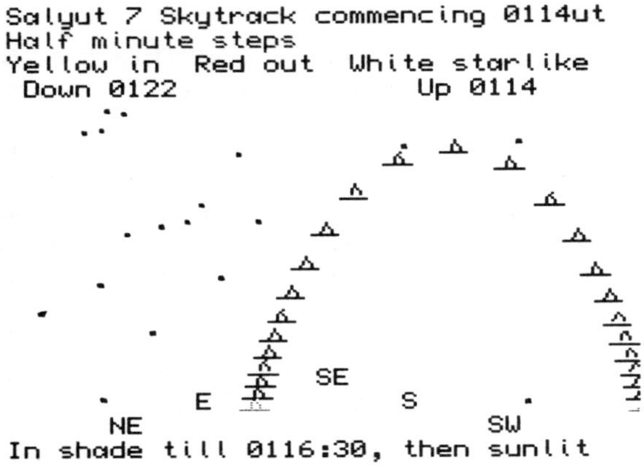

Fig 10.06: Display from a visual tracking program by SARUG showing times when Salyut 7 was observable during a transit of Scotland

In this example the space station used a bit of Scottish midnight Sun. As it came above the Scottish horizon at 0114 UTC it was not sunlit as it was too far south to see the midnight Sun, but by two and a half minutes (five markers later) it came into sunshine, actually seeing the Sun over the pole to its northeast. For the rest of the track until horizon at 0122 it was sunlit all the way. As the star map shows, for the last three minutes it tracked east below the square of Pegasus.

Detailed star and satellite maps

With a spacecraft like Salyut 7 or Mir, the cosmonauts often change the orbit, so if you use the spacecraft for experiments this can be a severe nuisance unless you have a way of keeping your spacecraft Keplerian elements orbit data right up to date.

Fig 10.07 shows the computer graphic display of a program which allows you to check orbit data directly against the fixed stars. The position of the spacecraft is marked by a cross, which in this case locates the spacecraft just east of the bright star Rigel in the constellation of Orion. Also seen are the other stars in Orion, included the close trio which make up the belt of Orion. By comparing this graphic with a visual test of the exact time the spacecraft passed this spot and how far away it passed by, a good check of Keplerian element accuracy can be made. Normally a spacecraft pass of this sort will allow timing of the passage of several different well-spaced stars, allowing accurate amendment of Keplerian elements to be made.

Some people supplement this experiment by taking photographs of the spacecraft against the stars, accurately recording the time the camera shutter was opened and closed. Aside from their obvious value for checking computer Keplerian elements, this type of experiment can check for spacecraft spinning and tumbling visually versus changes in its radio signals.

Other checks possible, using a combination of visual and radio operation augmented by real-time computer displays, are monitoring satellites as they cross into Earth shadow and observing visual and radio cut-off sequences, and features like solar cell performance, battery performance and satellite temperature change.

Satellites far smaller than Salyut can be checked visually. Even the suitcase-sized Uosats are plainly visible to sharp-eyed youngsters, whilst elderly authors have no difficulty seeing them in binoculars, particularly if they are monitored when due to cross a 'star gate' such as Castor and Pollux or the Yeds Prior and Posterior which grace the UK summer skies.

Satellite solar data

The Sun is responsible for most of the changes in the physics of near-Earth space. Sooner or later, any satellite experimenter or user will find that he needs solar data. Where is the Sun relative to the satellite? How does it illuminate (insolate) the satellite, altering its temperature and its solar cell current? When the satellite goes into shadow behind the Earth, how long does it stay there and how does this affect its power budget and its battery? All these questions and many more depend for answers on computer programs which provide a constant stream of solar data in several forms.

Figs 10.08 and 10.09 show typical displays for the Uosat Oscar 9 satellite. In Fig 10.08 the data is tabled in a constantly scrolling display, here interrupted to show the period from 1232 to 1310 on 14 July 1985.

The first three columns contain standard time and satellite sub-point latitude and longitude west; the succeeding columns all contain solar-relevant data.

The fourth column is labelled 'INS' for insolation angle, the angle between the Sun, the centre of the Earth and the satellite.

The fifth column, labelled 'Ef%', would in the case of a stabilised satellite report the effectiveness of solar illumination on the satellite's solar cells as a function of the angle at which sunlight strikes the cell faces. With Uosat we never know exactly where it is facing, so this column merely says 'SHD' when the satellite is in Earth shadow, and '+NK' for some illumination but incident angle on solar cells unknown.

The sixth column is labelled 'Sun', and it reports the

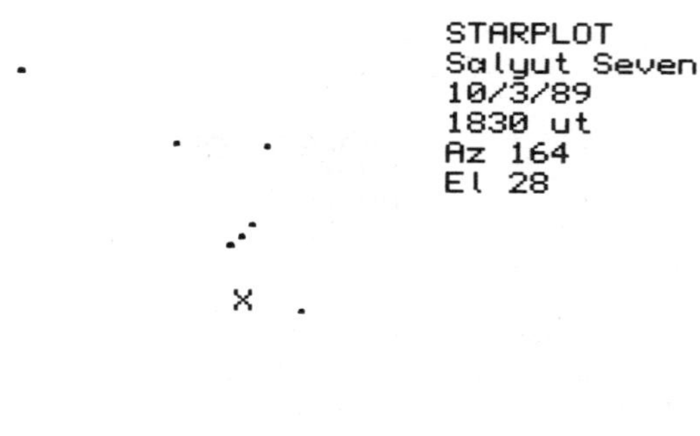

Fig 10.07: Computer visual plot of a Salyut 7 pass against Orion

UOSAT 1 ON 14/7/85

UTC	LAT	LON	INS	Ef%	Sun	Sat	ma
1230	30	111	88	+NK	111	91	7
1232	22	113	83	+NK	111	96	13
1234	15	115	79	+NK	111	100	18
1236	7	116	75	+NK	111	104	23
1238	0	118	71	+NK	111	108	29
1240	-8	119	67	SHD	111	112	34
1242	-15	121	64	SHD	111	115	40
1244	-23	123	61	SHD	111	118	45
1246	-31	124	58	SHD	111	121	51
1248	-38	126	56	SHD	111	123	56
1250	-46	129	55	SHD	111	124	61
1252	-53	131	54	SHD	111	125	67
1254	-60	135	54	SHD	111	125	72
1256	-68	141	55	SHD	111	124	78
1258	-75	151	57	SHD	111	122	83
1300	-81	174	59	SHD	111	120	89
1302	-83	224	61	SHD	111	118	94
1304	-79	265	64	SHD	111	115	99
1306	-72	281	68	+NK	111	111	105

Fig 10.08: Computer prediction of satellite in sunlight or shadow

footprint great circle angle the Sun can see at the satellite's height. This term is simply the solar footprint great circle angle added to the satellite footprint angle. In the case of a near circular orbiter like Uosat this angle shows little or no change, but an elliptical orbiter, eg Oscar 10, would show marked variation of this angle with time, because the size of the Oscar 10 footprint varies continuously as satellite height above the Earth changes.

The seventh column, labelled 'Sat', reports the great circle angle subtended at the Earth's centre by lines from the Sun and the satellite. Clearly, if this figure is less than the Sun figure in the previous column the satellite is sunlit. This column also gives an accurate idea of just when the satellite is approaching the edge of the sunlit zone. For example, at 1232 the footprint angle Sun is 111 and the satellite is 96 degrees from the sub-solar point, so 111 – 96 = 15 tells us it is well inside the sunlit zone. By 1254, however, this calculation Sun – Sat produces an answer of 111 – 125 = –14 degrees, so the satellite is now deep in Earth shadow.

The last column in the table reports time since perigee measured in units by 256, eg 0 or 256 = perigee, and 128 = apogee.

By contrast with the previous figure, Fig 10.09 presents the information graphically. Because we do not know Uosat Oscar 9's alignment precisely we can only give it an arbitrary 100% efficiency when in sunlight. The display was started at 1220 UTC. 20 minutes later the satellite went into Earth shadow, coming back into sunlight about 25 minutes

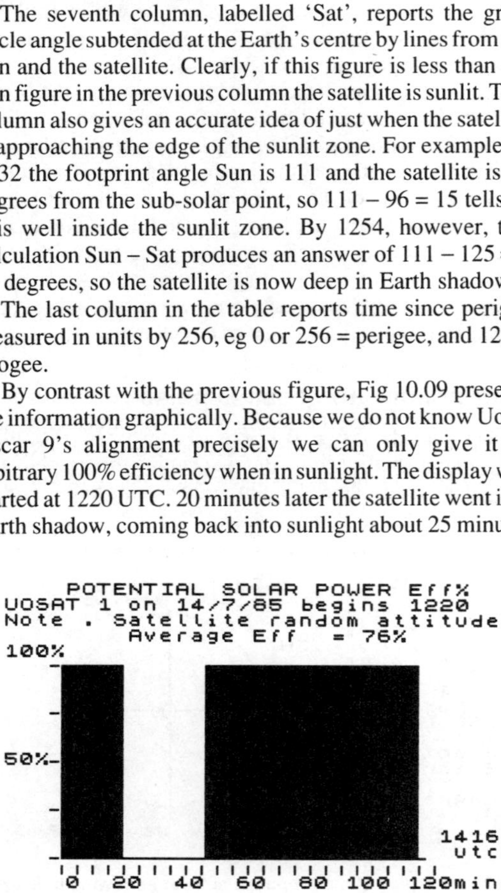

Fig 10.09: Graph of potential solar power of Uosat Oscar 9

or so later. This resulted in the satellite spending about 26% of the orbit in the dark.

Special computer maps

In radio propagation, the signal generally follows a great circle path in a straight line. When considering the propagation of HF satellite signals via the ionosphere, it is useful to be able to see the position of the satellite, the Sun and the part of the world lit by the Sun at both the ground level and satellite height. If this information can be put on a great circle projection map centred on the listening ground station, it may be possible to usefully analyse any results.

Fig 10.10 shows a computer graphic display of this type, again for Uosat Oscar 9. Uosat Oscar 9 had several HF beacons, with the one on 21.002MHz being the best performer. Signals from this beacon were received at times from remote parts of the world via ionospheric propagation. Signals from the west in the early morning, and from the south at local sunset, were frequently heard in the UK.

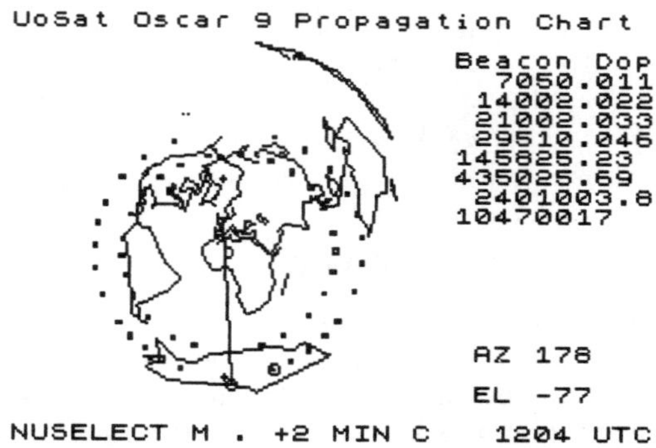

Fig 10.10: Uosat Oscar 9 HF beacon propagation great circle map

In the example shown, a line from the home station at the centre of the map projects south to the satellite positioned below the south pole. This line defines the great circle signal path from the UK and on its way south this line passes over Africa and the marker of the solar sub-point.

Circling over the edge of Antarctica, South America, North America, the Far East and the Indian Ocean are markers which show the location of the solar terminator: the dawn/dusk zone at ground level. Outside this circle the world is in darkness.

A second ring circling further out from the Sun covers Antarctica, the Pacific to the west of South America, North America and south of Japan and the Southern Indian Ocean. This is the solar terminator at the satellite height.

In the situation shown, Uosat Oscar 9 is in darkness near the South Pole, just outside the area sunlit at its orbital height. Given all this solar and positional data on the map, it is possible to examine the circumstances by which the Uosat 21MHz signal is propagated by the ionosphere onward to the UK.

The great circle projection map used here makes some of

Fig 10.11: Footprint of Moon on 20 June 1986 at 2100 UTC

the land furthest from the UK almost unrecognisable. The string-like lines around the top right edge are New Zealand. By using great circle plotting we keep the radio paths straight but we distort the geography of those places near the periphery of the map.

Additional software is available for actually predicting the HF radio propagation conditions on any path to or from the UK. This is useful for planning where signals are likely to be heard from, and for checking the accuracy of the predictions against actual times and places the satellite is heard from.

Moonbounce software

It is 40 years since the US first bounced radar signals off the Moon and back to Earth. Since then moonbounce communications have become a regular feature of amateur radio. Results are possible with relatively modest equipment, but a great deal of expertise is necessary in assembling the equipment, aligning it to maximum performance and employing a successful operating strategy.

Computer software is a must for any serious moonbouncer. All too often the Moon is obscured by clouds and cannot therefore be accurately pointed and tracked unless computed azimuth elevation data is available. Because of the high-gain antennas required, antenna beam widths are narrow, so pointing accuracy is essential.

Fig 10.11 shows a typical moonbounce graphic map. The Moon is shown over South Africa, and the lunar footprint is outlined by an arc of small circles.

The footprint stretches from South America, up to Scandinavia, and down to Western Australia. Any station in the footprint may be able to communicate with any other station in the footprint. Recommended azimuth and elevation are shown to enable accurate antenna pointing, and a time-of-day strip records that whilst South America, Africa and Europe are all wide awake, only dedicated Australian moonbouncers will be up after their local midnight.

Moonbounce amateur radio demands high technical competence and a wide knowledge of lunar and other astronomical conditions. Special graphic displays are available to show this data. Fig 10.12 shows one such display. First it says something about the Earth's ionosphere. Any signal from or to the Moon must transit the ionosphere, and where and at what incident angle this transit is made is very important. The lower the incident angle, the less the chance of effective moonbounce. The bigger these incident angles on the E and F layers, the bigger the likelihood of a reasonably transparent ionosphere and hence good moonbounce.

Much of the variation in ionospheric transparency is seasonal. It is clearly asking a lot to expect good moonbounce at 144MHz when sporadic E in the ionosphere is partially reflecting terrestrial 144MHz signals back to Earth. So daylight operation in the sporadic E seasons is questionable. Sporadic E is predictable to some extent and early warning is possible, so the program warns moonbouncers of times when it would be wise to check for SpE.

Another feature of moonbounce which the computer can predict is Earth-to-Moon distance. The Moon can be as near as 355,000km or as far away as 420,000km. So Fig 10.12 shows a path loss figure in decibels, and has a simple path loss 'thermometer' indicator showing when the Moon is near or far away. In the example quoted in Fig 10.12, we have a Moon near its perigee, so the Earth-Moon path is shorter than usual, and moonbounce is likely to be a little bit easier, with the 'thermometer' arrow down towards the negative, low path loss end of its scale.

The program has also checked to see whether the Moon is down the magnetotail from Earth, and reports that it is clear of the magnetotail. This may be a pointer to relatively undisturbed moonbouncing as the magnetotail is sometimes the scene of severe magnetic disturbance which moves charged particle plasmas up and down tail at high speed. So the magnetotail is a good place to avoid, especially at times of severe magnetic storms. A lot more experiment needs to be done before we are sure whether the magnetotail is a serious threat to moonbounce.

Moonbounce and cosmic noise

At the right side of Fig 10.12 is a 10 degree radius 'bull's-eye', centred on the Moon. Before printing this graphic, the computer has checked its catalogue of cosmic radio sources

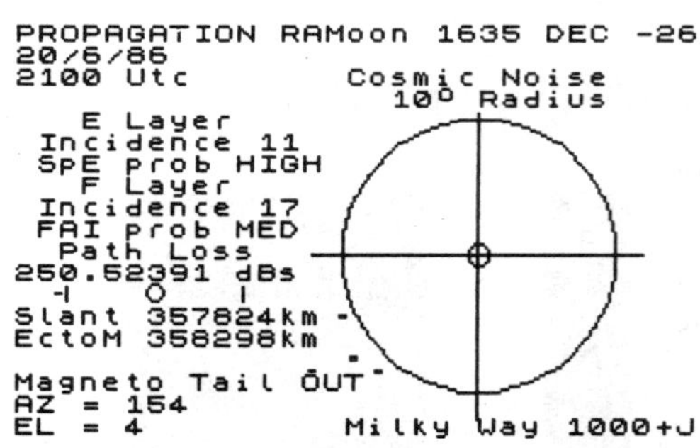

Fig 10.12: Display of moonbounce software showing bull's-eye chart, propagation conditions, path loss, Earth-to-Moon distance and Moon position in relation to the Earth's magnetotail

COSMIC NOISE TARGETS
at 2100 utc 20/6/1986

NAME	Janskys	Az	El
Cassiopea	11000	27.8	31.3
Sagittarius	9000	OUT	OUT
Cygnus A	8100	71.8	38.2
Taurus A	1420	OUT	OUT
M87 Virgo A	970	224	39.8

Fig 10.13: Table of radio sources which can be used for moonbounce equipment calibration

to see if any of them are within 10 degrees of the Moon's position, thereby constituting a possible degradation of the signal-to-noise ratio for any moonbounce at this time and sky location. In this example only one noise source, the Milky Way, is near the Moon's sky position. In this example the Milky Way is outside the bull's-eye at lower left, constituting no problem at this time. The statement below the bull's-eye confirms it is the Milky Way and gives the signal level it produces as 1,000+J, ie more than 1,000 Janskys. The chapter on amateur radio astronomy explains what Janskys are. With a power flux of 1,000+ Janskys the Milky Way can be a serious problem to moonbouncers when the Moon directly overlies part of this great edge-on 'catherine wheel' of stars.

Checking moonbounce equipment on radio stars

Unless moonbounce equipment is working at peak performance it is useless. Maintaining peak performance is therefore something of a problem. Many moonbouncers use the Sun as their radio test star. Unfortunately the Sun is a highly variable radio star, so it can sometimes be more confusing than helpful. Given a microcomputer and suitable software, the moonbouncer can check the performance of his equipment on half a dozen stable 'radio stars'. As Fig 10.13 shows, the name radio star is a bit misleading, because only one of the candidate calibration targets is a star; this is Taurus A in the Crab Nebula, which is the remnant of a star which went supernova. All the other moonbounce calibration targets quoted in Fig 10.13 are either whole galaxies, like our own Milky Way, composed of millions of stars, or they are active galactic centres like Sagittarius A, the active radio emitter at the centre of our Milky Way. Using this list, moonbouncers should have no difficulty checking their equipment performance.

Weather satellite pictures by computer

Many home microcomputers can be adapted to demodulation and display of Wefax weather satellite pictures. Some home micros require no extra connections or add-on electronics. Other micros have to be assisted by all sorts of convertors and sometimes quite complex hardware.

In many cases the microcomputer has insufficient memory to store a complete Wefax picture, so the user has the choice of buying supplementary memory, or of dividing the picture in half, storing it half at a time on tape or disc and replaying each half as required. In chapter 8, Fig 8.4.04a shows a typical half-picture from a NOAA weather satellite, demodulated by a Sinclair Spectrum without modems and transferred from the microcomputer's screen display to a dot-matrix printer. While this may satisfy those who simply want to explore the technique, its lack of contrast and generally low quality of reproduction will not satisfy weather experts, who desire a more impressive display of their favourite topic.

Automatic telegraphy

The biggest single growth area in amateur radio during the 1980s has been in the field of automatic telegraphy. The single most important reason for this has been the microcomputer. Hardware and software are available for most makes of computer and, as with weather picture decoding, the sheer volume of equipment modems and software available can be a confusing area for a beginner. Would-be users must check before they buy a particular microcomputer just what modems and extras are necessary before it can be regarded as a thoroughly useful auto-telegraphy terminal.

Both hardware and software requirements should be checked out, preferably on a friend's microcomputer, before parting with cash for your own purchase. Auto-telegraphy outfits can be quite cheap. This does not mean they are nasty and useless, but it can mean they use slow-to-load tape rather than instant plug-in ROM. Please take great care before you make any purchases in this field. Read what the specialised groups have to say, check the 'DataComms' column in back issues of *Radio Communication*, and take a good look at what your friends have got before you part with your cash.

Satellite data communications

Most modern satellites use some form of automatic telegraphy or data communications to get their information back to Earth. Navigation satellites use standard radio teletype formats, albeit coded and often in Russian, but this form of space data communications is expensive in terms of drain on the satellites' batteries and solar cells.

For the least loading of satellites' power supplies, phase-shift keying is the preferred data comms mode. Computer decoding of PSK telemetry is available in both hardware and software packages. Which of these you choose depends on your computer. Most home micros make a lot of radio-frequency noise, and direct computer decoding of a signal is impossible because you cannot hear the signal you want and have the computer switched on at the same time. Some home micros, particularly those built to US regulations, are relatively RFI-quiet. Computer RFI is discussed fully later in this chapter.

Coming on the satellite scene fast is packet radio. This is a computer-controlled message system which (licensing regulation permitting) can be almost automatic or, to use the more expressive phrase, unattended. All planned major packet satellites are being designed with the TAPR Tuscon amateur radio packet AX.25, level 2, version 2, protocol. It is essential that would-be packet users check that they are buying software or hardware for this protocol if they wish to use satellite facilities. There are other protocols in use elsewhere, but they do not work on satellites where international standardisation is all-important.

Packet radio looks like being the biggest change to amateur radio operating generally, and amateur radio satellite operating particularly, since the introduction of SSB voice. Software and hardware are already available for several microcomputers (do be careful checking for RFI and make sure you get the right AX.25 protocol system). It is difficult to estimate just how much packet radio will change operating patterns in amateur radio. As yet commercial radio is a long way behind, although packet techniques are well established in line communication telephone systems operations. For space radio operators the experimental content of packet operation is very high indeed, and given relatively relaxed licensing conditions, radio amateurs could achieve high levels of advancement in this field in the next decade.

Types of satellite packet radio networks

At this early point in the development of satellite packet radio, there are several system choices.

In its simplest form the packet signal is sent up to a satellite, which immediately relays it in the hope that the intended recipient of the message is listening to the satellite. This situation is fraught with 'ifs' and 'buts', and is not popular. What is needed as a first-stage improvement is a facility aboard the satellite to hold the message until down loading is requested by the addressee. This store-and-forward mode requires computer and memory facilities in the satellite.

The next desirable improvement is a computer-controlled access to the satellite memory, so that the satellite is not swamped by too many people trying to use it at once. Finally, and most controversial, is the requirement for unattended operation of the home station, so that a sender can make up his message, and if he finds access temporarily denied because others are already using the access and store facility, he can put his station on automatic, allowing it to up link with the satellite when access is available. The complement to this is unattended reception operation, with a likely recipient programming his computer to operate in his absence and down load any messages for him.

Store-and-forward is an essential feature for LEO satellites, if, say, communication by packet from the UK to Japan is desired, because these stations are never simultaneously in the approximate 4,000km footprint of these satellites. Why would anyone want to do this? A good example is the author and JR1SWB, who for years have exchanged satellite propagation and software data by the present-day, far-from-reliable channels. Given suitable packet hardware in space, daily exchange of up-to-date data becomes possible.

Fuji Oscar 12 satellite packet experiment

Satellite Fuji Oscar 12 was designed, built and launched by Japan in August 1986. It is intended as a test vehicle for packet radio, but it is not solely devoted to packet and this leads to some minor complications. The first of these problems is limited storage capacity. FO 12 has a megabyte of storage, and given some quite reasonable projections of potential user demand, this may prove to be far too small. But FO 12 is experimental and we cannot expect everything at our first attempt. A second problem arises because FO 12 shares digital and analogue facilities and, in a small suitcase-sized satellite such as this one, there is not enough power to run both systems simultaneously. Some of the features of this second problem were improved when FO 12 entered regular service, but the power supply problem was not completely eliminated and in November 1989 FO 12 had to be taken out of service due to lack of power. Despite this setback, FO 12 details in this book have been left unmodified because they form the perfect introduction to the next Fuji satellite, JAS 1-B, launched in February 1990. JAS 1-B is similar to FO 12 except in respect of power supply and memory, where its features have been greatly improved.

Strategies for optimising the chance that one's message will be safely delivered depend on the message staying in the satellite's memory until a firm opportunity to down load it to the intended recipient occurs. If the satellite is alternating one or two days of packet store-and-forward with one or two days of analogue voice transponder operating, the times when these changes occur must be considered.

Fig 10.14 shows a printout from one Oscar 12 tracking program, which offers a clear picture of when down loading of packets will be possible at a particular location. An asterisk in the callsign column of the place of interest, eg Japan, callsign JA, shows only one opportunity for down loading at 1520 UTC, whereas Hawaii (KH) has three opportunities at 1120, 1320, and 1540 UTC.

If this information is used in conjunction with the published times for changes from packet to transponder operation, it should be possible to find convenient up loading times just before these down load times in order to reduce the possibility of the message being in the satellite memory for a long time and being pushed out of memory by new messages before it can be delivered. A station in the UK with a message for Japan has to get his message in before 1520 UTC. He can use convenient up load opportunities at 1000 or 1200 UTC, with the later one being the one with the least time in satellite memory, ie at risk only once from likely heavy up loading over the USA at 1340 UTC. By contrast, the 1000 UTC load from the UK risks being bumped out of memory by two separate American up load opportunities at

1140 and 1340 UTC. Clearly, whilst packet storage memory is limited, the system is not completely reliable. None the less, it is an excellent start and provides lots of opportunities for amateur radio packet experiments.

```
 JAS 1 DumpSked begins 30/12/86
Time  S U4AZV9BJVKZKKKWWWWLP
 utc GMIAX4SUMYA63LGHL6042UY
1000 *****..................
1020 ......*................
1040 ...........*...........
1100 ............**.........
1120 ...............*.*.....
1140 ................*****..
1200 *.*....................
1220 ......*................
1240 ...........*...........
1300 ...........***.........
1320 ..............**.......
1340 ................*****..
1400 ...................**..
1420 ......*...............*
1440 ......*................
1500 ........*..**..........
1520 ..........*...*........
1540 ...............****....
1600 ..................***..
```

Fig 10.14: Fuji Oscar 12 data up and down loading schedule

Full details of Fuji JAS-1B (Oscar 20) and the other packet satellites launched in early 1990 (Uosat Oscar 14, Pacsat Oscar 16, Dove Oscar 17, Webersat Oscar 18, Lusat Oscar 19) are given in chapter 6.

Computer control of radio equipment

Space radio reception and communication is a field wide open to computer control techniques. The minimum equipment for this task is a microcomputer with a program-addressable serial port feeding a coupling device, often employing electrical-to-optical-to-electrical translation as a break in the direct electrical connection, before going on to couple with the station receiver or transmitter.

An increasing number of amateur radio receivers and transmitters are being sold already fitted with the facility to control them via a computer serial input, but there are a wide range of different standards, both between equipment manufacturers and even equipments produced by the same manufacturer.

Early computer controllable receivers and transmitters had few facilities. Receivers would accept commands to change frequency or modulation mode, but they would not pass back to the computer essential feedback commands such as AGC level, signal S meter level or squelch. So there was no way they could be used in any sort of auto-control loop, allowing scan, hold on signal, examine, continue scan, type sequences. This situation is changing slowly, but in regard to transmitters and transceivers it was even more unsatisfactory because few if any feedback features were available, and most important, some indication that when the remote computer told the transmitter to tune to a particular frequency, it actually went to that frequency and reported accurately that it had done so. Fortunately this situation is

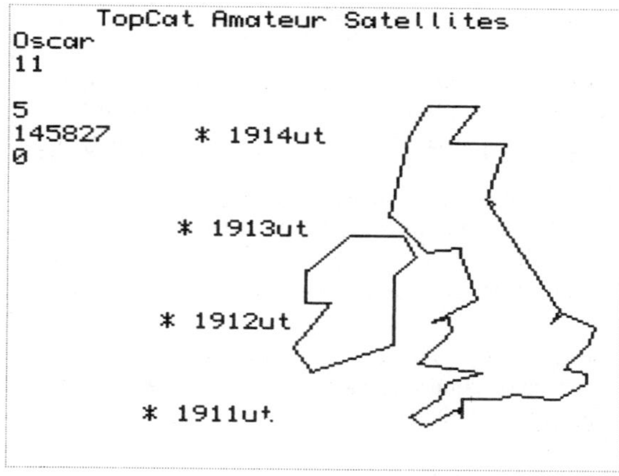

Fig 10.15: Computer display for automatic satellite tracking

changing but radio amateurs and space radio listeners should be careful that what they buy does what they want and is compatible with their station equipment.

Amateur space radio operation has often been described as a situation requiring an octopus using all its hands at once, in order to tune, transmit, train antennas, read the next azimuth, log what the other station is saying etc. This is a fair description, but it can be relieved by computer control. Fig 10.15 shows a computer display being used for real-time tracking and experimental work on satellite Uosat Oscar 11. Receiver frequency is being controlled and corrected for Doppler shift as the computer display highlights the changing position of the satellite relative to UK. Output to the antenna training loop keeps the antenna pointing at the satellite in azimuth and elevation throughout the pass. This particular combination of receiver, computer, software and antenna control is designed to operate for any existing Oscar or Radiosport satellite. But it is relatively unique, because on most computers the RFI generated by the computer completely blanks out most reception. A careful choice of computer was necessary before this scheme was successful. So far, only the Radio Shack Colour Computer, the CoCo as it is sometimes called, and the Sinclair QL have done the job successfully. Computer RFI will be reviewed in detail in a later section of this chapter.

With the appearance of computers which produce only low levels of radio frequency interference, it has become possible to explore several areas of active computer control of radio experiments. These new techniques include:

- Doppler correction of transmitter and receiver signals.
- Software controlled antenna tracking using computer-driven commercial rotators.
- Satellite experiment data reception and real-time plotting.
- Selective satellite monitoring.
- Automatic packet radio receipt, despatch and routing.

In addition, future developments are likely to be:

```
Today          22.1.86

  HF Propagation   Best time of year
                   154 cycle quiet

  Sporadic E  winter season moderate

  METEORS       Aurigids
   all day    Rate peak day
   Shower size         small

  DUCTING   small pos duct in Hipres


  Space Shuttle    Flight 51L
 Spartan TDRS, never in range of UK
 Amateur Radio unlikely
 SPACE Voyager 2 Uranus 22/24 Jan
```

Fig 10.16: Computer display of space activity diary

- Satellite detection classification and identification.
- Antenna polarisation optimisation.

Not all computers are RFI-quiet so it pays to shop around until you find one that is.

A space data computer calendar

Keeping a check of all the various kinds of space radio activity is a considerable task, but here again the ubiquitous microcomputer can lend a hand. Fig 10.16 shows a headline page for a typical day in the life of a space radio experimenter. Each day before operations start, the operator keys in the date and gets a printout similar to Fig 10.16, telling him that:

Northern hemisphere HF propagation is predicted good, with the 154-day cycle of solar flare activity predicted as quiet, so no solar storms are expected.

Sporadic E propagation in daylight is possible as the calendar shows we are in the winter SpE season.

Meteor activity is expected. The Aurigids shower is due to peak today. It is a small shower and produces only a few meteors, and it lasts all day.

Annual records of VHF/UHF propagation for this Scottish station in sight of North Sea and Irish Sea surface ducting indicate that if high-pressure, stable conditions are forecast, some surface ducting to Germany and the Netherlands in the east, or Spain in the south west, is possible.

Space shuttle activity for this day showed a flight into a low-inclination orbit, not in range of the UK. The flight carried no amateur radio.

Deep space activity was the day's priority item, with Voyager 2 closing in for rendezvous with Uranus.

Clearly amateur radio would take something of a back seat today as the operator concentrated on network TV reports of Voyager's progress.

Having got the daily bulletin, the operator can then go on to follow up the high points in detail, for example ask for more data on the Aurigids meteors, including a map of radiant elevation and azimuth versus time, plus a related effectiveness table for certain meteor monitoring stations, together with any data on any related comet, showing whether the comet was near Earth, with the possibility of an enhanced shower.

There is no reason why the program should not be gradually enlarged to control station equipment to search for auroras and report its presence or to check ionospheric transparency on a suitable geosat target. The presence of sporadic E could be actively checked as could scintillation measurements to explore solar wind enhancement and magnetic activity. Such data is readily available from experimental satellites and perfectly normal commercial and amateur satellites. Details of how to get some of this information are given in chapter 8.

Computer decoding and display of telemetry

Many satellites send data back to Earth in the form of telemetry, consisting of simple message blocks containing shorthand reports of the parameters they are measuring, both about themselves and about the physical parameters of the space around them. Most of the early amateur radio satellites used formats similar to the Radiosport format shown below:

RS7	K91	D80	O77	G01	U23	S19	W20
RS7	IK99	ID01	IO91	IG01	IU11	IS14	IW01
RS7	AK87	AD91	AO77	AG91	AU77	AS93	AW77
RS7	MK83	MD01	MO02	MG10	MU12	MS11	MW11

This telemetry block is sent in morse code at about 25wpm. It can be read by the operator and recorded manually, or it can be read by a computer equipped with morse reception software. Then, either the manual or auto-copy can be reviewed and translated by software which understands the calibration algorithms for each of the 28 data windows in the block. The actual contents code for each window is described in the experiment chapter of this book.

A more complex form of telemetry is used by more modern Oscar satellites. The University of Surrey satellites Uosat Oscars 9 and 11 have been specifically designed to measure complex space phenomena, and there is some excellent software available for UK microcomputers which can take the received PSK signal, decode it and then translate each separate data window into a parameter measurement statement. With satellite Uosat Oscar 11, the satellite can send down stored data. So it is capable of taking measurements all the way around the Earth and then down loading this whole orbit data to any receiving station. In the receiving station this data can be computer decoded and translated, and in some programs the computer can produce graphic plots of the way a particular measurement has changed as the satellite went around the world. Examples of this type of data output are shown in chapter 8.

In all cases, the major problem with automatic telemetry reception, decoding and display is computer-generated RFI.

It is therefore customary for telemetry users to separate their work into two distinct operations.

First the user makes a tape recording of the audio frequency signal produced by receiver demodulation of the satellite telemetry.

Only when that stage is complete does the user connect the tape recorder to the microcomputer, switch on the microcomputer for the first time, and successively load the telemetry decode and display program followed by the telemetry recording.

Telemetry decoding and display is a rapidly expanding field for amateur radio space experimenters. Many radio amateur and space radio listener stations now possess research facilities which begin to rival those in professional laboratories.

Computer-generated radio-frequency interference

Radio-frequency interference and poor EMC are problems well known to all radio amateurs. It is therefore rather galling that, after taking precautions to ensure that one's station does not cause annoyance to neighbours, one's own operating is disrupted by a badly screened home computer. The author suffers from a neighbour's games computer – the level of interference from this micro is such that almost all VHF frequencies are blocked irregularly by drifting signals, strong enough to completely destroy any chance of listening to satellites.

Many countries have regulations covering the screening of computers, the most well-known being the USA FCC regulations. In the UK we will have to wait until the EEC EMC Directive comes into force in January 1992. Until then, what can microcomputer users do themselves?

In regard to distant interfering microcomputers, directional receiving antennas cut out most of the interference except when the satellite being received is on the same azimuth bearing as the offending microcomputer. If the signal is being picked up by the mains supply, this can be suppressed.

However, neither of these cures works if the microcomputer is in one's own home, or worse still, actually alongside the radio equipment. You can of course shop around for a microcomputer which produces little or no RFI. These do exist, and typically they are American-built micros which have had to meet stringent US FCC regulations. The Radio Shack Tandy Colour Computer is usually sold with its screening and filtering intact. So it and its Dragon counterpart are among the favourite micros of the packet radio brigade, who must run the computer alongside the radio.

Most other 8-bit computers sold in UK are much too RFI-noisy to permit this. Some of them can be professionally screened, typically by zinc spraying the inside of the case, and plate screening the keyboard. They also need good earth connections inside and outside the micro case. However, be careful because any work of this sort usually revokes the guarantee.

Whatever you do, try to observe some if not all of the following rules.

(a) Check any prospective microcomputer purchase for RFI, particularly at HF and VHF.

(b) Check any prospective ancillary purchase for RFI. For example, some printers are noisy at VHF, producing drifting carriers at quite high power.

(c) If you already have your micro, shop around for professional RFI treatment. You can do it yourself but it is not easy and not always successful.

(d) Try writing computer software so that your micro avoids the noisiest of the RFI-generating sequences. For example, the Sinclair computers are noisy when they are flashing the cursor to prompt you to input the answer to a question. You cannot inhibit this directly in high level software, but you can program it to pause and wait for a key press before it goes briefly into the RFI noisy input mode.

(e) Modern 16-bit computers are much less RFI-noisy in general than older 8-bit micros. So if you have a choice, opt for 16-bit.

(f) Finally, and as a last resort, try all possible combinations of location for the radio and for the microcomputer, and pick the quietest one from the RFI point of view.

Computers in space

The modern spacecraft is a complex machine which requires a high order of operational flexibility in order to allow it to perform a wide variety of tasks. If possible, this flexibility should extend to allowing its functions to be altered by the up loading of new instructions, long after it has been launched. The evolution of onboard computers has been gradual but all-important. From simple onboard decoders and actuators which simply switch equipment on or off, on receipt of commands from the ground, we have progressed to highly flexible onboard microprocessors capable of controlling most if not all spacecraft functions. This total control was achieved initially via fixed software, often hardwired before launch, and this has gradually been modified to provide computer systems which are capable of being rewritten literally from the ground up, substituting new programs for old when the spacecraft is already far from Earth. Fig 10.17 shows a schematic of this type of system.

Satellite onboard computer construction

Professional and amateur radio satellite onboard computers have had quite different histories. In the professional world, reliability almost irrespective of cost has been the compelling requirement. This has led to a conservative approach to professional onboard computer design. Old-fashioned, well-proven systems have been preferred to untried state-of-the-art systems, and built-in redundancy, such as fitting three

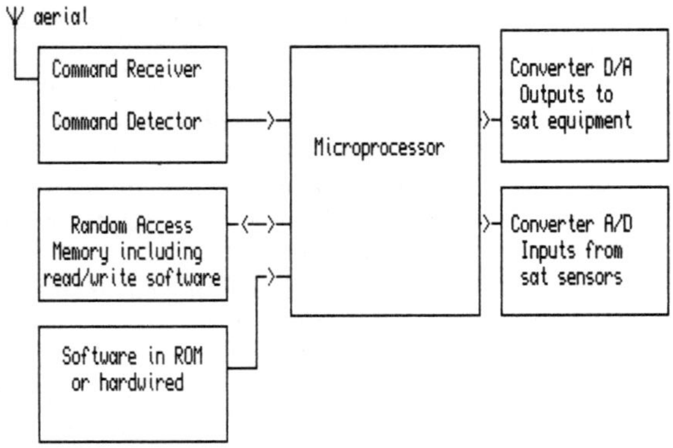

Fig 10.17: Satellite onboard command computer inflight-modifiable software

components instead of one so that if one or even two fail the system still works, has been commonplace. Indeed, most professional spacecraft have been fitted with at least two of everything, a policy which has paid handsome dividends in missions such as Pioneer and Voyager, which suffered major failures but have continued to fulfil mission objectives. This philosophy is altering as the new approach of redundant onboard computers and flexible rewritable software has proved its worth, but change is at a slow but sure 'no risks' pace.

By contrast, amateur radio spacecraft have weight and cost restrictions which force their designers to extract every last possible desired feature, using as little in the way of hardware as possible. Therefore inexpensive, high-performance components and circuits are in, and redundancy is out. Amateur radio spacecraft are built as close to the state of the art as money and time permit, a risk strategy which is unavoidable and which inevitably invokes the occasional serious penalty.

Onboard computer languages

As with all computer subjects there is no simple universal choice of which language to adopt for spacecraft computers. Initially all early onboard processors were programmed directly in machine code, and this continues to be the case in most professional work, but with the tremendous software load imposed by the space shuttle it soon became clear that, as with most ground-based work, space computer programs were somewhat easier to use if written in a high-level language (Fortran, Forth, Pascal, etc) and then assembled as machine code only when ready to be input to the spacecraft onboard computer.

As Fig 10.18 shows, this is only possible with major ground support facilities housing the necessary linkers, compilers, assemblers and editors, an arrangement which requires at least a powerful minicomputer. Fig 10.19 shows how this strategy leads to suitable facilities for in-orbit control and servicing of onboard software. This method of working allows everything to be worked out and tested on the ground before it is up loaded to the spacecraft, which is often millions of kilometres from Earth. There have been some spectacular successes with this approach. Voyager 2, the supremely successful visitor to Jupiter, Saturn, Uranus and Neptune, has onboard software which is totally rewritten for every new planetary encounter. So flexible is the Voyager computer system that it has allowed newer and more 'memory economic' features to be included in its software, features which had not even been thought of when Voyager was launched, many years ago.

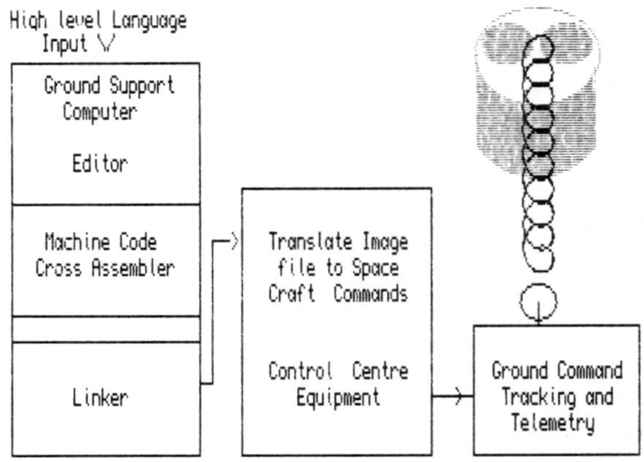

Fig 10.18: Ground equipment required for inflight modification of satellite onboard software

Clearly, enormous care is necessary. If you make a mistake in software sent up to a distant spacecraft the results can be fatal. All ground stations today use elaborate ground simulators to duplicate the satellites functions during software tests, but it is only a few years ago that changes in software back-up personnel on the Viking spacecraft mission allowed a fatal change to the software. Viking was reporting steadily from the Martian surface despite showing signs of battery deterioration. To counter this trend before it became a serious problem, the battery charge/load cycle

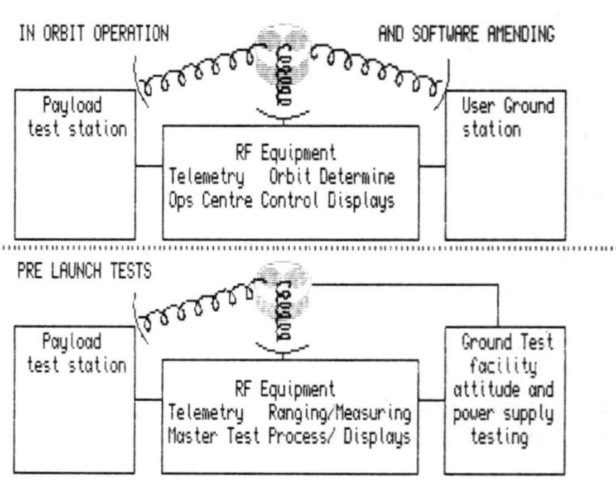

Fig 10.19: In-orbit operation and software amendment

was rewritten and was telemetered up to Mars. Unfortunately there was a mix-up regarding just what was where in the Viking computer memory, and the new battery routine was loaded into memory already occupied by the spacecraft antenna Earth pointing commands. The antenna pointing data was wiped out, and the Viking antenna stopped following the Earth. So though the new battery routine has probably kept Viking running to this day, it no longer talks to us. A sad end to a superb mission which had already exceeded the design life by about 10 times.

Unfortunately, the problems caused by the use of spacecraft computers with different high-level languages, and worse still different microprocessors with different machine-code formats, will not go away overnight. As with terrestrial use of microcomputers, standards are hard to set. Only in fields where coherent objectives are definable and enforceable from the top, eg US military and the European Space Agency, will sensible standardisation begin to appear.

The US military (but not Nasa, NOAA or the American scientific community) have settled on ADA, a high-level language derived from Pascal. The European Space Agency has gone one better and have produced EGSE communication standards (Electrical Test and Checkout Equipment) which, together with ETOL (European Test Operations Language), allows a wide range of compatibility between products of different nations, and different manufacturers and universities.

The European EGSE system recognises that onboard computer language, its ground testing pre-launch, its debugging post-launch, and any subsequent in orbit amendment are inseparable. The cost is high. Elegance is necessarily over-specified in order to include all levels of complexity of likely input. Indeed the ground based-computer facilities necessary to an individual university's programme of manufacturing experimental instruments for satellites using the EGSE protocol are at present more than some universities can afford.

None the less, this protocol and amendments thereof do point the way that radio amateurs will need to go in respect of both their own satellite launches and those they undertake in partnership with others, eg the proposed amateur space telescope. Radio amateurs may not be able to afford the elegance, but that is no reason for rejecting the good sense underlying these developments in standardisation.

Computers in amateur radio satellites

The early Oscar and Radiosport satellites used simple radio command actuated systems. With the move to more complex orbits and greater distance from Earth, which began with the Phase III satellites, a much more sophisticated approach has been used, leap-frogging in some respects much of what has been done in the professional satellite sphere. Oscar 10 (Phase IIIB) was designed from the start to carry onboard microcomputing equipment. The project was led by DJ4ZC of Amsat Germany, and was built around the use of IPS, a language derived from Forth.

This has had several interesting consequences. Oscar 10 failed to achieve its designed 60 degree inclination molniya type orbit. It instead took up an orbit of about 28 degrees inclination, which consequently was subject to severe precession of the orbit, taking the satellite through the densest parts of the Van Allen belts twice a day for months at a time. The result of this was severe radiation damage to the onboard computer memory, and loss of flexible command of satellite functions and attitude. Despite this setback, Oscar 10 has enabled radio amateurs to learn the hard way the problems and methods of debugging damaged in-orbit software/hardware.

As a consequence of this, the next satellite in line, Oscar 13 (Phase IIIC), had its original onboard computer memory removed and replaced by memory chips of far better radiation hardness.

A quite different approach was used by the University of Surrey, when they built Uosat Oscar 9. This craft was designed from the start as a satellite platform for experiments, both internal and external. The two microcomputers were designed both as experimental tools and experiments themselves and have demonstrated their worth 10 times over. Uosat Oscar 9 used a nice combination of 'belt and braces' redundancy to ensure that all will not be lost if either of these experimental microcomputers fails. In addition the careful use of this flexible onboard computer power gave Uosat Oscar 9 control of a far wider range of experimental modes and formats than has been achieved elsewhere. A full description of the Uosat Oscar 9 computers appeared in *Radio and Electronic Engineer*, Vol 52, nos 8 and 9, August/September 1982.

As demonstrated by Uosat, amateur radio groups are in a unique position. They can build in to their satellites not only lots of useful facilities and flexibility, but also genuine forward-looking experiments.

Writing computer programs

Programs relating to space radio usually require at least a minimum of mathematical ability at sixth form, high school senior or university level. Original programs are generally only written by people who are mathematically trained to this standard. In addition, it helps to have a professional background in astronomy or terrestrial/space navigation.

There are two possible courses for the non-mathematicians:

(a) Build your own programs on top of original mathematical algorithms written by others.
(b) Use a combination of other people's programs and your own further studies of literature of the type shown below.

Thousands of radio amateurs regularly follow route (a). The RSGB book *Amateur Radio Software* by John Morris, GM4ANB, contains two full chapters of space-oriented software with copious illustrations and explanations. Old editions of radio amateur magazines back to 1977, eg *Radio Communication*, *QST*, *73*, *Practical Wireless* and *Orbit*, have lots of useful articles. In particular, the W3IWI article in *Orbit* No 6, March 1981, is a superb introduction to the complexities of orbit-tracking calculations, and the regular *Radio Communication* column was also highly informative, particularly in regard to the non-mathematical sections of programs.

For those who wish to follow route (b), delving rather more deeply into the mathematics, the following are recommended as containing whole sections explaining orbital mechanics, solar, lunar and planetary motions.The first two books in this list should be given priority:

- *Satellite Experimenter's Handbook* by Martin R Davidoff, K2UBC, ARRL, 1985, ISBN 0-87259-004-6. Available from RSGB
- *Astronomical Formulae for Calculators* by Meuss, Willman-Bell Inc, USA
- *Orbital Motions* by A E Roy, Adam Hilger
- *Spherical Astronomy* by Green, Cambridge University Press

The last two books on the above list should only be tackled by those with mathematical ability to undergraduate standard.

Please remember that almost all published software is copyright. Reproduction of these programs in whole or part without permission is illegal. In the case of some radio amateur programs, eg the W3IWI program mentioned above, permission is sometimes given for single private non-commercial copies to be made. This right should never be assumed. Always check with the author before you produce a copy of part or whole of his program. In practice few authors permit copying, even of single copies. Under no circumstances is any author likely to permit commercial sales of copies of his copyright work. Copyright law applies in most countries of the world, so please take care.

Space radio software distributors

In general, commercial suppliers stick to the larger non-space market. Almost all space-oriented software is produced by individual radio amateurs or amateur astronomers, who distribute their English language work through the suppliers given in appendix 1.

For a regularly updated review of all available amateur radio software, readers should consult the Media Network publications of Radio Hilversum.

Notes for would-be computer purchasers

1. There is no such thing as a special amateur radio/space listener microcomputer. Purchasers have to accept that they must try to find the most suitable of the available general-purpose microcomputers.
2. As in racing, there are horses for courses. Micros with poor keyboards are no good for RTTY, telemetry decoding, packet radio etc. Micros with limited memories cannot handle big satellite graphic maps. Some micros have very flexible central processors with direct calls from high-level language to machine code, but most modern micros lack these facilities and therefore require all kinds of add-ons, eg modems and so on, before they will handle problems like telemetry decode, packet radio, SSTV, wefax etc.
3. Less than one radio amateur in 300 can write original microcomputer software. Everyone else has to rely on these few individuals. So never buy a computer until you assure yourself that it has software of the type you require, already written for it. Computers without software are expensive door stops.
4. The biggest range of software is available for the biggest-selling microcomputers. Never buy a microcomputer which is likely to have only limited sales, because no one will write software for it.
5. Never believe what a microcomputer owner tells you about his machine. He will never admit that it is a dud.
6. Never wait for tomorrow's machine. It will be years before it has any software and it may turn out to be a flop.
7. If your present microcomputer works well, keep it. Even if you buy a new computer, keep the old one and its software.
8. Always check out for RFI any prospective microcomputer or ancillary such as a printer.
9. Buying new software every time a new satellite is launched is expensive. Most software will work for all similar (same inclination, same period/orbits per day) satellites. For example Uosat software is usually good for NOAA, CosNav, Landsat etc. Salyut software usually works well for Mir, shuttle and Fuji Oscar 12.
10. Up to 1986, most computers were far more flexible than the average user required. They would run programs which everyone wanted, but they would also allow writing, editing and machine code development of software which less than one person in a hundred needed. Since 1986 a growing number of microcomputer products have been describable as 'Will run IBM programs and can do nothing much else'. Few if any of these clones have good write, edit or machine code facilities. So if you want to learn as you use, writing the odd program yourself, you should avoid these 'also rans'. Conversely if you are one of the great majority who will never want to write anything, these cheap clones are made to order for you, provided you realise that you will not get software written directly on them, your software must come via the original microcomputer off which these follow-ons were cloned.
11. Be careful with your advice, when you have bought a computer and are tempted to write to every software author in sight telling him it is time he woke up and

started writing for your super-dooper XYZ. A moment's thought may produce a more mature viewpoint, whereby the fact that you need him to write programs for you automatically means he must know a lot more about computers than you do.

12. Last but not least, for the software authors. You must accept that 99.99% of radio amateurs will ignore the above suggestions, and having bought the glossiest electronic doorstop in sight, they will descend on you demanding that you write for their computer. Never refuse them. Simply point out your inability to afford one of every micro in sight, and suggest that if they care to buy another of these superb micros and donate it to you, you may perhaps write the odd program for it!

Chapter 11

Meteors, comets, moons and asteroids

Meteors and meteor scatter

The Earth and eight other known planets circle our Sun in nearly circular orbits. Over the last 20 years, space probes from Earth have visited seven of these planets and their families of moons, giving us our first close-up views of their surfaces. It came as a surprise to many people that the great majority of these planets and their satellites are almost totally covered in craters, giant holes which have been gouged out of their surfaces by enormous bombardment or volcanic activity.

Our own Moon and the planet Mercury show this cratering clearly, and the Apollo flights to the Moon have allowed geologists to date this bombardment quite accurately. Most of it took place when our solar system was very young, between 4,600 to 4,000 million years ago, as the planets and moons 'collected' the debris left from the formation of the solar system. By about 3,300 million years ago, the amount of debris left was small, but even today there is enough of it around to give a slight chance of a collision with something every 100 million years or so. Indeed, the expectation for the Earth and Moon is that they will be hit by a body of 10km diameter or more at least once every 30 million years or so.

This present-day minimal rate bombardment seems to derive some of its material from the asteroid belts, a region between Mars and Jupiter where large amounts of space debris continues to orbit the Sun. Only when perturbed by Jupiter or some other large body are members of this belt deflected into orbits coming nearer the Sun, so it is not surprising that this happens only rarely. By contrast, however, there are other bodies which come from much further out in space, and which pass the Earth regularly. It is these comets which initiate the meteor bombardment of Earth which is of interest to us here.

Comets and meteors – the connection

The Earth on its journey around the Sun continually encounters numerous small particles, themselves moving along somewhat different, usually more elliptical, orbits around the Sun. Where the orbits of the particle streams cross the Earth's track, many of them are captured by the Earth and plunge into its atmosphere at high speed. The result is usually a complete destruction of the particle, producing a short trail of ionised gas. We call these particles 'meteors' or 'shooting stars'. The few amongst them big enough to survive the fiery passage through the atmosphere and get down to the Earth's surface are called 'meteorites'.

The collective name we give these particles before they hit the Earth is 'meteoroids', and their origins have recently been demonstrated to be the comets which regularly orbit through the inner solar system.

In 1985/86 Comet Halley, the best-known comet of all, was back near the Sun on one of its 76-year periodic visits. That particular visit was noteworthy for two reasons. First, the comet was a poor visual spectacle, and second, Halley was the first comet ever to be subjected to really close scrutiny by spacecraft cameras. This first close look was indistinct, but it did establish quite clearly that the comet was surrounded by a cloud of dust. In fact some of this dust had enough energy to knock the Giotto space probe temporarily off course.

It is this connection between dust and comets which is important in the discussion which follows. The dust is present in enormous quantities and, given the thousands of comets which have come past the Earth in the last million years, it is no surprise that our Earth runs into it continuously. The last incandescent moments of this comet dust, as it plunges into the Earth's atmosphere, is such that even dust the size of sand grains will produce momentary ionised trails capable of propagating low VHF radio signals, thereby providing the extremely interesting and useful phenomenon we call 'meteor scatter propagation'.

The firm connection between comets and meteor streams has been postulated for a long time, but it is only recently that this connection has been demonstrated beyond doubt. The proof has come from the infra-red satellite IRAS built and operated by a British/Dutch/American scientific collaboration. IRAS produced actual infra-red images showing the dust trails of several comets stretching millions of kilometres.

The orbital connection with specific comets was proved and the spatial location was seen to agree with the Earth orbit crossing points of the meteor streams associated with these comets. In one case, a comet and its dust stream was tracked for 80 million kilometres and the dust stream was calculated to contain 20 million tons of dust.

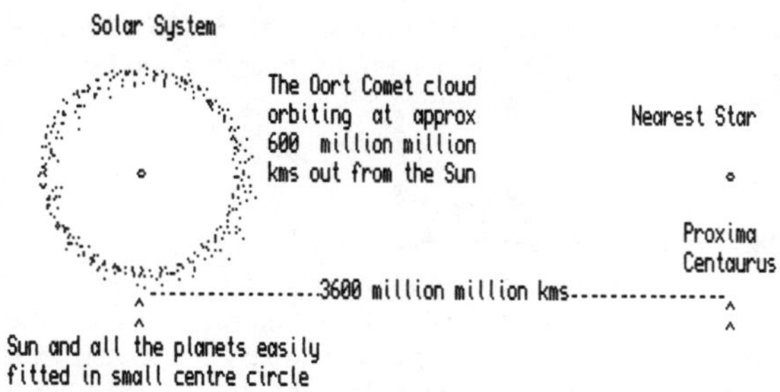

Fig 11.01: Representation of Oort Cloud and its position in relation to the Sun and Proxima Centauri

Cometary orbits

We can only make rough suggestions as to how the solar system comets were born. Theorists speculate that about a sixth of the way out from the Sun to the next nearest star, the comets orbit in their millions in what is called the 'Oort Cloud'. Fig 11.01 shows a representation of what the Oort Cloud might look like and its position in relation to the Sun and the nearest star Proxima Centauri.

In the Oort Cloud, the leftovers from the coldest outermost debris left from the dust and gas which formed our solar system have formed the dusty snowballs we call 'comets'. That cold icy material is relatively common, so far out from a star, was another of the surprises revealed by IRAS. Several of our near neighbour stars, including Fomalhaut, Vega, and Beta Pictoris, were found to have wide skirts on their IRAS images. When these features were checked by big optical telescopes, it was revealed that the infra-red returns orbiting these stars were clouds of dust, and in several cases much bigger chunks of material. To date nearly 40 nearby stars have been shown to have this orbiting cold matter.

In the case of our Sun and its comet cloud, the large separation between them means that the Sun's gravitational attraction on individual comets is very weak. The solar system must come close to other stars at intervals of perhaps

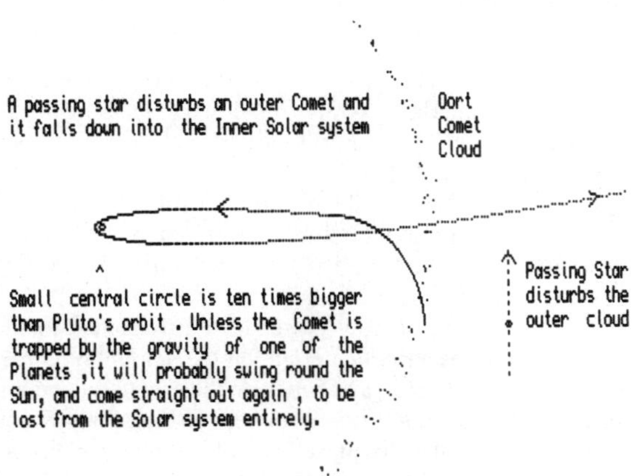

Fig 11.02: How comets fall towards the Sun

millions of years, and at these encounters some of the Oort Cloud comets may have their orbits seriously perturbed. Most will slowly drift away from the solar system, but a few will move slowly towards the inner planets. Fig 11.02 shows the path a disturbed Oort Cloud comet might follow.

It may take a million years for a comet to make its first journey in towards the Sun, and for most this will be the first and last visit to the inner solar system, for once it swings round the Sun it comes straight back out again and probably continues on, being entirely lost from the solar system thereafter.

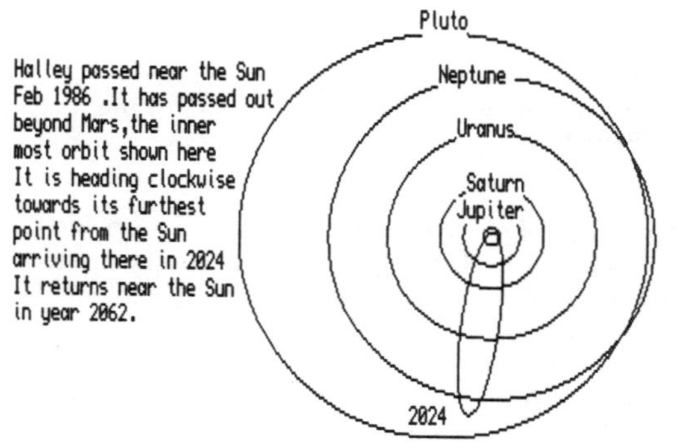

Fig 11.03: Orbit of Comet Halley in relation to orbits of the outer planets

A few comets, however, pass too close to one of the planets in the inner solar system. Perhaps this is what happened to Comet Halley about 10,000 years ago; maybe it passed too close to the planet Neptune, suffering such a change to its orbit that thereafter it was trapped in a relatively short-period 76-year orbit between Neptune and the Sun. Fig 11.03 shows the overhead view of Halley's orbit. It should be pointed out, however, that this view fails to show that the orbit actually goes far below the outer planets.

The same sort of capture scenario can be applied to virtually all the short-period comets, with Jupiter being the chief 'captor', with the result that many comets go no further out than Jupiter and therefore go round the Sun much more frequently than Comet Halley. Once captured, the life of a short-period comet inside Jupiter's orbit is short in terms of the age of the solar system. Every four years or so the short-period comet passes close to the Sun, suffering tremendous heating and losing millions of tons of its ice and dust. In consequence, gradually getting smaller, the short-period comet eventually disappears completely or perhaps leaves behind a burnt central core, as seems to have happened to the comet which gave birth to the Geminids meteor shower of December.

Comets and dust

The gradual boiling-off of the comet's ice and dust exterior has important consequences. The solar wind and radiation pressure modify whatever escape velocity the dust had from

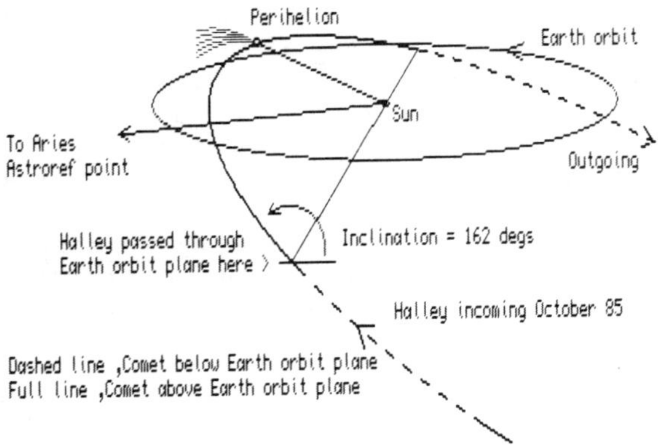

Fig 11.04: Comet Halley's nearest approach to Earth, October 1985 to April 1986

the comet, gradually, over several thousand years, slowing some material and speeding up other material with respect to the comet. All this material starts with the initially high orbital velocity of the comet and this is hardly modified at all, so the dusty material released by the Sun's heat can rarely escape from the comet's orbit, but it can spread until eventually it fills that orbit. Travelling with the comet's initial velocity of perhaps 100km/s, the dust can never really escape but in its spread around the orbit it is sometimes uneven, a situation which can change the character of the annual or biannual encounter of the Earth with its track. Eventually, as the comet's orbit becomes full of dust, the dust may even be sorted by size, with the smaller pieces on the outside of the track and the big pieces on the inside (the sunward) side.

Comet Halley dust

The cameras on the ESA Giotto spacecraft, which approached to within a few hundred kilometres of the comet, produced lots of evidence of the size and chemical composition of the dust particles being released by it. At this 1986 swing around the Sun, Halley did not pass anywhere near the Earth, so we did not experience any actual passage through the active regions near the comet. None the less, 1985 and 1986 were exciting because, as Fig 11.04 shows, the Earth passed near the comet's track in both October 1985 and in May 1986, giving rise to plenty of prior speculation as to whether the Earth would encounter a lot of cometary dust at these times.

Meteor showers and Comet Halley

Because of the proximity of Comet Halley to Earth in 1985 and 1986, there was a close watch on the regular meteor showers of May and October known to be associated with the comet. Fig 11.05 shows how the Earth's orbit comes close to the comet's track on 4 May and again on the 20 October each year. At these dates it must be reported that the meteor showers observed were not abnormal, except for the passage through the comet's track a little before its arrival on 4 and 5 May 1985, which produced a very good shower indeed.

Meteor showers

Most of the regular meteor showers occur every year at the same sidereal time and date, simply because the Earth in its orbit around the Sun crosses the same tracks at the same times each year. The two meteor showers associated with Comet Halley are encountered in early May when the Earth crosses a track which appears to come out of the sky from the region near the star Eta Aquarius, and therefore this shower is called the 'Aquarids'. As Fig 11.05 shows, this is actually the outgoing track of Comet Halley, and the associated incoming Halley track on the other side of the Earth's orbit produces a meteor shower which appears to come from the constellation of Orion and is therefore referred to as the 'Orionids', occurring around 20 October each year.

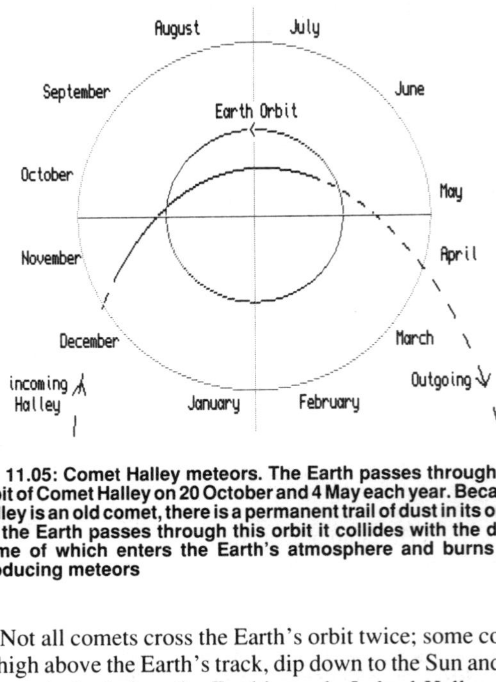

Fig 11.05: Comet Halley meteors. The Earth passes through the orbit of Comet Halley on 20 October and 4 May each year. Because Halley is an old comet, there is a permanent trail of dust in its orbit. As the Earth passes through this orbit it collides with the dust, some of which enters the Earth's atmosphere and burns up, producing meteors

Not all comets cross the Earth's orbit twice; some come in high above the Earth's track, dip down to the Sun and go out again far below the Earth's track. Indeed Halley is a famous comet simply because its track comes near the Earth and sometimes, but not always, gives a splendid performance as it goes around the Sun. Unfortunately 1986 was a return where it passed quite a long way from the Earth, so it was a relatively poor spectacle.

So this feature of how close the Earth comes to the comet's track has a marked effect on the amount of comet dust the Earth captures, and hence on the size of the meteor shower we see as shooting stars or hear on our radios. Some meteor showers, usually those from old comets such as the Geminids, are much the same year to year, because the dust is evenly spread around the comet's track. Other meteor showers, like the Draconids of 10 October, vary enormously from year to year, being best when the associated comet Giacobini Zinner is near the Earth. The famous Leonids shower of November is usually small, except that every 33 years it puts on a magnificent display.

So what we see as meteor showers is the product of comets formed in the early days of the solar system which fall in past the Sun, are captured by one of the big planets and thereafter are forced to go round the Sun in short-period orbits. Every time they pass the Sun, the heat boils off their icy dust mantle, releasing the dust to spread along the comet's track. Once or twice a year the Earth crosses that track and captures the dust. The dust is travelling at anything up to 100km/s relative to the Earth, and the enormous friction as it hits the atmosphere melts and totally destroys the dust grain, annihilating in less than a second a particle that had survived unharmed since the beginning of the solar system 4,500 million years ago.

Given a dust particle no bigger than a grain of sand, enough ionised plasma is produced from its millions of atoms to provide propagation for VHF radio signals for perhaps one second or two. How far the meteor penetrates the atmosphere before burning up depends on the angle at which it strikes the latter. Dust plunging straight in at high, near-vertical, incidence rapidly reaches the denser layers of the atmosphere and burns up, producing a short intense trail. By contrast, a meteor which hits the top of the atmosphere at a shallow angle heats up slowly, producing a long but very thin trail.

The bigger the dust grain, the longer and denser the trail it produces. Very small dust particles do not generate enough energy to be heated up to melting point, so they gradually slow up and come to rest in the atmosphere, perhaps taking several weeks to fall down to the Earth's surface. Big particles, particularly those which strike the atmosphere at a shallow angle, get very hot and lose a lot of their outer material, but they can survive to reach the Earth's surface. Falling quickly, they often make small impact craters, but these events are so rare as to make them of no value for VHF radio propagation.

Some meteor showers seem to travel much faster than others. The Leonids are very swift indeed, whereas the Geminids are extremely slow, often producing lazy slow-moving fireballs across the eastern winter sky, and giving good radio propagation. The diagrams in this chapter, from Fig 11.08 onwards, show a meteor shower calendar and report the characteristics of all the regular meteor showers.

Random meteors

It is now generally recognised that all meteors had their origin in comets, but in some cases the comet itself has disappeared, or the dust has been perturbed so far from its original orbits as to render its origins totally obscure. The result of this residue of old and forgotten comets is a steady slight infall of meteors every day of the year. This random streaming seems to be at its peak in June every year, when by coincidence the Earth passes through the orbital plane of

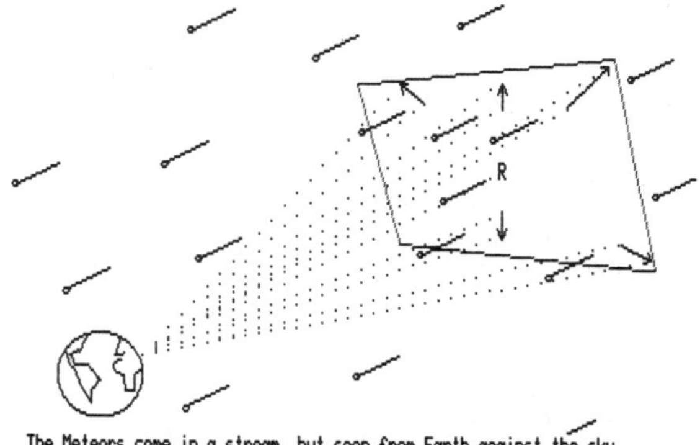

Fig 11.06: Meteor stream – radiant dispersal. The meteors come in a stream, but seen from Earth against the sky, perspective makes them appear to spread from a point radiant R

Jupiter around the Sun. This is probably no accident. Jupiter traps most of the short period comets and thereby constrains their motion in or near its own orbital plane in a fair proportion of cases. IRAS results have given us our first clear views of some of this dust. In addition to their activity peak in June, random meteors also have a daily peak at around 0600 local time. This is because the observer's station is at that time in a position of minimum relative velocity with respect to the random meteors, and hence more of them are captured over this 6am quadrant of the Earth. So 0600 local time is the best time to look for random meteor-scatter propagation.

Observing meteors by radio

The majority of meteors belong to showers. The calendar of Fig 11.08 gives details of when these showers can be expected and Fig 11.09 reports the particulars of individual showers. Much of this information is in astronomical terms which needs further explanation. First, the position the shower comes from in the sky, its so-called 'radiant', is given as right ascension and declination in degrees so that the point can be found on any astronomical chart. The meteor stream is in fact like a constant flow of traffic along a wide road, and you on the Earth are like a pedestrian trying to cross that traffic stream. As you cross, the cars/meteors seem to flash past you at every angle but, as you look away up the road they are coming from, the road and the meteor flow associated with it seem to come from a point, the distant 'radiant' of the meteor stream.

This radiant effect is important for meteor-scatter propagation because the radio antenna sees the ionised trails with the same perspective as the human eye sees the vehicles approaching along the road. Fig 11.06 shows this effect of perspective whereby the meteor trails all seem to come from the central radiant, some producing short points of light, others long visible trails.

A meteor coming straight at us appears as a point source

with no trail and that is how the radio antenna sees it, which is why pointing your antenna directly at the shower radiant is not good policy. By contrast, meteors well to one side or other of the radiant seem to produce long useful trails, and this is just how the radio antenna sees the situation and hence produces excellent meteor scatter results on bearings well away from the radiant. Indeed, it cannot be emphasised too often – do not point your antenna directly at the radiant; for best results aim off by at least 30 degrees of azimuth.

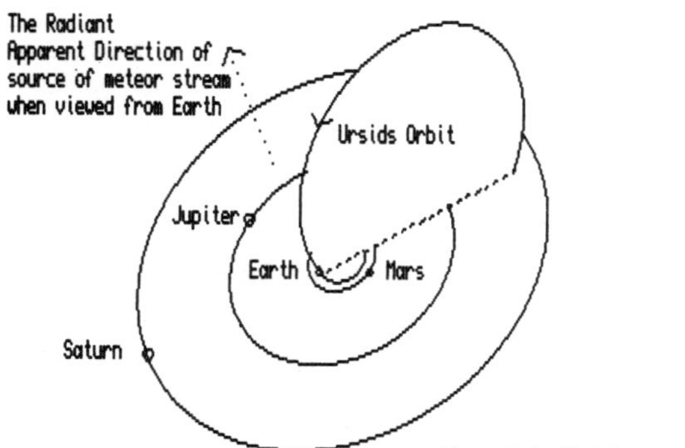

Fig 11.07: Ursids meteors orbit relative to Earth orbit plane

The second point of interest with regard to meteor radiants is shown in Fig 11.07 where the orbit of the Ursids meteor shower of December is shown relative to the Earth. We live on a rotating body (the Earth), so we turn with respect to the meteor shower radiant. If the meteor radiant is within 50 degrees of the pole star we will see the radiant all 24 hours of the day though it will circle our northern sky at one point directly high above us, then 12 hours later down on our northern horizon. This relative movement of the radiant across our sky is most important because it has considerable effect on the quality of the meteor-scatter propagation we get at different times of day (different locations of the radiant with respect to our station). If, as happens in many cases, the radiant is located more than 50 degrees away from the pole star, we will lose the radiant below the horizon for some part of the day. This again is vital information. Some important meteor showers have radiants with southerly declinations which means they only appear briefly above our southern horizons for a few hours each day.

The method used in this book uses graphics from a program by the author. For simplicity the ground station is assumed to be in central England. Fig 11.09vi shows a display for the two-hourly position of the radiant of the Eta Aquarids meteor shower of 4 and 5 May. On top of a map of the UK and western Europe, three circles of radiant elevation are placed around our English Midlands ground station. As the table of Eta Aquarid radiant position from the UK (printed by the side of the map) shows, the Eta Aquarid radiant is above the UK horizon only from just before 0400 UTC until just before 1200 UTC, its highest elevation being at about 0800 UTC when it is at 17 degrees of elevation, bearing a little west of south.

This low elevation is bad news for meteor scatter as will be explained later in this chapter. None the less, some results will undoubtedly be achieved between 0400 and 1200 UTC by pointing your antenna east, ie aiming about 45 degrees or more off the radiant. If, say, you wanted a Spanish contact, the best time would be just after 0400 UTC when you could aim south south west at about 60 degrees to the radiant. Thereafter the conditions towards Spain would get worse, but by contrast the best time for an Italian contact would be around 1000 UTC when you would be aiming well to the east of the radiant. Also hopefully clear from this map is that 0400 UTC would not be the time to make a schedule for tests with Italy. Fortunately the Eta Aquarids is a broad shower so it is likely to be at reasonable strength throughout its time above the UK horizon on perhaps both 4 and 5 May.

In complete contrast to the relatively lengthy Eta Aquarids, the shower shown in Fig 11.09i, the 3 or 4 January Quadrantids, is fast and furious. To use it properly you must know the sidereal time at which it is likely to peak (as discussed two paragraphs further on in this chapter), and you must concentrate your activity within two or three hours of that expected peak. Fortunately, as Fig 11.09i shows, the radiant stays above the UK horizon all 24 hours of the day, but again please remember that the azimuth bearings shown on Fig 11.09i cover 24 hours (because shower peak changes by roughly six hours per year), but you will only get the strong shower for, say, six hours, with the actual peak being over and done in an hour. Do not let this put you off; the Quadrantids is a magnificent shower but you must allow for the fact that, given a shower peak at 1900 UTC (as it was in 1986), at this time the radiant is low on the horizon, so the meteor trails you see or hear are poor. Four hours before shower peak, at 1500 UTC on 3 January 1986, the radiant was near its optimum elevation for a UK station, just below 40 degrees. This tendency for the shower peak to be poorly placed for the UK in some years has caused lots of misunderstanding.

The worst error which can occur when observing or communicating via meteor scatter is this failure to appreciate the effect of the changing position of the radiant. In a typical case an amateur astronomer reported counts of meteor pings observed from the Eta Aquarids whilst listening to a Polish FM transmitter. Each half-hour or so he tabled the number of separate times he had heard the signal, but unfortunately he made no allowance for the fact that the radiant started elevation 0 degrees, azimuth difference 40 degrees (rather poor), went through elevation 17 degrees and azimuth difference near 90 degrees (much better) at 0800 UTC, then went on to zero elevation and azimuth separation 60 degrees or so at 1200 UTC, again back to a poor situation. Given these changes, the fact that his count of meteor pings maximised between 0800 and 0900 UTC had little or nothing to do with the varying strength of the meteor shower, but an awful lot to do with the change in position of the radiant relative to the signal path. Please therefore be careful before embarking on this sort of exercise.

The Quadrantids meteor shower shown in Fig 11.09i is an extreme case. Its right ascension is 232 degrees and it declination is 52 degrees. This declination is important because it means that any station located at a northerly latitude above 28 degrees (ie 90 degrees – 52 degrees) can see the Quadrantids radiant all day. However, it also means that at 0800 UTC the radiant will be almost overhead, never a good position for meteor scatter (lots of short, intense pings and nothing else), then at 2000 UTC it is right down on the station northern horizon, which is bad news again. In between at 0200 and 1600 UTC the radiant is perfectly placed near 45 degrees elevation, and if the shower peak covers either of these times (it will not cover both), you should have the best meteor scatter of the year.

The meteor shower calendar

Fig 11.08 shows a calendar of meteor shower activity observable from the UK. The big showers, eg the Quadrantids, Perseids and Geminids, are printed in boxed capital letters. Less big, but still useful, showers, eg the April Lyrids and the Leonids, are shown in plain capitals. Moderate showers, eg the Orionids and the Lyrids of June, are shown with a capital first letter and the rest of the name in lower case. All the remaining small showers are printed in lower case.

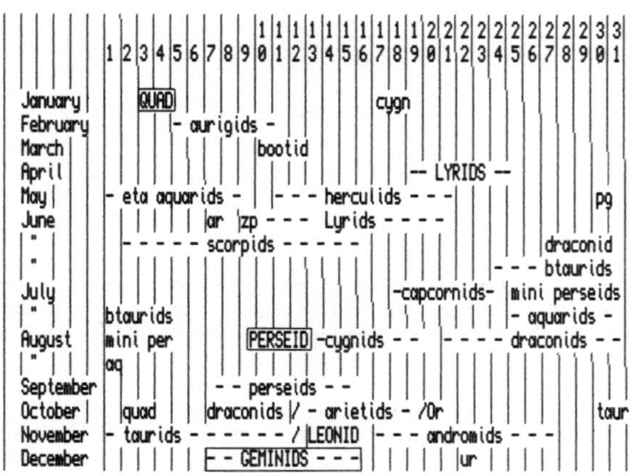

Fig 11.08: Meteor shower calendar

It is a good idea to check this calendar every day, eg if you look at the 7 June, the calendar reports two small showers, the Arietids and the Scorpids. To get further details of these showers, consult Figs 11.09i to xxx (over the page).

You should find the Scorpids on Fig 11.09ix and the Arietids on Fig 11.09x. The first thing of interest is that they do not conflict; the Scorpids are above the UK horizon from 2000 to 0200 UTC and the Arietids appear from 0200 to 1800 UTC. Neither shower is reported in glowing terms but the Scorpids may give contacts into Europe at their best around midnight and the Arietids are beautifully placed for Spain at 0600 or 1400 UTC with optimum radiant elevation. Europe to the east of the UK should be possible via any Arietids which appear around 1000 UTC when the azimuth difference is optimum and the elevation a little above its best position.

You should also note that, whilst the Arietids is a one-day only affair, the Scorpids stretch over 15 days and do not peak until 10 June. Being a mostly daylight shower, the Arietids have been poorly reported by visual observers, none the less they have performed quite well at times, albeit irregularly, as radio meteor-scatter sources.

Maximum effective meteor-scatter propagation

The geometry of meteor scatter requires that the meteor trail be tangential to an ellipse whose foci are the two stations communicating. This rather sweeping statement can be effectively summarised by saying that:

MS effectiveness = (Sin radiant el)*(Cos radiant el)*(Sin (azimuth difference between line to radiant and to other station))

or MS eff = Sin rad el * Cos rad el * Sin az dif

This equation maximises when radiant elevation angle is 45 degrees and azimuth difference to radiant and other station is 90 degrees.

Referring to Fig 11.09i, the maximum effectiveness of the Quadrantids is at 0400 when the most effective bearing for a communication path is 60 + 90 = 150 degrees azimuth = UK to Italy.

At 1400 the Quadrantids radiant is 304 az, 44 el, near maximum effectiveness on azimuth 304 – 90 = 214 = UK to Spain.

Meteor shower activity peaks

In addition to attempting to schedule your operations for times of maximum effective meteor scatter, it is also essential to appreciate that some powerful showers such as the Quadrantids only last for nine hours at most, with useful levels of possible activity being the middle six hours out of this nine-hour stretch. This adds a nasty complication for would-be users of meteor-scatter propagation, because the timing of shower peaks relates to a radiant in the sky, and locations in the sky keep sidereal (star) time and not UTC.

Sidereal time has no direct connection with solar mean time (the time we use on our clocks), and sidereal time does not have leap years. So to keep in step with the timings of meteor shower peaks, it is necessary to allow for the difference between the two time series. Table 11.01 shows how this affects the Quadrantids. The Quadrantids shower lasts only nine hours, so with the roughly six-hour per year stepping of sidereal time (no leap years), with solar mean

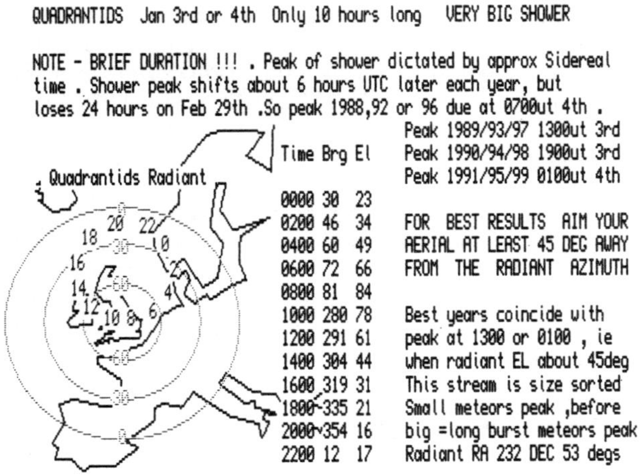

i

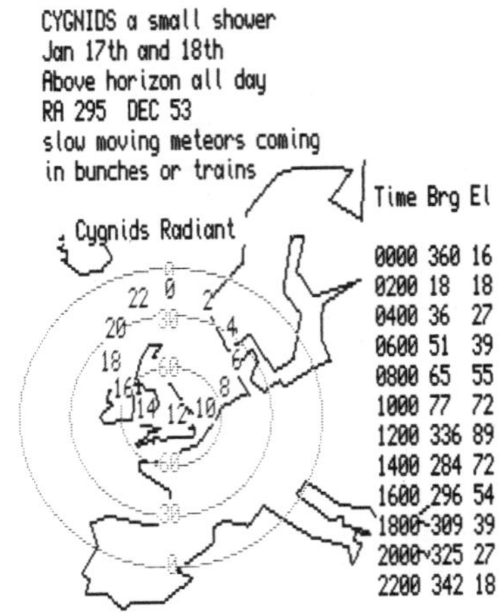

ii

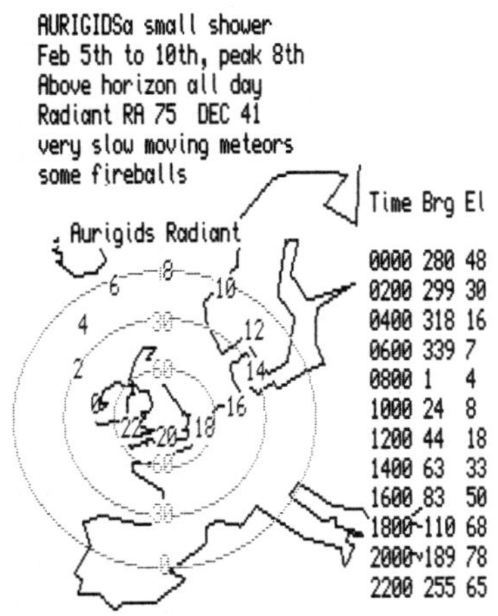

iii

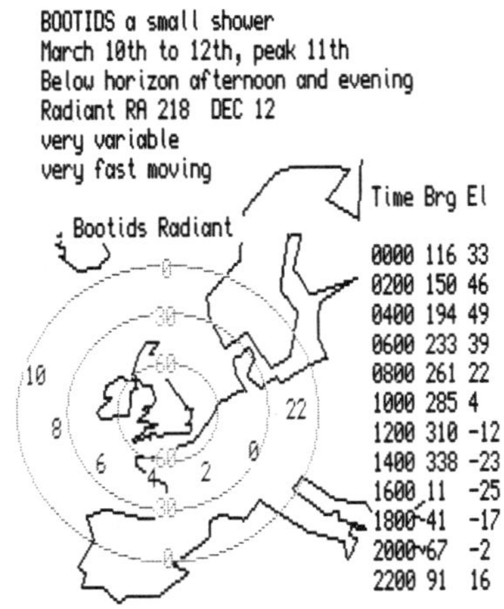

iv

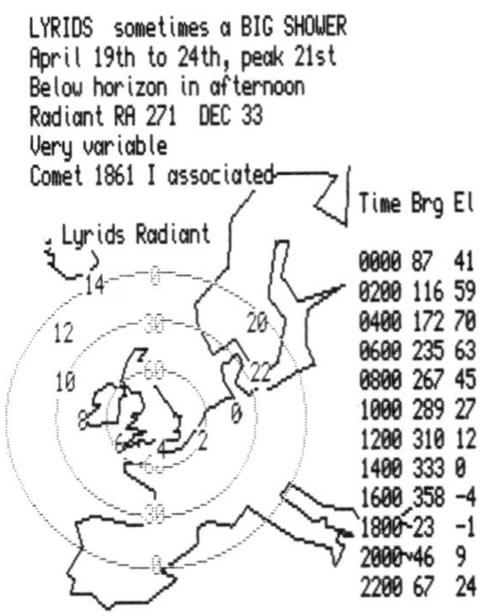

v

Fig 11.09i-xxx: Meteor shower data sheets. On the following pages data for the major meteor showers is given. They are arranged in date order, beginning with the first shower of the year (the January Quadrantids) and ending with December's Ursids. The circles superimposed on the map of western Europe show the angle of radiant elevation. Superimposed on top of this is a circle of times showing, at two-hour intervals, the position of the shower radiant

Table 11.01: Timings of Quadrantids shower peak

Year	Date	UTC time of peak
1988	4 January	0700
1989	3 January	1300 (1988 leap year, go back 1 day)
1990	3 January	1900
1991	4 January	0100
1992	4 January	0700
1993	3 January	1300 (1992 leap year, go back 1 day)
1994	3 January	1900

time (leap year roughly every fourth year) we get the timings shown in the table. Please note this time sequence is not very accurate, but this does not matter because changes in the Earth's orbit with respect to the meteor stream can also change these timings by an hour or so, and the changes are much more difficult to predict. So use this as a rough guide.

It is important to realise that if you apply this dating scheme to a meteor shower which occurs on or after 1 March, you make the jump back of one day in the leap year, not in the year after.

Irregular meteor showers

In the real world, no meteor shower behaves the same from one year to the next. Sometimes the Earth passes near the

AQUARIDS usually a small shower
May 1st to 8th, peak 4th
Above horizon only in morning
Radiant RA 334 DEC -2
Sometimes BIG when Comet
Halley is near Earth

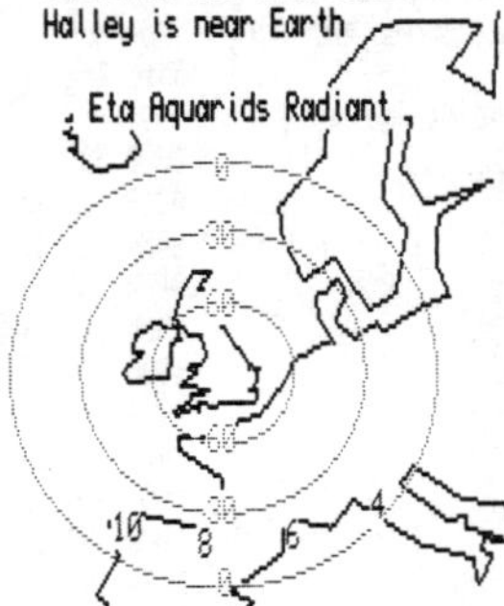

Time	Brg	El
0000	84	-30
0200	107	-12
0400	131	4
0600	157	15
0800	187	17
1000	215	11
1200	240	-3
1400	263	-20
1600	288	-38
1800	323	-53
2000	12	-57
2200	56	-47

vi

HERCULIDS a small shower
May 11th to 21st, peak 17th
Below horizon in afternoon
Radiant RA 247 DEC 28
swift moving

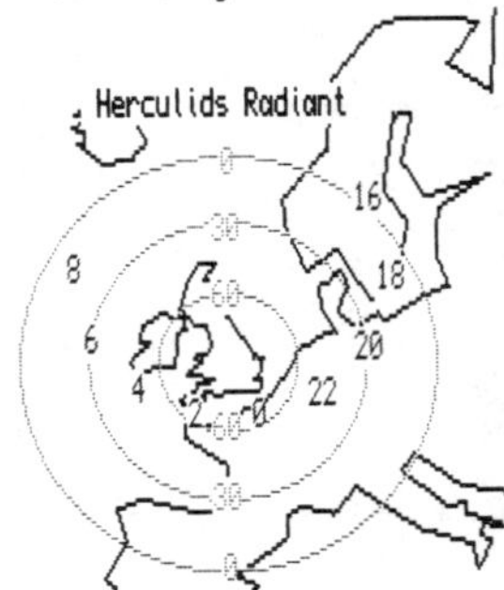

Time	Brg	El
0000	152	63
0200	213	63
0400	253	48
0600	278	30
0800	300	13
1000	323	-1
1200	348	-9
1400	15	-8
1600	40	0
1800	63	15
2000	85	32
2200	111	50

vii

PEGASIDS a small shower
May 30th
Below horizon in evenings
Radiant RA 333 DEC 27
very swift moving

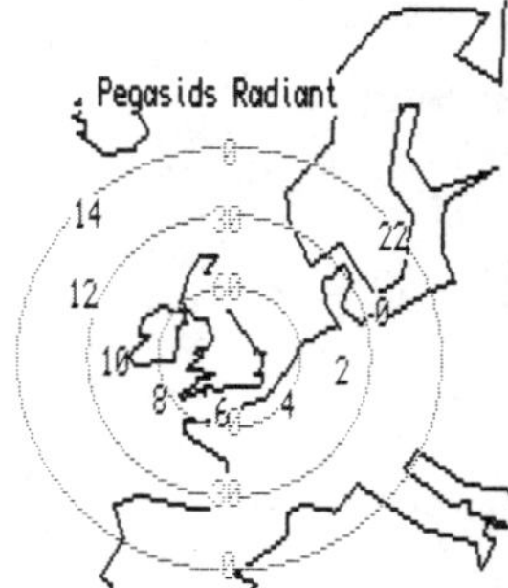

Time	Brg	El
0000	75	23
0200	98	41
0400	131	58
0600	187	64
0800	237	54
1000	267	37
1200	290	19
1400	312	3
1600	336	-7
1800	3	-10
2000	30	-5
2200	54	7

viii

SCORPIDS A small shower
2nd June to 17th June, peak 10th June
Not in daylight
Radiant RA 253 DEC -22
Very slow, some fireballs

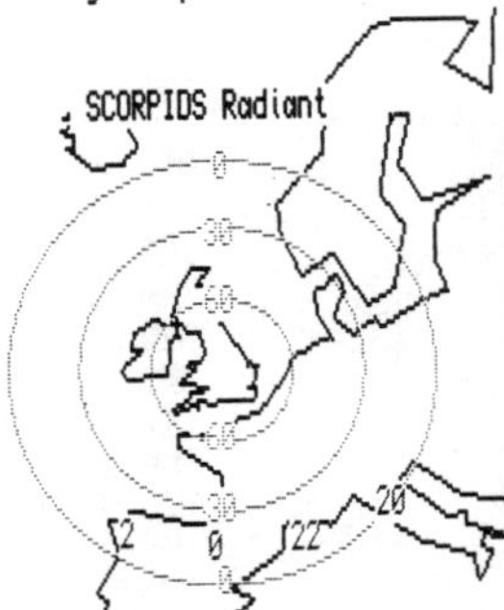

Time	Brg	El
0000	184	15
0200	212	10
0400	237	-3
0600	259	-20
0800	284	-38
1000	317	-54
1200	8	-59
1400	54	-50
1600	84	-33
1800	107	-15
2000	130	1
2200	156	12

ix

ARIETIDS a small shower
June 7th
Below horizon in evening
Radiant RA 45 DEC 23
Poorly reported shower

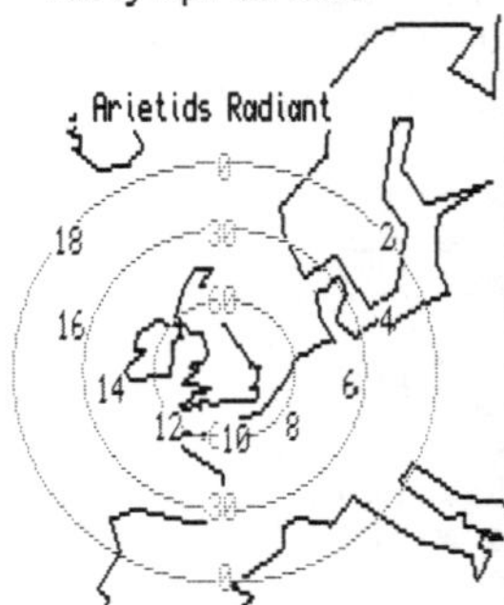

Time	Brg	El
0000	27	-10
0200	52	1
0400	75	17
0600	98	36
0800	130	52
1000	179	60
1200	229	53
1400	260	37
1600	284	18
1800	307	2
2000	332	-10
2200	360	-14

x

Z PERSEIDS a small shower
June 9th
Below horizon at night
Radiant RA 62 DEC 24
A classic daylight Radio Shower

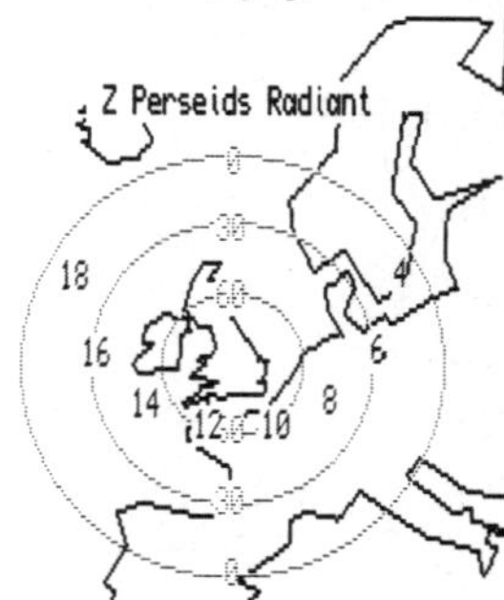

Time	Brg	El
0000	13	-13
0200	39	-4
0400	63	10
0600	85	27
0800	111	45
1000	151	59
1200	206	59
1400	247	46
1600	273	28
1800	296	11
2000	319	-4
2200	346	-12

xi

JUNE LYRID a small shower
June 10th to 21st , peak 16th
Below horizon in afternoon
Radiant RA 275 DEC 32
A shower with no obvious peak

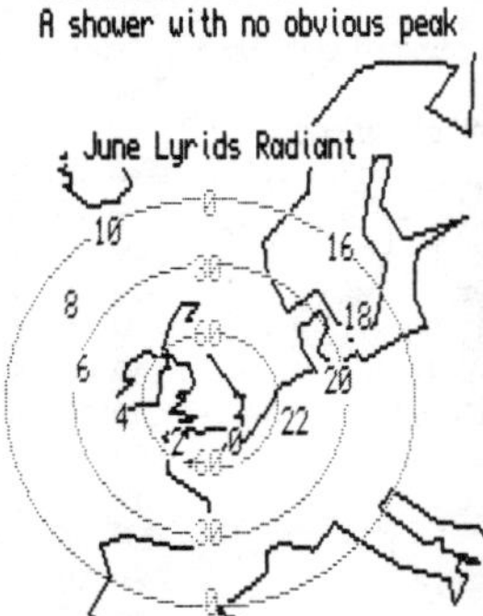

Time	Brg	El
0000	152	68
0200	219	66
0400	258	50
0600	282	32
0800	303	15
1000	326	2
1200	350	-5
1400	15	-4
1600	39	4
1800	61	18
2000	82	36
2200	108	54

xii

B TAURIDS A small shower
24th June to 4th July, peak 29th June
Daylight only
Radiant RA 87 DEC 23
Associated Comet Encke

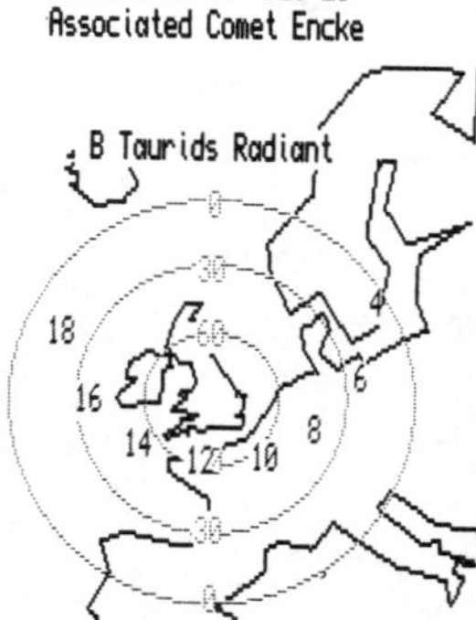

Time	Brg	El
0000	8	-14
0200	35	-7
0400	60	6
0600	82	23
0800	107	41
1000	143	56
1200	197	60
1400	240	48
1600	269	31
1800	291	13
2000	315	-3
2200	341	-12

xiii

June DRACONIDS A small shower
27th June to 30th June, peak 28th June
All day
Radiant RA 228 DEC 57
Associated Comet Pons Winnecke

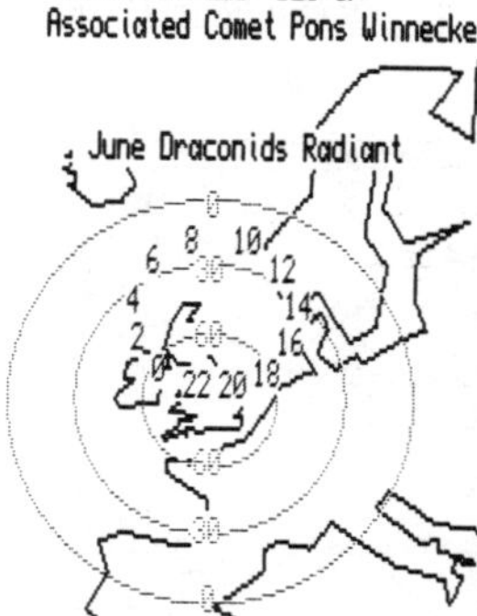

Time	Brg	El
0000	298	63
0200	308	48
0400	321	35
0600	336	25
0800	352	20
1000	10	20
1200	26	26
1400	41	36
1600	54	50
1800	62	65
2000	53	81
2200	301	79

xiv

CAPRICORNIDS a triple shower
July 18th to 30th July , 3 peaks
Evenings only
Radiant RA 304 DEC -12
Very Slow moving ,and bright
Possible product of several comets

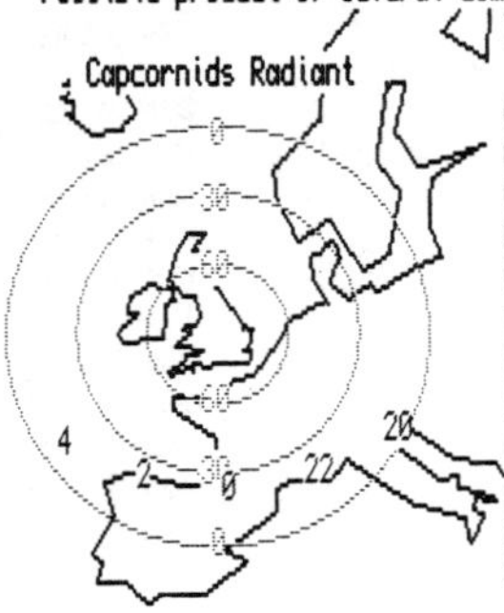

Time	Brg	El
0000	176	25
0200	208	22
0400	236	9
0600	260	-7
0800	284	-26
1000	314	-41
1200	355	-49
1400	38	-44
1600	70	-29
1800	95	-11
2000	119	6
2200	146	20

xv

D AQUARIDS A small shower
25th July to 1st August, peak 28th July
Not in daylight
Radiant RA 339 DEC -17
Slow moving, long trails

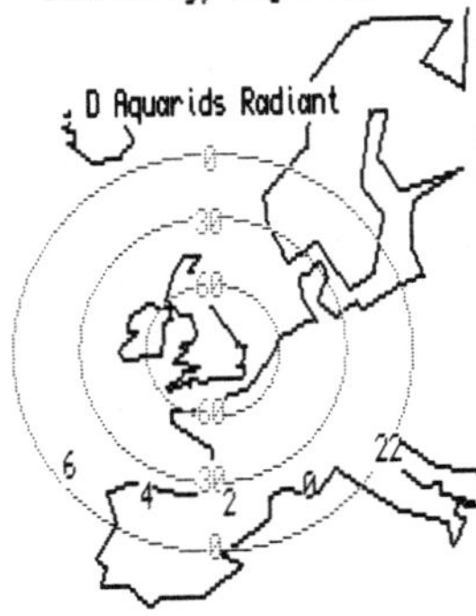

Time	Brg	El
0000	146	14
0200	175	20
0400	205	17
0600	232	6
0800	256	-11
1000	280	-29
1200	310	-45
1400	353	-54
1600	39	-49
1800	73	-34
2000	97	-16
2200	121	1

xvi

Mini PERSEIDS small preview of big Perseids
July 25th to 4th August , peak 30th
All day
Radiant RA 48 DEC 43
Very Slow moving ,has been quite
intense some years 30th July + 2nd Aug

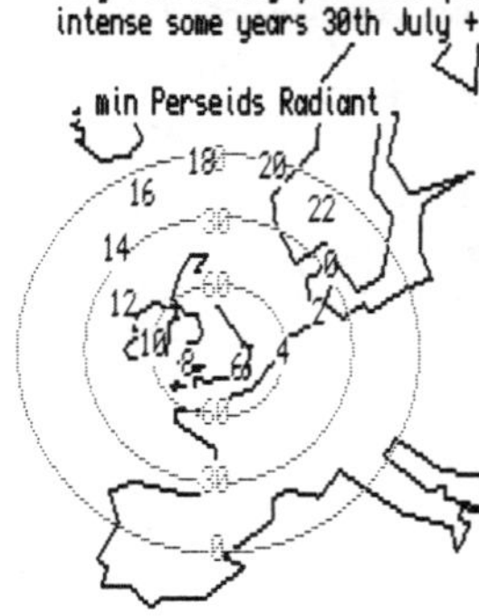

Time	Brg	El
0000	53	27
0200	71	43
0400	92	61
0600	136	78
0800	240	74
1000	273	57
1200	293	39
1400	311	23
1600	330	12
1800	352	6
2000	14	7
2200	35	14

xvii

PERSEIDS Aug 10th to 12th, peak on 11/12th Above horizon all day

NOTE - This is a regular shower which was good up to 1981, since then it has behaved very oddly . Associated Comet uncertain . The 24 hour aspect allows contacts to be scheduled for time of optimum elevation and azimuth

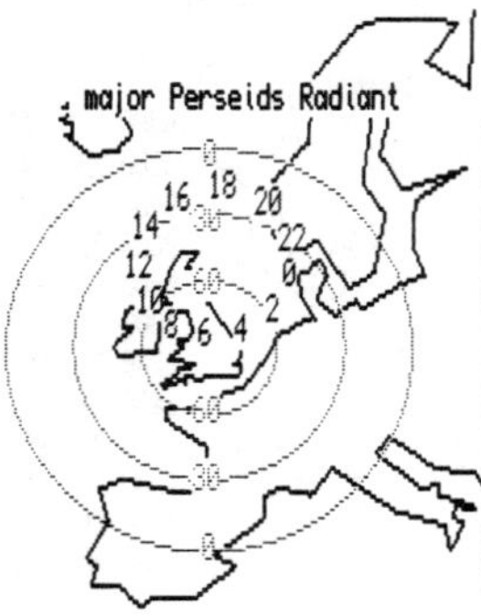

Time	Brg	El
0000	48	43
0200	59	58
0400	63	74
0600	339	85
0800	297	70
1000	303	55
1200	315	40
1400	329	29
1600	345	22
1800	2	20
2000	19	23
2200	35	31

Comet Swift-Tuttle, possibly associated has'nt reappeared so future is uncertain .

FOR BEST RESULTS AIM YOUR AERIAL AT LEAST 45 DEG AWAY FROM THE RADIANT AZIMUTH

Keglers comet due 1992, may be true progenitor , if so shower may improve late 80s This stream can have 15 min breaks with zero activity even at shower maximum . Radiant RA 45 DEC 57 degs

xviii

K·CYGNIDS small shower
August 13th to 20th , peak 15th
All day
Radiant RA 290 DEC 54
Slow moving

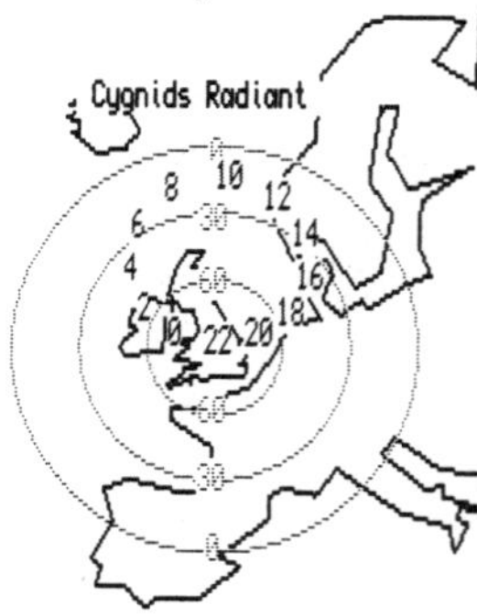

Time	Brg	El
0000	287	71
0200	298	54
0400	311	39
0600	326	27
0800	343	19
1000	1	17
1200	20	20
1400	36	28
1600	51	41
1800	64	57
2000	74	74
2200	313	88

xix

O and Z DRACONIDS small double shower
August 21st to 31st , peaks 22nd + 26th
All day
Radiant RA 291 DEC 60 , RA 263 DEC 62
Slow moving

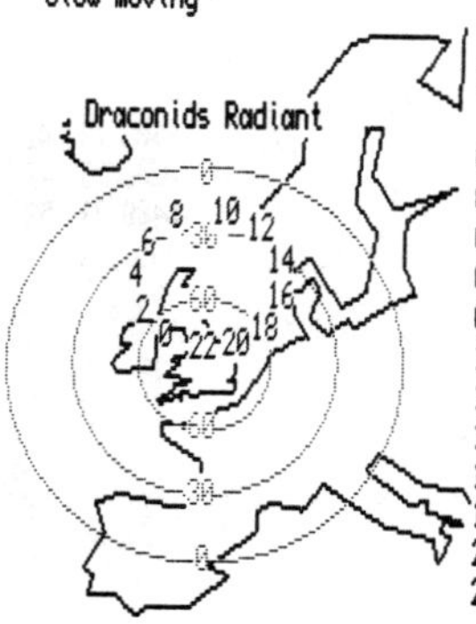

Time	Brg	El
0000	305	68
0200	309	53
0400	320	40
0600	333	30
0800	348	24
1000	4	23
1200	20	27
1400	35	35
1600	47	47
1800	54	61
2000	49	76
2200	331	81

xx

E PERSEIDS a small shower
September 7th to 15th , peak 11th
All day
Radiant RA 61 DEC 35
Fast moving

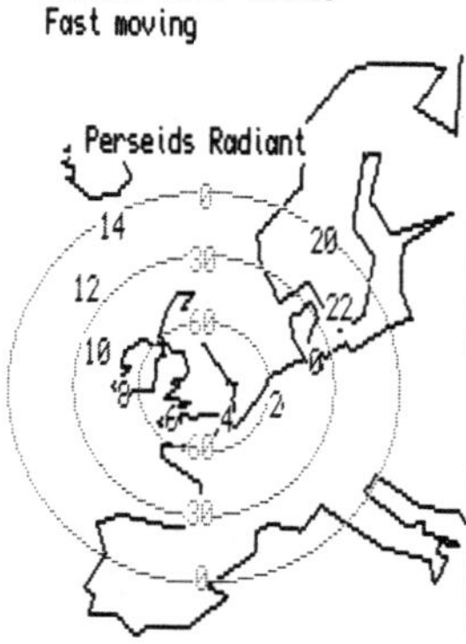

Time	Brg	El
0000	79	37
0200	103	55
0400	148	70
0600	223	68
0800	262	52
1000	285	34
1200	305	18
1400	327	5
1600	350	-2
1800	15	-1
2000	38	7
2200	59	21

xxi

October QUADRANTIDS ,a small shower
October 2nd
All day
Radiant RA 230 DEC 52
Slow moving
Very poor compared with January shower

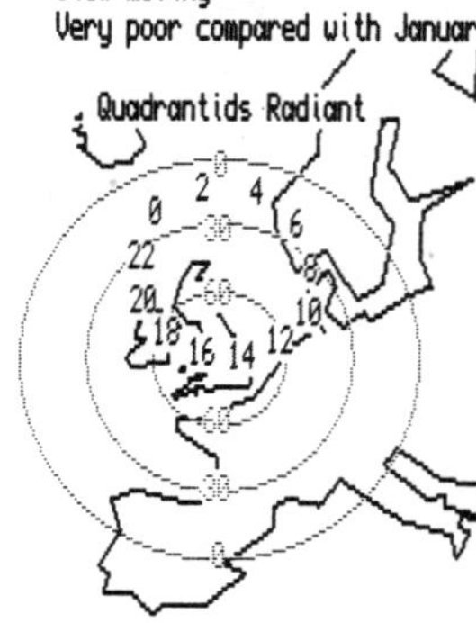

Time	Brg	El
0000	335	20
0200	353	15
0400	12	16
0600	30	22
0800	47	34
1000	61	49
1200	75	66
1400	90	84
1600	276	78
1800	289	60
2000	303	44
2200	318	30

xxii

DRACONID/GIACOBINIDS Variable
7th to 11th October, peak 8th + 10th Oct
All day
Radiant RA 262 DEC 54
Associated Comet Giacobini Zinner
Very good when Comet GZ is near Earth

Time	Brg	El
0000	321	30
0200	338	21
0400	356	17
0600	14	18
0800	31	25
1000	47	37
1200	60	52
1400	71	68
1600	66	86
1800	286	76
2000	295	58
2200	307	43

xxiii

ORIONIDS a very variable shower
October 18th to 20th , peak 20th
Not afternoons
Radiant RA 92 DEC 15
Earth usually misses path of associated
Comet Halley by a wide margin

Time	Brg	El
0000	101	27
0200	130	43
0400	172	52
0600	217	48
0800	251	33
1000	276	15
1200	299	-3
1400	325	-16
1600	355	-22
1800	26	-19
2000	54	-7
2200	78	9

xxiv

E ARIETIDS a small shower
October 12th to 19th , peak 18th
Early morning,evening and night
Radiant RA 42 DEC 21
Slow moving, some fireballs

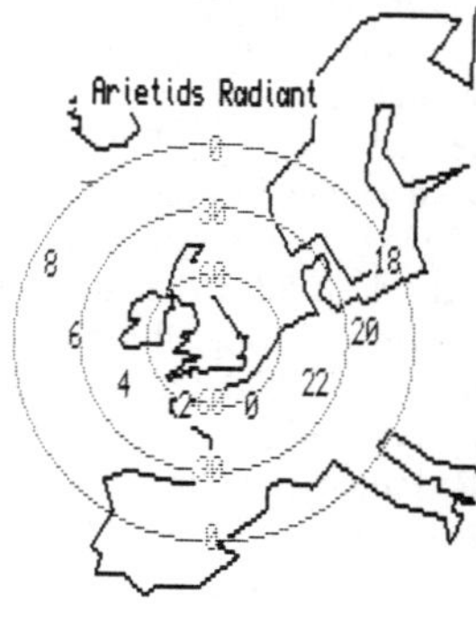

Time	Brg	El
0000	151	56
0200	203	57
0400	243	44
0600	270	27
0800	293	9
1000	317	-6
1200	344	-15
1400	13	-16
1600	40	-7
1800	65	7
2000	87	25
2200	114	43

xxv

E TAURIDS a small shower
October 30th to 12th November , peak 8th
Not in daylight
Radiant RA 64 DEC 22
Associated Comet Encke

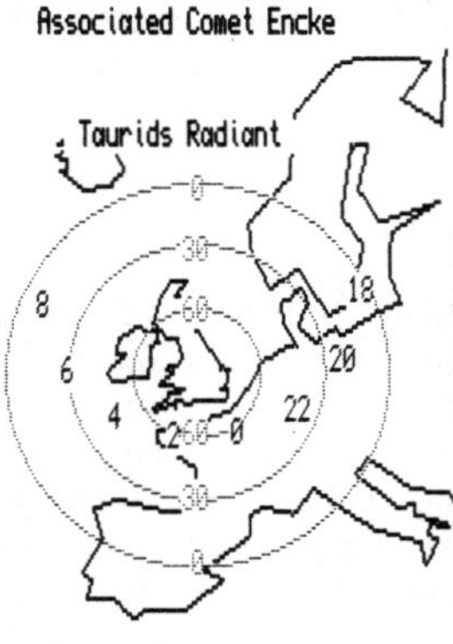

Time	Brg	El
0000	148	56
0200	201	58
0400	243	46
0600	270	28
0800	293	10
1000	316	-5
1200	343	-14
1400	12	-15
1600	39	-7
1800	63	7
2000	86	25
2200	112	43

xxvi

LEONIDS A 33 year super shower
13th to 15th November , peak 14th
Not in evening
Radiant RA 150 DEC 22
Associated Comet 1866 I
Next super shower 1998 or 1999

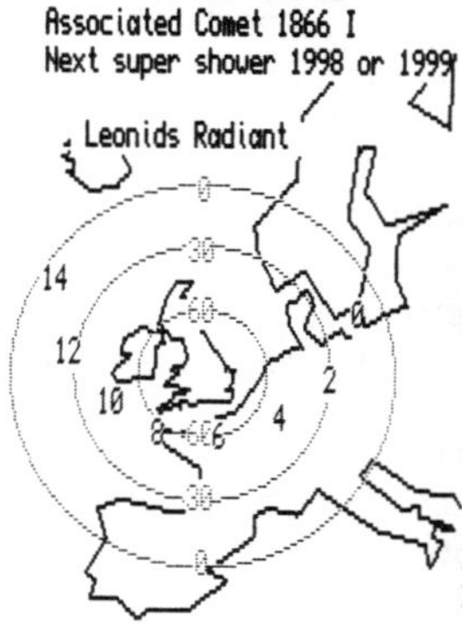

Time	Brg	El
0000	70	12
0200	93	30
0400	121	48
0600	165	59
0800	217	55
1000	253	40
1200	278	22
1400	300	5
1600	325	-9
1800	353	-15
2000	21	-13
2200	47	-3

xxvii

ANDROMIDS A very small shower
17th to 27th November , peak 22nd
All day shower
Radiant RA 25 DEC 43
Associated Comet Biela
Has been poor since 1980

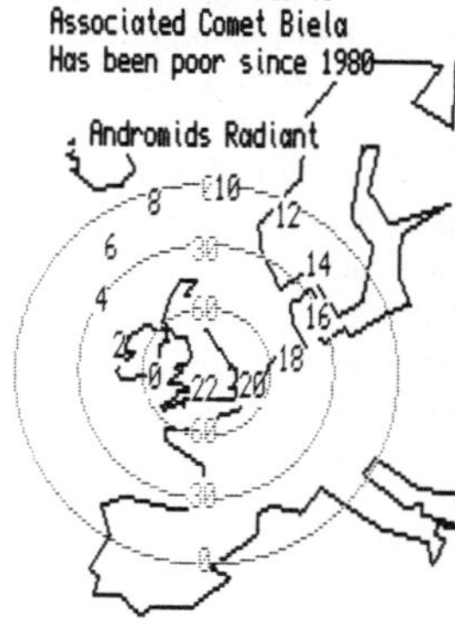

Time	Brg	El
0000	261	65
0200	284	47
0400	302	30
0600	321	17
0800	342	8
1000	4	6
1200	25	10
1400	45	21
1600	63	35
1800	82	53
2000	110	71
2200	203	80

xxviii

GEMINIDS Dec 3rd to 15th peak on 11/12th Below horizon in afternoon

NOTE - This is a regular shower which builds up gradually , to be at its best on the nights of the 12th, 13th and 14th . The all night aspect allows contacts to be scheduled for time of optimum elevation and azimuth

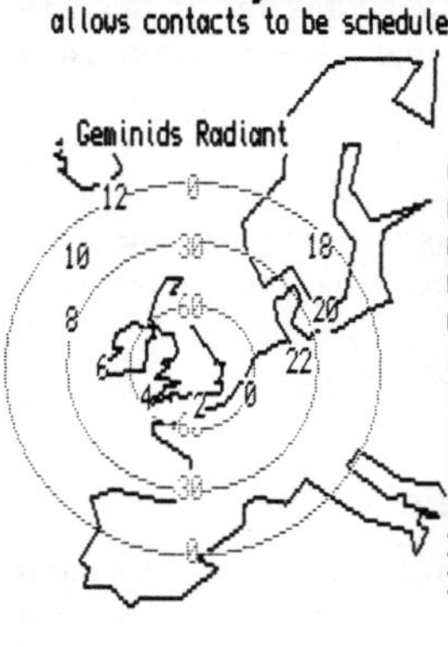

Time	Brg	El
0000	115	59
0200	171	70
0400	235	63
0600	267	46
0800	289	28
1000	310	12
1200	333	0
1400	357	-4
1600	22	-1
1800	45	9
2000	66	24
2200	88	42

Associated Comet now only a dead asteroid . So little annual shower size variation

FOR BEST RESULTS AIM YOUR AERIAL AT LEAST 45 DEG AWAY FROM THE RADIANT AZIMUTH

Geminid meteors often slow with some good fire balls giving long radio bursts This stream is size sorted Small meteors peak , before big long burst meteors peak Radiant RA 112 DEC 33 degs

xxix

URSIDS A small shower
22nd December
All day
Radiant RA 226 DEC 76
Associated Comet Tuttle 1939X
Radiant circles around the Pole Star

Time	Brg	El
0000	13	41
0200	20	47
0400	23	53
0600	21	61
0800	10	66
1000	352	66
1200	340	61
1400	337	54
1600	340	47
1800	346	42
2000	355	39
2200	4	39

xxx

centre of the meteor stream, sometimes it does not. In addition some parts of the meteor stream may be thinly dusted, whilst other parts are thick with dust. Some of this sorting of material may be predictable, because it appears in some cases to be caused by solar radiation pressure which pushes the smaller pieces of dust to the side of the track furthest from the Sun, leaving the larger pieces on the side of the track nearest the Sun. If the Earth goes right through the track from inside to outside, observers see this as a shower in which the big pings peak first, to be followed by a subsidiary peak of lots of smaller, shorter pings. Sometimes the Earth goes through the track off its centre, producing a meteor shower which features only big pings one year, and maybe only small pings the next year (this is often the case with the January Quadrantids).

A lot of evidence has been gathered in recent years regarding those showers which seem to go for years doing nothing, then suddenly produce a magnificent shower before returning next year to almost nothing. Donald Yeomans of Nasa's Jet Propulsion Laboratory in California has made a particular study of the Leonids shower of November. Every year there are a few Leonid meteors around 14 November, but records exist from 1833, showing that every 33 years since then, except for 1933, the Leonids have produced a super shower, much bigger than anything we normally see or hear. The last big Leonids in 1966 was a big shower, and the next is due in 1998 or 1999.

Yeoman's evidence suggests that the Leonids are at their best for six years either side of the year in which their associated parent comet, Comet Temple Tuttle, comes nearest to the Sun. The absolute peaks every 33 years seem to occur when the Earth's orbit takes it through the side of the meteor stream outside from the Sun, and behind the comet.

Recent evidence in regard to another irregular shower, the Draconids of 7 to 11 October, suggests that this usually weak shower is enhanced when the parent, Comet Giacobini Zinner, comes closest to the Sun. Up to October 1985 the Draconids were very rare but, as Giacobini Zinner approached the Sun, the shower produced an excellent display, which suggested that it may now be two separate streams, one of which peaks on the 8th and the other which peaks on 10 October. This double track is not really surprising, as in the early part of this century Giacobini Zinner went rather close to the planet Jupiter and suffered a distinct change in its orbit in consequence. This seems to have caused it to follow a new track, laying down a new dust trail. The old, pre-perturbation dust trail is still there, so we may now get two meteor showers from this comet.

Asteroidal meteors and fireballs

Examination of photographs and spectra of the rare meteors and fireballs big enough to survive in part, and hit the Earth's surface, suggests that these bodies are not of cometary origin and are quite unconnected with the familiar regular meteor showers.

The origin of the majority of the large stone and iron meteorites which reach the surface of the Earth is thought to be the asteroids which orbit the Sun in a belt between Mars and Jupiter. Perturbation by Jupiter and occasional collisions amongst the thousands of minor bodies in this zone results in some of them falling inwards towards the Sun.

In addition to the asteroid belt there are other sources of big meteorites on both the Moon and Mars. Recent examination of meteorites collected from the 'cold storage' of the Antarctic and Greenland icecaps shows good evidence for a small number of meteorites being of lunar origin, and an even smaller number being of martian origin. It is quite possible that these meteorites were catapulted into space by the impact of large meteoroids and perhaps asteroids with the Moon and Mars. Indeed, Mars' moons Phobos and Deimos are probably captured asteroids. Neither of these small bodies is in a completely stable orbit; both will collide with Mars in the next million years or so. The martian surface already has relatively recent cratering which, far from being unusual, has been the pattern for many millions of years.

Unfortunately, neither the large exotic asteroidal meteorites or the lunar or martian meteorites have any regular predictable effect on space radio. So they can be discounted for the purposes of this discussion of meteor-scatter propagation.

Meteor-scatter operating

The preceding paragraphs have shown how a would-be operator can use the meteor shower calendar, together with the reports of individual meteor showers, to prepare for a session of meteor-scatter communication. Advanced preparation can be tailored to preparing charts of times of likely maximum effectiveness on particular paths to particular distant stations. This planning can then be used as a basis for arranging schedules of operating with individual meteor-scatter (MS) operators via the HF meteor-scatter liaison nets.

Most MS operators prepare schedules of effectiveness and operating times for each major shower, and they go on to book particular time slots with distant operators some days or weeks before the shower event is due. In this way they have the clear knowledge that someone is probably listening at the other end of the path.

The actual operating periods themselves are usually planned to start on a given hour UTC, on a given frequency. Noting that at shower peaks designated meteor-scatter frequencies get crowded out, protocols have arisen whereby stations schedule contact tests on specific frequencies some way off the designated MS calling frequencies.

Preparing an MS schedule

To prepare a schedule for a prearranged MS test, the would-be operator must go on an MS liaison net, eg 14.340MHz at 1400 UTC on Saturdays. Having accessed the net, contact schedules can be arranged with other stations. The information which needs to be exchanged on this net is:

(a) Frequency
(b) Mode and speed of transmission
(c) Start time
(d) End time
(e) Who transmits first
(f) Duration of individual transmit periods
(g) Any special report codes

Transmit periods vary depending on likely shower conditions and operator preference. Periods of half a minute, one minute and five minutes duration are equally popular. Scheduled termination of an incomplete contact is usually set at one or two hours.

Meteor-scatter operating formats

A typical MS contact consists of:

1. Station A sends your call, his call, repeated for whole transmission. Station B listens.
2. Station B sends your call, his call, repeated for whole transmission. A listens.
3. If nothing is heard, opening procedure is repeated.
4. If both calls heard, recipient (eg Station A) changes. Station A sends your call, his call, plus report ... repeated
5. When B hears both calls from A he sends a similar report as above back to A.
6. If A hears report from B he acknowledges by repeating rr [report] rr [report] etc for his transmission period. If B hears A he uses a similar acknowledgement.
7. When either hears the rr report from the other he replies with rrr rrr rrr
8. Receipt of rrr at both ends signifies 'contact successful'.

Typical MS station facilities

The success of meteor-scatter communications depends to some extent on the sophistication of the operating procedure and station hardware. Military systems used to communicate between missile sites and their central command in the 'peak effectiveness' frequency band around 50MHz. The missile site receiver listens for an MS reception on the command beacon frequency. On receipt of the start of that reception it automatically transmits back along the same path on an adjacent frequency channel. The transmission is by high-speed telemetry on a 1kW transmitter feeding a 6dB Yagi beam antenna. Message transfer speeds are 400 words per minute or more, in order to make effective use of really short-duration meteor pings. Given these high speeds of transmission, plus use of optimum frequency and plenty of power, the delay time before a message is passed and received can be down to five or seven seconds, even at times when only random MS is anticipated.

Radio amateurs cannot always deploy techniques as sophisticated as this, and in addition they use lower power and generally tend to concentrate MS activity on 144MHz because the preferred 50MHz band is open to few countries and is restricted in regard to the transmit power which can be used.

As yet, the writer has not heard of radio amateurs using the 'automatic transmit on receipt of his beacon' format, but with computer-assisted callsign checking there is no reason why automated MS should not be the rule rather than the exception in the next decade. At present radio amateurs have mostly used tape recorders and automatic keys to generate morse at 45 to 200wpm. Here again there is lots of room for improvement, using computer-controlled automatic telegraphy or digital packets. Packet radio has excellent possibilities via meteor-scatter propagation.

One area where radio amateurs already match or better the professionals is in quality low-noise reception, though there is some difference of opinion in respect to where to point the antenna attached to your MS transceiver. Some amateurs favour pointing directly along the great circle path to the other station, whilst others favour going off the great circle several degrees towards the shower radiant.

It is possible to communicate by meteor scatter at 432MHz but this is really a case of doing things the hard way. In a similar vein, meteor-scatter propagation will often support SSB voice communication, but again results are markedly inferior to using telegraphy and the operator is more likely to get laryngitis than he is to get a contact. Multipath fading is a regular feature of MS returns which last for more than a second, so SSB operation can be frustrating.

For the future it must be said that MS in the automatic mode is perhaps the most reliable means of disaster/emergency communications we are likely to get for services in the range 500 to 1,500km, particularly where ionospheric propagation is impaired, eg in the event of a major nuclear accident. At the other end of the operating scale, any radio experimenter who lives in Europe and can receive 62.247MHz in the CW or SSB mode should, if he has not previously tried it, just connect an antenna and listen to this frequency.

The Moon

The Earth's Moon is likely to see a great deal of activity in the next 80 or 100 years. It is an excellent communications platform and, seen from the Moon's nearside, the Earth is a lunar stationary satellite, a situation which will undoubtedly lead to quite simple and effective communications for both professional/commercial interests and radio amateurs and space experimenters.

All this is in the future, so for this reason these developments are discussed in the chapter of this book which reports the likely course of future amateur radio developments. In this chapter only the present-day state of lunar amateur radio activity will be reported.

Moonbounce (EME) communication

Terrestrial stations on different continents are rarely if ever able to enjoy regular direct communication via line-of-sight VHF/UHF or via the ionosphere at HF. The advent of artificial Earth satellites has modified this situation, but even here there are problems. In low Earth circular orbit, satellites are 'seen' for only 20 minutes or less at a time, and are limited to a maximum range of 7,000km. Geostationary satellites are not yet available to radio amateurs, but there is one satellite which can passively relay signals continent to continent for hours at a stretch – the Moon.

'Oscar 0', as the Moon is sometimes called, was first used as a passive reflector of radio signals in US Army tests in 1946. By 1960 radio amateurs were regularly bouncing signals Earth-to-Moon-to-Earth (EME) on frequencies from 28MHz up to the microwaves. Initially this EME activity was confined to those who had the space to build large antenna arrays, but with improved electronics, this situation has gradually relaxed, so that by the 1980s EME activity was possible from backyard sites on every continent, with a strong UK contingent well to the fore.

The EME problem

The Moon is a long way away, orbiting between 352,000 and 420,000km from the Earth. The signal leaving the Earth has to pass up through a far-from-transparent ionosphere, suffering scintillation, Faraday rotation of polarisation and attenuation thereby. It then has a long path to the Moon, and gets there to find that the Moon is a very imperfect reflector. Only about 7% of the signal getting to the Moon is reflected, and even that is garbled by libration, the oscillating motion of the face of the Moon.

The Moon's surface is irregular, and this with the libration wobble imparts multiple reflections to the signal which add or subtract, one from one another, in an irregular sequence depending on the signal frequencies versus the lunar surface anomalies. Having been reflected from the Moon, this much-abused signal suffers further spreading and hence power loss on the path back to Earth. Once again it must pass through the ionosphere, suffering further Faraday rotation, before it gets down to the receiving antenna.In addition to these path losses, the Moon is quite a small-diameter target, and most radio amateur antennas have a half-power beam width broader than the Moon, so some transmitted power does not even hit the Moon and in the receive mode the antenna picks up sky noise from a wide area around the Moon.

It should therefore surprise no one that EME was pioneered by a relatively small number of radio amateurs, prepared to tackle its enormous challenges. Reviewing the EME scene in 1990, it is clear they have succeeded beyond even their wildest dreams.

The ionosphere and EME

The ionosphere is the biggest variable in EME operation; almost all other aspects of the EME path are predictable, the ionosphere is much less so. At low-frequency EME, from 28 to 432MHz, Faraday rotation is the single biggest problem. A 144MHz signal can experience up to four and a half rotations of polarisation on the way up through the ionosphere, and another up to four and a half rotations on the way back down again if the path to the Moon is at low elevation. Even high-elevation paths suffer roughly one and a half revolutions up and one and a half revolutions down of polarisation at 144MHz. Invariably the total revolution count is not a whole number, so what goes up has one polarisation, and what comes down a quite different polarisation.

At 144MHz this presents an almost insoluble problem. Installing circular polarisation is an enormous task on an already very large antenna. So most two-metre users accept that Faraday rotation will often interrupt EME operations. This makes sense for two reasons: first, the Moon is moving across the sky, so it is being seen through a different piece of the ionosphere every few minutes as the line of sight to the Moon swings across the sky. One minute Faraday causes loss of received signal, 10 minutes later a slight change in the path electron density changes the Faraday rotation so that polarisation, although rotated, is matched and communication is heard. The second reason is clear if we consider that when two stations talk via EME they use different ionospheric paths – if you are lucky polarities match.

For the 144MHz and 432MHz moonbouncer Faraday is a problem which most decide to live with if they use Yagi or loop array antennas. Any other kind of antenna is out of the question at 144MHz, but at 432MHz there is the option to use a dish reflector antenna, and if that is your choice you can relatively easily fit a rotatable central pick-up dipole. Then if you do not hear your own echoes, you can rotate your pick-up dipole between each transmission and reception interlude. If Faraday has caused a misalignment of transmitted and received polarisation, this should sort it out and allow you to hear your own signals. Signals coming from another station may also require you to rotate your antenna polarisation to match the incoming signal, during reception, going back to the polarisation the other chap can hear you on before you transmit again.

From 1,296MHz upwards Faraday rotation is much reduced and should cause no serious problems.

Scintillation affects EME signals only on their way up through the ionosphere and to a lesser extent as they pass through solar wind plasma en route to the Moon. Once signals are reflected from the rough, librating, wobbling lunar surface, they can no longer be said to be coming from a point source, indeed they are so spread and diffuse that the return trip down from the Moon and through the ionosphere cannot really have that much of an effect.

Other ionospheric effects on EME signals are far less predictable. Sporadic E seasonally affects the temperate zone daylight ionosphere, and this clearly reduces ionospheric transparency to the detriment of transiting EME signals. The effects of sporadic E can be reduced by scheduling EME activity outside the summer and winter daylight

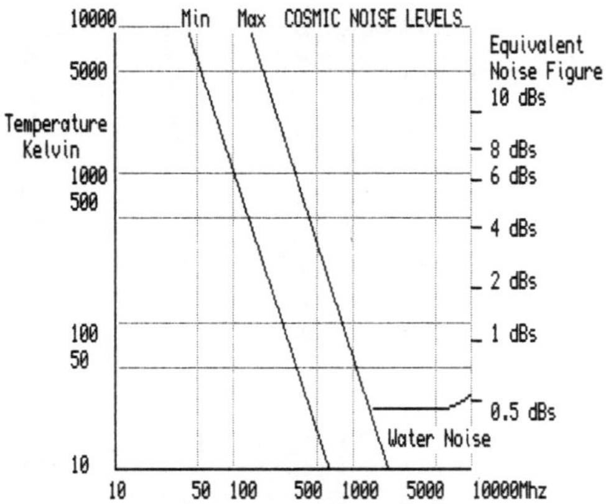

Fig 11.10: Graph of cosmic noise levels

sporadic E seasonal peaks. Low-elevation paths to the Moon are much more susceptible to SpE problems than high-elevation Earth-Moon paths, so periods when lunar declination is low and sporadic E is forecast should be avoided.

At frequencies from 1,296MHz upwards SpE is not a problem, but atmospheric absorption can be a source of difficulties on low-elevation paths to the Moon and should be avoided if at all possible.

EME and interplanetary propagation

The experiments in Earth/lunar space conducted by the American ISEE 3 satellite (renamed ICE satellite) clearly demonstrated the presence of dense concentrations of ionised plasma in the Earth's magnetotail. As yet there is no firm evidence correlating a disturbed magnetotail with EME propagation problems at the time around full Moon, when the Moon is in or near the magnetotail, but these plasma disturbances will probably be proved to cause some.

The lunar reflector

The empirical evidence from EME work suggests that the Moon reflects about 7% of an incident EME signal back in the direction of the Earth. However, the signal is no longer a single discrete wave; reflection from the irregular cratered lunar surface is complicated by the fact that this surface is continuously wobbling with respect to the Earth. This 'libration', as it is called, moves the Moon slowly from side to side, and up and down, simultaneously. So the signal coming back from this moving surface is travelling along multiple paths, causing selective fading effects when it arrives at the Earth station receiver.

Libration-induced multipath fading is less serious at the lower frequencies, with 144MHz not being seriously affected. At 432MHz the fading frequency can be at about 3Hz, whilst by 1,296MHz it will flicker at about 9Hz, a point at which it becomes a considerable nuisance. Unfortunately the situation is actually much worse than a simple regular periodic fading every ninth of a second – what actually happens, because of the irregularities in the lunar reflector, is that you probably get nine fades per second, but they do not occur regularly every ninth of a second, they occur at random, making dashes sound like dots and some dots disappear entirely.

As yet the author knows of no steps being taken to reduce libration-generated fading, but it has characteristics similar to the fading of geostationary satellite signals in sporadic E storms, and that can be overcome by using space diversity reception or frequency diversity reception. Whilst space diversity is almost certainly a non-starter – antennas are big enough individually, without suggesting that one now needs two of them, the same is not true for frequency diversity which might work well with FSK signal modulation, and the receiver picking the mark or space tone, whichever was instantaneously the better of the two.

Noise sources behind the Moon

Most EME antennas see a patch of the sky much larger than the Moon's half of one degree. In consequence any EME signal coming back from the Moon is often accompanied by a lot of unwanted sky noise. This natural noise originates in discrete sources, both in our galaxy and further out in the universe beyond. Fig 11.10 shows the average intensity of this noise at the frequencies of interest to moonbouncers but, as the sky map for VHF/UHF at Fig 11.11 shows, there are a number of very strong discrete sources of radio noise which often trespass into the moonbouncer's antenna beam. Any of these sources can be a big nuisance.

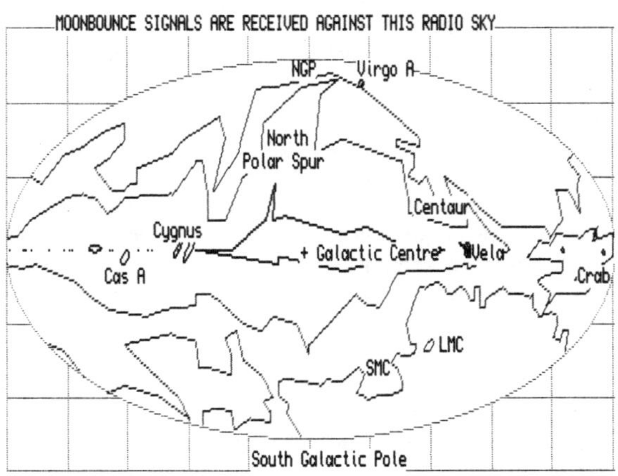

Fig 11.11: Radio source map of the sky. It is against this background noise that EME signals are received

Further information about these radio noise sources will be found in the computer chapter of this book. Discrete radio sources, such as the centre of our galaxy (Sagittarius A), the Crab nebula supernova remnant in Taurus, and the radio galaxies Cygnus A, Centauri A and Virgo A, must be taken into account in any serious EME work, and the best way to

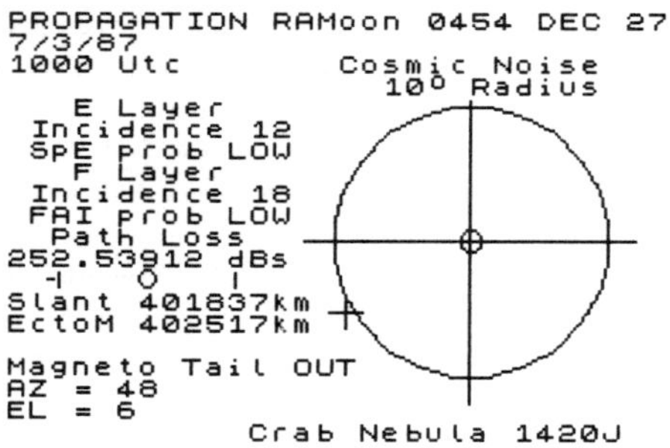

Fig 11.12: Bull's-eye computer display for EME

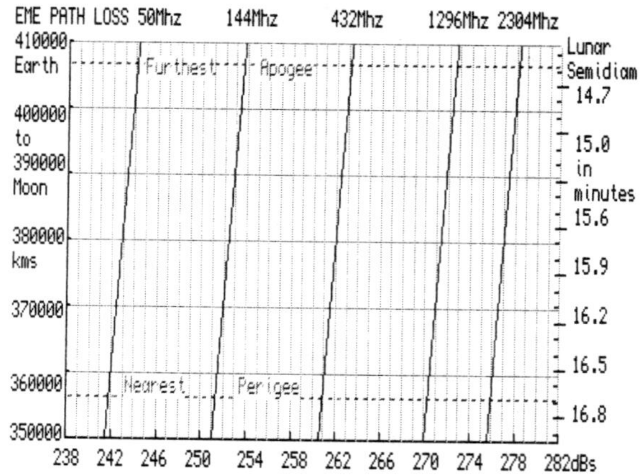

Fig 11.13: Graph showing two-way EME path loss

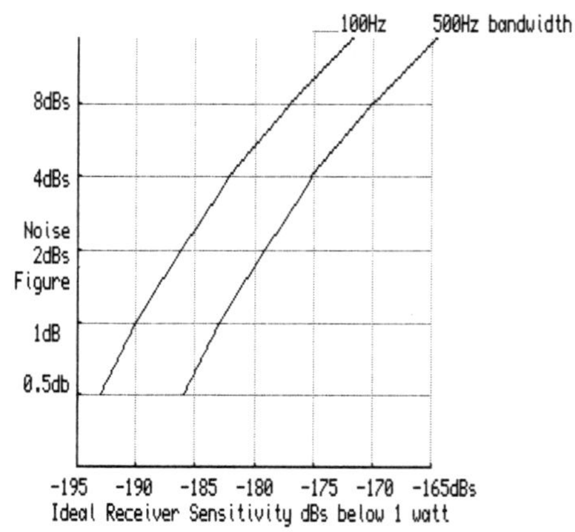

Fig 11.14: Graph showing ideal receiver sensitivity against bandwidth for EME operation

do this is by using a suitably programmed microcomputer. Fig 11.12 shows a typical computer graphic for EME activity on 7 March 1987 at 0910 UTC. The Moon is shown at the centre of a 10 degree bull's-eye, and at the lower left outer edge of the bull's-eye is a + sign in the position of the Crab Nebula radio source. In this example the Crab is probably too far away from the Moon to be a problem, and it is also still below the station horizon, noting that the Moon itself is only one degree above the latter. The statement '1,420J' refers to the power flux of the Crab in Janskys.

EME path loss

The Moon is in an elliptical orbit with respect to the Earth. The parameters of this orbit are variable, being affected by the gravitational pull of the Sun such that the distance from Earth to Moon can be as little as 356,375km at some minimal lunar perigees, or as much as 406,720km at some maximal lunar apogees.

This is a sizeable change in path length, so it must be considered when examining anticipated path loss on any particular day, noting that the change in path loss can be so great as to totally rule out any but the most sophisticated EME systems on some days. The first example which follows describes the operating conditions during the first successful EME communication test at 1,296MHz – it should be noted that this simple approach needs to be modified somewhat if modern high-sensitivity/low-noise receiver preamplifiers are available.

Equipment parameters were: transmit power about 500 watts, 2dB of antenna feeder loss, and a receiver using a parametric amplifier with 2dB of receiver front-end noise. Using Figs 11.10, 11.13 and 11.14 we get:

Path loss at Fig 11.13	= 271.07dB
Transmit power 500 watts	= 27.07dB
Feed loss	= −2dB
	= −246dB loss
Noise limit RX sensitivity	= −187dBW (bandwidth 500Hz) (from Figs 11.10 and 14)
RX noise factor 2dB	= 170K (from Fig 11.10)
Line loss 2dB	= 170K
Total 3.4dB	= 340K
Cosmic noise 1,296MHz	= 0.5dB (from Fig 11.10)

Reading across on Fig 11.14, 0.5dB = 186, 3.4dB = 176
0.5dB noise versus 3.4dB receiver

	= +10dB
Receive sensitivity	= -187 + 10dB
	= −177dB
Total antenna gain required	= 246 - 177dB
	= 69dB
Individual antenna gain	= 69/2
	= 34.5dB

In the actual successful test the antenna was a 6 metre dish rated at 35dB gain. So this test was very marginal. Table 11.02 reports another worked example.

Table 11.02: EME worked example – 750 watt transmitter at 432MHz to a dish antenna 25dB gain (circa 4 metre dish), listening for his own echoes

Transmit power 750 watts	= 28.7dB
Transmit feed loss	= –1dB
Transmit antenna gain	= 25dB
Total	= 52.7dB
Path loss (from Fig 11.13)	= –262dB
Signal return to antenna	= –209.3dB
RX antenna temperature	= 100K
RX feed loss	= 1dB
RX feed temperature	= 290K
RX noise figure (from Fig 11.10)	= 1.2dB = 93K
RX bandwidth	= 100Hz
Ts	= antenna T + (RX feed –1) * Feed T + RX feed * RX noise T
	= 100K+(1–1)*290+1*93
	= 193K
RX noise power	= 10 Log K * Ts * bandwidth
	= 10Log(1.38E–23)*193*100
	= –185.7
Sig/noise RX	= sig dBW + RX antenna gain – noise power
	= –209.3+25–(–185.7)
	= 1.4dB

Own echoes heard 1.4dB above noise. A typical marginal (will work if ionosphere is quiet) situation.

EME Doppler shift

The signal path length is constantly changing because Earth rotation is turning the ground station either towards or away from the Moon. To a far lesser extent the motion of the Moon from its perigee to its apogee is also a factor affecting signal Doppler shift. The combination of these two motions gives the ground station a velocity with respect to the Moon, measured at twice the distance closed per second, in the case of a single station listening for its own echoes.

In the case of EME communication between separate Earth stations, the Doppler shift depends on the rate of change of overall path length, station A to Moon + Moon to station B. Fig 11.15 shows a typical computer printout of anticipated Doppler shifts at 144, 432 and 1,296MHz, first for own station echoes, and second for a communication path from the UK to the Moon to New Zealand.

Fig 11.16 shows a graphic sketch of how these motions and resulting Doppler shifts are derived, noting that it is important to be able to predict Doppler shift because moonbounce is at best marginal, and the use of narrow-band filters can markedly improve reception. Knowing where to tune the narrow-band receiver is therefore very important.

EME antennas

Moonbounce antennas can be divided into two classes, dishes and big arrays. The dividing line usually occurs at 432 or 1,296MHz, with dishes above and arrays below these frequencies. Both dishes and arrays are practical at 432 or 1,296MHz. Both types of antennas have their advantages and disadvantages. Dishes can have rotating feedhorns to match polarisations or reduce Faraday effect, but they are expensive to build and need very strong and precise drive systems and sturdy supports. Antennas consisting of arrays of Yagi beams or loops are easier to build, but they can suffer badly from Faraday effect and they rarely survive for long in high winds.

```
            DOPPLER SHIFT
            -------------

      At 0910 Utc on 7/3/1987

Dopshift ur 2m
sig back to you = 0.124khz Up
Dopshift ur 70cm
sig back to you = 0.372khz Up
Dopshift ur 23cm
sig back to you = 1.117khz Up

Doppler to/from another station
Other Station
 Lat -41 Long 185

Dopshift 2m
him from/to you = .055khz Down
Dopshift 70cm
him from/to you = 0.163khz Down
Dopshift 23cm
him from/to you = 0.487khz Down
```

Fig 11.15: EME Doppler computer prediction

Because EME work is concerned with high levels of transmitted power and low levels of received signal, there is a natural tendency to try to solve both these problems by using the biggest possible antenna. Just what size is possible depends on several factors – the cost, the space required and the local weather patterns. The weather is the factor which should always be given priority – never underestimate your local weather.

Most UK EME sites experience 100km/h winds at least once, and sometimes three or more times a year, and 150km/h winds can occur at least once every four years in some parts of the UK. It must also be accepted that even if you build an extremely strong antenna, driven by battleship gun turret servo motors, there will be quite a few days each year when you will simply not be able to turn your monster

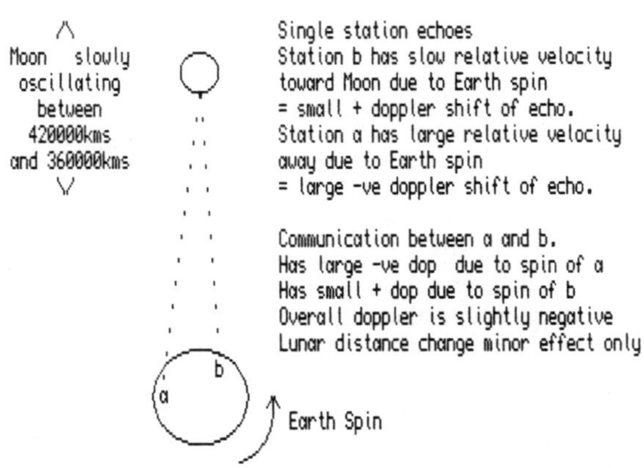

Fig 11.16: EME Doppler shift

antenna through the wind, and you will not be able to hold it at an angle to the wind.

Normal servos supplied for amateur radio antenna rotators are totally inadequate for moonbounce antennas. In one recent case in the UK, a four by 12 element Yagi array for 144MHz, placed on a 60ft extension tower, destroyed two elevation and one training rotators, sheared a large mast coupling and absolutely chewed up some half inch thick steel end stops before the owner gave up and changed to a massive non-'amateur supplied' antenna assembly and rotators. It is perhaps no coincidence that these problems usually occur with our regular March/April and September/October equinoctial gales. Unfortunately it is just these times of year which seem to be selected for moonbounce contests.

Equally important, whilst moonbounce antennas and fittings must be extremely strong and therefore extremely heavy, they must also be capable of pointing with extreme precision at a moving target. Most radio amateur antenna rotators are quite incapable of meeting these two requirements. The typical rotator offered for 144MHz antennas will run in to a designated bearing to within ±5 degrees at best from one direction only. Try running in from the opposite direction and it may achieve ±10 degrees on a good day. The problem is static friction, sometimes called 'stiction', and the amount of play in the gear chain, and this can only be overcome by using more complex servo drives featuring second- and third-order (velocity and acceleration) feedback terms in the servo loop. This sort of servo is not cheap but the strong accurate drive it provides is essential if you are to achieve consistent EME results.

Equally as important as strong accurate servos is the provision of accurate static and mobile alignment. In ordinary amateur radio work it is possible to use the 'near enough' approach to antenna alignment, but in EME work and indeed in any space work this approach is a waste of time. It is therefore vitally important that, when you align your antenna azimuth on north, you check that your antenna actually is pointing at the Pole Star. You can of course use a magnetic compass provided you know the local correction for magnetic to geographic bearings, at present about 7.5 degrees in UK, ie a magnetic compass points 7.5 degrees west of the true geographic north rotation pole). Most local Ordnance Survey maps give the up-to-date figure for this correction on the side of the map.

However, you should be careful, as the author found after half a day spent checking his antenna N, S, E, W on corrected magnetic compass bearings produced only confusing nonsense. It was noticed that as the magnetic compass was hand carried along a straight path towards a spot west of the antenna suitable for an alignment check, at every step, the compass gently shifted westward. The closer the compass was to a neighbour's wrought iron fence, the greater the error. So please be careful and if possible check out your alignment, not only pointing at the Pole Star, but also through the back of the antenna on the Pole Star, ie when your antenna is pointing south. You should also allow your antenna to run into north or south from both clockwise and anti-clockwise bearings with both short run-ins and run-ins from widely different bearings. You may be surprised how badly your servos perform on this test.

Many radio amateurs use on-site alignment checks for their big antenna beams. To make sure his 4 by 19 Yagi beams all point parallel to one another the author has a set of spots painted on the house wall. The antennas are set one at each corner of a two-metre square, so are the spots on the wall, and beyond the same spots over the house is a well-sited chimney on a very accurately measured bearing, as an additional check. In the centre of the four alignment spots is a fifth spot. This is used in conjunction with a polythene alignment pipe fixed along the centre of the antenna beam. It also provides a good confidence check, whereby when the antenna is pointed at the Moon in a clear sky, the Moon should be firmly centred in the pipe when the antenna is driven to its computer predicted co-ordinates.

Having got your antenna mechanical alignment perfect, how do you know the signal is going out along the mechanical alignment? In one never-to-be-forgotten check, a piece of visually perfect coaxial cable was found to be putting an 8 degree squint on the antenna main lobe. This was found by checking against the radio noise sources as described in the computer chapter of this book. All good moonbounce software should contain radio source antenna alignment check data.

No doubt there are radio amateurs who get moonbounce results now and again with a less than perfectly aligned antenna, but the Moon is only half a degree wide, so an error of two degrees equals four Moons. Indeed, this sort of error is often introduced electrically when radio amateurs do things which, whilst marginally acceptable at 2 metres, are not acceptable at 70cm.

The worst sin in this category is running the antenna feeder cables through the field of view of the antenna. Coaxial cable is unbalanced feeder, and virtually all 70cm antennas are less effective when having the equivalent of half-inch thick copper pipes taken at an angle through their directors. The result of this is a serious squint and reduction of performance. Fig 11.17 shows two ways to feed coaxial cable to a 70cm array.

EME transmitters

Most EME operators use the legally permitted maximum power. Signal-to-noise ratios are so small that any other policy is misguided. How the transmitter power is generated varies greatly with all the standard modes of amplifier design featuring somewhere, but one thing they all have in common is a clean clear stable frequency transmission. Chirps and harmonics merely waste power, and moonbouncers cannot afford to waste a single watt.

EME reception

Low-noise preamplifiers located right up on the antenna itself are an absolute 'must' for regular moonbounce work.

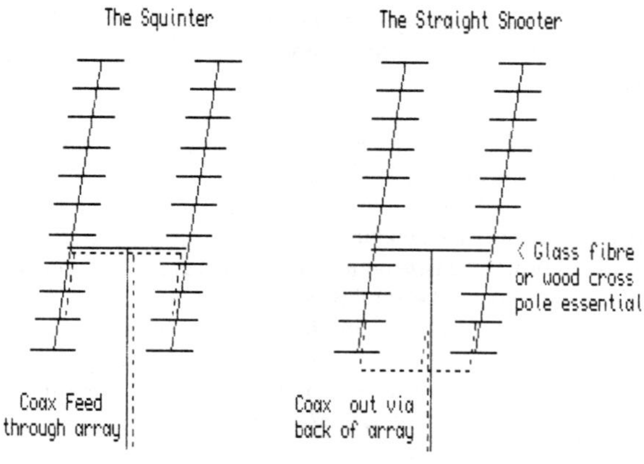

Fig 11.17: How to avoid UHF antenna array squint

Equally important, the sensitive GaAsfet-preferred preamplifier should be protected by positive pre-transmit switching. Voice/signal operated switching to transmit with the receiver preamplifier still in line is a sure way not to get moonbounce contacts. The transmitter must be positively switched off, before the receiver preamplifier is switched on to the antenna, and when the listening period is over, hard positive switching should be used to take the preamplifier off the antenna, and only when it is completely clear should transmitter HT be applied.

Every centimetre of coaxial cable and every joint or junction is a source of signal loss. So these features should be minimal in front of the preamplifier, and they should be used as sparingly as possible thereafter. If it is impossible to put the preamplifier on the antenna, the coaxial connection from the antenna to the preamplifier should be as short as possible and it should use the highest-quality low-loss coaxial cable available.

Almost any kind of superheterodyne receiver can be used. Combinations of preamplifier and convertor, eg 432 to 28MHz, are available. Where possible convertors with low oscillator noise are preferred, and if the signal from the antenna is immediately down-converted further feeder losses are minimised. The receiver itself should be comfortable to use; it is possible at, say, 432 or 144MHz to use a standard amateur radio receiver but the author's personal preference is on-the-antenna conversion in a Jamsat preamplifier convertor to 28 or 26MHz, feeding the shack receiver which has slow-motion Eddystone-type tuning, and a narrow-band CW filter of 500Hz or tighter: 200Hz or 100Hz if you find you are comfortable with tighter (more prone to ring, and harder to tune) really narrow filters.

EME ALMANAC DATA

Date	Trans	EL	Rise	Set	Ang
1/3	1342	33	0746	2000	15.9
2/3	1429	40	0751	2129	15.6
3/3	1514	46	0756	2257	15.4
4/3	1600	52	0802	....	15.2
5/3	1647	56	0812	0024	15.1
6/3	1737	60	0825	0149	14.9
7/3	1827	62	0847	0311	14.8
8/3	1919	62	0921	0422	14.7
9/3	2010	62	1015	0516	14.7
10/3	2101	60	1126	0551	14.7
11/3	2149	56	1246	0612	14.8
12/3	2235	52	1410	0625	14.9
13/3	2320	47	1534	0635	15.1
14/3	....	0	1658	0640	15.2
15/3	0000	41	1820	0646	15.3
16/3	0044	35	1944	0651	15.5
17/3	0127	28	2112	0655	15.6
18/3	0215	22	2243	0702	15.8

Fig 11.18: A page from an EME almanac data program

Tracking the Moon

The first requirement is a microcomputer and suitable software. Fig 11.18 shows a page print from a computer-generated lunar almanac. Using this display the EME operator can look ahead and plan his operating schedule to fit his free time periods when the Moon is near Earth. For example, big Ang = semi diameter in minutes of arc, with good high elevations, occurs in this example around 1342 UTC on 1 March. Based on the almanac data EME schedules can be fixed with other moonbouncers, using the HF EME liaison nets.

LUNAR TRACKING DATA 7/3/1987

UTC	AZ	EL	EtoM km	AngDiam
0600	359.5	-6.9	402071	0.49532
0615	2.8	-6.9	402101	0.49528
0630	6	-6.7	402130	0.49525
0645	9.3	-6.4	402157	0.49521
0700	12.5	-6	402187	0.49518
0715	15.7	-5.5	402216	0.49514
0730	18.8	-4.9	402242	0.49511
0745	22	-4.2	402271	0.49507
0800	25.1	-3.3	402300	0.49504
0815	28.2	-2.4	402326	0.49501
0830	31.3	-1.4	402355	0.49497
0845	34.3	-0.3	402383	0.49494
0900	37.3	0.9	402409	0.4949
0915	40.2	2.2	402437	0.49487
0930	43.2	3.6	402465	0.49484
0945	46	5	402490	0.4948
1000	48.9	6.5	402517	0.49477
1015	51.7	8.1	402545	0.49474
1030	54.5	9.7	402570	0.49471

Fig 11.19: A page from a typical lunar tracking data program

Fig 11.19 shows a page from a typical lunar tracking program. The Moon comes above the station horizon at 0900 UTC on an azimuth of 37.3 degrees clockwise (east) of north, the moon is a long way away, near its apogee range 402,409km, and small diameter 0.4949 degrees. Please note that this is twice the semi diameter given by the almanac. The almanacs have for centuries used the older term 'semi' or half diameter because this was the way the old astronomers measured it: by obscuring half the moon's image with a semi-circular metal 'standard moon'. For moonbounce reflection the diameter in degrees given here is more appropriate. They both say the same thing, but the difference in style can be confusing.

There is little or no point trying to do Moon tracking without computer predictions. The Moon is far too small a target to be tracked by guess-work. SARUG supply Moon-tracking software; the address is given in appendix 1.

EME operations scheduling

Moonbounce operating is clearly likely to be successful when the Moon is nearest to the Earth, ie has a big angular diameter. The higher the elevation angle to the Moon, the less likely the signal will encounter problems in the ionosphere, equally the further removed from the summer sporadic E season the more transparent the ionosphere, with the added attraction late at night that the ionosphere will be particularly quiet.

Please remember that you must also take into account the conditions at the other station. Your night is New Zealand's day, so there is no gain in arranging a UK night-time schedule with New Zealand. Equally there are sociable and there are unsociable times of day, so you need to make sure you are not getting your opposite number in the EME schedule out of bed at his 3am. The map at Fig 11.20 sorts out this type of problem and it also tells you who is able to see the Moon at the same time as you can see it.

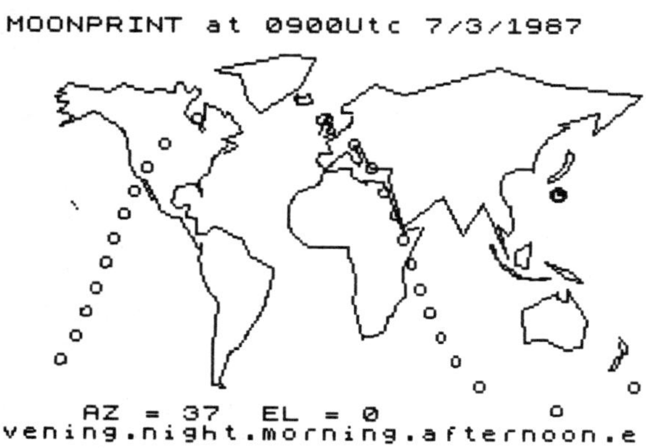

Fig 11.20: Moonprint – who sees the moon

In the example in Fig 11.20 the Moon is far to the east of the UK, just south of Japan. The UK is just coming into the western edge of the lunar footprint, whilst the eastern edge of the footprint runs up the Pacific Ocean to include Alaska and western Canada. This is clearly a time when a UK station able to access the Moon on his horizon, far to his east at great circle azimuth 37 degrees, can if he is lucky talk to Australia, New Zealand, most of the south and all of the north Pacific, including Hawaii, Canada and Alaska. In practical terms the low elevation makes good moonbounce from UK most unlikely, but it would be worth a try.

Because of the need to schedule contacts for times when other people are free, weekends and holidays are usually good moonbounce days. So there are lots of things to consider before you go on the HF net to arrange your proposed schedules. Given good computer data, however, this should not be a problem. Indeed it is advisable to run the computer as you make the schedules so that as you fix a schedule you can model it on the computer and check that it makes sense.

The actual operating features will be confirmed on these HF scheduling nets. What you need to confirm with each station is:

(a) Frequency to be used (remember to check Doppler).
(b) Start time UTC.
(c) End time UTC.
(d) Who starts the schedule.
(e) Length of transmission/listening period.
(f) Modulation mode to be used.
(g) Whether standard or modified procedure to be used.

Always come on schedule early to make sure your equipment is warmed up and will not drift in frequency.

EME operating procedures

These procedures are not fixed; at the same moment you will hear signals from the Moon using different formats. The whole format is given here, just do not be surprised if you hear large parts of it omitted. The better the moonbounce conditions the freer the procedure.

The transmit and receive period are usually set at one or two minutes duration. Who transmits first is decided when you fix the schedule. Transmit speeds of about 10 wpm are the norm, shorter dots are easily lost, so high speed lids are incoherent. In some but not all procedures, the first half of your transmit periods you send repeats of both callsigns, in the second half you send reports if appropriate.

Standard reporting procedure uses a dash code, again because dots get lost due to libration fading:

T one dash repeated slowly = signal detected
M two dashes = letters or portion of calls copied
O three dashes = both calls and report copied
MT two dashes one dash = nearly solid copy
5 five dots = solid copy: forget the code, use morse

By this system an O plus both calls received at both ends results in RRR being sent. RRR both ways confirms successful moonbounce QSO.

In practice many operators use Os or nothing at all; the other codes T, M, MT are rarely heard.

If you hear nothing, please check likely Doppler shift. Fig 11.15 shows a typical computer printout of Doppler data. This program works out Doppler from, and to you, from a second station anywhere in the world, provided that station has a clear view of the Moon (and so do you).

EME listening and learning

Would-be moonbouncers are urged to get in touch with local moonbouncers to find out when they are likely to be operating. They can then listen in to these contacts and see what they hear. If your local moonbouncer is willing, you may find it useful to visit his shack during EME activity – it may surprise you to hear how weak the return echoes

Table 11.03: Radar observation of asteroids and comets to 1987

Name	Range	INT time	Wavelength	Station
Asteroids				
7 Iris	–	–	–	–
16 Psyche	250 million	30min	–	–
97 Kylotho–	–	–	–	–
1862 Apollo	8 million	55s	–	–
1915 Quetzalcoatl	–	–	–	–
Eros	?	–	–	Arecibo
Comets				
Grigg Skjellerup	500 million	–	12.6cm	Arecibo
Kouhoutek	Unsuccessful			
D'Arrest	Unsuccessful			
Bradfield	Unsuccessful			
Comet IRAS	450,000km	8.5min	12.9cm	Mojave
Comet IRAS	450,000km	2.3min	3.54cm	Mojave
Comet Encke	?	?	12.6 & 3.5cm	Arecibo

really are. Indeed no one should expect to hear anything of moonbounce unless his hearing is good and well practised at copying weak morse way down in noise.

Asteroid and comet signal reflections

One area where there may be progress in amateur space radio concerns asteroids and comets. In the simplest terms these objects have already been the target of Earth radars as reported in Table 11.03.

To get some idea of why these meagre results take such a lot of power (eg Mojave 400kW to 64 metre dish), consider an object 30,000,000km from Earth. The object is 1km in radius and it reflects about 10% of the radio signal which hits it. Using X band (3.54cm) because it is far more sensitive (bigger dish gain), it would take five hours of reception before a signal to noise ratio of 2 could be achieved.

This is a typical asteroid target. By contrast Comet IRAS was a once in 10 years event where a sizable body came within 450,000km. So that is why it proved to be such a good target. However, Comet Encke echoes received on the massive 300 metre dish at Arecibo were only barely discernible above the noise. Comet Encke is a much more typical cometary target than is Comet IRAS.

The clear story one gets from this data is that where these comet and asteroid echoes were seen, they were only seen after long integration times, where the signal was allowed to build up for minutes or hours before it could be recognised. This is not the way to communicate! So no one should expect to make easy communications use of asteroid or comet reflection.

That is not the end of the story. Comets offer some intriguing communications possibilities as natural maser amplifiers, and asteroids which visit the inner solar system inside the Earth's orbit have potential for both repeater and asteroid settlement communications. All this is perhaps possible in the not-too-distant future. What has to be firmly said about the here and now is that asteroids and comets are at present not very suitable targets for amateur radio space experimenters.

Chapter 12

Amateur radio astronomy

We live on a small planet, circling around a modest star which is located in an outer arm of the spiral nebula we call the Milky Way. Figs 12.01 and 12.02 show our situation. We are far from the centre of the spiral, so we see it much as a fly on the spoke of a wheel sees the wheel. As we look towards the centre we see the hub and the far rim of the wheel; as we look out in the opposite direction we see the nearer rim out beyond us.

Fig 12.03 shows the inward view we see as we look south on a September evening at about 2100 UTC. Turning this figure over we see the view we get that same evening by looking north out towards the outer rim of the Milky Way spiral. At other times of day and other times of year we see the same band of stars, but instead of going right overhead as it does on a September evening, it slopes at an angle to the vertical. So whenever the night is dark and the sky is clear of clouds, the broad star-studded band of the Milky Way is plainly evident, particularly if you get away from street lights.

Optical astronomers got the telescope 400 years ago, but it was not until about 70 years ago that our true situation in the Milky Way galaxy was appreciated, and it then took a further 30 years before astronomers were convinced that out

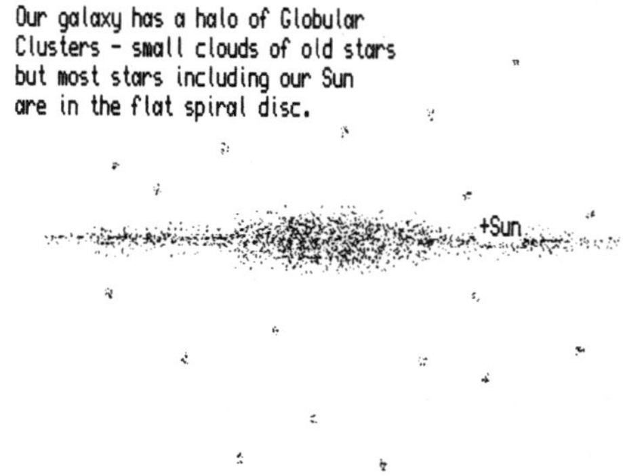

Fig 12.02: Side view of the Milky Way galaxy

beyond our Milky Way were millions of other galaxies, some spiral-shaped like our own, some elliptical, and some quite irregular in shape.

In making these discoveries astronomers used the narrow band of the electromagnetic magnetic spectrum we call 'visible light', that part of the spectrum our eyes are sensitive to, but already by the 1780s astronomers realised that

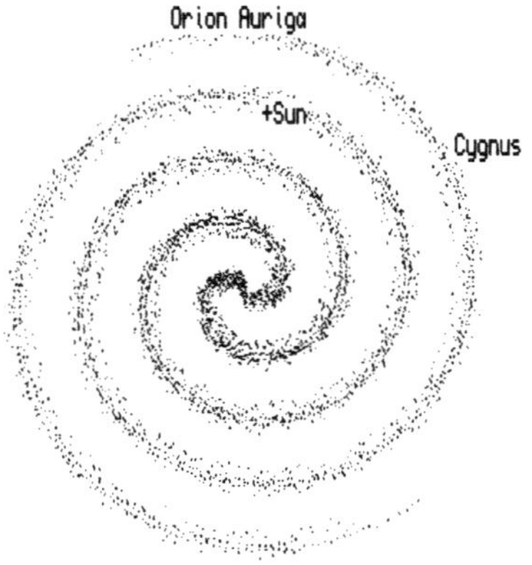

Fig 12.01: Plan view of the Milky Way galaxy, showing the position of the Sun, Orion, Auriga and Cygnus. Because we live in this galaxy, we are not at present sure of its precise shape and form. The view from Earth is badly obscured by gas and dust clouds in and between the spiral arms

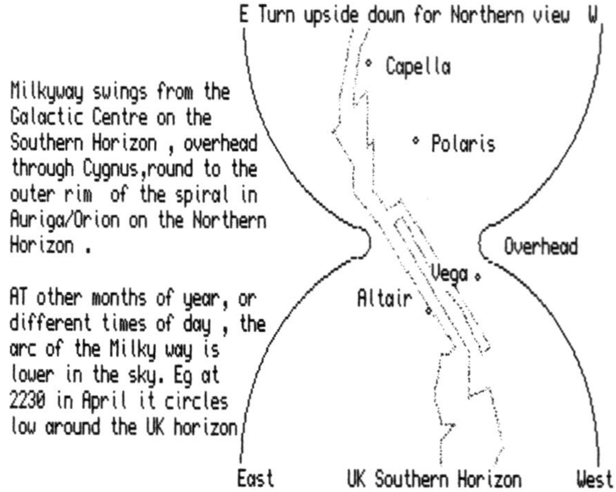

Fig 12.03: The inward view of our galaxy as we look south on a September evening at about 2100 UTC

there were probably signals at other wavelengths coming down from the stars which we cannot see. Herschel then proceeded to demonstrate this by using a glass prism to split sunlight into its rainbow colours, and placing a thermometer in the invisible area below the red end of the rainbow spectrum, he proved there was something there which heated the thermometer and caused the mercury to rise.

This infra-red experiment by Herschel was as low as he could go in frequency and he simply had no way of detecting what sort of radiation lay below the infra red in frequency. So would-be experimenters had to wait until the late 1800s for radio wave detectors to be invented before this part of the spectrum could be opened to study.

Left to the astronomers, radio would not have been detected even then, because astronomers saw no reason to stop their interesting experiments with starlight, particularly when the radio apparatus then available gave only the crudest images and certainly could not resolve anything so minute as a star.

Karl Jansky

Whether astronomers were interested or not, the pace of radio developments increased sharply in the 1920s. Radio amateurs could not be spared the highly commercial medium waves, so they were allowed to operate in the unwanted shortwave bands. What happened then is history. Radio amateurs quickly demonstrated that the shorter wavelengths above 80 metres could provide superb low-power communication worldwide, and in face of this demonstration the commercial stations soon began to set up their own shortwave wireless stations, amongst the first of which were those operated across the Atlantic by the Bell Telephone Company of America.

Bell scientists soon noticed that amongst other things, the performance of their shortwave links was conditional on the level of noise, and this noise was variable. They reasoned that if the sources of the noise could be identified it might be possible to design narrow-beam antennas that picked up the wanted signals but excluded or reduced the noise. A young Bell scientist called Karl Jansky was given the somewhat unpopular task of trying to identify these shortwave noise sources, and just by chance the Sun was at its sunspot cycle minimum, so the frequency he chose was open to the universe, unimpeded by the ionosphere.

Using a former potato field at the Bell Laboratory at Holmdel in New Jersey, Jansky built a massive Bruce curtain, vertically polarised beam antenna. The antenna was mounted on a wooden frame supported by four Model T Ford car wheels, and the wheels were set to allow it to run in a circular track driven by a motor so that it took 20 minutes for a full 360 degree rotation, ie three rotations each hour. The antenna was designed to receive at 20.5MHz with a 20 degree beam in azimuth and elevation – because of ground effects the elevation pattern was probably aligned at about 20 degrees elevation. Fig 12.04 shows a schematic of the antenna.

The signals from the constantly turning antenna were taken about 80 metres to a small shack containing a stable sensitive 20.5MHz receiver whose output was integrated over about 10 seconds and then fed to a pen recorder. Fig 12.05 shows a typical pen recorder trace for one hour. At first Jansky classified his signals as near and distant thunderstorm noise plus a steady unknown hiss. It was this hiss which produced the regular curves on the recorder trace.

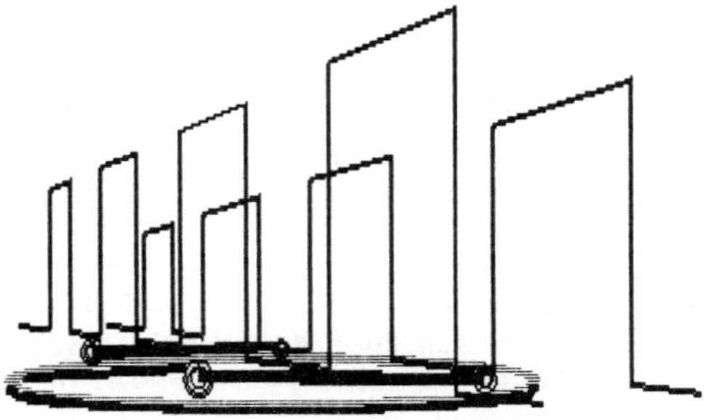

Fig 12.04: Karl Jansky's rotating 20.5MHz antenna for the first radio astronomy experiment in 1932

The interference from local thunderstorms and, via ionospheric propagation, of distant thunderstorms was reasonably well known, but the hiss which seemed to peak in one part of the sky was a new feature.

It happened by coincidence that the part of the sky the hiss came from was also near the location of the Sun, and Jansky at first went along with the idea that the Sun might be the source of the signal. What he did not know was that the Sun was in that part of the sky as a seasonal visitor and behind the Sun was the true source of the signal, the Milky Way.

Fortunately, Jansky continued to observe as winter 1931 changed to spring 1932, and gradually he became aware of two things. First, the Sun was moving further and further from the bearing of the unknown signal and, more important still, the time at which the peak of the unknown signal

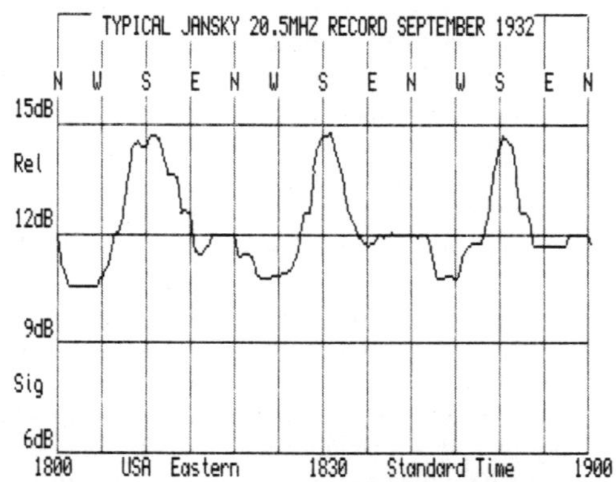

Fig 12.05: Type of pen recording obtained by Jansky on 20.25MHz

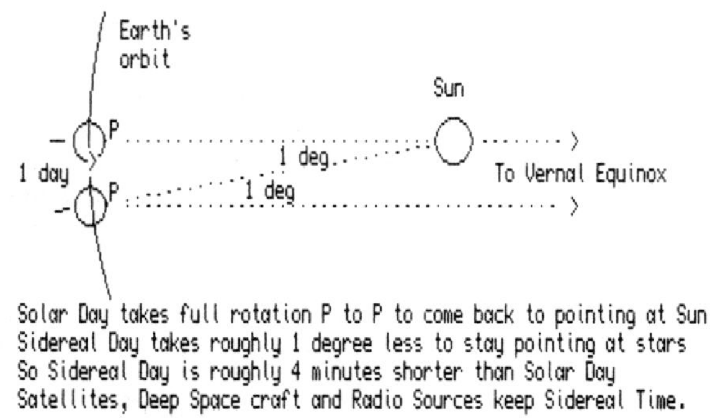

Fig 12.06: The difference between mean solar time and sidereal time

passed south of his antenna was getting four minutes earlier each day. Not being an astronomer, Jansky asked his friend Melvin Skellet to explain this feature of his data and, based on what his friend told him, Jansky realised he was monitoring a signal which kept sidereal time.

Fig 12.06 shows why it is necessary to use a different time for tracking the stars. Our normal mean solar time averages out the time intervals between the Sun passing over our station meridian; sidereal time relates to a system which is not orbiting with the Earth so the Earth's single orbit round the Sun each year is not added to the roughly 365 Earth rotations in a year. The difference of about one orbit in 366 accounts for the roughly four minutes of time per day by which sidereal star time runs ahead of mean solar time. So if something keeps sidereal time it is away from Earth, out in space.

Jansky did not have the assistance of modern computers, so his simple pen recordings are not easy to interpret. Fig 12.05 shows what he got in a typical one-hour session in which his antenna scanned around the sky three times. From the record it is clear that at 1810 EST as his antenna turned through south it crossed a strong broad signal source. At 1830 EST the antenna crossed near the same source again and at 1850 EST it crossed near it for a third time. Clearly the 1810 EST crossing when the signal is strongest fits in well with the suggestion that a source is highest in the sky as it crosses south of a northern hemisphere station. In fact Jansky's antenna beam elevated a little too high to cross the actual centre of the Milky Way, the centre proper passing slightly below his antenna beam, getting weaker each subsequent rotation as the source elevation decreased, pulling it further below the antenna beam.

Today it is possible to give Jansky's data to a microcomputer and produce a sky map. If Jansky's antenna could have seen the whole sky, the map he would have got would have resembled Fig 12.07, with the heavy dark centre showing the powerful radio emitter at the centre of our galaxy. Though Jansky lacked a computer he was able to show quite clearly that he got his biggest signal when the centre of the Milky Way passed just under his antenna beam. He also showed that other views looking through other parts of the Milky Way, some a long way from its centre, produced a

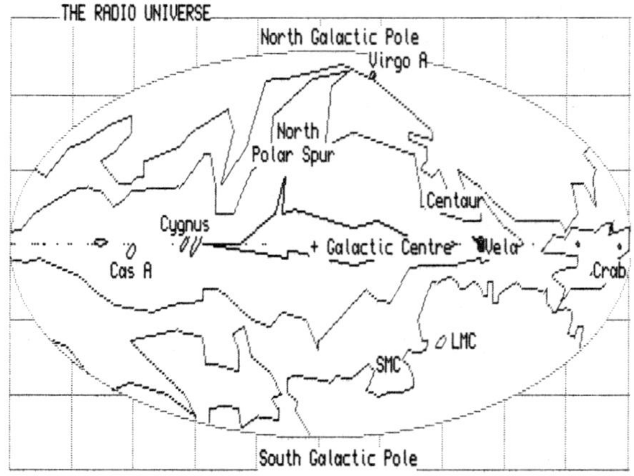

Fig 12.07: A simple map of the radio universe

signal as the thin plane of the galactic disc crossed his antenna beam. We now know that his data showed evidence of other discrete sources of radio signals set apart from the Milky Way. Of these the remote galactic source Cassiopeia A is most clearly shown, but Jansky cautiously kept his message to the fact that he was 'seeing' the Milky Way by radio.

Anyone who tries to repeat Jansky's experiment should note two things: first he took his records at solar sunspot cycle minimum when the ionosphere was relatively transparent at his chosen frequency of 20.5MHz, and second the picture is slightly complicated by the fact that no one spot on the Earth can see the whole of the sky. This latter fact means that a portion of the southern sky containing the Small and Large Magellanic Clouds – two medium-sized companion galaxies of our Milky Way, plus the star fields of Centaurus and the Southern Cross, are never seen from northern Europe. Fig 12.08 shows the gap in the map for northern stations. To see or to radio monitor this part of the sky it is best to go to Australia or South America.

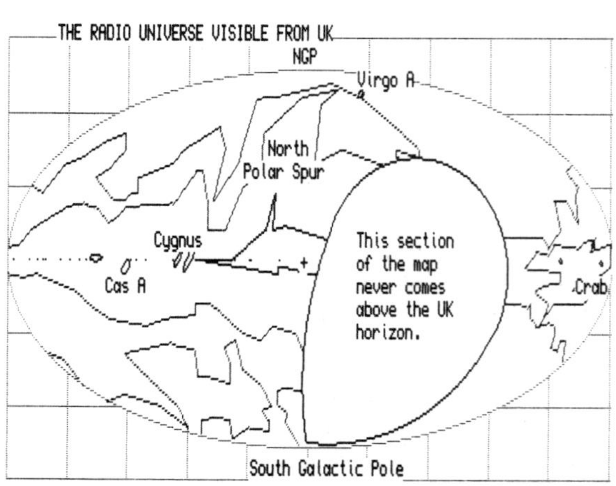

Fig 12.08: The radio universe visible from the UK

The map shown in Figs 12.07 and 12.08 has the rough contours which should be recorded by anyone repeating Jansky's experiment, but it should be appreciated that the discrete sources shown require rather better resolution (narrower antenna beam width), than Jansky had available when he made his great experiment.

Grote Reber, W9GFZ

Jansky's results were of little commercial value, so after publishing them in *IRE Proceedings* for 1932, 1933 and 1935, he went on to other work. However, his work was not wasted: he had lectured around the United States and had inspired several future radio astronomers who would eventually take his work further than he could ever have dreamed.

There was a pause, however, and it was not until 1940 that radio astronomy experiments were taken up by Grote Reber, a professional radio engineer and radio amateur. Reber realised that he needed narrow-beam antennas to get a clearer picture of the radio sky, and to this end he built a large parabolic dish antenna.

Using this antenna, Grote Reber was able to scan the sky at several VHF, UHF and lower microwave frequencies, and in so doing he obtained clear evidence of discrete radio sources such as Cygnus A, and he was able eventually to produce the first useful map of the radio sky. Reber's principal contribution was that he was able to convince professional astronomers that the use of radio beams could give us a new window from which to observe the universe. That Dr Reber's 1940 paper was published in the *Astrophysical Journal* says a great deal for its editor, the astronomer Dr Otto Struve. Astronomers at that time were singularly uninterested in the vague picture of a radio universe, and Dr Struve realised that future work might change this view completely. Despite misgivings he preferred to publish a promising paper that might be wrong, to not publishing a paper that if right was epoch-making.

Publication of Dr Reber's paper coincided with the beginning of a particularly dark period in the second world war but, as events were to prove, Dr Struve had indeed published a paper which would revolutionise our view of the universe, and several famous astronomers such as Walter Baade and Rudolph Minkowski read the paper and decided that radio astronomy would be at the top of their agenda when the war ended. In addition, the paper was read in German-occupied Holland by Professor Jan Oort and what he did produced almost immediate results.

The hydrogen line

In the darkest days of the second world war, Professor Oort at Leiden University in Holland tried to keep his students busy. Practical work was out of the question, but theoretical work was possible, so Professor Oort set his colleague H C Van Der Hulst the task of investigating, by theory alone, whether any of the common atoms or molecules likely to be found in space might at times radiate discrete radio signals. Laboratory experiments had shown that energy changes in atoms or molecules are restricted to fixed levels. Much as a lorry carrying sacks of coal over a bumpy road may at times lose coal by the sackful, so an excited atom induced to change or spontaneously changing to a lower energy level will lose energy in fixed packages, whilst radiating at a fixed frequency where energy is related to frequency of radiation by the formula:

Energy = frequency * Planck's constant

$$E = \nu * h$$

For atoms these changes can involve energies of the order of 1E–11 ergs, ie about five electron volts, with radiation being at high frequency, ie light.

For molecules these state changes involve much lower energy level of around 1E–17 ergs, so the radiation is at a much lower frequency in the microwave or UHF radio spectrum.

Van Der Hulst was able to show that the common gas hydrogen in its neutral (un-ionised) state had just such an energy change when the magnetic fields created by its rotating positive central proton and, by its orbiting negative electron, changed from parallel to anti-parallel. Left unmolested in the cold of otherwise empty space, a hydrogen atom would flip perhaps once in several million years, but in denser clouds of galactic hydrogen, it was possible that collisions would lower the time between flips to perhaps once every 50 years. So dense clouds of countless millions of neutral hydrogen atoms might produce a detectable radio signal. The frequency to listen for came out of the formula: it would be 1,420.403MHz plus or minus Doppler shift, due to cloud relative motion with respect to Earth. At the end of the war, Leiden University published details of this suggestion.

The reception of the hydrogen line

For several years after the war, professional experimenters attempted to receive the 1,420MHz signal but no one succeeded until 1951, when Harold Ewen at the Harvard Lyman Laboratory used a sensitive microwave receiver fed from a large fixed horn antenna sticking out of the laboratory window.

Fig 12.09 shows a schematic diagram of his apparatus, which detected the passage of the Milky Way across the sky outside the window. With modern equipment the Ewen experiment should be amenable to duplication by any well-equipped amateur radio station.

The catalogue of atomic and molecular radio lines

Since the discovery of the hydrogen line, radio astronomers have located hundreds of different atomic and molecular emission lines and, for a full catalogue of these, readers are

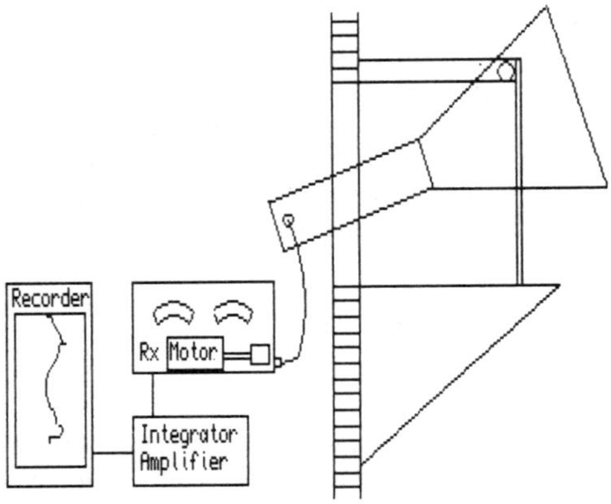

Fig 12.09: Schematic diagram of Ewen's equipment used to detect the hydrogen line in 1951

recommended to consult *Radio Astronomy* by John D Kraus, Cygnus Press.

The most important of these lines are those concerned with organic molecules. Indeed, there are some astronomers who believe we will identify the major organic molecules of life in the radio signals from space. Other molecules of importance are the molecules such as the OH water radical which supports maser action – microwave amplification by stimulated emission of radiation. The OH radical radiates a quartet of frequencies just above the frequency of the hydrogen line and it is an excellent maser. If one adds the intriguing fact that Comet Halley and most other comets seem to produce prodigious amounts of the OH radical, it could well be that comets will one day be used as natural radio amplifiers.

Galactic and extragalactic radio sources

Grote Reber was the first man to recognise the existence of discrete radio sources in our galaxy, and in space beyond our own galaxy. Given the improvements in receiver performance since his day, there is no reason why modern experimenters should not find and use these sources for equipment testing and experiment.

Unlike the Sun, which can vary enormously in radio signal strength in a relatively unpredictable fashion, most galactic and extragalactic radio sources are relatively steady signals. It is therefore much more sensible to use them for performance tests of moonbounce equipment.

The Sun as a radio star

Many early radio experimenters tried and failed to detect radio signals from the Sun. Jansky did his famous experiment at solar cycle minimum, so it is not surprising that he found nothing. Thereafter several experimenters in the microwaves reported hearing the Sun, but it was not until

Table 12.01: Useful galactic and extragalactic radio sources

Source	RA	DEC	Type	Janskys
Cassiopeia A	350.25	58.55	supernova remnant	11,000
Cygnus A	299.44	40.6	distant galaxy	8,100
Sagittarius	265.6	–28.901	centre of galaxy	9,000
Taurus A Crab	82.875	21.97	supernova remnant	1,420
Virgo A M87	187.075	12.66	distant galaxy	970

1 Jansky = 10^{-26} W/m²/Hz

1942 that there was firm evidence that our Sun was a radio star.

Operators on the great radar chain that had just helped the RAF to win the Battle of Britain were worried in February 1942 when all their radar displays were jammed by noise. Only after careful checks was it established that the problem was the Sun, and not the enemy. After the war this information was published and the experiments which followed soon revealed that whilst the Sun was not generally a powerful radio emitter, it was a highly variable one and because it was close to Earth, its peak variations were very noticeable.

If the Sun emitted radio waves simply because it was hot, it could be expected to stick close to the black-body radiation curve for a object at a temperature of 6,000 degrees Kelvin. At times, however, the Sun emits radio signals as if it were a black body at 10,000 million degrees Kelvin, and even when it is quiet the Sun behaves as if it were a lot hotter than 6,000 degrees Kelvin in respect of frequencies below 30GHz. Fig 12.10 shows the Sun's radiation profile.

Solar radiation modes

The Sun in its quiet mode at sunspot cycle minimum is a stronger-than-expected emitter of radio waves because the area from which the radiation occurs is much bigger than the

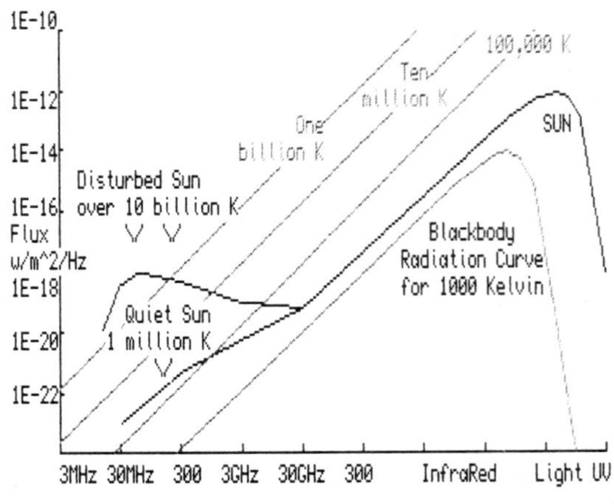

Fig 12.10: Radiation profile of the sun compared to that of a black body

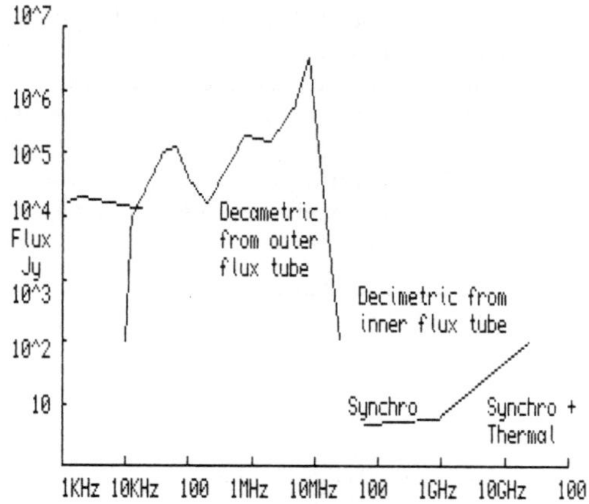

Fig 12.11: Graph showing radio emissions from Jupiter

relatively small disc we can see. The difference can be as much as 15 to 20 times bigger in radius than the visible Sun.

As the Sun begins to climb from sunspot minimum towards its cycle maximum, roughly four years after minimum, it begins to develop sunspots.

These spots, or to be more exact the areas of the Sun high above the yellow 'plages' (French for beach), which are found around the spots, radiate strongly, and it is this radiation which we measure at microwaves and report as solar flux.

At solar minimum the reference value of solar flux can go as low as 65 units, whilst at one or two extreme solar cycle maximums the flux level has risen to 350 units or higher. This flux level is a good guide to HF ionospheric propagation.

Over and above the rising flux level as the Sun cycles towards maximum, there is an increase tendency for the Sun to radiate large amounts of additional radio energy in bursts. Intense sets of burst usually follow flares in the solar outer layer we call the 'chromosphere'. These flares have tremendous energy, and some of the big ones can reach the explosive equivalent of 2,400 million million tons of TNT ie, 240 million hydrogen bombs. Needless to say these explosions have an enormous effect on the solar wind and, when they reach the Earth, on radio propagation and our weather.

There are several different types of solar flares with widely different patterns of radio emission, but all of them are easily monitored. One method for doing this monitoring is described in chapter 8.

Radio emission from the Moon and the planets

The Earth, Moon and solar system planets have temperatures between 50 and 700 degrees Kelvin. As the emission curve of Fig 12.10 shows, this results in most of their radiation being in the infra-red part of the electromagnetic spectrum, but this emission can be greatly attenuated if they possess atmospheres.

Jupiter radio emission

Jupiter is a strong radio source. Fig 12.11 shows that its emission spectrum includes kilometric radiation at 3 to 300 kHz, decametric radiation at 3 to 40MHz and decimetric radiation at 100MHz to 3GHz.

Jupiter's radiation was first detected by Burke and Franklin in 1955, when they found it to be a strong fluctuating signal source in a broad band around 22MHz. Subsequent experiments showed that the Earth's ionosphere was blocking some of these signals, and when the ionosphere is transparent these Jupiter bursts can be detected down to 3MHz and up to a maximum frequency of about 40MHz. Later it was discovered that Jupiter radiated kilometric and decimetric signals. Fig 12.12 shows a side view of Jupiter, locating the sources of some of these signals.

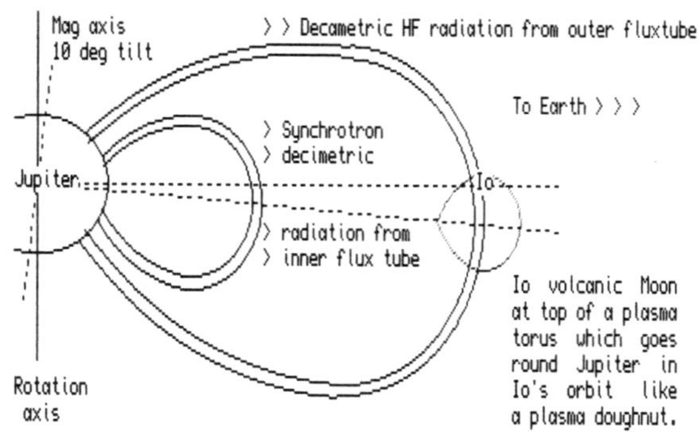

Fig 12.12: Radio emissions from particles in Jupiter's magnetic field

The Jupiter radiation at shortwave, around 18 to 22MHz, can easily be detected by a simple loop antenna and a shortwave receiver. Best time to listen is at night when the ionosphere is transparent at these frequencies, after first checking that Jupiter is above your horizon.

Practical amateur radio astronomy

Radio amateurs and space radio experimenters can duplicate, and in several cases expand, the original experiments of Jansky, Reber, Ewen and the rest. In addition some of the major radio sources in our galaxy, such as Cassiopeia A, Virgo A, the Crab Nebula, and Sagittarius A are easily detectable from the UK using moonbounce-type antennas and receivers. For those who need them, amateur radio software programs are available for locating all these objects.

Nearer to home, interplanetary radio sources such as the Sun are easily monitored on simple 144MHz amateur radio equipment, and Jupiter's HF bursts are clearly detectable on a simple horizontal loop antenna feeding a standard short-wave receiver. For experimenters prepared to build special equipment, particularly antenna arrays, pulsar reception is quite possible using a low-end VHF receiver. At VLF it can be anticipated that Nasa will continue to fly 'get-away special' packs, capable of monitoring and relaying VLF from space to Earth via UHF.

In co-operation with other space experimenter groups, it is possible that radio amateurs may share in projects such as a solar wind driven spacecraft capable of slowly leaving the solar system, relaying VLF and other interesting observations perhaps from outside the solar system. Indeed, wherever one looks the facilities exist, or can be produced, whereby radio amateurs can play a major part in the exploration of space.

Chapter 13

Future of amateur radio in space

Getting amateur radio into space

To be assured of even the smallest place on the road to space, amateur radio groups must prepare for any and all opportunities. There will be obvious amateur radio niches on each stepping stone along the way, and amateur radio should be prepared in advance to take advantage of these by having suitable equipment ready to go. Sites for beacons, radio relay of scientific experiments and emergency/disaster relief equipment will be forthcoming, but will only be taken up if the hardware is ready because the opportunity had already been anticipated.

No one is going to give amateur radio a free ride into space, simply to allow radio amateurs to waffle for hours, but services like recreational amateur radio for isolated space stations must not be overlooked with, if necessary, organised amateur radio footing the bill for equipment. If amateur radio has stated its intention to assist with these sorts of facilities we may be able to make a better claim on the limited transport available.

In the paragraphs which follow an attempt is made to suggest what organised amateur radio should prepare for at each stop along the way.

LEO amateur radio equipment

There is a continuing need for simple equipment in this area. Satellites carrying any or all of the following facilities will be required for several decades, but equally important will be the growing requirement for fixed space station recreational, emergency and scientific equipment.

(a) Satellite transponders: 2m up, 10m down and 2m up, 70cm down, for voice, RTTY, AMTOR, ASCII and packet communications.
(b) Store-and-forward packet satellite facilities.
(c) Multi-sensor experimental packages of the Uosat type, aimed at secondary/high school and university undergraduate studies of space topics.
(d) Beacons for experimental study purposes.
(e) Bulletin boards carrying space-related information.
(f) Relay facilities for spaceborne radio receivers of VLF, LF, MF and lower HF bands.
(g) In the ionosphere, free and towed satellites carrying beacons for E and F layer studies.
(h) Space station amateur radio recreational and science facilities.

General comments on LEO requirements

There will be a continuing requirement for low Earth orbit satellite transponders of the simplest kind. The preferred modes of operation would be mode A (2m up, 10m down) and mode J (2m up, 70cm down). Low duty cycle modulation types should be the rule, eg CW, SSB and packet.

Satellites in low Earth orbit carrying large memory (greater than 20 megabytes) with store-and-forward packet capability are required, using mode J (2m up, 70cm down) or mode L (23cm up, 70cm down).

Perhaps the most important feature of all in LEO is the continued availability of increasingly sophisticated multi-sensor experimental satellites of the Uosat type. With features of interest to newcomers to space science, these satellites could be the cornerstone of educational training in space topics. In the past these satellites have not always been able to provide dedicated scientific beacons, in that where beacons have been present they have been heavily modulated, greatly reducing their usefulness for ionospheric studies and the informative computer-controlled differential Doppler studies. Beacons should wherever possible be unmodulated except as required by international regulations in respect of periodic identification signals.

Telemetry of all kinds should be excluded from satellite beacons, and placed on separate discrete carriers at frequencies well away from beacon channels. Equally important, multi-frequency beacons should where possible be genuine single harmonic source, phase-locked signals. An excellent model for a successful family of beacons was provided by the outstandingly successful DOD P76 satellite. Provision of a microwave frequency in a beacon family should be made if at all possible, with the frequency not less than 5GHz, allowing it to be free of most scintillation problems and therefore useful as a reference.

Where possible, receivers aboard satellites should relay VLF, LF, MF and low HF reception to Earth via UHF FM links to permit regular monitoring of radio astronomy and

Earth magnetosphere signals at these frequencies, which are normally blocked by the ionosphere and do not reach the surface. LF radio astronomy is an almost totally unexplored field, with some of the experiments which have taken place in the past being totally under-publicised, and hence almost wasted.

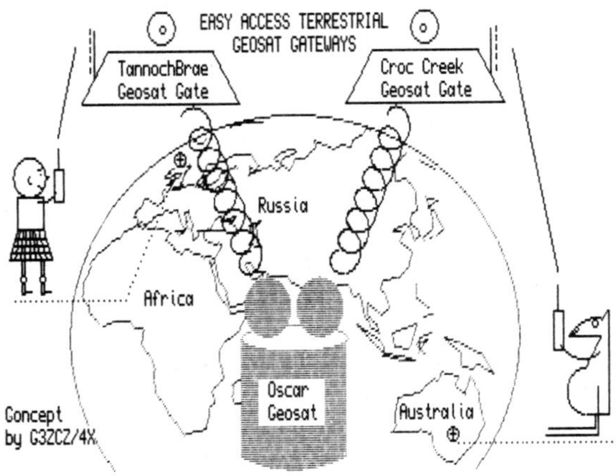

Fig 13.01: Easy-access terrestrial gateways using geosats

Satellite bulletin boards transmitting digitalker speech and PSK automatic teletype or computer formats are required in low Earth orbit. Subjects for bulletins should be space science data oriented, eg solar activity reports, solar flux readings, spot counts, coronal holes, filaments, flares and general solar wind enhancement. In addition the bulletins could include terrestrial features such as polar activity reports, magnetic storm data and equatorial and polar zone scintillation data.

Despite 30 years of satellites, we know very little about the Earth's ionosphere. Space shuttle 'get-away' packages, Salyut Iskra release packages, and the proposed families of towed satellites offer unique opportunities for studies in this field. Equipment for the above experiments and, most important, full advanced publicity for these experiments should be given the highest priority. In the past expensive packages have been released with details known only to the builders and a few associates, despite the totally unclassified nature of this work.

Amateur radio authorities have to break down the barriers which at present inhibit timely early release of information on projects of this type. Liaison channels already exist for discussion and dissemination of information about both Soviet and American space station amateur radio facilities. Sometimes in the past, as with the shuttle plasma packages, the space authorities have given all necessary information, but it has not been released by amateur radio authorities, perhaps because they thought it too technical for their members. This lack of foresight and confidence must be corrected.

High-altitude elliptical orbits

Geostationary satellites are not always the best way to serve communities at middle and high-latitude locations. For many years the Soviets have used the molniya orbit to provide satellites in highly elliptical orbits which appear to hover above high latitudes for six to eight hours at a time before dropping quickly down round the Earth and back up into a new high-latitude hover, four hours or so later.

The satellite requirements in the molniya type orbit are numerous, and include much the same requirements as those requested for low Earth orbit, plus special high-altitude and long-access time features such as cameras for polar zone studies and network facilities for international amateur radio communication links.

The geostationary orbit – future requirements

The geostationary orbit is highly suitable for communications facilities. The fact that the satellite in geostationary orbit appears to be stationary as seen from Earth allows it to be used for high-volume, fixed communication links using microwave frequencies. This opens up the possibilities for a whole range of communication formats from simple person-to-person voice or packet message exchange, through to intercontinental geosat-to-geosat links on a 24 hour a day basis.

In particular, the geostationary comsat allows simpler access, with no need for constant antenna tracking, and no serious Doppler effects. This can be taken to the point where special terrestrial 'gateway' terminals located near centres of population can be accessed by ordinary repeater techniques, with the gateway doing all the hard work of pointing its antenna accurately at the geosat, using the right up link frequency, and connecting the caller to other 'gateways' around the world. Fig 13.01 shows a graphic presentation of this concept, which was first described by Joe Kasser, G3ZCZ/W3.

Geostationary satellites (particularly those with gateways) offer extremely useful international communication facilities at times of natural and man-made disaster. It is perhaps important that all geosat facilities be designed with this type of public service facility given top priority. This should in no way reduce their usefulness for ordinary amateur radio traffic, but it is important that we do not go the other way, designing satellites which are complicated to operate and therefore are less-effective public service aids.

The provision of experimental beacons at HF and VHF frequencies is often forgotten when geostationary satellites are designed. This is an important omission: geostationary satellites simply by their 'stay in one place' advantage offer a unique platform for long-term studies of fixed paths down through the ionosphere. As with LEO satellites, unmodulated CW carriers are the preferred mode if science information output is to be maximised.

Beyond the geostationary orbit

Above Earth orbit a whole new set of site considerations and science opportunities appear. The factors most likely to influence choice of equipment site location are likely to be:

(a) Accessibility to men and materials.
(b) Location in respect of important communication paths.
(c) Potential for useful scientific experiments of all kinds, not just radio science.
(d) Local strength and cyclic period of solar illumination.
(e) Local temperature range.
(f) Local radiation environment.
(g) Physical nature of site – rock, regolith, ice etc.
(h) Local ionosphere or atmosphere if present.

Equally important, the actual hardware used at remote space sites will require quite different characteristics from terrestrial or satellite equipment. The main features of any specifications for space hardware are likely to be:

(a) Maximum emergency and life-saving potential.
(b) Long life expectancy.
(c) High order of reliability, with double or treble redundancy of all major components.
(d) Simplicity of function.
(e) Simple installation requirements.
(f) A wide range of fail-safe design features.
(g) Zero pollution potential (chemical or electronic).
(h) Very rugged shockproof construction.
(i) Remote on/off shut down facilities.

It is particularly important that amateur radio designers avoid problems caused by using advanced, untested designs.

Several major satellite failures in the recent past can be put down to the use of exotic, relatively untried, state-of-the-art systems, and in a different sphere, to lack of manufacturing quality control. Belt and braces techniques are to be preferred to design elegance, simply because the latter is a totally unnecessary risk. Indeed, even interplanetary radio communications and science pose no problems of marginal conditions demanding ultra-high performance – in fact they demand quite normal signal powers and techniques, well within our present capabilities.

Table 13.01: Worked example – signal path propagation, Earth to Moon

P = 0.5W transmitter power
D = 1m dish diameter at each end of path, aperture 50% effective
S = 3dB signal-to-noise ratio required at receiver
W = 0.03m wavelength
B = 2500Hz bandwidth
T = 250K, system temperature in degrees Kelvin

num = (P*.5*PI*D*D/4*.5*PI*D*D/4)/(S*1.38/1E23*T*B*W*W)
Range in kilometres = ((num)^(.5))/1E3 = 575,418km

Conclusion: 50mW at 10GHz to a 1m dish is adequate for communication to or from the Moon at apogee 420,000km

Lunar surface – equipment requirements

Table 13.01 is a worked example showing the requirements for a typical Earth-to-Moon or Moon-to-Earth SSB voice communication link at a frequency of 10GHz. The maximum Moon-to-Earth separation reaches about 420,000km at maximum lunar apogee. This gap can easily be crossed by a 50mW signal feeding a 1 metre dish at the transmit end, coupling to a similar 1 metre dish and modestly noisy receiver.

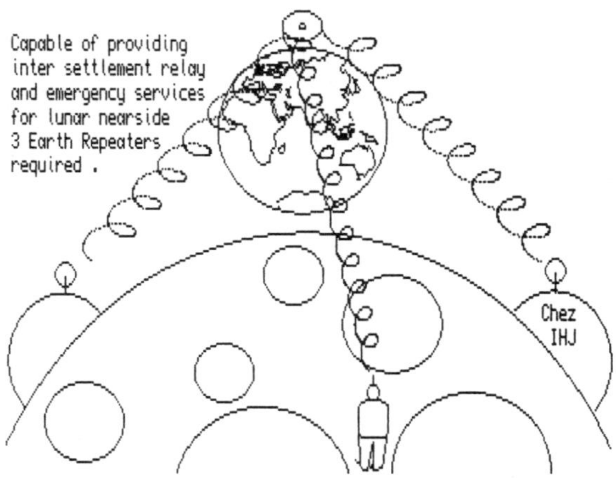

Fig 13.02: Using an Earth-based repeater for inter-lunar base communications

So there is nothing extraordinary facing us about Earth-Moon activity. Lunar communications are quite different from moonbounce, which has to contend with enormous losses at a relatively poor reflecting lunar surface plus a double transit of the Earth-Moon path.

The Moon is an excellent site for experimental beacons reporting lunar conditions back to science groups on Earth, but whilst repeaters on the Moon relaying Earth communications back to Earth are perfectly feasible, they are hardly appropriate use of the amateur radio spectrum. Once permanent lunar settlement begins, amateur radio will be able to offer excellent recreational communications for isolated nearside lunar settlements and, perhaps more important, will be able to offer simple Earth surface lunar repeaters connecting lunar settlements which are not line of sight with one another. Indeed these reverse repeaters could be a useful contribution by terrestrial radio amateurs to lunar emergency communications. Fig 13.02 shows a graphic scenario for this type of service, whereby a lunar nearside surface user could use a helmet radio to raise an Earth surface repeater which then alerted lunar-based emergency teams to his problem.

A lunar surface beacon

The initial requirements are for a simple digitalker broadcast of short-duration lunar surface science bulletins, plus an unmodulated carrier broadcast to permit terrestrial Doppler and differential Doppler experiments, ionospheric transparency experiments, and simple lunar emergency communications.

Specification: to include solar-powered, battery-supported supplies driving a 5 watt or less microwave transmitter, modulated by digitalk or PSK telemetry, or unmodulated CW. The antenna could be a simple flat phased array placed on the surface. The whole package to have access for emergency use as a transmitter.

Suitable items for telemetry reporting would include solar cell current, battery voltage, battery current, transmitter power, solar wind monitor, magnetometer, moonquake reporter and lunar temperature reporter.

In addition to beacons, lunar settlements will require access to Earth surface educational and recreational facilities. As lunar settlement expands, opportunities for amateur radio will appear in all these niches.

Appendix 1

Useful addresses

The **Radio Society of Great Britain** is the national society which represents all UK radio amateurs. It seeks to promote the position of the amateur service on the radio spectrum and liaises with the Radiocommunication Agency of the Department of Trade and Industry and other government departments. It publishes a monthly magazine, *Radio Communication*, which features a satellites column.

Radio Society of Great Britain
Lambda House
Cranborne Road
Potters Bar
Herts EN6 3JE

AMSAT UK is the national society specialising in amateur satellite matters. It has approximately 3,000 paid-up members. It produces a bimonthly magazine *Oscar News* and runs a net three times a week on 3.780MHz at 1900 local time Monday and Wednesday, and 1015 local time Sunday. AMSAT UK can provide satellite tracking software, Keplerian orbital elements, telemetry data formats and other satellite information. The most important function of AMSAT is the building of new satellites. AMSAT UK accepts donations which go to the development of the amateur radio satellite service.

AMSAT UK
94 Herongate Road
London E12 5EQ

The **British Amateur Radio Teledata Group (BARTG)** specialises in data communications.

Mrs P Beedie, GW6MOJ
Ffynnonlas
Salem
Llandeilo
Dyfed SA19 7NP

The **British Interplanetary Society** is an independent body promoting study and development of astronautics. It was founded in 1933 and became the UK national society for astronautics in 1945. It issues two periodicals: the *Journal of the British Interplanetary Society* and *Spaceflight*. It is the ideal body for those interested in the wider areas of astronautics and space exploration.

British Interplanetary Society
27-29 South Lambeth Road
London SW8 1SZ

The **Remote Imaging Group** specialises in weather and Earth satellite survey experiments. The Secretary is G8XTW.

Secretary, Remote Imaging Group
14 Nevis Close
Leighton Buzzard
Beds LU7 7XD

The **Commodore Radio Users Group** has amateur radio software available.

Commodore Radio Users Group
69 Irvine Drive
North Clippens
Linwood
Paisley PA3 3TB

The **Sinclair Amateur Radio User Group** (SARUG) provides space experiment programs for the Sinclair range of computers including satellite and Moon-tracking programs.

Sinclair Amateur Radio User Group
3 Red House Lane
Leiston
Suffolk IP5 4JZ

AMSAT NA, the North American branch of AMSAT, covers much the same areas as its UK counterpart. It produces the fortnightly *Amateur Satellite Report* and runs a Sunday net on 14.282 and 21.280MHz at 1900 UTC. This net is also relayed by Oscar 13 mode B on 145.957MHz and mode L on 435.888MHz.

Other nets
AMSAT International, Sunday 1800 UTC, 21.280MHz
AMSAT International, Sunday 1900 UTC, 14.282MHz
AMSAT European, Saturday 1000 UTC, 14.280MHz

Amsat Software, at the same address, has a wide range of space software for IBM, Apple Macintosh, Commodore 128 and Amiga, Radio Shack TRS, Texas Instrument and Atari microcomputers. Please send three IRCs with any enquiry.

AMSAT NA
PO Box 27
Washington DC
20044
USA

AMSAT HQ has good IBM software for Dove telemetry decoding. Please send three IRCs with any enquiry.

AMSAT HQ
850 Sligo Avenue
Silver Spring
MD 20910
USA

A **Uosat data booklet** is available from:

Uosat Spacecraft Engineering Research Unit
Dept of Electronic and Electrical Engineering
University of Surrey
Guildford
Surrey GU2 5XH

Appendix 2

Glossary

Altitude Satellite height above the Earth.

AOS Acquisition time of satellite at horizon.

Apogee The most distant point from the Earth for a body orbiting the Earth.

Argument of perigee The angle measured in the direction of satellite motion, around the orbit plane from the right ascension northerly crossing of the equator to the perigee. This one of the Keplerian orbital elements. It is expressed in degrees and sometimes written as the greek letter ω.

Ascending node The point in a satellite's orbit where it crosses the plane of the equator in a northerly direction.

Azimuth The angle measured clockwise in the observer's horizontal plane from the North Pole to the line of sight to the satellite.

CPA Time of a satellite's closest approach to the observer's station.

Declination Angular distance of an object from the celestial equator. The celestial equivalent of latitude.

Descending node Point on an orbit where a satellite crosses the plane of the equator in a southerly direction.

Elevation Angle of an object above the observer's horizon.

Epoch time This is the time at which the Keplerian orbital elements were taken and to which they refer. For example, Epoch 90 38.75 refers to year 90, day 38, and 0.75 of a day, which translates to 1800 hours on 7 February 1990. Epoch time should not be confused with the astronomical term 'epoch' which refers to the time at which given star positions are accurate.

Equatorial plane An imaginary plane extending from the Earth's equator into space.

EQX An abbreviation for equator crossing north bound.

First Point Of Aries This is a reference point in the sky based on the position of the Sun as it crosses above the equator in a northerly direction at the time of the spring equinox. This is the sky reference point from which the right ascension of a star or a satellite is measured.

Footprint The area beneath a satellite within which it can contact ground stations.

Geostationary orbit A satellite placed in an orbit at a height of 35,680km (22,300 miles) above the Earth will orbit once every day. If the orbit has zero inclination with respect to the equator the satellite will appear to be above the same point all the time. Used for communications satellites.

Geosynchronous orbit Similar to a geostationary orbit, a geosynchronous orbit does not put satellites in the same point of the sky all day. Instead the satellite with an orbital inclination greater than zero will move about the sky relative to a ground station, but will always be at the same point in its orbit at the same time each day. Used for military satellites which patrol a given viewing area, and scientific satellites which can be contacted by scientists in different continents during their respective working days.

Inclination The angle measured anti-clockwise up from the equator to the satellite's ascending orbit plane. One of the Keplerian orbital elements.

Keplerian orbital elements A set of co-ordinates which provide data to allow the calculation of orbital motion.

LOS Loss of satellite time, at horizon.

Mean anomaly (1) When used as a Keplerian orbital element the mean anomaly specifies the angle in degrees measured at epoch time that the satellite has moved around the orbit since passing through perigee.

(2) When used to report the times of satellite operational mode switches it is expressed as a number, based on the orbital period divided into 256 equal units of time. Therefore 'mean anomaly 128' refers to apogee and 'mean anomaly 0 or 256' refers to perigee.

Mean motion The number of orbits a satellite makes in one Earth day.

Orbital plane An imaginary plane containing the Earth's centre and the satellite's orbit.

Oscar Orbiting Satellite Carrying Amateur Radio.

Perigee The closest point a body orbiting the Earth comes to the Earth.

Period The time it takes a satellite to make a complete orbit of the Earth. 'Nodal period' refers to the time between north ascending equator crossings and this is generally what is meant by the word 'period'. The term 'anomalistic period' is a more accurate way of describing an orbit because it allows for the drift of perigee which occurs in most satellites' orbits.

Right ascension of the ascending node A Keplerian orbital element used to fix the orbit's position in space with reference to the angle between the ascending equator crossing and the First Point of Aries reference. In satellite work the RAAN is written in degrees but in astronomy it is quoted in hours, where 24 hours equals 360 degrees.

Slant range Distance between satellite and ground station. As the satellite and Earth are moving asynchronously this will vary with time.

TCA Time of a satellite's closest approach to your station.

Telemetry Coded information received from satellites giving details of the environment inside and outside the spacecraft.

UTC Universal Time (Co-ordinated) which for practical purposes is the same as Greenwich Mean Time or UK Winter Time. For UK Summer Time, add one hour to UTC.

Index